The Life-Style Violent Juvenile

By Roosevelt 10X Yamamoto

The Life-Style Violent Juvenile

The Secure Treatment Approach

Andrew H. Vachss
Juvenile Justice Planning Project

Yitzhak Bakal
Northeastern Family Institute

Lexington Books
D.C. Heath and Company
Lexington, Massachusetts
Toronto

Library of Congress Cataloging in Publication Data

Vachss, Andrew H.
  The life-style violent juvenile.

  Includes index.
  1. Juvenile corrections. 2. Rehabilitation of juvenile delinquents.
3. Juvenile delinquency. 4. Juvenile justice, Administration of. I. Bakal,
Yitzhak, joint author. II. Title.
HV9069.V23   365'.42   77-2520
ISBN 0-669-01515-6

Published simultaneously in Canada

Printed in the United States of America

International Standard Book Number: 0-669-01515-6

Library of Congress Catalog Card Number: 77-2520

To Richard Soney Allen, the best face-to-face professional in the field of juvenile violence I have ever known, and to the residents and staff of Andros II (1972).

Contents

List of Figures

Foreword

If prisons—as Dostoevski said in the nineteenth century and Winston Churchill in the twentieth—are the gauge of the level of a civilization, then the manner in which we regard and handle the truly violent offender is the touchstone of the correctional system itself.

This is particularly true with regard to the violent juvenile, who is today the object of a higher level of public fear, political demagogy, and legislative effort than in any prior period. Progress in the direction of reform within the correctional system is not an easy path—the pendulum is, regrettably, a more accurate metaphor for describing our attitudes towards the treatment of the convicted adult or juvenile offender. Today's swing of that pendulum is ever more toward the punitive. Incarceration is increasingly advocated as the only—and the best—instrument for dealing with the law breaker, short of capital punishment, which is itself winning ever wider support.

This is exemplified in the 1978 gubernatorial campaign in Massachusetts where the most successful contender in the recent primary urged the restoration of the death penalty and the imposition of mandatory sentence laws for repeated offenders, including juveniles. His victory exemplifies the support that such repressive programs seem to be gaining everywhere.

Meanwhile our senior senator calls for "significant punishment," tantamount to a jail term "in a special facility" for violent juvenile offenders, thus echoing the threat of a recent president that, "If juveniles are big enough to commit vicious crimes against society, they are big enough to be punished by society."

Such declarations by persons in high office are being written into legislation. Witness the recently enacted New York State law empowering the transfer of cases of children as young as thirteen to the criminal court; authorizing their appearance before the grand jury, making them liable to indictment; and allowing them to be confined, by age sixteen, in adult correctional facilities.

The crimes that may invoke these adult criminal procedures and penalties include those which characterize the violent young offender: homocide, arson, kidnapping, rape and other serious sexual offenses, burglary, and robbery.

No reference is found here to "aid, encouragement, and guidance," which has been the basic philosophy of the juvenile process since 1899, nor to "need and condition" rather than the nature of the act committed, as the proper guide to court action in behalf of juveniles.

As the authors of this book correctly point out, any attempt to assay the characteristics of the "violent offender" is fraught with tremendous prospects of error. A leading publisher of works in criminology recently announced the imminent release of no less than nine works devoted exclusively to the "dangerous offender." Society sees serious juvenile misconduct as a peril to personal safety and community stability. No more than 6 percent of young people charged with delinquency can be called "violent," yet, despite their small percentage, these deeply disturbed young people are responsible for as much as two-thirds of the total of serious offenses committed by persons under the age of seventeen.

Sodom and Gomorrah were doomed for want of ten men who were without sin. Today, many in high places in academia, law enforcement, corrections, and our state and national legislatures stand ready to jettison all the advances made in the past hundred years of special handling in the juvenile justice system in order to ensure that this 6 percent do not go unchecked.

The authors rightly stress that if the truly dangerous offender can be culled from the mass of juveniles charged with delinquency, the way will then be clear to reduce drastically the number of institutional slots currently used for the warehousing of their less seriously delinquent peers. Our states vary widely in their use of noncustodial facilities for delinquents. According to a 1975 national survey, six states confine *all* delinquent children committed to state care. At the other end of the scale, Massachusetts confines only 6 percent in institutions. The remaining 94 percent are out in the community in a wide variety of facilities, including their own homes, halfway houses, group and foster homes, camps, and special schools.

For even the most violent and dangerous young offender, unless he is to be locked up for life as the recently enacted New York State statute authorized, will sooner or later be set free. And, as the authors of this book make abundantly clear, imprisonment teaches young people nothing as lasting or helpful to their continued criminal behavior as the lessons learned from their confréres in confinement. It is an old saw that prisons are institutions of advanced studies in the finer points of crime. This is compounded today by unprecedented brutality between guards and inmates as well as between inmates; the prevalence of sexual abuse, individually and en masse; and traffic in alcohol, drugs, and even weapons.

Despite the fact that it has the lowest incarceration rate for juveniles of any of the fifty states, Massachusetts has seen no concommitant increase in its crime rate. The state-wide murder rate, which stood at 134 in 1974 (two years after the juvenile training schools in Massachusetts were closed) fell to 76 in 1977—close to a 50 percent reduction. At the same time a Department of Corrections preliminary study revealed a drop in the percentage of prisoners received at adult correctional institutions who have had early delinquent records.

What price imprisonment of children, then? If we can carve away from the total adjudicated juvenile population those in need of intensive therapy, and provide them with secure and meaningful programs under highly skilled and carefully selected personnel, we can continue and extend the resort to nonincarceration for the 90 percent plus of all other young offenders. Intensive care, such as herein described, costs four or five times more than custody in the average training school. But if we expend the higher amount for a very small number, we shall, in the long run, make extraordinary savings in correctional dollars.

The decision six years ago to close the Massachusetts juvenile institutions was spurred by the finding that the longer children had been confined, and the more stringent the conditions under which they had been held, the higher was their recidivism rate. From a Borstal school for girls in distant New Zealand comes a confirming datum: disciplinary reports dropped from 859 to 32 and absconders dropped from 10 to 0 when the average length of stay was reduced from 12 months to 6 and the resident population was reduced from 78 to 54.

It would be a *reductio ad absurdum* to state, on the basis of such findings, that if all penal institutions were to be abolished then crime would disappear. But the reciprocal is valid enough because the best of today's reform schools daily graduate boys and girls back into our communities who are more criminally wise, more dehumanized, and more convinced of their innate worthlessness than when they went in.

Delinquents, says Erik Erikson, are convinced that they are incapable of ever producing anything of value. The youngster who has been sorely abused throughout his life may feel that the only recourse left to him is to give as good as he has received. To abuse such a person, however outrageous his resultant behavior, by imposing more of the same treatment he has already received at the hands of society, is to doubly victimize the victims of the racism, injustice, and discrimination, which is characteristic of the minorities who fill our ghettos. Like "Pirate" in the Introduction, they turn their hatred of themselves outward into hatred of society.

So this book is most timely in its reasoned and carefully developed plan for alternatives to present dealing with the seriously disturbed young people whom we call violent offenders. It is also, appropriately, a follow-up to an earlier book by Yitzhak Bakal, *Closing Correctional Institutions,* which describes the Massachusetts experience. Taken together, these books can provide information and encouragement to all who, with the authors and with this writer, advocate a moratorium on new penal construction, leading to the ultimate reduction in total cell capacity for all offenders, juvenile and adult.

Benedict S. Alper
Visiting Professor of Criminology
Boston College

Acknowledgments

Literally hundreds of individuals materially assisted in the preparation of this work, far too many to properly list in this limited space. For reasons of confidentiality, many cannot be identified, as will be apparent from an examination of the text. Others have been fully identified in the appendix of interviews. The following people provided a wide variety of assistance in the preparation of this manuscript, ranging from professional input to research to physical labor; our special thanks to: Colonel Nyati Bolt, Roger Friedman, Myrtle Horrington, M.S.W., Pamela Jordan, Robert John Lewis, Marvin R.X. Mathis, Walter Lee McGhee, Detective Warren McGinniss, Ralph C. Pino, and Anthony M. Traini. It should, however, be noted that the authors alone are responsible for the opinions and conclusions of this work.

The John Hay Whitney Foundation (Robert Gangi, field representative) provided fellowship assistance to Andrew H. Vachss from 1976-1978; the New York Foundation (Fred Brancato, program director) provided a grant to the Juvenile Justice Planning Project from 1977-1978. Both grants enhanced both the quality of the finished product and the speed with which it was delivered to the public. Our thanks also go to Frank Dobyns, director of the Arca Foundation, for his advice, encouragement, and assistance throughout the preparational period.

Special Acknowledgments

Daniel Bumagin designed and prepared the concept renderings of the Secure Treatment Unit.
Jim Procter was the primary manuscript editor, from rough draft to finished product.

Introduction

Public reaction to crimes of violence has always been characterized by a mixture of fear, fascination, and a strong need for retaliation. Such emotionally charged responses render any objective treatment of the subject difficult, if not impossible. Theories on crime causation have also been hotly debated by criminologists and social scientists. Students of this subject can't help but be struck by the extent, diversity, and contradictions of these theories.

Nevertheless, criminologists studying the etiology of violence fall into two general groups. One group of investigators has focused on the individual violent offender, attempting to explain such behavior in individual, personal orientation. Inquiry into the offender's heredity/biology/psychosocial development generally assumes that the answer to such behavior can be found within the individual. Such theories use the medical model as their point of departure and assume that abnormalities and illness are at the base of such behavior.

Another diametrically opposed point of view is held by the second group of criminologists who assume that sociological and cultural factors are the underlying causes of violent acts. Most current theories of the etiology of violence take the second position as their point of departure. Terms such as "socialized delinquents" or the "subculture of violence" became the cornerstone of theories explaining delinquency and violence in youth.

The lack of congruency between these two approaches suggests that it is one thing to explain the violent behavior of one individual person and yet it is another thing to explain violence among youth. These are two different and often uncomplimentary levels of analysis of the problem.

This book deals with intervention strategies for treatment of the life-style violent youth. Such youth's behavior cannot be explained by analyzing only his personal, individual behavior but must also include analyzing the subculture he follows. In explaining the subculture of violence, sociologists describe these youths as ones who identify with neighborhood codes and value systems, that support, enhance and give specific direction to violent behavior. Such theories see the violent offender's aggression as part of his personality and most often cannot be explained as an emotional disturbance.

Even when an emotionally disturbed youngster joins and participates in violent acts, it is the group subculture that directs, controls, and molds the youth's behavior. Theories explaining violence among youth suggest that rebellion often directs such behavior. Violent juvenile offenders' behavior, according to one investigator, Albert Cohen, can be explained by the youths' rejection of the value system and the behavior taught them by schools. It is a kind of reverse behavior to the one taught by the school. Thus impulsiveness and need for instant gratification, becomes the dominant mode of behavior.

Another theory argues that violence among youths is a form of masculine protest. Youngsters who grow up in fatherless homes, often controlled, supervised and directed by females at home and at school, resort to behavior that could validate their role as adult males. This involves drinking, fighting, and sexual conquests (including violent behavior against women). Vandalism can certainly be explained as a form of proving one's manhood and masculinity. Similarly, assaults on women, the elderly and children shows a strong preoccupation with needs for power while mugging and armed robbery are acts to achieve specific economic results.

Shaw and McKay in their classic work *Juvenile Delinquency in Urban Areas* discovered that over a period of thirty years in one neighborhood in Chicago, the delinquency rate among juveniles remained high despite the changes in population. Thus, certain economic and sociological conditions, (not the individuals), kept the level of delinquency high.

Criminologists studying the violent subculture emphasize that the group codes of behavior have a strong impact on the individual. Violent behavior as such becomes a learned process and there are rewards for excelling in such activity. Members of such groups do not feel guilty about their acts because they have developed attitudes and have acquired strong identification with such goals.

Marvin E. Wolfgang describes the subculture of violence as: "congested groups of people sharing a belief, a value system, and a set of attitudes and habits concerning the ready resort of violence in a setting where violence is indeed not only tolerated, but often encouraged and sometimes required in certain kinds of interpersonal situations."*

Despite their small percentage, the life-style violent youths are the source of much fear and anxiety. Public concerns are not unfounded. Since they tend to act as a group, these youths can grow in number and become more dangerous and threatening in those places where anomie and other sociocultural disintegration are present. Furthermore, we are referring to youth who can unleash irrevocable damage upon helpless and innocent people who need to be protected from them.

Intervention strategies with the life-style violent youth must be found and this book provides a detailed plan for such strategies. It must be stressed that lack of approaches and policy of action have been one of the main reasons for the public's lack of confidence in the juvenile justice system.

The proposed Secure Treatment Unit described in this book stands in sharp contrast to the conventional way of dealing with such youth. These children have generally been warehoused in secure settings where they graduate into more delinquency and violence. They enhance their reputation and enrich their contacts. They are either oppressed or treated with a laissez-faire attitude and end up getting more freedom to do what they please, thus crystalizing their belief that might makes right.

*Marvin Wolfgang, "Contemporary Perspectives on Violence," in *Violence and Criminal Justice*, ed., Duncan Chappell and John Monahan (Lexington, Massachusetts: D.C. Heath and Co., 1975).

The Secure Treatment Unit described in this book does not separate between treatment and security. No treatment and rehabilitation can be provided without the protection for all residents. Without such security we are forfeiting the basic human need and rights of the inmate. Such secure settings should provide not only controls, limits, and discipline, but also nurturance and positive reinforcement. Too many controls will bring repression and too little will invite violence and delinquent subculture. The balance is crucial. A swing in any direction destroys the program's effectiveness. Planning is of the essence. A secure setting that is poorly planned and sloppily run will quickly become destructive and despite all good intentions, stigmatizing and repressive. It is important to note that this unit's main goal is to change youth's behavior and violent behavior is a primary target for change. This largely calls for reeducation and not therapy, and demands a high degree of staff training supported by a network of services within and outside the unit.

This book has involved many years of planning. It is based upon the authors' experiences in working with hard core youths at the Andros program in Massachusetts and subsequent years of research including interviews with violent youths, evaluations of programs, attempting to provide care in secure settings and setting community-based network for delinquent children and their families.

The book starts with an interview with a youth who is a gang member in New York City. This interview provides a unique and rare look at this young person's thoughts, ideas, feelings, attitudes, and ways of operation. We strongly felt that such a presentation can introduce the readers very quickly to the dilemmas and complexities of dealing with these kinds of youths. The book is organized from the general to the specific. It starts with a short overview of the juvenile justice system, then proceeds to describe some of the basic characteristics of the lifestyle violent juvenile.

In chapter 1, there is a discussion of "waiver" as a way of ignoring the problem of such youths rather than dealing with it. The rationale to providing a closed setting is outlined in subsequent chapters. The remaining chapters describe the need for maximum security, the concept of differential treatment, and the planning of a secure treatment facility. There is a thorough discussion of the way the unit operates, including intake, population size, staff training, as well as many aspects of treatment, education, and other programmatic considerations.

The book also contains case histories, a detailed architectural plan showing the physical plant, and charts outlining different phases of treatment. Unlike other books which are general and theoretical on this subject, this book makes an attempt to provide a detailed and specific plan of action. It is our feeling that this would be one way to push the act of the care and custody of such youths from theory into practice. It is our hope that those who are interested in the subject can use it as a point of departure for experimentation and further study.

Since institutionalization has generally produced poor results the question is what are the possible outcomes of the Secure Treatment Unit. It is this author's opinion that these youth need confinement, even if it is just for society's protection. Furthermore, research has generally been referring to negative results of training schools and detention centers where warehousing has been the main intervention strategy with little or no attempt to have an impact upon these childrens' emotions, attitudes, belief system and their way of operation.

Thus, with proper planning and intervention as described in this book, positive results are very possible indeed.

Interview with "Pirate"

The following interview between Andrew Vachss (V) and "Pirate" (P) took place somewhere in New York City in 1977. Names and locations have been changed to preserve confidentiality.

V: Under what circumstances did you first make contact with the Blood Devils? How did it come down?

P: Well, years back, I was in the Young Hawks gang; I was a War Counsellor. We bumped against each other once in a while, and most of them I met by face, and recognized their faces when I got locked up . . . cops had grabbed a couple of us, but we never got acquainted to know each other until I left the Young Hawks and I moved out [to another neighborhood] and I met the Blood Devils.

V: How did you become a member?

P: I did a lot of crazy shit.

V: Can you explain any of that?

P: The President had something for you to [to do] to get into it at a certain position . . . you had to do something, and I wanted War Counsellor, so I just had to arrange a meeting with another gang . . . go by myself and actually set it up . . . and I did.

V: That was your only initiation? That was all you had to do?

P: Well, I had to do other things. Like go to Central Park and rape . . . which I did. Mug somebody. And the last, what they call your Last Performance, is we went downtown to the white folks neighborhood and I did pretty nasty things, I beat this white dude with a baseball bat that had nine-inch nails across. All they wanted was to see if I had the heart to do something so I wouldn't be able to back out [at a later date].

V: Did you do these things acting with other guys, or did you do these things alone?

P: Well, they were there.

V: They were there to observe you?

P: Yeah. But I guess I did it because I really wanted to get into them. I felt if I don't they'll think a lot of other things about me which I know I'm not, so I just went . . . it happened.

V: But then they became convinced, right?

P: Yes.

V: Were these particular acts the first time you did any such things? Was that rape the first rape you ever participated in?

P: No.

V: Was hitting somebody with a baseball bat the first time you did that?

P: With a baseball bat? Yeah.

V: Was the mugging the first mugging you were involved in?

P: No.

V: How old were you when you first got involved with this type of activity?

P: Eleven, maybe ten.

V: When you were that age, and you were engaged in this type of activity, did you act alone or with other individuals?

P: Well, there was a whole bunch of us just being together. We was always together. And we noticed that a lot of people would come out with gangs, and if you weren't in one and you were just walking, that they would beat you up and I mean really hurt you, and you know I was tired of getting hurt, you know, for no reason. So I decided to hurt people. And we decided to get just a certain gang together with that name [Young Hawks].

V: That's the way you saw things; that you would have to hurt people or they would hurt you?

P: Right.

V: Is that the way it still is?

P: In most places, I hear it is.

V: When is the first time you came into contact with the police? How old were you?

P: Eleven, twelve.

V: What was the charge?

P: They accused me of suspicion of beating up this old man with a couple of other guys. And I was there, but I know they didn't see me and I figured I'd get away from there quick so they asked for my mother and I told them she was out. And I needed somebody old to get me out [to claim he was a relative or guardian] so we always had somebody old in the crowd, that can just go there and talk some shit and get us out. Most of the time it was easy, I would just be locked up in a room [at the local precinct] and there would be signing of papers and I would get out.

V: That was at the precinct, right? What about the Youth Center?

P: That's worse than the streets. I mean if you were there, if you would just get there . . . they would cause some kind of initiation and get a couple of guys in a corner and just boogie on you. And boogie on you good.

V: Did that happen to you?

P: It happened to me, yeah. I had to make up a choice. See, I was in C-2, and there was this room with around twenty-nine or thirty people, young dudes, and every day that I was in there, I was even . . . I would like a couple and dislike a couple. And the ones that I disliked, I had to do something about it.

V: What did you do?

P: I fought a lot. I mean I used to hit them with a lot of different things. I hurt them a lot. Just to show them that I wasn't the type of person you could push around that easy.

V: How long were you there?

P: One year. One year for being in Central Park. See, I had just gotten out of school and we went down to the Park, and there was a couple of us and we all ran, and somebody got hurt . . .

V: How bad?

P: They say it was bad. I mean whoever got hurt, I don't know . . .

V: You didn't do this particular thing?

P: No. and I was caught. When they took us in, they recognized me by the clothes I was wearing and the way I was dressed and I was just sent in.

V: Who does most of the violence in your organization, the older guys or the younger guys?

P: The younger guys. I mean, the older guys, most of them just like to lay up with their lady, like to settle down. The young guys are just trying to keep what they been fighting about for quite a while.

V: How much do you understand about the criminal law? Let me ask you this question: when you are under sixteen, do you know that you can not be sent away to an adult prison? Do you know that?

P: Yeah.

V: But you know that *now* you can, right? In other words, if you are caught after the age of sixteen . . .

P: Seventeen!

V: Sixteen!

P: I don't know. I guess that would be what they call your first offense . . . so you wouldn't go in?

V: You wouldn't go in?

P: I am *asking*; you wouldn't go in?

V: Sure you would. If you are past the age of sixteen even by one day, you're the same as an adult, and if you were to commit an act of serious violence, you could certainly be incarcerated. Does that surprise you?

P: Yeah. At that point, you're an adult?

V: Yes.

P: So . . . you'll go in mostly with anything anyway. They'll put you some-where . . . a reform school and being in jail is practically the same thing.

V: You think you could do time as an adult, right?

P: Yeah. If it's worth it.

V: What would make it worth it? Give me some examples of what would make it worth it.

P: Hurting somebody who's hurting me or my people or done something that we disagree with completely. I would go out and . . .

V: How about someone who hasn't done anything to you?

P: To me personally?

V: To you or your people. A rape of somebody that you never saw before . . . is that worth it?

P: I won't think about it. If I have to, I wouldn't think about it. I'd just do it.

V: What would be the circumstances that would make you do it? What kind of situation would you have to be in?

P: Not a deep one. I can hurt you for any reason, if I dislike you for the reason, I'll do it. If it's small and I dislike it, I'll hurt you.

V: Do other people have the same attitude towards you? In other words, do people just hurt you . . .

P: They've done it. I've walked the street and just because I walked on the wrong side of the street or because I wore my jacket a different way I've gotten hurt. Actually hurt. And I feel they've done it to me, I've learned, through the people I am with, if you are going to live and survive out here, best do it that way.

V: Hurt people before they hurt you?

P: If you got the chance, yeah.

V: Do you figure just about anybody would hurt you if they got the chance?

P: That's right.

V: The police would hurt you?

P: Police would hurt me.

V: Regular citizens would hurt you?

P: They've done it.

V: What would you do if you got arrested tomorrow for something serious like a robbery or a rape?

P: What would I do? I wouldn't do nothing.

V: You'd just go along with whatever happens?

P: That's right. Try to keep it away from these people as much as possible.

V: How are decisions made inside the Blood Devils? How do people decide on what happens?

P: We have on the table six people, and we are the ones who sit and talk.

V: You are one of the six, right?

P: Right. And we'll try to bring it down to the easiest thing of talking but if like a President and a Vice President says "No" and four of us says "Yes," we have to vote it again for the simple reason that they are up there. And we respect them.

V: Are you going to be up there?

P: If they need me and I got the chance, yes.

V: Do you expect that to happen?

P: It will happen.

V: What's the difference between your gang and the Savage Skulls?

P: They'll do things we probably wouldn't think of doing . . . like going out and blowing clubs for one person.

V: Blowing up the whole club because of something one person did?

P: Because of one person, right. And we disagree with that completely. Letting youngsters go out for us is out. I wouldn't let nobody thirteen or ten years old go out and hurt somebody for me and then just stand there. I would do it myself.

V: But the Skulls will do that?

P: Yeah, to keep as tight as they are, that's the only way they would be able to do it. Sending the youngest out and getting probably caught or hurt and still have a chance to be together, than if they sent somebody who is seventeen, eighteen years old. He gets caught and his chances of coming back is not very good.

V: Are there ever any major disagreements among members of the same organization? What happens if two guys in the Devils disagree heavily on something?

P: Well, they would have to settle it one or another way. If they disagree with it, depending on what it is . . .

V: Say an argument over a girl. How is that settled?

P: That's stupid.

V: So that doesn't happen?

P: It happens. It has happened. And they've gone out and beat each other's brains out, and after that they'll pay a lot of punishment. We'll pay them a lot of punishment. I mean I can hurt someone for doing something stupid, I don't care how close he is to me.

V: Do you have brothers and sisters?

P: I have a younger brother, and two older brothers.

V: What do your older brothers do?

P: I don't know; I never bothered getting into their life.

V: What about your younger brother?

P: He tries to follow steps.

V: Your steps?

P: Yeah.

V: You expect him to be in the Devils?

P: Yeah. If he keeps on following me, he will get there. And if he has a reason to be there, he'll be there.

V: What do you see yourself doing two years from now?

P: I don't look in the future.

V: Six months?

P: Well, six months from now, it will probably be summertime and we'll probably have a bigger organization than we have now.

V: You expect to recruit more people during the summer?

P: Most of the summers we usually do. Guys that feel that they can do things, they just don't know where to do it and how to show they can do it, and we'll take a crack at it. We'll see. But it will be a while before we can say he's in with us completely. And we've bumped into guys that we've taken cause they're big and they're strong and they've turned us down.

V: Is it O.K. for them to turn you down?

P: It's not for me. If they turn me down, something behind it. There's something behind everything.

V: So what do you think is behind that?

P: Guilt. I mean he turns me down when I feel I need him. If I can help it he won't be able to turn nobody else down.

V: What about people who simply don't want to be in the Devils but live in your territory? Is that permitted? Do you let people be neutral?

P: We don't have too many of those. Old people only. Most of the youngsters that live in my neighborhood are all in this. This is about the only way we can protect what's ours.

V: What is yours?

P: We have a territory [of about twelve square blocks] but we've managed to get around with other clubs near us. We got into them for them to feel we're brotherhood with them. And we'll be there if they need us, but we don't depend on them. If we know there's something going to go down hard, I wouldn't depend on the boys down the street because I know they feel if they are going down to somebody else's territory and they don't belong there, they won't go. I don't feel that way. If you need me, wherever it is, I'll be there if I can. I'll make it.

V: Is your organization almost exclusively Hispanic . . . are there mostly Latin men in your organization . . . do you have alliances with all-black clubs?

P: There was a couple of them. I mean down on the East River Drive. There's a couple of them. But they all break off by themselves. They will do two or three things at most and then they'll break off by themselves. They won't be able to handle it or . . .

V: They'll stop short at certain things?

P: Yeah. So we just don't bother with them. They don't exist anymore.

V: What would you call the most notorious club in the City right now?

P: There's a couple of them. The Bronx has got them all. I'm going to get a chance to move up there myself.

V: You want to move to the Bronx?

P: Yeah. I'm staying . . . my mother threw me out of the house and I'm staying with my grandmother in the Bronx, and I don't communicate with the people out there because I know what they do and I know how they act. But I feel the way I got into the Blood Devils I'll get into anybody else's gang. It will take a lot more but I'll be able to handle it.

V: How do you support yourself? Do you work?

P: No.

V: Do you go to school?

P: No. I don't bother. I mean they don't get me nowhere. They don't get nobody out here nowhere.

V: So how do you support yourself?

P: I support myself by the people out in the streets.

V: Steal?

P: I steal. I rob. I mug. I manage to get around.

V: And you will continue to do so . . .

P: For as long as it takes.

V: Is there any kind of job that anyone could offer you that would motivate you to want to quit what you're doing now?

P: No.

V: No kind of job at all?

P: No.

V: Two hundred dollars a week?

P: No. It's going to take me away from the thing I grew up with. The thing I feel. It's probably going to put me into a different person. I don't want that. I'll probably get hurt out here. The way I am now, I'm secure, I'm protected, I know there can't nothing happen to me. I mean I will probably get locked up but once I come out with the faith my people got towards me and the respect that we all got I can always turn around and say "Well, here I am. I'm back." And they're going to treat me the way they were treating me when I left them. They'll still be there. Everyone who's out there protecting what they want and what they feel belongs to them, they're going to keep it and they're going to try to keep it for as long as they can.

V: Do you think this situation with the fighting clubs is going to continue in the City?

P: Yes.

V: We used to have a whole lot of it . . . remember in the fifties, I guess you heard about it, it used to be the whole thing, right? And then it seemed to disappear . . .

P: It didn't disappear. It's just that we have it now in a completely different form. We've changed. We're not out there, like in the fifties, they had a lot of brothers with leather jackets and motorcycles and that was their transportation; that was their everything. They wouldn't do nothing unless they were on their motorcycles and so on. Everything has changed. If you want to do something and deeply inside you want to do it; you're going to do it. You cross the river and won't wet your pants; you'll do it. You'll get there.

V: What is your ambition? Eventually you'll be President of the Devils, or maybe join one of the Bronx clubs, right? What about after that? Do you have any ambitions about consolidating different clubs?

P: You can't. Too many people out here don't agree on what we people really feel. As long as they disagree with it, we won't be as together as we want.

V: What are the basic disagreements? What do people mostly disagree on?

P: Your attitudes, the way you do things. They disagree with the way you rip off somebody. They disagree with the way you rape somebody. They want to do it this other way. They want to get rid of it completely. That's out.

V: You're drawing the line at homicide; is that what you're saying?

P: No. I would kill if it's necessary. I mean I'm going to do something and I'm doing it for my pleasure and for what we know I'm going to rape somebody. And if I rape her and it turns out in the situation that I got to get rid of her, I'm going to do it. But I'm not going to do it because I finished doing what I wanted to do. Dump her in the river cause I finished laying her and she was no good. Hell with her. Dump her. No. You rape her. I'll rape her. I'll let her go if she be still. It won't bother me. She'll recognize me as much times as she wants. But I know a girl won't put me for rape.

V: She wouldn't testify against you?

P: No.

V: Why?

P: She wouldn't. If she would she'd be a fool. If it really came down to it and she had to testify she'd be a fool. She'll be losing maybe two lives. Keeping it the way it is, I'll hurt her once in a while, because it's in me, and they'll probably tease her and scare her, but she won't lose her life just like that.

V: You're not just talking about a girl from the neighborhood . . .

P: Any girl. No. I mean I'm going to do something with the protection of the Blood Devils. Now, if I rape her, she knows it's not no city kid who feels like raping her. It's somebody . . . they look at us like evil, nasty, dirty. Hell, I really don't care. But if I rape, and I just rape you, and you catch me and you recognize me in the paper and you say "Well, that's him," everybody knows you pointed me out. If I get in trouble, I mean if I do go in, and they know I don't want to be in there, they're going to do something about it. I have that confidence. They are going to do something about it.

V: Has this happened in your experience?

P: Yes. We've hurt a couple of people.

V: Are there any people whom you would respect and leave alone who are not members?

P: My mother and father. That's it. Well, Turk here [indicating another person in the room]. He's not in with us. I mean he's got his own head, and he understands us and he met a couple of guys that so far they find him cool. They . . . and I like him; he's alright. But I wouldn't hold myself from doing something against him if he hurts me, or hurts any of us.

V: What if you don't know him; if you have no contact with him at all?

P: You mean I'm going to hurt somebody and he's in the way?

V: No, no. He's just not involved. Let me give you an example. O.K.? We met today. You and me, right? Now you see me on the street tomorrow; are you going to attack me?

P: No.

V: Why not?

P: I'm not like that. I'm not going to attack just for attacking you. I just like you. But I'm talking here and I know what's the reason and I'm not going to go outside tomorrow and lay for you and say "well this man is this and he's that and I don't dig him." I won't get rid of you. You ain't going to hurt me. I know. I was told by Brother Turk. You ain't going to hurt me.

V: So you respect his word?

P: Yes. Now if you were to come up to me and say "Pirate, you going to rap on this and this, but watch what you say" and put me in the position that I got to be checking myself out a lot because of someone, I don't give a fuck who he is, if you push me far enough, I'll probably hurt you.

V: Everybody's like that, aren't they? I mean that's just not you. I'm the same way; everybody's the same way. Everyone has a limit, right?

P: Yes. But you have your limit like "I don't like him and if he fucks with me I'm going to hurt him; I don't like you; if you fuck with me, I'm going to hurt you" but you'll probably go up to the person and talk with him and bring up a conversation. I'll see you in the street and you can call me and I'll see you but I won't stop in the street and talk to you.

V: What are your requirements for someone to be friends with you? Let's say that I wanted to be your friend. What is it I would do?

P: I would keep you around me for pretty long to see what type of person you really are.

V: So only people that would hang out with you every day?

P: Every day.

V: And you don't have friends outside of that?

P: No friends. I know people outside of that. And the people I'm with every day is like a dollar in my pocket everyday, and that's your friend. Somebody you go outside and you meet and you know him because you read his name and he probably asked you . . . he's not your friend. He's just a two-way mirror. You're looking at him and there's somebody in there looking at you that doesn't like you and just don't know how to come out.

V: You believe most people don't like you?

P: Most people don't like me.

V: Why?

P: I been trained, and I look at somebody and he'll look at me and I can sense it. I can actually hear him say to himself "I don't like this guy" and it don't bother me. I know he's thinking that. It's just that I guess I would prefer it more if you would just kind of come out with it. If you didn't like me you would give me the same looks I gave you and you would react to me the way I reacted to you. If you're going to insist on me knowing that you don't like me and you're going to try and be sweet to me, I know you're going to be playing something else, and I'm going to find out what it is.

V: But you think the average person has some kind of game, some kind of reason for doing what he does, right? And this is what you've seen and observed with your own eyes, right? It's not just a feeling . . .

P: A lot of guys do things because mostly they feel one way and they do things another way. I mean my mother threw me out. That is something that I never thought she would actually do. But she threw me out. She disagreed with what I am. That's what I learned. I've been out here and that's what I learned. How to be what I am now.

V: Did you learn anything about being the way you are now while you were in those training schools?

P: Even if you got busted stealing your first pocketbook, and they put you in there, by the time you come out, I don't care if it's two weeks, three weeks or what, you're going to feel that you belong to some kind of organization, and it's going to be completely different. You are going to want to experience it and really kind of . . . I mean, I was in there, and the time I was in there, I heard guys saying "I do that and I do this" and I never got out to there. And yet they felt so big and I wanted to get there. I came out and I came out with the will power of doing whatever I wanted to do. If I needed money and I couldn't get it in no other way but to snatch it off somebody or hustle for it, I'll do it. To satisfy myself, I would do it, cause that's what I learned in there . . . satisfy yourself first and the people you really think about and you'll probably be somewhere. And you'll be together. I have had rice, beans, bread, water. Everyday I am out here in the streets, most of it I get from friends of mine, girls that are in the neighborhood, and we manage to tease them or order them to get us a plate of food. And them knowing us, they'll do it. Not because they are scared of us but they know the situation we're in. They wouldn't turn us down. No, because they know they will help. "You're a devil! Why should I feed you?" It's not like that. "You're a devil and I'm going to feed you, but it's not because I like you or anything like that. I am going to feed you because we are together. I know you would do the same thing for me." I mean somebody comes up to me and says "Pirate, I am going to need this for this and I can't do it on my own"; I'll do it with him. I'm going to do it with him. I'll go as far as I can with him, as long as he's pleased and as long as he knows that whatever he needs he's got somebody to come up to. I'll hear "you ain't got nobody to come up to." People be going to school most of their lives, and they come out here to earn a couple of dollars for themselves, and they don't get a damned thing. I'm better off than they are. I go out here and I want to buy me a pair of pants, or I want to do something, I'll rip off anything I want to rip off. Grocery store, snatch pocketbooks, wallets. Open it up and have a couple of dollars in there, and I'll get what I want. Most people out here, they hustle all day . . . all day, everyday of the week, and they don't come home with a damn thing, and they don't know what to say. I know what to say if I ain't got the money. I just say "try harder, man" but I'll get it and I usually do. I came here because Turk told me what was going on and what was involved here. I figured, you know, it's easier than hanging out in the street and checking somebody coming out of a bank. I mean, I could stand out there and look at somebody coming out of the bank, and without seeing what he got, I'll rip him off.

V: Have you learned to be able to tell which people are coming out there with money and which aren't?

P: Definitely.

V: Sometimes people go to put money in, right?

P: You learn. You see that. You can be a person that I want fifty dollars. That's a person you rip off for fifty dollars. Hell, you'll never get nowhere. I have observed banks, I have seen old people, young people, rich people, put money, take money out of the bank, and I've even named them. I've given their names and told them, actually saying that money is nice. And I'll get it some way. I need fifty dollars and I know I can rip off this apartment over there then I'm going to do it, and get fifty dollars for whatever it is, stereo, TV anything. As long as I'm pleased, as long as I got something I can give to somebody, to please somebody that's real close to me, that's all we really need . . . to pile up the little grains of rice and pack them together. And that's us right there.

V: When you're going to take somebody off, do you try and make a judgment as to how hard it's going to be? Do you try and pick easier targets?

P: You don't. You can't think at things like that. No. You just . . . you want to rip somebody off and somebody's coming, all right . . . that's your victim. If you let it pass and you rip the second person off, he probably won't have nothing and the person in front of him already seen this. So just the first chance you get you do it. And do it the way it comes down. If I grab you to your throat, and you're going to kneel on the floor, then you're giving me a better chance. Because all I got to do is keep you there. Now if you're one of them people that like to move your arms a lot, while you're moving your arms and hurting me in my face with that, I'm going to get your money. But I'm going to hurt you for hurting me.

V: What happens if the person just surrenders? Just says "take my money?"

P: I take it.

V: And that's it?

P: That's it. And I go. But if he tries something I'll hurt him. I have something in seeing blood. I guess that's why they call me Pirate. I like blood. I won't cut you after you give me your money, quietly. Sooner or later you're going to have to go and say "I seen him." But if you try and get smart with me and after you gave me your money and I turn around and run, and you're going to come over here and chase me, or try to grab me while . . . you're putting your own life in danger. That's the way I look at it.

V: How do you feel about people committing crimes against you personally?

P: That's just the way they are.

V: You don't have any hostility towards them?

P: I mean I walk and somebody rips me off; he's going to rip me off. I'm going to try and not get ripped off, but the guy will probably rip me off. I'm not going to just sit down and stand for it. He ripped me off.

V: You'd just go with it?

P: Yeah. If I can get my hands on him, I'll do it. If I know what's happening, I'll get to it. But if I know I can't get to it and we've decided that there's no way you can get to that person, well, hell, it happened, man, and it's over. I don't mean that if you see him again you can't do it to him or you can't remember. I've remembered a lot of guys who've hurt me. Just for the hell of it. See me walking down the street and kick me, man, stomp on me. I haven't been able to do anything. We've talked about it. I've described the person, exactly who he is, and we've gone all the way down about how it come out. You can't touch him. And you're furious! "Why can't I touch him?" He grabbed me. You can't touch him. And the reason comes out. You just don't touch him.

V: What could be some of the reasons that you can't touch him?

P: He's somebody else in another brother gang. A brotherhood gang; he belongs to somebody in that gang. I won't be able to go up to him and stab him for taking my money, because you're hurting one of your own, and they might know that too, but they might just feel "I don't care." That's what we ain't got in common. And that's why we can't really get together. I mean, if we could just say "He's my brother, but he ripped me off," I could sit down with you and tell you "Let's talk about it; why did you rip me off?" He come up to me and tell me "I know you had this and, all right . . . but if you're going to come and say I ripped you off and you're not allowed to rip me off. . . ." That's out. We are real basic with the things that we do. We do them, but we don't do them in stupidity ways. We won't try to hurt; you don't try to hurt yourself when you do things, or the person you're doing it . . . just do it and be satisfied. And that's all.

V: You're talking about justice now, right? How do you think things should be done? Let say somebody breaks in my house, rapes my wife . . . what should I do?

P: You seen "Death Wish?"

V: Yes.

P: You would go out and look for that person. Protect yourself as best as you can. Now you'll find him and you'll get him. If you're going to hide away from everybody else and you're going to let nobody find out exactly what happened, you might as well just say "Here I am; take me now," because they're going to take you. There's going to be somebody that's going to see you and he's going to remember you shot this guy because he raped your wife and so far you've been hiding. He's going to bang you. He's going to get rid of you good. And he's going to feel happy and he's going to try everything he can so that his people could feel happy you're rid of. You're gone too. Now if you come out and find the person and you hurt them, and you actually go through meeting somebody and actually saying "Look, I hurt this person because he hurt my wife, and I know where he was and I know who he is and I just disliked him" and you actually come down . . . a lot of people are scared of doing things like this. They are afraid they are at the end . . . after somebody tells them they can go, they'll be stabbed in the back. But that's not true . . .

V: You say that everybody out there will hurt you?

P: Somehow. If they get the chance.

V: There's different ways that people can hurt you. I mean, there's ways besides violence that they can hurt you.

P: Definitely. I mean you got people who are in a back table sitting down, white collar, black suit, and that bastard's going to hurt you. When you face him, no matter how sweet you look, no matter how innocent you look, he's going to hurt you somehow and that hurt is taking you away from what you really want . . .

V: What about the people who are in business to protect you?

P: Who are there to protect us besides our own people?

V: What about if you get arrested? Wouldn't a lawyer protect you?

P: I don't know. I haven't gone that far. I wouldn't trust a lawyer. I can't trust anybody. I just got to trust the people I live with. Like the people I actually see going through it everyday and they are accepting it. I mean they are actually surviving out there. I started thinking about things like that ten years old, eleven years old. I realized you can't trust nobody out there. I used to be walking around, cut out of school, didn't have nothing to eat for breakfast. Walk inside a restaurant and just walk around the table and see a dollar seventy-five lying there and that's yours. Take it gladly and walk out. You got a dollar seventy-five. Two hours later you got a cop busting you and grabbing you and he actually requesting that you try and get away from him . . . and they still hurting you by being there asking you so many questions "why I ain't got school today?" and still they hurting you, knowing they going to put you somewhere, everybody's going to find out what you did that day. Your mother find out, your father find out, your teachers will know you got locked up. Why? Because the son of a bitch didn't want to let you beat it, didn't want to let you walk the streets and actually mind your own business and just let him pass by. No, you're a youngster and you belong in school and the law says you belong in school, and the law's wrong. They don't care what the law says; if you don't want to go to school, you don't go to school. I didn't go to school. I didn't like school.

V: Do you read?

P: Magazines, comic books, yeah. Those are the things I spend time with.

V: Do you teach the younger ones; you do any kind of teaching?

P: Yeah. Open up a switchblade fast enough. Run. Zig-Zag. Dodge. Rip off pocketbooks. Quick. That's about all I can . . . that's all the skill I got to teach that I know of. I mean I can't actually sit down and tell somebody "let's do this and let's do that and this is the way you do it." You tell me to teach them how to open up a blade, and I'll teach them how to open up a blade. I'm going to teach them to use it the correct way. And probably at the time I'm doing it, he'll probably feel like he's going to become somebody, like I felt I was going to become somebody in there [the state training school]. I felt I was going to become Pirate, the fastest blade. The fastest dude with a blade. And even now, I feel I'm the fastest dude with a blade.

V: When did you first start to feel that, while you were inside?

P: Yeah. Right in there. When you actually be using it more and trying to find something that's as good as a knife or scissors. Cut a pair of scissors in half, split them in half. Just have something you can actually pull out and show them there. You're not going to let them step all over you just cause you smaller, just cause you Spanish or whatever.

V: If someone says to you "I like you; I respect you," you don't trust that, right?

P: I don't buy that. No. You actually got to show me. And I'm not going to tell you show me you like me. You got to show me your way and if I like your way and I feel that you're a person with a good reason and understand somebody else's thing, so time will pass then I will . . . but I can't say you come up to me and say you're a nice guy, Pirate. That's out, you don't understand me at all. But what has to be done, I'll tell them to do it. I can't see myself being a War Counsellor and just cause I need those papers picked up I'm going to pick up the papers. Just go over there and straighten out them books. I don't go for none of that. I mean, I'm going to look at you. You're a person who likes to play around with guns; you know a lot about guns. You could fire an M-16 or a rifle pretty good. So every time I get my hands on a weapon I'm going to make sure you get that. Because that's what you know. Me, I know how to play around with a blade, get in and out with a blade. I've learned things from old people in the streets that've gone half their lives doing what I'm doing now. And they still doing it but in other ways and I just pick things up from them. And they let me know a lot. They know everything I want to know. I don't have to sit down in no room with a blackboard, or to listen to nobody else, or do what they tell me to do. I just do what I feel I want to do and just learn how to do it.

V: Is there anything you want to say before we close this up?

P: No. Just that the Blood Devils are where I belong and it's going to take a lot more than people out here in the streets to convince me that there's something else inside the apple they call New York City.

1

The Life-Style Violent Juvenile: An Overview of Treatment

Overview

Although today's media coverage of violent juvenile crime has never been more intense, the problem of the violent juvenile offender is by no means a recent phenomenon.

> Juvenile delinquents appear . . . to be increasing in numbers; certainly their crimes have increased in violence and [literally] drip horror.[1]

Variations of this quotation have appeared frequently in recent months. Both print and electronic media have increased their coverage of juvenile crime to the point that public perception has been heavily influenced. The average citizen would hardly react with surprise to any new mention of a "juvenile crime wave," and many informal surveys[2] have revealed that fear of juvenile criminals is a major factor in the perceived decrease in the quality of urban life.[3]

But those who believe that this really represents a *new* wave of juvenile violence and who, as a result, forcefully advocate a return to the "good old days" of juvenile justice would be well-advised to read the footnote accompanying the above quote—the *Time* magazine article was written in 1954![4]

The history of American juvenile justice is not linear, as the media might have us believe, but circular. The juvenile criminal has not changed, only our society's response to him. The purpose of this work is not to trace the history of the juvenile justice system in America. It is sufficient, for our purposes, to briefly recount some of the major stages in its development:

1. Juvenile criminals are not differentiated from their adult counterparts: the "crime equals time" mentality.

2. The common law "rule of sevens" is applied,[5] wherein a child below the age of seven was conclusively presumed to be incapable of criminal intent or behavior; a child up to the age of fourteen was presumed capable, but such presumption was rebuttable by evidence; and a child past the age of fourteen was presumed to be an adult for purposes of criminal justice treatment.

3. Around the turn of the century, reformers agreed that the then-prevalent practice of mixing young offenders with hardened criminals was vicious, dangerous, and degrading to both its juvenile victims and the society which endorsed it.[6] Those children who somehow managed to survive adult incarcer-

1

ation became, of necessity, as hardened and as dangerous as their fellow prisoners.

4. The Juvenile Court Act of 1899 (Illinois) established a separate system of "treatment" for juvenile offenders; the emphasis was to be on the so-called "rehabilitative" aspects of intervention rather than on retributive punishment.

5. Gradually, the juvenile justice system grew to be a separate and distinct entity, complete with specialized courts, specialized "services," and specialized institutions. The Juvenile Court Act was widely adopted in other jurisdictions, and the mad rush to differentiate juveniles from adults was expressed in an entire new vocabulary: defendants became "respondents"; a verdict of guilty became "a finding of delinquency," and so forth.

6. Although there remained a rough correlation between type of offense and dispositional response, children tended to be institutionalized for activities ranging from truancy to homicide in the same "training schools."

7. Following World War II, "juvenile crime waves" were a frequent target of media attention. The gang wars of the 1950s (notably in New York City) and the 1960s (notably in Chicago) were widely reported and there was a strong public outcry for "get tough" measures from the courts, the police, and the legislature.

8. By the middle of the 1960s, institutionalization was still commonplace, and virtually every jurisdiction had a network of "training schools" for young offenders.

9. But juvenile crime continued to (apparently) increase, and a new breed of reformer began to insist that the juvenile prison, as a "cure," was far worse than the disease. Knowledgeable observers were quick to point out that the over-whelming majority of America's life-style criminals[7] had served a prior appren-ticeship in juvenile institutions.[8]

10. Such juvenile prisons came to be (rightfully) characterized as "crime factories" and "sodomy schools," and the demand for their reformation or abolition spread.

11. Once the juvenile institution itself came to be thought of as inherently criminogenic, the demands for reform crystalized around the phenomenon known as "de-institutionalization."

12. Originally aimed at so-called "status offenders" (such as truants, runaways, and "stubborn children"), the concept eventually expanded to embrace *all* juveniles.

13. The resulting emphasis on "community-based corrections," (together with the vastly increased availability of federal funds for such purposes), required the system to discover alternatives to institutionalization. Among those were group homes, foster homes, halfway houses, advanced probation services, diversion programs, and a great variety of other, non-incarcerative, options.

14. And today, in the midst of de-institutionalization efforts, the circum-stances outlined in no. 7 have again produced a market for "get tough" measures

so that the cutting edge of "new" juvenile strategies is now expressed in legislative efforts to *increase* incarcerative possibilities for juvenile offenders.[9]

The public (and perhaps the juvenile justice profession) quickly, and conveniently, forgets that juvenile crime has been a virtual constant in the fabric of American life for at least the last century.

This book must be viewed as a working proposal for change (complete with professional and technical recommendations for implementation of such change), and not as a legal brief which requires proof beyond a reasonable doubt of each assertion upon which the central premises rest. For example, it is necessary to admit the existence of certain "givens" to conserve time and space and to proceed directly to those proposals that will be viewed as more controversial. To those criminal justice professionals who want to "look at the numbers" before agreeing to any of the basic premises which we use as a departure point for our proposals for change, we would ask only that this work be evaluated in terms of the solutions it offers, not the problems it describes.

Therefore, we take it as a given that the problem of violent juvenile crime is a major source of public concern, and that constructive criticism of the juvenile justice system must be based on political as well as professional considerations. The latter theme is the thread that runs throughout our work: no solution is practical if it cannot be implemented and our goal is not to define utopia but to shed some light on a future that does not necessitate a trip back through a most unproductive past.

The Life-Style Violent Juvenile

Life-style violent juveniles have an effect on the juvenile justice system, and on society in general, greatly disproportionate to their actual numbers. Everything the juvenile justice system has come to hold sacred regarding the uniqueness of juveniles and the necessity of formulating specialized treatment alternatives for them is threatened by the actions of a tiny minority—the life-style violent juvenile offender.[10] This tiny minority (and society's response to it), has so colored public opinion as to cause it to lapse into a state of irrationality. Utterly without advocates because their crimes take them out of the realm of sympathy for children,[11] such juveniles are an embarrassment to a system founded on essentially humanitarian principles. In fact, many of the fervent advocates of juvenile justice reform have based their positions on a negative view of the "treatability" of offenders such as "Pirate," the youth whose interview introduced this book. For example, those advocating the separation of status offenders from delinquent (criminal) offenders are quick to point out the very real dangers to status offenders, both physical and psychological, which come from an enforced association with hardened criminal types.

When we speak of the life-style violent juvenile, we are not referring to a murky, ambiguous classification. The juvenile whose criminological, social, and economic life-style is marked by chronicity of (often escalating) violence tends to precipitate out of any known system of measurement. Perhaps the most frequently cited study in this area is Professor Marvin E. Wolfgang's Philadelphia Cohort Analysis.[12] Here, ten thousand juveniles were tracked to age eighteen in an effort to determine actual accountability for juvenile crime in a single community. The findings included this startling fact: those juveniles committing five or more offenses represented only 6 percent of the entire population surveyed, yet this *same* 6 percent accounted for approximately 66 percent (!) of all violent crimes attributed to this group.

The chronic, violent offender continues his disproportionate impact on society and the criminal justice system as he ages. The Prosecutor's Management Information System (PROMIS) research project[13] bluntly states:

> [A] small number of individuals represent a significant portion of the prosecutor's and court's workload not to mention the disproportionate impact those recidivists have on citizens who are the victims of crime.[14]

The same report cites Professor James Q. Wilson's analysis of priorities in criminal justice:

> Most serious crime is committed by repeaters. What we do with first offenders is probably far less important than what we do with habitual offenders.[15]

Not only does the life-style violent juvenile impact disproportionately on the criminal justice system, but the high degree of visibility attached to his criminal behavior by the media also impacts disproportionately on public perception, political response, and results in changes in our methods of responding to the crisis he represents.

When we speak of chronicity of violence, we must look to life-style, not to a single espisode. Throughout this work, we will be referring to the "life-style violent juvenile." This juvenile is a youth whose life is characterized by chronicity of violence, not a youth who had a single violent episode in an otherwise relatively nonviolent existence. Violence *as a life-style* is what concerns us. We would not require adjudication of an individual's life-style as a prerequisite to commitment to the proposed Secure Treatment Unit.[16] But we do wish to focus exclusively on those juveniles to whom violence is a primary means of self-expression, not those juveniles who commit any single act defined as "violent" by the legislature. This is not to say that those individual juveniles who do commit single episodic acts of violence are not fit candidates for specialized treatment. However, the purpose of the proposed Secure Treatment Unit (STU) and the purpose of the planning expressed in this work is to seriously intervene in a chronic, escalating pattern of life-style violent behavior which has implications for the future as well as for the present.

The life-style violent juvenile is characterized by a distortion of societal values, a commitment to immediate gratification, and a (reinforced) alienation from societal structures and institutions. Our target population will probably have been previously institutionalized, will almost certainly have come to the repeated attention of the juvenile authorities,[17] and most likely will have functionally (if not actually) left school some years prior to the adjudication. And, regardless of his personal family constellation, he will most likely relate to a gang of similarly inclined youth as the major reference point in his life. To the urban juvenile gang member, traditional concepts are redefined by the peer group so that they surface in aberrant ways. To such a juvenile, gang rape is not antisocial, mugging is not wrong, and tomorrow is dimly (if at all) perceived.[18] Life is controlled by anonymous institutions and agencies, including landlords, the welfare department, the police force, and the judicial system. Life is a lottery, and gratification delayed is probably gratification denied. Role models are armed robbers, pimps, narcotics dealers, and extortionists, and emulation of such models begins as fantasy, proceeds to peer-level imitation, and finally ends as active participation.

When the juvenile justice system *does* intervene in this chain of inevitability, it tends only to reinforce the validity of this youth's models and he is bombarded with similar, noncompeting messages throughout his juvenile years. If a child is incarcerated because he stabbed another child, and finds himself in an institution in which skill with a knife is the only way to avoid sexual exploitation by those larger and stronger than he is,[19] what is reinforced is *not* the unacceptability of using a knife to enforce one's will on others, but the unacceptability of leaving survivors to complain to the authorities.

The life-style violent juvenile is educated to the use of exploitation to gratify his peer-directed desires. The juvenile who embraces life-style violence perceives few options in his word; he will either exploit or be exploited, and the way to avoid the latter is to amass sufficient skills in the former. An individual who is not habitually exploited is visible only to the extent that he can advertise his strength. There is a corresponding emphasis on such advertising symbols as clothes, jewelry, cars.[20] Life to such a juvenile is a mystery: he sees no causal relationship between (his) acts and consequences. In his world, everybody commits crimes: some get caught, even fewer are punished. The punishment itself is so remote in time and possibility as to almost entirely dilute any effectiveness it might have.

"Dangerousness" cannot be the sole criterion for inclusion in the "life-style violent juvenile" population. Not only is this quality difficult to properly diagnose,[21] *dangerousness can also be learned, and there is ample evidence that the most fertile ground for the growth of this personality characteristic may be found within juvenile institutions.* That any institutional population contains both the exploited and the exploiters is an accepted fact,[22] and the thrust of many liberal arguments is that certain classes of juveniles should not even be *exposed* to such a system. Although there is now (or should be) virtually universal agreement that status offenders should not be housed with criminal offenders, restricting potential intake to juvenile "criminals" will not result in the isolation of dangerous offenders from those not dangerous.

Even if categories such as "dangerous" and "not dangerous" are initially viable, segregation according to such labels will not directly attack the exploiter-exploited hierarchy prevalent in all closed settings. There are two basic reasons for this statement:

1. "Dangerousness" (particularly *institutional* dangerousness) cannot be directly predicted from the criminal activities which originally brought the offender into contact with the juvenile justice system; and
2. Even if such a prediction *were* possible, dangerousness in an institutional setting is an *evolving* characteristic which is often a form of adaptive behavior rather than an expression of a personality trait.

Prediction of human behavior is a woefully inexact science even when the analyst has all the facts. And when such facts are unavailable, the word *prediction* is not justifiably used since the "analysis" is nothing more than random guesswork, colored by an individual's own prejudices and misconceptions.

A criminal defense attorney related the following incident which illustrates this point. A nineteen-year-old defendant[23] was charged with harassment[24] and attempted simple assault[25] because he hurled a half-full bottle of soda at a young woman riding past him on a bicycle. The attack was apparently unprovoked, and the attorney interviewed the defendant to ascertain if the young man's action might have had some justifiable (or even rational) basis.[26] In response to questioning, the youth replied:

> Sure I did it. That bitch was secretly laughing at me . . . they *all* laugh at me behind my back! Women are always doing that to me . . . I should have broken her goddamned head for making fun of me . . . One day they're all going to see it don't pay to laugh at me like they do . . .[27]

Would any rational person conclude that this youth was "not dangerous"? Yet the acts with which he was charged appear common on their surface, and to be the most minor in nature, certainly not warranting incarceration or even "treatment" of any kind.[28] Our society generally has concluded that an individual is not dangerous until he has actually committed a dangerous act, and we must endorse this conclusion since the consequences of prediction as a criterion for incarcerative treatment are too frightening to contemplate.

Yet there is another side to the coin of prediction that must also concern us. A young man was living in his home with his mother and two younger sisters. His father was deceased and his brother was working in another state. The young man was seemingly well-adjusted, up with his class in school, and had a noncriminal circle of friends and associates. His older brother suddenly returned to the home and assumed a strongly authoritative role in the household. His disciplining of the young man was frequent, physical, and harsh. The young man ran away from his home and quickly became involved with a roving street gang of slightly older youths, all of whom had previously served time in juvenile institutions. After two weeks of living with this group in an abandoned building, the young man returned home to visit his mother and found his older brother had departed as suddenly as he had appeared, allegedly to work in another state. The youth was welcomed home by his mother and sisters and quickly settled into his former routine. His mother had notified the school authorities that the young man had been "visiting relatives" out of state so he was not suspended for his lengthy absence.

Soon, however, he was visited by the gang with whom he had lived for the past weeks. He was told that he owed them his share of the food they had consumed while living together. When he replied that he had no money, he was pressured to come with them, saying that they had a "job" to do and his share of the proceeds would extinguish his "debt" to them. When the young man initially refused, the other youths told him they would get the money "one way or another," and his resistance was overcome.[29]

The "job" turned out to be a purse snatching. The gang drove up to a deserted bus stop and noticed an elderly woman waiting with a shopping bag and a pocketbook. The young man was told that his role was to run up to her and grab the shopping bag and to continue running around the corner where the others would be waiting in the car. Again he protested, and he was told that they needed the money, and if they could not get it the proposed way, they would have to take whatever they could find in his mother's house.

The young man did as he was told, and successfully snatched the shopping bag. As he was running down the street, the gang attacked the women in an attempt to steal her pocketbook, which she was by then tightly clutching. The altercation resulted in the woman being violently thrown to the ground, where she struck her head on the curbstone. She died in the hospital the next day, and arrests soon followed. The young man was charged with homicide as the "perpetrator" of the attack, while the others, far more sophisticated in dealing with the criminal justice system, pleaded guilty to attempted unarmed robbery.

The young man was adjudicated a murderer,[30] and placed in a secure facility after one year of "close detention"[31] awaiting the placement. Although decidedly *not* dangerous when first arrested, he clearly required treatment because of his deep-seated feelings of remorse and guilt. When those feelings were not only ignored but actually scorned in his new environment, the young man displayed sufficient adaptability so that, by the time he was placed in "secure treatment," he was a full-fledged thug with the affect and attitude of a life-style violent delinquent.

Had a genuine analysis been completed and its recommendations implemented, the young man would not have been considered dangerous to society. But a cursory reading of his criminal justice "contacts"[32] might well have reached the opposite conclusion. A system which labeled purely on a legal definition of physical acts then proceeded to suffer the effects of its own labeling.

This young man was ill-equipped to survive in the predatory jungle of a maximum-security detention facility, and he ironically found that his reputation as a "killer" was all that stood between him and sexual attack by others. Given his limited options, the young man began to assume the only self-protective role available to him and, with the passage of time he assimilated this role so well that he was actually fearful of displaying any deviation from the stereotype. In fact, when first interviewed, the young man refused to admit he even knew how to read and write! He had *learned* to be dangerous, and learned very well indeed.

We cannot hope to predict dangerousness from labels.[33] Therefore, we must concede that isolating only those juveniles who have violent criminal records will not result in the isolation of all those who are, in fact, actually dangerous. We must also conclude, and concede, that the nature of our criminal justice system is such that some juveniles will be incarcerated in spite of the fact that they are not dangerous in any way. Political realities being what they are, we are well aware of the fact that all candidates for incarceration in the proposed Secure Treatment Unit will not meet the criterion of dangerousness. We are also aware that potential candidates for incarceration will not all be life-style violent juvenile offenders. At a later point in this book, we will discuss the secondary diagnostic level that has been built into the Secure Treatment Unit in order to mitigate the difficulties inherent in any diagnostic system that attempts to make judgments based on either statutory labeling or prediction of dangerousness.

Waiver

Current criminal justice systems provide a variety of options for the treatment of the life-style violent juvenile offender. Before there can be any meaningful discussion as to what results we want when addressing the problem of the life-style violent juvenile, we have to decide which component of the criminal justice system will be relied upon to produce that result. Options as to placement/treatment break down into three broad categories:

1. The existing juvenile justice system.
2. A specialized component of that same system.
3. The adult correctional network.

Currently, options 1 and 3 are being invoked with almost total regularity. This regularity has become so pronounced that option 3 is generally seen as *part of* option 1.[34]

For the life-style violent juvenile, the "waiver" system has emerged almost to the exclusion of all other options as society's choice. It is a well-known but rarely discussed fact that virtually all juvenile justice statutory schemes have some provision for removing certain juveniles from the juvenile network and treating them as adults.[35] This process, called "waiver," "transfer," "certification," or "bind-over,"[36] among others, generally amounts to an even greater exercise of discretion than is common in an already criteria-less system. The process may be prosecutorial, judicial, or legislative, but recent decisions of the United States Supreme Court have mandated certain "safeguards" before it is actually utilized.[37] Whether or not these safeguards adequately protect the rights of the juveniles involved is beyond the scope of this work. What does most urgently concern us is the professional and political implications of "treatment" of juveniles in an adult correctional setting.

The popularity of waiver is not based on its success rate in treating the life-style violent juvenile offender. It is virtually impossible to logically conclude that the waiver of a juvenile into the adult correctional network is based on rehabilitative grounds. In fact, the very *possibility* of rehabilitation in such a setting is now uniformly denounced, and such authorities as the Federal Parole Board are now giving weight to *immutable*[38] factors in their release decisions. Even the American Bar Association (ABA) is advocating terms of no more than five years as *punishment* for any crime, with exceptions only for "dangerous" offenders.[39] Noting that "professional" criminals may be given longer terms under the ABA standards, it is possible to conclude that the adult correctional network is seen as a place of incapacitation and deterrence-based punitive activity *only*. We can find no evidence whatever that adult prisons offer greater rehabilitative possibilities than their juvenile counterparts, and we feel comfortable in concluding that those juveniles singled out for adult correctional treatment are those juveniles the system considers to be "beyond rehabilitation." Indeed, the criteria articulated by the United States Supreme Court in *Breed* v. *Jones*[40] specify the juvenile's "non-amenability to rehabilitation"[41] as a prerequisite for treatment as an adult.[42] Given the weight of the evidence, we would conclude that the decision to treat juveniles within the adult correctional network is an admission of failure and an expression of an entire system's desire to "cut its losses."

There appears to be no correlation between genuine diagnosis and adult incarcerative result. Moral and philosophical objections aside, there are serious pragmatic difficulties with the acceptance of a waiver approach. Even if the "untreatable" juvenile is to be phased out of the juvenile justice system and treated as an adult, we will continue to find ourselves with juveniles who meet the same criteria, but who lack the chronological age to justify similar treatment. New York State, for example, has no waiver provision and, therefore, no juvenile under the age of sixteen may be treated as an adult regardless of the criminal acts committed.[43] Yet no professional would claim that this cutoff point at age sixteen is based on scientific/criminological data or analysis. New York's law simply expresses a moral judgment, a judgment that is coming under increasing fire from the media as the public perception of another juvenile crime wave continues.[44] In a non-waiver jurisdiction, the life-style violent juvenile, acculturated to the relative nonconsequences of the juvenile court, quickly becomes an incarcerated felon shortly after he reaches the cutoff age.

Whether or not a jurisdiction has a waiver statute on its books, there is *always* an age at which the law provides a way by which a youth may be incarcerated with adults. Whether this is accomplished by actual waiver, or by automatic statutory cutoff, the result is virtually the same. None of these systems provide specialized treatment in an incarcerative setting for those youth who appear to fit the description of the life-style violent juvenile offender.

The use of waiver is a confession of failure and an attempt at divestiture of the problem by the juvenile justice system. But the real weakness, the essential fallacy in the argument for waiver is this: we exempt juveniles from the adult correctional consequences of their acts on the grounds that they lack sufficient life-experience, intelligence, and maturity to be held fully responsible. In effect, "juvenileness" is a form of the "diminished capacity" defense. Although we (as a society) do not excuse the criminal acts, we believe the acts have a different motivation and etiology than the same acts committed by adults, and we attribute this difference to the essential immaturity of the juvenile offender. There is ample evidence to support the view that the ability to change behavior and attitudes is inversely correlated to the longevity of those behaviors and attitudes, and that young people are sufficiently "unformed" so as to make them more susceptible to rehabilitative influences. The juvenile justice system basically exists as a monument to that point of view. Yet examine for a moment the waiver process: a child of fifteen who is deemed to be culturally, socially, experientially, and intellectually immature suddenly acquires sufficient maturity by an act of criminal violence![45] This position is the height of absurdity, yet it is, in effect, *the* position of the advocates of waiver.

Since this position must fall when faced with even the most superficial analysis, we are left with the concept of punishment as deterrence, or punishment as revenge, or punishment as a means of achieving incapacitation.

Deterrence is possible only for certain types of behavior,[46] and functions best in an atmosphere of immediacy. Such is not possible in today's criminal justice system which represents, especially in the lower criminal courts, nothing so much as a lottery. Incapacitation can be sufficiently accomplished within a proper juvenile justice network[47] and revenge as a concept must be dismissed if only because it has proven to be counterproductive and evocative of counter-revenge by the predator-turned-victim.

The logical result of an overall reliance upon waiver as a treatment tool for the life-style violent juvenile is a specialized treatment unit run by the adult department of corrections. We submit that if waiver were invoked in sufficient numbers, we would eventually create, almost *de facto,* the kind of specialized placements (*not* treatments) that we advocate for the life-style violent juvenile.

No prison warden wants very young men in his care. They create serious problems, both as aggressors and as potential victims.[48] The correctional establishment's response will be to create settings which functionally segregate the young offender,[49] not because of rhetoric about so-called "specialized treatment" but simply due to the necessary management objectives of an adult institution. Our advocacy of a Secure Treatment Unit option as part of a continuum (network) of services in juvenile justice is founded on the principle that there really *are* no other options that possess even a hope (much less an expectation) of returning life-style violent juveniles to society as less dangerous individuals than when they were removed.

The Closed Setting

Despite arguments for total de-institutionalization, treatment in closed, secure settings is a necessity for the life-style violent juvenile. The need for closed, secure treatment institutions is *not* rooted in repression and a desire to punish. What must be clearly understood are the consequences of *not* providing such specialized facilities:

1. A return to waiver across the board;[50]
2. A dangerous mixing of criminological types within single settings;
3. The collapse and failure of the alternative methods of treatment because of the contamination factor;[51]
4. The continuing problem of a system that returns dangerous juveniles to communities in far more dangerous condition and, at the same time, continues to incarcerate nondangerous juveniles within its "programs."

But the need for specialized institutions is not the only need of a system attempting to cope with the problems posed by the life-style violent juvenile.

Such a closed setting cannot be used indiscriminately, and it must be controlled, through intake, by the strictest criteria. And even if such a specialized facility *is* constructed, and even if such a facility is properly utilized by the courts, it must be understood that no institution is, in and of itself, a program. It is but the *housing* for such a program.

Any new system designed to impact upon the problem of the life-style juvenile offender must first be evaluated on its actual service-delivery ability. It is vitally important to understand that a "get tough" policy founded on a simple-minded return to past methods of juvenile "justice" can, at best, duplicate the counterproductive disasters of the past. Readers of this book must understand that they have a fundamental role as *consumers* in our criminal justice system. This system is purchased with their tax dollars (and occasionally with their property and their lives) and returns only more vicious, more hardened, and more competent criminals. If General Motors built cars that worked as well as our juvenile justice system, it seems safe to say that most Americans would be driving Fords by now. Even in the noncompetitive world of human services, it is an understatement to say that the American juvenile justice consumer is being short-changed. It is the thesis of this book that the American consumer, and not the American criminal justice professional, has the strongest vested interest in a juvenile justice system that protects society at all levels.

The present juvenile justice system has no such ability. The cornerstone of the juvenile justice system is the concept that the system itself exists to serve the best interests of society. The reasoning is that the best interests of our children are the best interests of the larger society. We have no strong argument against this concept. Our argument is, rather, with those who would maintain that the current system is in anybody's best interests. Juvenile justice thinking has always been reactive: abuses are uncovered, investigations (usually inspired by the mass media rather than the allegedly "self-policing" human services profession) are begun, and solutions are sought. Whether legislative or administrative, all such solutions have this in common—they are political in nature and in motivation, and thus very limited in potential for success.

Superficial analysis would appear to reject any form of closed, secure setting for juvenile delinquents. If this work were to be a polemic describing a rehabilitative utopia for the life-style violent juvenile, we could conclude any discussion as to the necessity for maximum-security incarceration with the argument that such a facility is "not appropriate to the needs of the child." It is this sort of language that permeates juvenile justice legislation and that might lead a casual reader to conclude that "adult" concepts such as retribution and punishment are beyond the pale of those who work with juveniles.

Similarly, the media would have us believe that to be a juvenile in a major urban area is to hold a virtual license to rob, rape, and murder. Yet any working professional will readily admit that the effect of the juvenile justice system on violent delinquents has been to expose them to even greater viciousness than they themselves displayed, perhaps in some insanely misguided notion that when conditions within juvenile institutions are ugly enough, the juvenile will "reform" because of a fervent desire to avoid being returned to the same place. However, when such "reasoning" *does* penetrate the psyche of the violent juvenile, it is likely to turn a routine arrest for a minor offense into a homicide of the arresting officer. The juvenile may have left the institution vowing never to return, but this is a vow to "hold court in the streets" rather than to conform his daily behavior to acceptable standards.

But a strong case can be made for the proposition that maximum security can, in fact, be in the best interests of the child. We accept, as a basic premise of the organizing that is a necessary component of any social change in America, that individuals and agencies often do the right thing for the wrong reasons. It would easily be possible to justify the construction of a Secure Treatment Unit on purely therapeutic grounds. It would be possible to justify construction purely on the ground that the policy of absorbing life-style violent juveniles into a service continuum that does not feature such a placement/treatment option impacts heavily on that system and creates dysfunction to an alarming degree. It would be possible to justify such a unit on the ground that its very presence will greatly contribute to decrease in the use of waiver by any given jurisdiction.[52] It would be possible to justify such a unit on the ground that it guarantees a significant increase in physical safety to the general public.

But, in the real world, we find that rationales such as the "best interests of the child" are often a sham,[53] and that rhetoric often runs far ahead of reality in the treatment of *any* juvenile. We conclude that a failure to make a *political* case for the construction of a Secure Treatment Unit is a failure to look objectively at the obstacles facing its advocates.

Politically, a Secure Treatment Unit is an important step forward. Following the construction and maintenance of such a facility, juvenile court judges will no longer be forced to institute waiver proceedings against juveniles whose violent acts have inflamed the community. No longer will otherwise-relevant community programs be forced out of business because of their inability to adapt to the treatment requirements of a special population; no longer will de-institutionalization be the scapegoat of a system which has been a failure since its inception. Without a "maximum-security" unit that serves as a visible monument to the seriousness with which the community views violent juvenile crime, rehabilitation of the juvenile justice system is doomed to failure.

Political Considerations

A Secure Treatment Unit is a political, as well as a criminological, necessity. Just as experience has educated us to the necessity of a Secure Treatment

Unit, experience has also taught us that such an institution must have a political viability of its own to reach reality. Fortunately, the concept of "maximum security" (either our working definition or the one popularized by the media) has tremendous political value. A frightened public wants reassurance that dangerous juveniles will be off the streets and within a program that will, at least temporarily, incapacitate them. This is an area of need which cuts across all social and political philosophies: whether one believes a violent juvenile should be punished, treated, rehabilitated, or subjected to societal revenge, there is universal agreement that the price of allowing dangerous juveniles to remain at large in our communities is too high. A Secure Treatment Unit has a political viability in its very visibility. It stands as a symbol to potential offenders and the public alike that we as a society have a response to violence that categorically condemns such behavior.

The mass institutionalization of juveniles has proved itself a failure. The key to understanding our position in this regard can be found in our position on juvenile institutions and institutionalization in general. That position is simple indeed: we are totally opposed to the use of institutions for either treatment or confinement for the overwhelming majority of juveniles. We believe that institutions are not necessary for the protection of the public, contribute little or nothing to the proper care and treatment of juveniles, and exhibit their own unique syndrome of negativity that stamps a child initially and follows him for the rest of his life. We take it as no accident that almost all of this country's major life-style criminals began a career while incarcerated as juveniles. This list is virtually endless, and includes such notorious individuals as Carryl Chessman, Carl Panzram, Albert DeSalvo, Joe Barboza, and Charles Manson. Surveys of inmate populations in adult maximum security prisons show that most prisoners incarcerated for serious crimes that were part of a criminal life-style served an initial apprenticeship as juvenile prisoners.[54] We characterize the juvenile institution as criminogenic in design and iatrogenic in accomplishment. We ardently support the concept of de-institutionalization and we advocate its adoption throughout the nation.

However, a small, highly selective institution for the life-style violent juvenile is nonetheless a necessity. But as former and current participants in a de-institutionalized system,[55] we have learned that there is a small percentage[56] of life-style violent juveniles who *cannot* be treated outside a closed setting. Because such juveniles require specialized programs and specialized settings, the consequences of a failure to address these needs is the systematic destruction of all the other specialized services a proper juvenile justice network will provide for the rest of the juvenile offender population. A halfway house which requires a "commitment to nonviolence" on the part of its residents cannot function with individuals incapable of such commitments. Its response to episodes of violence is simply to expel the offender.

In a system which lacks a programmatic response to violent behavior, the supposedly negative sanction becomes, instead, a positive reinforcement, and we find the most dangerous juveniles being released *because* of their inability to function within "nonviolent" programs.

Even Dr. Jerome Miller, the "Father of De-institutionalization" for juvenile offenders in this country, has finally concluded that a system that provides no institutionalization (closed settings) whatever is deficient in its responsibilities to society and to the juveniles themselves.

> If I were to set up a model [deinstitutionalized] system [today] I would have at one end a very limited system of small, locked facilities for really dangerous kids . . .
>
> I would have something for the really dangerous kid and I would want to make it very clear that a dangerous kid is a kid who's committed a violent act, period. Not someone that we think *might* be dangerous, or someone who's *possibly* dangerous, or someone who's dangerous to *themselves,* but someone who's killed someone, someone who's raped someone, someone who's maimed someone and shown by what they *did* that they're dangerous.[57]

The popular demand for "get tough" treatment of violent juveniles is now very powerful, but still unfocused. Yet, in spite of its political viability, the concept of a Secure Treatment Unit will not achieve political strength while the public remains so placidly undemanding of its elected officials. The "get tough" rhetoric often appears sufficient to satisfy a public that responds to slogans without requiring solutions. (See illustrations.) For example, in New York, following a wave of media attention, there were numerous political demands for fingerprinting of juveniles, for trial of juveniles to be handled by special prosecutors from the District Attorney's Office,[58] and for specialized secure treatment of hardcore violent offenders.[59] All of these demands have been met without the construction of a single specialized program (much less facility) to accomplish the goal of protecting society. Most of the rhetoric has focused on detection, rather than on behavior change. Yet the most notorious offenders have been those that were in the custody of the authorities many times before they achieved media prominence.[60] Fingerprinting an eleven-year-old child may satisfy the public's desire that the child won't "get away with something" in the future, and may guarantee that such a child will become "known" to the responsible agencies each time he commits a new offense, but it will accomplish nothing in terms of reversing what now appears to be an inevitable march towards life-style criminal violence.

The demand has not yet focused on Secure Treatment Units because more facile solutions are far less expensive. Why then has there been no political demand for a Secure Treatment Unit to serve both the public and this specialized population of juveniles? The answer is simple: previously mentioned political

Copyright 1977 New York News Inc. Reprinted by permission.

solutions have about them one area of viability that construction of a Secure Treatment Unit cannot hope to match—they cost nothing. Screaming "get tough!" costs nothing. Construction of a specialized facility[61] and payment of salaries can be a major expense. We will deal with the cost-effectiveness of a Secure Treatment Unit as part of a network continuum of care in a later section but, for now, we want to focus on why such an institution has not received the political support an observer might expect.

The concept of a fully functional Secure Treatment Unit has failed to mobilize political support simply because of the population it is designed to serve. As a minority-within-a-minority, the life-style violent juvenile is not only the least likely to become a therapeutic "success," he can also be the most highly visible failure. As a result, programming and planning for such juveniles is distinctly not a high priority. Politicians are likely to be perceived as "soft" on juvenile crime when they advocate special programs for such offenders. It is

Copyright 1977 New York News Inc. Reprinted by permission.

possible to obtain precisely the same political mileage from inarticulately screaming "get tough!" as it is from innovative (and often expensive) programming.

Political considerations aside, treatment of the life-style violent juvenile is a difficult, unpopular, and often unrewarding task. Life-style violent juveniles require a disproportionate investment of the "ergs of energy"[62] available within any therapeutic staff, and the potential rewards are low. Danger of violence is omnipresent, and recruitment of staff tends to lag behind that of all other programs. Why innovate for violent juvenile offenders when it is possible to receive the same per capita funding for innovation with children exhibiting less demanding problems? And although there is some residual sympathy for those children in trouble with the law for the first time, or for relatively minor offenders, the public attitude towards our target population is overwhelmingly punitive.[63] A truly innovative program for the life-style violent juvenile offender contains "punishment" as an integral part of the therapeutic process, but the program itself is not punishment per se. Explaining this to a layman often sounds as though the advocate for the program is blind to reality, and believes "there's no such thing as a bad boy." And selling *that* concept in 1979 is next to impossible.

But the public has proved itself to be dangerously shortsighted in its view of treatment for violent juveniles. Ironically enough, the same lack of a sense of the future that characterizes the life-style violent juvenile contributes to the inability of the general public to perceive the necessity of specialized programs for that same population. Specialized programs are dimly perceived as some form of soft liberal approach, and the extraordinary amount of funding necessary is automatically resented. Thus, there is no political viability and no political support. But if the public were aware of the fact that juvenile prisons (as currently constructed and managed) can never be anything but crime incubators and that regardless of how harshly the great majority of juveniles are punished, they will reenter society as more competent criminals, then public attitudes might radically change.

The public believes that no method of treatment has been able to rehabilitate violent juvenile offenders, but the public has failed to pursue a better future as it conveniently forgets the mistakes of the past. Because the "good old days" of juvenile justice produced some of this country's most dangerous criminals, a return to the practices of that era will not yield a different result today.

Notes

1. Robert Linder, M.D., "Rebels or Psychopaths," *Time Magazine,* December 6, 1954.

2. In 1977, a Harris Survey asked more than 1,000 adults their opinions on juvenile crime. The results of this survey showed that more than half of those queried felt that juvenile crime had increased in the past year. Almost half of those surveyed were in favor of changing the current law and lowering the age limit to allow for adult prison sentencing for teenagers 16 or younger. (As reported in the *New York Post,* May 9, 1977.)

See also, Public Opinion About Crime: The Attitudes of Victims and Nonvictims in Selected Cities, Criminal Justice Research Center, Albany, New York (1977); James Garofalo, Project Coordinator. This study is an analysis of the National Crime Survey Attitude and Victimization Data project, supported by LEAA grant no. 75-SS-99-6002.

An Overview of Treatment

3. *See,* for example, editorials such as "Of Crime and Punishment," *New York Post,* November 5, 1975, which reads, in pertinent part:

> A sense that juvenile crime has become epidemic here is shared by countless New Yorkers. It is a virulent, deadly plague. Both the causes and the treatment are in daily dispute. . . . There has been a[n] . . . increase in fear, particularly among the aging, because of a widespread conviction that dangerous juvenile offenders are being routinely returned to the streets after brief terms in jail, or none at all. . . . The need for quarantine [incarcerative isolation] is inescapable if we are to begin to lift the shadow haunting our streets.

4. Today's version of the "current" situation has not changed to any appreciable extent. Following is a quote from "The Youth Crime Plague," *Time Magazine,* July 11, 1977, p. 18. Reprinted by permission from *Time,* The Weekly Newsmagazine; copyright Time Inc. 1977.

> People have always accused kids of getting away with murder. Now that is all too literally true. Many youngsters appear to be robbing and raping, maiming and murdering as casually as they go to a movie or join a pick-up baseball game. A *new,* remorseless, mutant juvenile seems to have been born, and there is no more terrifying figure in America today. [emphasis added]

5. New York State is one of the few jurisdictions that retains the common law presumption of incapacity as the only "competency" defense available to a child above the age of seven charged with a criminal act; the American Bar Association Juvenile Justice Standards Project considers the age of ten to be the threshold for assuming criminal responsibility [Tentative Draft—1976—Vol. IV, p. 7] and other jurisdictions concur.

And even in New York State, some responsive jurists have held that the defense of lack of capacity owing to immaturity shall be available if "proven factually" notwithstanding the applicable statutes. *See, Matter of Andrew M.,* Kings County Family Court, J. Gartenstein, as reported in *New York Law Journal,* November 18, 1977, p. 1 ff.

6. *See,* for example, Charles W. Tenney, Jr., "The Utopian World of Juvenile Courts," 383 *The Annals of the American Academy of Political and Social Science* 101 (1969). But for a theory which holds that the juvenile court system was never intended to be progressive at all, *see* S.L. Schlossman, *Love and the American Delinquent—The Theory and Practice of "Progressive" Juvenile Justice, 1825-1920,* (Chicago: University of Chicago Press, 1978).

7. The life-style criminal offender is distinguished from the episodic offender, and also from the offender whose motivations may be attributed to mental disease or defect. Also called "career criminals," "professional" crimi-

nals, or "intensive offenders," such individuals' cultural and social activities and relationships cannot be separated from their criminal behavior.

8. One noted commentator traces the evolution of the Chicago Vice Lords (also known as the Vice Lord Nation, and the Conservative Vice Lords), one of the most notorious street gangs of the 1960s, as follows:

> It is generally stated that the Vice Lord Nation—referred to by Vice Lords as a "club," not a gang—originated in 1958 in what is usually called "Charlie Town," the Illinois State Training School for Boys at St. Charles, Illinois. In St. Charles the inmates live in what are called "cottages." The Vice Lords began in Harding Cottage, which housed the toughest boys in the institution. The club was started in the Lawndale area of Chicago in the fall of 1958, following the release of several members.

From The Vice Lords: Warriors of the Street by R. Lincoln Keiser. Copyright © 1969 by Holt, Rinehart and Winston, Inc. Reprinted by permission of Holt, Rinehart and Winston.

9. From "Juvenile Justice in State "In Disarray,' Official Says," *The New York Times,* March 2, 1976 © 1976 by the New York Times Company. Reprinted by permission.

> The most outstanding of the recommendations made by the commission of the American Bar Association is that juvenile-sentencing practices be reversed and that judges make their decisions according to the seriousness of the crime rather than what they feel are the "needs" of the offenders.

From Ernest van den Haag, *Punishing Criminals: Concerning a Very Old and Painful Question,* (New York: Basic Books, 1975), at p. 249:

> After the age of thirteen, juveniles should be treated as adults for indictment, trial, and sentencing purposes. . . . [T]here are more offenders among juveniles. They are the product of the leniency of the law—of the privilege granted them—as much as anything else.

And, for an unusually-reasoned discourse, from a column by William F. Buckley, Jr., in *The New York Post,* August 11, 1977:

> There being no way to make parents responsible for the behavior of their children when there are no parents (it is estimated that over 50 per cent of black teenagers in New York City live without one or more parents) legal distinctions between children and adults should be abolished where there are no parents; and where there are parents, they should be abolished after repeated offenses.

The authors take the position that the logic, much less the constitutionality of Mr. Buckley's "position" does not merit much discussion.

10. *See,* for example, Nicholas Pileggi, "How Fifteen-Year-Olds Get Away With Murder," 10 *New York Magazine* 36 (June 13, 1977), detailing the career of convicted murderer George Adorno; and Neal Hirshfeld, and Michael Daly, "He's 15 and He Likes to Kill—Because It's Fun," *New York Daily News,* June 29, 1978, which provides a chronology of the criminal career of another infamous juvenile, Willie Bosket. This youth committed two murders and attempted another half-dozen before his sixteenth birthday. In New York, he must be treated as a juvenile.

11. The following is a description of a juvenile gang attack, written by Captain Tom Walker, former commander of New York City's infamous 41st Precinct in the South Bronx, known to locals as "Fort Apache." First published as "The Seige of Fort Apache" in the February 23, 1976 issue of *New York Magazine,* the original article was expanded into a book, *Fort Apache,* (New York: Thomas Y. Crowell, 1976):

> Armed with shotguns and knives, [the youth gang] stormed into [the victim's] apartment. First they tied him to a chair and forced him to watch as they repeatedly raped his wife. Then they cut her savagely with their knives. Finally, they placed a shotgun between her legs and pulled the trigger. Perhaps [the victim] felt some sense of gratitude when they turned the shotgun on him and papered the walls of the apartment with parts of his arms and chest.

12. Marvin E. Wolfgang, Robert M. Figlio, and Thorsten Sellin, *Delinquency in a Birth Cohort,* (Chicago: University of Chicago Press, 1972).

13. *Curbing the Repeat Offender: A Strategy for Prosecutors,* a report by the Institute for Law and Social Research (INSLAW), National Institute of Law Enforcement and Criminal Justice, LEAA, U.S. Department of Justice, U.S. Government Printing Office Stock No. 027-000-00576-4, (1977).

14. Ibid., p. 9.

15. From: James Q. Wilson, *Thinking About Crime,* (New York: Basic Books, 1975), at p. 199.

16. "Life-style" is far too vague a description to warrant penalties under the law and, as will be found to be commonplace with Secure Treatment Unit philosophy, we accept *both* sides of the proposition: (1) no commitment to the Secure Treatment Unit will be permitted simply on a finding that a defendant displays a "criminal life-style," actual criminal *convictions* must support any such commitment; but, (2) commitment to the Secure Treatment Unit *will* be acceptable even *absent* such a finding if the juvenile is convicted of substantive criminal acts of a serious nature.

17. Wolfgang et al., note 12, *supra*, at p. 252:

It appears that the juvenile justice system has been able to isolate the hard core offender fairly well. Unfortunately, the product of this encounter with sanctioning authorities is far from desirable. Not only do a greater number of those who receive punitive treatment (institutionalization, fine or probation) continue to violate the law, but they also commit more serious crimes with greater rapidity than those who experience a less constraining contact with the judicial and correctional systems. . . . [I]t is clear that, if a selection process is operating which routes hard core delinquents into the courts and correctional institutions, no benefit is derived from this encounter, for the subsequent offense rates and seriousness scores show no reduction in volume and intensity.

18. *See,* for example, the attitude and outlook displayed by "Pirate," the juvenile gang member whose interview provided the introduction to this work. *See also,* Michael Pousner, "The Savage Kids," an investigative series in *The New York Daily News,* Part Two, November 15, 1976. Copyright 1976 New York News Inc. Reprinted by permission.

"Everything's impulse, you just don't think about what you're doing when you do it." That's Eddie Pagan's explanation for many of the juvenile murders, rapes, and muggings today. Pagan, a one-time leader of the Savage Immortals youth gang, appeared before Bronx Supreme Court Justice Francis Bloustein last Tuesday and pleaded guilty to manslaughter in the death of a Bronx social club owner.

19. T. Robert Clements was recently paroled from a life sentence in New Jersey and is awaiting release from a Pennsylvania prison. He literally grew up in the juvenile prison system, having first been incarcerated at age nine. In a lengthy interview (set out in detail in the appendix), he describes an incident which occured during his first week of incarceration in Pennsylvania's notorious Camp Hill Reformatory:

The first time I was involved in a sex thing, I was in the shower, and a few guys came in and jumped me . . . Now I picked up a mop wringer. I put one guy in the hospital, and I went in the hospital myself, because I got beat up real bad too. But after that, nobody bothered me anymore. Sex wasn't worth it.

20. Unemployment has sharply decreased those symbols formerly produced by more acceptable role models such as the debt-enslaved factory worker who drives a new car. The juvenile sees only the car, not the debt.

    See also, "New Green Sneakers and Other Lessons of the Street," a 15-part series broadcast by WCBS Radio (51 West 52nd Street, New York City, New York 10019) between January 24, 1977 and February 11, 1977. Written and broadcast by Irene Cornell. The following is an excerpt from a conversation between Detective Irwin Silverman of the Bronx (New York) Senior Citizens Robbery Unit and an unnamed juvenile offender:

Det. Silverman: How many pairs of sneakers can you wear at one time? Can you wear two pairs at one time?

Juvenile: No, but look, see, you know . . . when they [other juveniles] be gettin' that money buyin' new sneakers, you know, they don't be wanta wearin' the same old sneakers every day. They wanta change like, you know, they wear a pair of black pants, they wanta wear a pair of black sneakers, you understand.

Det. Silverman: Why's that so important? Except you wanta show off to people that "Look, I got green sneakers one day, and red ones tomorrow?" Is it important that you wanta go to jail, for that?

Juvenile: Look, see . . . them people, you know—people say "Yeah . . . that boy know how to dress. That's right. He know how to dress, you know." People like to hear that! You understan'?

21. *See,* for example, Stephen E. Schlesinger, "Prediction of Dangerousness in Juveniles," 2 *Crime and Delinquency* January, 1978, at p. 48:

Predictors of violent behavior identified by previous researchers were not substantiated by this study. Future efforts to predict dangerousness will probably meet with similar success. We may be wrong in our definition and study of dangerousness as an isolated factor, and the very state of the art in predicting such behaviors may well be moribund. Perhaps we should reconsider our conduct as professionals in light of this rather dismal state of affairs.

If we cannot reliably predict violent behavior, how can we justify our continued detention of juveniles evaluated as violent? Can the use of unsubstantiated and demonstrably unreliable techniques be professionally and ethically justified? And how shall we balance the right of individuals to remain free from the control of others and society's need to protect itself from those few who will become violent? The fairness of present policies is dubious.

22. *See,* Clemens Bartollas, Stuart J. Miller, and Simon Dinitz, *Juvenile Victimization: The Institutional Paradox,* (New York: Sage Publications, 1976), especially part 2.

23. The youth is described as a "defendant" and not as a "respondent" because he was being tried in the adult system.

24. New York Penal Law section 240.25 (1967). Harassment is a violation (below a misdemeanor) and is punishable by a maximum of 15 days imprisonment and/or a fine of $250.

25. New York Penal Law section 110/120.00 (1967). Attempted Assault in the Third Degree is a Class B misdemeanor (the lowest severity) and is punishable by a maximum of 90 days imprisonment or one year's probation, and/or a fine of up to $500.

26. Because of the attorney-client privilege, both the names of the attorney and the defendant have been omitted, and the circumstances have been slightly altered. The interview was primarily to ascertain if the perpetrator and the victim were acquainted with each other and, if so, the facts and circumstances leading up to the events.

27. A verbatim recounting by the defense attorney who explained that he found the defendant's words and manner so frightening that he had no difficulty in recalling the exact words used.

28. In this case, the sentence was an Unconditional Discharge following a plea of guilty to simple harassment. It should be noted, however, that the severity of the criminal justice system's response is correlated here with the accuracy of the defendant's aim. Depending on the injuries sustained by the bicyclist, the offenses chargeable against the bottle-thrower range from a violation punishable by a maximum of 15 days in prison to a major felony (attempted murder or actual homicide) punishable by up to a life sentence.

29. It is apparent that the prior institutional experience of the other youths was an asset in their attempts to force this young man into criminal activity.

30. More properly phrased, the young man was "adjudicated a juvenile delinquent by virtue of criminal acts, to wit, homicide."

31. As opposed to a "shelter care" facility which is more akin to an open setting. The "close detention" was, in fact, maximum-security incarceration. Were he an adult, his preplacement period would count as "jail time" and come off his maximum sentence. But, as a juvenile awaiting a treatment placement, this time (since it was not, in itself, "treatment") did *not* so count.

32. The juvenile version of a "rap sheet" or "yellow sheet," renamed in line with the juvenile justice system's philosophy of euphemism in all things.

33. *See* note 21, *supra.*

34. Dale Mann, *Intervening with Convicted Serious Juvenile Offenders,* Rand Corporation (1976).

Our interest has been in serious juvenile offenders, yet we have been unable to uncover a single program which focuses primarily on treating [such] youth. [at p. 70]

Our persistent question "Who is doing a good job with serious juvenile offenders?" regularly brought the same negative or puzzled response. While some programs *include* serious offenders . . . there are no programs of concentrated assistance specifically for this group. [at p. 71, emphasis added]

35. Joseph N. Sorrentino, and Gary K. Olsen, in their article entitled "Certification of Juveniles to Adult Court," in 4 *Pepperdine Law Review* 497 (1977) explain the transfer provisions of those three states that do not currently authorize the juvenile court to waive its jurisdiction at pp. 500-501:

> Vermont does not provide for transfer of cases originally brought in the juvenile court. But where a child is transferred from the criminal court to the juvenile court, the latter may retransfer the case upon a finding that the child is not in need of juvenile treatment and rehabilitation . . . Vt. Stat. Ann. Title 33 Section 655 (1973).

> In Nebraska, the county attorney, not the juvenile court, decides whether the child may be tried as an adult. But the child may petition the court for transfer back to the juvenile system. Neb. Rev. Stat. Section 43-202.1-2 (1971).

> New York has no transfer statute. New York Penal Law Section 30 (McKinney 1909) states that no criminal responsibility attaches to acts of those under the age of 16 at the time of commission . . .

Mark M. Levin, and Rosemary C. Sarri, *Juvenile Delinquency: A Study of Juvenile Codes in the U.S.* (Ann Arbor: The University of Michigan Press: 1974), at p. 18:

> In nearly every state, the juvenile court is empowered to weigh certain competing policy objectives listed in the statute and make a determination that the juvenile would be best tried in the criminal system.

36. Although often used interchangeably, these terms are distinguishable from each other to a limited extent. Juvenile court "waiver" actually refers to a *divestment* of jurisdiction by that court. The case is then Transferred, after Certification that appropriate findings have been made so that the adult courts properly have jurisdiction. In Massachusetts, for example, a juvenile is said to be "bound-over" for trial, reflecting the actuality of an indictment in the natural course of prosecuting those felonies felt to be suitable subjects for trial in the adult forum.

While most statutes tend to use several or all of the terms, common usage in the individual state tends to dictate the use of one term to the virtual exclusion of the others.

See also, Wallace J. Mlyniec, "Juvenile Delinquent or Adult Convict— The Prosecutor's Choice," 14 *American Criminal Law Review* 29 (1976).

37. Starting with Kent v. United States, 383 U.S. 541, 86 S.Ct. 1045, 16 L.Ed.2d 84 (1966), the Supreme Court has attempted to delineate the due process requirements necessary for the "waiver" decision. The leading case at

this time is Breed v. Jones, 421 U.S. 519, 95 S.Ct. 1779, 44 L.Ed.2d 346 (1975). Most court decisions focus on the juvenile's actual criminal conduct, both current and past, and his "amenability to rehabilitation" (which some jurisdictions extrapolate strictly *from* the criminal acts themselves).

38. Those factors that cannot be changed by the passage of time, such as race, sex, past criminal offenses, age at time of crime, etc. *See, Ad Hoc Parole Committee Public Information Report #1: The Parole Denial Process in New Jersey,* (New York: The Arca Foundation, 1975) for a detailed analysis of the use to which such factors are put by a paroling authority.

39. American Bar Association Project on Minimal Standards for Criminal Justice—Standards Relating to Sentencing Alternatives and Procedures, Part II, Statutory Structure and Judicial Discretion—Range of Alternatives (1968):

> 2.1 General principles: statutory structure. . .
> (d) It should be recognized that in many instances in this country the prison sentences which are now authorized, and sometimes required, are significantly higher than are needed in the vast majority of cases in order to adequately protect the interests of the public. [Except for a very few particularly serious offenses, and except under the circumstances set forth in section 2.5(b) (special term for certain types of offenders), the maximum authorized prison term ought to be five years and only rarely ten.] Sentences of twenty-five years or longer should be reserved for particularly serious offenses or . . . for certain particularly dangerous offenders. For most offenses, on the other hand, the maximum authorized prison term ought not to exceed ten years except in unusual cases and normally should not exceed five years.

40. *See* note 37, *supra.*

41. *Breed* at 523. The Court cites the finding of the Juvenile Court that, in accordance with California Welfare and Institutions Code section 707 (supp. 1967) [the applicable law *at that time*], the Respondent (defendant) was "not . . . amenable to the care, treatment, and training program available through the facilities of the juvenile court . . . "

42. Senate Bill S.1437, 95th Congress, 1st Session, was introduced by Senators McClellan and Kennedy on May 2 (legislative day, April 28), 1977. Entitled "A Bill to codify, revise, and reform Title 18 of the United States Code and for other purposes." Section 3603, subtitled "Juvenile Delinquency Proceeding," speaks, at (b), to the criteria for waiver:

> (b) Criteria.—In making the determination required [for transfer to adult jurisdiction], the court shall consider and shall make findings of fact on the record with regard to:
>
> (1) the nature and circumstances of the offense;
> (2) the age and social background of the juvenile;
> (3) the extent and nature of the juvenile's prior delinquency record;

(4) the likelihood of reform of the juvenile prior to his majority;
(5) the availability of programs designed to treat the juvenile's behavioral problems;
(6) whether juvenile disposition will reflect the seriousness of the juvenile's conduct, promote respect for the law, and provide a just response to the conduct of the juvenile.

43. There seems little question that this "liberal" provision of the law will not survive an election year. The New York law, which does not permit "adult" criminal justice treatment for a juvenile under the age of sixteen also does not permit juvenile treatment for any person *past* that age. When "waiver" comes to New York (as we believe it will), will the jurisdiction of the juvenile authorities be extended into the adult areas to create a genuine overlap?

44. *See,* for example, "How Teens Beat Criminal Raps," a front-page, bold headline story in the *New York Daily News* by Michael Daly, April 17, 1978.

45. On June 26, 1977, a seventeen-year-old runaway from the Lad Lake Home (for emotionally disturbed children) in Wisconsin was being held in the Maury County Jail in Columbia, Tennessee. He was confined to a padded cell in the jail, apparently because he displayed overt signs of the behavior which occasioned his original confinement as an emotionally disturbed juvenile. The youth, Andrew Zimmer, allegedly set fire to his cell, and 42 people died in the resulting blaze. He now faces a hearing to determine if he should be tried (on 42 counts of manslaughter) as a juvenile or as an adult.

46. *See,* Robert Waelder, "Psychiatry and the Problem of Criminal Responsibility," 101 *University of Pennsylvania Law Review* 378 (1952) for an excellent discussion of types of criminal behavior that would lend themselves to deterrence. Dr. Waelder divides criminal behavior into three basic areas: "Dangerous vs. Not Dangerous," "Treatable vs. Not Treatable," and "Deterrable vs. Not Deterrable," and recommends the use of actual "punishment" only for those behaviors which display a "Deterrable" aspect.

47. A "network" of services implies some form of treatment/placement/ service intervention at any point within the continuum of behavior for which a specific modality may be designed. A juvenile justice network, to be considered complete, would contain some form of incapacitative treatment, even in a "de-institutionalized" system.

48. From an interview with a New York State correctional officer who then held the rank of captain, January 1978. The officer has requested that his identity remain confidential:

> Listen, anytime you got kids [the speaker is referring to youth between the ages of sixteen and eighteen; no younger individuals can currently be incarcerated with adults in New York State] you got grief. They get into all kinds of crap on the street and they keep it right up when they come in the institution. Always fights, rapes, sodomies, screaming . . . it never stops.

Nobody in their right mind wants to work in a place with kids . . . the older men [prisoners] don't even want to do *time* with 'em.

One of those little yo-yos takes more time and trouble than a whole tier full of regular cons.

49. Some examples are the Adolescent Remand Unit at Rikers Island (New York), the Duell Vocational Institution in Tracy, California, and the Mansfield Reformatory in Ohio.

50. Defense attorneys in Massachusetts, for example, have complained that since de-institutionalization (from 1970 to the present), the lack of "secure institutions" in the juvenile system has motivated judges to "bind over" juveniles on the ground that certain offenders cannot be safely held or treated in community-based facilities.

See, however, Lloyd E. Ohlin; Alden D. Miller; and Robert B. Coates, *Juvenile Correctional Reform in Massachusetts,* a Preliminary Report of the Center for Criminal Justice of the Harvard Law School, prepared under LEAA grant number 76-JN-99-0003, at p. 17:

Many youth clearly and obviously belong in community placements. Some clearly belong in secure settings.

One danger is that the courts, lacking what they believe to be secure commitment facilities, will bind over youth considered dangerous or disturbed to adult courts. These might result in confinement in an adult jail or prison. So far (through 1973) this has not happened.

51. Local non-secure programs forced to assimilate violent or dangerous juveniles will find their original programs and goals so distorted by the need to adapt to such juveniles as to threaten their very survival. *See* interviews with Dr. Jerome Miller and William Jesinkey, appendix.

52. *See,* Theodore Levine, "Community-based Treatment for Adolescents: Myths and Realities," 22 *Social Work* 144 (1977) at 144:

Some children have so little regard for themselves, for their peers, and for the community that a closed, secure setting is required to contain them. Such youngsters, regardless of the legal designation placed on them, cannot be helped in an open, community setting.

The view that some children require treatment in closed settings (a view to which we subscribe) requires that any juvenile system which desires to retain responsibility for *all* juveniles must have access to such a setting or lose some juveniles to adult corrections. *See also,* note 50, *supra.*

53. H. Ted Rubin, "The Juvenile Court's Search for Identity and Responsibility," 23 *Crime and Delinquency* 1 (1977), at p. 4, quoting Francis A. Allen,

The Borderland of Criminal Justice (Chicago: University of Chicago Press, 1964), p. 51 ff.:

[I]t is ... both inaccurate and deceptive to describe the operation of the juvenile court ... as the exercise of a rehabilitative or therapeutic function. These [violent] cases are being adjudicated by the court for one principal reason: because they involve disturbing and dangerous behavior on the part of adolescents which the community must respond and attend to, for it is behavior that threatens the security and well-being of the community. The primary function being served in these cases, now and for what is likely to be an extended period in the future, is the temporary incapacitation of children found to constitute a threat to the community's interest. In short, the value advanced is not primarily that of the welfare of the child adjudicated a delinquent.

See also, Schlossman, note 6, *supra.*

54. *See,* for example, *Ad Hoc Parole Committee Report* #1 note 38, *supra,* Table XIII, p. 24.

55. The authors were intimately involved in the "Massachusetts Experience" of de-institutionalization. Dr. Bakal was assistant commissioner in charge of institutions under Commissioner Jerome Miller and was largely responsible for the actual closing of Massachusetts juvenile prisons; he now directs the Northeastern Family Institute of Marblehead, Massachusetts which operates a wide variety of community-based residential and nonresidential programs for the Massachusetts Department of Youth Services. Andrew Vachss directed Libra, Inc., a community-based reentry program for former prisoners, was deputy director of the Medfield-Norfolk Prison Project, a paramedical and resocialization program for prisoners from the Norfolk Prison Colony, directed Andros II, Massachusetts' only (at that time) maximum-security treatment unit for juveniles, and has served as a consultant to both DYS and NFI since that time. Other members of the Juvenile Justice Planning Project's (see ch. 4, note 83, *infra*) Consultant-Advisory Board who have been intimately involved in that experience are: Dr. William Madaus, former assistant commissioner of DYS and currently director of the Northshore Guidance Center, Salem, Massachusetts; Dr. Jerome Miller, formerly commissioner of DYS during the de-institutionalization period and currently editor of *Institutions, Etc.* [IE], an investigative newsletter on institutions and alternatives; Ralph Pino, Esq., a former floor counselor at Andros III, now a partner in Pino & Shea of Essex, Massachusetts and current legal consultant to NFI, Gregory Torres, formerly administrative director of Andros II and now the juvenile justice specialist for the Massachusetts Committee on Criminal Justice; and Anita S. Weissman, Esq., formerly floor counselor and staff historian for Andros II.

56. This is, amazingly enough, one area that has escaped the onslaught of the statisticians, and no precise figures are available. Although it is generally

conceded throughout the profession that the percentage is "small," guesstimates vary with the political philosophy of the individual and tend to expand or contract depending on the available alternatives (number of secure treatment beds, etc.).

57. Interview with Dr. Jerome Miller on the grounds of the Cornwall Heights (Pennsylvania) Security Treatment Unit, July 27, 1976, see appendix for complete text.

58. Formerly, all prosecutions of juveniles were handled by attorneys from the Office of the Corporation Counsel, whose expertise was largely in the civil law field. The use of assistant district attorneys is only for "designated felons" under New York's Juvenile Justice Reform Act of 1976. However, many commentators believe that no matter how skilled the prosecution, the system will continue to misfire. Elizabeth Fass, a corporation counsel attorney in New York's Brooklyn Family [Juvenile] Court, stated: •

If Clarence Darrow were reincarnated, and put in the role of prosecutor-persecutor . . . nothing would make any difference under the sentencing structure that we have had and that we have now under the law. For instance, I have a list of every homicide that we have had in 1976. We lost only one on the law—on a question of law. The problem is not with the trial of the cases. What happens after you place a child? And I say to you, what difference does it make who tries a case, if when it's all said and done, you send a kid to Goshen [N.Y.'s "secure" facility for juveniles], let's say, a secure facility, and he goes home for Christmas, and kills somebody else. Or, as happened here with the two rapes I had, he turns around and rapes a kid.

From: "New Green Sneakers and Other Lessons of the Street," note 20, *supra*, part 11, February 7, 1977.

59. Such demands have come from virtually all areas of public life. Some advocates for treatment of serious juvenile offenders as adults include the New York City Taxi Drivers Union (Editorial "The Time Has Come!" in the *Taxi Drivers VOICE*, September 28, 1976), the Transit Authority Patrolmen's Benevolent Association (*New York Daily News*, January 18, 1977, p. B2), trial judges (New York Supreme Court Justice Alvin F. Klein, as quoted in the *New York Law Journal* of April 4, 1977, p. 1), politicians (State Senator Ralph J. Marino, writing in the February, 1977 issue of *Trial Magazine* at p. 25), and, lest any reader think that such demands are limited to New York City (or even the United States), commentators on foreign criminal justice systems (Francis Cowper's "London Letter," a column of the *New York Law Journal*, November 22, 1976 at p. 2).

60. Recently, journalists have been able to penetrate the alleged wall of secrecy which protects an individual's juvenile record from public scrutiny. In addition to the George Adorno case, see note 10, *supra*, journalists have

uncovered past criminal records of juveniles in other jurisdictions. For example, the recent fervor in Chicago involves the case of one Clifford Finley. Disclosures of this defendant's (most recently charged with attempted murder, armed violence, aggravated battery, and attempted armed robbery) past record, an alleged violation of the Illinois Juvenile Court Act, have sparked judicial efforts to hold the media accountable; *see* "Chicago Press on Carpet Over Juvenile Records," an article in the *Chicago Sunday Sun-Times* by Michael Zielenziger, July 2, 1978 at p. 40.

61. *See,* for example, H.B. Bradley, "Community-Based Treatment for Young Adult Offenders," 15 *Crime and Delinquency* 359 (1969) at p. 361:

> Because of the tremendous expense involved, we are not about to fundamentally redesign our inadequate or downright archaic institutions . . .

62. We are indebted for this term to William Jesinkey, director of Advocates for Children of New York and coauthor (with Jane Stern) of *Lost Children,* a research report supported by a grant from the John Hay Whitney Foundation of New York (and available from that source). Mr. Jesinkey, a veteran child-care professional, explains:

> I think that what [a violent juvenile] does is he blows apart programs. Programs have so many ergs of energy, in terms of staff, in terms of the intensity and training of staff . . . They have a maximum level of what they're able to handle in terms of numbers and in terms of quality. Qualitatively, these [violent] children go beyond that and start to draw all energy towards them. The rest of the system starts to collapse and you see morale go down among kids, among staff. Programs disintegrate down to the least common denominator, which is absolutely the opposite of what you're supposed to be doing.

> Interview, November 4, 1976 (full text in appendix).

63. Among countless cases, we note, for example, that a seventeen-year-old youth has been sentenced to death for the murder of a state trooper in Oklahoma. The youth, Monte Lee Eddings, is awaiting appeal. A sixteen year old had been sentenced to death in Pennsylvania, and was spared the possibility of execution when that state's death penalty statute was found to be unconstitutional.

2 Considerations in Treatment of the Life-Style Violent Juvenile

Diversion and Rehabilitation

The needs of the first offender, while arousing greater sympathy in the public, are actually less urgent. There is a great deal of sympathy among law enforcement personnel for so-called "diversion" programs. There is almost general agreement that a juvenile's first contact with the criminal justice system should be his last, and there is realistic support for the proposition that resources should be allocated in terms of *prevention* of delinquency as well as for its treatment. Unfortunately, this farsighted approach instantly becomes myopic when confronted with the life-style violent juvenile who has *already* committed a serious crime. How does one "divert" such an individual when he has already crossed the line dividing the vandal and the truant from the robber and the murderer? The fact is that it is at *this* point that divergence is the most important! Not diverted, this juvenile finds himself on a one-way street marked "inevitability," with way stations of release to the community followed by criminally violent episodes followed by additional incarceration.

It is necessary to decide whether or not diversion (from a criminal career) is possible for the life-style violent juvenile. We must make an operational judgment as to life-style violent juveniles, and we must live by such a judgment. Either an offender is already a lost cause, (at which point he should be waived out of the juvenile system and incarcerated forever as an adult), or he can still be diverted from a criminal career.

When we speak of diversion from a life-style of criminal violence we are in danger of being caught up in a morass of definitional difficulties. Before proceeding further, we must discuss the concept of rehabilitation, upon which all juvenile justice treatment is based.

Terms such as "rehabilitation" must be operationally defined. One reason that criminology (especially that portion which purports to deal with juvenile delinquency) lags behind other disciplines in terms of scientific acceptance is that its terminology is often media-inspired and media-defined. Terms such as *recidivism, juvenile delinquency, maximum security, rehabilitation,* and *community-based corrections* are rarely operationally defined, and the public perception of such terms tends to become fixed by the context within which they were originally introduced.

The strict definition of "rehabilitation" as a return to a former, functioning state, is inappropriate when applied to the life-style violent juvenile. The concept of *rehabilitation* is supposedly the very foundation on which the juvenile justice system was erected. It would be difficult to find a single piece of juvenile legislation that does not contain this word, yet it clearly means different things to different readers.[1] We take the word *rehabilitation* to mean the return to a former state of existence or achievement. To us, it evokes a sense of restoration or reestablishment. So defined, the concept has a certain limited utility in describing a once law-abiding individual who, for one reason or another, deviated from his usual practices into criminal behavior. The goal with such an individual would logically be to restore him to his former state of existence. But the essence of such a definition is that the individual targeted for rehabilitation previously exhibited a life-style that was acceptable (or, at least, not dangerous) to society. Without this condition, rehabilitation as we define it would not only be fruitless, it might even be dangerous when applied to the life-style violent juvenile.

Once the former "whole" state of the life-style violent juvenile has been examined, it is clear that the medical model of rehabilitation is wholly inappropriate in treatment of this population. The life-style violent juvenile lives a feral,[2] atavistic,[3] existence. He is responsive only to immediate situations and not to any larger societal pressures. Very often he is hostile, fearful, and (as a result) dangerous. At some point in his progression towards adult criminality, the "system" intervenes. If this intervention is chronologically early enough for the child to be treated as a juvenile under the law, he is to be dealt with in a rehabilitative fashion. And now we ask: can we seriously state that the goal of *any* rational therapeutic system is to return this juvenile to his former state of existence? We think not. It is our belief that concepts like rehabilitation are medical, and not social, in their underpinnings. If an individual were to lose the use of his arm in a railroad accident, we might be accurately describing an actual process if we were to call his hospital therapy (designed to help him regain the full use of that arm) as rehabilitative. But our goal with the life-style violent juvenile is not to return him to former behavior, but to give him the means, motive, and opportunity to participate in the *changing* of such behavior.

Whether a juvenile continues along the life-style of criminal violence is often determined by whether or not he is incarcerated while still a juvenile. In his famous *Delinquency and Drift*,[4] Matza postulates that *most* juvenile offenders literally mature out of (or drift away from) criminal activity and that only a small percentage continue on criminal careers as they near adulthood. Although this natural drift would seem to argue against the need for any formalized divergence programs, we would not support such a position because one of the major factors in the process by which a life-style violent adult criminal is created is a critical period spent incarcerated as a juvenile. Although studies have yet to be fully developed in this area, the evidence, at a practical level, of a direct correlation between juvenile imprisonment and later life-style adult criminality is overwhelming. As one of the authors explained in an interview:

> We have never produced, to my knowledge, a single heavyweight life-style criminal—throw out the Charles Whitmans and the Sons of Sams[5] the looney-tunes nobody can predict—who didn't serve an apprenticeship in the juvenile joints.

> Look at literally thousands of "professional"[6] criminals, the bank robbers, institutional armed robbers, organized crime soldiers, hit men, pimps, and so on . . . [y]ou will find "reform" or "training" schools as the thematic thread throughout all their backgrounds.[7]

But for those juveniles who precipitate out of any possible divergence system, some form of institutionalization is inevitable. The violent juvenile, is, then, a prime candidate for various intervention strategies. Indeed, our self-interest demands that such resources as we have in this area be fully focused on this special population of offenders. But the Secure Treatment Unit is primarily designed for those juveniles for whom standard intervention (such as diversion) is far too late. Those juveniles who have precipitated out of the social matrix into life-style violence are the same individuals who will dominate our courts and correctional systems as adults. They will continue to precipitate out of any correctional system into which they are thrust by the criminal justice agencies, and the "hard-core" label will follow them throughout their careers. To such an individual, homicide is the most likely culmination of a criminal career, and many commentators are taking the position that incapacitation of such human beings is probably more effective, in societal terms, than any rehabilitative service now available. In *Criminal Careers of Habitual Felons,* the authors state:

> [I]f an objective of sentencing is to prevent future crime by incapaci-tating high-risk offenders, our data suggest that it is counterproductive to concentrate on older habitual offenders. The greatest effect in crimes prevented would come from imprisoning the younger, more active offenders, since individual offense rates appear to substantially decline with age.[8]

But this country's most notorious criminals seem to have been produced *by* juvenile incapacitation, and not because such incapacitation was not utilized.

Charles Manson said, "you can see me in the eyes of your ten year olds."[9] His quote seems almost an unholy echo of the speech by Carl Panzram, certainly one of the most vicious murderers the juvenile justice system has ever produced. Panzram, who was executed for the murder of a federal prison guard in 1930, admitted to more than twenty homicides, several hundred acts of arson, and in excess of a thousand acts of forcible sodomy on youthful victims. First incarcerated in a juvenile training school when he was eleven, Panzram spent the rest of his short life either in prison or committing acts certain to guarantee his return. His fundamental philosophy of life was simply that "might makes right," a philosophy he claimed to have learned through various brutal (and brutalizing) experiences in juvenile institutions. The way Panzram explained a criminal career that would shock even the most case-hardened professional, was simply to state:

> I have done as I was taught to do. I am no different from any other. You have taught me how to live my life, and I have lived as you have taught me. If you continue teaching others as you have taught me, then you as well must pay the price, and the price is very expensive. You lose your all, even life.[10]

Incapacitation

Although some juveniles have demonstrated by their acts that some form of institutionalization is necessary, it is a costly and ineffective procedure to opt for mere incapacitation as a treatment goal. If the goal of a nonutopian criminal justice system may be described as reduction of crime to a point at or below the tolerance level of society, it may be necessary to employ some sort of criminological triage in dealing with offenders. The PROMIS people bluntly express this proposition as follows:

> The greater the prosecutor's desire to affect the future crime rate, the more weight he or she will give to the indications that the defendant is a repeat offender.[11]

Since the typical resident of the proposed Secure Treatment Unit is a bona fide member of that population which will inevitably become the life-style criminal of tomorrow, spending time and money on him is certainly justified. Although an exact actuarial prediction is almost impossible, it can be safely stated that any life-style violent juvenile who is somehow diverted from adult career-criminality represents a major savings to society in both social and economic terms. Contrast for example, the social and economic differences between the following scenarios:

1. Juvenile [A] exhibits a chronic, escalating pattern of criminal violence from age twelve to fifteen. He is continually incarcerated in a variety of training schools until, while on parole, he commits a robbery-connected homicide. Waived out of the juvenile justice system, he is convicted as an adult and sentenced to a life term in the state prison. He serves approximately thirteen years on this sentence prior to parole, at a cost to the taxpayers of roughly $15,000 per year. He is released as a confirmed life-style criminal, now armed

with far more sophisticated criminal techniques, access to like-minded career criminals on the streets, a certain knowledge that he can "do time" and survive, an enhanced criminal reputation, and the certainty that he will return to prison.

2. The same juvenile, instead of being waived out of the system at age fifteen, is sent to a Secure Treatment Unit for a term not to exceed five years. The cost will be roughly $60,000 per year, which represents, on a surface analysis, a net loss to society in dollars. However, the expectation that this individual will be released *without* a commitment to life-style criminality and with serious noncriminal survival tools at his disposal has a value that we cannot accurately express in dollars. If, in fact, he does not become an adult criminal repeater, the savings to society are incalculable.

Note: Even the incarceration of waived juveniles will still result in the eventual release of a *young* offender. Thus, the cultural influences that might induce "drift" away from a criminal life-style, or the "burn-out" on which the proponents of "waiver" to adult incarceration seem to be relying, certainly will *not* operate when the "learning environment" is an adult correctional institution.

The "pure incapacitation" option is a last resort when applied to juveniles. To justify its use, we must first conclude that any form of genuine reformation is impossible. There is nothing inherently reformative in prolonged incapacitation; indeed, there is much to the contrary. The incarcerated juvenile finds every negative aspect of his former street existence exalted by the prison: physical strength, speed and dexterity with a knife, stealth, and cunning are all highly-prized attributes, and the quality of an individual prisoner's life is directly related to his skill in the use of violence. Crime is rampant inside a prison: theft, sexual assaults, extortion, brutality, and homicide are far more commonplace than in even the most violent community in the outside world. Personal safety is an art form, not a protected right, and mere survival often depends on the practice and execution of criminally violent skills. The idea that regimentation, tight security, and total control of human beings will change their behavior for the better has been utterly disproven by generations of negative results. In fact, the concepts of incapacitative incarceration and criminal inevitability are intertwined. The former is justified only on the ground that rehabilitation is largely a myth.

The fact that reformation occasionally does occur, in individual cases, within a purely incapacitative environment is not a refutation of the above principles. If reformation *does* occur, it is self-induced and is based, as it *must* be, on internal motivation. Maximum security is a crucible that occasionally produces remarkable individuals.[12] The emergence of these individuals, however, into the mainstream of society should not be credited to any inherently rehabilitative properties of the institutions that formerly housed them. Whatever personality or behavioral changes emerge with the released offender probably occured in spite of, not because of, the prison environment. Sequence does not infer causality: because [A] *follows* [B] does not mean that [A] was *caused by* [B].

The proposed secure treatment unit offers temporary incapacitation as a necessary predicate to the potential for reformation. The proposed Secure Treatment Unit appears to endorse incapacitative incarceration, but that appearance is largely illusory. Incapacitation is accepted as part and parcel of any overall schematic on the basis that "environmental therapy" cannot occur in a predominantly negative environment: the subject/participant must be continually exposed to therapy *before* he makes the commitment to meaningfully participate. If this commitment never materializes, the Secure Treatment Unit still expects a degree of de-escalation of criminal violence merely by exposure of the residents to alternative methods of doing business; and the incapacitative "goal" is met during this period. However, the major investment required to support a functioning Secure Treatment Unit is only partly repaid by incapacitation of dangerous juveniles; it will be largely repaid by providing those socialization and habilitation opportunities simply not available in the juvenile's "natural" environment. The Secure Treatment Unit, in the final analysis, offers at least a *potential* for substantive change in the attitudes, values, and behavior of the life-style violent juvenile, and it is this potential that justifies the required investment of time and money. Absent the death penalty, our current criminal justice system offers no genuine incapacitative ability in terms of the life-style violent juvenile.[13] And since this type of individual supplies the major source of raw material[14] for the adult habitual offender (or career criminal),[15] the Secure Treatment Unit expects to dramatically and substantially intervene in a way never before contemplated.

The Needs of the Child: Consequences

The needs of the child must be strictly defined when that child is a life-style violent delinquent. Regardless of actual intent, no juvenile justice legislation would be rhetorically complete without language insisting that the "needs of the child" are to be predominantly considered in any action taken by the authorities. In the 1970s, such language is generally seen by the public as a dependent variable of concepts like "punishment" and "security." Similarly, advocates of treatment and advocates of security are likely to see themselves in opposing roles. However, the fact is that the "needs of the child" need not be equated with what some are now calling the "dictatorship of the delinquent," and the concept of a Secure Treatment Unit cannot be placed in perspective without a thorough analysis of the "needs of the child" as operative language.

We take it as an accepted professional fact that no child needs maltreatment, or brutal conditions of confinement, or deprivation of basic human rights. No child needs to be recklessly endangered, and all children require basic irreducible minimums of adequate care, regardless of what criminal acts they may have committed.[16]

When operationally defined, societal needs and those of delinquent children may well converge in certain cases to indicate incarceration in a secure treatment facility. But we do not leap a chasm of logic to the proposition that no juvenile needs incarceration. Before we even speak of the interests of society, we have to accept the fact that the best interests of our children *are* the best interests of our society. We further have to accept that most of the children now in society will grow to a form of adulthood, and mistakes not rectified in childhood will exacerbate with age. We can embrace the ideal of "least restrictive alternative" when deciding which placement/treatment options to exercise with life-style violent juveniles. But we also realize as part of that concept that sometimes the least restrictive alternative that makes sense involves and requires secure placement.

Although many life-style violent juveniles appear to escape the criminal justice consequences of their acts, it should be understood that this escape is, at best, temporary. Nonrestrictive placement is clearly *not* always in the best interests of any juvenile. For a small, but definite, percentage of juvenile offenders, *any* non-secure placement will serve as nothing more than a temporary stop on the road to maximum security incarceration in an adult facility.

Not only will we have failed to adequately intervene in negative behavior, we will have also transmitted a message of acceptance that somehow radically changes when a certain predetermined age is reached. A juvenile who has been acculturated, through frequent court appearances, to an attitude of nonintervention on the part of the judicial system, is likely to be surprised to the point of systemic shock when the first actual intervention results in a long prison sentence. The ability of the life-style violent juvenile to perceive the future is severely limited at best,[17] and to expect such offenders to alter their life patterns because of the knowledge that society will respond differently when they "mature" is totally unrealistic. When the juveniles fail to perceive as we demand they perceive, we drop the rhetoric of "treatment" and substitute the reality of vengeance as expressed in our "normal" method of doing business in the adult world of criminal justice.

Although a failure to perceive consequences is one characteristic of the life-style violent juvenile, his adult counterpart suffers no such deficiencies. Plea bargaining has contributed to a mythology that crimes have a certain secret "weight" not expressed in the criminal law. Experienced defense attorneys will speak of what a given crime is "worth" in a given jurisdiction,[18] and equally experienced defendants will become outraged if the prosecution and the judiciary insist on playing the game by the written rules.[19]

While adult correctional consequences for criminal behavior are expressed both in terms of length and place of incarceration, juvenile consequences generally vary only as to the latter. Since length of incarceration is almost infinitely variable in juvenile institutions,[20] only the place of incarceration has any significance as a transmitter of messages. Adult correctional schemes partially succeed in transmitting messages by length of incarceration: there is a rough correlation between the type of crime for which convicted,[21] and the number of years the defendant can expect to serve in prison. Therefore, it is generally not considered necessary to place different classes of felons in different institutions,[22] length of sentence serving as the dividing line for treatment purposes. But, even in adult corrections, management problems are routinely transferred to other institutions,[23] and the intensity of incarceration often depends on the crime for which convicted.[24]

But for juveniles, it is not uncommon for those convicted of homicide to be incarcerated with those convicted of acts that would be misdemeanors (or no crime at all) if they were adults. We are assuming, for the purposes of this work, that virtually all jurisdictions have (or should have) eliminated the practice of housing status offenders with criminal offenders.

What is the message thereby transmitted? We have told the life-style violent juvenile that his acts of criminal violence are perceived by the larger society in much the same terms as we perceive acts of petty criminality by those juveniles housed in the same institution. Upon release, the life-style violent juvenile persists in his behavior until he crosses the chronological (or, in some jurisdictions, the community tolerance) barrier, and *then* the message is finally received for the first time—often in the courtroom itself.[25] And, of course, by then the message is too late to be effective.

Varying the site of incarceration is a more viable method of imposing and communicating consequences than is varying the length of incarceration. Critics of the current system claim that the only way to impress society's anger on the juveniles involved in heavy criminal activity is to incarcerate them for long periods of time.

We disagree. One of the functions of the Secure Treatment Unit is purely symbolic: *only* violent juveniles are incarcerated within its walls, and the message is quite unmistakable. Society views the activities of *those* juveniles quite differently from those of lesser offenders.

Another function of the Secure Treatment Unit is to respond to the need of the child for limit setting, *before* limits come to be set in terminal fashion. To the juvenile offender engaged in a "program" where each participant progresses at his own rate towards release, the message is that his prior criminal behavior is not the real issue. The conceit in such a program is that the juvenile is "not together" and needs to become so before he can be discharged. This means only that the juvenile must learn a new set of institutionally adaptive behaviors, *not* that he must learn a new way of doing business on the street.

By contrast, the Secure Treatment Unit provides graduated levels of social and environmental options that are directly correlated with graduated levels of functioning and responsibility, and increased demands for actual performance.

A program may make the same claims, but a program is a unified whole, not a series of separate and distinct units. Unlike programs, the Secure Treatment Unit will mandate certain minimum periods of incarceration regardless of any "progress" made within its walls by its residents. This is accomplished by use of a *curriculum* which requires a certain number of participant/hours for completion. It further requires that completion is not to be viewed as "final" until discharge; the resident may have to complete a portion of the curriculum more than once; until he "passes." This passing, unlike that of our current school system, is *not* based on the amount of time invested, but on actual achievement.

It is necessary to affirmatively state at this point that the Secure Treatment Unit will *not* be a reenactment of the so-called "Defective Delinquent" statutes such as those in Maryland whereby a juvenile can be held until he is "no longer a danger to himself or others."[26] This purely medical model we have rejected, and we accept that some residents will simply "max out" of the Secure Treatment Unit by virtue of completing the period of incarceration to which sentenced by the court. If the courts cooperate, this minimum period will be sufficiently long to motivate the residents to work within the curriculum to achieve its benefits.[27] If the period is too short, participation may be severely limited. However, given the climate of the times, our only real fear is that the minimums may be set too *long* to be effective.

Maximum Security

When listing the requirements for institutional treatment of the life-style violent juvenile, the term "maximum security" often surfaces. Yet it is clear that this term is rarely used by correctional authorities solely to indicate the ability to prevent escapes. In line with our position that only operational definitions are of value in proactive planning,[28] it is our contention that "maximum security" is too amorphous a term to warrant inclusion in a service-delivery plan for our target population. If maximum security is defined as that kind of system which effectively prevents incarcerated prisoners from escaping, most of this country's large-scale penal institutions would amply qualify. Although not unheard of, escapes from such prisons are extremely rare, and successful escapes rarer still. Yet is is useful to note that most of these prisons allocate a section of their interior space to confinement of prisoners in a manner far more rigorous than is prescribed for the rest of the population. No matter what such an area is called,[29] the fact is that its goal is never the mere prevention of escape from the prison itself. The raison d'etre of such segregated areas is to protect residents from other prisoners (protective custody), to protect the rest of the prisoner population from the residents of the segregated areas (administrative segregation), or to isolate the residents as a form of *increased* punishment (solitary confinement).

In correctional thinking, maximum security is perceived as a degree of custody in excess of that which is required to keep the prisoner within the walls of the institution. Although local jails, (charged with the responsibility of holding defendants prior to trial, or holding convicted prisoners awaiting trial on other charges), can maintain a high security area on the ground that such inmates constitute a greater threat to escape, the typical walled institution cannot sustain such a rationale.[30] This is, however, apparently no barrier to the construction and maintenance of such specialized internal facilities. Instead of an "escape risk" rationale, prison administrators rely on the concept that virtually all human rights are "privileges," and that deprivation of such privileges is an appropriate response to negative behavior within the institution. The appellate courts have recognized the multifaceted deprivations inherent in *any* form of solitary confinement and have addressed themselves to these issues in decisions setting forth minimum standards for such incarceration,[31] and specifying the procedure(s) that must be adhered to as a minimum requirement before such isolation may be legally imposed.[32]

But although the appellate courts are (relatively) quick to intervene in procedures perceived as purely punitive,[33] they are less quick to act when the same procedures are described as treatment.[34] In recent years, a great variety of inhumane acts have been perpetrated on prisoners "for their own good," and the courts have usually responded only when the therapeutic value of the treatment has been proven to be nonexistent.[35]

Utilization of maximum-security procedures for punishment purposes reinforces the "might makes right" mentality. This, in turn, reinforces the attitude that revenge is sufficient justification for any act. Even leading advocates of punishment per se freely admit that unless the punishment is perceived as directly and fairly related to the specific acts performed by the recipient of the punishment, the punishment itself will be counterproductive. There must be a direct relationship between acts and consequences if the consequences are to have an effect on future acts. Ironically, when punishment is seen as nothing more than revenge, it finds its strongest endorsement among those who are most likely to suffer from it. The so-called "psychopath" who views humans as mere objects is very likely to respond with demands for vengeance when confronted with the prospect of violence against himself or others close to him.[36] Indeed, the ability to recognize the need for revenge, and the ability to successfully carry it out is often viewed as the most distinctive mark of masculinity among the life-style violent juvenile's peer group. Author Floyd Salas describes this phenomenon accurately and significantly in his "novel" entitled *Tattoo the Wicked Cross*.[37] In the following excerpt, a juvenile prisoner is attempting to cheer up (and motivate) his younger friend who has just been gang-raped while in the "training school." The young man tells his victimized friend the following story:

> Well, man, I knew some pachuco dudes once. You know, some real pachucos, Mexicans, bad actors with pachuco crosses on each hand. And this one pachuco, name of Hector, he used to wear a great big silver cross around his neck, and even had a six inch cross tattooed on his chest, and he was the baddest, coldest, revenge-gettingest dude I ever saw. Man, listen to this, he said and Aaron lifted his head higher on the pillow.
>
> Once I escaped from a foster home over in River County. They put me there after my second burglary job because my old man had taken off on my mother when I was about ten. Well, anyway, I was cutting across country to stay off the highways and clear of the Highway Patrol when these Chicanos in a fruit picker camp took me in. I stayed a whole week with them, and when I was there, I saw this Hector corner a guy who had given him the finger with both hands from a passing car full of guys from another camp. That was about a week before I got there, and he got this dude and slapped his face about ten times, and, then, talking some kind of fantastic Mexican slang, he made the guy kneel down and cup his balls in his hands without squeezing them. Do you know what that means?
>
> Spittle bubbled in the corners of Skip's mouth, but unwilling to pause for a long breath, let alone an answer, he gasped a whistling short wind and kept talking.
>
> Man, when you grab a guy's nuts, you gotta squeeze them or you're a punk, a bitch, a whore. And this guy practically cried. He begged and begged Hector, and said he'd do anything for Hector except that. But Hector, and, man, his arms were as big as tree branches from picking fruit all his life, man, Hector, he made the guy cup 'em or fight. And the guy lifted his hand right up between Hector's legs and held him, man, and when he did, Hector spit in his face for doing it, man. Now, tell-me-like-it-is, man. Is that revenge, man? And just for a guy giving you the double-barreled finger? Revenge, man. Wow!
>
> That's revenge. Yeah, now that's really revenge, man, Aaron agreed, and [he fantasized] the Buzzer [the leader of the gang of rapists] . . . on his knees before him, pink palm upraised, gingerly cupping the crotch of his dungarees. I'd love to make the Buzzer do that in front of everybody, and I'd love to spit in his face.[38]

But the response of the juvenile justice system has been to simply rename those concepts which have proved to be counterproductive. Calling maximum security a form of treatment is not only hypocritical, it is dangerous. The "punishment perceived as treatment" paradigm is most dangerous in the juvenile system because this system has historically permitted abuses and deprivations that would not be tolerated within the adult correctional network. Those punishments and deprivations have flourished under the same rationale that, until quite recently,[39] allowed a juvenile to be found guilty and sentenced without the legal and procedural safeguards that we take for granted in the adult system. And even today, when a great many of those safeguards have been incorporated into the juvenile system,[40] it is a fact that benign rhetoric often cloaks the most serious abuses.

A gross example of the free reign given juvenile authorities may be found in an examination of the history of Patuxent Institution in Maryland.[41] Under that state's so-called "Defective Delinquent" statute, a child may be incarcerated for the rest of his natural life regardless of the criminal acts that first brought him to the institution. Since the prison was seen as existing for the good of the prisoners, any prisoners retained past the point where an adult could legally have been held for the same offense were thought of as being "served" by this continued incarceration. Even a hard-liner might balk at a life sentence for petty theft, but when such a sentence is called treatment, it finds support from even the most liberal sources.

Similarly a juvenile prison superintendent may say that his institution is run on the "cottage plan," but the observer can often find the institution's "disciplinary cottage" if he looks hard enough. And, the superintendent who claims that solitary confinement has been abolished within the walls of his institution should always be asked to show the observer the "quiet room."

At this point, it is necessary to differentiate between the *planning* value of the term "maximum security," and its *political* value. Those jurisdictions planning a complete service-delivery system for the life-style violent juvenile will find the term unwieldy at best; it lacks the self-definition necessary to guarantee a narrow range of compliances and its flabbiness virtually invites abuse by administrators. However, the political value of this term cannot be overestimated. In a country where violent juvenile crime is seen as perhaps the worst menace to our desired way of life, maximum security is a most reassuring sounding solution. In truth, what we propose is to reverse past negative practices by utilizing the same semantic tactics: just as vicious, deprivatory punishments were permitted when they were called treatment, it is our goal to institute the most progressive, *habilitative* system and to partially grease the skids of public acceptance with terms such as maximum security. However, unlike past practices, our intent is not to mislead the public, but to protect and benefit it. Maximum security, in the sense that the residents are prevented from escaping, *will* be guaranteed in our design; yet the sensory and emotional deprivations (now perceived as an inherent part of maximum security) will *not* be present.

What sounds like a contradiction in terms is, instead, merely a proper use of those terms.

Differential Treatment

The concept of differential treatment of residents, while variously interpreted, is standard procedure in most institutions. The concept of differential treatment of inmates within the same prison (or residents within the same program) is not new. In fact, such differential treatment is generally accepted as a (negative) fact of life by residents in any institutional setting. Inmate analysis of the motivation for such differential treatment ranges from the elemental ("the guards just don't like me"), to the mildly sophisticated (racist, political, or self-interest motivations of staff), to the near-mysterious (self-perception as a human being destined from birth to be ill-treated).

The so-called "convict code" was originally evolved to combat the divisive effects of differential treatment. There is little question but that differential treatment was originally designed as a tool to combat inmate unity. Prisoners treated in exactly the same (inhumane) fashion will display greater solidarity than those whose treatment depends strictly on their compliance with institutional goals. In the past, prisoner peer pressure was designed almost solely around the need to combat differential treatment by the management authorities; thus the strong sanction against *any* form of cooperation with the power structure.[42] There were, of course, self-serving aspects to each side's position: the administration claimed to utilize differential treatment so as to be able to properly reward those inmates showing progress towards "rehabilitation" and conformity to institutional rules, but actually utilized such treatment to "divide and conquer" the convict population. And convict leaders utilized the "code" (especially those strictures against informing) to protect their own interests while allowing prisoners of lesser status to suffer the consequences of their refusal to cooperate.

In the resulting contest, differential treatment emerged the victor, and the "code" itself is now virtually nonexistent. The rhetoric of rehabilitation has combined with the continuing management need for a divided population of prisoners, to gradually erode old concepts of inmate solidarity to the point where most veteran observers now believe the code no longer exists.[43]

> When I first went down [became incarcerated] in the 50's, it was unheard of to even be seen *talking* to a screw [guard].[44] And a rat [informant] was the lowest form of life; cons wouldn't even *drink* behind scum like that.[45] And if it became a known thing that a guy *was* a rat, he'd have to lock up [seek Protective Custody] if he wanted to live. It wouldn't matter who he ratted out, *anybody'd* shank [stab] him just to be doing it. It was the right thing to do, you know? And he'd be in P.C. [Protective Custody, also occasionally called "Punk City"] for life. He could never walk the yard.

But let me tell you something. I don't know if we're getting a different type of con, or if the screws are winning, or what, but it's different today. Now a guy will come in here *bragging* that he's a fuckin' rat . . . and to be seen talking to a screw is *nothing*. Everytime something goes down [happens], the kites [secret notes to the administration; sometimes signed and sometimes not] *fly*.

I'll tell you the truth; I can't do time no more. Especially with all those young fools running around in here. I never thought I'd see this, but I think the administration is finally running this prison.[46]

Of course, this path to control was not always smooth. Many of the techniques of differential treatment backfired, (if their goal was to increase intraprisoner hostilities). Designation of certain prisoners as more dangerous than others often proved to be more of a status symbol than a divisive tool.[47] Although such individuals ostensibly were to receive less of the "rewards" of prison life, the fact was that other admiring prisoners were quick to pass along goods and services to which such special-status prisoners were not entitled.

However, with the tremendous increase in popularity of the indeterminate sentence, parole became the most important issue in adult corrections. The more narrow the range of release-options (for example, "flat-time" sentences or terms such as "from 5 to 7 years"), the less impact the *potential* for differential treatment had on the prisoner population. The converse of this principle also quickly became obvious to correctional observers. It is no accident that the California penal system, which featured the ultimate in indeterminate sentences such as "from one year to life," became notorious for the constant inmate warfare within its institutions.[48]

In many ways, the indeterminate sentence is the ultimate in differential treatment in that it opens up wide vistas for this possibility. Although the indeterminate sentence was generally held to be rehabilitative in intent, the idea being that prisoners progress at individual rates and should be responded to and rewarded in terms of those rates, it is possible to hold a distinctly contrary view of that intent. Mark J. Lerner, of the New York State Board of Parole, states:

The notion of indeterminate sentences being a treatment modality, with parole board discretion coming into play to decide when treatment has been completed, was adopted from penologists of the mid-nineteenth and early twentieth centuries [citations omitted]. This idea was founded not on scientific studies, but on religious beliefs [citations omitted]. Contemporary efforts at providing a scientific framework for this century-old misconception have generally proven to be failures [citations omitted]. Actually, the concept of the indeterminate sentence was originally introduced in the late eighteenth century [citations omitted] as a method of mental punishment that was thought to be more severe than the physical tortures then in vogue. Hence, the indeterminate sentence originally was proposed in a deterrence model but redefined by penal "reformers" as a treatment tool.[49]

Although any adjudication of juvenile delinquency gives rise to indeterminate sentencing, differential treatment did not prove as effective a tactic when used against a juvenile offender population. The correlation to the juvenile justice system is obvious: indeterminate sentences were based on the rehabilitative model. In fact, such sentencing was based on the "medical model" of treatment: prisoners were socially "sick"; they were capable of being "cured"; and some were "cured" at a faster rate than others. Those who achieved this cure earlier than others were, correspondingly, released at an earlier date. Virtually *all* juvenile sentences are, by their very nature, indeterminate. But the prospect of earlier release did not prove to have the same controlling effect it did in the adult system. Those juveniles who found themselves doing time with older convicts quickly proved to be a source of difficulty for both the administration and their fellow prisoners:

> The worst fuck-ups are *always* the kids! It takes them *years* just to settle down and realize they're going to be here a while.[50]

Confronted with the very real difficulty of controlling a largely unstable population of juvenile offenders, the "treatment" and "custody" blocs within the juvenile institutions were forced to come to the bargaining table and mutually agree on a new system of control.[51] The bastard offspring resulting from the backroom liaison between these two forces was a new concept of differential treatment. This treatment was designed to channel the acting-out aggressive-violent behavior of juveniles back against the prisoners themselves, with a corresponding increase in manageability.

Although generally expressed in nonpunitive, treatment-oriented terms, this differential treatment often had a vicious aspect to it, as in the "cadet captain" or "cottage duke" models.[52] Yet even the most therapeutically described differential treatments had precisely the same actual motivation: to produce a more tractable, governable, quiet population of prisoners.[53]

Management concerns always predominated in juvenile institutions of the past,[54] and similarly predominated in both versions of differential treatment. Although the cadet captain model was based on the proposition that juvenile offenders were savage beasts capable of control only with physical violence, it was also so obvious a technique that reformers were quick to condemn its use. The popularity of "rehabilitation rhetoric" has ebbed and flowed in adult corrections, but it has been constant in the juvenile justice system. Management personnel were forced to evolve new techniques that would give them the control delivered by the old system, but which would lend themselves (on paper) to the rhetoric of the new. Soon, differential treatment began to assume innovative new "therapeutic" forms.

The new forms of differential treatment promised some innate reform of the old system. Although certain behaviors would still be singled out for rewards, proponents of the new systems claimed that the *kind* of behavior rewarded would be radically different. For example, no longer would a resident of a training school rise to a position of power over other residents because of his (physical) contribution to the overall peace and quiet of the institution. Since this contribution was based on intimidation of (and physical violence directed against) other residents, advocates of the new systems believed that the keepers would look at *individual* behavior and hold each resident responsible for his own actions. The theory was that if proper behavior were rewarded, the same management objectives (a smoothly run, quiet institution) could be achieved. What would be the benefit to an institutional thug of keeping the place quiet if each resident were individually rewarded? The thug would be rewarded only for his *own* quiet behavior, and would theoretically not reap dividends from the quiet behavior of others.

However, many institutional programs failed to functionally distinguish between two basic types of intimidation observed by their staff members: one type was designed purely as a manipulative tool, with the intimidator understanding that staff rewards would flow from his ability to "run" the institution; but the other type was concerned only with his personal status and gratification, and used physical intimidation as the quickest means to that end.

The older systems found it unnecessary to distinguish between those two basic motivations, because either motivation produced exactly the same behavior in the resident population—the few would control the many (by force) and management objectives were thereby enhanced. The new systems were supposed to bring about a clarification of the motivations of the intimidators/exploiters. The belief was that those residents with purely manipulative motives would change their behavior when the manipulation was not rewarded, and that those whose motives were more emotional/social would persist regardless of exterior "rewards." The problem was that even with this distinction, the system itself had no means by which to deal with the latter group.

Another way to look at the perception of two different types of institutional intimidator/exploiters is to examine the motives for unarmed (or "strongarm") robbery. One perception is that the robber is motivated strictly by the opportunity of obtaining money for his efforts. Such individuals, if supplied with sufficient funds, allegedly would cease their criminal activity. Yet another perception is that some psycho-emotional need of the robber is satisfied by the physical attack itself. It is commonly observed that many teenage robbers assault their victims *following* the robbery itself. The lack of necessity for this action (in purely financial terms) gives rise to the belief that some strongarm robbers are not economically motivated. Needless to say, treatment of these two distinct types of robbers is vastly different and a purely statistical analysis of the underlying criminal acts as "robberies" is insufficient as a diagnostic tool.

It was the expectation of the planners of the new reward systems that the system itself would act as a diagnostic tool, separating those physical intimidators/exploiters who acted for the sake of the activity itself from those who acted in the hope of institutional rewards. However, the juveniles' *perception* was key to the viability of the new systems. Therefore, any failure of the institutional intimidators/exploiters to perceive that their behavior would have a negative effect on their opportunities for release tended to negate any value possibly attached to a diagnostic separation of the divergent motivations for their behavior.

Additionally, the planners ignored the complexities involved in what they saw as a "free choice" area. Some juveniles joined the ranks of the intimidators/ exploiters so as to avoid classification as potential victims. Others "found themselves" after a period of exploitative activity and concluded that such activity was the most pleasurable they had ever experienced; such residents obviously could not be motivated to change their behavior by the promise of release. And other juveniles, those with powerful personalities and leadership qualities, simply adapted to *any* new environment by attempting to rise to whatever positions of strength and control that environment offered. Such juveniles lack the perception that they could *change* environments and are commonly described as individuals who "could have been bank presidents if they'd been born in a suburb."

Although given various names, the new systems and techniques were all designed around the purchase (with good behavior) of rewards (in terms of goods and services). The new systems had various names. Some were called "token economies,"[55] others were called "point systems"[56] or "levels systems."[57] All were designed around the concept that residents would progress at individualized rates and that verbal recognition of this progress was less important than tangible reward. Stipped of therapeutic verbiage, these systems allowed residents to "buy" specific items and "privileges" by accomplishing specified, approved behaviors which were to be recorded by staff. However, once the items purchased were introduced into the general stream of commerce within the institution, possession and enjoyment continued to be governed by *past* systems of intimidation and exploitation. This applied, as will be seen, equally to privileges.

The success of such systems was to be based on the conceit that staff (1) is able to properly criteria-ize those behaviors and (even more difficult) those attitudes which merit reward; (2) is able to achieve a standard of consistent and unbiased observation which will properly detect and record those behaviors deemed worthy of reward and punishment; and (3) will, in fact, base all such rewards on the disclosed criteria *and* the actual behavior of the residents.

Inevitably, those activities deemed worthy of reward by staff would be those which advanced the management objectives of the institution. The first-mentioned difficulty can be overcome only in terms of justice, not in terms of therapeutic value. Justice is assured, in a philosophical sense, merely by the *establishment* of criteria for judgment and evaluation of behavior, with the caveat that this sense of justice applies only when the established criteria are disclosed to the resident population *prior* to an individual's entrance into the program. The inherent fairness of granting more "points" for "dealing nonviolently with a conflict situation" than "going to bed promptly in the evening" can never really be disputed, so long as all residents are informed, in advance, of the rating system. However, the *actual* value of specific behaviors in terms of therapeutic goals is nearly impossible to calculate, and staffs' management bias always creeps in. The result is that behavior which increases the manageability of the institution is more highly rewarded.

It was equally inevitable that some "proper" behavior would go unrewarded and this difficulty is never surmounted in actual practice. Staff continues to rely on sporadic observation, buttressed by reports from the residential population itself. Probably less than 10 percent of all behavior that takes place in a typical institution is actually observed by staff; the remainder is deduced from a variety of easily-subverted reporting mechanisms.

Staff, of course, quickly evolve ways of rewarding those juveniles who help "manage" an institution. Even when the criteria for "correct" behavior are overtly disclosed, there is always sufficient flexibility in the design so that certain favored residents can still be inappropriately rewarded for "assistance" in management of the institution itself.

In response to new treatment techniques, new exploitation techniques develop. With new goods and services introduced into the economy of the institution, veteran exploiters among the resident population simply evolved new means to achieve their old ends. It was common for observers to note that the occupants of the higher "levels" (which allowed greater access to highly prized privileges such as weekend furloughs) were generally those who would have been the "dukes" in the older systems. Although hard-core corruption (such as a resident bribing a staff member to fabricate and record certain "positive" behavior) was certainly not widespread, varieties of soft-core corruption (such as a staff member recording nonexistent positive behavior as a reward to a violent resident who "assisted" staff in keeping the institution quiet) became more commonplace. Although some of the systems attempted to realign institutional values with the promise of rewards (such as extra "points" for informing on another resident, phrased in euphemisms like "intervening in a potentially dangerous situation for the good of the community,") peer pressure still controlled, and informants were still rewarded *sub rosa* (by giving them "points" *actually* earned for informing, in the guise of rewarding more acceptable, but nonexistent, behaviors). Also, since there was always an attempt to measure and reward "attitudes," there was a great deal of flexibility built into all the new systems.

But to the residents, the promised new systems were nothing more than old wine in a new bottle, and old habits and ways of doing business were not significantly altered. Regardless of the rhetoric in which the new systems were cloaked, the residents quickly perceived that institutional management objectives remained the top priority, and those residents who contributed to the manageability of the institution were still rewarded. If, for example, a resident could earn some new clothing by virtue of good behavior, there was nothing to prevent this resident from "lending" his new clothing to an institutional "heavy" who had earned no such reward himself. Simply stated, there was no real correlation between justifiable possession and the *continuation* of such possession. In other words: business as usual.

Those new systems that attempted institutional "self-government" often simply increased opportunity for exploitation. Even more susceptible to corruption were those systems that relied on a form of approved self-government for institutional residents. These systems first renamed the institution a "therapeutic community," announced that the residents "shared common concerns," and permitted them to "vote" on such matters as the distribution of privileges. Needless to say, those physical and social pressures that operated prior to the advent of the new system were not altered in any significant way. In all fairness, we should note that the "therapeutic community" idea(l) has been somewhat successful in many other settings, and with many other kinds of "patients." Our commentary is addressed to those juvenile *prisons* which housed life-style violent juveniles. Such institutions have proven themselves to be poor candidates for transformation into therapeutic communities.[58]

With the possible exception of outright release to the community,[59] any rewards dispensed by the new systems simply fed the commercial stream of the institutional economy and were redistributed according to the prevalent power-relationships. Tangible evidence of enhanced status remained under the exclusive control of the inmate population because all residents, regardless of staff-assigned status, shared the same quarters. The new systems never impacted on the individual life-styles of the residents, and all continued to be governed by past models of exploitation and manipulation.

But in rejecting past models for treatment of the life-style violent juvenile, we do not reject the possibility of reformation, nor even the use of differential treatment to accomplish that end. Although we have been highly critical of the so-called rehabilitative models on which juvenile justice has been historically based, and although we have pointed out the failure of differential treatment to accomplish any goals but those of institutional management, we have not gone so far as to embrace the proposition that life-style violent juveniles are beyond any treatment whatsoever. Nor have we accepted the proposition that punishment and incapacitation are the only achievable goals of an institution for such individuals. Our positions are far from inconsistent. The real inconsistencies lie with planners and managers of the past, for they merely displayed the reality of simple-minded punishment cloaked in the rhetoric of rehabilitation. And, as a consequence, they achieved the benefits of neither one.

Yet if we reject the notion that pure punishment/incapacitation is the only achievable goal, what remains to be tried? Recognition that juveniles are individuals who will progress (and retrogress) at differing rates forces us towards the adoption of a treatment plan that not only permits, but takes advantage of this important characteristic. And if we summarily reject the *past* forms of differential treatment, what can be utilized as a substitute?

Notes

1. The *Dictionary of Criminal Justice Data Terminology,* (Search Group, Inc., U.S. Department of Justice, Washington, D.C., 1976) for example, omits this term entirely.

2. The Chicago Vice Lords, see ch. 1, note 8, *supra,* even call their violent forays into the community "wolf packing":

> "Wolf packing" is somewhat similar in form to strong-armed hustling. However, the aim is different. Strong-armed hustling is concerned with making money, while wolf packing is primarily for enhancing a rep[utation]. Wolf packing was explained to me in the following way: "Wolf packing—like for instance me and some other fellows go out and knock you down 'cause we feel like it. That's what it is. I might take your money, but I really want to kick some ass anyway, so I decide to knock the first thing in my way down." [at p. 35.]

And other groups of violent juveniles seem to have adopted similar terminology for similar acts:

> Everyone walked in cliques [inside the institution], groups of from about five to thirty guys. The younger kids always walked in big bunches. Individuals or weak groups walking along got rat-packed [attacked by a group], pressured out of their canteen draw, or stabbed right in the hallway. A strong group wouldn't be bothered. This was called the wolf code; and the blacks' clique was the Wolf Pack, strongest group in Tracy [Correctional Institution].
>
> James Carr, *Bad (An Autobiography),* (New York: Herman Graf Associates, 1975) at p. 60.

The authors find it strange that when we discover "wolf children" in the wilds of Europe, no expense is too great for society to "socialize" them to our ways. But when we find "wolf children" in the wilds of the South Bronx, our societal response is that such children are incapable of any type of reformation.

3. Lewis Yablonsky, *The Violent Gang* (Baltimore, Maryland: Penguin Books, 1973), at pp. 55 ff., quotes the father of a youth murdered by a New York City street gang viewing the juvenile killers of his son:

They are monsters—in my mind I classify them as savage animals. That's all. I don't think that they have any civilization in them. I just think they're two-legged animals. They haven't any concept of living with other people, outside of to show that they can do something worse than the other or to claim any sort of notoriety. . . . This [the murder of his son] is pure jungle activity.

4. David Matza, *Delinquency and Drift,* (New York: John Wiley, 1964).

5. Whitman's crime (the "Texas Tower Massacre") was certainly episodic, but the homicides committed by David Berkowitz, while extending over a period of time, were so psychotically motivated as to remove them from any possible description as "life-style" crimes.

6. *See,* ch. 1, note 7, *supra.* But the life-style chronic violence of the juvenile offender population has impacted even on our definitions of "professional" crime. As one scholar reports:

Traditionally, by examining their characteristics . . . criminologists have seen professional criminals as those who have criminal values and engage in non-violent, skillful, specialized pursuits for long periods of time with lessened likelihood of being caught, prosecuted, or incarcerated. Contemporary professional criminals are conceptualized in a different way. [A]n emphasis is placed on crime being an occupation without the requirement of the criminal being relatively skillful at the same time. Thus, they are conceptualized as being generalists operating in loose associations, no longer unified by normative proscriptions or status.

Gregory R. Staats, "Changing Conceptualizations of Professional Criminals," *Criminology* 49 (1977), at p. 63.

7. Jim Procter, "Study Says Juvenile System Needs Overhaul," in the Jackson, Mississippi *Clarion-Ledger,* October 24, 1977, p. 1.

8. Joan Petersilia; Peter W. Greenwood; and Marvin Lavin, *Criminal Careers of Habitual Felons* (Santa Monica, California: Rand Corporation, 1977), at p. 120.

9. Manson's statements constantly refer to his early imprisonment as the cause of his later criminality. He has often said "The State is my Father," and occasionally refers to himself as "The Graduate."

See, for example, V. Bugliosi, and C. Gentry, *Helter Skelter,* (New York: W.W. Norton & Co., 1974) and Ed Sanders, *The Family,* (New York: Dalton, 1971).

10. T.E. Gaddis, and J. Long, *Killer: A Journal of Murder,* (Greenwich, Connecticut: Fawcett Publications, 1970) at p. 9. Copyright © 1970 by Thomas

E. Gaddis and James O. Long. Panzram's attribution of his life-style vicious criminality to juvenile imprisonment can be readily seen in the following statements from the same work:

> They trained me all right in that [Minnesota State; Red Wing, Minnesota] training school. There during my two years I was trained by two different sets of people to have two different sets of morals. The good people tried to train me to be good and the bad people did train me to be bad. The method that the good people used in training me was to beat the goodness into me and all the badness out of me. They done their best but their best wasn't good enough to accomplish what they set out to do. The more they beat me and whipped me, the more I hated them . . . [at p. 23.]

> Oh yes, I learned a hell of a lot from my expert instructors furnished to me free of charge by society in general and the State of Minnesota in particular. From the treatment I received while there and the lessons I learned from it, I had fully decided when I left there just how I would live my life. I made up my mind that I would rob, burn, destroy, and kill everywhere I could as long as I lived. That's the way I was reformed in the Minnesota State Training School. [at p. 29.]

11. Note 13 (ch. 1), *supra,* at p. 13.

12. For example, Robert Stroud, the famous "Birdman of Alcatraz"; George Jackson, author and social commentator; *see,* for example, *Soledad Brother, The Prison Letters of George Jackson,* (New York: Bantam Books, 1970); Robert John Lewis, an unjustly imprisoned teenager who became a major force for social change in New Jersey (former Director of the Ad Hoc Parole Committee and current Director of the Glassboro State College Prisoner Re-Entry Program), and Carryl Chessman, whose *Cell 2455, Death Row* (New York: Prentice-Hall, 1954) gave us some penetrating insights into the etiology of the life-style violent juvenile.

13. Jack P. Gibbs, "The Death Penalty, Retribution, and Penal Policy," 69 *The Journal of Criminal Law and Criminology* 291 (1978), comments at p. 292:

> [I]ncapacitation is a dubious rationale for the death penalty, for there is no compelling evidence that the execution of all convicted murderers would reduce the murder rate appreciably. Indeed, the repetitive rate for murderers appears to be very low [the author here cites, for example, Waldo, "The 'Criminality Level' of Incarcerated Murderers and Non-murderers," 61 *Journal of Criminal Law, Criminology, and Police Science* 60 (1970)]. Hence it could be that the murder rate would be reduced appreciably only by the prevention of first offenses. So, paradoxically, while the death penalty incapacitates absolutely, its effect on the crime rate *through incapacitation* may be inconsequential. (emphasis in original).

14. Some of the major organized crime figures who began their careers in juvenile institutions are Joe Barboza [*see,* Joe Barboza, (with Hank Messick),

Barboza (New York: Dell Books, 1975)], Ira Pecznick [*see* Paul Hoffman, and Ira Pecznick, *To Drop a Dime* (New York: G.P. Putnam's Sons, 1976)], and Joseph Luparelli, [*see,* Paul S. Meskil, *The Luparelli Tapes,* (Chicago: Playboy Press, 1976)]. And juveniles are used by older criminals well before they themselves reach adulthood, a practice that has been in existence for many decades:

> At the time of the study a member of this gang, only twelve years old, was in the juvenile Detention Home on charge of participating in a thousand-dollar robbery. He said that the other members were trying to put the responsibility on him. It is said that the leader's custom is to commit crimes and then make the smaller boys bear the brunt of the punishment.
>
> Frederic M. Thrasher, *The Gang* (Chicago: The University of Chicago Press, 1927) at p. 260.

> When they [junior gang members in the South Bronx] got older, and after undergoing a brutal initiation or carrying out a dangerous assignment designated by the senior gang president, they graduated into membership in the regular gang. Gang presidents often used younger members to do the shooting when someone was to be killed. That way, if the police arrested several gang members for the murder, the kid would confess and get off with a sentence to a juvenile home.
>
> Gary Hoenig, *Reaper: The Story of a Gang Leader,* (Indianapolis/New York: The Bobbs-Merrill Company, 1975) at p. 49.

> "You take a 30-year-old guy who's about to be charged with a murder that happened three years ago," says a defense lawyer. "He goes to an 18-year-old kid and pays him $1,500 to confess. Since the kid was a juvenile at the time of the murder, nothing can happen to him. Everybody comes out happy. The kid gets status as a killer and a lot of money. The cops clear a case. And the real killer gets away with it."
>
> "Hordes of Teens Beat Serious Raps," by Michael Daly, *New York Daily News,* April 17, 1978, pp 3 ff. Copyright 1978 New York News Inc. Reprinted by permission.

15. As this type of offender has come to be known in prosecutorial circles.

16. *See,* for example, American Bar Association Criminal Justice Section Project on Standards Relating to *The Legal Status of Prisoners,* Tentative Draft, 1977.

17. This inability to perceive the future is, in fact, a social/cultural disability, not an organic one. It partially explains why any form of deterrence other than that which is *immediately* applied will probably fail with this group but, at the same time, it offers genuine hope for eventual reformation in a controlled environment where the life-style violent juvenile can be trained to lengthen his perceptions.

18. This "weight" may vary radically even among neighboring jurisdictions with precisely the same statutory scheme. For example, an armed robbery committed in Manhattan is "worth" less penal time that the same crime committed in the neighboring county of Queens. And it is common to observe that rural areas of a state are more likely to heavily penalize crimes than their urban counterparts. Unfortunately, this "weight" seems to vary more according to individual prosecutors and the quality of the available evidence than according to the severity of the crime. *See,* for example, Mark Schorr, "Blood Stewart's End," *New York Magazine,* March 27, 1978 at p. 58 for an analysis of the "weight" of certain sex crimes in New York City.

19. A young defendant known to us was a relatively notorious thief, largely to support a serious narcotics habit. While on parole from a burglary conviction, he was apprehended asleep in a stolen car, the back seat of which was filled with stolen property. He was found to have a handgun in his possession and several "bags" of heroin. Following his (by now automatic) plea of guilty, he listened to the prosecutor ask for a sentence of 4 years and immediately jumped up and exclaimed:

You motherfucker; all that shit [the various crimes] was only worth a deuce [2 years in prison]!

20. Juvenile incarcerative statutes rarely specify precise terms for specific criminal acts. Even New York State's much-touted Designated Felony Act simply provides (for those juveniles convicted of committing any one of several Class A felony acts) that:

(i) The respondent shall be placed within the division for youth for an initial period of five years.
(ii) The respondent shall initially be confined in a secure facility for a period set by the order, to be not less than twelve nor more than eighteen months.
(iii) After the period set under clause (ii) of this paragraph, the respondent shall be placed in a residential facility for a period of twelve months.
(d) Upon the expiration of the initial period of placement, or any extension thereof, the placement may be extended, on a motion of any party, the division for youth, or the court, after a dispositional hearing, for an additional period of twelve months, but no initial placement or extension of placement under this section may continue beyond the respondent's twenty-first birthday.

Family Court Act of the State of New York, Section 753-a (enacted 1976, effective 1977).

21. Note, not crimes actually *committed,* especially important in plea bargaining situations, although the Parole Board occasionally "makes up the

difference" between pleaded-to crimes and actual criminal conduct by denying parole based on the "seriousness of the offense."

22. Although some states have relatively sophisticated penal networks (such as New York and California) and make some attempt to locate prisoners in facilities deemed appropriate to their criminal acts, other states have but a single maximum-security facility to which all convicted felons are sentenced.

23. Norval Morris, and Gordon Hawkins, *The Honest Politician's Guide to Crime Control,* (Chicago: The University of Chicago Press, 1970), at p. 199:

> [A]ll in all, the most positive criterion for selection of an inmate [by a given institution] will be the urgent strength of the desire of the warden of another institution to get rid of him!

24. Incarcerative possibilities range from solitary confinement through maximum-medium-minimum security to "honor farms," "work camps," and community-based facilities. Often benefit/privileges such as work release or "study release" (to a local college) are correlated directly to the seriousness of the prisoner's original offense, and some jurisdictions statutorily exclude certain classes of criminal offenders from participation in "outside-oriented" programs.

25. It is, tragically, not uncommon for a youth formerly acculturated to juvenile court dispositions to be thunderstruck when he receives a long-term sentence to an adult facility. One juvenile, a veteran of literally dozens of strong-arm robberies in New York City, reached the age of sixteen and pleaded guilty to a similar crime in the adult court. When told he would have to serve a sentence of up to 15 years, he turned to his defense counsel and said "Just for that [the robbery]?"

26. The Maryland Code, Article 31B, "Defective Delinquents," defines the candidate for such treatment as:

> An individual who, by the demonstration of persistent aggravated antisocial or criminal behavior, evidences a propensity towards criminal activity, and who is found to have either such intellectual deficiency or emotional unbalance, or both, as to clearly demonstrate an actual danger to society so as to require such confinement and treatment, when appropriate, as may make it reasonably safe for society to terminate the confinement and treatment.

See also, Linda Sleffel, *The Law and the Dangerous Criminal* (Lexington, Massachusetts: D.C. Heath and Co., 1978), at p. 49.

27. The planned curriculum for the Secure Treatment Unit involves several complex steps. Although its potential benefits to the residents of the facility are great, a too-short period of incarceration will permit the residents to retain their subcultural focus to the point where anything resembling voluntary participation is unlikely.

28. Since proactive planning purports to focus on the *future,* it requires *working* definitions of terms and concepts to be effective. Vague concepts such as rehabilitation will not adequately provide the foundation of a plan designed to solve problems that have yet to emerge.

29. Some common terms are "The Hole," "Management Control Unit," "Adjustment Center," "Administrative Segregation," "Lock-up"; the change in terminology does not reflect a change in attitude from one institution to the next.

30. Jails, because of their particular function, must anticipate a much higher degree of inmate traffic in and out of the institution on a daily basis. Typically, they are located in urban areas for immediate access to courthouses, and do not lend themselves to more intrusive forms of physical security (such as gun towers, etc.). An isolated, walled institution should be able to adequately prevent escapes without utilization of a special internal unit to serve that function.

31. *See,* for example, Jordan v. Fitzharris, 257 F. Supp. 674 (N.D.Cal. 1966) and Sostre v. McGinnis, 442 F.2d 178 (2d Circuit. 1971).

    See also, Thomas B. Benjamin, and Kenneth Lux, "Constitutional and Psychological Implications of the Use of Solitary Confinement," 2 *New England Journal on Prison Law* 27 (1975).

32. *See,* for example, Morris v. Travisono, 310 F. Supp. 857 (D.R.I. 1970), and *In Re* Owens, 9 CrL 2416 (Cook County, Illinois, 7/9/71).

33. *See,* for example, Gates v. Collier 349 F.Supp. 881 (N.D. Miss. 1972) and Holt v. Sarver, 309 F.Supp. 362 (E.D.Ark. 1970), *aff'd* 442 F.2d 304 (8th Cir. 1971), for court decisions outlawing previously accepted practices such as corporal punishment and gun-carrying convict/guards.

34. David J. Rothman, "Historical Overview: Behavior Modification in Total Institutions," 5 *The Hastings Center Report* 17 (1975) at p. 23:

> While the federal courts have struck down as unconstitutional many prison practices, from prohibitions on letter writing to barbaric solitary cells, they have often done so because they could find no rehabilitative purposes to the measures. But these decisions leave the door wide open to procedures that can enter under the guise of rehabilitation.
>
> The institution at Patuxent [see note 24, *supra*], for example, has won numerous legal contests because the judges were impressed with the good intentions of its administrators and the number of professionals on its payroll. [*id.* at 23, but the author warns that:]
>
> If we are incarcerating people for treatment purposes, then let us measure the effectiveness of treatment, not hide behind the claim that these people [the inmates] are dangerous. [*id.* at 23]
>
> If Patuxent officials tell us that some persons, who at another institution would have been incarcerated for thirty years, leave their institution in only five, we must remember to ask about the others,

those who might have been confined elsewhere for only five, and ended up spending thirty years at Patuxent. [*Id.* at 24.]

35. The case of Knecht v. Gillman, 488 F.2d 1136 (8th Cir. 1973) and 14 CrL 2282 (CA 8, 12/5/73) is most illustrative. Inmates of the Iowa Security Medical Facility (a prison) were forcibly injected with apormorphine, a drug which induced violent vomiting and also had some cardiovascular effects, every time they violated the "behavior protocols" of the institution. Prohibited behavior for which this "therapy" would be applied included not getting up promptly, giving cigarettes to other prisoners, talking against orders, swearing, and lying. The drug was injected by a "nurse," intramuscularly, and with force if necessary. This was blithely described as "aversive therapy" based on "Pavlovian conditioning."

After taking testimony, part of which defended the "therapy" and part of which characterized it as "worse than a controlled beating," the court held:

> The use of apormorphine, then, can be justified only if it can be said to be treatment. . . .
>
> At the outset we note that the mere characterization of an act as "treatment" does not insulate it from eighth amendment scrutiny. in *Trop v. Dulles,* 356 U.S. 86, 95 (1958), the Supreme Court stated that the legislative classification of a statute is not conclusive in determining whether there had been a violation of the eighth amendment [which prohibits Cruel and Unusual Punishment] . . . .
>
> Whether it is called "aversive stimuli" or punishment, the act of forcing someone to vomit for a fifteen minute period for committing some minor breach of the rules can only be regarded as cruel and unusual unless the treatment is being administered to a patient who knowingly and intelligently has consented to it. [*id.* at 14 CrL 2282]

See also, David Goldberger, "Court Challenges to Prison Behavior Modification Programs," 13 *American Criminal Law Review* 37 (1975) and, Willard Gaylin, and Helen Blatte, "Behavior Modification in Prisons," 13 *American Criminal Law Review* 11 (1975). For a case involving juveniles, *see* Nelson v. Heyne, 491 F.2d 353 (7th Cir. 1974).

36. *See* interview with Nicholas Pileggi, Appendix.

37. Floyd Salas, *Tattoo the Wicked Cross* (New York: Grove Press, 1967).

38. Ibid at pp. 300-301. Reprinted by permission of the author.

39. The leading cases establishing constitutional and procedural rights for juveniles are less than a dozen years old. The major procedural breakthroughs date from *In re* Gault, 387 U.S. 1, 87 S.Ct. 1428, 18 L.Ed.2d 527 (1967) and *In re* Winship, 397 U.S. 358, 90 S.Ct. 1068, 25 L.Ed.2d 368 (1970).

40. The major exception being that juveniles have been held *not* entitled to

a trial by jury; McKeiver v. Pennsylvania, 403 U.S. 528, 91 S.Ct. 1976, 29 L.Ed.2d 647 (1971).

41. *See* note 26, *supra*. Patuxent Institution, as described in the annotation to the Maryland Code Annotated, Article 31B, Section 1, was "established and opened on January 1, 1955 and has been characterized by the [Federal] Court of Appeals as 'neither a prison, a hospital, nor an insane asylum, but an institution which exercises some of the functions of all three.' Director of Patuxent Institute v. Daniels, 243 Md. 16, 221 A.2d 397 (1966)."

> In the last twenty years, there has been a growing disillusionment with the indeterminate sentence. Patuxent Institution inmates despise the indeterminate sentence because, in a situation already charged with uncertainty and tension, it adds the worst uncertainty of all: the release date. The indeterminate sentence forces Patuxent inmates to play the treatment game, which, for some, is demeaning, for others, self-destructive, and for still others simply a waste of time. In the eyes of the inmates the indeterminate sentence becomes not the motivating force in improving oneself, as its adherents claim, but the motivation for playing the game necessary to achieve the ultimate goal of freedom. Regardless of how the indeterminate sentence looks on paper, it becomes something quite different in the operation of a place like Patuxent. The indeterminate sentence is self-defeating as a rehabilitative device.

> E. Barrett Prettyman, "The Indeterminate Sentence and the Right to Treatment," 11 *American Criminal Law Review* 7 (1972), Abstract S 12021, from 5 *Crime and Delinquency Literature* 183 (1973).

42. We exposed a veteran professional criminal (in the old sense) who had served numerous terms as a juvenile and as an adult, to the "Staff and Inmate Attitude Perception Survey in Shirley, Cottage Nine [the maximum-security unit of Massachusetts' major juvenile training school]." (This study, by Robert B. Coates and Alden D. Miller, entitled *Youth Reactions to Programs in the Massachusetts Department of Youth Services Institutions 1970-1972,* was copyrighted 1972 by the Center for Criminal Justice, the Harvard Law School.) We asked him to compare his own attitudes to those of the incarcerated juveniles. He was somewhat taken aback by the (relatively) high tolerance the juveniles had for such behaviors as associating with guards and informing; his own reactions to such behaviors having been violently negative. When asked to explain the apparent discrepancy between his attitudes and those of current juvenile prisoners, he replied "Just give them time." The interviewers (Andrew Vachss and Anthony Traini) did not ask if a pun was intended.

43. Those prisoners interviewed who insisted that some sort of "code" does continue to exist were quick to state that only members of their particular subgroup could be expected to adhere to it.

44. In New Jersey prisons, guards are called "cops"; in New York they are

called "hacks"; in Massachusetts, "screws." However, we have noted a national trend towards adopting a form of the New Jersey model, and guards are referred to as "the police" in many other institutions.

45. A reference to a practice still common in southern prison camps where known homosexual prisoners are forced to carry their own drinking cups into the fields because the other prisoners will not permit them to use the common cup. This practice allegedly stemmed from fear of venereal disease being transmitted.

46. Interview with a prisoner at Trenton State Prison, 1975. Identity not disclosed at interviewee's request.

47. For example, in the late 1930s, those prisoners in the Louisiana State Penitentiary (Angola) considered to be extremely dangerous were forced to wear straw hats and red bandannas and live in special "Red Hats" quarters which were not closed until 1972. Such prisoners were generally respected by the rest of the population as "stand up" individuals, and supposedly were able to avail themselves of most prison goods and services through cooperative fellow prisoners.

48. *See,* for example Edward Bunker, "War Behind Walls," *Harper's Magazine,* February 1972, p. 39 ff. and, Carr, note 12, supra, and George Jackson, note 12 *supra.*

49. Mark J. Lerner, "The Effectiveness of a Definite Sentence Parole Program," 15 *Criminology* 212 (1977) at p. 213.

50. Interview with a prisoner at Walpole (Massachusetts) State Prison, 1971. Identity not disclosed at interviewee's request.

51. The authors do not allege that anything so formal as open bargaining between the two blocs took place; it was obviously an evolutionary process by which current practices came to fruition.

52. "Cadet captains" were more common in institutions which functioned on a paramilitary model, complete with marching in formation and drilling with inoperative wooden rifles, such as Camp Hill Reformatory in Pennsylvania. The "cottage duke" is the juvenile equivalent of the county jail "barn boss," and his status, while less formally recognized by management, is no less dependent on his personal combat skills.

53. Paraphrasing one veteran correctional officer, in a system which does not permit heavy hardware (such as shotguns) inside the institution, control of the many (prisoners) by the few (guards) must always rely on "divide and conquer" to some extent.

54. Mann, ch. 1, note 34, *supra* at p. 70:

> The place of detention is frequently governed by management concerns regardless of the presenting offense—"troublemakers" get locked up; "good timers" have fewer restraints. . . . [T]he issue of offender management can sometimes obscure the distinction between serious and not so serious offenders, thereby clouding an analysis of what works with whom.

55. This system, which provides "play money" in the form of "tokens" that can be exchanged for privileges or tangible items, is actually most favored at schools for the retarded as a means of teaching the residents our economic system as well as motivating their achievement.

56. Another form of the "token economy," the major difference being that no tangible "tokens" are provided, only a "score sheet" for each resident maintained by the staff.

57. Popular in therapeutic communities (including those in voluntary mental hospitals), they sometimes combine the "point system" whereby the resident must accumulate a given number of points to move up to another level (of privileges, rewards, and permitted behaviors).

Note: some would say that the whole juvenile justice continuum is nothing more than a "levels system" (in a hierarchy model of services, *see* figure 4-1).

Some institutions have "level systems" not based on achievement, but on characteristics of individual residents found in response to testing:

> There are four levels in the school [Goshen Training School, New York State], based on reading skills. The lowest is group seven, which ranges from kindergarten to just below the third grade; the highest . . . covers the fifth to eighth grades.
>
> Joseph B. Treaster, "State Delinquent Center: No Punishment or Reform," *The New York Times,* March 2, 1976. © 1976 by The New York Times Company. Reprinted by permission.

58. The *intent* of society is so clearly expressed in the architecture of juvenile prisons and in the personalities of the keepers that the "sense of community" so desired for therapeutic purposes is extremely difficult to attain. In addition, such "communities" require a degree of voluntariness to function effectively, and those juvenile prisons which punish refusal to participate in the program with the usual methods find themselves right back to running a penal institution in short order. Additionally, therapeutic communities have always relied on expulsion in the case of uncooperative or disruptive members; no such sanction is available in a prison setting. Such limited successes as have been noted have been when those prisoners desiring to participate can be isolated from the remainder of the population.

59. There is no showing that the increased possibility of earlier release to the outside community by compliance with new institutional goals had any effect on behavior of life-style violent juveniles. With a characteristic "here and now" focus and a limited ability or willingness to perceive the future and long-term goals, the life-style violent juvenile is a poor motivational candidate in such systems.

3 Considerations in Planning a Secure Treatment Unit

Planning

Criminal justice planning has repeatedly come under heavy criticism as reactive, proposal-oriented, busy-work. Before proceeding with the specific plans for the proposed Secure Treatment Unit, it is necessary to anticipate some potential criticisms of any such planning. The Law Enforcement Assistance Administration (LEAA), operating through a variety of state and local units, has certainly provided the major financial impetus to criminal justice planning in the past decade. This agency has repeatedly come under fire,[1] because the bulk of its money seems to have been expended on "reactive" and "policy-blind" planning. Critics claim planning has not been solution-oriented and actually only serves to document what the consumer population (including crime victims) already knows. The Honorable David L. Bazelon[2] recently stated that "American criminology is obsessed with numbers,"[3] and admonished the profession to spend less time arguing over methodologies of data collection (which have produced conflicting reams of statistics), and more time producing some answers. As we now define "reactive" planning, we are basically speaking of locking the barn after the horse has been stolen (and re-sold across the state line). Thanks to LEAA, virtually every state has a master plan of some sort. This plan is largely financial; it "prioritizes" anticipated federal grants in terms of criminological "needs," which are, in turn, largely based on a statistical analysis of prime figures, which are themselves open to criticism.[4] Al Bronstein, of the American Civil Liberties Union Prison Project, openly accuses American criminologists of being panderers to the legitimate fears of a frightened public.[5] The real creativity in the criminological profession is often expressed in the authorship of proposals-for-funding, and little money is available for the kind of "proactive" planning the serious members of the profession are now routinely demanding.

If the membership of the human services profession is to continue to insist on respect from the general public, we have to move beyond the incessant documentation of common knowledge and into the realm of active, implementable solutions.

It is therefore necessary to examine whether such criticisms fairly apply to the planning that produced our version of a Secure Treatment Unit. So how does the proposed Secure Treatment Unit fit into these requirements? Surely, documentation of the fact that we have a serious juvenile crime problem is only wasted money. Isn't the construction of a maximum-security intensive treatment facility for life-style violent juveniles also reactive? Are we not merely planning for events that have already taken place? Shouldn't we be working strictly in the area of prevention and diversion of juvenile offenders? Or perhaps more to the point, shouldn't our efforts be concentrated on those social and economic conditions that *produce* juvenile crime?

The answer is a resounding "no!". To see the problems raised in pure proactive planning in proper perspective, it is useful to examine another area of criminal justice in which reform is long overdue, and trace the proximate consequences of a purely proactive stance. Probably no agency impacts more heavily on the lives of adult prisoners than the parole board. The unbridled discretion of this body has come under strong, and justified, fire from critics, scholars, and practitioners in the field.[6] The fact that it is usually the function of the board to actually set sentences, coupled with the fact that prediction of human behavior has proven to be nearly impossible, has created a situation of unrest behind prison walls.[7] As jurisdiction after jurisdiction recognizes the impracticability of the current paroling system, the movement towards "flat-time" systems has gained strength. Under such a system, parole would either be eliminated entirely, or reduced to a very narrow function, operating only in certain institutions and on certain types of criminal behavior.[8] This sort of planning is proactive; a new method is proposed which will radically alter some of the identified negative aspects of the former system. Without making any value judgments, it is necessary to ask one significant question: if we switch to the flat-time system for all incoming prisoners, under what system will the *current* population be handled? Any prison administrator will be quick to state that a population governed (in terms of potential for release) under different systems at the same time will be inherently unstable and difficult to manage. Remember, when a paroling scheme is changed, it is also necessary to alter the statutory sentencing scheme of that jurisdiction. If, for example, homicide was formerly punished by a term of from ten years to life, with parole eligibility vesting after the ten years, it would now be punished by a term of fifteen years flat, with reductions in sentences only for "good time" and/or "work time." Some prisoners would benefit from the old system; some would benefit from the new.

Simply stated, any human services proactive planning that ignores an existing population of clients is nothing but an exercise in semantics, and should not be called a plan at all.

Purely proactive planning with life-style violent juveniles ignores the present population of such juveniles, and it is this population that provides the impetus for the planning in the first place. The crux of the matter is this: even with the most advanced commitment to proactive planning possible, there will be an existing pool of human beings who have already proceeded beyond the point before which the proactive planners hoped to intervene. And any successful planning effort must incorporate this pool, because we cannot simply write off such individuals. In statistical terms, such a write-off might be feasible (we simply start with another blank sheet of paper); in human terms, it is not. If we plan only for the *future* life-style violent juvenile, we doom most of those currently in that category to a life-time of treatment within the adult system, and we doom a huge pool of potential victims to the future attacks of those so treated.

The public will not accept purely proactive planning in the area of violent juvenile offenders. The public will not accept causation theories rooted in the social and economic problems of our country. The public wants something done *now*. The public wants action focused in terms of its own safety and well-being, and tolerance of massive social engineering is extremely low.

The proposed Secure Treatment Unit is reactive in focusing on the present population of life-style violent juveniles, but it is also proactive in the solutions it offers to such a population. The proposed Secure Treatment Unit is a proactive plan in that it anticipates a continuation and expansion of a trend towards life-style juvenile violence. It is proactive in that it anticipates the desperate need for solutions other than those now in operation. It is proactive in that it offers a genuine hope for change in what has been a headlong slide into helplessness.

The proposed Secure Treatment Unit is also reactive in that it acknowledges the immediacy of the *current* need. It is reactive in that it accepts the fact that massive social engineering (even if it ever materializes) is far too late for those juveniles already committed to a life-style of violence against society. It is reactive in that it recognizes that a solution-demanding public must be heard and responded to. And it is reactive in that it draws its impetus from what *is* happening, not from what *will* happen.

Secure Treatment

Functional definitions of secure treatment tend to be vague to the point of obscurity. Our concept of rehabilitation (which we define in terms of habilitation/socialization/reformation) has been previously discussed. And just as we seek an operational (and necessarily narrow) definition of that concept, we also seek a narrow definition of the framework within which this much-vaunted process is to take place. In reviewing statutes, professional literature, and actual practice, we cannot find a working definition of what we call a "secure treatment unit." The recent New York State Juvenile Justice Reform Act,[9] for example, limits its definition to:

> Secure facility. A facility in which the juvenile delinquent may be placed [under this article] which is characterized by physically restrictive construction, hardware, and procedures, and is designated as a secure facility by the Division for Youth.[10]

This description not only fails to describe the process that is to take place within the unit, but even fails to provide us with a clue as to the structural/architectural features necessary to accomplish a legislatively mandated goal.

The proposed Secure Treatment Unit is, by contract, a highly specific, maximum-security facility. Until we arrive at an actual description of programming and therapeutic content,[11] we will be satisfied with another working definition. The Secure Treatment Unit is a maximum-security institution. This means that one of the primary goals of the structure itself is the prevention of escape. It will be a locked setting externally, which means that control of passage from the inside to the outside will be in the hands of staff personnel only. However, the internal options will range from fully locked (isolation areas) to fully open, and there will be a high degree of resident participation in the selection of those options.

Maximum security, as a functional concept, protects residents from each other as it protects society from residents. Moreover, it should be understood that we consider maximum security to be a two-sided coin. Not only must the public be safe from the residents, the residents must also be safe from one another. Adult prisons usually achieve the former, but fail miserably in the latter.[12] Whether the failure to provide even minimal safety for inmates of adult correctional institutions is by accident or design is beyond the scope of this work, but it is indisputable that many of this country's maximum-security prisons make it impossible for an inmate to "do his own time."[13] Dr. Daniel Jacobs, a former psychiatrist at the federal penitentiary in Milan, Michigan, and now director of the Cambridge Court Clinic in Massachusetts, tells us:

> Maximum security has had, it seems to me, a bad connotation. We always think of the worst prisons. If by maximum security we mean maximum security for each youth in the setting, where he can learn, develop, explore his problems without having to worry about being raped or assaulted, *that* kind of maximum security, I would certainly be in favor of it. If we also mean an environment in which youths understand that if they cannot control their own violent or aggressive behavior, there are people and environments which will help them control it, so that nobody need fear that their crazy, violent, suicidal inclinations will get out of hand, so they can feel secure that somebody will be there—if things do get out of control. That kind of maximum security I'm all in favor of. I guess also if you're going to deal with very, very dangerous people, the surrounding community is going to have to

feel that you're in control of the situation. If you just mean guards who are going to patrol up and down, that kind of maximum security has not been very effective.[14]

The safety of each individual juvenile within the institution is an absolute prerequisite to treatment. The necessity of providing safety for individual residents goes beyond the basic human right to physical protection from violence. Dangerous environments produce dangerous responses. When we add to this equation the fact that our population will consist largely of juveniles whose previous violent criminal acts were in part motivated by situation-response, we see the vital necessity of providing this physical safety. When we speak of treatment for such youngsters, we understand that control of their environment is the most critical issue. Without such control, the residents respond to a set of rules the observer will never find in written form. A former inmate of a juvenile institution, (and now a maximum-security prisoner serving a life sentence for homicide)[15] described the techniques for survival in a facility where personal safety is a personal responsibility. In speaking of his introduction to Trenton State Prison at age eighteen, the prisoner explains:

> There was a particular man there that knew my father when he was younger and he came to me and he said "Look, the only real advice I can give you is to take this," and he had something wrapped up in a magazine. He said, "The first real trouble, you have to pull his head off, go to the lock-up for a year, and you'll have no more trouble." So when I took this particular item that he handed me it was wrapped up in a Life Magazine and a piece of old newspaper. I laid it on my bunk and when he later went away I opened it to see what it was; it was a 12-inch knife. And he said that this was the only way I could survive Trenton State Prison at that time . . . it turned out that he was right.[16]

Fear also causes dangerously violent behavior. Human beings are more comfortable when limits are set on behavior. Although they thereby relinquish certain proscribed behavioral options, they receive, in turn, assurances that such behaviors will not be visited upon them. To be sure, as one examines the societal progression from *malum in se*[17] through *malum prohibitum* legislation,[18] one finds less consent to have one's behavior be so governed, but there appears to be a strong consensus that rational human beings would prefer to exist within a structure that prohibits, and responds negatively to, crimes of violence.

A Secure Treatment Unit that does not provide safety for its residents promotes a culture of violence which will inevitably destroy the very goals upon which the institution is founded. We have learned that much violent behavior within institutional settings is a desperate, nonverbal attempt to learn whatever limits *do* exist. Many juveniles *want* to be stopped, and escalate their negative behavior until they are. This escalation has a testing affect to it that cannot be rationally ignored. When confronted in group or individual therapy, institutionally violent juveniles give a variety of rationalizations for their behavior. Persistent and intelligent focusing on motivation often reveals that the juveniles perceive themselves as existing within a "might makes right" hierarchy where status or position is temporary at best. Just as the ghetto youth seeks visible symbols to refute his actual powerlessness (such as obviously expensive clothing),[19] the institutionalized youth seeks to physically dominate and exploit others as a visible symbol that he is not, and cannot be, exploited himself. It is clearly insufficient to attack the amorality of such reasoning if the environment itself gives the lie to the therapist's position. But it *can* be said that "might makes right" is a dysfunctional way to behave. It can be demonstrated that such behavior is self-destructive; it is not necessary to attack it on purely moral grounds.[20] The juvenile who makes a total investment in this philosophy leaves himself open to the same lack of protection he exploits in others. A posture of enlightened self-defense can be shown to be the most functional way to behave *only* if the institutional mores and procedures actually support this premise.

Although every institution (as every street gang) will contain individuals for whom exploitation and violence hold an almost magical allure, the majority of residents will participate in exploitative violence only as a form of self-protection, although it may be perceived otherwise by uninitiated observers. But we cannot hope to distinguish between these types of juveniles without the actual existence of other behavioral options that are themselves perceived as functional and socially acceptable by the resident population.

In an environment where individual safety is not guaranteed, the inmate who exhibits skill in the use of violence is guaranteed both power and prestige. Institutional rapes, for example, are generally perceived as (homo)sexual attacks.[21] Most of the time, they do not properly fit within this category. This behavior, which is so typical of juvenile institutions, is motivated by the same displaced aggression and need to avoid exploitation by others that motivates violent behavior on the street. There are no elderly citizens to mug inside an institution. Goods and services, however, are no less highly prized. The source of such goods and services is largely *within* the resident population, (even though the origin might be the institution itself), and the life-style violent juvenile readily turns to sources of power and prestige that have served him in the past.[22] If an institution, by its structures and procedures, provides ready access to exploitative opportunities, the message to the juvenile is the same one he received on the street. Such activities are forbidden (in some distantly removed place that he does not occupy and to which he is denied admittance), but they are clearly sanctioned and acknowledged (if not overtly approved) by the same power structure so long as the behavior does not reach beyond its "acceptable" limits.[23]

The analogy between the street and the institution is obvious. The juvenile court returns the life-style violent juvenile to the streets after only a short period of incarceration. Similarly, the juvenile institution returns him to the resident population after a short period of isolation or solitary confinement. Although both methods of transmitting "correct" societal messages have failed, it would be the height of fallacy to conclude that longer periods of confinement or isolation would transmit the message with any greater clarity.

Unless there are immediate (societal or institutional) consequences to the use of violence, the benefits of its use will outweigh any dimly perceived risks. The analogy is as follows: the juvenile who follows an elderly woman home from the supermarket and pushes in her door, and physically attacks her in order to obtain money knows that he is committing a crime.[24] But he also knows that the chances of immediate (or even future) consequences are remote. This is not the product of a rational, intellectual balancing of risks against potential gains, but the product of cultural knowledge. Immediate consequences are outside his experience. He knows of many others who have committed the same acts he is about to commit, and he knows that he sees these same people (dressed in the fruits of their labor) every day. He also knows that someday he will go to prison, and his real concern is that he go to prison for a crime of some seriousness,[25] thereby preserving the same status he now displays with material goods. The message he receives, and in turn transmits, is not that robbery by violence is necessarily approved, but that it is expected. That same juvenile, when he is finally institutionalized, finds himself in a similar environment to the one he left on the streets. There are rules, to be sure. But those rules are made by nonparticipants in his existence, and noncompliance is met with the same response as the mugging. That is, consequences (if any) are remote and are not considered. The unprotected old woman and the unprotected juvenile resident are alike—access to both is virtually unlimited, peer approval of violent acts against them is assured, and societal response is so uncertain as to be beyond perception. Furthermore, the fourteen year old who successfully mugs an elderly victim can find his newly acquired money summarily taken from him by older gang members, or even by adult members of the criminal community. The thought of turning to the police or to any established agency is beyond the youth's comprehension (just as many juveniles are literally shocked to learn that a mugging victim has made a complaint to the police), and his options are to live with this exploitation of "his" property or to seek revenge. The extent to which he is able to avoid such exploitation (or, in the event it does occur, to accomplish significant revenge) is the extent to which his status within the peer community remains intact and grows.[26] When the same juvenile is institution-alized, he soon learns that there is a pool of individuals within the prison who may be exploited, and that his status among those who are not to be so treated is partly dependent on his ability as an exploiter himself. The same message, the same results.

Thus we conclude that double-edged maximum security is the only way to sufficiently control the living environment of the life-style violent juvenile. We cannot hope to rationally analyze, much less change, behavior which is situationally responsive unless we also control the situation.

Recidivism

The goal of the traditional training school, to decrease recidivism by making the initial experience intolerable, proved counterproductive on many levels. One of the earlier "rehabilitative tools" employed by the training schools was to induce in the prisoners a profound desire never to return. This would presumably motivate the released juveniles to lead a righteous existence so that the possibility of return to the institutions would not arise. However, this technique backfired in several ways.[27]

A juvenile about to be apprehended during the commission of a relatively minor infraction might escalate the offense seriously by resisting arrest, often with violence. The *objective* was to avoid a return to the training school, the *result* was to guarantee a return. And some of the more vicious juveniles, some of the juveniles who were most committed to a life-style of violence, found themselves a home in the training schools. Here was an environment where violence was a way of life, and where status and prestige (including access to goods and services) were available in direct proportion to one's ability to exercise and utilize violent behavior.

This goal presupposed that the juveniles believed an option not to return to the training school really existed. This method failed to recognize the total sense of inevitability that comes to characterize the life-style violent juvenile very early in his development. The possibility of avoiding additional incarceration never impacts on the attitudes of such juveniles, and their behavior therefore does not change in response to that which they do not perceive. Too often, a juvenile merely hopes to return to the training school with increased status as a result of criminal acts on the street.

> When I was first in Lyman School, I was about the smallest kid there and they made me sleep next to the toilet in the dorm.[28] I made up my mind that when I went back there it wasn't going to be me sleeping there, no matter what.[29]

This goal also ignores the fact that most life-style violent juveniles do not find institutionalization so intolerable, at least not the institutionalization to which they have been accustomed by the juvenile justice system. Even the pain of deprivation inherent in any institutionalization is perhaps overperceived by the average middle-class citizen.[30] For the life-style violent juvenile, incarceration not only enhances prestige on the street,[31] it also serves as a training ground in more sophisticated criminality. As one former juvenile prisoner (now serving a life sentence for a narcotics-related homicide) put it:

> Let me tell you something, man. Except for women, you know, I had everything I wanted in there after I got a rep. The first time there wasn't shit, but I knew things would be boss when I went down again. The Man didn't bother our clique, you know, and things were cool.[32]

The Secure Treatment Unit is faced with a conflict between primary and sophisticated efficiency. The "primary efficiency" goal is typical of social services in general, as exemplified by standard "welfare" practices. The concept of making social services unpalatable is surely not new. The primary-versus-sophisticated efficiency may be seen by an examination of the Welfare Department in any large city. The primary efficiency advocates believe in making the entire experience a negative one, so replete with difficulty, pain, and bureaucratic red-tape that the recipient is somehow motivated to get a job and never return to the welfare rolls. But the advocates of more sophisticated efficiency will actually increase services to the recipient population, recognizing that removal from the welfare rolls comes about on a permanent basis only when the former recipient is able to earn a functional living. A welfare recipient offered a standard of living only pennies above his current rate is unlikely to be sufficiently motivated to make a move in his own behalf. But those recipients who can achieve a significantly higher living standard will be so motivated. Since the great bulk of welfare recipients are, in fact, minor children, each recipient who is introduced to full employment and self-maintenance status actually represents many individuals no longer dependent on public assistance, and the generational cycle of welfare recipience may therefore be permanently interrupted.

Most social work is stop-gap, stemming-the-tide, "crisis intervention" on an ongoing basis. What is so unique about the proposed Secure Treatment Unit is that it addresses both the individual offender and the larger problem at the same time, thus avoiding the built-to-fail, planned obsolescence model of social intervention on which most reform is based.

Sophisticated Efficiency

Sophisticated efficiency, as applied to institutional treatment of life-style violent juveniles, is clearly more difficult, but also clearly more productive in the long run. Of course, sophisticated efficiency is the more difficult to achieve, and requires a greater commitment than merely making things difficult for a hapless recipient (or inmate, or resident). The line between motivation and harassment is sometimes a thin one, and it is a rare caseworker who walks it consistently. Such caseworkers are often accused of coddling welfare clients, but those caseworkers may be the only ones seriously attacking a multigenerational economic and social problem that threatens to bankrupt some of our major urban areas.

So it is with the juvenile institution. Some citizens who examine the plans contained in this book will immediately accuse the authors of being "soft on juvenile crime" because of the many facilities and services built into the concept of the Secure Treatment Unit.

Yet nothing could be further from the truth. It is our intention to provide conceptual plans for an institution that is expected to have a materially interruptive effect on juvenile violence, and we recognize the fact that *no* therapy can be effective without the cooperation and participation of the patient. The features of the Secure Treatment Unit are not designed to placate recalcitrant juveniles, but to maximize the opportunities of the treatment staff to intervene in a life-style that now threatens all citizens.

Notes

1. *See,* for example, "LEAA: Restructuring Alone Won't Do The Job," 63 *American Bar Association Journal* 472 (1977), and 21 *Criminal Law Reporter* 2041 (1977):

> Attorney General Griffin Bell has ordered a thorough examination of the Law Enforcement Assistance Administration with a view to determining how the agency can be improved . . .
>
> Bell has repeatedly criticized LEAA's performance and has stated that he regards reform of the agency as one of his top priorities . . .
>
> The [Washington] Post, quoting unnamed Justice Department sources, reported that the aim of the study would be to de-emphasize LEAA's billing as an organization capable of eliminating crime. Rather, it would focus on a limited range of problems where the impact of its program would be susceptible of measurement.

2. Chief Judge of the United States Circuit Court of Appeals for the District of Columbia.

3. During a Plenary Session of the American Society of Criminology Annual Meeting in Atlanta, Georgia, November 19, 1977. The topic was "Public Policy and Crime Control"; Moderator, John Conrad, Academy for Contemporary Problems.

4. For example, in Walter B. Miller, *Violence by Youth Gangs and Youth Groups as a Crime Problem in Major American Cities,* (Cambridge, Massachu-

setts: Center for Criminal Justice, Harvard Law School, 1975), at p. 33, the author speaks to the problems engendered by a reliance on statistical "analysis" as it relates to his area of interest, youth gangs:

> With regard to the manipulability of gang-related statistics, descriptions of the process of deriving figures for each of the four largest cities—New York, Chicago, Los Angeles, and Philadelphia, suggest that in all four cities the process of deriving publishable statistics involves objectives other than that of providing systematic and accurate data. In all four cities at least some of these influences can appropriately be designated as "political." This finding lends support to a recommendation to be forwarded in a subsequent report, that federal influence, resources, or both be directed to developing and implementing modes of gathering information about gangs which might serve to transcend, to some feasible extent, the influence of political considerations on data-gathering operations.

Questions such as "If reported crime increases, is a jurisdiction experiencing more criminal activity or the results of a better reporting system?" have never been satisfactorily answered, and to assume that self-interest plays no part in data gathering would be inexcusably naive.

5. Speaking in response to Judge Bazelon, *see* note 3, *supra*. Mr. Bronstein's remarks were entitled "Corrections Policy: Pandering to the Public About Prisons."

6. *See*, for example, Kenneth Culp Davis, *Discretionary Justice, A Preliminary Inquiry,* (Chicago: University of Chicago Press, 1971); *Ad Hoc Parole Committee Public Information Report #1*, ch.1, note 38, *supra*; Karl Menninger, *The Crime of Punishment* (New York: The Viking Press, 1968) at 82 ff; and Andrew H. Vachss, "Parole As Post-Conviction Relief: The Robert Lewis Decision," 9 *New England Law Review* 1 (1973), among others.

7. *See*, for example, Griswold, Misenheimer, Powers, and Tromanhauser, *An Eye for an Eye,* (New York: Holt, Rinehart, and Winston, 1970); *see also,* ch. 2, note 48, *supra*.

8. *See*, for example, Maine Revised Statutes Annotated, Title 17-A, effective May 1, 1976.

9. *See* ch. 2, note 20, *supra*.

10. Family Court Act of the State of New York, Section 712(j); enacted 1976, effective 1977. But were such a facility actually to be constructed, the proposed definition of the Task Force on Secure Facilities (Massachusetts), might be more appropriate:

> A *Secure Treatment Program* is one which provides the care, maintenance, and treatment for, and which contains or holds, youths who have demonstrated, in prior commitments to DYS [Department of Youth Services] or by the actions which are the basis for their present commitment, that:

a. They pose a danger of serious bodily harm to others, which cannot be averted or controlled in a less secure setting; or

b. They engage in a pattern of persistent, uncontrollable and serious offenses and it has been demonstrated that a less secure setting cannot control and treat them.

"The Issue of Security in a Community-Based System of Juvenile Corrections," *The Final Report of the Task Force on Secure Facilities to Commissioner John A. Calhoun,* L. Scott Harshbarger, Chairman, November, 1977, at p. 18.

11. *See* chapter 6, *infra.*

12. *See,* for example, T. Plotkin, "Surviving Justice: Prisoners' Rights to be Free from Physical Assault," 23 *Cleveland State Law Review* 387 (1974); Gresham Sykes, *The Society of Captives* (Princeton, New Jersey: Princeton University Press, 1958); and H. Toch, *Living in Prison—The Ecology of Survival,* (New York: Free Press, 1978).

13. An often-repeated assertion by current prisoner interviewees from various jurisdictions.

14. Interview, November 10, 1976, see appendix for full text.

15. And for both successful and unsuccessful escape attempts. The interviewee is now in medium-security custody for the first time following false accusations by the officials in another prison (of narcotics traffic controlling). Following a polygraph examination, he was found to be innocent, and sent to medium security as a "reward."

16. Interview with David Guy Baldwin, Rahway (New Jersey) State Prison, July 21, 1976, *see* appendix for full text.

17. *Black's Law Dictionary* 4th Edition (St. Paul, Minnesota: West Publishing Co., 1968) defines this term at p. 1112:

A wrong in itself; an act or case involving illegality from the very nature of the transaction, upon principles of natural, moral, and public law . . .

18. Ibid:

A wrong prohibited; a thing which is wrong *because* prohibited; an act which is not inherently immoral, but becomes so because its commission is expressly forbidden by positive law . . .

19. *New York Daily News,* April 3, 1978. Copyright 1978 New York News Inc. Reprinted by permission.

Sporting $300 suits, $100 shoes, cashmere sweaters, diamond pinky rings, and 14-carat gold medallions, the twins [the infamous Timmons Twins, the subject of more media ink than Al Capone because of their notorious records of juvenile violence; they have been called the "inventors of the push-in mugging" and are now both serving adult prison terms for robberies of different victims. Ronald Timmons sparked massive political debate when it was learned that he was free on low bail following a charge of armed robbery and assault on an elderly victim. The media disclosed that he had been involved in a homicide of an elderly victim when he was a juvenile, *see* note 59, *supra*] still slept in stairwells and subsisted on potato chips and soda.

There is evidence that this attitude does not change when the life-style violent juvenile is incarcerated; *see* Bartollas et al., ch. 1, note 22, *supra*.

20. Secure Treatment Unit philosophy and operating procedure requires that the consequences for every single act of violent aggression (against other residents or against staff) be spelled out to the juveniles. This is not a lecture on "right" and "wrong," but a clear statement of the risks involved in such behavior.

21. Although such attacks *could* have a sexual motive, the usual motives are: aggression, exploitation, and dominance. For the majority of attacks, any "homosexual" aspect is probably more attributable to the group participation than to anything else.

22. Generally, physical violence: singly or as part of a group. While some juveniles obviously join institutional gangs for protection, others join (or start) such gangs as an extension of their own hostility and aggression. The same motivations for joining and participating will be found in the outside communities.

23. The "acceptable" limits vary from institution to institution, but almost never "permit" physical attacks on staff members. Additionally, they will vary among individual staff members; *see* chapter 4, *infra*.

24. The methodology of the "push-in" mugging is generally as follows: the perpetrator waits outside a store, bank, supermarket, or other place where people might cash checks or spend money. He then selects a likely-looking victim (with particular attention to advanced age or physical infirmity) and follows the victim home. If the victim proceeds directly home, the perpetrator will follow through the front door and get on the same elevator. He will then watch which floor the victim selects, and himself select the floor just below. After he leaves the elevator, he will race to the stairs and be on the next floor before the elevator arrives. Just as the victim enters his or her own apartment, the perpetrator will shove both victim and door, slamming the door behind him. He has now isolated a completely defenseless individual and can proceed to rob (and/or physically attack) without fear of disturbance. If, for some reason, another (physically stronger) party is present, the perpetrator will simply flee, knowing the prospect of apprehension is virtually nonexistent.

25. As one informant told us:

The first thing they ask you in there [the juvenile institution] is what your beef [crime] is. If you have something chump, like some rookie rip-off [most likely a purse-snatching] it's like you're nothing. But the brothers who did homicides and heavy shit like that *already* have something just behind having so much heart [courage].

Conversation with W.T., 1976.

26. In *Tattoo the Wicked Cross,* ch. 2, note 37 *supra,* the protagonist (Aaron) deliberately poisons the institutional soup to revenge himself against his rapists as previously counseled by his friend. His act results in the death of three juveniles, one his tormentor, and another his friend. In the scene set out below, he is awaiting a court decision as to placement, having already confessed to the crime. His girlfriend is allowed a brief visit with him, and tries to persuade him to "cooperate" with the authorities.

"John [Aaron's older brother] says that if you'll only co-operate, the case can be transferred to juvenile court, where you'll get Youth Authority [remain in the juvenile system], and—"

"And they'll send me to a state reform school instead of San Quentin until I'm twenty-one, and then send me to San Quentin," he said huskily, hating her for helping them, but using the hate to put himself beyond her pleas.

"No, John says—"

"John sent you, didn't he? He told you to write, didn't he? I wondered how I got a letter so quick," he said . . .

"Well, let me tell you something. I'll get Youth Authority anyway, because of my age. And let me tell you something else. Because of my age, they can't put me in Que."

"Que?"

"San Quentin, and let me tell you something else. They can't snuff me, either."

"Snuff you?," she asked.

"Gas me, baby! They can't give me the gas chamber. And let me tell you something else . . .

Do you know that I've got a great rep now? Do you know that all the guys in the DT [Detention Area] come around to my isolation cell and talk to me through the window? Do you know that all the guys in Whittier and Preston [large-scale juvenile "reformatories"] have heard about me and are hoping that I'll get sent to their joints? Do you know—?

"Do you know that I'm Big Time now? That nobody will mess with a killer? Do you know that no matter where I go, I'm going to do Good Time? Good Time? . . . ."

27. *See,* for example, Roy Lotz; Robert M. Regoli; and Phillip Raymond, "Delinquency and Special Deterrence," 15 *Criminology* 539 (1978) at p. 546:

[W]hile arrest and conviction are outcomes sought by no one—[previously incarcerated] training school boys or other—the prospect of either outcome may strike *less* fear in the boys who have already experienced training school. It may be somewhat less humiliating to them, less upsetting to their friends and relatives (to whom this kind of trouble may be nothing new). [emphasis added]

See also, the following statement by Dr. Paul Hahn, Chairman of the Corrections Department at Xavier University in Cincinnati:

There is no way a child who has been deprived of almost every basic need of the human spirit for years and who tells us through his behavior that something is wrong in his life will be scared into behaving by the possibility of a jail sentence.

21 *Criminal Law Reporter* 2041 (April 13, 1977), reporting on "The Effectiveness of Correctional Programs" at the Fourth National Conference on Juvenile Justice in Orlando, Florida.

28. The dorm consisted of a single, rectangular room, with toilet and shower facilities off to one side. However, during the night, the only toilet facility available to the juveniles was a single urinal placed in the middle of the floor.

29. Interview with F.M., 1972, identity not disclosed at interviewee's request. F.M. began an incarcerative career as a young child (age nine) and eventually served more than forty years in state and federal institutions. His criminal behavior was limited to armed robberies, assaults in the course of such robberies, and escapes from prison.

30. *See* note 27, *supra.* This is not to suggest that *actual* pain is less, only *perceived* pain. Since incarceration in some form or another is perceived as inevitable by the life-style violent juvenile, and since he is likely to be re-united with the same peers he had on the streets, the sense of deprivation is perhaps lessened. *See also* note 31, *infra.*

31. Some observers believe that a "successful" juvenile incarceration is almost a prerequisite to urban gang leadership. In addition, the prisoner who "stands up" to imprisonment enhances his prestige with peer groups both inside and on the streets. "Heart" ideology, the position (and proof) that the juvenile fears nothing, is also enhanced by proof that the juvenile faced up to imprisonment without complaining. *See also,* Sykes, note 12, *supra,* p. 99 ff.

32. Interview with G.T., Newark, New Jersey, 1974. Interviewee's identity not disclosed at his request.

4 Staffing and Operation of a Secure Treatment Unit

Contracting Out

The threshold question in the management of a Secure Treatment Unit is simply this: Who shall the managers be? Shall they be civil servants, or private vendors? The concept of "contracting out" is not new to American criminal justice. When a system finds itself required to provide services for which it is not physically equipped, a portion of the system's budget is then allocated to such services, and the money so allocated is paid directly to a private vendor. This funding is sometimes on a "per head" or "per bed" basis, and it is sometimes granted in exchange for broad-based services not necessarily tied to a specific caseload, such as providing counseling to youth in trouble.

Before making any decision as to the viability of contracting out, it must be understood that this description has, in the past, been used to cover a range of abusive systems. The long history of criminal justice contracting out has not always been an illustrious one. Sometimes a state agency finds itself without budget allocations sufficient to even house and feed (much less treat) prisoners entrusted to its care. At such times, the prisoner's labor has been a medium of exchange, and it was not uncommon for southern landholders to lease prisoners from the state to perform farming tasks. The landholder would contract to provide "room and board" to the prisoners, and the state would require the prisoners to work on the patron's land. Although this was not, strictly speaking, the providing of "services" to the prisoners other than room and board, (the rehabilitative value of manual labor not having been established by any scientific testing), it was a fact that a state employing such a system could provide a form of incarceration at little or no cost to its taxpayers. Indeed, some prison systems even managed to show a profit,[1] and ironically enough, such states appear to be among the most progressive in the granting of specialized privileges with a rehabilitative flavor.[2] Perhaps the leading jurisdiction in this category is Mississippi, which even permits conjugal visiting,[3] although the rehabilitative value of this privilege is certainly open to discussion.[4]

The above-described systems were a form of contracting out only because of the existing state of affairs. The prison was not *supposed* to provide any form of rehabilitative service; therefore, it was legitimately able to pass along any responsibility it had for the prisoners to another entity (the farmer) who, by feeding the prisoners, met the same standards established by and for the state.

The farmer was paid for his services with the prisoners' own services, and the general perception was that this method was absolutely cost-free. Taxes remained low, because the prisoners achieved a form of self-maintenance, and nobody appeared to be the loser. Of course, such a system had the effect of depressing wage rates for the nonprisoner farm workers, and it certainly only exacerbated the bitterness and hostility the prisoners felt at their treatment. Such a system also invites corruption, and permitted prisoners with access to money to avoid any of the negative aspects of incarceration.

Contracting out in the southern prison systems reached the height of dangerous absurdity when convicts were employed as prison guards. This, of course, saved money since the prisoner-guards were not paid in cash. The task of guarding the prisoners was contracted out to this new breed of "correctional officer," with the result being a system so vicious, so degrading, and so dangerous to human life that the federal courts abandoned their traditional "hands-off" posture in a series of sweeping decisions which have largely eliminated the convict-guard from the southern prison camps.[5]

The juvenile justice system has also utilized contracting out as a means of providing many varied services. The juvenile justice system has made far more extensive use of contracting out than most other social services. The rhetoric of rehabilitation has resulted in a continuous demand for a wider variety of specialized services, and various states have found it more economically feasible to allow private vendors to fill the many gaps in the treatment continuum. Most of the group homes or halfway houses are operated by private agencies, and some jurisdictions even employ private vendors to establish and maintain a foster home network for status offenders.[6]

Juvenile de-institutionalization, for example, seems almost to require contracting out and, in particular, the contracting out of a secure facility. There is a strong correlation between the extent of a jurisdiction's commitment to de-institutionalization and utilization of private vendors to provide services. A state with such a commitment generally closes its training school network first,[7] and later discovers a small percentage of juveniles for whom institutionalization is either therapeutically or politically mandated.[8] Since resurrection of a complete training school to house only a small percentage of a former population is economically infeasible (besides giving aid and comfort to opponents of de-institutionalization), the private vendors find themselves in a powerful position. Additionally, private vendors who have established alternative methods of treatment for juvenile offenders are generally united in their demands for a "secure" institution with which to threaten those residents of their facilities who don't "function within the program." This demand is further underscored by a desire to restrict their own individual intakes to those juveniles felt to be suitable to their programs.

Contracting out (as opposed to civil service) provides a greater opportunity to hire and maintain top-quality staff. A state agency will enjoy many significant advantages in contracting out for services to juveniles. Unlike civil servants, employees of private agencies can be discharged relatively easily, and cost overruns are the sole responsibility of the private agency, thereby permitting more precise budget allocations. As civil servants acquire tenure and seniority, their pay must be increased. This is, again, not the situation with private agencies which necessarily subsist from contract to contract.

The private agency can offer much greater flexibility in compensation, not being bound strictly to longevity as a determinant of salary. Employees of such agencies are rarely unionized, and tend to see their employment as temporary in nature rather than as a life-time attachment. Even those employees who seek a career in human services are unlikely to expect to serve that entire career with a single agency. Among individuals in the human services profession, private agency employment is more highly prized since it carries with it the aura of nonbureaucratic, innovative programming, and the employees see themselves as reformers, not wage slaves who must bear the responsibility for the errors of the past. Promotion is much freer in such agencies, opportunities for advancement greater, and youth more highly prized. Finally, such agencies are seen as less prone to overt patronage, and it is not always necessary to "know someone" to be considered for employment. And the private agencies traditionally have been far more receptive to hiring people on a part-time basis,[9] and to placing less emphasis on items like a past criminal record.

In a state that uses civil service rather than private vendors, a secure facility tends to be staffed by the least skilled and least dedicated of workers. Of all the services for which a state juvenile justice system can contract out, a Secure Treatment Unit is perhaps the most suitable. In the past, assignment to a state training school, for example, was among the least desirable for civil servants. Few, if any, volunteered. We have personally observed occasions where civil servants assigned to a secure facility have viewed the transfer as punitive,[10] as was reflected in the work attitudes displayed. A Secure Treatment Unit's population is more likely to require specialized skills which would not be available in the civil service ranks: psychotherapy, remedial reading, and occupational therapy are more likely to be handled on a consultant basis by a state agency, and a private vendor can provide such services more easily and economically.

Finally, because state training schools traditionally have been located in outlying areas, away from urban centers, they tend to be staffed by civil service personnel from the local area who will be extremely reluctant to relocate to a single, statewide unit. Although such individuals tend to quickly rally political support *against* de-institutionalization, the *real* issue has nothing whatever to do with treatment methodologies; the issue is employment. Just as LEAA, ostensibly designed as the ultimate national crime-fighting weapon, really served the public interest only by fighting the unemployment of white-collar professionals; anti-de-institutionalization forces are often far more concerned with the loss of local jobs than they are with the impact of any new treatment modality on society in general.

De-institutionalization of training schools raises the issue of civil service employment survival. A jurisdiction that has closed its training schools will be faced with an impossible dilemma if it chooses to utilize existing civil service staff in a small "secure" unit. The closing of the training schools will produce unemployment in an area once thought to be immune from layoffs and discharges,[11] and, in spite of the relative undesirability of the assignment, competition for staff slots in the new unit will be keen. Since far less personnel will be required, those civil servants with the greatest seniority will have to be selected regardless of suitability for this particular assignment. Flexibility in the hiring of staff is thereby diminished, or lost entirely, and the new unit will be handicapped before it opens its doors.

In fact, the process of de-institutionalization has highlighted many of the weaknesses inherent in civil service and many of the problems in the transition to contracting out. For example, the use of civil servants in so-called "new" programs decreases the likelihood of outside funding for such programs.[12]

Finally, those who really count in this area, potential funders, may view the transfer of civil servants from a closed-down training school to a new secure facility as merely a cosmetic change. Much de-institutionalization was actually nothing more than "grants chasing" by state agencies that saw the writing on the wall. Professional support for de-institutionalization was manifested in the funding priorities of the federal government, and virtually any jurisdiction could count on "block grant" money to open up alternative facilities. Therefore, many such facilities were opened, and new programs continued to crop up in a period of unemployment. State agencies that had their patronage wings clipped by economic necessity saw a new way to provide employment without tapping the state coffers. LEAA became more effective in fighting unemployment than in fighting crime. Now that secure treatment has become a priority, (or, at least, the serious juvenile offender has become a priority), we can expect the proposal writers to be busy. And proposals that propose to do nothing more than rehire discharged civil servants from the closed-down training schools will not enjoy the same success as those that propose an entire new way of doing business.

Similarly, the hybrid process of the state providing civil servants as part of its responsibilities to a private vendor has proved dysfunctional. Many private vendors will be prevailed upon to accept some former civil servants as the state's "in-kind" contribution. This would be intended to reduce the actual amount of money passing from the state to the private vendor, and would permit the state to retain civil servants for a longer period of time. Although this plan has a surface attractiveness, it is doomed to failure since a civil servant "bloc" in the secure facility will not only be resistant to innovative change, but will come with an unquestioning belief that the old training schools *were* successful. They are likely to perceive all deviations from that model as something to be resisted. If the private vendor is given no greater rights than the state formerly held in terms of discharge and employee discipline, the civil servants can be counted upon to pose serious problems for the staff as a whole. In addition, civil servants will retain all previous vacation rights and schedules, and will force management of the new unit to accommodate them to the exclusion of other staff.[13] A concerned state which wants to make arrangements for the continuation of civil service personnel should do so in other areas, perhaps in other agencies, and totally avoid the attempt to intermingle such staff with that of a private agency.

Performance Contracting

Once past the initial question of whether to contract out a secure treatment unit for life-style violent juveniles, a state must then determine what kind of contract is the most effective. Crucial to the question of fiscal effectiveness in contracting out the care, custody, and treatment responsibilities for the life-style violent juvenile population is the method of determining compensation. Clearly, a system whereby the private vendor agrees to assume responsibility for all such children, without specification as to number, cannot succeed. A per capita rate must be established to avoid dilution of services as numbers increase. In addition, a firm intake policy must be established and enforced so that the agency responsible for treatment will have a realistic opportunity to succeed.

A per head system of per capita funding rewards faulty placement procedures by encouraging sloppy intake, overcrowding, and retarded release. The threshold question in per capita funding is whether the agency will be paid per head or per bed. Under the per head system, the agency is paid a daily, weekly, or monthly rate for each juvenile physically in its care. The rate is established on a yearly basis, and is divided by the actual number of days spent in the agency's care. This puts pressure on the agency to fill its facilities at all times, thereby retarding the release process until suitable "replacements" are found.

An observer might wonder if this observation is valid, since all other programs in the same state will be clamoring for admission slots for their own candidates. Why should a Secure Treatment Unit concern itself with the prospect of *ever* having an empty bed? But if the Secure Treatment Unit's self-interest lies in accepting only *certain* juveniles, then it will want to wait until such juveniles are on an approved preadmission list before discharging any of its current residents. (This statement is not intended to be deliberately cynical; the survival of any Secure Treatment Unit will depend, in part, on the political dexterity of its management, and such management will be fully aware that the self-interest of community-based agencies will demand ready access to the Secure Treatment Unit. If management simply announces the availability of a bed within the unit, it can rest assured that "suitable" candidates will be produced by the rest of the system within the hour).

Another problem with per head systems is one that rarely surfaces in the planning literature. This is the temptation to take more juveniles than the planned-for capacity to increase the profit-margin of the agency. This "one more won't hurt" attitude is often expressed in the most humanistic language, but a properly designed program will suffer if additional residents are added past the parameters of the original plan. This, in turn, leads to designing a program with sufficient "flab," making the inevitable extra admissions more easily absorbable. "One more won't hurt" always leads to two more, or three more juveniles. Retreating from *that* point becomes difficult since a precedent has been established and the private vendor will not want to antagonize its patron, the state agency.

Another problem with per head funding is the tendency of unit directors to do favors for other agencies by "temporarily" accepting a juvenile for treatment to "take the pressure off" the referring program. The unit could then be forced to perform this same favor for other agencies, until the original limit is routinely exceeded. Sometimes, units agree to accept extra-capacity juveniles as a means of solving their own fiscal management problems. With a strict budget,[14] the unit director often finds himself unable to grant deserved pay raises or to purchase vital equipment. Since no additional funds are forthcoming from the state, the only solution is to accept more residents to increase revenue while holding costs at the former level. Such a program could profit financially but lose therapeutically. A properly designed contract will simply not permit this option.

A per bed system of per capita funding will substantially reduce the incentive to overcrowd. If a unit is funded on a per bed basis, it will receive a flat sum of money based on the space it lists as "available" annually. If the space is not filled, the agency will still receive the same amount of money but, if the space is filled to capacity, there will be no financial gain to the unit. On the surface, this would seem to encourage the unit to keep its population as low as possible, and we maintain that this is not a negative goal in and of itself. There is universal agreement that only a small percentage of convicted juvenile offenders actually require Secure Unit incarceration, and we would want to avoid giving a financial incentive to agencies that would increase this number without therapeutic justification. Nevertheless, we realize that all vacuums *will* be filled, and we would expect a unit compensated on a per bed basis to be filled as quickly as one compensated on a per head model. But, with the per bed system, the unit has no vested interest in adding additional charges to its roster.

A per bed method of contracting out would also help minimize possible conflicts of interest and other forms of "soft" corruption. Under such a method of payment, no individual or agency would have a vested interest in channeling additional residents into the facility, and income would remain relatively inflexible, regardless of outside input. Thus, a sentencing judge who was a member of the corporation which managed (or owned) the Secure Treatment Unit could agree to placements within that facility without leaving himself open to charges of conflict of interest . . . the unit would show the same balance sheet at the end of the year regardless of how many juveniles were referred to it. Such a practice is, of course, not recommended: even though the Secure Treatment Unit would not require a "full house" to earn the amount of funding allocated to it, continual underutilization would certainly militate against extension of the unit's contract with the state. The vested interest therefore is not actually eliminated, only lessened somewhat. But we would be naive in the extreme were we to ignore the potentiality for such conflicts, and a per bed method would minimize them.

While per bed funding places more pressure on the intake procedure, such pressure can be utilized to reinforce the identity and function of the unit itself. Administration of a per bed funding system requires more skill than a conventional per head variety. A facility so managed will be under extreme pressure to fill to capacity, and the administration will be continually faced with the task of defining, and redefining its objectives to other agencies in the treatment community. It is one thing to tell the director of another program that you have no vacancies, and that you'll put his agency's candidate on your waiting list; it is quite another to openly admit that you are under capacity but that the proferred candidate is not suitable for admission to your unit. This forces the Secure Treatment Unit to criteria-ize its intake policy, and to expose that intake policy to a basically adversarial system. In our opinion, such requirements will only strengthen the Secure Treatment Unit, since this is but one aspect of the overall contracting out system that we recommend—performance contracting.

The first task in designing a performance contract for a Secure Treatment Unit is to define the goals of the secure treatment unit itself. Although the concept of performance contracting is not new, it requires a new working definition when viewed in a human services context. Unlike the construction of a building, where materials can be specified and the contract (properly) awarded to the lowest bidder, human services contracting does not lend itself to such simplistic decision-making on the part of the purchaser.

The abbreviated goal of the Secure Treatment Unit must be the de-escalated use of violence by the juveniles under its care. A gross de-escalation in violence as a response to all stress situations and as a (perceived) major economic necessity is the unit's real goal. We seek to increase the life-style violent juvenile's repetoire of responses to stress and to need, not to eradicate all traces of the behavior which brought him to our attention. Advocates of community-based treatment are enamoured with statements such as "for what it costs to incarcerate a juvenile for one year, we could pay his tuition at Harvard," but they seem to ignore the fact that mere payment of money will not transform the life-style violent juvenile into a college student.

Incorporating the traditional "cost-benefit" analysis into such a contract may be counterproductive. Human service contracts are generally expressed in numbers, not in terms of results promised. Indeed, the entire profession overrelies on quantitative measurements as a means of "proving" everything from an academic hypothesis to the need for a federal grant. LEAA, for example, attempts to inject a cost-benefit analysis in its response to some proposals in spite of the fact that the actual accomplishments of a successful criminological intervention cannot be so measured. A brief case history will illustrate the point:

> Sam J. was originally committed to the care and custody of the Department of Youth Services in the Commonwealth of Massachusetts as a delinquent child at the age of eleven for involvement with a group of other children in a series of burglaries.
>
> He served a sentence at the Lyman School for Boys and was paroled. He was returned to the same institution within three months following a finding that he was delinquent by virtue of several armed robberies; again as a participant with other boys.
>
> Remanded to the Shirley Industrial School for Boys, Sam was a frequent resident of its infamous Cottage 9, a "disciplinary cottage" designed to isolate and punish dangerous juveniles within the institution.
>
> Following his release from Shirley, Sam continued to be involved in serious street crime, and was arrested for participation in a homicide. Again, he was returned to Shirley, and again he was continually violent and assaultive.
>
> While on parole from his last release, Sam shot and killed another youth following a fist-fight. He was sent to Andros II when Shirley closed pursuant to a state-wide de-institutionalization program.
>
> At Andros II, Sam caused considerable problems for staff and other residents, but also responded well to treatment and gradually improved to the point where release was recommended.
>
> Almost eighteen months following his release, Sam was arrested as a passenger in a stolen car. He was not carrying a weapon, and did not resist arrest. As a first (adult) offender, he was placed on supervised probation, and remains free in the community to this day.
>
> Viewed in purely statistical terms, this juvenile was a recidivist.
>
> Viewed in pragmatic terms, he was a success.[15]

A Secure Treatment Unit must be contractually bound to provide specified goal-oriented services. Viewed realistically, performance contracting in terms of a Secure Treatment Unit provides certain guarantees that basic irreducible minimums will be established, respected, and maintained. It is not enough for a private vendor to say that it will provide "care, custody, and treatment" for a given number of juveniles over a specified period of time. Without an operational definition of the words themselves, the door is open not only to abuse, but to benign neglect. Dr. Jerome Miller has proposed allowing each juvenile to be the individual purchaser of services he needs through a "voucher system."[16] Although this radically progressive idea is not likely to be implemented for economic (among other) reasons, it clearly illuminates past problems in contracting out. If all the private agency is going to guarantee is a form of custody, it seems that the old state institutions were more economically viable, and that the purchaser (that is, society) is merely paying a premium price to guarantee the same humane conditions that the old system *should* have provided. But if the private agency is going to provide essential services with anticipated results, then such services have to be clearly spelled out, and the maintenance and extension of the contract has to hinge on actual delivery.

The performance contract must contain an evaluation procedure to determine if services are actually provided and whether those services are accomplishing agreed-upon goals—"monitor-ability." This is not to say that we believe a Secure Treatment Unit should be evaluated in terms of statistical criteria such as a so-called "recidivism" rate, but rather that it should be evaluated on two basic levels. First: what services does it actually provide, and, second: of what value are those services? In past contracts, a generalized value was placed on treatment processes with no correlation asked or expected to result. An academic judgment was made as to the value of the proposed services and, following this "validation," the services were contracted for by the state agency under the assumption that they would be continually provided as part of a "process." For example, if group therapy is considered by the grantors to be of value, grantees may expect funding by saying that group therapy is the form of treatment to be employed. But where in such contracts does it specify the number of hours of exposure *each* resident will get to this therapy, the qualifications of the therapist, and the criteria the vendor itself uses to measure success or failure of its program? The concept of "informal, one-to-one counseling" is more vague and difficult to pin down, and even those programs that reveal a schedule of activities do not covenant that *all* residents will be so involved. A program that does not disclose to its sponsor what its reaction will be to incidents of violence *as part of the program* is not contracting for specific performance, but only for performance in the unlikely event that the residents fail to exhibit the behavior which brought them into the program in the first place!

Contractual specification in terms of a program's responses to violence on the part of its residents is vitally important in the juvenile justice sphere. Our profession is often prone to semantic tricknology, and calling solitary confinement "the quiet room" is *not* a sufficient change from our old methods of doing business to warrant professional respect, much less funding by a jurisdiction concerned with the welfare of its children and the safety of its citizens.

Another method by which the concept of performance contracting is perverted is the listing of heavily credentialed "consultants" to the program. It is all too easy, for example, to call someone a program consultant when he is actually a proposal writer or a fund raiser. Unless the impact of their contribution is graphically demonstrated, and unless there is a showing that their input actually filters down to the residents, the vendor has really done nothing to justify the expense of such individuals. A list of publications in the field may be impressive, but a Secure Treatment Unit is a front-lines type of operation, and some translation from theory to practice should be demonstrated as a condition to its continued operation.

While specification is essential in a performance contract, it must also be recognized that there is a limit as to what such specification can accomplish. It must be absolutely clear that a program which lacks specification of its treatment plan is, in reality, only agreeing to warehouse children. Although the program may, in actuality, accomplish far more than this minimal "goal," it is a fact that such accomplishments cannot be *compelled* by the written instrument that governs the relationship between the parties. Once again, politics rears its ugly head because such contracts are really contingent on the political strength of the vendor, not on any specific performance. If the grantor does not specify the results it wants, it has failed to live up to its essential responsibility. And the responsibility conveyed by law to a youth service agency should *not* be considered fulfilled simply because a private vendor has contractually agreed to assume that same responsibility. Performance can be contracted out, but responsibility remains in the hands of the vendor *and* the governmental agency. Anything else is unacceptable, because only the governmental agency can have the overview necessary to guarantee the establishment of a network of services, the continuum of care that is the bedrock of a genuine juvenile justice system.

A workable performance contract should be a blueprint of the Secure Treatment Unit itself. True performance contracting requires a degree of specification heretofore unknown in the human services profession. Rather than merely specifying the staff-patient ratio, a true performance contract will indicate the job descriptions of each and every member of the staff, and the ratios will be expressed in terms of actual activities, not merely in terms of time spent on the unit. For example, if there is to be an educational component to a Secure Treatment Unit, the number of classroom hours to which each resident will be exposed must be spelled out, together with the number and qualifications of those staff who will be participating in this particular endeavor.

A daily census, which is normally required of all public and private institutions, will specify not only how many residents are physically present on the unit each day, but what they are *doing* on the unit. For example, a resident will spend a certain percentage of his (24-hour) day in his room, a certain percentage in classrooms, a certain percentage in therapy, in recreation, at meals, and so forth.

The intake procedure and criteria will be described in contractual terms so that there is a decision made prior to any admission, and so that this decision itself defines the working relationship between the Secure Treatment Unit and the state agency. This contractual specification will go a long way toward defining the use the state intends to make of the Secure Treatment Unit. If the unit is to be used as a mere dumping ground for those juveniles considered ineligible for treatment within an otherwise de-institutionalized system, the contract will reflect this attitude by granting the state total control of intake. A garbage can is not allowed to make decisions as to its own contents. Conversely, if the Secure Treatment Unit is to be an integral part of a statewide continuum of care, as part of a network of services, the contract will reflect this perception by permitting the Secure Treatment Unit to define its admission criteria in such a way that the endorsement of the state agency is guaranteed. By use of performance contracting, the private vendor will be able to evaluate the state's attitude towards the Secure Treatment Unit prior to accepting the responsibility of its juvenile referrals.

If the Secure Treatment Unit is to enjoy even a minimal chance of success with life-style violent juveniles, the sponsoring state agency must be committed to performance contracting, and to the very performance the contract requires. This concept, perhaps more than any other, will establish the crunch-point of professional programming for the life-style violent juvenile. If the state agency adopts a form of the "low bidder" mentality, it will be heavily biased in favor of the private vendor that agrees to surrender all control of intake. However, if the state sees the Secure Treatment Unit as a necessary component of its own network, as a *partner* in treatment, fully entitled to the respect and attention it deserves, control of intake will continue to be negotiable, and the Secure Treatment Unit's policies will be guaranteed a full and fair hearing. Under such a system, the state will focus on the programmatic aspects of the unit, rather than the convenience it will provide to other programs, and the state will evaluate the unit in terms of its effectiveness with its target population, *not* in terms of the pressure it takes off the rest of the system.

A Secure Treatment Unit, anchored by a performance contract, also requires a public educated as to its own self-interest. The performance contract is a sword that cuts with both edges. It guarantees the state agency a certain level of performance by the private vendor, and it also guarantees the private vendor certain operational considerations necessary to achieve its own goals. A performance contract should incorporate evaluative criteria since this area is the subject of far more discussion than illumination. While this tends to hold the Secure Treatment Unit close to a previously established standard, it also protects the unit from newly imposed criteria for which it was not originally designed. Such a contract puts an additional burden on both parties: a state agency will have no media problems in funding a Secure Treatment Unit that promises to provide "complete rehabilitative services," and a Secure Treatment Unit itself will have no difficulties meeting such vague criteria. But a state which agrees (or admits) that realistic goals are necessarily somewhat short of "complete rehabilitation" runs the risk of media criticism, and this is a risk that many jurisdictions are not ready to assume. Therefore, part of a performance contract is basic salesmanship. The public can accept such a contractural relationship only if it has been educated by the appropriate authorities as to the *actual* problem, and to the realm of the possible. Grossly raising expectations is not only cruel, it works against any realistic goals of the state or the unit itself. Anyone who believes that a functioning Secure Treatment Unit will somehow transform life-style violent juveniles into "taxpaying citizens" will be disappointed. If the public is helped to understand that the de-escalation of life-style violence is difficult and time-consuming work, however, it can look upon the Secure Treatment Unit as a *necessary* investment, and respond to it accordingly. Performance contracting strips away much of the proposal-oriented rhetoric and forces the participants and observers alike to look at what the parties *themselves* expect to happen as a result of their mutual efforts.

By specifically outlining such procedures as public visitation of the Secure Treatment Unit, performance contracting can help to insure that these procedures are designed to further the proper functioning of the unit rather than to satisfy political needs. Performance contracting also tends to reduce the individualized negotiations and behind-the-scenes battling that can occur when state agencies and private vendors form a relationship. For example, the right to "visit and inspect" the premises is never spelled out in the usual contract, and the unit tends to be publicly visited in direct proportion to the impression it is likely to make on outsiders. The Secure Treatment Unit will have a strong interest in restricting the number of visitors. In contrast to the "concept house" which specifically gears a part of its total program to the indoctrination and entertainment of visitors, a closed unit will find that its own specialized programs tend to be disrupted by frequent visitation.

On the other hand, the Secure Treatment Unit cannot be allowed total autonomy in this area, since the unannounced visit is an excellent method of curbing abuse, and of chilling its recurrence. Therefore, rules and regulations as to outside visitation and observation should be established by contract. Visitors could, for example, be restricted to state-appointed evaluators, and the Secure Treatment Unit could require that such evaluators remain on the unit for a specific minimum period of time to insure that their recorded impressions are based on more than fleeting observations. In addition, in spite of the vested interest in correct evaluation, access to the residents themselves should be restricted, both to protect their privacy and prevent disruption of the program.[17]

The extent to which evaluators disclose the criteria on which they propose to base their evaluation is the extent to which the evaluation will be fair, unbiased, and useful.[18] If the evaluators simply have instructions from the state to "go and take a look around," the Secure Treatment Unit will be forced into a public relations posture that will detract from its own programs. No evaluator should be permitted on the site of the program merely to confirm or deny his *own* particular view of how things should be done unless those biases are disclosed prior to his visit and their efficacy tested in a hearing before the appropriate authorities. The unit should also be informed as to the extent of the evaluator's own experience with similar operations. For example, it was quite common at Andros[19] to be visited by "evaluators" whose sole criteria for evaluation appeared to be the extent to which the program was "noninstitutional."[20] This was *not* one of the program's self-perceived goals, and is so broadly worded that it is to be doubted that *any* program would adopt it. Consequently, the evaluations could often be couched in negative terms in spite of the fact that the program was an operational success. On the other hand, if the evaluator's bias is in favor of pure security, it might be possible for a totally negative program to receive an excellent evaluation simply because it had a record of no escapes. Neither result is desirable.

Too often, evaluative biases reveal only a superficial understanding of program requirements. Some evaluators are in favor of the employment of former prisoners[21] in working with hard-core delinquent youth. Such evaluators are likely to ask only how many such individuals are on staff, and never inquire into what characteristics beyond prior imprisonment make the employees especially suitable for this kind of work. Although this is not the forum to relitigate *Bakke,* quota systems have no place in human services.

The contract must require that the basis of any evaluation is the extent to which the Secure Treatment Unit fulfills the performance contract. The solution is to have the evaluation performed in terms of how close the actual program lives up to its contractual obligations. In such a system, the greater the specificity with which the program's obligations are stated, the greater the degree to which the evaluators can achieve the goal of objective, accurate evaluation. This permits the program to consistently work towards the *same* evaluative standards, and not merely adapt its program around the occasional visit of an evaluator.

As a secondary function, such a system of evaluation would serve to check and balance the criteria and standards specified in the performance contract itself. Contractually established evaluation standards produce another significant advantage. If the program indeed lives up to its contractual criteria in terms of performance without effectuating those kind of changes and improvements which the state agency desires for the target population, we will have achieved an evaluation of those criteria. As a result, changes could be made in the standards required. A performance contract, therefore, not only simplifies evaluation, and tends to eliminate bias, it further provides a means of assessing the criteria on which the program itself was initially evaluated.

Finally, the performance contract must be sufficiently fluid to correct (through further contracting) any defects spotlighted by the Secure Treatment Unit evaluators. At some point, we would hope that the state agency and the Secure Treatment Unit organization would arrive at mutually satisfactory criteria for evaluation, but the performance contract should be seen as a tool towards that end, not as the end in itself.

Intake

Control of Intake is a behind-the-scenes battle with political and economic implications far beyond its surface significance. Who controls Intake? This question is relevant whether one is discussing a foster home network for abandoned and neglected children or a maximum-security institution for aggressive/violent juvenile offenders. Control of Intake is hotly debated and vigorously contested throughout the juvenile justice profession, yet the general public has difficulty perceiving what the fuss is all about. If the juvenile justice "system" is committed to the care, custody, and treatment of *all* children within its jurisdiction, what does it matter which agency or institution has the responsibility for any given child?[22] There are three basic reasons for the endless disputes about Intake procedures in juvenile programming:

1. Such decisions are rarely made by an individual agency; they are usually a composite of several inputs, and political strength is equally as important as the suitability of a given placement.

2. Many agencies and institutions view children placed in their custody strictly in terms of their "manage-ability," and find it extremely difficult to later transfer such children if they prove troublesome. Therefore, the goal is to summarily exclude from initial Intake any juvenile thought to be a potential source of problems.

3. The "purchase of care" agencies and institutions are paid at a per capita rate which is *not* adjusted to the difficulty in management or treatment of an individual child. The rate is established based on the general services provided by the program. The economic and therapeutic interests of the agency therefore dictate against the acceptance of any juvenile who might cause disruption or force the program to devote a disproportionate amount of time and energy to his treatment.

The closer the treatment facility gets to maximum security, the less it is generally concerned with Intake Control. In most systems, the "secure setting" (or training school) is seen as the "bottom of the barrel," the one location which effectively takes a juvenile out of the transfer-eligible pool.[23] In fact, this management-motivated mentality is even expressed *within* maximum security juvenile facilities in some jurisdictions, since such institutions have the power to enforce a transfer to an adult facility.[24] The very concept of Intake Control seems foreign to an adult correctional system. Whoever heard of a prison rejecting a candidate for admission because he did not satisfy the institution's Intake criteria? Such criteria as do exist are purely statutory in form: commission of certain crimes guarantees admission to certain institutions,[25] and "poor institutional adjustment" in that prison guarantees transfer to either a specialized unit of that same prison,[26] or to another institution specifically designed to deal with such problems.[27] Although management personnel in adult corrections are rarely heard to demand a voice in Intake, placement in one institution over another is deemed to have such serious consequences[28] that the United States Supreme Court has required procedural safeguards before such administrative transfer is effectuated.[29]

Private vendors often employ intake control so as to populate a Secure Treatment Unit with their own rejects. The average secure facility is not perceived as a placement/treatment option whose specialized elements might be especially designed to aid in the rehabilitation of certain juvenile problems. Rather, it is perceived as either punishment or banishment, and is employed as a behavior-control threat by staff in other programs.[30] This not only stigmatizes the role of the staff in the Secure Treatment Unit, but virtually guarantees that any new admission will have both a hostile and cynical attitude towards whatever program does exist in the new facility.

New admissions will be hostile because they view the transfer as punishment, and cynical and unresponsive because they view the secure facility as a last stop within the system. The staff is generally quick to point out that the (new) institution still retains some significant controls, among them the aforementioned threat of transfer to adult corrections and direct control of the prisoner's release date. The prisoner perceives that he was placed in the new, secure institution because he was a "bad inmate," and eventually refocuses his energies on release by acquiring the appearance of successful institutional adjustment.

Unfortunately, we have learned that the so-called "model prisoner" is often a dangerous, maladaptive human being. Adjustment has no value for him unless seen as a reaction to a situation. Therefore, good adjustment to a negative situation is often a counter-indicator of adjustment to the outside society.[31]

In fact, many maximum security juvenile prisons are run on such a rigid pro-management model that the inmate who terrorizes others into a semblance of obedience and good behavior is often prized and promoted. One former prisoner remembers his juvenile incarceration like this:

We had what you call a Cadet Captain; he was the duke of the dorm . . . which means he was the strongest guy there. The Man put him in charge and he could do what he wanted to do . . . if you had candy, it was *his* candy, you know? And for some of the boys, they had to give up a lot more than candy. His job was to keep the place real clean, and real quiet, and the Man didn't care how he did it. As soon as I dug what was happening, I made my move and then *I* was the fucking Captain.[32]

The "reject" system is only one indicia of the hierarchy (as opposed to network, or continuum of services) model prevalent in the juvenile justice system. To return to our original question: if there is indeed a total juvenile justice "system" which collectively assumes total responsibility for all juvenile offenders in its jurisdiction, why does it matter so intensely which component of that system has the actual treatment responsibility for a given individual? The answer to that question cannot be found because, in fact, no such system exists. Rather than a continuum of services which would work together to jointly address the multi-problem juvenile offender's (and society's) needs, we have instead a distinct hierarchy of placement/treatment options, with significant gaps between those options. A juvenile found to be behaviorally inappropriate for a given placement will manifest himself as a management problem if actually placed there, and will eventually be passed *down* the hierarchy to the maximum-security alternative—regardless of the behavior that caused his original incarceration. Figure 4-1 illustrates the contemporary (hierarchy) model, while figure 4-2, in dramatic contrast, illustrates the systemic continuum of services model we propose.

Under a hierarchy model of services, intake and discharge are plagued with competing self-interests. The hierarchy model poses still another administrative problem, one with serious treatment consequences. Under this model, the self-interest of the institution is to limit intake as much as possible, while increasing discharge (if under a civil service system with a fixed budget and no financial relationship between the number of residents and the compensation received), or to establish the full number of "manageable" residents and restrict *both* intake and discharge. However, the self-interest of the governmental youth agency is to open intake as far as possible (to offer management alternatives to all other programs within its system) and restrict discharge until the residents reach statutory maturity, at which point the system is no longer responsible for them.

The reasons for the latter restriction (in a hierarchy model) are simple enough: just as community-based programs have rejected management problems among juvenile offenders, they are equally adamant in refusing to accept "graduates" of maximum-security units now on their way back "up" the system's hierarchy of treatment. This appears to be more of a *self*-judgment than

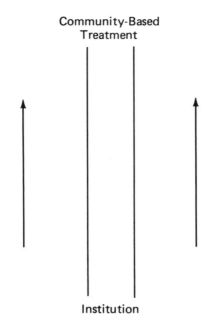

Figure 4-1. Contemporary (Hierarchy) Model of Services

a judgment of the maximum-security unit's ability, since the majority of juveniles in the maximum-security unit were originally referred there simply because they presented management problems to the community-based facilities. A juvenile that could not function in an open setting is far *less* likely to do so after being exposed to a continual period of institutional treatment. Ironically, some of the most dangerous juvenile offenders are therefore released *directly* to the community, rather than through a halfway house or other graduated alternative.[33]

Figures 4-3 and 4-4 below illustrate the difference between the self-interest of the institution and that of the governmental youth agency in a standard hierarchy model, while figure 4-5 illustrates the proper relationship in a network (continuum of services) model.

A network (continuum) of services treatment model demands a collective, criteria-ized decision on each individual placement, with appropriate compensation to the accepting agency based on the particular attributes of the juvenile placed. Under a continuum of services model, the system itself accepts the responsibility for the individual juvenile offender, and the placement/treatment decision is made by all components of that system, acting collectively. The

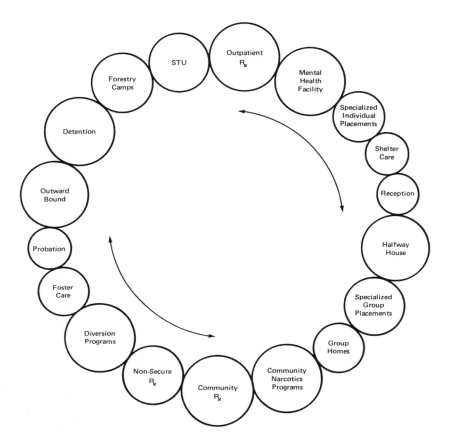

Figure 4-2. Systematic Continuum of Services Model

authors are not so naive as to assume that this method will magically eliminate
the self-interest of the varying agencies, but we believe that this method would
enforce the establishment and maintenance of admissions criteria in *all* programs, not just those offering "secure" treatment. Although placement agencies
in the juvenile justice system have been traditionally reluctant to articulate their
actual admission criteria in specific terms, we maintain that a systemic responsibility for all juveniles would eventually produce this articulation by the process
of precedent. An agency that accepts a given juvenile who seems to have
essential characteristics in common with another whom they refuse to accept
will assume the burden of explaining its decision to the representatives from the
other programs. This process, gradual though it may be, is perhaps the only
viable method of discovering those juveniles for whom no treatment program

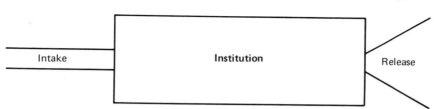

Figure 4-3. Self-Interest of the Institution, in Standard Hierarchy Model

actually exists. A new agency, then bidding to establish such a program, will have committed itself to the acceptance of such juveniles. Given sufficient time, and sufficient sincerity, a genuine network of services covering all treatment needs of a jurisdiction's juvenile population can be established.

Such criteria as are established can then be used as a baseline to establish the compensation required to maintain each individual program, thereby enforcing at least a modicum of fairness in the placement decisions. For example, if a participant in the network refuses to accept a juvenile on the ground that he has committed a violent act, such a program cannot later lobby for admission of another juvenile who appears to pose no management problem but who has also committed a similar violent act. The *actual* criterion, that of manageability, will have been exposed by the program's actions, and a form of continuing criteria-ization will emerge. Thus, if a program's *actual* admissions standard is the ease with which they can manage a given juvenile, that program cannot expect to be compensated at the same level as those programs that accept juveniles in the unmanageable category.[34]

These criteria, through discussion and actual use, will increase in specificity, and we will avoid the practice one commentator calls "creaming"[35] in the selection process.

The Secure Treatment Unit will function far more effectively under a network of services model. In addition, a network of services model presupposes a solid

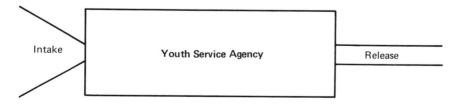

Figure 4-4. Self-Interest of the Governmental Youth Agency, in Standard Hierarchy Model

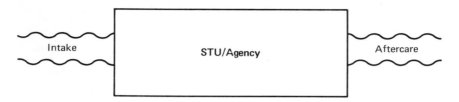

Figure 4-5. Institution-Agency Relationship, in Network Model

commitment to treatment, not just devotion to management objectives. Therefore, if the Secure Treatment Unit is continually employed by the other programs because of the specialized treatment it offers, the perception of this unit as "the bottom of the barrel" dumping ground will be changed, and so will its allocation of funds. A network of services model stands for the proposition that the life-style violent juvenile impacts on all programs within its borders, and acknowledges that such other programs cannot unilaterally withdraw from all treatment responsibility for this population, *especially* on an after-care basis.

If working with such juveniles is more difficult, the staff-patient ratio must be reexamined. And member agencies in the network of services should not be heard to protest against increases in such a ratio since they are subscribers to a philosophy that demands *treatment* of such offenders, not just mere warehousing.

And, most significant of all, a network of services model means that the Secure Treatment Unit is merely one of many placements that can be utilized on a dynamic, ongoing basis. Under such a model, a juvenile could be placed initially in a community-based treatment center, temporarily housed in the Secure Treatment Unit, and returned to the original placement after a period of intense work. Similarly, a juvenile statutorily assigned to the Secure Treatment Unit could remain on the unit a relatively short time and then be placed in a community-based facility during the rest of his commitment to custody. Staff would be elevated in their ability to treat the "whole child," not just by the wider range of interconnected options but by the professional option of working within more than a single setting during their period of employment. This is one proposed solution to the ever-present problem of "staff burn-out," and one which merits considerable discussion by those responsible for the performance of an entire system. To be sure, it does require a commitment to totality of treatment now lacking in the component members of juvenile justice "systems," but the enforced process of criteria-ization earlier described should reduce some of the barriers to interagency employment that now exist.

The network itself will greatly benefit from continuum of services methodology through minimization of existing agency power-blocs. Finally, under the proposed network of services model, it would be far more difficult to establish individual fiefdoms of power within the system. An "established" agency would theoretically have no more power than a new community-based program in controlling Intake, and no less weight in the allocation of new resources. Too many jurisdictions have adopted a so-called "purchase of care" model of de-institutionalization by merely transferring the governmental agency's power to a giant private agency. This perversion of the ideal of permitting responsible community agencies to plan for (and work with) juveniles from their own areas is accomplished by demanding "start-up costs" from each "purchase of care" candidate. Of course, those agencies with other sources of funding, (especially established religious organizations), will be easily able to comply with this requirement, while grass roots organizations will not. The old adage "it takes money to make money" is no less applicable to social services, and every attempt should be made to involve local organizations in planning and programming. Calling a national organization a local agency simply because of its street address is like calling a multinational corporation a neighborhood business simply because it maintains a branch office in a given community. For a network of services model to be effective, there has to be across-the-board allocation of *opportunity* to individual agencies, with an emphasis on those agencies that have significant local roots. Of course, the major obstacle to the establishment of this highly preferrable model would be the existence (and resistance) of civil service, as discussed earlier in this work.

Is a statewide diagnostic center the answer to intake problems? Would it really be a necessary component of a network of services? At first glance, a central diagnostic center seems the most appropriate way of settling any network disputes as to which placement/treatment option a given juvenile will be initially referred. Under such a system, each newly committed juvenile is sent to the center for a period of diagnostic evaluation during which he is tested and his behavior monitored. Unfortunately, in a multi-option network system, the diagnostic center is required to make too many judgments in too short a period of time. In a large jurisdiction, the center itself would have to be mammoth merely to house all new admissions and, as a result, there would be heavy pressure to reduce the stay of each individual so as to increase the manageability in the center itself. A statewide diagnostic center might become the largest institution of all. We maintain that it is dysfunctional to mix juvenile populations (in terms of personalities and offenses committed), and a large diagnostic center would have no choice but to engage in this practice.

It is already well accepted that status offenders should not be mixed with criminal offenders, but we are equally opposed to indiscriminately mixing juveniles whose only common characteristic is "criminal" behavior. The institutional-management problems of housing juveniles ranging in age from twelve to eighteen are monumental, and we consider the proposition that basic criminality acts as a leveler of age differences to be ludicrous. For example, would any competent professional seriously maintain that a thirteen-year-old car thief is an appropriate companion for a seventeen-year-old murderer?

The task of matching an appropriate placement to an accurate diagnosis would actually be impeded by a central diagnostic center. Leaving aside the enormous management problems inherent in such a large and diverse population, two additional factors oppose the creation of a central diagnostic facility:

1. Such centers cannot observe behavior in any realistic way and are forced to rely on standardized tests which may or may not be relevant to the assessment needs of any particular program. A juvenile might have grave difficulty adjusting to the original institution (the diagnostic center) so that it might be thought that placement in an open setting is not indicated. But the juvenile's problem may be within the institution *itself,* and a community-based placement might be the *most* appropriate.

2. Matching the needs of the juvenile with the appropriate placement[36] presupposes that the diagnostic center has the most up-to-date and comprehensive understanding of the workings of each individual program. Yet is is a fact that many professionals are more capable of *running* a program than of writing descriptive literature about their efforts, and the quality of the information on which the diagnostic center would have to rely to make the appropriate "matches" would be, at best, highly suspect.

Programs that are functioning ethically and effectively serve as de facto diagnostic centers. Each individual program/placement really serves as its own ongoing diagnostic center. If the juvenile is found to be inappropriately placed, the option is to re-place him (still within the continuum of available services). If, in fact, the juvenile is found to be unmanageable within a community setting, he has virtually diagnosed himself by virtue of his behavior. Similarly, the Secure Treatment Unit could have a "rejective" option *upwards* in that a child might be found to be in a sufficiently advanced state of socialization so that a closed, intensive setting is not required.

This requires the strongest ethical commitment on the part of the individual program directors. The Secure Treatment Unit should not retain a juvenile simply because he poses no management problems, if his condition does not require intensive treatment. Similarly, the community programs should not reject a juvenile simply because of unwillingness to extend their resources with a difficult case. Only if individual programs see themselves as part of a unified whole will this philosophy be implemented.

The role of the Secure Treatment Unit's individual diagnostic center will be thoroughly explained when we discuss the inner workings of that unit.

Regardless of the path by which the juvenile reaches the Secure Treatment Unit, the unit itself must make a preliminary diagnosis as to inclusion or exclusion of that juvenile. The concept of diagnosis *within* a Secure Treatment Unit is unique; it is a process of exclusion rather than actual analysis, and it requires input from a variety of sources. When a juvenile is admitted to the unit, the origin of that admission will never be a factor in exclusion or inclusion. Depending on the statutory scheme which governs a particular jurisdiction, a juvenile may be admitted to the unit from a juvenile court, a criminal court, a so-called training school, a nonresidential juvenile placement, a detention facility (secure or non-secure), or even a mental hospital. There will be no assumption that the diagnosis of the initiating institution is totally credible since the Secure Treatment Unit is designed to be self-diagnosing. We take it as an operative assumption that some juveniles *will* be inappropriately referred to the Secure Treatment Unit, whether because of professional diagnostic disputes or gross self-interest on the part of other programs.

Some factors will be automatic grounds for exclusion. It is the exclusionary process that will eventually determine if a juvenile is to continue within the Secure Treatment Unit. Some exclusions are virtually automatic, and do not reflect on the actual suitability of the juvenile for Secure Unit treatment. For example, individuals with active tuberculosis or other communicable disease would be excluded because such juveniles would pose a continual danger to other residents. On the other hand, those short-duration illnesses which could be treated in an infirmary setting would not be grounds for exclusion, and the architectural design of the unit anticipates the recurrence of such cases and makes provision for their temporary (medical) isolation.

Other conditions will also result in virtually automatic exclusion and *are* directly related to the ability of the Secure Treatment Unit to respond to a given individual juvenile. Examples of such conditions are severe mental retardation, (*not* learning disabilities),[37] or those extraordinary physical handicaps that make participation in any program impossible.[38]

One criterion for acceptance by the Secure Treatment Unit would be a series of convictions for behavior exhibiting a chronicity of (possibly escalating) violence. It is also vitally important to establish some baseline criminality as a prerequisite to admission. Although no rational person would consider commitment of a status offender to such a specialized facility, experience has taught us that "liberal" laws may be construed in repressive ways. Experience has also taught us that prediction of dangerousness[39] is a task beyond the ability of any of our scientific disciplines.

We would further insist that the threshold criminality necessary for (consideration for) admission be statutorily defined. The ideal candidate for admission to the Secure Treatment Unit will be a juvenile exhibiting chronicity of violence, usually in an escalating pattern, who functions asocially in terms of the larger society but who does function at a minimal level within his own peer group.[40] We are looking for assaultive behavior, and it is this violence towards other human beings that must characterize the successful admission. Once this threshold is actually crossed, the statutory distinctions between crimes is less significant. The push-in mugger who viciously and needlessly attacks an elderly victim is not criminologically different from the perpetrator whose similar attack results in a homicide. This distinction is not a moral or legal judgment, but a criminological analysis based on the realities of the human condition. The human skull ranges in solidity from that of an egg shell to that of cast concrete, and the perpetrator who smashes a victim on the head with a blunt object can have no way of knowing what the proximate result of his behavior will be. The criminal codes thus distinguish assaulters purely on the basis of random chance: one defendant is charged with a felonious assault, another with a homicide. Similarly, the codes do not meaningfully distinguish between the mugger who uses force to overcome resistance to robbery (a purely economic motive) and the mugger who attacks his victim *following* an already-successful robbery. Both crimes are "robbery by violence," yet treatment of the individual perpetrators may be vastly different in tone, technique, and duration.

A possible exception to the requirement that admission-mandated violence be supported by actual criminal convictions is for those over-institutionalized juveniles whose chronically violent behavior began following incarceration. There will be one obvious exception to the rule of requiring threshold criminal convictions for admission to the Secure Treatment Unit. This will be the juvenile who was originally incarcerated (possibly as a status offender) at an especially young age who, after years and years of institutionalization, has changed into the exact prototype of the life-style violent delinquent we described earlier.[41] This juvenile probably will emerge as a so-called "management transfer," and it will be the philosophy of the Secure Treatment Unit to accept such children without reservation since it is our operating thesis that they are among the *most* likely to pursue a life-style of adult criminality unless substantial intervention is instituted.

The Secure Treatment Unit must accept the fact that some juveniles will plea bargain out of eligibility for admission. This analysis would not be complete without a brief discussion of a practice which impacts on all future admissions to any Secure Treatment Unit—plea bargaining. In a jurisdiction where only designated crimes are fit grounds for secure treatment and confinement,[42] defense counsel (once having passed the first hurdle, that of "transfer" to the adult system) will find that the dispositional options to which the defendant is potentially exposed are a far more significant factor than guilt or innocence. Although the practice of plea bargaining in the juvenile courts is not as widespread or as all-pervasive[43] as in the criminal courts, it certainly does occur, and with apparently increasing regularity. What is the result if an assaultive offender "bargains down" to a section of the juvenile law which does not permit Secure Treatment Unit-type confinement? In our opinion, the result *must* be that the juvenile avoids the prospect of such treatment, regardless of the actual criminal acts which brought him to the attention of the court. There is even a school of thought which holds that many prosecutors willingly participate in such bargaining with the not-cynical assumption that the juvenile's criminality will continue unabated and that his *next* appearance will be, by virtue of age, in a criminal court with adult correctional consequences.[44]

This possibility presents a moral dilemma to the conscientious defense attorney. The philosophical-moral dilemma of the concerned defense attorney is almost immeasurable in such a situation: what are the "best interests" of such a juvenile? Take, for example, the problem of a defense attorney in a non-waiver jurisdiction such as New York.[45] A juvenile four months short of his sixteenth birthday[46] is charged with robbery-by-violence and assault with intent to commit murder as the result of an attack on an old woman in her apartment. The prosecution offers a plea of assault in the second degree, which is *not* a designated felony in that jurisdiction. If the plea is accepted, the juvenile cannot be housed in a Secure Treatment Unit[47] and most likely will be released from custody some months past his sixteenth birthday. Suppose further that the juvenile has told his attorney that push-in mugging is the way he earns his living and that he expects to continue this practice indefinitely. If the plea is accepted, the juvenile's next arrest will probably be for the same crime, but he will be tried in an adult court. Rather than facing a maximum sentence of 1-3 years as a juvenile designated-felon, he will then face a maximum of 25 years as an adult assaultive robber.

The attorney is not a social worker. He is not required to predict future behavior of his clients, and he must concentrate all his energies on the best result immediately possible[48] for his client. Yet the attorney viewing the vicious chain of inevitability in which this juvenile is a participant must sometimes wonder what his role really *is*. Is he just another cog in a machine that seems designed to produce adult criminals, or can he view the "best interests" of the juvenile on a long-term basis? This book suggests no answers to this question, and the point is raised only to illustrate that no statutory scheme, no matter how well intentioned or perfectly drafted, can guarantee either the inclusion of all life-style violent juveniles in the Secure Treatment Unit or the exclusion from that unit of those juveniles who would be better served in another setting.

Population Size

In addition to Intake control, there must be a fixed limit on population size in the Secure Treatment Unit. Control of Intake is, of course, meaningless unless there is also control of population size. This control need not, and perhaps should not be in the hands of the Secure Treatment Unit exclusively, but it must be firmly established *prior* to the initiation of any of its programs. If the number of residents is to be flexible, and under the control of any outside authority, both architectural and programmatic structures will find themselves transformed past the point of usefulness. It is an ugly truism in the juvenile justice profession that all institutional vacuums will be filled. If we construct an institution for the care of fifty residents, the observer can be well assured that no *less* than fifty residents will ever occupy the available space. This, in itself, does not represent a significant problem to intelligent planning. Although our proposed Secure Treatment Unit has space for fifty residents, "space" is not an all-encompassing concept. Rather, space is separately allocated in terms of the functions it may be called upon to serve, and there is sufficient "over-design" in the facility to serve a population that will habilitate at individualized rates.

This population limit must be contractually predetermined to protect it from predictable, inevitable pressures. If the number of residents is not agreed upon, (and contractually bound) prior to the beginning of the program, it will be political power that will actually determine the size of the population. Political pressure will be a fact of life regardless of contractual stipulations limiting total size, since there will also be pressure on the Secure Treatment Unit to move current residents out to make way for juveniles who other programs and other judges are demanding be admitted. If the release decision remains in the hands of a specially designated body of professionals who have no other ties into the system,[49] we are confident that such pressures can be resisted. But we are equally certain that the Secure Treatment Unit will never have the political strength to resist special-interest demands for intake or release if the number of residents is not contractually set.

Absent such a limit, overcrowding would prevent the proper functioning of the Secure Treatment Unit. The arguments against overcrowding are numerous: such conditions are physically and emotionally dangerous to residents and staff alike, they are unhealthy in the extreme, and they are the kiss of death to any therapeutic program. But the greatest danger involved with placing an excess number of residents in a Secure Treatment Unit is simply that large numbers require the kind of institutional management objectives that run counter to the specialized treatment necessary for the life-style violent juvenile. This kind of juvenile, more than any other, readily adapts to standard penal institutions, and finds his stunted, distorted view of the world reinforced in the resulting "might makes right" culture. And those juveniles with gang affiliations entering a standard institution will find the gang remains the dominant force in their lives even while incarcerated.[50]

As an institution changes, because of overpopulation, from a Secure Treatment Unit as we define the term to a large warehouse of life-style violent juveniles, staff will increasingly rely on residents themselves to control the population. We will then have business-as-usual, with no surprises for the juvenile population and no hope of serious intervention in their lives. Planning will change its priorities from therapy to day-to-day survival, and long-term planning will be shelved while the unit concentrates on continual crisis-intervention. Human interaction will be forced to give way to institutional control needs, and the only real differences between the specially designed Secure Treatment Unit and the usual juvenile training school will be the greater success of the former in preventing escapes.[51]

For many people, this latter success will be a sufficient accomplishment. The protection of the public will be temporarily assured. Unfortunately, the emphasis will be on the temporary aspect of that assurance, while the viciousness from which the community sought protection will be honed and perfected during the period of incarceration. We see no functional difference between a bomb dropped from an airplane and a time bomb hidden deep within a city, especially if the time bomb is far more deadly.

Architectural design cannot prevent overcrowding, although it can make it more difficult to achieve. In our discussions with architects and planners, we learned that it was possible to build an institution that would be "utterly unsuitable" for more than a pre-designed number of residents. But we also know that "utterly unsuitable" will not remotely deter special interest groups, and we believe strongly that construction of a specialized Secure Treatment Unit should not even be attempted unless there are enforceable agreements limiting the size of the resident population.[52]

The Secure Treatment Unit is specially designed to utilize "space" within the treatment model. Limiting the size of the resident population is absolutely key to the success of the Secure Treatment Unit because the concept of "space" is itself a program tool. Residents must have space within which they feel (and are) completely safe. They must have privacy, but privacy that does not readily lend itself to criminal activity. They must be able to *acquire* additional space as they progress through the program(s), and they must learn to utilize space intelligently.

This means that the Secure Treatment Unit, which cannot control the total amount of space once the institution is constructed, must be able to control the number of residents so that the necessary ratios are maintained. Flexibility of available space is the key to program success, and sufficient flexibility has been planned into the proposed structure. But that flexibility is a function of the number of residents; if control is relinquished over that number (the amount of total space being finite), the flexibility is lost in direct proportion to the loss of control.

Therefore, the commitment to limiting resident population size is a primary requirement of any jurisdiction willing to give the Secure Treatment Unit the fair trial it deserves. Chief among the commitments a sponsoring jurisdiction *must* make if the Secure Treatment Unit is to have a realistic opportunity to succeed is the commitment to hold the number of residents to the amount planned for at the beginning of the construction. A (relatively) large institution can utilize many specialized services with a high degree of economic feasibility; but smaller units are universally conceded to be more functional in terms of therapeutic treatment. The proposed Secure Treatment Unit combines both features, but the balance is a delicate one and overcrowding would diminish or destroy many of the unit's special advantages.

Staff Bloc-ing

A significant barrier to the proper functioning of a Secure Treatment Unit is the traditional conflict between staff "blocs" found in any conventional juvenile institution. We have formerly stated that control of Intake is not only vital to the establishment of a functioning Secure Treatment Unit, but is also a significant contributor to the elimination of the so-called "management mentality" prevalent in the standard training school. Since we maintain that avoidance of this mentality is necessary if anything resembling treatment is to occur, we want to closely examine those internal staff conflicts that characterize the standard institution and grossly inhibit therapeutic goals.

Primary among those conflicts is that between security and treatment blocs. Standard juvenile institutions contain staffing "blocs" with distinctly separate identities and felt needs. Each bloc continually lobbies for what it perceives to be its own self-interest, and can be counted on to at least passively resist procedures and innovations perceived as contrary to such self-interest.

The most obvious conflict is between the advocates of "security" and those in support of "treatment." The conventional wisdom is that innovative programs are an automatic threat to custody/security considerations, and that heightened security must be equated with antitherapeutic goals.

The security and treatment blocs tend not only to have differing attitudes, but also to have different histories and job goals. The usual pattern is that the custody/security bloc preceded the treatment bloc in term of service. The treatment bloc is usually composed of "nine to fivers" and consultants, who generally feel morally and professionally superior to the security bloc. The treatment bloc is apt to think of itself as reformist, working against difficult odds in an essentially negative system, while the custody/security bloc is apt to blame the treatment bloc for any new difficulty in management.

While the treatment bloc tends to receive greater recognition (including higher salaries), the custody/security bloc tends to do the bulk of the actual work in a standard training school. Usually the rhetoric is all treatment-oriented, the proposals are written in therapeutic language, salaries are heavily slanted in favor of the treatment bloc, and only the custody/security bloc is required to work late shifts and weekends.[53] Often the newly hired treatment staff owe their employment to a wave of outrage over prior conditions, and arrive with a newly named therapeutic modality designed to radically alter the behavior and personalities of juveniles in their care. The custody/security bloc tends to be scapegoated for the institution's past failures. If the new methodology *also* fails, the custody/security bloc will be blamed for resisting the reformers' efforts.

The custody/security bloc also tends to have far greater power and control within the institution. But while the rhetoric is treatment, the reality is security, and custodial considerations generally have the last word in decision making. The reality is simply that the institution can continue to function (as perceived by the outside community) in the complete absence of the treatment bloc, and it cannot do so if the custody/security bloc is gone. Treatment is secondary to control, and control is in the hands of the custody/security bloc. Although the release-oriented resident[54] might well welcome the advent of a system whereby discharge is related to a series of therapeutic goals, such residents are in the minority[55] and, in any case, are rarely in a position of power within the resident population. Rewards and punishments are actually controlled by the custody/security bloc, especially when the immediacy of such rewards and punishments is a consideration.[56] To the residents, the treatment bloc seems oriented around a world that the residents simply do not understand. After all, the failure to perceive the future in any realistic sense is a major distinguishing characteristic of the life-style violent juvenile, and the treatment bloc seems to lack the "here and now" focus to which such juveniles primarily relate.

The power of the custody/security bloc is communicated to the residents through overt control of rewards and punishments. Even the flow of goods and services, (both approved and contraband[57]), is controlled by the custody/security bloc. And, in spite of rhetoric to the contrary, the resident cannot perceive an actual relationship between "good" institutional behavior and earlier release. The fact that the more institutionally dangerous residents are often rewarded gives increasing weight to the proposition that *real* control is determined by what takes place in the cells and in the corridors, not in the front office.

The treatment bloc tends to retreat from physical confrontation within the institution. The custody/security bloc believes it is needed by the treatment bloc, but not vice versa. Usually an accommodation is reached whereby the treatment bloc physically retires to certain designated areas of the institution, and confines its input to written recommendations and highly structured counseling, while the custody/security bloc makes all the operational decisions. The custody/security bloc also has ample means to enforce its will when its authority is challenged,[58] while the treatment bloc is virtually powerless. This situation is reinforced by the division of labor within the institution. If a member of the treatment bloc is physically attacked by a resident, or even if a resident becomes unruly during treatment, it is assumed that the custody/ security bloc will be called in immediately. The treatment bloc often feels that physical participation is not its role, and the custody/security bloc considers the treatment bloc to be individuals who lack the skill and the will to deal with violent juveniles in "the only way they understand."

The treatment bloc further contributes to this schism by opposing any treatment attempts by the custody/security bloc. This unwillingness to physically participate in these inevitable aspects of institutional life is only one component of the schism between treatment and security blocs. Often an institutional guard has sincere feelings of empathy for his juvenile charges. He believes that the juvenile could benefit from advice or counsel from someone like himself, especially when he sees certain of his own life experiences as being in common with the behavior which brought the juvenile to the institution. He therefore tries to form a relationship beyond that of "prisoner" and "jailer." But such relationships are discouraged by the treatment bloc allegedly because the guard is "unskilled" in the human services profession. The guard's tentative overtures are met with scorn, contempt, and rejection by the treatment bloc, and his stereotype of the "holier than thou," inexperienced, rhetoric-crazed liberal is once again reinforced.

Each side continually attempts to co-opt the other's functions. Both sides overextend themselves in the struggle for supremacy. The custody/security bloc demands the right to distribute medications,[59] and the treatment bloc demands that security personnel intervene each time a resident becomes violent.

The director's power is undercut by the necessity of having to bridge this schism. The director of an institution is also viewed in terms of his identification with, and loyalty to, a given bloc. He is either "treatment-oriented" or "security-minded." Staff quickly learn that proposal writers don't run the show once the funds are granted, and the director finds that management of the institution is largely a matter of maintaining the shaky accommodations between the two blocs. Clear-cut choices are rare, but when they are necessitated by events, the custody/security bloc can count on a base of community support beyond the reach of the treatment people.

Finally, because civil service places a major premium on longevity of service, it is obvious that the custody/security bloc will also be the most powerful (in terms of seniority, promotions, titles, and so forth) in any standard institution.

A Secure Treatment Unit must plan against bloc-ing if it is to have a hope of success. Once part of the institution's life-style, bloc-ing is virtually immune from eradication.

Our experience has taught us that solutions to the above problems do exist, but, like Intake control, they must be determined prior to the opening of the unit.

As part of such planning, all staff should be hired at approximately the same time. There should be relatively equal seniority and no former civil servants from other institutions. The first step is to hire the entire staff at about the same time, with seniority stemming directly from participation on this particular unit. It must be a strictly private operation, run on a "purchase of care" model, with state input being confined to an overall supervisory capacity. The importance of adhering to this model cannot be overemphasized.

If the state, for example, decides to partially staff the Secure Treatment Unit with civil servants from another institution,[60] the result will be that some members of the new unit's staff will look to a higher authority than the director for control. It bluntly means that hiring and firing, a potent personnel tool, will not be in the hands of the individuals responsible for the successful functioning of the unit. This is not to say that former civil service employment should act as a disqualification from employment at the Secure Treatment Unit, only that such employees must first relinquish (either by resignation or leave of absence) the civil service seniority and protection they formerly enjoyed as a condition of employment. Otherwise, the unit will have more than one class of employee, and the tensions associated with employment in such an institution will be intolerable.

Staff functions cannot be divided into treatment and security. All staff must be responsible for, and participate in, both. But even if this minimal requirement is met, the new Secure Treatment Unit is still doomed to repeat the mistakes of the past if staff are hired specifically to perform security or treatment tasks. The abrupt departure from past ways of doing business must start with the concept that *all* staff are there to perform *both* functions, (indeed, that both functions are completely interrelated), with responsibilities and division of labor occurring on a dynamic, as-needed basis.

In a properly functioning Secure Treatment Unit, "treatment" staff will be expected to respond to physical emergencies without waiting for the designated "security" personnel to appear. The therapeutic milieu of the unit will be maintained at 3:00 A.M. as well as during "counseling hours." Just as treatment staff will be required to participate fully in all aspects of institutional life, no personnel will be hired strictly to perform security tasks. In-service training and outside professional/academic opportunities[61] must be provided to all staff so that personnel can fully participate in the therapeutic process on an ever-increasing basis. The teams must become a single team, with a dual goal—security cannot be ignored, and is the key to successful operation and survival. But security in the absence of treatment is nothing more than a repetition of past failures, and this concept must be clearly communicated to all staff.

This uniformity of purpose will communicate itself to the residents in terms of consistent rewards, punishments, and consequences. This method will enable staff to provide a single, ongoing, and consistent message to the resident population. No longer will different blocs, different shifts, and different individual staff members permit different behaviors, and opportunities for manipulation will be decreased correspondingly. This is not to say that staff individualities will be obscured in the headlong rush to provide uniformity of treatment, since the human qualities required of a competent worker in such a facility require in themselves a significant degree of individuality.

Consistency does not require rigid, authoritarian modes of personnel control, but it does demand uniformity in distribution of privileges and uniformity of consequences for proscribed behaviors.

This requirement of consistency is most important when expressed in the institution's response to violence. Since the Secure Treatment Unit is structured around the problems of life-style violent juveniles, no consistency is possible unless there is a uniform response to violence on the part of the residents. We have, in the past, been highly successful in disclosing our philosophy directly to the residents. This philosophy is as follows: violence is not a preferred form of work. No staff member is hired for his or her ability to *be* violent, and we take it as a baseline goal that all residents will be protected *from* violence. This means, however, that violence will not be permitted against residents by residents either. As a result, each resident chooses the amount of violence necessary to restrain himself, and he makes such choices through his own behavior.

A resident will be prevented from using violence by the use of only so much force as is necessary to achieve this prevention. For example, if a resident is in the process of assaulting another resident, the extent to which he requires physical restraint is the extent to which he refuses verbal demands to cease his behavior. But the period of verbal negotiation is also directly correlated to the intensity of the initial physical attack. Verbal threatening of one resident by another can be dealt with verbally: the degree of actual physical intervention by staff will be strictly determined by the resident's own use of physical force. Staff will break up a fist fight in a different manner than an assault with a weapon.

Group staff participation in such on-the-spot prevention will actually decrease the amount of physical force required. Also, by the use of complete staff participation, the danger of physical injury to staff and residents alike is greatly diminished. A resident refuses to surrender a homemade knife and return to his room: if an *individual* staff member tries to enforce the unit's rules, either he or the resident will almost inevitably be hurt.[62] But, if a *group* of staff members participate in the process[63] the odds are heavily in favor of resolution without injury to anyone.

Group participation makes the discouragement of violence societal and programmatic, not just individual. There is another, equally important effect of this group participation/intervention in violent behavior. The message transmitted by the intervention of a single staff member is that *this* staff member will not *personally* tolerate certain behavior; but the message from group participation is that the resident's violent behavior is *programmatically* unacceptable. This is most significant, since once this message is actually absorbed by residents (with continual reinforcement by staff), the level of violence within a Secure Treatment Unit will drop predictably. Much of the staff-resident violence in a typical institution comes about because residents tend to individualize staff responses to negative behavior, and to "pick their shots" in terms of who to attack. Often, a custody/security bloc will use the residents as a form of testing behavior of its own, selecting staff members on the basis of their ability to "handle themselves." When the residents are confronted with a collective response to violence, they begin to perceive that staff solidarity is based on a mutual therapeutic goal, and not just on peer-recognition of physical strength.

Much of the violence displayed by the life-style violent juvenile is simply behavior adapted to environment. Establishing programmatic responses to all forms of resident behavior has both treatment and management implications. The life-style violent juvenile is not unable to adjust to his surroundings; quite the contrary. Much of the violence that characterized his life-style while on the streets is adaptive in nature, not self-motivated.[64] A portion of this adaptation may be attributed to the reward-punishment set established by any inner-city ghetto, while an additional portion may be attributed to peer pressure. This peer pressure will remain operative even inside the walls of an institution,[65] and attempts to substitute staff as "role models" are almost always doomed to failure.

Individual staff members functioning as role models cannot counterbalance the effects of peer pressure on life-style violent juveniles. Only a programmatic response to behavior can hope to achieve that end. Why is this so? An individual staff member's presence is limited to the length of a work-shift, and staff cannot be expected to match individual tenure of employment with the residency of a given juvenile. As one institutionalized juvenile put it:

> Yeah, [X] is my main man. If I was on the bricks [free], I'd live just like him. He has my respect right down the line. But [X] don't have to live *here*. If he did, I don't think he'd come off the same.[66]

Even an excellent role model, (like [X] in the above quote, who impacts upon the residents' life and consciousness even while he is outside the institution), must constantly compete with an environment whose very flexibility works against the transmission of consistent messages.

One form of divisiveness which inhibits a programmatic response is that which exists between various work-shifts. Not only do staff blocs with varying orientations and self-interests transmit different messages to the resident population as to what is permitted and what is not, but different work-shifts often adopt individual personalities of their own. And even within the shifts, individual personalities develop based on which behaviors will be tolerated, overlooked, condoned, or even supported. Just as residents tend to group together on the streets and within the institutions, so do staff who share similar backgrounds, interests, and temperaments. Requests for transfers from one shift to another are quite common in the formative stages of any new institution, and informal leadership matrixes form despite any attempt to impose structure strictly through job assignment.

Shifts tend to develop individualized personalities, complete with varying attitudes and activities, giving separate shifts separate, and sometimes competing, functions. In the standard institution, the first shift tends to be less tolerant of acting-out behavior (even that which falls well short of actual violence) because the "nine to fivers" or the "professionals" will be present. Such professionals tend to evaluate staff performance in terms of how well controlled the residents appear to be. Conversely, the second shift tends to have a recreational, or activities, focus and horseplay which would not be tolerated on the first shift tends to be more acceptable to its staff. The second shift tends to be more participatory in that it will mold activities around what is interesting to staff, as well as to residents. Thus, each second shift will have staff members ready and willing to play basketball each evening, and other members all-too-willing to spend each evening watching television with the residents. Those second shift members with a counseling orientation are told that it is necessary to "tire the kids out" so the third shift's task of getting the residents into their rooms and to sleep is made easier. Staff with such a counseling orientation tend to gravitate towards the first shift, where there is a greater emphasis on cerebral activity and a greater opportunity to attract the attention of the professionals who could intervene in a request for a change in job descriptions. Since activities tend to be compulsory on the first shift and voluntary on the second, the entire second shift tends to be more accommodating to the residents, and there is a general attitude of permissiveness an observer will not find earlier in the day.

Similarly, the third shift tends to be characterized by an emphasis on security. The third shift wants to keep things as quiet as possible. The residents are usually locked into their rooms, or dormitories, for the evening. Although fights are more likely on the second shift, serious violence and suicide attempts are more likely on the third. Since the latter causes the most problems for staff, and since "the kids are supposed to be in bed anyway," custodial considerations are given first preference.

The requirement of staff cohesiveness within a work-shift sometimes only heightens the individuality and isolation of the separate shifts from each other. Of course, each shift impacts upon the others, and a lack of programmatic unity will exacerbate an already tense environment. For example, if the third shift is lax about getting the residents to bed because of an inability or unwillingness to enforce rules, the first shift will have a correspondingly difficult time getting the residents up in the morning.

It is easy enough to manage juveniles if no pressure is brought to bear upon them, so it is not uncommon to find weaker staff members permitting residents to watch television on the third shift until very late. Or, if the second shift simply chooses not to interact with the residents and locks them into their individual rooms for the entire shift, the incoming third shift will be faced with restless, bored, and angry residents who will bitterly resent any attempts to bed them down for the night.

Structural solutions (such as assigning the second shift the task of getting the residents settled down for the night, and the third shift the task of getting them up in the morning) are useless, since the change-of-shift is a time of considerable movement and activity within the institution, and residents quickly learn that this represents an excellent opportunity to act out. As one resident of a maximum-security institution told us:

> If you want to get down [fight with another resident], the Second Shift is the time to make your move . . . with all the running around and screaming and shit, nobody pays too much attention. But *forget* about it when [Y]'s on duty . . . that motherfucker's not going for *anything*.[67]

Consistency as to the life-rules of the Secure Treatment Unit is as important for individual staff members as it is for entire work-shifts. Just as differing shift mentalities are contrary to the goal of a unified program, individual differences among staff members in terms of their responses to residents' behavior can also have a negative overall effect. Too often, certain staff members will be perceived as softer than others, and staff attitudes are generally transmitted to all residents within a few weeks. This is acceptable only within strict tolerances, and the bottom line is, once again, the life-rules of the Secure Treatment Unit.

One temptation for weaker staff members is to allow residents who present potential control problems to control others. The life-rules of the Secure Treatment Unit must be observed at all costs. These rules present a problem for both inferior and superior staff members, but for widely different reasons. An inferior staff member will attempt to placate the residents past the point of programmatic tolerance. Such a staff member will tell a particularly dangerous resident that he may do as he wishes, so long as no problems are caused for the individual worker. This, naturally, means open season on the weaker residents, and our definition of maximum security cannot be maintained in such an atmosphere. This institutional practice of management by use of the most dangerous residents is common in both juvenile and adult corrections. One former resident of several juvenile and adult prisons described the Intake process as follows:

> When I came to the joint the first time I had a reputation as a real bad-ass . . . I was so used to getting beat on that it didn't frighten me too much anymore, and I expected the screws [guards] to treat me like shit. But almost as soon as I got off the New Line [holding area for recently admitted prisoners], this Sergeant came up to me and said "Find a kid [passive homosexual partner] and settle down and don't make trouble for me and I won't make no trouble for you. You got a lotta time to do and there's no sense making it hard on me, 'cause then I'll make it hard on you." And it was true; they didn't give a fuck what you did so long as you weren't looking to escape or get physical with a screw.[68]

An institution-wise resident will soon spot such inferior and weak staff, and carefully "pick his shots" when moving into the area of negative behavior.

By observing the weaker staff members, the resident perceives that the institution itself permits such negative behavior as the weaker staff members allow. The message to the resident is that society (the institution) disapproves of his negative behavior within the institution only in the abstract, the same way that mugging is theoretically disapproved of by the larger society but certainly condoned (and even expected) by his peer group in the local community. When you ask former residents of institutions if staff knew of sexual attacks by "booty bandits"[69] on weaker residents, the response is always the same: "They *had* to know."[70] Because there are really no secrets within the closed society of an institution, the assumption is that the behavior that goes on is the behavior that is permitted. Although this could result in a "well managed" institution (no escapes, no riots, and so forth), it also reinforces the world view that brought the life-style violent juvenile to the institution in the first place.

A strong staff member can similarly undermine programmatic response by insisting on individual confrontation of negative or violent behavior. Even the most superior staff members can contribute to an antiprogrammatic set of responses to negative behavior. If the life-rule is (as we recommend) that all violence by residents be met with maximum and immediate staff response, then the staff member who insists on "going one on one" with a violent resident undercuts the staff member who summons help when confronted with a similar situation.

The excellent staff member, who is willing to confront negative behavior alone, soon finds himself isolated from such activity by the residents, and those staff members actually observing the institutional rule of *collectively* responding to such behavior find their actions met with scorn. It is necessary for even the most physically powerful or courageous staff member to fully subscribe to the life-rules; even when confronted by a resident who he could easily overpower, he must summon assistance so that the resident perceives the response to his behavior as programmatic. Society (the Secure Treatment Unit) disapproves of his behavior, not just an individual staff member. The "might makes right" mentality is thereby dealt a serious setback.

One technique necessary for the avoidance of bloc-ing among individual shifts is complete avoidance of the use of "casual" labor as institutional staff. There are many techniques that may be utilized to minimize the phenomenon we call "bloc-ing" of institutional staff. These are extremely important when the goal is to promote programmatic, societal responses to residential behavior. One such technique is the elimination of the use of so-called "casual" labor in the Secure Treatment Unit. "Purchase of care" agencies often find that they can hire a core staff to perform professional tasks and hire the rest of the required personnel on a day-to-day basis. This is far less expensive, but always costs more in the long run. "Casuals" generally do not receive health insurance, are not given vacation or sick leave, and some are not even covered by unemployment insurance or workman's compensation, and so represent an attractive alternative, to accountants. But it is virtually impossible to develop the unity necessary to provide a safe atmosphere (much less a therapeutic one) when issues such as job security continue to surface. Additionally, the opportunities for corruption are numerous since casual employees are not hired based on their performance or ability. They are all equal in the eyes of management and the decision as to which employees to utilize on a given day is not considered crucial. Casual employees are transients, and cannot be relied upon on a long-term basis. In-service training may be wasted on such staff, and the message to the resident is one of impermanence.

Such staff may be controlled not in terms of their job performance but in terms of their loyalty to individuals, something that should be avoided for obvious reasons. The very concept of a "shape up" as a hiring practice in human services is contrary to its major tenets.

Using a shift liaison can encourage unification of the program. Additionally, the position of "shift liaison" should be established by the Secure Treatment Unit. The function of the liaison is to integrate the needs of the unit with the needs and abilities of each shift, so that a unified attitude and response-pattern can be developed. The shift liaison is not an advocate for any particular shift, but serves as an ombudsman for all employees. His own shift may be from the middle of the first shift through the middle of the second shift, with the second liaison shift coming from the middle of the second shift through the middle of the third. This not only breaks up shift loyalties, it also provides management with a perspective not usually available. The shift liaison is not a supervisor, but an observer-reporter-analyst, and the presence of a person not emotionally and socially aligned with a given shift will have a chilling effect on negative staff behavior within that shift.

Partial shift rotation can decrease shift loyalties while increasing loyalty to the overall program. Also, attempts must be made to move staff from shift to shift on an overlapping basis. For example: 20 percent of the third shift could go to other shifts every six months. This would not only serve to break up developing blocs, it would also give all staff an institutionwide perspective. Part of shift loyalty is developed by the feeling that one shift is the most important to the functioning of the entire institution. Different shifts require different perspectives (but all require a unified agreement to follow the life-rules of the unit), and this can be developed only by observation and participation. No staff manual can convey this message.

Management must refuse to comply with initial staff preferences for shift assignment. Placement decisions as to individual shifts must be made by management without regard to the personal preferences of staff members. Management will be confronted with staff who live in the same apartment building who want to share rides to work. Management will also face the situation of married couples who want to work different shifts, with personnel who hold other jobs, those with school commitments, and so forth. However, the needs of staff must be subordinate at all times to the needs of the unit. And if one staff member is permitted to work on a given shift for any reason, it will not be long before other staff members (rightfully) demand the same treatment.

Management must establish sufficient salary levels so that it will not be necessary to accommodate staff in terms of personal requests. Most institutions yield to such staff requests as assignment to a particular shift simply because institutional requirements are low, and so is institutional pay. In a functioning Secure Treatment Unit, both staff qualifications and compensation should be high. Professional managers cannot rely on a continuing employment shortage in this country to provide qualified staff at low rates.

Once a policy is established with a state's rate setting commission or equivalent body that personnel costs are X, all increases have to be predicated on that base-line figure.[71] Setting X too low initially makes management's task extremely difficult and should be avoided.

Seemingly innocuous personal preferences of staff members can have significant and far-reaching consequences on an institution's overall program, and must therefore always remain subordinate to that program. The management problems inherent in allowing staff members to choose their own shifts on the basis of personal preference may be illustrated by a common institutional situation. Several of the staff on the second shift ride to work in one employee's stationwagon. He is the only one of the group that has a car, and they all contribute to the cost of gas. This arrangement avoids reliance on public transportation and is more comfortable for the staff, especially in the winter. But when the employee who owns the car has trouble with it, the entire group is late to work. Management is understandably annoyed because this puts a heavier burden on the previous shift (the rule generally being that one shift cannot be discharged until the full complement of the succeeding shift is actually present in the institution), and tells the group that they are individually responsible for getting to work on time.[72] This group of staff members, penalized as a group, tends to draw together as a group, and the shift-bloc mentality is only reinforced. Such individuals will bitterly resent transfers to other shifts, especially if the other shift is one they have been habitually inconveniencing by their tardiness. The result will be more staff problems, and less time to concentrate on the problems of the residents.

Structure and Function

Just as a Secure Treatment Unit cannot function with staff divisiveness, it cannot function in a physical structure that contradicts program goals. Even assuming a staff composed individually of the finest human services professionals, with a collective mentality that contributes to the unification of the Secure Treatment Unit's goals, the unit cannot hope for success unless control of the environment is also established and maintained. Although our profession gives lip service to statements such as "structures influence functions," the rhetoric is rarely expressed in the architecture of juvenile institutions. In fact, structure and function have been traditional adversaries much like security and treatment, but the structure-function conflict (unlike security-treatment) is impossible to adjust after the fact.

Even the finest therapeutic program can be at least partially defeated by a negative physical environment. We cannot understand how professionals can speak of "milieu therapy" and mean only the attitude of the therapists themselves. Structures impart a message of their own, and materially contribute to the quality of the work performed within them.

The possible aesthetic value of one structure over another is clearly not the key to the significance of that structure in programmatic terms. Our position in this regard goes well beyond the conventional wisdom that tells us certain colors are more depressing than others and that close confinement is contrary to the goal of promoting a more healthy social attitude. Creating a physical environment that is aesthetically pleasing (usually to the designers; rarely to the inhabitants) is completely insufficient. And even if such a creation did have therapeutic value, planners consistently ignore the fact that their lovely structures are intended for human habitation. Since involuntary institutional habitation is quite often destructive, there is no guarantee that even a beautifully designed institution will maintain its appearance over the years.

The structure of a Secure Treatment Unit must not only provide protection against escape, it must also provide personal security for each individual resident. Institutions that have been designed to hold prisoners against their will have been generally successful in meeting that goal. Escapes from maximum-security institutions are relatively rare, and usually short-lived. However, since we have redefined "maximum-security" as providing full security for individual residents[73] as well as for the outside community, we reject past structures as wholly unsuitable. The reasons for this may be found by examination of the Incident Reports[74] in any such institution. Violence between prisoners, sexual assaults, and suicides are common, especially in adolescent facilities. It is certainly true that if residents are to be allowed to interact with one another, heavy reliance must be placed on *human* security, not just that provided by hardware. The common assumption is that when violent incidents do occur, the personnel security has been lax. But while mindful of the fact that many institutional personnel are less than zealous about protecting the human rights of residents, we also realize that the physical plant often contributes to a lack of security. A resident of one state institution described conditions there as follows:

> If I got a beef with you, and I'm looking for you in this joint, you got no place to hide. There's all kinds of places here where the police [guards] can't see . . . it's a real killing ground and there's plenty of guys here who know it. That's why life is so cheap in this place.[75]

A structure designed to humiliate will produce hostility and violence as additional by-products. Many of the features of a standard juvenile institution seem deliberately designed not just to contain, but to humiliate. Residents are subjected to group bathrooms, group showers, and a complete lack of control over their individual living situations.[76]

The shower room is one of the most dangerous places in a closed juvenile institution:

> The shower room is the perfect place for a take-off [sexual assault]. First of all, the hacks don't go inside with us, and it's so fulla steam and all that they can't even *see* inside. O.K., then remember that those walls are *hard,* man, and you don't need a shank [prison-made knife] if you tell a punk you'll bash his head into the walls. And that soap's just as

good as grease [vaseline or K.Y. jelly, the preferred lubricants for homosexual assaulters; designed to protect the rapists and not their victims, its mere possession is contraband in some institutions] and there's all this fuckin' noise and guys millin' around and all. Besides, you don't wear no clothes in there, right?[77]

The majority of guards are not eager to work on patrol inside institutional shower rooms (and we would be interested in the motives of those who are).

Part of the motivation to viciously exploit other youths stems from the total lack of control each resident has over his own life. When external forces control even such minutiae as access to bathroom facilities, a common response is to attempt to exert dominance over other residents as a (sometimes vicious) affirmation of status and self-worth.

This responsive form of hostility is analogous to the physical phenomenon occuring when cigarette smoke is blown through a narrow tube; the smoke actually accelerates in speed.[78] Hostility, narrowly channeled (so that it almost *must* be directed against other residents) is all the more violent as a result.

A danger-inducing structure also produces fear which, in turn, produces and escalates violence. Life-style violent juveniles are especially dangerous when they are frightened, and nothing is more frightening than the unknown. Security is a laughable concept in a closed institution that is actually fully accessible to aggressive/violent individuals. As residents fail to perceive safety in their environment, they act increasingly violent—partly to reaffirm their tenuous control over themselves and partly to extend the institution to its limits so as to learn what those limits actually are.[79]

While a constant, uniform structure limits program options, a graduated, variable structure can geometrically increase such options. Still another major problem with standard institutional structures is that they are so utterly uniform in internal design. There are no options *within* the facility in terms of placement or treatment (except for solitary confinement or one of its many euphemisms). This forces the entire population to be environmentally rewarded at about the same pace, and is contrary to the principle of individualized progress. The concept of environmentally rewarding residents is a new one, and should be discussed in greater detail. In the proposed Secure Treatment Unit, the resident will gain increasing control over his environment as he progresses through a variety of available program options. As he gains increasing control, he will be forced to make decisions and choices to maintain that control, so that the resident is in the constant process of movement.

For the Secure Treatment Unit, "after-care" will not be the major factor it was supposed to be in other institutions, because the discharged residents will be much older than those leaving other placements. Unlike the standard situation, a model inmate will not be promoted within the program, and institutional adjustment will not be a program goal. As the resident adjusts and masters a given set of circumstances, his physical environment will change to the point where he sees eventual discharge as just another step in a process in which he himself is a participant, not a passive recipient.

The ideal is to design the structure to serve the program, not to make the structure itself the goal. A major goal of the proposed Secure Treatment Unit is not merely to combat the negative effects of inadequate structures, but to utilize structure in new ways. It is, for now, sufficient to say that we expect structures to be designed around the functions they are intended to serve. However, it is important to note that the success of the Secure Treatment Unit is not *wholly* dependent upon designing and building new structures; rather, we believe that intelligent rehabilitation (here used in its proper context) can serve both needs. The programs, policies, and procedures of the Secure Treatment Unit can to some extent be adapted to virtually any structure, and could lend themselves to a "rehabilitated" training school as well as to a "ground-up" design. But needless to say, the more minimal the conflicts between structure and function, the greater the opportunity the Secure Treatment Unit will have to succeed.

There is nothing magic, and much that is destructive, about renaming an institution a "program." Virtually all institutions currently refer to themselves as programs. Just as adult prisons are now called correctional facilities, and solitary confinement is now called the quiet room, juvenile training schools are responding to the need for media-marketing. Although federal or foundation funding is relatively unknown for training schools, it is quite common for "innovative new programs." Since proposal writing is often, in reality, commercial advertising (containing no contractual guarantees of performance),[80] it has often been thought necessary to rename an existing institution.

Sometimes, there is a minor attempt to change the game as well as the name. Institutions set up programs that provide a path to the front gate based on a "point system" or "individual evaluations" by counselors or a committee. Yet the idea of a program remains an idea, not a reality. Juveniles are quick to learn the rhetoric of the new system. Even illiterate juveniles seem to possess a remarkable grasp of street terminology that impresses outsiders as being akin to a second language. An institution-wise juvenile will be quick to tell visitors "I'm not doing time here; I'm helping myself in the program," but he will be equally quick to confide that "it's all another hustle."[81] To the juvenile, all that has occured with the inauguration of the "program" is a new set of parallel language descriptions for structures and events that have not changed at all. Calling a prison guard a correctional officer or an inmate counselor does not automatically bring about a change in his behavior. Failure to change behavior when nomenclature is changed contributes to the cynicism that pervades any juvenile institution.

Juveniles tend to have as much faith in the rehabilitation of institutions as society has in the rehabilitation of juveniles. The fact is that the juveniles themselves are no believers in rehabilitation! If names are changed and one is to believe that behaviors and attitudes also change (there having been no change in personnel), one must accept that people are capable of changing their own behavior. And, to the juvenile prisoners, staff attitudes don't change. The idea that an authoritarian guard can become a warm and concerned counselor is scorned by the juvenile population. The same reaction comes from the larger society when professionals speak of changing the behavior of their juvenile charges by exposing them to a different system of treatment. This underscores our emphasis on the need for realistic goals throughout the planning of the Secure Treatment Unit.

The past choice between traditional training-schools and community-based settings necessitated a choice of evils. One of the major arguments against juvenile training schools is that they were functionally ungovernable and psychologically destructive. Individualized treatment was impossible because of the sheer numbers of juveniles contained within a relatively small area, and management concerns (always a factor in any closed setting) mushroomed with the size of the population. Stripped of its verbiage, community-based programs offered two things: (1) increased opportunity for contact and interaction within a community, thereby overcoming the sense of isolation/alienation inherent in institutionalization; and (2) small numbers of people in small settings. Yet those advantages had to be weighed against the economic feasibility of placing major resources into a small setting.[82] Elaborate vocational programs, for example, were unsuited to small settings because the machinery had to be duplicated for each and every program, thereby greatly increasing the cost. So the large institution was almost always better equipped, and the community-based units were forced to rely almost solely on personnel to accomplish their objectives.

A cluster system within a larger setting mitigates the above evils while providing an effective means of differentiating between residents' progress. We propose, for the Secure Treatment Unit, to answer the objections of advocates of both placement alternatives and, at the same time, to provide the kind of differential treatment options, with the juveniles as primary participants in the selection of such options, that will enable a treatment program to function in effective ways. We propose a relatively large institution broken into "clusters" of housing, with some services and facilities shared and others unique to each cluster.

While the unpopularity, funding difficulties, and disutility of large institutions are evident, there are also many valid objections to the use of small modules for violent juveniles. We cannot ignore the fact that the words *large institution* run distinctly counter to the current thinking in our field, and automatically discourage many potential grantors from the private sector. The only disclaimer we can offer is that our vision of a large institution is simply any institution that is not small, a concept we define as housing a maximum of twelve residents.

At the Juvenile Justice Planning Project's Intensive Conference in 1977,[83] there was almost unanimous agreement that smaller modules are far more effective in accomplishing both treatment and custodial objectives. Conference participants were then asked to list their objections to establishing small modules for the treatment of the life-style violent juvenile. The responses included the following:

1. Too many jurisdictions misperceive the actual number of juveniles who require a locked, secure long-term setting. With the establishment of a small unit, it would be quickly filled, and pressure would be brought to bear for the construction of more units.

2. As a result, the number of juveniles treated in such a setting would be virtually unlimited, leaving the possibility of Intake control breakdown and wholesale incarceration of juveniles; thus threatening any attempts to establish a basically de-institutionalized juvenile system.

3. The principle of "least restrictive alternative" would not tend to be followed in such a situation, since we agreed that all institutional vacuums will eventually be filled.

4. There would eventually occur a prioritization of the small units, with a de facto rating system whereby some of the small units took hard-core violent residents and others did not.

5. This could result in some of the small units being used exclusively for treatment of those juveniles who would not even be *candidates* for institutionalization in another system.

6. Statewide de-institutionalization goals could be crippled, perhaps permanently.

7. Unless "purchase of care" arrangements were reached with several *different* agencies, the extensive use of smaller units could have one of the following results:

a.   One private vendor could gain a stranglehold on the state's department of youth services by controlling institutions and programs throughout the state; or

b.   The smaller units would be quickly staffed with civil servants who would then retain a strong vested interest in keeping them open even if the need for them was nonexistent.

8. Allocation of resources would be a severe problem. One could justify putting a swimming pool into a large institution, but several swimming pools hardly seems cost-effective.

9. Small modules would not offer sufficient internal treatment options, thus exacerbating the problems of incorrect initial diagnosis, response to negative

behavior, and ability to provide a clear sense of individual progress for each resident.

10. Small modules could not provide sufficient "steps" in the treatment process, and after-care would continue to be a major difficulty.

11. Small modules capable of only one program would place too much pressure on the unit itself. A resident could either complete the program and be released to still another unit, or fail to complete the particular program of the small unit to which he was assigned (regardless of the suitability of the match between the needs of the resident and the small unit's program) and remain in an untreated state.

The Secure Treatment Unit eliminates these problems by centralizing the small modules within one institution, and by ordering them progressively so as to accomplish treatment goals. It was finally agreed that our concept of a Secure Treatment Unit designed around several clusters, or "units," of progressive treatment offered the only possible solution to the stated objections. With only one such unit (with actual size to be adjusted to the population base of the sponsoring jurisdiction), problems of mislabeling would be minimized. There would be no real pressure to construct additional units because of the relatively high cost. Intake control could be centralized, and criteria-ized, thus allowing a uniform policy for the entire jurisdiction,[84] insuring that one region would not be permitted to "stack" the unit because of its own attitude towards juvenile crime.

Statewide de-institutionalization goals would be *advanced,* not retarded by such a unit, and judges would not be forced to commit juveniles to adult facilities in response to societal and political pressure.

Full allocation of available resources in a single Secure Treatment Unit would permit high utilization of such resources, since cost-effectiveness would be increased. Internal treatment options could be maximized in such a setting, and a clear sense of progress could be provided while requirements for after-care alternatives would be greatly lessened.

Rather than diminish the goals of de-institutionalization, the Secure Treatment Unit may be its salvation. Even if the proposed Secure Treatment Unit manages to walk the tightrope between reactive and proactive planning to the satisfaction of potential critics, it will still come under fire from those advocating juvenile de-institutionalization across the board, and also from advocates of a total moratorium on all prison construction.[85]

The first criticism is easily answered. Professionals in the field now concede that without a Secure Treatment Unit somewhere in the network picture, life-style violent juveniles will contaminate programs and eventually precipitate out into adult corrections. Even if the use of waiver were not on the increase (and we believe it is, politicians being what they are), the public outcry against juvenile violence has reached a fever pitch and the political response cannot be too far behind. If the juvenile justice profession's demand for separate treatment for juveniles is to be based on respect for the profession's abilities in this area, the treatment must include that category of juvenile "delinquents" that frighten the public the most. We believe that the profession's commitment to its own specialized treatment modalities and structures is sufficiently strong to provide all the motivation necessary to accept full responsibility for the life-style violent juvenile offender.

The second criticism is, in fact, another form of the argument in favor of de-institutionalization. It holds that we already *have* enough penal institutions, and that construction of new facilities will only encourage the institutional option when other alternatives might be more suitable. As we have previously stated, vacuums tend to be filled, sometimes beyond their original capacity. Yet our position—abolition of state training schools for the overwhelming number of juvenile offenders and, at the same time, construction of Secure Treatment Units for far smaller numbers of serious violent offenders—is not inconsistent with the above rationale.

After years of careful study and personal observation, we have concluded that most training schools are constructed in such a manner that physical rehabilitation of the institution is nearly impossible. Many of the treatment plans we feel are necessary to achieve even minimal success with our selected population are predicated on control of the design of the facility. Despite our belief that portions of our plans could be adapted to any structure, it is only by new construction (or extensive rehabilitation of existing facilities) that the varying goals be achieved. For example: if a standard training school were to be physically rehabilitated, its original use would be disguised, but not changed. It would still be "available" for the large-scale incarceration of juveniles should the (political) need arise.

Construction of a Secure Treatment Unit would additionally insure a jurisdiction's real commitment to treatment of the life-style violent juvenile within its juvenile justice system. But construction of a Secure Treatment Unit would not lend itself to political expediency. Its designed-in capacity could not be exceeded without significant expenditure of new money, and the initial large expenditure would stand not only as a jurisdiction's commitment to progressive treatment of the life-style violent juvenile, but as a deterrent to dismantling or conversion to other forms of treatment.

The real political value of the community-based programs is the ease with which they can be dismantled. The low initial capital outlay plus the multi-use capacity of any structure that could house a community-based non-secure treatment alternative makes it an attractive candidate for sacrifice to political whims. The Secure Treatment Unit would represent a position from which it would be far more difficult to retreat, and would pragmatically as well as symbolically commit a jurisdiction to giving treatment of the life-style violent juvenile the fair trial it deserves.

Notes

1. The southern prison camps in Louisiana (Angola), Alabama (Kirby), Arkansas (Tucker and Cummings), and Mississippi (Parchman) are all said to actually produce a net profit from the prisoners' labor. Louis X. Holloway (Faruq Muhammed), *Parchman Genocide* [unpublished manuscript, portions of which have appeared in 10 *New England Law Review* 143 (1974) and 45 *Mississippi Law Journal* 757 (1974)], at p. 106:

> This work [the work of the prisoners on the farm] had absolutely nothing to do with rehabilitation. They [the prison managers] want slaves, and slaves they have been getting.

The fact that Parchman, (a giant plantation of 21,000 acres) exists only to provide a profit to the State is supported by the Transmittal Letter for LEAA Consultant Committee: *Interim Report on Mississippi State Penitentiary*, p. 2, as cited in David Lipman, "Mississippi's Prison Experience," 45 *Mississippi Law Journal* 685, 699 (1974):

> [T]here are three basic philosophies so fundamental to the existing system [at Parchman], which continue to perpetuate the problems existing today . . . (1) That the prison system must operate at a profit at any cost; . . .

2. Specialized privileges with a rehabilitative flavor include furloughs, "time-cuts" (a process by which a sentenced prisoner can petition a board for a reduction in penal time without the necessity of appealing to the courts on the grounds of "excessive sentencing"), compassionate leave, "Christmas" leave, work release, etc.

3. Other states, such as California and Massachusetts, also permit some form of conjugal visiting, although to a more limited extent.

4. Louis X. Holloway, "Sex at Parchman: Conjugal Visiting at the Mississippi State Penitentiary," 10 *New England Law Review* 143 (1974). The author is a former prisoner at Parchman. His basic arguments against the rehabilitative value of conjugal visiting reflect those of the profession: it unfairly discriminates in favor of married inmates; it is handled on a purely discretionary basis, generally as a reward for labor in the fields; it is conducted under demeaning and degrading conditions; it has proven of little or no value in halting homosexual attacks; and home furloughs are far more sensible in all respects.

See also, Michael Braswell, and Paul DeFrancis, "Conjugal Visitation: A Feasibility Study," 1 *Georgia Journal of Corrections* 171 (1972), as abstracted under Number S 11833, 5 *Crime and Delinquency Literature* 258 (1973):

> Although conjugal visitation is helpful, it is still somewhat demeaning to the inmate and his family. The quarters are private, but the setting is artificial and creates some degree of anxiety in both parties. Also creating anxiety is the knowledge of the inmate and his family that they are on display to inmates and staff.
>
> Furlough visitation, on the other hand, can take place in a more private and natural setting with the furlough program's costs absorbed by the inmate's family. Conjugal privileges are not accessible to single male or female inmates . . .

5. *See,* Holt v. Sarver, and Gates v. Collier, ch. 2, note 31, *supra.*

6. The Northeastern Family Institute, of Marblehead, Brockton, and Salem, Massachusetts, operates a foster-home network for the Department of Youth Services in Region IV of that state. This network includes Intensive Foster Care (with specialized counseling and a low caseworker-client ratio), Foster Care direct placement, home selection, counseling of foster parents and children, court advocacy, and interconnection with the Institute's Experiential Learning Program.

7. As did Massachusetts. The training schools are generally the subject of the most intense media focus, evidence the greatest abuses of human rights and, at the same time, tend to be scapegoated for the failures of an entire system. And, for dramatic impact, nothing tops the physical closing down of an institution. *See,* for example, Yitzhak Bakal, *Closing Correctional Institutions: New Strategies in Youth Services,* (Lexington, Massachusetts: D.C. Heath, 1973).

8. Again, as did Massachusetts with Andros I.

9. As opposed to "temporary" or "casual" employees, see chapter 4, *infra.*

10. Since most training schools are regionalized, it is difficult to determine if the perception of the transfer as punitive was attributable to the type of facility to which transferred or to the greatly increased distance from the workers' homes. However, it is only fair to note that many civil service workers have stated that they much preferred working in a standard training school to a community-based facility because of what they saw as a grossly permissive attitude on the part of management in the latter units. But although many workers agreed that training school employment was satisfactory, they were all adamant that they would not want to work in such a place unless provision for transferring out the "hardcases" was maintained. The Secure Treatment Unit would have no such provision.

11. At one time, civil service was felt to be free from even the possibility of lay-offs or outright dismissals due to lack of funds. And training school employees felt even safer than other civil servants because of the relative undesirability of their employment; there were always few applicants for such positions. However, in today's climate where we have seen lay-offs of civil servants such as policemen and firemen, no such illusion can be reasonably maintained.

12. It is difficult to sell "innovative, new programs" which may be perceived by the potential grantor as nothing more than an attempt to keep civil servants on salary without the necessity of the local government paying the tab.

13. In such a situation, there would be two classes of employees: those of the private agency who have agreed to salary scales, vacation schedules, and benefit packages as they were hired, and civil servants whose union has previously negotiated a contract binding on the state. Such civil servants will have, for example, a contractual right to x number of vacation days (and probably a prohibition against accumulation), management will be forced to build its schedules around their rights, probably to the dimunition of the rights of its own employees. This differential treatment of employees will doubtless have the same effect that differential treatment of inmates was designed to have: divisiveness. *See* chapter 2, *supra.*

14. The administrator of a "purchase of care" institution will find him- or herself without allies should a budget increase be sought. Many of the "purchase of care" contracts are let on the ground that they will cost the state less than prior methods of doing business. In addition, rates are generally established by law, and are not flexible. If the private agency overestimates its needs, it will be the loser in a bidding war; if it underestimates its needs, it will be caught short at some point during its operations.

15. Lamar T. Empey, *A Model for Evaluation of Programs in Juvenile Justice,* University of Southern California, January 1977 (National Institute for Juvenile Justice and Delinquency Prevention, LEAA, U.S. Department of Justice), at p. 11:

> The measurement of outcome, to be most fruitful, should be concerned not merely with recidivism. Indeed, if the experimental strategy is to receive a definitive test, outcome should be measured in terms of intermediate goals.

If the Secure Treatment Unit is to reduce life-style juvenile criminality, it must specify the methods it intends to use to achieve that result. We can then check to see if such methods were actually utilized, and *then* measure outcome. If goals are not met in spite of actual utilization of the methods proposed, the methods *themselves* have been evaluated, not just the outcome of a particular program.

16. From interview of July 27, 1976, *see* Appendix for full text:

It would seem to me that it would be a lot healthier if we said [to a juvenile ordered to be incarcerated by a court] "You're sentenced to that status, you would have to be in a locked setting. Now here is someone with brochures, a consumer of human services, you go out and visit—what the upper class have always done—you visit these four locked settings, and you and the trained citizen-consumer decide which one you want to go to. And you'll take the State's money with you there. We'll pay for it. Now if you find yourself unhappy and mistreated there, during your time of incarceration, we'll have a grievance procedure, so you don't leave impulsively. You can't just get mad at a staff member and walk out the door and go elsewhere. There'll be a grievance procedure, and you sit down, and if, after the grievance procedure, you've decided this place is no longer for you, you can take the State's twenty or thirty thou and you can go to another approved locked program." Those places which can't keep their kids, can't keep their money.

17. There is a difference between evaluating a program as to compliance with standards (more in the nature of inspection and certification than actual evaluation) and attempting to measure effectiveness and outcome. The former type of evaluation will necessitate direct contact with the residents on occasion to insure that irreducible minimums of care and treatment are provided. But the more in-depth contacts necessitated by the second type of evaluation must be restricted (in frequency, if not in length) to insure that the programs within the institution have the opportunity to establish and maintain continuity.

18. *See*, Empey, note 15, *supra*.

19. For a detailed journalistic account of this period, *see* Eric Best, "Andros: An Alternative for Dealing with Juvenile Problems," 2 *Prisoners' Digest/International* 1 (1973).

20. The original evaluators were fervent supporters of the Massachusetts de-institutionalization philosophy prevalent at that time. Since institutions were per se "bad," the extent to which a program was noninstitutional was the extent to which it was "good." For example, home furloughs were thought to be an excellent method of mitigating the horrors of institutionalization, and we were asked "how many residents are given furloughs?" without any background as to the therapeutic (or, in the case of some residents awaiting "bind-over," legal) appropriateness of such an activity for a given resident.

21. Another bias of the Massachusetts evaluators with whom we spoke. Andros II was often misperceived as having an "all ex-con staff"; while this was never accurate, it carried significant weight with some evaluators.

22. Marc LeBlanc, "Theory, Research, and Practice: An Interaction to be Developed," 15 *Canadian Journal of Criminology and Corrections* 13 (1973) at

p. 24 [translated from the original French], Abstract S 11966, as cited in 5 *Crime and Delinquency Literature* 227 (1973).

> Transforming criminology into a technological science by means of research entails the risk of losing sight of the human being. This danger is compounded by the fact that crime is a *political* concept: since each political regime defines its own criminality, criminology can easily become a political *tool.* We cannot be sure that all criminals are maladjusted individuals rather then agents of social change. Who defines the criteria of a criminal personality? The distinction between crime and deviance, between concern and control, between punishment and treatment, between criminology and repression is always *politically* defined. [emphasis added.]

23. That is, transfer *within* the juvenile justice system, not "transfer" *to* adult criminal jurisdiction. There appears to be an inverse correlation between transfer options within the system and transfer of juveniles *out* of the system entirely.

24. *See,* Bartollas *et al.,* ch. 1, note 22, *supra,* at p. 109:

> Staff . . . are able to place considerable pressure on the aggressive "heavy" by threatening to prolong his institutionalization, by threatening to transfer him to an adult reformatory, or by promising to give him institutional privileges.

25. Those jurisdictions that offer a range of custodial security from maximum through minimum generally have a classification procedure which determines where a prisoner will serve, depending on crimes for which sentenced. And the federal system differentiates among types of offenders by selection of penal sites. Several jurisdictions specifically state that certain types of behaviors (notably sex offenses) must be treated in specific facilities designed for that purpose.

26. In an adult prison, this would be an isolation unit; in a juvenile system (perhaps), an isolation "cottage."

27. For example, Massachusetts used to maintain a "Departmental Segregation Unit" (DSU) at Bridgewater for those prisoners who could not be controlled even inside the isolation unit (Block 10) of its maximum security prison (Walpole). A similar unit, called the Institute for Juvenile Guidance (IJG) was maintained on the grounds of Bridgewater strictly for juveniles who could not be handled in the juvenile equivalent of the adult system (Cottage 9 at Shirley). The shared site gave juveniles at the IJG a clear view of their future.

28. These consequences could include: loss of "good time," gross reductions in available privileges, decreased access to (increased distance from) family and community, decreased educational and vocational opportunities, physical danger, and negative reaction by the parole authorities.

29. Wolff v. McDonnell, 418 U.S. 539, 94 S.Ct. 2963, 41 L.Ed.2d 935 (1974); *see,* for example, Barbara Ann Morgen, "Wolff v. McDonnell: The Handwriting on the Prison Wall," 10 *New England Law Review* 509 (1975).

30. Dr. Jerome Miller describes how de-institutionalization in Massachusetts altered this threat-therapy:

> That's the . . . problem we had in Massachusetts, initially . . . with the Concept Houses, the self-help drug houses. Because although they mouthed the therapeutic philosophy, they all depended on the slammer, "If you don't shape up here, kid, in you go." Now the older programs, the more mature programs, learned to adjust to the fact that we didn't have slammers for kids, and they learned to keep kids in their programs other than through threats, and they did better . . .
>
> But a lot of them, it seems to me are very phony. They play both sides. They talk about how bad prisons are, how we need to get more Group Homes, how we need to get more therapeutic communities, but when push comes to shove, they like to use the prison as a means of motivating someone to stay with their program.
>
> Interview, July 27, 1976, *see* Appendix for full text.

> 31. Poor institutional adjustment is a goddamned farce! This place is a cesspool; it's full of degenerates, rats, and bastards who'd shank you for a couple of packs [stab you for a couple of packs of cigarettes; the common medium of exchange in a maximum security prison where mere possession of "soft money" is usually contraband]. The day I learn to "adjust" to this place is the day they should *leave* me here.
>
> Interview with deliberately unnamed prisoner, Rahway State Prison, 1970 (as part of a study of the actions of the New Jersey Parole Board); first quoted in "Parole As Post-Conviction Relief: The Robert Lewis Decision," *see* ch. 3, note 6, *supra.*

32. Interview with a former inmate of all the juvenile prisons in Illinois' vast network (Audy Home, St. Charles, Sheridan, and Pontiac), later convicted of homicide and served a life sentence, now on parole. Identity not disclosed at interviewee's request, 1972.

33. Robert Herbert, Journalist, interviewing Judge Isidore Levine (Queens County Family Court, New York City), *New York Daily News,* March 6, 1977. Copyright 1977 New York News Inc. Reprinted by permission.

> [Judge Levine] said there have been instances when the Division for Youth, which is responsible for custodial care, has asked for permission to parole a youngster because "they couldn't control him." The judge shook his head, "They can't control him, so they want to put him back on the street. I wouldn't issue an order like that."

34. Those juveniles considered to be "unmanageable" will naturally require more staff per resident, special facilities, and specialized programs. Compensation for such efforts should be higher than for those programs which need not make the same investments. If a program professes to accept "hardcore" juveniles but, in actuality, excludes juveniles on grounds of unmanageability, it cannot rationally expect the same compensation as a program which, in fact, accepts *all* referrals, since the latter program will soon find itself a natural repository for those juveniles the other programs cannot, or will not, handle.

35. Dr. William Madaus, commenting at the Juvenile Justice Planning Project's Intensive Conference, June, 1977, New York City. He is referring to the practice of filling a program with those juveniles who are likely to present the fewest management problems, and deliberately rejecting all others.

36. One juvenile may "need" a secure placement strictly on grounds of manageability; another may "need" a secure placement because of the intensive programming offered; yet these two juveniles may not "need" the *same* placement.

37. *See,* for example, Charles A. Murray, *The Link Between Learning Disabilities and Juvenile Delinquency: Current Theory and Knowledge,* (Washington, D.C.: U.S. Government Printing Office, 1976).

38. For example, the need for an iron lung, or the need for routine kidney dialysis.

39. Mann, ch. 1, note 34, *supra,* at p. 45:

Given the enormous mechanical and ethical difficulties of accurately predicting violence [citation omitted] we need to rely on interventions which do not depend on predictive schema. We can, for example, focus on those juveniles who have *already* demonstrated that they are repetitively dangerous . . . If we were to adopt a policy incarcerating those who appear to present a danger to public safety *and* are multiple offenders, while treating others in community-based facilities ranging from totally open to relatively tight security, we might be able to improve both our effectiveness and our efficiency.

See also, Schlesinger, ch. 1, note 21, *supra.*

40. David C. Raskin (Principal Investigator), *Psychopathy and Detection of Deception in a Prison Population,* [Report No. 75-1, Contract 75 NI 99-0001, Department of Psychology, University of Utah, (1975)], lists, at p. 3, "subcultural delinquency" as a *counter-indicator* of psychopathy. Our observations would tend to confirm this, with the caveat that most urban juvenile gangs with a serious commitment to violence have, at their functional core, members who display the lack of empathy, contempt for others, flatness of affect, and utter self-absorption that comprise some of the characteristics of the psychopath.

41. *See,* for example, case history no. 5, chapter 5, *infra.*

42. For example, besides the court-mandated "waiver" criteria, *see* notes 35 and 37, (ch. 1), *supra,* statutes such as New York's "designate" those criminal acts which allow the respondent/defendant to be "treated" in a secure facility. The designated Class "A" felonies are: murder in the first and second degree, kidnapping in the first degree, and arson in the first degree. The other designated felonies are: assault in the first degree, manslaughter in the first degree, rape in the first degree, sodomy in the first degree, kidnapping in the second degree (with force), arson in the second degree, robbery in the first degree, and any attempt to commit a Class "A" designated felony other than arson; Family Court Act of New York State, section 712(h).

Note: sale of narcotics is *not* a "designated felony" in New York State, a jurisdiction which boasts America's most severe penalties for this offense among adults; *see* ch. 2, note 14, *supra.*

43. Some juvenile court judges apparently feel there is something distasteful about overt plea bargaining. Such judges expect a plea of guilty (or, "an admission to the petition") absent any prior agreement as to disposition, since they represent that any disposition handed down will be in response to the "needs of the child."

44. During a conversation with a police officer outside of court in 1972, one of the authors was bluntly told that the officers were "just waiting for this punk to turn seventeen." Many police officers believe that the juvenile court system is a "slap on the wrist" waste of time, and "cures" or changes nothing in a juvenile's behavior. Of course, many police officers believe the same about the adult system.

45. Given the political/media climate (and the fact that this is an election year), New York's status as a "non-waiver" jurisdiction may not survive the publication date of this book. *See* ch. 1, note 43, *supra.*

46. In New York, no juvenile, regardless of criminal acts committed, may be treated outside the juvenile justice system until he has reached the age of sixteen. And, once past sixteen, he may not be treated within the juvenile system regardless of circumstances. There is no prosecutorial, legislative, or judicial discretion in the New York system at the present time.

47. *See* note 42, *supra.* If the accepted plea is not to one of the designated felonies, the juvenile is exempt from such specialized treatment.

48. *See* Marion C. Katzive, *A Caseworker's Guide to the New York State Juvenile Justice System,* (New York: Vera Institute of Justice, 1976), at p. 21:

> Some law guardians [defense counsel in a juvenile proceeding] believe there is a difference between the job of law guardian and that of counsel in a criminal case. When a youngster appears to be in need of treatment, their objective would be to secure treatment for the client, even at the cost of a court adjudication.
>
> Other law guardians, particularly those affiliated with the Legal Aid Society, are more defense oriented. They will bend all efforts toward

avoiding adjudication on the theory that the court process is never in the child's best interests and that services should be provided outside the court process or not at all.

See also, "Advocate or Sociologist: What is the Role of the Defense Attorney in Juvenile Court?," 1 *The American Journal of Trial Advocacy* 311 (1978).

Some defense attorneys believe that the juvenile court forum must provide a two-tier protection to the defendant. Not only must the defendant be afforded the full panoply of constitutional rights available in an adult court, but even if convicted, the disposition must reflect, as accurately as possible, the actual facts in the case. Therefore, although the polygraph (lie detector) is generally not admissible in the criminal courts, some attorneys have advocated for its use on *disposition* to avoid the possibility of unjustly incarcerating an innocent juvenile. *See,* Ralph C. Pino, "The Polygraph as a Dispositional Aid to the Juvenile Court," 9 *New England Law Review* 311 (1974). From an interview with Charles H. Zimmerman, chief polygraph examiner for Scientific Security of Boston, Massachusetts and a nationally known expert in the field, December 23, 1976. (Interviewers: Andrew H. Vachss and Ralph C. Pino):

V: Now, when you gave us your basic criteria for fit subjects [for polygraph testing], I heard nothing in that criteria that would seem to exclude juveniles. Is that true?

Z: No, I do not address myself only to adults. Juveniles, obviously, are testable within certain degrees. I personally have tested youngsters as low as eleven-twelve years of age. But the point is that you must make sure that the individual is amenable to it and understands the scope of what you are trying to do.

V: Let me ask you this. What probative value . . . do you think a top-quality professional polygraph examination would have in a juvenile court, in your experience?

Z: You are talking now about postconviction, presentencing?

V: Yes, I am.

Z: And we are talking about the facts of that particular crime itself?

V: Yes.

Z: Well, I have tested in that area. Obviously, that's the last stand that [defense] counsel can normally take, and the last input he has into the judge's ears. Assuming there is a clarity of issue; there is a quality of issue; if there is a strength and/or distinction of issue; if the individual has said "I did it alone" and the investigation discloses that it could have been done by two or more people, then obviously to enlighten the judge, of whether or not this person is telling the truth, or whether or not this technique does or does not support the candor of the particular statement, or the answers at least, to the questions that he is being asked, could be very enlightening for the judge. It has been so in my experience anyway.

V: How influential was that enlightenment? Once the judge was given this new information, do you feel that influenced his later decision on disposition?

Z: Yes, it did.

Although this is not the proper forum to fully discuss the issue, the authors are well aware of the potential damage in trying to "treat" an innocent juvenile. We fully endorse the principle of top-quality, professional polygraph examination in all juvenile cases where truth appears to be the major relevant issue. Whether such an examination, and its results, may be introduced into evidence depends on the fluctuating state of appellate law, but we believe that such evidence should always be admissible on disposition, *after* a finding of delinquency and prior to actual sentencing.

49. *Not* a "parole board" or similar body of individuals. We believe that this body should be composed of a rotating pool of professionals in the juvenile justice field, and that their decisions should be supported by *written* reasons for grant or denial so that a body of precedent can be established and so researchers can study (and eventually recommend improvements in) the decision-making process.

50. *See,* for example, James B. Jacobs, "Street Gangs Behind Bars," 21 *Social Problems* 395 (1974).

51. Since the proposed Secure Treatment Unit would not be run on the so-called "cottage model" but would be, in fact, a maximum-security walled institution, we would expect a non-escape record roughly parallel to that of an adult secure facility.

52. We believe the same restrictions should apply to "rehabilitation" of existing structures, even though commentators who have focused on the high cost of construction have extolled the virtues of this process. *See,* Bradley, ch. 1, note 61, *supra,* continuing from the same quote:

> . . . but we can drastically redesign our organizations at relatively little expense in ways that support effective change processes in spite of limitations imposed by physical plant.

Positions such as the one taken above generally have been read to be supportive of physical rehabilitation of facilities as a compromise position between building new structures and simply altering "program" in existing structures.

53. There seems to be a prevailing mentality among "treatment" people that professional services are just not required outside of "regular business hours" as far as institutions are concerned. When we assumed control of the maximum-security Andros II, we announced that one counselor was going to be transferred to the third shift in order to achieve a better personnel balance. The counselor indignantly refused, saying "I'm not a guard."

54. This type of resident generally does not manifest himself until well into his period of confinement in a secure facility. The only "motivation" required of

residents in such facilities is to behave themselves as far as interaction with staff is concerned.

55. Lack of future orientation has previously been cited as a distinguishing characteristic of the life-style violent juvenile, but it also applies to many other juveniles whose criminality (and commitment thereto) is not so pronounced.

56. The custody/security bloc is omnipresent, and less likely to hold long discussions before punishing a resident. This bloc is also far quicker to utilize actual physical abuse, and controls distribution of such items as cigarettes, T.V. privileges, access to recreation, etc.

57. Contraband is always first defined by each separate institution, and then redefined by individual staff members. It can range from the obvious (weapons, narcotics, etc.) to the ridiculous (after-shave lotion, curtains, photographs).

58. Both the treatment bloc and the custody/security bloc implicitly believe that the former cannot function in the institution without the latter. It is possible to bait a violent resident into attacking a member of the treatment staff by suggesting, for example, that this "social worker" is holding up the resident's release. And those residents who run afoul of the security/custody bloc will quickly find themselves subjected to far more misery than the treatment bloc could ever impose. But the real strength of the custody/security bloc lies in its access to all residents at all times, during all activities (both approved and theoretically disapproved).

59. This is one of the most potentially dangerous (both therapeutically and physically) of the many concessions often made to a powerful custody/security bloc; see ch. 2, note 35, supra.

60. A not uncommon practice, and certainly one that was adopted in Massachusetts to soften opposition to de-institutionalization programming. The spectre of unemployment was more threatening than any "soft" treatment of juveniles, and civil service employees were retained in every way possible. Some were, in fact, paid to stay home while a suitable placement for them was sought.

61. Even including sabbatical opportunities for staff who have served a given period of years and who make a commitment to serve an additional period upon return.

62. In such a "one on one" situation, there is too much ego investment, and too great an emphasis on physical strength as a determinant of result. Once a staff member is absolutely committed (usually following a period of verbal confrontation and/or threatening) to a given result, he must achieve that result or risk serious loss of face. In a serious situation, such as possession of a knife, the staff member cannot retreat and, to enforce the institutions rules, might have to resort to far greater physical force (or violence) than would be required if a number of staff participated.

63. In such a situation, we utilize the "mattress" technique whereby

trained staff each take one end of a standard gym mat and slowly approach the juvenile holding the knife. If he continues to refuse to drop his weapon, his escape paths are blocked and the juvenile is forced against the wall using the mat. Thereby effectively "pinned," trained staff can literally "roll" him into his room, force him to the floor, and approach his disarmament without danger to the juvenile or to staff. Also, simply speaking, nobody can look in all directions at once and, perhaps more importantly, a juvenile does not face loss of status when he "surrenders" to a *group* surrounding him.

64. *See,* note 40, *supra.* There is no question but that many "violent" juveniles are only adapting to conditions (in their home communities or, subsequently, in institutions) and not expressing their own individual commitment to this behavior. These are, however, often the marginal members of violent subgroups and not generally those characterized as "life-style violent juvenile offenders."

65. *See,* Jacobs, note 50, *supra*, and Carr, ch. 2, note 2, *supra.* For an interesting description of the extent to which peer pressure can motivate participation in violence even among those not previously so disposed, *see* Don Moser, *The Pied Piper of Tucson,* (New York: New American Library, 1967).

66. Interview with D.J., 1972, at that time a juvenile institutional resident. Identity not disclosed to protect interviewee, who is currently an adult prisoner and a parole candidate.

67. Interview with L.W., 1972, at that time a juvenile institutional resident and now serving a life sentence for homicide committed during the course of a robbery. His identity has been withheld at his request.

68. Interview with G.G.K., 1971, a former resident of several juvenile and adult institutions, recently violated while on parole (from an extortion conviction) for possession of firearms. Identity not disclosed at interviewee's request.

69. James Carr, note 2 (ch. 2), *supra* referred to himself by this term. It is also mentioned in Bartollas et al., ch. 1, note 22, *supra,* and is still in common usage in such institutions as Attica.

70. Interview with "Gypsy," a former juvenile gang member who served a life sentence for a gang-related homicide, *see* appendix for full text:

They had to know. Because not to know would have shown a gross ignorance on their part. They had to know—but I don't think they were too concerned.

This sentiment is almost universally shared by current and former inmates of penal institutions, adult and juvenile. The interview with "J" (see appendix for full text) expressed it in words which seem to echo Gypsy's:

Well, you had to know what was going on. Especially if you were in a cottage, because they had steady cottage officers, and very few times you would get a relief [staff substitution], and if they didn't know what was going on, then they're dumber than some of these people they say are dumb . . .

71. In spite of the great publicity surrounding so-called zero-based budgeting, it appears that the majority of jurisdictions continue to operate on the same old model, with increases in the previous year's budget being the continual bone of contention.

72. In addition, it is difficult to summon much righteous indignation at a resident's failure to return promptly from a furlough when the resident knows that habitual staff tardiness is tolerated.

73. Sykes, ch. 3, note 12, *supra*, at p. 78:

> The prisoner's loss of security arouses acute anxiety, in short, not just because violent acts of aggression and exploitation occur but also because such behavior constantly calls into question the individual's ability to cope with it, in terms of his own inner resources, his courage, his "nerve." . . . These uncertainties constitute an ego threat for the individual forced to live in prolonged intimacy with criminals, regardless of the nature or extent of his own criminality . . . . His expectations concerning the conforming behavior of others destroyed, unable and unwilling to rely on the officials for protection, uncertain of whether or not today's joke will be tomorrow's bitter insult, the prison inmate can never feel safe.

74. The analogy is to the "Unusual Incident Reports" required of therapists making their rounds in a mental hospital. All institutions have some method, regardless of name, for listing incidents of violence so that "investigation" may proceed. In most penal institutions, every violation of the institutional rules results in a written "charge" against the inmate, and these too are part of such reporting.

75. Interview with an inmate at Walpole State Prison (Massachusetts), 1974. Identity not disclosed at interviewee's request.

76. In many institutions, residents are permitted to carry cigarettes, for example, but not matches. They must make a specific request to a staff member every time they wish to smoke. Some institutions do not permit individual ownership of such items as toilet paper.

77. Interview with a former inmate of Dannemora Prison (a.k.a. Clinton Correctional Facility), New York, 1975. Identity of interviewee not disclosed at his request.

78. The "Venturi Effect."

79. If a human being is summarily thrust into a completely dark room, his first instinct is to tentatively reach out his hands to find out where the walls are. If no walls are palpable to his touch, he moves more freely about the darkened room, still looking for the limits of his new environment. The vagueness as to behavioral standards, and the failure to disclose consequences for acts that characterize the standard juvenile institution are just another form of this darkness, and the violence of the residents often another form of the reaching out. This is not to say that limit testing is the motivation of *all* incarcerated juveniles, but it is a factor for some of them.

80. Or, at least, no *enforceable* right to performance, since specification is not usually supplied by the grantee, nor required by the grantor.

81. These two apparently conflicting statements were made in the presence of one of the authors during a visit to a community-based residential treatment facility in Pennsylvania in 1971. The name of the speaker was never learned, but he seemed to be the "official greeter" for the program. The first statement was made publicly, the latter privately.

82. A swimming pool makes good sense when dealing with institutional-size populations. The cost-per-resident is relatively low initially, and is amortized over a short period of time. A swimming pool in a small, community-based facility would not enjoy these economic advantages. The same statements may be made about almost any expensive piece of equipment or specialized service—utilization by large numbers of residents reduces cost-per-resident, and makes the expenditure seem more palatable.

83. New York City, June 1977, *see* ch. 1, note 55, *supra.* Participants were: Daniel Bumagin (senior planner, city of Lawrence, Massachusetts, Community Development Department and planning/design consultant), Yitzhak Bakal, Richard Child, Esq. (professor, New England School of Law), Arthur M. Holsborg (director, Westchester County Office of Criminal Justice Planning), Dr. Daniel H. Jacobs (director, Cambridge Court Clinic and professor, Harvard Medical School), Robert John Lewis (then director of the Ad Hoc Parole Committee, Camden, New Jersey), William C. Madaus, Ed.D. (director, Northshore Guidance Center), Cornell A. Royal (then with the Interpublic Group of Companies), Dr. Walter A. Stewart (New York Psychoanalytic Institute), Gregory Torres (juvenile justice specialist, Massachusetts Committee on Criminal Justice), Anthony M. Traini, Esq. (an attorney in private practice in Boston; formerly deputy director of Advocacy Associates), Anita S. Weissman, Esq. (now an attorney in private practice), and Andrew H. Vachss.

84. Which is not currently the case. Observers in large states routinely report that attitudes towards juvenile crime, by the public, the police, and the judiciary, vary radically throughout the state. The proposed system would, of course, only control Intake at a point rather far along in the system, it would have no impact on discretional decisions earlier on (such as whether or not to prosecute, whether or not to arrest, and whether or not to opt for an incarcerative disposition).

85. *See,* for example, *Should We Build More Prisons?*, A Debate between John P. Conrad, Senior Fellow, Center on Crime and Justice, The Academy for Contemporary Problems, and Milton G. Rector, President, National Council on Crime and Delinquency, (Hackensack, New Jersey: National Council on Crime and Delinquency, 1977).

5 Classification and Application

Case Histories

A brief look at some typical future candidates for placement within the proposed Secure Treatment Unit: a practitioner's version of "constructing a typology." The following are case histories of violent juvenile offenders known to the authors for the past several years; they have been abbreviated since each file would run several dozen pages at a minimum. In examining these histories, the reader is urged to pay the closest attention to similarities in *statutory* criminality as contrasted with the radically differing paths *to* that criminality. These histories do not purport to amount to a typology of the violent juvenile offender, and there is no claim that they are based on statistical data culled from thousands of files. The intent is only to provide a more intimate view of the violent juvenile offender and his special characteristics.

At the conclusion of this section, we will discuss implications for treatment and a broad attempt at a functional form of classification.

Case Number:	1
Name:	Raymond W.
Age:	17
Family Composition:	Mother
	Brothers (two, aged 21 and 10)
	Father (whereabouts unknown; departed 12 years ago);
	Stepfather (of youngest brother; also listed as "whereabouts unknown" by mother to avoid "hassles" by the Welfare Department; actually a local community resident, but not residing in the home).
Family Income:	Public Assistance
School:	No known attendance since age 9
Residence:	Inner-city housing project
Age First Arrest:	10
Current Charge:	Homicide

Raymond's school history was marked with turbulence; he was suspended at age 9 for repeatedly fighting with other students, and the suspension ran several weeks past the legally permitted period because his mother never responded to written requests from the school authorities to come down and discuss the situation. There was no follow-up by the school, and the home was never visited.

The only available report card from Raymond's school was from the second grade. He received a marking of S (for Satisfactory) in all subjects, including Deportment.

At age 10, Raymond was arrested inside a sporting goods store; he had apparently been boosted over the transom by older boys, but he refused to identify them to the police. Taken to the detention center, he was attacked by a group of older inmates who were awaiting trial on armed robbery. The actual motivation for this attack is still unknown; however, Raymond acquitted himself so favorably that the other inmates desisted without the need for intervention by the guards.

Because of his "recalcitrant attitude" and because his mother told the juvenile court judge that she "couldn't do nothing with him," Raymond was sentenced to a state training school. His training school record shows repeated "disciplinary action" (unspecified) for fighting, and Raymond once spent 10 days in "isolation" for another unspecified offense. He was paroled at age 12 and returned to his home.

Raymond was returned to the same training school about 6 months later; this time the charge was mugging. Again acting in concert with older boys, Raymond was attacking elderly people on the streets of the downtown business district. Although linked to a series of such crimes, and a suspect in a number of push-in muggings within his housing project, Raymond was actually convicted ("found to be delinquent") of only one offense. Again, he refused to name the other participants.

Back in the training school, Raymond was moving up in the institutional hierarchy. He had grown considerably since his last incarceration, and the crime for which he was returned was higher in status than his original offense.[1] This institutional period was marked by his overt membership in an exploitative institutional gang, and he spent almost half of his two year incarceration in the school's disciplinary cottage. According to the training school's records, he was too disruptive to be allowed to attend classes, and he was a suspect in the gang rape of another inmate. Again paroled; Raymond returned to his home community.

Returned to the same institution for a violation of his parole (being a passenger in a stolen car), Raymond quickly proved to be beyond the control of the institutional authorities and he was transferred to a high-security installation in another part of the state. Once more, he joined an institutional gang, and once more he became totally enmeshed in the institutional subculture. Raymond now sported tattoos on both arms, (his initials on one arm, and the name of the institutional gang on the other), and he continued to physically mature. When asked about his period of adjustment to the new training school, Raymond told an interviewer:

When I first got to [Training School], I was the littlest there, but I wasn't the littlest with my hands . . . I had to show those suckers that I wasn't goin' for lollypops [sexual seduction] or rip-offs [forceful sexual threats or actual rape], and I knowed how to do that. But when I got to ["Secure" Training School] I already had a rep behind the Dragons [the gang from the first institution] and there was like already a place for me.

At age 16, Raymond shot and killed a rival gang member in a dispute over the proceeds of a narcotics transaction. He had been out on parole less than 3 months.

Case Number:	2
Name:	Sam J.
Age:	16
Race:	White
Family Composition:	Mother
	Father
	Sister (19)
	Brother (20)
Family Income:	Both parents employed full-time
School:	Completed 9th grade; dropped out
Residence:	Parents own their own home in a working-class section of the city.
Age First Arrest:	14
Current Charge(s):	Robbery, A.D.W.

Sam was an indifferent student until high school, at which time he began to fail in all subjects. He then started to spend all of his time in his room, and displayed an interest only in cars. Unlike many of his contemporaries, Sam was never involved with stealing cars or joyriding, but he was arrested on the report of several other boys and found guilty of a string of burglaries of private houses.

Placed on probation, he was arrested again within 2 weeks and, this time, sent to the state training school. Sullen and aloof, Sam was the target of frequent taunts from other inmates, to which he did not respond. Although compliant to staff direction, he preferred to spend all his time in his cell listening to a portable AM/FM radio he had sent to him from his home. However, when one of the older prisoners attempted to "borrow" the radio, Sam stabbed him with a sharpened screwdriver he had managed to conceal. After he emerged from solitary, he was allowed to maintain a distance from the other inmates, and several of the other white youths in the institution made friendly overtures. Sam soon joined an institutional gang of whites and, although outnumbered by the black inmates, this gang generally held its own in the constant warfare between the groups.

Sam escaped from the institution 2 weeks prior to his parole hearing, was recaptured at his own home (he told his parents that he had been paroled), and returned to the same institution. Upon this return, a black youth told him he had been a chump for coming back so quickly, and it took several guards to restrain Sam who attempted to strangle the other youth.

Paroled 3 months later, Sam was arrested for strong-arm robbery of a gas station attendant and for assault with a deadly weapon (a tire iron) on the same victim.

When placed in the Detention Center to await trial, Sam's first action was to punch a black youth who, he said, "looked at me funny."

Case Number:	3
Name:	Louie S.
Age:	16
Race:	White
Family Composition:	Mother
	Father
	Brothers (4, age range: 38 to 22)
	Sisters (2, aged 26 and 20)
Family Income:	Father's employment
School:	Dropped out in junior high school
Residence:	Parents rent a large apartment above a store in a residenial/commercial section of the city.
Age First Arrest:	13
Current Charge(s):	Attempted Murder

Louie was born and raised in a so-called "Italian ghetto" in a large urban community. Although none of his older siblings had any previous contact with the authorities, Louie's parents were so angered by his acting out in school that they removed him and placed him in a Catholic Protectorate when he was 11. He apparently behaved well there (no records are available) and returned to his family at age 13. He was almost immediately suspended from junior high school for a series of fights both during and after school hours. He returned to the school openly carrying a rifle he took from his father's closet, and was arrested only after a 2-hour seige in the guidance counselor's office. Placed on probation after a lengthy hearing in juvenile court (at which time his parents promised to secure psychiatric treatment for their son), Louis was arrested that same week for attempting to steal a car.

Remanded to the detention center, Louie's behavior was so overtly threatening, (the major threats being to return to the center with a gun and "blow away" various staff members), that he was placed in Isolation for several days.

Sentenced to a state training school, Louie's behavior continued to be threatening and violent. Louis insisted on being addressed only by his last name, and dismissed his repeated fighting by saying "I just don't like niggers, none of us do." When pressed for an explanation as to who "us" was, Louie went into a twenty-minute tirade, the essence of his outpourings being that he wasn't a "rat" and that he would never talk about such things to the authorities.

Interviewed by a specially assigned social worker, a report was given to the institutional staff that stated Louie was suffering from "homosexual panic."[2] This observation was somehow shared with Louie, who soon escaped and made good his threat to return to the institution with a gun. This time, shots were fired before Louie was subdued.

While awaiting trial on a charge of attempted murder, (after a transfer hearing to decide that he should be treated as an adult), Louie was held in a maximum-security detention facility. His obsession with guns (and now explosives) was frightening to staff, who avoided him whenever possible. When given the opportunity to make an "unsupervised" phone call as a reward for good behavior, Louie telephoned a staff member's wife and told her there was a bomb in her husband's car. His affect became almost totally that of a movie gangster, and he professed not to understand verbal communications from "outsiders."

When interviewed prior to his trial, Louis said:

Hey, I know I'm going to [State Prison]. Where else would they send a guy with my record? That's fuckin' O.K. with me, Jack; I got people up there who'll take care of me.

Louie now spends most of his time in his cell, reading comic books and writing lengthy threatening letters to various prominent individuals in his community.

Case Number:	4
Name:	Max R.
Age:	15
Race:	Hispanic
Family Composition:	Mother
	Father
	Brother (24)
	Sisters (3, age range: 17 to 22)
	Only two youngest sisters still live in the family home.
Family Income:	Both parents employed in same factory.
School:	Completed 8th grade.
Residence:	Parents rent an "attached house" in a racially mixed urban community.
Age First Arrest:	12
Current Charge(s):	Attempted Robbery, Assault, Narcotics

Max first began exploration into narcotics while a junior high school student. Prior to this experimentation, he had been arrested on two occasions for "loitering" in a local poolroom; both arrests were "adjusted" at the police station when his parents appeared immediately and expressed appropriate concern. Attempts by his parents to involve Max in a local church group were rebuffed by the youth, and the heavily physical discipline applied by his outraged father seemed to have no effect on his behavior. It became common for Max to return home late at night, and the school authorities eventually stopped notifying his parents of habitual truancy.

When family conflicts over his behavior would spill over into beatings by his father, Max would often simply disappear from his home for several days, and he ignored all referrals to neighborhood counseling programs.

Max was arrested during an attempted robbery of a "decoy cop."[3] When questioned at the police station, he freely admitted that he needed money to buy heroin. Found by the juvenile court to be a Person in Need of Supervision (PINS) by virtue of narcotics addiction, Max was sent to a group home that specialized in the treatment of adolescent addicts. He walked out the front door after a four-hour stay and simply returned to his home. There was no response from the authorities, (a dispute later arose as to where the responsibility for this lack of response should be placed), and Max continued his former life-style.

Shortly afterwards, Max was arrested in the act of mugging an elderly man in a hallway. The victim had resisted, and Max had fractured two of the man's ribs before he was pulled off by the arresting officers. Remanded to a secure detention facility, Max was forced to "kick cold" in a holding cell. He emerged after 4 days somewhat weakened but apparently no longer physically addicted. Interviewed prior to his court appearance, Max blamed the victim for resisting so violently, and claimed that he didn't want to hurt anyone unless he was forced to.

Sentenced to the state training school, Max quickly challenged the leader of the dominant institutional gang; Max was the winner; the loser was hospitalized. Soon Max settled down to a routine of lifting weights and victimizing other inmates and was a "good parole candidate" when he was isolated for assault on an institutional staff member in a dispute over which program to watch on television.

He now faces additional assault charges and is awaiting transfer to an "adult reformatory."

Case Number:	5
Name:	Elmer R.
Age:	15
Race:	Black
Family Composition:	Father (left the household approximately 8 years ago)
	Mother
	Sisters (19, in the home
	22, left with father)
	Brothers (2, in the home
	20, left with father)
Family Income:	Mother's employment (housekeeper)
School:	No attendance shown.
Residence:	Family rents top floor of a three-family house.
Age First Arrest:	Never arrested.
Current Charge(s):	None pending.

At age 7, Elmer's mother brought him to juvenile court and signed a petition stating he was a "Stubborn Child" and that he was in need of "guidance, supervision, or control" by the court. She asked the court to incarcerate her son to "teach him a good lesson" and "help him see the way of Jesus." The court refused this request, and ordered a Social Investigation.[4]

The investigation revealed that the mother was "religiously obsessed"; she was found to be a member of an obscure religious sect to which she voluntarily contributed a significant portion of her meager income. She told the investigators that she did not want her son adopted, or placed in foster care, but only sent to prison for his "crimes." She refused to specify the nature of the crimes, but was quite willing to make repeated court appearances to expound upon her religious convictions and the necessity for locking up her son. Attempts to contact the boy's father were fruitless. Elmer was placed in a foster home and his mother stated "I wash my hands of the whole affair."

Elmer quickly proved to be unmanageable in the foster home and, after repeated attempts at placement within the foster care network, he was transferred to a juvenile detention facility to "await further placement action." When teased by the other residents of the facility, Elmer would fly into an uncontrollable rage and, in spite of his small size, the others were reluctant to physically attack him because of the ferocity and disregard for consequences he displayed.

He was repeatedly beaten by the detention center staff, often with a leather strap, and he responded with escalating rage until he would lapse into unconsciousness. Although this at first frightened the staff into stopping the beatings, they soon learned that he would quickly recover and the pattern of physical abuse continued.

Considered "un-placeable," Elmer was finally sent to the state training school which, at that time, indiscriminately mixed status and delinquent offenders ranging in age from 8 to 17.

In the school, Elmer's awesome rages increased with repeated beatings, and he soon became an object of hate and fear to staff and residents alike. A nurse prescribed heavy doses of tranquilizers, and Elmer's diet of thorazine increased weekly. Since the medication was dispensed by the staff, Elmer was often given doses far in excess of any medical need and a pattern soon emerged: Elmer would slowly emerge from a tranquilizer-induced comatose state and, as his muscle tone and visual perception returned, he would immediately attack any human within range. The steady doses of medication and the physical abuse seemed only to increase his physical strength and, by the time he was 13 years old, he had the physical appearance of an adult.

Numerous attempts to place Elmer failed; he was diagnosed as "retarded" although he had never attended so much as a single class in any school, but the state school for the retarded rejected him because of his violent behavior. A similar rejection came from the state mental hospital since its "childrens' ward" was "not suitable" for violent individuals. Even the training school could not handle Elmer, and he was eventually transferred to maximum security where he spent most of his time locked in a cell, heavily sedated.

Those inmates who preyed upon him when he was comatose (even to the extent of extinguishing lighted cigarettes on his arms) soon found that he would take violent revenge on those rare occasions when the medication wore off and the staff was too slow with replenishment.

Finally, he fractured a guard's skull with repeated punches, and the local police had to be called in to restrain him. Transferred once again, this time to the state's most restrictive placement for juveniles, Elmer is now considered to be a nonfunctioning animal whose self-control does not even extend to his own bowels and bladder.

However, the diagnosis of mental deficiency must be questioned in light of a report given by a guard from Elmer's last institution:

There's no way that boy's retarded. One time he comes into the office and *asks* for his medication. Now usually we got to have three, four people hold him while he gets a shot, but this time he *asks* for the pills, right? So, like idiots, they give them to him. Then he walks down the hall smiling to himself and looking in his hand . . . and one of the big guys that's always fucking with him comes up and asks what he's got. Elmer tells this gorilla that he's got some *speed,* that we gave it to him to have him lose weight. So this gorilla immediately bogarts [threatens] Elmer and makes him turn it over. If this fucking moron was even thinking he would have known there's no way you going to *make* Elmer give up nothing . . . but anyway, he scarfs down the pills and he's out like a light. We had to take him to the Emergency Ward and he almost died . . . I mean, Elmer gets a *heavy* dose, man. Now tell me how some fucking *re*tard is going to pull off a move like that!

When he reaches statutory adulthood, Elmer will be "paroled" to the community unless a mental hospital can be located that will accept him.

Case Number:	6
Name:	Roberto A.
Age:	15
Race:	Mother, Puerto Rican
	Father, White
Family Composition:	Unknown
Family Income:	Unknown
School:	No known attendance
Residence:	Unknown (see history)
Age First Arrest:	10
Current Charge(s):	Homicide

Roberto was first incarcerated at age 10 when he was found living with several other young people in an abandoned building. Their loose federation appeared to be supporting itself by petty thievery and begging. When questioned by social workers, Roberto described himself as a "trick baby" (an accidental child resulting from intercourse between a prostitute and her customer), and claimed he did not know how to get in touch with any relatives.

While being held in detention, Roberto was allegedly raped by an older inmate, but he refused to identify the older boy and no charges were ever brought. He later escaped from the detention center and has been free since that time. A juvenile court warrant was issued, but will not be served since Roberto's only known address is the place from which he escaped. During the several years he has been on the streets, Roberto has supported himself through homosexual prostitution. For some time, an older man arranged "dates" for Roberto, but in the past year he has been out on his own, "free-lancing" in the same profession. Roberto was apparently arrested at age 14 upon the complaint of a former sex partner who claimed Roberto had stolen his wallet. Roberto gave a false name, the address of what turned out to be a vacant lot, and listed his age as 20 on the police forms. He was released after 7 weeks in jail when the complainant repeatedly failed to show up for court appearances.

During an argument with another male prostitute over the proceeds of a cocaine transaction in which they were both to share, Roberto stabbed and killed the other youth. Aware of the consequences of his acts in terms of the criminal law, Roberto has given the police his correct age, and he is now awaiting trial in a juvenile detention center.

Case Number:	7
Name:	Chris T.
Age:	16
Race:	Hispanic
Family Composition:	Mother
	Father (unknown)
	Brother (25; now serving a sentence of 10-20 years in the state prison for armed robbery).
	Sister (22; current whereabouts unknown)
Family Income:	Public Assistance
School:	Completed 5th grade.
Residence:	Shares 3-room basement apartment with mother in large tenement.
Age First Arrest:	12
Current Charge(s):	Arson, Homicide (Felony Murder)

Chris was first arrested at age 12 for a series of push-in muggings in his community; he was also charged with the attempted rape of one of his victims, and rape and sodomy charges against him were dismissed after another victim failed to testify.

He was sent to a state training school and served an uneventful two years. Since his release, he has been an active member of a local street gang and has amassed a record of 21 arrests, none of which have resulted in additional incarceration.

For a cash payment of one hundred dollars, Chris "torched" a building in his neighborhood. He was paid the money by the adult leader of another street gang, who claimed that one of the youthful residents of that building had broken the windshield of his car. The adult gang leader applied to Chris' gang president for "justice and vengeance" and this president made the arrangements.

Chris broke into the unoccupied basement of the building with a 5-gallon can of gasoline. He simply poured the gasoline over the floor, climbed out a window, and tossed a lighted rag into the basement. Three adults were trapped on the top floor of the building, unable to reach the fire escape because the protective gates on the windows had been rusted shut. Chris has been sent to a state diagnostic center to determine if the arson was part of a psychiatric pattern, and he will be sentenced to a juvenile institution when the diagnostic period is completed.

Case Number:	8
Name:	Toby A.
Age:	18
Race:	White
Family Composition:	Unknown; raised in an orphanage, then placed in a series of foster homes when not adopted; then in a "protectorate."
Family Income:	Unknown (see history)
School:	Completed 4th grade.
Residence:	Variety of state institutions.
Age First Arrest:	11
Current Charge(s):	Homicide, Armed Robbery.

Toby has been a so-called "state kid" in that his entire background and upbringing have been arranged by the state authorities. Originally an abandoned child, Toby was placed in an orphanage in "pre-adoptive" status; when no adoption was forthcoming, he was placed in the state's foster care network, and he lived with seven different families, with occasional returns to a religious protectorate when his behavior proved difficult to manage for the foster parents.

At age 11, Toby ran away from his last foster home. He was arrested about 6 months later during a gambling raid on a local "after-hours" nightclub. Toby had been selling newspapers, shining shoes, and generally making himself useful to the minor league criminals who frequented the club. The police were originally willing to simply tell him to "get home," but when he couldn't give an address, he was held for investigation ... which revealed his actual status. Returned to state custody, he was transferred from the foster home network to a training school, where he continued to act as a protégé of an older, more criminalized group of youthful offenders.

After an abortive "escape" attempt (during which he was captured by one of the older inmates),[5] Toby was placed in solitary confinement for 3 weeks. Upon emerging, he quickly distinguished himself by a willingness to fight older inmates, and was repeatedly beaten by both these inmates and the guards. The guards later explained the beatings by saying that Toby would not obey even the simplest order and had to be forced into a semblance of compliance with the institutional rules.

Toby escaped again, at age 14, and participated in a long series of "cowboy-style"[6] armed robberies of local businesses. Again easily captured by the police, Toby loudly proclaimed next time he would "hold court in the streets," and was beaten by the arresting officers when he resisted being handcuffed.

Remanded to "secure detention" while awaiting trial for armed robbery, Toby and four other boys attempted to escape by overpowering a guard. Their escape was foiled at the outer door by an incoming "change of shift." Toby's arm was broken during a fight with the incoming guards.

Found guilty of the armed robberies, Toby was offered probation if he would reveal the names of the other participants, some of whom were apparently of adult age. Toby refused, and was sentenced to the state training school's maximum unit for an indeterminate period. Toby's behavior there was so violent that he was paroled after only 4 months,[7] and he returned to his old haunts and old habits.

At age 16, Toby was arrested in a public park with a handgun, and several hundred dollars in his possession. He was wearing four heavy, studded rings on each hand, to give the impact of "brass knuckles" when he clenched his fists. Although the authorities were unable to connect him with any specific robberies, his parole was violated and he was again returned to the training school. His violent behavior in the institution resulted in continual threats to transfer him to an adult reformatory, but he was instead paroled at the end of 3 months.

Within 2 weeks of his release, Toby and 2 other young men were surprised by an off-duty policeman as they were backing out of a liquor store they had just robbed. Shots were exchanged and the officer and one of the youths were killed. Toby is now being held prior to trial as an adult for first degree murder.

Case Number:	9
Name:	Henry B.
Age:	17
Race:	Black
Family Composition:	Mother
	Father (whereabouts unknown)
Family Income:	Mother does factory work, supplemented with Public Assistance during periodic layoffs.
School:	Completed 8th grade.
Residence:	4-room apartment, large multiple dwelling, inner city.
Age First Arrest:	17
Current Charge(s):	Rape, Sodomy, assault (multiple counts)

A student of limited ability but above-average interest, Henry was placed in the "slow classes" in grade school and, once so tracked, was given a number of regular "social promotions" through the 9th grade. At age 14, he was arrested for an attempted burglary and placed on probation. This probation was violated several weeks later when he participated with four other boys in a purse-snatching which resulted in serious injury to the elderly victim.

One of the other boys assured Henry that this case would never come to trial and, following his advice, Henry simply did not appear on his scheduled court date. No warrant was issued for his arrest, but Henry was picked up during a "sweep"[8] of a street corner and found to be holding a "gravity knife."[9] This time, he was remanded to the secure detention unit and held for 3 months. Finally adjudicated a delinquent, Henry was sent to a training school and served one year, during which time he was no problem to the institutional authorities. Although placid and easily led by others, Henry appeared to spend more of his time listening to other youths than in acting out, and was generally classified as "no trouble" while incarcerated.

Upon his release, Henry became a full-time burglar, with some degree of success, employing techniques he had apparently learned while in the training school. At one point in his burglary career, he entered a top-floor apartment and surprised a sleeping woman. The woman was extremely frightened and begged Henry not to hurt her ... Henry repeatedly raped and sodomized the woman, remaining in the apartment for several hours. He stole some money and a portable radio.

Henry then began a series of house invasions, and his apparent targets were women living alone. Apprehended on his way out of a project by a housing authority policeman, Henry immediately confessed to a string of 11 such rapes, and he was subsequently identified by 4 of his victims. Although Henry kept insisting that he entered the apartments to steal, he admitted that he never entered an empty apartment after the first rape.

Henry has been sent to the state diagnostic center to await an "appropriate placement."

Case Number:	10
Name:	John W.
Age:	16
Race:	White
Family Composition:	Mother
	Father
	Brother (15)
Family Income:	Father's employment (Manufacturer's Representative; self-employed).
School:	Completed 10th grade.
Residence:	Private home, mid-affluent suburb.
Age First Arrest:	16
Current Charge(s):	Homicide (3 counts).

An average scholar and a fine athlete, John was popular with a small group of his contemporaries and well regarded by the faculty of his high school.

A chronic bed-wetter at age 10, John seemed to have conquered this problem, and he displayed none of the problems that seemed to characterize the general student population in his community: this community had recently become aroused over reports that students were excessive abusers of alcohol and "soft" drugs. Since there has been minimal agency involvement in his life, very few facts are known about his early childhood development. However, John's father was known as an "aggressive go-getter" in the business community and it was clear that his family had high expectations of future performance from their sons.

Three weeks ago, John returned home early from school after complaining of a headache. He apparently entered the house and searched his parents' bedroom for some time. He then loaded a deer rifle he had been given for his 16th birthday and sat down in the living room. When his mother returned from picking up his younger brother from an after-school activity, John shot and killed them both.

He remained by the bodies until his father returned to the house, and shot his father too. The police noted that his father had been shot several times, and theorized that the boy must have stopped to reload at some point.

John then shot himself in the side, but the wound was not fatal. He first told the police that a burglar had surprised the family and shot them all before escaping, but later changed his story and admitted the homicides. John is now in close detention, with a posted suicide watch, and his attorney has announced that John will enter a plea of "not guilty by reason of insanity" at his upcoming trial.

Case Number:	11
Name:	Percy S.
Age:	17
Race:	White
Family Composition:	Mother
	Father
	Sisters (2, aged 11 and 6)
Family Income:	Father's employment (Plumber, self-employed).
School:	Completed 6th grade.
Residence:	Private house (tract); middle-class suburban community.
Age First Arrest:	13
Current Charge(s):	Rape, Sodomy, Sexual Abuse (multiple-counts)

An indifferent student (although not retarded and with no marked learning disabilities), Percy often came to the attention of the school authorities because of his habit of setting small fires in and around the school building. Percy was also a suspect when a puppy was found tortured to death, but he vehemently denied involvement and the matter was eventually dropped.

Percy was arrested at age 13 for forcibly "fondling" a neighbor's 6-year-old daughter. Again, he denied the acts, but was remanded to the state training school as a "sex offender." His parents did not appear in juvenile court until threatened with a summons, and they claimed they had insufficient funds for a legal defense. No home investigation was made prior to his commitment. The probation interview with his father gave a portrait of a decent, hard-working man who was utterly dumbfounded by his son's bizarre behavior.

At the training school, Percy withdrew from all interaction with the other residents, and quickly acquired the reputation of being a "rat" because of his constant desire to spend time with male staff members. He was gang-raped in the shower room and, although he informed on each and every perpetrator, no concrete action was taken by the staff since it was believed that no physical force was used and that Percy may have willingly participated.

Percy was paroled a short time later and returned to his home. The school authorities refused to accept him back as a student and he spent all his time inside the house. At the age of 15, he forcibly raped his 5-year-old sister, causing serious injury. Although the young child's story was confused and incoherent, the physical injuries were obvious and, in view of Percy's past record, he was returned to the training school. At the insistence of one staff member, a home investigation was launched, but the parents refused to cooperate in any way, even after being told that the length of their son's confinement could well hinge on their participation in his treatment. Percy's counselor later learned that the boy's father repeatedly beat the young daughters for the slightest infraction of his "rules," and that the mother was also a frequent target of physical abuse. Percy, on the other hand, had never been physically disciplined by anyone in the household. The oldest daughter stated that her father routinely committed a variety of incestuous acts with her and her young sister, and further stated that Percy knew of this relationship.

Percy began to hallucinate freely; he often said that Jesus Christ was speaking to him, and that he was acting as he was ordered to do. Shunned by the other residents, Percy spent most of his time in his room, refusing to come out for showers or recreation. He continued to be eager to speak with male staff, but most staff found him so personally offensive that no solid relationships were ever formed. Months later Percy joined a mass escape from the recreational yard. He was apprehended less than a mile from the institution when the screams of a 7-year-old girl attracted the attention of neighbors. Returned to the institution,

Percy regaled the other residents with tales of the "rape" he had committed . . . the story he told was essentially factual, except that the age of the victim was changed to that of an adult.

Percy was again involved in group homosexual behavior while in solitary confinement, again informed on the other participants, and, this time, was isolated from all other residents.

He now speaks lovingly of the time when he will "grow up" and enter the armed forces and be a soldier. A hand-lettered notebook found in his cell was full of graphic descriptions of various sexually oriented tortures.

The staff consensus is that Percy is incurably insane, dangerous to the outside world, but a "good inmate" and really no trouble to them. The only problem with Percy is that his very presence seems to provoke violence from others, and he must be isolated at all times. He is currently awaiting trial for the last sexual assault.

Which of the juveniles described in the case histories would be referred to the Secure Treatment Unit? The answer to this question, given the social and political climate in 1979, must be a somewhat cynical "all of them." Assuming, as we have advocated, that no statewide diagnostic center exists, the criminal acts of all of these juveniles, standing alone, would pressure local authorities to push for incarceration.

Although even a brief glance at the minimal information contained in the case histories would indicate substantial variance in etiology of criminality, we insist on working within a non-utopian format, and we are well aware of the reluctance (if not outright refusal) of mental health facilities to accept juveniles whose behavior pattern exhibits violence towards others.[10] Assuming further that waiver will not be invoked against any of the aforementioned juveniles, we can now begin to see some of the functional aspects of the Secure Treatment Unit's physical and programmatic design.

Which of the juveniles would be likely to remain with the Secure Treatment Unit and be integrated into its programs? At first blush, Roberto, Toby, Max, Raymond, and Sam appear to be classic life-style violent juvenile delinquents (or, depending on one's perspective, "intensive offenders").[11] Their criminality appears to be both chronic and escalating, prior incarceration seemed only to exacerbate their negative behavior, and the predominant influences in their lives appear to be cultural, social, and economic. Given only the brief information presented, it is more likely than not that they would be considered appropriate candidates for the Secure Treatment Unit programs.

It is important to note at this juncture that these juveniles would not be required to "make a commitment to the program"; they would not be required to sign some sort of bogus "contract" with the program,[12] and they would not be told they had been found "qualified" for admission. They would be entering an institution that *contains* a variety of programs, with specific and defined curricula for each separate unit. They would also be informed, pursuant to whatever local statutes were in effect, that there was a certain minimum period of incarceration, which would not (and could not) be altered regardless of their behavior. (The significance of this position will be detailed as we later discuss Unit Two of the Secure Treatment Unit.)

Percy appears to be psychosexually motivated beyond a reasonable doubt; arguably, the same motivations and etiology could be applied to Henry, and, to a lesser degree of certainty, to Louie.

There would seem to be little argument that John is mentally disturbed and was responding to serious inner compulsion. And Elmer, although institutionally *created,* is not a criminal in any real sense of the word; yet it appears that treatment outside an institution is currently impossible.

Assuming that the final decision is to include Henry, Elmer, and Louie within the program, and to reject Percy and John, what happens to the latter two juveniles?

Various (seemingly conflicting) schools of thought can be stretched to rationalize the politically expedient incarceration of a given juvenile. The case histories represent only a partial view of the many divergent routes to Secure Treatment Unit incarceration. Although there is a growing body of opinion supporting the proposition that the length and severity of juvenile incarceration should be directly proportional to the seriousness of the offense,[13] the proponents of "purely rehabilitative" intervention have not folded their tents. In fact, these ostensibly opposed camps often manage to reach the same conclusion by different rhetorical paths when the result to be achieved is politically mandated.

Such an expediency exists when a juvenile is chronically violent, even if such violence occurs solely within an institutional setting. For example: Elmer has committed no serious crimes against the outside society, and the observer would expect that the "least restrictive alternative" camp would vehemently oppose his incarceration in a Secure Treatment Unit. Similarly, the observer would anticipate that the "just deserts" proponents would be opposed to incarceration on the ground that "crime" and "time" should be proportionately matched. Yet, in Elmer's case, both camps demanded Elmer's continued incarceration: those expressing a rehabilitative philosophy claimed that Elmer was beyond the control of community-based facilities, and could only be rehabilitated in a closed setting. Those promoting the "crime equals time" mentality took refuge in Elmer's "dangerousness." Both paid homage to the political necessity of incarcerating Elmer; this juvenile would impact upon the system in grotesque and obvious ways if permitted to remain "at large" outside the institution, and the management concerns of the remainder of the juvenile justice system required that Elmer be kept apart from all other programs. The "rehabilitative" proponents, while loudly announcing that Elmer was living proof of the failures of a training school system, still recognized that his current dangerousness was a fait accompli, and that it was impossible to retrace or restore his life. Elmer, in other words, was a functional write-off, and the rehabilitative contingent felt that its energies were more profitably invested in other juveniles with a more favorable prognosis. And the "just deserts" people were not prepared to simply release Elmer to the community for fear that his violent behavior would call into question the very efficacy of incarceration for very young children . . . since Elmer was demonstrably *made* dangerous while being "treated."

So long as the juvenile is in fact chronically violent, the Secure Treatment Unit must respond to such expediency and accept him for admission. It was in the self-interest of neither group to release Elmer; it was in the self-interest of neither group to place him anywhere in the juvenile justice system except a secure unit; and, although each group would supply a different rationale for its decision, both arrived at the same conclusion. Any Secure Treatment Unit plan that fails to make provisions for the Elmers of this world is doomed to failure. Regardless of the strength of Intake procedures, regardless of the political clout of an individual unit, regardless of any diagnostic decisions made inside the unit, the Elmers of the juvenile justice system will be incarcerated so long as we continue to allow the process of creating dangerousness to continue, without intervention, for the years and years it takes to develop such an individual inside our institutions.

Regardless of (short-term) political expediency, the Secure Treatment Unit must maintain the integrity of its Intake criteria in order to assure its own (long-term) survival. The Secure Treatment Unit must consider its *own* survival and, to do so in pragmatic fashion, it must be relatively ruthless in its Intake decisions. A common argument from the system to the institution is: "If you don't take him, where will he go?". And the Secure Treatment Unit's response must be, to the extent it is politically permitted, "That's not *our* problem; that's *your* problem!"

The Secure Treatment Unit that allows itself to be used as a garbage pail for the rest of the juvenile justice system will have tremendous political utility, and its survival will be assured. But its failure will be equally assured, and this choice represents the major decision that will determine the future of any new unit. A juvenile such as Raymond *must* be accepted if the unit is to be taken seriously by the profession: as a life-style violent delinquent, Raymond is what the Secure Treatment Unit is all about. And, equally important, a juvenile such as Percy must *not* be accepted, since his criminal acts are so obviously and hopelessly intertwined with psychosexual dysfunctioning as to make treatment inside the unit utterly impossible. The unit is predicated on attacking life-style violence which is culturally, socially, and economically motivated; its treatment plans, its staff, even its very architecture is designed to directly intervene in cultural/social patterns and to teach new life-style survival skills to its residents. It is not a psychiatric facility; it is not a therapeutic community; and it is not prepared to refocus its entire program to accommodate the needs of a deeply disturbed and, possibly, untreatable individual.

Just as the unit is, in effect, asking society to choose long-term goals of safety, peace, and behavior-change over short term goals of punitive incarceration, the unit itself must choose long-term goals of survival by performance rather than survival by political acceptance. A Secure Treatment Unit which accepts a juvenile like Percy because the system finds this to be useful is insuring only its short-term survival. When the Percys are included, the unit ceases to function as a change-agent in the life-style which brought the majority of juveniles within its walls and serves instead only as a "bottom of the barrel" for a system that continues to endanger society far more than any individual juvenile criminals. Similarly, a Secure Treatment Unit that refuses to accept the Raymonds exposes itself as something less than a front-line warrior in the struggle against juvenile crime and violence. This unit will also survive, but not for long. Its task can be performed with far less cost, and the value of the task it has relegated to itself is greatly diminished.

The Secure Treatment Unit's survival depends as much upon its acceptance of the juvenile whose violence occurs solely within an institution as it depends upon rejection of the juvenile whose violence is motivated by psychosis. So far, the choices appear to be simple; the decisions appear to be almost preordained when viewed in terms of survival and viability. Yet a juvenile like Elmer presents the most serious problems even for the unit committed to long-term survival for itself and long-term success for its programs, because Elmer, although not a fit candidate for any Secure Treatment Unit that now exists or is likely to exist, *must* be accepted as a resident!

The Secure Treatment Unit, by rejecting the psychotic juvenile, forces the appropriate authorities (within the mental health field) to be accountable for such cases. Part of the functional goal of the unit is to force the remainder of the system to perform; to strip naked the sham and rhetoric of the proposal writers and clearly expose those components of the juvenile justice network that are evading or failing in their appointed tasks. If there is no mental health facility that will accept Percy, the system is clearly at fault. If there is a facility that, on paper, should accept Percy, it cannot be permitted to slide out from under this obligation simply because its director can put the magic initials M.D. after his name. If there is no mental health facility for those juveniles who express their mental illness in violence, the system must produce one, or stand damned before the public as completely inadequate. The unit will be totally counterproductive if it serves as a hiding place for juveniles like Percy. Such juveniles *do* exist; such juveniles will continue to exist, and simply hiding them within a system and allowing them to fester is more than a disservice to the public—it is nothing less than the cold-blooded and deliberate construction of a time-bomb guaranteed to claim its victims in society.

But the Secure Treatment Unit cannot use the label of "insanity" to reject juveniles who appropriately belong within its custody. Elmer represents no such easy answers. Although he is arguably dangerous, and although he arguably needs close supervision and confinement, he does not appear to be a candidate for a mental health facility. Elmer has responded to the culture in which he was raised, the culture of the institution. And although it appears ironic that an institution must be used to counteract that very culture, such an analysis nevertheless has merit: Elmer, regardless of his path to this status, *is* a life-style violent delinquent and he diagnostically belongs within the Secure Treatment Unit. And Elmer also *politically* belongs within the unit, because the survival of the unit depends on its profile in the professional and public communities—the unit can legitimately refuse to accept Percy, and it should do so. But when the unit refuses a juvenile like Elmer, it calls many of its own goals and abilities into question and the spectre of mental illness should not be used to shield the unit from its own responsibilities.

Mental illness is culturally, not biologically defined. Many readers might say that Pirate is certainly insane; after all, would any sane person act as he does? But there is an argument that actual insanity is exhibited only by a total inability to assimilate cultural and social messages and, by such standards, Pirate is far from insane. This is not a plea for "understanding" of antisocial cultural patterns; not at all. No society can tolerate acts dangerous to its own existence merely on the grounds that such acts constitute the beliefs of one of its segments. But to call Pirate insane is to ignore reality and, worse yet, to surrender any hope of substantial change.

Those juveniles whose culture gives rise to a life-style of violence must be accepted by the Secure Treatment Unit, whether such violence takes place on the streets or within another institution. The Secure Treatment Unit must either impact on the lives of juveniles like Pirate, or disappear—while teams of criminologists preside over the corpse with dubious analysis and copious statistics, and the public continues to live in fear. And, if this happens, the movement to lower the age of "juvenileness" will continue to gain momentum, and we will eventually end up with an expansion of one of America's greatest failures: the penal system.

Elmer was no less culturally produced than Pirate; he is no less a fit candidate for the Secure Treatment Unit. And if the unit wants to be heard with respect when it rejects Percy, it must not dilute the strength of its own analysis by rejection of juveniles like Elmer.

Funding, and the withholding thereof, are increasingly being used as a sanction against service-delivery agencies in the child-care field. The survival of the Secure Treatment Unit must be based on its acceptance by the larger community. The public grows increasingly angry at unfulfilled promises, and there is a growing feeling that maybe federal funds are not "play money" after all. Although many child-care agencies have sufficient political insulation to protect them against the consequences of substandard performance, this insulation is subject to increasing pressure as the need for drastic change becomes more apparent. The less the behavior of the cared-for children impacts upon the public consciousness, the safer the agency is from discipline by society's appointed watchdog, the legislature. However, even the "low profile" children have their advocates, and these advocates are increasingly turning to the concept of reducing or eliminating funding as a sanction. The American Bar Association recently reported:

> Law Professor Patrick Keenan of the University of Detroit says federal money is being used to maintain juvenile offenders in "hellholes" in which they are subjected to physical abuse, solitary confinement, and drugs. To end abuses, said Keenan at Washington, D.C. hearings organized by *Children's Express,* a publication put out mostly by children, reformers must trace the funding to its source and either control it or threaten to cut it off.[14]

In the treatment of the life-style violent juvenile, such sanctions are directed at the results rather than the methods employed. This attitude probably reflects less on the population of any future Secure Treatment Unit than on any other program, agency, or institution for juveniles. The reader will note the tone of outrage directed at the quality and type of treatment afforded the population of the "hellholes"; there is no expressed outrage at the results or end products of this treatment. And, for the life-style violent delinquent, the public is far less concerned with methodology than with results. An angered public might be convinced that vicious and outmoded methods of treatment are, in fact, dangerous to that same public in that they produce a more dangerous class of criminal upon release, but arguments against a certain form of treatment on purely humanitarian grounds are likely to fail miserably. Public acceptance of the Secure Treatment Unit will be based not on perception of the humaneness of its methods, but on perception of the success of such methods.

Such sanctions apply equally to the field of criminology as they do to specific service-delivery agencies. Criminology is perceived by the public largely as an investigative science. It is perceived by the profession as scientific investigation. But neither the public nor the criminal justice profession perceives criminology as a viable tool in fighting crime, and the American public is past the point where it can be placated by heavily funded studies.

Criminology's failure stems from its inability to consider crime as a socio-political phenomenon. It is illusory that the proliferation of criminological institutes and studies will compensate for the depletion of conventional criminology. On the contrary, the sophistication of "methodologism" has contributed to the emptiness of contemporary criminology. Criminology has been unable to deal with the problem of crime.[15]

A functioning Secure Treatment Unit will profit rather than suffer if sanctions are applied to the failure to produce results. The Secure Treatment Unit makes two promises to the public: (1) it will successfully incapacitate the life-style violent delinquent for a minimum period,[16] and (2) it will produce a de-escalation of life-style violence in the released offender. The simplicity of the promise does not detract from the difficulty of its implementation.

Pragmatic Considerations

The proposed Secure Treatment Unit is designed as an exportable model, not unique to any one jurisdiction. The proposed Secure Treatment Unit is not keyed into any one jurisdiction. Political considerations will dictate the final form of the unit, and the speed with which it is implemented, but we anticipate that *some* form of this solution will eventually be adopted in most areas. Therefore, the intent is to design a fully exportable model with sufficient inherent flexibility to satisfy the requirements of jurisdictions as varied as New York and Utah.

The Secure Treatment Unit attempts to produce (from a population of life-style violent juvenile offenders) individuals who can exist and function within society without constant eruptions of violence. The goals of a functioning Secure Treatment Unit are to de-escalate the use of violence as a tool of self-expression and employment by the life-style violent juveniles who live within its walls. Reentry survival for Secure Treatment Unit graduates depends almost totally on this reduction in life-style violence. However, survival without the constant use of criminal violence again depends on the employment capability of each graduate, and this capability is partially dependent on both cognitive and affective skills which are developed in the unit's varied curricula. Figure 6-8 illustrates the relative importance of the new attitudes and skills, in terms of the emphasis placed on these areas as the juvenile progresses through the Secure Treatment Unit's individual living-clusters.

Notes

1. *See* ch. 3, notes 25, 26, and 31, *supra.*
2. This report was prepared by a sympathetic social worker who tried to

lobby for Louie's placement within a psychiatric, as opposed to penal, facility. In plain language, the social worker explained that Louie had self-perceived "homosexual tendencies," and reacted (violently) to them by "proving" he was as masculine as the next resident. In his current environment, masculinity was so closely associated with serious violence that Louie's behavioral options were thus limited.

3. A common technique in New York City, and a special favorite of the Transit Authority Police. The "decoy" is a police officer, dressed to resemble a drunken derelict. The decoy lies down (on a convenient bench or on the floor) with a dollar bill prominently protruding from a breast pocket. When the "perpetrator" grabs the dollar bill, the "back up team" moves in and an arrest for "robbery" is effectuated. Such arrests are routinely bargained down to petty offenses in Manhattan, but are treated less leniently in other counties. The practice has been held *not* to constitute "entrapment."

4. A "Social Investigation" in juvenile court is analogous to a "Pre-Sentence" investigation in the criminal courts. It is generally performed by a probation officer, and is often dispositive of a juvenile's future. It is heavily emphasized in the juvenile forum (since the court is responding to the "needs of the child" and not merely inquiring as to past criminal conduct).

5. In some training schools, especially those run on a strict "cadet captain" model, prisoners who captured a runaway were often rewarded for their efforts, sometimes by actually being paroled. It was not long before exploiter/intimidator inmates forced weaker prisoners to "attempt escapes" so as to reap those rewards.

6. This style of armed robbery is generally considered to be the mark of a rookie in the field: it involves virtually no planning, and simply requires a firearm, a target (preferably a liquor store or a gas station) and a getaway vehicle.

7. *See* ch. 4, note 33, *supra.*

8. "Sweep arrests" generally represent attempts by the police to respond to community complaints about illegal street activities. Usually, they are focused on prostitution or narcotics traffic, and anyone caught in the sweep "net" is subject to arrest. The New York Civil Liberties Union is currently challenging the validity of the practice, representing a plaintiff arrested in a prostitution "sweep" who was not, in fact, a prostitute. The sweep that occasioned Henry's arrest was an attempt to clean up a "bad corner" (although all such sweeps do is move the illegal activity to another site).

9. This knife is activated (opens) with a flick of the wrist as opposed to a mechanical device (switchblade). Commonly believed to be legal, it is, in fact, illegal in New York (PL section 265.01).

10. This was a repeated problem during the operation of Andros II, and some mental health facilities baldly disclose "violent behavior" as a criterion of intake exclusion.

11. *See* Petersilia et al., ch. 2, note 8, *supra,* at p. 97:

We perceived the intensive type as the more professional offender whose criminal activity seemed to be sustained and consciously directed, with deliberate attention paid to avoiding arrest. We perceived the intermittent type as an offender who did not view himself as a professional criminal; whose criminal activity was more irregular and opportunistic; and who was less heedful of the risks and consequences of criminal acts and more prone to arrest.

12. Such a "contract" is literally not worth the paper it is written on; in fact, it has a *negative* value, for the juvenile resident is quick to observe how some residents' "contracts" are more strictly enforced than others. Also, those programs that utilize such "contracts" can always kick the violator out of their facility; the Secure Treatment Unit has no such option.

13. *See,* for example, van der Haag, ch. 1, note 9, *supra.*

14. 64 *American Bar Association Journal* 662 (1978).

15. Manuel Lopez-Ray, "Criminological Manifesto," 39 *Federal Probation* 18 (1975) at p. 22, as abstracted in 8 *Crime and Delinquency Literature* 201 (1976), under S 16891.

16. Elyce H. Zenoff, and Alan B. Zients, "The Juvenile Murderer: Who is He and What Do We Do About Him?" (Paper presented at the American Society of Criminology Annual Meeting, Atlanta, Georgia, November 19, 1977), at p. 9:

[E] valuation of empathy is critical when assessing these youngsters. Its absence signals continued risk to the community. If the capacity for empathy is lacking, not even the most intensive therapeutic program can provide it. [N]on-empathic males have a poor prognosis for successful reentry into the community. They have a history of repeated violent offenses despite the fact that there has been psychiatric intervention. They require long-term institutionalization.

6

A Walk Through a Planned Secure Treatment Unit

The Secure Treatment Unit: A Structural Overview

A conceptual rendering of the Secure Treatment Unit, as seen from above, is given in figure 6-1. The viewer will immediately note the direct departure from the cottage-style juvenile institutions of the past, and will note some similarity to maximum-security adult institutions in that the structure is surrounded by a massive wall which is much higher than any of the structures it encloses.

However, a closer inspection will reveal that there are several separate and distinct living units within the wall, and that the wall itself houses both life-support and therapeutic/recreational/educational/vocational structures. The Juvenile Justice Planning Project long ago concluded that a viable treatment unit must have the *internal* ability to move residents within its own structure; it must have the ability to reward progress, the ability to temporarily separate given individuals, and it must have a variety of specialized programs (each with its own goals and requirements) all within the same total unit. The Secure Treatment Unit, as conceptualized in figure 6-1, answers these needs.

The Secure Treatment Unit is a maximum security structure (as defined in chapter 5) in that a high priority is placed upon retention of residents within its walls; it is maximum security in that its residents are there on a purely involuntary basis; and, perhaps most important of all, it is maximum security in that the residents are assured a degree of security from one another.[1] The external security is obvious to the viewer, but the internal security features will not become apparent until we examine the individual units via the blowups provided in figures 6-1 through 6-10.

The structure provides small units with individualized programs such as might be advocated by those in favor of community-based corrections for juveniles. It provides a ready means of transfer between programs according to the needs of both residents and management, such as might be advocated by those individual community program directors who believe the power to transfer is essential to maintenance of control over their resident populations. It provides the variety and scope of services advocated by those who understand that a mere warehouse will only delay violence temporarily, rather than work towards its eradication; and it provides such services in a far more cost-effective fashion than would be possible if the smaller units were to stand individually in separate locations. It provides the ability to transmit and reward a sense of progress by individual residents; it provides a means of control over one's environment to be

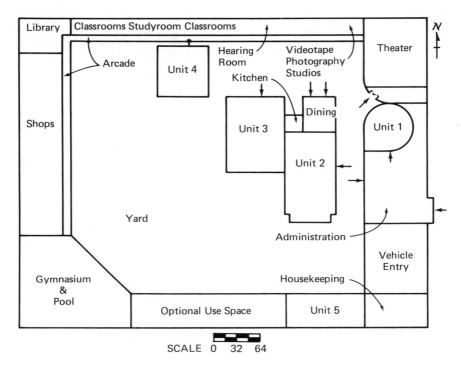

SCALE 0   32   64

Figure 6-1. The Secure Treatment Unit

shared by both staff and residents alike. And it stands as a visible symbol to the community of a jurisdiction's commitment to serious intervention in life-style juvenile criminality.

What follows is a necessarily brief "walk-through" of the Secure Treatment Unit (STU). We will trace the path of several different potential residents simultaneously as they progress through the STU as a means of illustrating the unit's unique features. However, it should be understood that the relationship between structure and function is a variable one, and that an essential feature of the STU is its adaptability to varying inputs. The walk-through is generalized; it would be specific only for a specific individual and rigidity is *not* a characteristic the designers have sought or, hopefully, achieved.

The residential candidate enters the Secure Treatment Unit: We will assume, for the purposes of this narrative, that all the juveniles whose case histories preceded this section have been referred to the STU by an appropriate court. Some will have come directly from the courthouse (such as Raymond), some from other institutions (such as Elmer), and some from other facilities (such as John, having been found "competent" at a mental health diagnostic facility). This is not the place to discuss the legality of transfers like Elmer because, as practitioners, we are well aware that legal maneuvers are time-consuming and that any functioning unit will have to deal with new arrivals whose very presence on the unit is being litigated elsewhere. All the juveniles in the case histories will be placed *somewhere* within the system, and we are assuming at least a temporary Secure Treatment Unit placement, for illustrative purposes only, not as a prediction or value judgment of the efficacy of such placement.

All new arrivals will enter through the Vehicle Entry located at the lower right quadrant of figure 6-2, the blow-up of the Administration Area (first floor). The viewer will note that the unit utilizes an "air-lock" system, which simply means that only one door is open at any one time. As the transport vehicle enters the proper area (following a closed-circuit telephone contact with Control), an electronic eye trips a Polaroid camera and the vehicle is photographed so as to include its license plate; the time of arrival is superimposed on the photograph. This is to eliminate any possible institutional responsibility for lapses of time involving the transportation of a juvenile. (For example, if the juvenile has been taken into custody and his attorney has notified the authorities he is not to be questioned, many jurisdictions simply do not permit *any* questioning even if *Miranda* warnings are given and acknowledged.[2] If the transportation journey is to take approximately one hour, and the time of leaving the original holding area is logged, the actual time of arrival will indicate the actual elapsed time in transport, thereby preventing any allegations that there were unscheduled stops along the way, presumably to question the juvenile.) In addition, the STU keeps such records so as to establish some baseline times from point of entry to admission to the Medical Unit. Such baselines are important in order to continually monitor efficiency and to make valid predictions as to the feasibility of accomplishing varying tasks within specific time frames in the future.

Once the transport vehicle has entered the proper space, the outer door closes behind it. Control, (speaking through a speaker system into the entryway), then directs the transport officers to step out of the car with the juvenile and to stand in plain view. The juvenile is to be handcuffed at this point (although he will undoubtedly have been handcuffed throughout the journey), and the officers are directed to stand away from the car with its doors closed. They are then directed to walk towards the door to Control, and their movements are monitored through a large lexan[3] window located in the wall between Control and Vehicle Entry. If there is any movement from the transport car after the officers and the juvenile have begun their walk towards the door, the door remains closed and the room remains sealed until a suitable explanation is forthcoming. Assuming no movement, the officers and the juvenile are passed through the door into Control. At this point, Control will call for two staff members from the Medical Unit whose task it will be to accompany

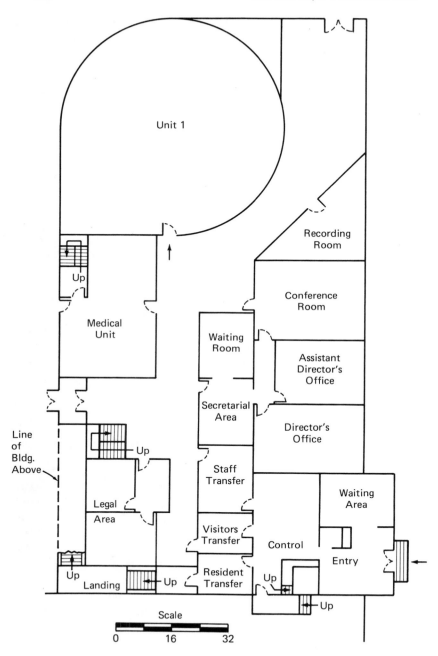

Figure 6-2. Administration Area

the juvenile from Control through the Resident Transfer area through the connecting corridor and into the Medical Unit. The officers may not go beyond Control unless they surrender their weapons, and most will elect not to do so. In Control, the transport officers officially sign over custody to the Unit, and are free to leave once the Vehicle Entry area is cleared for departure using the same procedures (including a departure photograph). The handcuffs are removed in Control, and the two staff members take the resident into the Resident Transfer area where a thorough search is completed. At the point where the handcuffs are removed, there are two transport officers, two staff workers, and a minimum of two Control personnel present, thereby minimizing any difficulties with a last-minute escape attempt, and minimizing any potential physical disputes between the juveniles and the transport officers.

After the search, the resident is escorted down the corridor to the Medical Unit, where he will undergo a complete medical examination. The STU is particularly concerned with communicable diseases, and the resident will be tested for the presence of syphilis, gonorrhea, tuberculosis, and other common illnesses. No new residents will be accepted during "change-of-shift" or when there are visitors in the Administration Area so as to minimize the possibility of conflict.

The Medical Unit: The Medical Unit serves not only as a medical diagnostic area, but also as a temporary infirmary for those residents who can be successfully treated within the Secure Treatment Unit. The Medical Unit is not a hospital, but it will be equipped with everything necessary to provide emergency treatment. Because medications are necessarily present, as well as surgical instruments, hypodermic needles, and other items likely to be highly valued by (and potentially dangerous to) the resident population, it is designated a high-security area. Therefore, in keeping with Secure Treatment Unit philosophy, security will be provided by *personnel,* not just by hardware.

The resident will be isolated in the Medical Unit for approximately two to five days, depending on the sufficiency and recency of prior medical diagnostic workups. During this time, he will also be evaluated by the resident psychiatric staff, and a final determination will be made as to whether or not to involve him in the unit's overall program.

We will assume, for the purposes of this illustration, that the STU would accept Raymond, Sam, Max, Roberto, Chris, and Toby without question. The unit would have questions about Louie, Henry, John, Percy, and Elmer. We will further assume that the unit would eventually decide to accept Louie, Henry, and Elmer, and exclude John and Percy.

Unit One: Those juveniles accepted by the STU would leave the Medical Unit directly for Unit Two. Those not accepted proceed to Unit One, and it is this unit we will examine first.

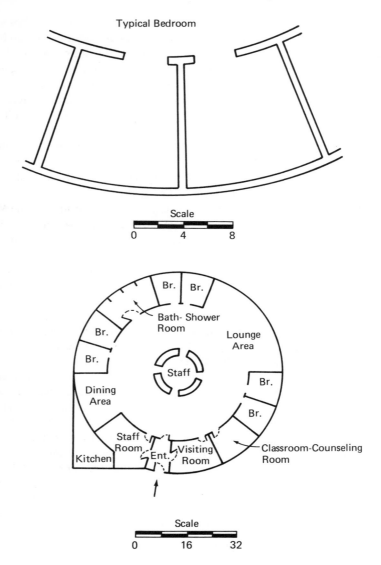

Figure 6-3. Unit One

Unit One (see figure 6-3) is a multipurpose structure, designed to care for and hold juveniles placed within it for a variety of reasons. But its unifying theme is security and safety; it is designed so that escape is virtually impossible, and so that it is equally impossible to commit an act of violence against another resident. Unit One is small and circular specifically so that there are no sharp corners behind which to hide; the staff area is designed so that staff sit or stand facing each other, with each staff member having the obligation to cover his partner's back. Space for the residents to circulate is deliberately limited, and there is a strict, inviolable limitation of one resident to one sleeping area. The walls are all covered in a material such as Royalite, a firm yet slightly yielding material designed to absorb tremendous impact without injury. There is a plexiglas dome over the unit, set some 35 feet above ground level, to provide natural light, and recessed lighting is used in each bedroom and throughout the remainder of the unit. There is no access between Unit One's kitchen and the dining area other than a serving window which is large enough only to admit stacked trays, and kitchen staff do not enter the rest of Unit One. Maximum surveillance of the residents is possible (and mandatory) at all times, but a degree of privacy is provided by the structure of the bedrooms, which are equipped with sliding doors controlled by staff. The only room furnishings are a concrete platform bed which is part of the structure itself, topped with a special innerspring mattress permanently sealed in a "breathing" but untear-able vinyl, and a similarly bolted chair with similarly constructed padding. Desks and easy chairs are provided in the Lounge Area only. The bedrooms draw light and air from the bubble-type skylight that covers the entire unit. This skylight, although permanently set in place, has openings to increase ventilation as required. The unit has a central heating and cooling system. The high ceilings not only chill the possibility of escape (which, even if accomplished, would still leave the resident safely inside the overall structure of the STU), but add to a sense of spaciousness.

In addition to physical security, Unit One has special procedures, such as not permitting more than two residents in the bath/shower rooms at the same time, utilizing easily breakable plastic eating utensils, and constant movement and alertness of staff.

Residents will be in Unit One for one of three major reasons:

1. "Turn-around" residents who will eventually be placed in another facility by virtue of being found unsuitable for the Secure Treatment Unit (STU) *at Intake* (it will *not* be used to house residents to be transferred from the STU's *program* to another institution because such an option simply does not exist. For example, Percy has been found unsuitable for the program within the STU, but another placement has not been located immediately. He cannot be temporarily placed with Unit Two, because that unit functions on an established curriculum, and Percy would not only be disruptive, but would force the staff and program into adaptive behavior of their own, something to be avoided at all costs. So there must be a safe place for Percy to await a transfer. We would advocate a legislative rule requiring that such turn-arounds be housed no more than five days within the STU and that, following that period, it be mandatory that the state authorities retake jurisdiction. However, we also strongly believe that the time spent waiting for that transfer should not be "dead-time" and even Unit One has a program of its own. Percy would be visited by counselors on a

regular basis; he would have the opportunity to interact with staff and, to a limited extent, other residents, he would be given the opportunity to express his feelings (and his fears) about the new placement to which he would be sent, he could be visited by his family or representatives of other programs or agencies, and his time would be productively occupied. The STU also believes that it could materially assist other potential placements by continuing its psychiatric workup while the turn-around resident was within its care.

2. Suicide threats: those residents who had actually attempted, or threatened, suicide would be placed within Unit One. Unit One is uniquely designed to prevent suicides because of the lack of opportunity, the lack of sufficient materials, and the training of Unit One staff. But suicide prevention will not consist of mere security; again, there will be an opportunity for the counseling, therapeutic, and psychiatric staffs to speak with the potential suicide on a regular basis to help him work towards the point where he can rejoin the other residents in whatever unit he was living at the time he made the suicidal gesture.

3. Violence: the Secure Treatment Unit *expects* violence from its residents (see Unit Two, for example) but that does not mean that a climate of tolerance for such behavior exists. Most violent behavior will be dealt with on the unit where it occurs, in accordance with specific procedures and response-patterns which will be an integral part of the training. However, in the event that an episode of serious violence (such as a stabbing, or an attempted rape) does occur, there must be a mechanism by which the perpetrator can be temporarily removed from his living unit and involved in a period of counseling, analysis, and discipline. Unit One meets all these criteria: access to the individual will be vastly increased, his ability to act violently towards other residents will be decreased; and the very fact of his presence on the unit will serve as evidence of a radical change in his status and treatment.

This does not mean that Unit One will serve as a "punishment block," or the modern equivalent of a disciplinary cottage; it will not be any form of solitary confinement or isolation, and the resident will be continually involved in a program, but it will be the program of Unit One, not the program of the unit from which he was removed. Rights and privileges which the resident enjoyed on the other units will not be available within Unit One, and any resident placed on Unit One for reasons of violence must be returned to Unit Two when his stay is over regardless of which unit he resided in at the time of his acts.

Assignment to Unit One is seen as temporary; it will not be possible for a resident to spend his entire stay at the Secure Treatment Unit within Unit One. Of course, it is conceivable that some residents will return to Unit One time and time again, but the goal of the unit is to impact against the subculture of violence, and the continual resident of Unit One will not find his return greeted with cheers by an admiring group of peers.

The most important feature of Unit One is that it is itself a program, not merely a housing unit with a high emphasis on security and safety. The temporary resident of Unit One is no less a fit subject for counseling and rehabilitative services; his presence in the unit simply indicates that he is not responding to the other units and his removal is both for the benefit of himself and his fellow residents. The resident may perceive his removal to Unit One as punishment, and the designers are quite comfortable with this possibility. The fact is that there is a component of punishment in the removal, just as there is a component of punishment to the initial assignment to the Secure Treatment Unit. The most important aspect of the removal is that there is a direct causal relationship between a resident's actions and the STU's response. It is too well established to require documentation that certainty and speed of punishment act as a deterrent, not severity. The life-style violent juvenile has been acculturated to a world where punishment is arbitrary and capricious—he is punished when he doesn't deserve it, he is not punished when he does—but there is no functional relationship between acts and consequences. Unit One *is* a consequence: forseeable, real, and quickly implementable. Unit One *is* a deprivation, although some critics will immediately point out that deprivation is a relative term and that residents of Unit One are certainly treated better than most residents of cottage-based training schools.

To avoid the capriciousness that is the hallmark of a random system, no resident will be transferred to Unit One because of the use of violence without a hearing, in a special room provided for this purpose in the north wing of the STU. In this hearing the resident will be represented by a counselor of his choice from the staff. It will be an adversarial procedure in that he will have an opportunity to confront witnesses against him and to be heard. No transfer will take place unless in the judgment of the hearing officer a distinct violation of clearly disclosed rules has actually taken place.

At this point, we should note that many of the problems inherent in prison hearings will not be present here. Typically, such hearings consist of an informant's testimony, with the identity of the informant being concealed to protect him from retaliation. With his identity concealed, he cannot be cross-examined, and such hearings tend to be relatively pro forma matters. Within the Secure Treatment Unit, no such procedure is possible, because transfer to Unit One is based *only* upon demonstrable evidence of violence or other violation of the STU's life-rules.[4] No informant's testimony is ever permitted in such matters, and it is the task of the staff to be sufficiently vigilant to detect such violations themselves. No institution will ever be conceived that lacks informants; it is not necessary for the STU's administration to recruit such individuals for they serve at their own pleasure and for their own reasons. However, informants probably do more to confound administration than to assist it, and the STU will not be run in such a manner as to encourage or reward informing. The hearing is necessary to impart a sense of justice, and as a check-and-balance on the staff members actually making the complaint. Since only the most substantive violations are punishable by transfer to Unit One, it is unlikely that the world of innuendos and hints will surface to punish a wrongdoer incorrectly—so, if a staff member lodges a complaint found to be unwarranted, he will find that "the door swings both ways."

Unit Two: Those residents who pass immediately from the Medical Unit into Unit Two will find themselves in the heart of the program. Unit Two (see figure 6-4) is designed around the principle that resocialization, not rehabilitation, is a necessary component of the future street-survival of the life-style violent juvenile. Here the emphasis is on affective development, or the way in which the

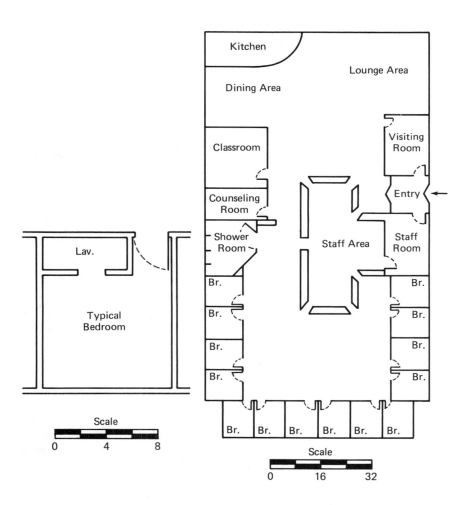

Figure 6-4. Unit Two

juvenile presents himself to the outside world. This unit is physically designed to prevent serious and dangerous violence, but also to provide a learning laboratory within which the resident can experiment with functional ways of surviving without the constant employment of violence. The unit is *not* simply a larger version of Unit One; the opportunities for interpersonal violence are greater, and the degree of staff surveillance/supervision is somewhat lower. The staff-resident ratio is highest in Unit One, and drops with each succeeding unit. However, the opportunity for violence is somewhat illusory: heavy hardware is not utilized to prevent personal contact between residents, yet staff is ready, willing, and able to immediately and effectively intervene when violence does appear. Without this opportunity, there can be no real learning experience for the life-style violent juvenile; if he is so restricted by hardware (for example, as in solitary confinement) that violence is physically impossible, he can never learn how to function in an environment (such as any community) where such restrictions are not part of the overall life-style.

This is not to say that Unit Two encourages violence between residents. Unit Two is designed as a testing/learning environment, and staff are armed with the expectation that the residents are more prone to violence than to any other method of settling disputes, gaining access to goods and services, and achieving prestige and status. The difference between Unit Two and the residents' home communities (and between Unit Two and other institutions) is that the violence to be expected on Unit Two will not be without consequence. The life-style violent juvenile cannot, at the beginning stage of his development and socialization, learn from books, or from lectures. He can only hope to learn from experience and, indeed, his current method of doing business is a product of that experience. If all possibility of interpersonal violence is suppressed, the juvenile will simply focus on how to subvert any system devised to contain him—and intervening in secretive violence is very difficult indeed. But if the juvenile is presented with what he originally perceives as an opportunity to conduct business-as-usual, he will avail himself of this chance and reveal himself in the process.

By revealing himself, he will also expose himself to sanctions. And, perhaps for the first time in his life, the juvenile will find that the sanctions are a direct consequence of his acts and, even more importantly, that their severity varies with his attitude towards them. For example, if one resident is attacking another resident, there will be immediate intervention. The extent to which the resident resists that intervention is the extent to which that intervention will be physical. But we want to be clear that no physical "discipline" will take place on this unit, or in any part of the STU. No physical punishments will be utilized at any time, it being our belief that such punishments are degrading and counterproductive.

However, this is not to say that there will be no physical response by staff when the situation demands such response. And there is no promise that either staff or residents will be entirely exempt from physical injury. We believe that the possibility of serious injury can be greatly reduced through the employment of proper techniques,[5] but anyone who would guarantee that our contemplated population could be housed on a long-term basis while being subjected to the stress of confinement and the tension of "treatment" without occasional violence resulting in injury would be a fool.

Indeed, some environmental stress will be deliberately introduced on Unit Two. Since affective development is a key ingredient of the program in this unit, there will be deliberate pressure placed on given juveniles who have revealed their individual "triggers." If a juvenile has repeatedly displayed an inability to react to certain stimuli without serious violence, those very stimuli will be deliberately introduced to test the effects of socialization and affective development as he progresses.

There will be no attempt to measure affective development; we leave that to the fund raisers and their ilk. Rather, instead of an ill-defined "program," Unit Two will have a specific *curriculum*. Simply stated, this means that all residents will have specific tasks to complete before being deemed eligible for Unit Three. It additionally means that some will complete those tasks more quickly than others; that some will not complete those tasks at all. But the philosophy of the STU demands that there be no "social promotions" within its walls; there will be no rewards to residents for acting like "good inmates." Progress will be based on actual accomplishment, not effort (or the appearance of same).

The curriculum in Unit Two will require x number of hours exposure to various inputs and, when this exposure is fully completed, the curriculum will be deemed fulfilled and the resident can move on to Unit Three. It sounds simple: but the problem in forward movement will be that some juveniles will not tolerate the exposure quietly; some will react with violence and some will react with fear. This response will inhibit participation (which must be voluntary), and, as a result, some will be extremely slow to complete the curriculum.

Unit Two will have heavy emphasis on the life-rules of the institution: no violence, no coercive sex, and no drugs. Contraband such as weapons will come under the ban against violence and will be spelled out under the full disclosure method of treatment.[6] This method simply takes nothing for granted; it assumes no operational assumptions on the part of the participants in the treatment and, in turn, promises no surprises to such participants when sanctions or rewards are distributed.

The goal of this unit is not to have the residents memorize a complex set of rules, but to live by basic rules in an assimilative, behavioral way. There will be no written or verbal tests of newly acquired skills and knowledge, but there will be constant (and escalating) experiential testing. Part of this testing will be deliberately confrontive, and part will be forceful (and sometimes forced) examination of values and attitudes. It is not enough for the STU to post rules against sexual assaults; it is not even enough to punish the perpetrators of such assaults; it is not enough even to ruthlessly expel the sexually assaultive culture from within the walls: it is also necessary to ensure the residents that they enjoy a degree of safety from such attacks so that they will not need to arm themselves or be constantly on the alert and, perhaps most important of all, it is necessary that former perpetrators of such acts (in other institutions) have the opportunity to examine their motivations and to be confronted about their attitudes.

The sexually assaultive juvenile who tells others that his behavior is motivated by lack of access to women is a liar; and he must be confronted with his lies if he is to change the behavior. The juvenile who attributes such behavior to peer pressure must be helped towards the strength to resist that pressure. The juvenile who correctly understands his motivations, and expresses them by seeking a more secure place in the exploitation hierarchy of the institution must be shown that such behavior is maladaptive in *this* environment and will be dealt with severely. And the former victim of such assaults who now seeks to change his status by assaulting those weaker than himself, or who fears a repetition of the attacks unless he "switches from catching to pitching" must be given programmatic (as opposed to merely verbal) assurances that he is, perhaps for the first time inside an institution, free to act as a human being without risk to himself.

We have found it is far easier to confront negative behavior as it happens, and to deal with its implications during the fallout from the actual event. Life-style violent juveniles are notoriously unable to abstract; this is not an intellectual deficiency but a cultural one. Such a juvenile is reality-oriented to the nth degree, and his behavior has been orchestrated along similar lines. The STU cannot hope to teach abstract morality; but it can hope to teach a functioning morality similar to that which evolved in primitive societies for their own protection. A juvenile forcibly restrained from the act of injuring another resident will not perceive that his actions were "wrong," but only that they displeased the ruling forces of the institution. If the stakes of this game are sufficiently raised, he will desist from this behavior because the price is now too high. But his attitude will not have changed. There are those who might argue that behavioral change is sufficient, as exemplified by this perhaps allegorical story recounted by a street worker to a group of juvenile gang members:

> When I went to college in the South it wasn't like it is now; being black meant you just plain had less rights than the next man.
>
> Now the college was just outside of this little town, and every Friday night these white boys from the fraternities would cruise on into what they called "Niggertown" (which was the black part of this little city) and raise hell . . . they'd smash windows, get drunk, beat on people, and they even raped a girl every now and then.
>
> Now they'd go *every* Friday night, right? One night they all go down there and, when they get back to the college, they find that two of their guy's are missing. The police found these two guys the next day, lying in some alley with their heads chopped off.
>
> After that, they never went into Niggertown again.

The juveniles immediately reacted to the story. Most expressed satisfaction at the results with comments such as "that was righteous work!" and "good for the motherfuckers!"

But the skilled counselor then led them to an examination of their own actions, the very actions that had brought them into repeated trouble with the law. And he asked: if that response was considered appropriate, then wouldn't it be just as appropriate for local community residents to kill some of the juveniles who had been terrorizing their communities? Reactions to this were mixed: but most of the juveniles continued to defend their actions on the ground that they had terrorized their *own* communities, not some foreign area. The counselor pointed out that the actions of the white fraternity members were patently against the law; but that didn't stop them. And he pointed out that those actions were completely eradicated without a single change in the law. "It's just that the people in Niggertown upped the stakes, right?" The juveniles could see where the conversation was going, and became vehement and uncomfortable, and the group broke up with several individual argument/discussions among the juveniles themselves. When the counselor was asked why he didn't "bring the discussion to a conclusion," he replied that his goal was to give the residents "something to think about," and he expressed the belief that "they'd be back" to continue the discussion on their own. He was correct.

But even as Unit Two is working on the affective development of its residents, it is ever-mindful that certain aspects of protective security cannot be ignored. Therefore, for certain key areas, security is both designed-in and staff-provided. Take, for example, the shower room. (See figure 6-5.) One veteran prisoner reacted to our proposed re-designs by saying:

> Man, I don't know *what* some of them jockers [aggressive homosexuals] would do if there was showers in each room like you say. I guess they'll always find *some* way, but that'd make it tough on them.[7]

The Unit Two shower room is specially designed, with partitions to separate individual residents, and utilizes a V-shaped base so that a single staff member can easily observe the entire room. Its walls will be lined with the same material used in the Unit One rooms, and access will be limited to four residents at any one time. Because of the room's special design, the four residents will be, in effect, showering individually, and will remain separated by the waist-high partitions throughout. The showers will be open and available during certain morning and evening hours, and residents will be accommodated on a "first come-first served" basis. This will (as is typical of Secure Treatment Unit innovations) increase management burdens on staff, but, at the same time, provide more real-world (and hence less institutional) experiences for the residents.

The reason for the specially designed shower room is not just to prevent

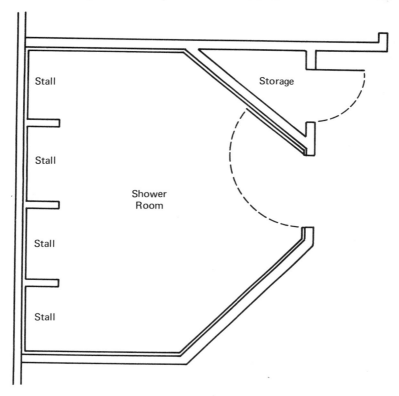

Figure 6-5. The Shower Room

sexual assaults. As with many features of the Secure Treatment Unit, it is designed to transmit the continual message that certain behaviors will not be tolerated, even *sub rosa,* within its boundaries.

There is no question but that institutional design will influence institutional behavior. There is no question but that some institutions appear to have more suicides than others, and some institutions are more prone to escapes. While it is true, as one of our sources previously stated, that individuals seeking to do damage to themselves or others will "find a way"[8] in spite of any precautions, our concern is to make that objective as difficult as possible. But our primary emphasis is on the peer-influenced marginal juvenile who can be deterred from negative action by structure as well as by physical intervention. As previously stated, the goal is not the utter elimination of negative behavior, but the elimination of that behavior which could have serious consequences *within* the institution while, at the same time, working on other violent behaviors with a view towards de-escalating their later appearance on the streets.

A closed institution may adopt one or more of the following response-attitudes towards resident violence:

1. Approval
2. Total inaction
3. Prevention (by structure or personnel)
4. Intervention
5. Punishment

An institution that adopts either (1) or (2) above is probably also in the process of *utilizing* resident violence, either as a form of management control or as a means to attack potential inmate solidarity. An institution that employs (5) exclusively will find the deterrent properties of pure punishment somewhat deficient. Indeed, most institutions that actually employ options (1) or (2) or both, would claim that option (5) is its chosen method.

The Secure Treatment Unit makes its heaviest investment in options (3) and (4), with strongest emphasis on the latter. If option (3) is totally successful, we will have achieved only the kind of arrested development of violent behavior that some institutions erroneously label "success" in treatment. Unless life-style violent juveniles experience, and learn from, specialized and skillful *intervention* in violence, unless they perceive violence as something less than a successful tool, the Unit will have only delayed the inevitable. Since we believe that the net effects of the Secure Treatment Unit will manifest themselves in the larger society, and not within the institution's walls, this would not be acceptable.

Unit Two places relatively low emphasis on education per se for the same reason that it has low expectations in terms of so-called "rehabilitation" at this level. It is our belief that *no* change is possible without the active participation of the juvenile himself, and Unit Two is dedicated only to achieving a suitable "state of readiness' for such participation. Reduced to simplistic terms, there are two basic methods to induce behavioral change in humans: one way is to channel the behavior by the systematic narrowing of options so that the recipient (*not* participant) is more or less forced into what is deemed a suitable path; the other way is to systematically expand the individual's optional range of behaviors to make him aware that there are more paths to his perceived goals and felt needs that he formerly realized. Unit Two attempts to distinguish between behavior and motivation, and further attempts to distinguish between those juveniles for whom behavior *is* motivation (such as Percy) and those for whom behavior is controlled by his motivations (such as Max). There are those individuals who pursue socially acceptable goals (such as the acquisition of material goods) in antisocial ways (such as robbery). Such individuals, when made aware of the risks and consequences inherent in their behavior, can be motivated to experiment with new methods of achieving their desired goals. And there are those for whom motivation and behavior are indistinguishable, such as the acting-out sex offender, where socially acceptable attainment of goals is virtually impossible.[9]

The life-style violent juvenile generally falls into the former category. Of course, not all motivations are as readily distinguishable from behavior as those of the thief: many life-style violent juveniles are equally motivated by a need for peer acceptance, an inability to perceive consequences *or* the future, and, finally, fear in all its forms. Unit Two is designed to reduce fear (but not to induce complacency), to enhance the ability to perceive the future (by both accelerating and escalating consequences of behavior, both positive and negative), and to utilize several methods of impact on peer pressure, including peer-group therapy, role models, transference, and individualized counseling.

In most juvenile training schools, there are at least two operating sets of rules: management sets up the most visible rules, and the inmate subculture establishes still another functioning set. Since the inmates generally manage the institution, the inmates' subcultural rules generally are more closely obeyed. This is not, however, to say that management concerns are ignored, since the institution will manage to enforce its self-interest through the process of creating (and occasionally destroying) inmate leadership. For example, all institutions have rules against forcible rape, yet many permit (or even encourage) this practice as a way of placating the most powerful inmates. Those inmates, in turn, focus their energies on exploiting their fellow prisoners, and cause no difficulties for management. James Carr, a veteran California prisoner later infamous for his assaultive confrontations with guards and other inmates (and since murdered while on parole) described the reaction of a juvenile institution when he and his fellow exploiters had raped another inmate:

> Hocker [a guard] was fiendish. He'd put us in AC [solitary] for ripping off [raping] Abernathy, yet he threw Abernathy in there too. And right in with the rest of us, *not* in protective custody, thereby setting us all up for a repeat performance.
>
> Abernathy never came out of his cell, but a week after we arrived we discovered he was right down the tier from us. Most everyone started harassing him right away, calling him "girl" and "punk" and yelling how they'd kill him; but I wrote him a real nice letter about how it's cold-blooded what had happened, and what we're gonna do is clear it all up since it's no use us fighting among ourselves. Come to the yard tomorrow, I told him, and we'll resolve it.
>
> Abernathy found us at the domino table. I slapped him on the back in greeting. Lee-Bug [a confederate] told him he wanted to talk things over in the latrine. When they got there, Lee-Bug slapped him around and raped him. Then we ran a train of twenty guys through there. By the time we were done it was time for lockup.
>
> Abernathy came out of the latrine looking highly confused. Spotting the cop on yard duty, he ran over and hugged him, crying that he'd

been raped. The cop freaked out, yelling, "Let go of me!" Only after he'd peeled Abernathy off did he ask what'd happened.

"They RAPED me!" the kid sobbed. The cop asked where; Abernathy replied that it was in the latrine. But the cop wouldn't go for that, because if it got reported it would mean he wasn't doing his job. So he told Abernathy to shut up and go to his cell.

Lee-Bug smiled and said to the cop, "I don't know what's wrong with that kid, boss."

Abernathy never came out of his cell again, and gradually went out of his head. He never saw a soul—people just took out their frustrations by yelling down the tier at him. Pretty soon he was shitting on the floor and pissing in his pants. The shrink examined him and had him shipped off to Atascadero [a California institution for sex offenders!] .[10]

Carr's attitude towards this incident is typical of the life-style violent juvenile with heavy institutional experience: the strong survive, the weak go under; might makes right; the institution will let you do as you wish if you don't make trouble for the authorities. As Carr's "career" progressed institutionally, he acquired a political focus to his actions (including a close friendship with George Jackson while in Soledad and San Quentin). Although the viciousness of his actions while a juvenile were obvious, he seemed to inspire no anger or even animosity among the guards; but as his actions changed from the grossly exploitative to the political, he quickly became the object of institutional and authoritarian anger and went from being a "good inmate" to a frequent inhabitant of solitary confinement. So long as his violence was turned against other inmates, it was tolerated and even encouraged; when it turned against the ruling structure of the institution, it was dealt with ruthlessly.

Unit Two will not tolerate exploitative behavior; neither will it tolerate attacks on staff members. As a result, staff on Unit Two will be personally engaged in physical interaction with the residents to a far greater degree than in most training schools; the price of refusing to allow residents to run amok is actual participation in the process of stopping this behavior. It is not an easy way to manage an institution; left to their own devices, all inmate populations will self-structure, and violence (against institutional personnel) will be thereby minimized. Violence between residents will, however, be a constant factor.

To avoid self-structuring (around a subculture of violence and exploitation), Unit Two will publish, display, and enforce a conspicuous set of rules that might seem puzzling, or even repressive, to the uninitiated observer. For example, no borrowing of any personal possessions will be allowed by and between the residents. Some might say that such a heavy restriction interferes with personal interactions, and is likely to inhibit the kind of friendly gestures that youth would naturally make towards one another. However, "borrowing" is often nothing more than a euphemism for outright extortion, with the extorted victim having to choose between losing his property or informing. In fact, one whose valuables (even, for example, a portable radio) have been taken is given very limited options within a conventional training school: he can either do nothing in response, accept the exploitation, and the accompanying loss of status, and at the same time prepare himself as best he can for the inevitable escalation of that exploitation once his new lowered status becomes apparent to the rest of the population; or he can inform on the perpetrator of the theft, exposing himself to ridicule, even lower status, and possible physical danger (if, in fact, he is not simply ignored by institutional personnel who tell him "that's *your* problem"); or he can physically attack the perpetrator and, if successful, regain not only his lost property but his lost status. All things are brutally proportional inside a juvenile prison: if a youth has his radio stolen, socially acceptable revenge might consist of a (successful) physical attack against the thief; and if a juvenile is raped, appropriate revenge could be *no less than* stabbing the perpetrator, with homicide certainly not beyond the expectations of all involved.

With no borrowing permitted, mere possession of something that does not belong to a given juvenile subjects him to punishment regardless of any explanation and regardless of the source of that explanation. A cynic will immediately point out the possibility of "planting" such contraband on an enemy; and we concede that this possibility exists. Unit Two is not designed (and cannot be designed) to functionally exclude all possibilities of negative behavior. Some behaviors, like sexual assaults, will be suppressed by staff or architectural design, or both; some behaviors, such as petty theft, will be limited to the extent possible; and some behaviors, such as direct physical attack unaided by weapons *will* happen: both against other residents and against staff.

Unit Two will not expect to eliminate such expressions of violence, but will use those expressions as tools, as jumping off points to express the new culture of the institution and to express, in the most graphic terms, the consequences and risks inherent in such actions.

The reader will note that, unlike Unit One, residents of Unit Two have individual toilet facilities (although shower facilities are still shared). This is not a reward for being in Unit Two since the great majority of the residents will never have seen Unit One: Unit Two is where the process *begins,* and the individualized toilets are designed to provide privacy and safety for the residents. Certain basic human rights: family visitation, uncensored mail, adequate food, light, air, space, cleanliness, and recreation are to be guaranteed to all residents regardless of their behavior while in the STU. Deprivation of basic human rights accomplishes nothing and only underscores the feelings of hatred and the desire for revenge that are already brewing in our residents. Such punishments are ineffective, because they are not perceived as punishments but as the expression of the will of a stronger force.

Unit Two is fully self-contained because it is, as we previously stated, a learning laboratory for the residents—and the main thing to be learned is a form of socialization that permits human interaction without the use of violence as a tool. The unit is designed so that activities are omnipresent. We want to avoid the usual picture of television-sedated juveniles free to establish and maintain their own culture and hierarchies without impact by the staff. To this end, another rule is simply that the television set is not to be turned on during the daylight hours (that is, before suppertime) for any reason. Similarly, the recreational facilities (such as table tennis, billiards, games, and so forth) can be utilized only during specified hours. Access to the gymnasium and the pool are similarly restricted, as is the use of the yard. These devices could be rehabilitative aids, or they could be ways of avoiding staff responsibility. Rather than constantly monitor the ways in which they are utilized, we choose to restrict the utilization, leaving the burden on the staff to involve (not entertain) the residents during the remainder of their working hours.

Unit Three: When juveniles have completed the curriculum on Unit Two, they are eligible for admission to Unit Three (see figure 6-6). This unit represents some radical departures from the previous unit in terms of design and program. First of all, and most obviously apparent to new residents, is the fact that the space allotted to each individual is vastly increased (see figure 6-7). Rather than occupying a single room (or, if you prefer, cell), the juveniles now occupy mini-suites that are completely self-contained, including stall shower facilities. A separate dining room is provided *off* the unit, which accommodates all residents from Units Three, Four, and Five. Unlike Unit Two, Unit Three has three floors, and is designed to resemble, in so far as is practicable, a small apartment complex. The extra room and features are not solely to reward successful completion of Unit Two; they have other, more far-reaching uses as the following exerpt from an interview with a veteran prisoner reveals:

> You want to know what an institutional man is? He's the kind of guy who comes in here talking about he's going to get him some pussy when he hits the bricks . . . but you talk to him just before he goes home and *now* he's talking about getting some ass. This may sound the same thing to *you*, O.K.?, but to *me* he's saying he's developed a taste for boy-butt after being here so long. And another way to recognize this guy on the street; he'll *always* rent him a furnished room, or maybe a studio apartment or something like that. But *always* one room, you understand? He's too used to the joint to deal with more than one room. The institutional man lives *here*, you understand? Being on the bricks is nothing but a vacation for him; they might as well keep his fucking room waiting for him.[11]

Most management-motivated institutional personnel actually have a strong vested interest in the creation of the "institutional man." Such a prisoner tends to be tractable and compliant, "does his own time," and is never an administrative problem. The STU cannot afford such management-motivated investments

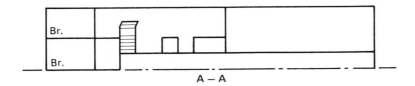

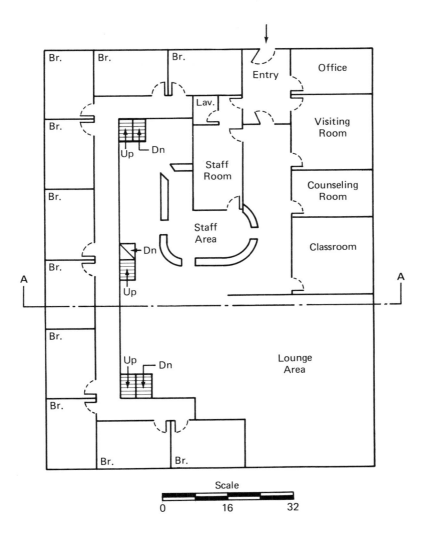

Figure 6-6. Unit Three

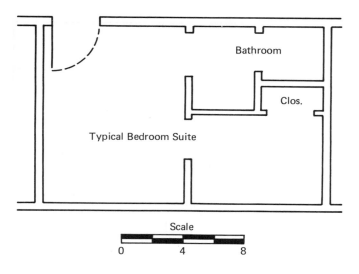

Figure 6-7. Individual Space in Unit Three

because the product of such an investment is a juvenile whose actual dangerous-ness to society is not decreased, but potentially increased. Part of the prepara-tion for the outside world is knowledge of more than institutional life. This is one of the many focuses of Unit Three. Another, no less important, focus is the emphasis on vocational and educational training. When affective development and socialization are sufficiently advanced, the resident will be placed in a combined work/study situation within the STU. Residents of Unit Three will have more of life's privileges, and more of life's responsibilities too. For example, residents of this unit will be permitted to select their own furniture from a list of available items when they enter the unit for the first time. This furniture will be new, and will belong to them. If they move to Unit Four, they will take it with them; if they move back to Unit Two, it will be placed in storage. If they destroy it, it will not be replaced.

In addition, residents of Unit Three will work in one of the shop assignments, and will be paid according to their worth on such assignments. Progress will be measured individually, and the emphasis will be on those trades which can readily translate into paid employment in their home communities: auto-body-fender shop repair, basic electricity, plumbing, carpentry, printing, and general maintenance. Those who refuse any work assignment will be returned to Unit Two, however a resident may choose to work part of the time and attend school for the remainder. No resident will be permitted to remain on Unit Three without *some* ongoing investment in work and study,[12] but such residents will enjoy increased social and recreational opportunities as well. The correlation to the real world is both obvious and intended. For example, the visiting room on Unit Three is far more spacious and well-furnished than that on Unit Two; there is increased opportunity (due to the spaciousness and the layout of furnishings) for privacy, and residents may receive visitors other than immediate family members and attorneys. For a mother who has never had an agency report on her son that was not utterly negative, it will be a genuine shock to visit him on Unit Three and note the immediate and obvious improvement in his surroundings. When she questions her son as to the reasons for this drastic improvement, he will be able to tell her (with complete honesty) that this improvement is directly attributable to his own progress as a human being. The message should have far greater impact than any written report, no matter how positive.

While on the subject of visits, we should state at this point our position regarding the STU's involvement in such activities. We firmly believe that the STU must not only provide as liberal a visitation policy as possible, but that its out-reach component must physically transport family members to the unit. Why do we take this position? The only way to learn if family members are genuinely interested in the welfare and progress of their son is to provide maximum opportunities to express that interest. Too many juveniles do not receive visits simply because their parents lack the financial resources to make the trip. This is, in fact, one of the few arguments in favor of community-based programs for life-style violent juveniles with which we agree. Equally important, however, are those parents who have no interest in their children and use the difficulty of visitation as an excuse. Only by directly providing visitation services to the home communities can the STU assist concerned parents in their common goal of rehabilitation and, at the same time, learn which parents can be relied upon to participate in the continuing program after the juvenile is released. The significance of this latter judgment will become more apparent as we discuss Units Four and Five.

Unit Three is a better place to live than Unit Two and it is intended to be so. It represents a legitimate step up in the overall institutional hierarchy, and each step up represents in itself a step away from conventional institutional norms. While the emphasis here is on cognitive and vocational learning, affective development and experiential learning continue to play significant roles. Figure 6-8 illustrates the changing significance of the various roles as the resident progresses through the STU.

Unit Three further provides a testing ground for the socialization process that was initiated in Unit Two. Holding a "job" in a traditional institution usually requires very little in the way of good work habits (although many promoters of this much overrated rehabilitative tool will speak in glowing terms of "learning the importance of showing up on time ready to work" in spite of the fact that institutions rarely permit an inmate the freedom of movement to do anything *but* "show up on time").

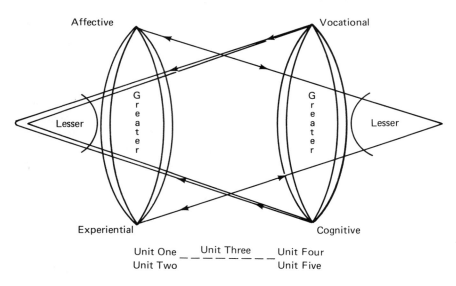

Figure 6-8. Changing Emphasis of Developmental Inputs as the Resident Progresses Through the Secure Treatment Unit

The residents of Unit Three will be exposed to vocational requirements which are a close approximation of any outside experience. Pay scales will be adjusted in terms of the resident's value to each work assignment, and that work assignment will function as a profit-making business. Of course, residents will not experience some of the negative aspects of outside employment—they will not be laid off because of lack of work, and working conditions will doubtless be superior to many they might encounter in the community. But their pay will be correlated to their ability: a resident who exhibits skill in carpentry will be moved into the more complex aspects of that shop, and will be paid accordingly. And a resident who either refuses to work, or displays an attitude inconsistent with that which would be tolerated on the outside, will be dismissed. A resident dismissed from one shop will have the opportunity to work in other shops, but the choices within the STU (as the choices in the real world) are somewhat limited, and a work assignment is a requirement to remain on Unit Three.

One of the essential problems of any closed institution is the lack of communication between residents and staff. The more liberal programs attempt to solve this problem by "opening the lines of communication" through a variety of verbal mechanisms: encounter groups, "community meetings," general discussions, and scheduled counseling sessions. The STU proposes to add a new dimension to communication by allowing the residents to indicate their positions in nonverbal fashion. Too much premium is placed upon the ability to articulate, and we are not interested in developing more members for the "new breed" of institutional man:

> The "new breed" knows how to play the man's game. If there's a new [therapy] group, this guy's in it. If there's a new way of talking, this guy's down with it. If it's in to call niggers your "black brothers," that's O.K. with him. This guy goes to school, takes all kind of correspondence courses, gets chumps to write to him off those lists [names of "persons interested in correspondence with prisoners" posted on a board in the "center room"], puts fucking *ads* in the paper asking for people to write to him [a sample ad: Black male Scorpio, 5'11" 175 lbs, into music, philosophy, good smoke and good people. Presently incarcerated. Would like to hear from concerned people, especially women. Age, race not important]. He goes to the [Parole] Board and confesses to everything he ever did in his miserable-ass life . . . and they deny him anyway. What a joke, right? You give some guys enough pills to swallow, or iron to push, or bullshit groups, and they're *happy* here.[13]

This new breed finds its counterpart in the juvenile institutions in young men who quickly learn the jargon of the "therapeutic community." This inmate knows that he cannot display rehabilitation too quickly; that he must be part of a "process" before his success will be institutionally endorsed (rewarded with release). Some of the old-style training schools are susceptible to a resident simply bulling his way out the door with violent behavior; others require a verbal commitment to T-group values, and a period of reformation in which the resident "gains insight" into his behavior and the reasons behind it.

But the life-style violent juvenile is not capable of playing a new game; the new game being tentatively offered (by people he does not understand and in ways he does not comprehend) is not necessarily too complex, it is simply too far removed from the present—the only dimension which he has ever occupied.

Although part of the socialization process in Unit Two would be dismissed by society as "game playing," the fact is that such new methods of behavior will still be in the experimental stage for the STU residents. The truth is that society has no reason to inquire beyond the bounds of behavior: motivations, predictions, and attitudes are beyond the legitimate concern of a society that is contracting *only* for a de-escalation in chronic violence. In fact, if residents who departed from "therapeutic communities" continued the same methods of negotiating with the system that helped them win an early release, society would be, by and large, completely satisfied. Unfortunately, such adaptive behavior does not continue past the bounds of the former "community" because the culture of that community does not sufficiently imprint itself to survive the transition back to the streets.

This latter point emphasizes the real interrelationship between Unit Two and Unit Three. To some extent, Unit Two is an artificial environment; there are forces of protection, sanction, reward, and punishment always hovering within arms length of each resident: consequences follow acts with almost frightening regularity, and behavior seems limited as, in reality, options are increasing. But Unit Three does not provide the same degree of custody, security, pressure, and instant-response. The opportunity to revert to old ways of doing business seems to be surfacing once again, yet the sanctions are more real-world than on Unit Two. Residents on Unit Three face loss of job, loss of better housing, loss of status, and so forth. But they also face a form of incarcerative treatment if violence is their response to this loss! Put another way: if a resident on Unit Three acts out within certain limits, he faces some temporary sanctions (such as loss of pay); if he escalates the acting out, he may face transfer to Unit Two; and if he returns full-scale to his former life-patterns and resorts to violence in a serious fashion, he faces transfer to Unit One for a period to be determined by the seriousness of his infraction. No resident will be transferred from Unit One to Unit Three, but the stopover on Unit Two can be as long or as brief as the resident chooses. The analogy here is to the amount of violence necessary to restrain a resident when he himself acts violently: the resident will determine this amount by his response to those staff members whose duty it is to restrain him. This participatory control over his own destiny will be one of the most difficult lessons for the life-style violent juvenile to absorb and understand.

The new dimension in communication we spoke of earlier is essentially nonverbal; the exact opposite of that demanded by the "therapeutic community." For example, the resident who finds the program on Unit Three to be beyond him, and who longs for a return to Unit Two, must have a way of expressing these feelings nonverbally. The resident may feel that to express such feelings is to display cowardice, or to exhibit himself as a "chump" who does not know enough to take advantage of what is being offered him. Or he may have some vague feeling that he was actually benefiting from the Unit Two curriculum and that he should have remained longer. The STU is designed as a series of freestanding units within a wall; the resident in the position we have described can make an "escape gesture" by leaving his room (or even his living unit) without permission. This is an obvious breach of the institution's rules, and it permits the resident to say what he could not say otherwise: that he wants out of his current environment (without risking the loss of status that would accompany such a *request*). Of course, the resident who "escapes" from his living unit is still well within the wall that surrounds the STU, and he will be picked up by staff members within a short period of time. Some judgment is, of course, necessary by staff to distinguish between the "gesture" escape and one sincerely motivated by a desire to leave the institution entirely. In many ways, there will be a testing period of attempted escapes until the information filters down to the population that such attempts are doomed to failure. It will be at that point that staff is more readily able to distinguish between gesture and serious action.

Units Four and Five: Progress to Units Four and Five (see figures 6-9 and 6-10) is based on less precisely measurable criteria than progress from Unit Two to Three. There will be a minimum period required to complete the vocational apprenticeship period and the educational period (since we endorse the belief that an individual who cannot read, write, and compute basic arithmetic will join either the victim or the predator pool in society, and our residents have already indicated their preference in such matters) and, of course, behavioral requirements will be higher in Unit Three. But Units Four and Five are actually prerelease areas, and a resident will not be moved to those living quarters until such time as he is ready for release. Given emerging legislative requirements for minimum periods of incarceration of certain juvenile felony offenders, it is possible to hypothesize that some juveniles will be legally ready for release while still on Unit Two, while others will be emotionally, socially, vocationally, and psychologically ready for release prior to the time when such release is legally permitted. The minimum period of incarceration will be fully disclosed to each resident upon admission to the STU; the unit will not rely on the fact that they hold the resident's release at their whim to insure proper behavior, since it is this type of speech which the life-style violent delinquent has been acculturated to ignore. Nor will we hope to rely on after-care programs, unless such programs contractually guarantee acceptance of the STU's graduates. Units Four and Five are, as we said, parallel programs, the only difference between them being the community release plan of the individual resident. Those residents with a reasonable expectation of being accepted back in their original home, or in a foster care or group home situation in the community will complete their sentences in Unit Four. And those who will be released outright, without supervision other than that minimally supplied by the parole authorities will be released from Unit Five. It is to be expected that the older residents will be the more suitable candidates for Unit Five, but this is not to be an inflexible rule.

Only residents of Unit Five will be on work release status, since maintenance of suitable employment in the outside community is considered absolutely essential to their survival as noncriminals. It is *not* expected that such residents will be subjected to peer pressure to bring contraband into the institution since, unlike most conventional work release situations, these individuals will be among the most veteran residents, without even the opportunity to interact with those residents of either Unit One or Unit Two. However, the STU will not rely upon this assumption and the full range of security procedures and hardware designed into the Secure Treatment Unit will be utilized to prevent this occurrence.

The program in Units Four and Five is almost essentially vocational/educational, with vastly decreased emphasis on the affective and experiential (see figure 6-8). However, as in all units, the counselor-on-the-floor will always be available, and the full range of support services of the STU will similarly be available. The difference is that, at this point in their development, the residents will be expected to initiate most such contacts themselves.

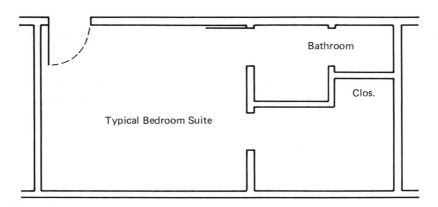

Bathroom

Clos.

Typical Bedroom Suite

Scale

0   4   8

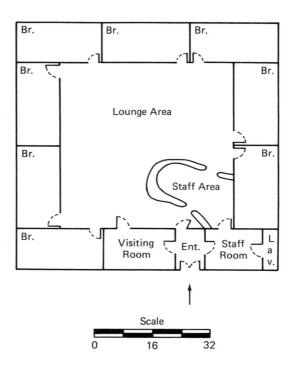

Br. Br. Br.

Br. Br.

Lounge Area

Br. Br.

Staff Area

Br.

Visiting
Room   Ent.   Staff
Room

L
a
v.

Scale

0   16   32

Figure 6-9. Unit Four

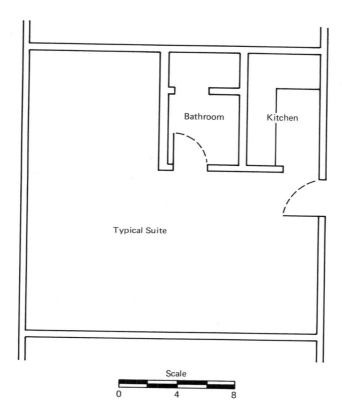

Figure 6-10. Unit Five

Because the Unit Five program is oriented more towards street-side survival, the living units will have individual kitchens. The residents on Unit Five will still be eligible to use the institution's dining facilities but, like staff members, will be expected to pay a minimum fee for each meal consumed, from their work release wages. They will also be expected to contribute to the cost of transportation to their work sites, work uniforms and tools, and other incidental expenses. Additionally, some portion of their salaries will be deducted and placed in a savings account each week, both to provide some "gate money" upon release and to acquaint them with the habit of regular, systematic savings. Residents of Unit Four will be eligible for weekend furloughs to their home communities, but only to those living sites that have already accepted them for residence upon release. These weekends will not be granted as a reward for good behavior, but will be automatic features of residence on Unit Four. Although there might be some community reaction to home visits from this population, it should be remembered that, in all probability, no juvenile will be released from the institution for any such purpose until at least a full year of incarceration has been successfully completed.

The progression from unit to unit within the STU carries with it the extension of privileges, increased access to goods and services, and increased opportunities in many spheres. It probably does not correlate with actual date of release, and we accept the fact that some juveniles will be released from units other than those designed as prerelease. However, it is our belief, based on the truly "hard data" of personal observation and experience, that the goal of early release is a poor one in terms of increasing the probability of street survival after that release. Only the motivation of an improved life-style is likely to carry over into community living, and it is our intention to enhance that motivation for the STU residents.

Staff

Staff Training: Although we have attempted to emphasize the pragmatic over the utopian through this book, there is one area in which the ideal should be pursued as vigorously as possible—staff training. The human services profession has always relied heavily on in-service training of those already on staff, and on-the-job (OTJ) training as a means of breaking in new members. We do not propose to comment on the effectiveness of such methods, especially since most human services operations are ongoing and cannot be interrupted for a training period. However, the Secure Treatment Unit is a new concept, and we hope we have dissuaded jurisdictions from simply attempting to engraft Secure Treatment Unit methodologies onto an existing training school.

We don't expect to be able to start with a blank piece of paper with the new unit. We hope jurisdictions will see the merit in new construction, but we are somewhat resigned to the prospect of rehabilitating existing structures. However, we do insist that the new unit be permitted a period of specialized training, on the new site, *before* the residents arrive. Much of the therapy and treatment that will take place within the STU is, in effect, cultural. All institutions quickly acquire a cultural identity of their own, and we need the opportunity to establish that culture in a relatively unpressured atmosphere. The training must provide the opportunity for new staff to learn the new system, and to learn the new structure; and experience has taught us that in-service training in a maximum-security institution is a most difficult task. We expect training to be ongoing, cumulative, and responsive to emerging needs of the institution. But the baseline training, the acceptance and understanding of the life-rules of the STU, and the specific intervention techniques and response-patterns can only be learned before the residents arrive. A culture for the unit will be established, and the first arrivals will have the heaviest impact on the establishment of that culture.

We are now working on a complete training package for the staff of the Secure Treatment Unit, and the differing philosophies and approaches of various members of our planning board continue to surface. But there is unanimous agreement that we must establish the basic training before the residents arrive, and that any jurisdiction serious about its commitment to treatment of life-style violent juvenile offenders within its juvenile justice system will permit the training of Secure Treatment Unit staff to begin at least ninety days before the arrival of the first resident.

Staggered Shift Changes: Unlike conventional institutions where "change of shift" takes place en masse, the STU will change *half* of each shift at a time, with each unit having separate, staggered hours. This will provide a constant flow of personnel through the administration building, to be sure, but it will greatly minimize the disruptions, and possible dangers, that accompany a massive change of personnel for the entire institution at one time.

There is an additional purpose to the staggered change of shifts. The Administration Building contains a Recording Room; this room consists of several chairs, each facing a voice-activated microphone, and each sealed within its own soundproofed booth. As each staff member leaves his shift, he will be required to briefly enter the Recording Room and simply dictate his daily observations (of individual residents, group activity, staff participation, or anything else that impacts upon the quality of care within the STU) into the microphone. The staff member will not control the recording apparatus in any way; the actual tape cassettes will be on the second floor of the Administration Building so that he will be unable to erase, rewind, or in any way manipulate the recordings. Each will be "signed" by voice, and dated, and will be transcribed the following day by the secretarial staff. Our experience with institutional logbooks has led us to the conclusion that only this method will produce a participatory record of the institution and its residents. A written report is far too cumbersome, and its length will vary with the motivation and education of individual staff members.

In addition, because written reports constitute a continuing document open to all, there are two problems: (1) staff members, having read what previous staff wrote, are subjected to peer pressure and often are reluctant to disagree with their fellows (conversely, some are all-too-eager to do so, truthfulness or relevancy notwithstanding); and (2) there is a serious problem of confidentiality. The recording method will answer these basic objections and provide the administration with an ongoing observational record of the residents' progress. Writing reports has become, in our opinion, too "professionalized" and the value of a report should not be judged on its grammar, spelling, and organization but on the clarity and insight it displays. Many staff members who are fully qualified to work within the STU will lack the formal education necessary to prepare written reports, and some will be needlessly intimidated by the prospect. However, the conversational style acceptable in the dictating booth will break

down some of these barriers, and the STU's sources of information will therefore
not be restricted to the professional staff.

Formal Education of Staff: A word here about professionals and paraprofes-
sionals and other such distinctions between staff members. It is our opinion that
professionalism implies commitment and competence, not training or education.
To be sure, the term speaks to knowledge and ability, but it does not speak
strictly to formal education. The counselor-on-the-floor is the strength of the
STU; he or she is the friend-advocate-therapist-role model that will determine
the final outcome of all the effort and attention lavished on the design,
construction, and program of the unit. Distinctions among such staff on the
basis of formal education are dysfunctional. This applies to matters of salary as
well as to matters of prestige.

Female Floor Counselors: In the same vein, we have found that the presence of
women as floor counselors is absolutely required for the success of the STU. A
good part of the socialization process necessitates development of an affect and
style appropriate to interaction with women in the community. This skill cannot
be taught by lecture, as is the case with most STU teaching/training/learning. It
can be assimilated only through a large variety of experiential factors, and
personal interaction is high on this list. Nothing destroys negative stereotypes
like observation and participation; seeing the role modeling counselors interact
with female staff is only one way of learning for the residents, seeing themselves
interact with female staff is another. It has been our experience that residents
desire such interaction. For example, one female staff member at Andros was
friendly, intelligent, and quite willing to converse with any resident who
respectfully requested some of her time. But any conversation that took a
disrespectful tone was abruptly terminated. Because conversation with this
young woman was desirable to the residents, they soon found themselves
modifying their conversational styles in order to continue to have such
opportunities.

But women have a role in the STU that goes beyond breaking stereotypes
and modifying temporary social behavior. Our society offers few all-male
environments, and the life-style violent juvenile is certainly unlikely to locate
one other than in another institution. Any form of socialization that does not
include interaction with women is deficient, artificial and unlikely to prove
useful in the outside world. The presence of women, in a variety of roles,
underscores the STU's commitment to a real-world orientation, and enables the
transmission of messages at a deeper level than any lectures or counseling could
provide.

For example, the gang stereotypes of masculinity are inherently challenged
by the female staff member who responds to a juvenile who expresses an interest
in such "unmasculine" pursuits as writing, or art. Since our thesis is that much

of the life-style violent juvenile's community behavior is, in fact, adaptive in nature, we seek to build on this adaptive ability by opening up new opportunities and new heights of behavior for such adaptation. The presence of female staff adds to such opportunities and is, therefore, a necessity.

Additional Considerations

The Videotape Studio: The Videotape Studio, located in the north wing of the STU's wall, serves several purposes. We have found it to be a most useful therapeutic device, utilizing its instant replay capability to "see ourselves as others see us." It also enables us to prepare special training packages in the studio and display them to staff at various times, thereby eliminating the necessity of calling the entire staff in at any one point. It allows us to exhibit training materials from other agencies, and to export our own material. We can also tape special events directly from the television networks to allow residents to view material that they might have missed because of strict curfew requirements.

We also envision the use of videotape in training residents for future careers. Although we earlier spoke disparagingly of those who comment that we could send a juvenile to Harvard for what it costs to incarcerate him, and although we heavily emphasize the pragmatic at all times, this does not mean that we intend to denigrate the innate capabilities of our residents. Surely, some of them will display the native intelligence and motivation to pursue careers other than those available within the institutional walls. Trained videotape technicians, for example, continue to be much in demand. We also envision journalistic training, using the electronic media, and we plan to provide "hands-on" experience for those juveniles interested in the field. We can tape athletic events and dramatic shows put on by residents within the walls, and we expect to involve residents in all phases, from camera work to editing.

Institutional Jobs: This is consistent with our philosophy that each of the vocational areas will be run as though it were an independently operating business. Residents will be trained in more than auto mechanics. They will also learn what it takes to actually run their own small business. Again, we realize that we are providing a continuum of available knowledge, and that not all residents will pursue this continuum to its conclusion. But the availability of more information and knowledge than the individual currently possesses will serve as a consistent motivating force. Unlike most institutional "jobs" (read: work assignments), a resident will not be fully trained within a week and merely involved in the same, boring repetitive work from then on. It takes a prisoner only several days (at most) to learn to operate a license plate making machine and, as one veteran convict said "there ain't too many jobs like that on the streets." As with progress, as with restraint of violence, as with education: the resident will determine how far he goes, and how far the STU goes along with him.

The availability of all institutional jobs will be disclosed, as will the criteria necessary to be accepted on such assignments. If, for example, only residents of Unit Four or Five are eligible for videotape training, all residents who are initially exposed to the workings of this machinery while in therapy on Unit Two will be made aware of this opportunity.

Optional Use Space: There has been disagreement among the planners as to potential uses of the Optional Use Space in the south wing of the building. Some of us believe that residents could benefit from exposure to work assignments such as a dog training and breeding operation, believing that involvement in the fundamental life process would be extremely beneficial. Others feel that this space must be left vacant for now, to be filled in by the expressed needs and wishes of the residents themselves. This faction believes that residents should not be so limited in choice of careers, and that several residents of Units Four and Five might decide to go into business in an approved venture that would take place behind the wall. Any jurisdiction adapting these plans would make that decision depending on a variety of factors that are beyond the scope of this work.

It is also our belief that the STU might offer valuable services to its surrounding community. Many of the ultramodern facilities within its walls might not be available in the local community, and we see no reason why this community could not utilize the facilities in a manner fully consistent with security considerations. This is an area that requires additional exploration in individual jurisdictions, but we want only to emphasize at this point that we believe in using what we have to the fullest extent. If the fullest possible use of the Secure Treatment Unit's facilities increases community acceptance of the institution, or provides an opportunity for social interaction between community residents and those of the unit, all the better. But we frankly believe that neither goal need be an absolute prerequisite to the use of our facilities by the outside community, simply on the theory that failure to use that which is available constitutes unacceptable waste.

Conclusions

One final word on life-style violent juvenile offenders. Much of what has been written in support of treatment of juvenile offenders within the juvenile justice system has been predicated on a kind of ecological reasoning—juvenile offenders are thought to be appropriate candidates for criminological "recycling" back into the larger society if properly "treated" by the system. But the life-style violent juvenile is not considered to be such a candidate: this special offender cannot be recycled and, like any other waste product, is thought to be suitable only for disposal—in this case, into the adult correctional system. Unfortunately for the ecological theorists, some "garbage" just won't stay buried, and putting a life-style violent juvenile offender into the adult correctional system makes as much sense as burying nuclear waste in the backyard! The "fallout" implications are obvious and frightening, and were, in fact, the inspiration for the planning that went into the Secure Treatment Unit.

The concept renderings are just that: illustrations of the concepts on which the proposed Secure Treatment Unit is to be structured and managed. They are not cast in concrete as to structure, it is the principles we hope to have expressed that are important.

If this book inspires any jurisdiction to actively plan for the care, custody, and treatment of the life-style violent juvenile offender within its juvenile justice network, we will feel rewarded for the years of effort that have gone into it. But it is our sincere feeling that the time for planning is well past; the life-style violent juvenile commands our attention and our intervention, and Secure Treatment Units are the *only* hope of the juvenile justice system if it wants to retain the responsibility for its most dangerous and highly visible charges.

Notes

1. *See*, People v. Unger, 21 *Criminal Law Reporter* 2113 (Illinois Supreme Court, April 5, 1977). Unger was charged with escape from an "honor farm," to which he had been transferred from the (supposedly tougher) state penitentiary. He was 22 years old, weighed 155 pounds, and was, by his own account, a poor fighter. At his trial for escape, he testified that he was assaulted and sexually molested by three other inmates. He thereafter continued to receive sexual assault threats from other prisoners. When it was learned that he reported the assault, he was threatened with death. He testified that he escaped the farm to save his life, but he had not actually reported any of the prior assaults or threats. He was apprehended two days after his escape, still dressed in prison clothes. The appellate court found that the lower court erred in instructing the jury to disregard any *reasons* for Unger's escape and to look only at whether or not he *did* escape. *See also,* People v. Harmon, 53 Mich.App. 482, 220 N.W.2d 212 (Mich., 1974) for a holding of duress as a defense to a charge of escape, and State v. Green, 470 S.W.2d 565 (1971), Seiler, J., *dissenting.* For a maximum-security prison to actually achieve this personal safety for its residents would be a massive step forward in juvenile corrections. Sexual assaults have taken place in jails, prisons, holding pens, and even in transport vans on the way to jail. *See,* Davis, "Sexual Assaults in the Philadelphia Prison System," in *Muckraking Sociology: Research as Social Criticism* (1972), and People v. Lovercamp, 43 Cal.App.3d 832, 118 Cal. Rptr. 110 (1974).

2. *See,* for example, *In re* Dino, 23 *Criminal Law Reporter* 2225 (Louisiana Supreme Court, May 8, 1978), which is one of the latest decisions to hold that a juvenile is, by virtue of his special status, unable to waive his rights to have advice of counsel prior to making any statements; *see also,* People v. McClary, 22 *Criminal Law Reporter* 2304 (Cal.Supr.Ct. 1977) and People v. Maes 22 *Criminal Law Reporter* 2245 (Cal.Sup.Ct. 1977).

3. Or any other bullet-proof transparent material.

4. Such life-rules must always be simple, direct, and capable of immediate understanding and assimilation by the resident population. At Andros II, they were: No Violence, No Sex, and No Dope.

5. *See,* for example, ch. 4, note 63, *supra.* The techniques must be taught during the period of time when the Secure Treatment Unit is empty, before the residents arrive for the first time, as we recommend in chapter 6, *infra.*

6. Full disclosure simply means that no resident will be subjected to punishment for any behavior not previously stated to be incorrect. However, it also means that any behavior which *has* previously been so covered will be the subject of immediate and certain consequences. In short, there should be no surprise at either the fact of reaction to certain behaviors, nor the severity of that reaction. The idea is to limit the fear that comes from vagueness, and also the exploitative and manipulative opportunities that vagueness always provides.

7. *See* ch. 4, note 77, *supra.* This quote is a continuation of a speech by the same interviewee.

8. Interview with a veteran of maximum-security incarceration in four different states, 1975, identity not disclosed at interviewee's request:

> If a guy wants to hang up [hang himself], cut up [slash his wrists], or take a flyer [leap from an upper tier to the floor], how you gonna stop him? There's *always* a way. When I was a kid, I heard about this guy up in the Death House at Sing Sing. He wanted to cheat the State, see? Check out himself, not be fried like a fuckin' egg. So he saved all his matches for months, then he pulled off the hollow iron bed support and stuffed hundreds of match heads real tight inside. Then he just put his head next to the radiator with this little pipe bomb and went to sleep. About an hour before they went to get him, it went off and blew a nice hole in his head. I love that story.

9. We are not prepared to say "completely impossible" so long as there are practitioners in the field attempting new solutions and new methods of treatment. *See,* for example, Edward M. Brecher, *Treatment Programs for Sex Offenders* (National Institute of Law Enforcement and Criminal Justice, LEAA Grant No. 75-NI-99-0125, to the American Correctional Association, 1978).

10. Carr, ch. 2, note 2, *supra,* at p. 65.

11. Interview with a prisoner at Trenton State Prison, 1972. The identity of the interviewee, who is now on parole after serving a sentence for kidnapping and robbery, has been withheld at his request.

12. There is virtually unanimous agreement that education is an integral part of any rehabilitative scheme for juvenile offenders. Mann, ch. 1, note 34, *supra,* at p. 52, in his survey of American programs, found

> schooling practices that are more consonant with what is known about human behavior and learning psychology appear to be largely confined to the *less* serious juvenile offenders.

> The schooling applied to serious juvenile offenders is similar to the state of the art in American public schools in the 1940s. [emphasis added]

13. Interview with an inmate at Greenhaven Prison, 1974. Identity not disclosed at interviewee's request.

Afterword

Late this summer, after this manuscript went to the publisher, the New York State Legislature, acting in Extraordinary Session, enacted chapter 481 of the laws of 1978. Known as the "Juvenile Offender Law," this act, which became effective on September 1, 1978, gives the criminal courts *original and exclusive jurisdiction* over certain violent juvenile offenses. These offenses include murder in the second degree for those juveniles aged thirteen and older, and the crimes of kidnapping 1, arson 1, assault 1, manslaughter 1, rape 1, sodomy 1, burglary 1 and 2, arson 2, robbery 1 and 2, attempted murder 2, and attempted kidnapping for juveniles aged 14 and over.

Unlike conventional "waiver laws," New York's new statute does not provide for a full hearing before a case is transferred from juvenile to adult jurisdiction. However, juveniles under the age of sixteen still will not be incarcerated with adult offenders, but can be transferred to such facilities upon reaching that age.

This new statute has yet to be tested in the appellate courts, and will doubtless be the subject of countless analytical articles in the appropriate journals.

The place of incarceration for this special class of juvenile offenders has not been announced, nor are we aware of any specialized programming available for this group.

Appendix

This section consists of interviews with the following individuals:

1. Dr. Jerome Miller
2. T. Robert Clements
3. William J. Jesinkey
4. "Gypsy"
5. Dr. Daniel Jacobs
6. Raymond Kiidh Gilyard
7. Lieutenant Arthur Holsborg
8. Dr. Walter A. Stewart
9. Judge Shirley Wohl Kram
10. David Guy Baldwin
11. Dr. Yitzhak Bakal
12. Nicholas Pileggi
13. "J"
14. Ramon Jimenez, Esq.
15. Dr. William Madaus
16. Professor Richard B. Child

Interview between Andrew Vachss (V) and Dr. Jerome Miller (M), with Comments by Robert John Lewis (L), on July 27, 1976.

Jerome G. Miller, D.S.W., was commissioner of youth services for the Commonwealth of Massachusetts during its nationally noted de-institutionalization of juvenile prisons. Since that time, he has served as commissioner of the youth services agencies for Illinois and Pennsylvania. Dr. Miller is currently the director of the National Center for Action on Institutions and Alternatives in Washington, D.C. and editor of its investigative newsletter, *Institutions, Etc.* (IE).

V: You've been nationally associated with de-institutionalization in juvenile prisons and it's pretty much assumed that you are the foremost advocate of this method of doing business in the juvenile corrections field. Following several years experience in several states, have you in any way changed your mind about the viability of de-institutionalization?

M: No, Andy, I don't think so in any basic way: I think that the way we did it in Massachusetts is probably the only way it can be done—rather quickly and fast. I would do a few things differently. I would not have relied so much on group homes. If I were to set up a model system I would have at one end a very limited system of small locked facilities for really dangerous kids. For the state of Massachusetts no more than forty beds, for instance: and then I would have almost no group residential care.

V: Can you define residential care?

M: Well, like group homes. I'd have a few, perhaps, but I think I would stress a great deal more advocacy programs, specialized foster care, transitional living, like that proctor program they have for girls where they get apartments and move in with staff and then staff move out when the girls are ready to make it on their own. I think that all that spectrum in between is kind of nonsense. I would have something for the really dangerous kid and I would want to make it very clear that a dangerous kid is a kid who's committed a violent act, period; not someone that we think might be dangerous, or someone who's "possibly" dangerous or some one who's "dangerous to themselves"; but someone who's killed someone, someone who's raped someone, someone who's maimed someone and shown by what they did that they're dangerous.

V: When you say "dangerous," are you differentiating between a physically dangerous kid and a psychotic kid, for the purposes of this institution?

M: I would be talking really about a kid who has been violent on the street, in terms of violence toward another person.

V: And you wouldn't put in there, in that same population, a kid who was schizophrenic?

M: It's hard to say. I wouldn't design a program like that for a schizophrenic kid. However, if you had a schizophrenic kid who had maimed someone, then I think that program ought to be able to relate to that kid. I don't think that we ought to have programs that exclude kids because of diagnosis, because otherwise we'll get caught up in the same bind mental health is, where they play diagnostic games and use that as a means of rejecting kids.

V: Okay, who should decide? Let us say, just for the sake of argument that we have such an institution. Right? It contains forty-fifty kids. Who should decide, and how should they decide, which children go in this place?

M: I think in corrections it could be decided within the law, and thereby within an intake policy procedure. I think that if you decide, for instance, that this is a place for violent kids who have demonstrated violence, that should be the only criterion. The program should be able to adjust and develop for that kid. Now, I realize that presents a problem because you can't have a program that will absorb every kid terribly easily. But on the other hand, if you look at the total state system there are no such programs and the rejectable kid then gets rejected as "unfit" for all existing programs. Somewhere the buck stops, and it seems to me that you could develop this system.

V: You're talking about an institution that would not have its own intake controls.

M: It would have intake controls in terms of policy, and in terms of numbers.

V: But they couldn't reject a kid on the grounds they couldn't work with him.

M: Right. Exactly. They would say that this is an institution, say for kids who have committed murder, in a violent sort of way. I'm not talking about some kinds of murder but, you know . . .

V: That's a good point. Not to sidetrack you, but what about the kid who's involved in a homicide, say in a gang situation, and himself wasn't morally culpable, or ethically culpable, but was legally culpable.

M: Well, I'd come at it both ways. I would do this: I would say that the institution would take that kind of kid, but that the judge could use something else, or the court could use something else. In other words, if I were to redo the recent New York law around juvenile justice, for instance, I would say that X institution's intake policies are such they'll take nothing below a certain level of violence. In other words, we won't take a kid who's a pain in the ass to the court or keeps running away from places. We will take kids on murder, on rape, and say on second or third robbery with a weapon, or clearly violent sorts of crimes. We will take those kids. However, you don't have to use us, you can use options, and I would allow that institution to have some sort of arrangement with the court whereby they could negotiate that kid out or negotiate that kid into another program. But I don't think that institution should be allowed to simply reject a kid and say we've got nothing, forget it, because in most states that will mean nothing else will be done.

V: Now what about the type of a kid—and I'll mention a name on the tape that will be deleted in the transcript—what about M.M., a kid who is not violent, but who will not stay in an unsecured cell?

M: That's a problem. Don Russell, that psychiatrist up in Boston who has written a great deal on the violent juvenile felt that certain car thieves are more violent than so-called violent kids. I'm not so sure I follow that.

V: Do they belong in the same institution with kids that have been involved in homicides and rapes?

M: I don't think so. I think others would argue they do. I think that there ought to be another kind of program that perhaps we haven't developed for these kids. My experience with these kids is that they never worked out anyway, in a secure unit. You keep them for a while and then they go out and cause a lot of problems.

V: So, security extinguishes the function of security.

M: Which isn't very helpful, and I think it probably criminalizes them a lot more. They get a bigger rep in their own head about what they're all about by associating with kids on really violent stuff. I would like to see for those kids a different kind of system, whereby if we had to, we got someone on their left arm around the clock and I think we could buy that sort of security—because really you're talking about keeping someone from jumping in a car and going a hundred miles an hour down a back street or something, and high speed chases and the possible injury that results out of that.

V: What about the description of most maximum security—in fact, I'd say all maximum-security institutions either juvenile or adult, as criminogenic in and of themselves?

M: Well I think that's true. I know that people these days are saying, I think Van den Haag and James Q. Wilson, have said that there's no evidence that prisons are criminogenic. That's a comment you always would get from someone who's never been in a prison. I can't imagine anyone going to a prison and saying such nonsense. Even in studies on rehabilitation not working, which I think are not terribly objective anymore, (I used to think they were better than I do now, having spent more time looking at it), they've overlooked certain research. There's some research by a guy by the name of Lamar Empey done in Utah, admittedly, which is certainly not New York City, but there's some seeds of research there, it would seem to me, hold some water. What he found is, when they moved from institutions to community-based programs, there was a drop in recidivism among the kids in community-based programs, for a while. Then, a year or two later, recidivism was at about the same rate as kids in institutions. It was taken to mean therefore the community-based programs were no better than the institutions. Now what Martinson overlooked, and I think must have consciously overlooked it, because it's clearly in the literature, is that Empey then did a five-year follow-up, and what he found is that the kids in the community-based programs were dramatically better off than the kids in the institution programs, five years later. Now they got back in trouble in terms of strict recidivism, they were repeating, but it *de-escalated*. They didn't get worse.The type of crime de-escalated and it sloughed off. Whereas, the kids that went the prison route, it kept adding on, kept getting deeper, and deeper, and it got more and more violent, and I think that that's where the Massachusetts thing will prove out after five, six years. I don't have any doubt at all, if they can sustain it, it will be a better system.

V: I agree with you that the Massachusetts system would prove that, if it were accurately studied. I'm not at all convinced that the studies that have been going on are as objective as we'd like them to be.

M: I don't know. I think the Harvard Studies are going to be all right. I really do. They've been very, very objective. In fact, they've been very aggravating at times. Like on their recidivism stuff, I felt that they went to press too early, and they did it to be sure that people knew they weren't playing games in a sense. But I think they feel, as well, now that they did go to press too early on it, because everyone's hopes gets raised and they get knocked down and then everyone runs with the ball. Their sense of public relations isn't terribly good, but that goes with being a good researcher, I guess.

V: Well, speaking about a sense of public relations, assuming that you've concluded that after these years and these various situations that at least one maximum security setting is indicated; is that conclusion entirely criminological, or is it partly a political conclusion?

M: Both. I think there's no doubt you have to be able to relate to the political call for retribution and all, and it's a dangerous sort of game to relate too much to it. You can get caught on the dilemma of the punishment versus rehabilitation, because people really do like to punish kids, and they really do like to scapegoat and put it to them, and a locked facility will be generally touted in those terms. I guess what people really like, is they like punishment *called* rehabilitation. They would like you to have a locked facility that you call rehabilitative, but deep down they know you're really putting it to them, and that's the dilemma of prisons. I mean they talk about all their rehabilitation programs, everybody knows, deep down, if they look, that its a Dachau village mentality: it's how you can sit in the village and know what's really going on out there, but pretend that you don't.

V: Are you somewhat soured on the whole *parens patriae* mentality of juvenile corrections?

M: Well, I'd do away with juvenile courts totally, if I could. I would substitute some sort of citizens committees . . .

V: Would you be appointing your citizens committees from the same housing areas?

M: From the same locale, yes.

V: Wouldn't that have the effect of institutionalizing a whole bunch of kids?

M: If I had it my way, of course, I'd put very firm restrictions on it. I would only allow a kid to be incarcerated for a very serious violent crime, first off, and I would insist that the committee have shown that they'd tried other options at great length. The courts have never done that. And then I would hold, rather than the kid responsible totally, I'd hold the *agencies* responsible to prove whether or not they did indeed give the services.

V: When you hold an agency responsible, would you hold them responsible financially?

M: Yes. And there are ways to do that within government, because you control the purse strings.

V: Performance contracts?

M: Sure. But you see that's never done. For instance, say you get Johnny Smith in some kind of trouble, brought back into court, and the court says, "Well, we're going to send him to Camp Hill Prison. Now, because we've tried probation twice, and we've tried X group home, and he's cut out." Now, what they very seldom would do is bring X group home in and say, "Well, tell me how many hours you spent with this kid, this week. Who saw him when? What did your staff do? What is their background? How much time did they spend? How many courses did they give?" Courts don't do that. They take the word of the "vendor" if you will, that the kid isn't getting with the program. And as a result they go after the kid, and I think that that's not a legitimate thing.

V: To what extent would you enforce this?

M: Well, I'd cut off money. I'd close places down.

V: How far does this go down? For example, you've been an advocate in the past of using so-called ex-offenders, which is not a term we like, but former prisoners, as therapeutic agents. Do you have that same philosophy still?

M: Oh. Yes. I think that's worked out well.

V: How do you respond to this criticism that I've heard, and the criticism is that the former prisoner is either the very best or the very worst possible person to put in a juvenile situation. Depending on the individual?

M: Well, I don't think that's true. I think you get about the same spectrum you do with regular staff. You get some real losers and you get some real winners and you get a lot in between, who win part of the time and lose part of the time, and I think you have to just set a program around peoples' strengths. But I think, as well, that if you get a good group of people that have been in trouble before, and who know the system, that you can get a little cooler approach to things, a little less uptightness around certain things, and it seems to me they can handle things much better. If they don't, you have problems, and I'm not talking about guys who've been in trouble, getting in trouble again. That's a problem, but not a major one. I think the major problem around ex-offenders is getting people who've been so socialized to the correctional system, that although they mouth a whole rehabilitative or change program, are very much like old-time guards underneath—and when pushed, have really come to buy the prison mentality that you control people by giving them a kick in the ass or throwing them in the hole.

V: We've seen that happen.

M: Yes.

V: Now, how would you propose to control that. For example, let us say that you were going to subcontract the work of running a small secure institution, and I was coming to you and saying I want to run such an institution. What would you require of me in terms of the staff I was yet to hire?

M: Well, there are two ways you could go. One is you could develop a kind of regulatory system, of regular inspection and people coming through. They would include some former offenders, and some people who are not part of that system, and I think that would help. Another way, which would probably be a more radical way, would be to rather than have one fifty bed institution, to have three twelve- or fifteen-bed institutions, and then to give vouchers to the kids. If I were to look to an ideal system, it would be something along those lines. It would have to be well thought through. Let me give you an example: There has always been in this country, decent care for dangerous violent people of the upper middle class, right? Even in the middle 1800s, there were decent mental hospitals for wealthy people, even when the other mental hospitals were terrible. Now I'm not saying they were terribly effective, but they never mistreated people. Friends Hospital in Philadelphia always had a petting zoo for patients and open visiting and little or no use of restraints at a time when the state hospitals were throwing them in holes and straitjackets. There were always decent places for people who could afford it. Now, the question you have to ask is "why?" and "what kept them decent?" Because large state institutions always get worse relative to the society at large. They seem never to get any better: they get a little better for a while and then they get worse, and then they mistreat people. And I think the difference is that with the private places, that are privately funded, the people can take their twenty or thirty thousand and walk out the door: and even if they're on a court commitment, in fact there's an eminent senator's daughter at a very eminent private facility in Boston, who's committed what would be a murder in any other terms. Now that person is not going to get mistreated at that private hospital because if she were, even though the court has ordered her to be in a locked setting, the senator would take his money and put her in another locked setting. He'd move her to Menninger's or to Chestnut Lodge, or whereever. So, they're never going to toss her in a hole when she gets obstreperous. Now, it seems to me that's the kind of thing we need in corrections. I won't deny the court the right of saying, "This kid is dangerous and cannot be on the street." All right, he's got to be in a locked setting for a given period of time,—but it would seem to me that it would be a lot healthier if we said "You're sentenced to that status, you would have to be in a locked setting." "Now here is someone with brochures, a consumer of human services, you go out and visit—what the upper class have always done."—"you visit these four locked settings, and you and the trained citizen consumer, decide which one you want to go to." "And you'll take the state's money with you there." "We'll pay for it." "Now if you find yourself unhappy and mistreated there, during your time of incarceration, we'll have a grievance procedure, so you don't leave impulsively." "You just can't get mad at a staff member and walk out the door and go elsewhere." "There'll be a grievance procedure, and you sit down, and if, after the grievance procedure, you've decided this place is no longer for you, you can take the state's twenty or thirty thousand and you can go to another approved locked program." Those places which can't keep their kids, can't keep their money.

V: How would you answer the natural criticism, which is that because of the economic competition, certain institutions would evolve that are absolute zoos, where there's open sexuality, there's narcotics in the place . . .

M: Well, I think there's that danger, but I don't think people generally tend to pick places that will tend to hurt them. That will happen now and then, but I would trust, and I think with some reason, the ability of people to pick better places.

V: Isn't it possible to combine both your ideas? There are certain minimal standards that you can enforce by inspection . . .

M: Oh, you've got to. I would still do that. I didn't mean that I wouldn't keep certain minimal standards, and keep our regular inspections going, by all means. But, I would also give the people the authority to move about. It's the argument the teachers have used against the educational voucher system, that there'll be a lot of hustlers getting people to go to poor schools. That may happen for a while, but after a while, people catch on, and the hustler doesn't succeed. It's an interesting thing because we've always been unwilling to give to the poor what we would anticipate and expect for ourselves. If I had thirty thousand and had a troubled kid, I would do a hell of a lot of shopping before I'd give that thirty thousand to someone. I know I wouldn't just give it to the state and send him to an institution.

V: Well, you're taking it a step further, because you're not presupposing here that the family would have the thirty thousand to keep if they did not put the kid in the institution, because that could happen too.

M: That would be another possibility. I think the only way you could sell it politically would be to do something á la Nader, and train lay people as consumers of human services, and give them some of that authority.

V: Well, I can see your argument is probably a valid one in the sense that society in general is the consumer of the criminal justice system. And to the extent that it doesn't work, we all pay for it, perhaps physically.

M: Sure. But I would, for instance, if a kid doesn't have a family, say, or he's got a destructive family, because kid's families would just as soon see them rot in jail, or they'd pick a lousy place. I think that we should have trained lay people to do for these kids what any well-educated middle class parent would do for their kid. There's a frankly, middle-class bias to it á la Alinsky's middle-class bias, in the sense that that's where the power is in a competitive market, the middle class are the people who know how to play that very well, and I think we've got to get those skills to the kids who are caught in this system. I would design, frankly a middle-class thing, whereby, I could give a good goddamn whether the person who was the kid's advocate was a wealthy suburban lady. She might be better able to ask those questions of the service giver than a poor person would. She might be better able to hold a social worker accountable in the same way she would if she were putting out the money. Now we've also got to train families of the poor to ask those questions. To hold that system accountable, because the way it is now, it's a seller's market. It's a vendor's market. The people who evaluate and decide whether the service is good are the same people who give it, or it's their peers in the child-care field, or in the correctional field, and they set their own standards and they make their own careers thereby.

V: In the same place they might even be consultants.

M: Yes, that's right. They rub each other's back. That's why we never regulate these places effectively.

V: Are you envisioning at some point an actual degree-granting procedure whereby there would be academic degrees in the evaluation of human services?

M: Yes. I think you could say academic degrees. Or you could even run very decent short-term training programs and give certificates of some sort, before people could get into it. It really wouldn't take a hell of a lot of training. You would teach people how to tour an institution, how to ask which questions, how to find out whether service-givers are following through. I wouldn't allow someone to say "Well, we give vocational training." I'd want to know who gives it, and when and how many hours a week, and the track record in job placement, and how well do you know this kid, I'd ask all those questions. People are not trained to ask those questions, and the kids do not dare ask those questions, generally, because they're liable to be scapegoated. When a kid bombs out of a program, those questions are never asked in the average courtroom. Generally, a person comes in from the program who will say "This kid never got with the program," and list a series of incidents or wrongs that the kid supposedly engaged in, but that program is not held accountable. The only time that program is held accountable is when it is a group like an ex-offender group or if it's a new group which isn't established.

V: Would it be fair to say, unequivocally, that if a child is raped in an institution, it's the fault of the institution?

M: I would say in most cases. I would say a good example in the institution we were talking about, there was a,—you couldn't call it a rape,—well, you could, depending on how you viewed it—in which a kid here, when he came in the door, was a rather naive kid from a rural area. The word was put out that he was an easy mark because he had been known from a training school to be used by other kids for a screw. He was approached, apparently, by some kids, and he made an arrangement to meet one of them. The one, then showed up with three or four others, and within like thirty feet of a staff member, who was around the corner, he was raped over a period of two or three days a number of times. You could call it rape and you couldn't because he never yelled, and he never said anything to anybody.

V: But didn't he perceive that it would do him no good to yell and scream?

M: Probably. There's no question that it was a result of poor supervision in the program, and a lack of program itself. On the other hand, the fact that it was found out was some indication of some good things in the program. Because some of the other kids brought it to the attention of the staff, and it was worked with the kids, and it worked out reasonably well. So that it wasn't like a prison rape where a guy's dragged under a staircase and raped, and the whole system plays into it. I don't know how you expect to avoid problems when you lock everybody of one sex in a big building. Unless you've got some kind of really dynamite program around the clock, you're just going to have a lot of problems.

V: The only quarrel I have with that is that when I was at Andros, we didn't *have* a dynamite program.

M: You had a lot of active programs. And it wasn't real large, either.

V: Oh no, it definitely wasn't.

M: You weren't talking about a hundred in the building or that sort of thing.

V: I'm assuming—I'm not talking about now, I'm talking about in the future—in other words, if we were to have an institution of no more than thirty-five or forty kids,—

M: You shouldn't have any rapes.

V: Would it be fair to say also that we shouldn't have any suicides?

M: Sure.

V: Would it be fair to say we shouldn't have any stabbings?

M: Well, if it's a good program, you shouldn't have any of that. You shouldn't have any of what's routine in the prison. Now Camp Hill, I would guess a rape a week, unreported. A rape a month, reported.

V: In other words, when we're setting up criteria for institutions, including a voucher system and an inspection system, we can also say that there are certain overt, large kinds of acts, that would brand the institution as not working properly?

M: Yes. In large institutions, that's part and parcel of the place. You wouldn't have the institutionalized violence either. You wouldn't have the hole, right? You wouldn't be dragging people off in handcuffs in the middle of the night to stash them here or there, or beating people or making them run down a line, or things like that. That's the institutionalized violence, which is kind of the backdrop to the rape, is in many ways causative of the rape . . . I mean, to suggest that a place like Camp Hill could exist without rapes is nonsense.

V: What about this? I personally believe that the homosexual rape that takes place in juvenile institutions is not sexually motivated at all.

M: I think that's true. I wouldn't say "at all," I'm sure people get off on it. There's some sex in it, but I don't have any question at all that it's basically violence. And it's related to the institutionalized violence that undergirds prisons.

V: You use it as a control mechanism, right?

M: Yes. Well, I've seen some prisons where it's used as a means of control by the guards and the administration, right. Joliet, for instance, where they put six and seven in a hole together, in a dark unlighted hole. The hole there was a dark room, there's no bars, solid steel cages, no nothing, meals slid in. The way I saw it used when I went through there I couldn't imagine that facility not being used to control inmates, whereby known homosexual rapists would (it's not a good word, homosexual rapists, because they're usually heterosexuals who are raping in a homosexual way) who are put in a room, and then a victim put in with them if he's out of line. Well, the way—you can play it like an accordion, in terms of the themes and the variations, once you have that kind of institutionalized violence.

V: Don't you have cadet captains? Anytime you have a duke system that's recognized like that . . .

M: But they all have them, though, don't they. I don't know of a prison that doesn't have a duke system. The runners, for instance, at Camp Hill—they call them tier boys—open and lock the cells. Control the mechanisms. Now officially they'll say they can't unless a guard is there. That's nonsense. They can, they can set them so people can go in and out, and they can set people up, and they can set people up for planning things. Well, you know, the same routine. And that just goes with the barter system, and the whole craziness.

V: Now isn't that a continual rewarding of the "might makes right" kind of syndrome?

M: That's right. That's right. And it's a reinforcement of the worst impulses that we have. It's a reinforcement of the worst. Personalities, you think, tend toward health generally, if given a chance. Prisons tend toward destructiveness, if given a chance. It's like Zimbardo's studies. You know those studies, where he placed college students in "mock" prisons and they acted sadistically as "guards" and had emotional problems as "prisoners." Well, that's a classic sort of a study, and I think it's true, that they make people worse.

V: Do you think that that study was valid?

M: I had problems with some of the methodology, but I on the basis of my own experience, I would certainly say that his findings are unquestionably correct.

V: I think his findings were correct. I had real problems with the speed with which he claimed things happened.

M: I don't know. Middle class kids that have not been subjected to that kind of experience tend to disintegrate more quickly. It's like middle-class gangs. I did a study on middle class gangs. All-white gangs in the Bethesda-Chevy Chase area a few years ago. And one thing that characterized middle-class gangs was that when they got caught they all snitched on one another. The whole thing collapses very quickly.

V: You think that's a middle-class attribute?

M: Not alone. But I think it's probably more characteristic.

V: If that was the case, I would assume that middle-class kids are less able to do time.

M: I think that's true.

V: So there's something about the whole experience of not having money in this country that prepares you to do time?

M: I don't think it prepares you to do time in the sense that you should do time, but I think that it's not as foreign to a person from the prison of the ghetto. To move into the prison of the prison, and that's why a lot of the terms—the prison terms and street terms—are identical. When you read some of George Jackson's stuff, for instance, and they talk about "the man," and they talk about this and that. It's very difficult—the lingo, the whole structure and all, of the way in which the ghetto's perceived, is very similar to the way in which the prison's perceived. And the authorities act in much the same manner. It's not any less harmful or hurtful to the poor, but in many ways, I think they deal with it in a healthier way. Do you see what I mean?

V: I do. And I want to ask you something about that. One of the criticisms about counseling youths, is that if you run a viable juvenile prison system, and it's really working, you have the effect of "declawing" these children who have to return to that same environment. Do you have a response to that?

M: I'm not sure I understand that. In other words, if you put a kid in an institution for a while, and then release him, that you've declawed him?

V: Yes. If it's a good institution.

M: Oh, I see, I see. Then he doesn't have the skills to deal with the street. Okay. No I don't think so at all. I think, well, what you've done, if it's good—and I don't know many good ones—say a good program, not a good institution but a good program, is that you've given him additional skills, so that he can use his street skills in a smarter way vis-à-vis the whole middle-class society. I mean, what characterizes poor kids is that they don't have the options the middle-class kid has and therefore they're stuck with their way of handling it. Now, a middle-class kid, if he's bright and if he's been educated to all the manipulations of the middle class, can play it both ways. He may be able to be a little street wise, or he can learn that, but he also knows how to play Mr. Superstraight. Lower-class kids may not know that. You learn that if you've been around the courts long enough. You know enough to say "yes, your honor," and "no, sir" rather than "yeah" and what have you. But a lot of kids, the first time around are gulped up in that right away. They don't know how to dress right when they go into the courtroom—when I say dress right, I mean to say dress to please a middle-class judge, because he's the one who's going to put it to him. The middle-class gangs that I worked on, they were pros in court appearance and court behavior, and their parents had briefed them on how to say you're sorry and you're penitent, even though you aren't. They learned all those skills, all the Watergate skills, and in a sense, those things have never been made available to poor kids.

V: Those are viable things or valuable things, that should be made available to poor kids?

M: Hell, yes. And then you've got the option of using them. And then, in a sense, your crime is more responsible, if you will; if you then want to go one way, you can go that way and then you ought to get punishment if you do. But the problem with most of the people caught in the system is that they never had that choice. They were forced into situations where they could only go one way, and in a sense their crime is irresponsible as a result.

V: In the situation where you're going to create a viable institution, a small institution to deal with a certain type of criminal behavior by kids, it goes without saying that you have a socioeconomic mix in that institution.

M: Yes. You'd have to.

V: It's not necessarily something that you would create, it would just have to happen. Especially because of the fact that some types of crime, such as murder, tend to cut across class lines, a lot more than armed robbery does.

M: That's true, although the chances of your getting a cross-class group is a little less, because the courts tend to work out quiet arrangements, even on murder. But I would think any decent institution should go across class lines, for violent kids because there are violent middle-class kids, and violent upper middle-class kids. It should be multiracial, and I would even go so far as to say that it ought to be coed eventually, but I realize that that presents problems.

V: I think we'll leave that for another time. I could see where that could lead to some heavy difficulties—some very heavy difficulties.

M: It could get into heavy difficulties. But the coed aspect, if it's well done, can reduce the violence. You get out of the machismo stuff.

V: I agree with that, because that happened at Andros. No question about female staff, it certainly decreased the level of violence, and increased certain interpersonal and social skills that were important.

M: You know, at the very least, you've got to have a sexually integrated staff. In that kind of environment.

V: You're not, I take it, in favor of all-black institutions, all-Hispanic institutions.

M: Oh no, no I'm not. If that's the way the country's going, and if that's the way it's going to be, one would be in favor of that. But given this situation, I don't think you could even say that, now that I think about it. Because you would always have a certain group controlling the power anyway, and an all-black institution within the correctional establishment means self-determination for blacks, the same way George Wallace means it in Alabama, when they let a certain area of the city murder and rape and do whatever they want, and stand outside and leave it alone..

V: You mean like that benign neglect kind of nonsense?

M: Yes. By neglect, you define a "certain element" as "animals" and you forget them so long as they don't touch our pure white folks. And I think that there's even that element when they talk about conjugal visits in prisons. It has a zoo-like, "let's bring in the gals that service the studs" kind of thing. And even though the idea is a very good idea, the way the prison establishment would use it could be very destructive.

V: One of our consultant-advisors, Louis X. Holloway, was a prisoner on a Mississippi plantation for five years, and he described conjugal visits as the way you service a mule.

M: Well, that's exactly right.

V: In fact, for many, many years whites were not permitted conjugal visits in Mississippi, just blacks, and the conditions under which the conjugal visits take place, including observation, of course, tend to enforce that mentality.

M: It's a whole craziness. And unless the motivation's well-understood, the programs don't mean anything.

V: Do you believe with me that conjugal visitation will do nothing whatever to decrease rapes inside an institution.

M: Yes. I don't think it would decrease it. They're more related to violence.

V: You couldn't really establish conjugal visitation for juveniles without an extreme amount of difficulty.

M: If we were in Sweden we might.

V: In Sweden you might. Here, you'd be violating the law every time it happened.

M: In Sweden, if you know, or maybe if you don't know, you can have a girl friend visit. And it's done in a respectful way with private cottages.

V: But see, that's not necessarily the hallmark of a progressive system, because Mexico has exactly the same system. Because the only place that they have conjugal visiting in a heavyweight sense here in this country is Mississippi.

M: That's right. The issue of conjugal visits—conjugal visits themselves don't mean a hell of a lot. It really isn't a basic reform.

V: Could you envision a maximum-security institution, a secure setting for juveniles, from which there would be no furloughs?

M: No. I could envision a *kid* who could not have a furlough, but I would never want to envision an *institution*, because then you would have to fit the kids to fit a policy. I could see where that tradition might build up if you had certain kinds of kids for a given period of time. But, I would never want to see any institution where any kid might not fit the rules. In other words, at some time, you might want to do it differently, and if you get a tradition around no one ever having furloughs, then you're bound to have problems.

V: I take it, from your statements and from my knowledge of you, that you're against this so-called "medical model" of juvenile rehabilitation.

M: Yes. I don't think it's very appropriate.

V: Can you explain why?

M: Well, it's too narrow. And the whole rehabilitative model, I don't think it has been very appropriate for these kids. It's too narrow a model. Too restrictive. If you look around this country at the very worst institutions for adults, the worst imaginable institutions, the most repressive, brutal, etc., they are generally medically run institutions for the criminally insane. Where you have the combination of corrections and medicine, usually run by M.D.'s, they're the worst. Lima, in Ohio, Bridgewater in Massachusetts, Farview here in Pennsylvania, they're unbelievably bad. The medical model may fit for a broken leg, but for these other issues, it's far too authoritarian and it's far too trusting of the system.

V: Then you would have a similar feeling towards pure chemotherapy?

M: Yes.

V: Toward aversive therapy?

M: Toward aversive therapy, definitely. I see no place for aversive therapy in corrections. Aversive therapy, even if I believed in its effectiveness, and I think part of the problem is that it *might* be effective, has no place in corrections. The only place that I can see it having a place is with totally voluntary patients. If someone wants to go out and get themselves a shock for bad behavior, that's their business.

V: But that's not really possible in corrections, to be noncoercive.

M: That's right. That's why I say it has no place in corrections at all. Even though a person may say he's doing it voluntarily, he just isn't. Promises are made. Things are perceived in such a way that if I do this it may mean I'll get out, so that as long as you have captives, I don't think you can ever use aversive therapy.

V: Now, I was in places—I was in Pennsylvania—do you know the [name deleted] joint?

M: I know *of* it, but I don't know it.

V: When I interviewed the kids there, they all said we're here voluntarily, we're not doing time, we're here to be helped. A very routinized kind of mystique, which was totally unimpressive to me. Frightening to me actually, because in fact, under closer examination they were there as an alternative to Camp Hill.

M: That's the problem we had in Massachusetts, initially, if you remember, with the concept houses, the self-help drug houses. Because although they mouthed the therapeutic philosophy, they all depended on the slammer, "If you don't shape up here kid, in you go." And it's across the board— Odyssey, Marathon, Synanon—it's across the board. Now the older programs, the more mature programs, learned to adjust to the fact that we didn't have slammers for kids, and they learn to keep kids in their programs other than through threats, and they did better. And as time went by, certain of them did very well with our kids. But a lot of them it seems to me, are very phony. They play both sides. They talk about how bad prisons are, how we need to get more group homes, how we need to get more therapeutic communities, but when push comes to shove, they like to use the prison as a means of motivating someone to stay with their program.

V: Have you somewhat soured on the therapeutic community model?

M: Yes. But I've soured on them in terms of coercing kids into them. The same way with group homes. Group homes can get just as demanding. Because we don't have any real consumerism in this field, because the vendors make all the decisions, there's a whole escalation of things, whereby the threats are always there. I'll give you an example. If you took Phillips Exeter Academy and had nothing but captive freshman class, brought in in handcuffs and told they had to be there, it wouldn't matter what kind of faculty you had: as time went by it would deteriorate, because you make decisions at most comfort to yourself, no matter who you are, and people can't depend on your altruism twenty-four hours a day. And it tends to work against the better care of the kids. Just that status of being a captive and having to stay in a place against your will does something to the staff.

V: Do you believe that the average child that's been involved in a crime of violence can sufficiently internalize the fact that he has lost a couple of his options. Not all of them.

M: Well I'm not saying that certain kids can't be locked up or shouldn't be.

V: And that's the option I'm talking about. In that sense he can't control the situation. Even if he were the primary consumer, he's going to be locked in the same place.

M: Right. But if you could build an element of choice into that, into at least saying which place, that might be of some help.

V: Well, didn't you have kids trying to bargain with you, like after you were commissioner.

M: Yes, like people would always say, my social worker friends, even would say, "well, you're being manipulated" and "the kids are running the system, and they're playing a game on you" and all of that. But see I don't mind that because that's none of my business whether the kids wants to play a game on me or not. I could care less. What I care about is whether he's getting in further trouble or not, and if I can keep a kid out of trouble by playing a game, great. Sometimes it works, sometimes it doesn't. It's a whole series of games, and I don't mind that. I'd say now and then you like to tell a kid that you know he's playing a game. But if he wants to, you're willing to go with it. I wouldn't want a kid always to think he's conning me. But I know, when I was in the service, for instance, screening airmen in a psychiatric clinic, some guys who really despised the service, and couldn't make it very well, you knew there was a way to get out, and that was by going through the psychiatric clinic and getting say a character disorder diagnosis. I had no problem with if a kid wants out badly enough to—but then I would want to say to the kid, "I don't believe this diagnosis, you don't believe this diagnosis, here's what it is, now this is what will happen if you get it. There will be this little number on your discharge, and it will bother you around jobs and all, now you weigh whether you want to take that or whether you want to stay in. If you want to take that I've got no problem."

V: And kids went both ways.

M: Sure. And I think that it's done regularly. It's done regularly in the service. There is no such thing as a character disorder. It's a nonsense diagnosis. It's an administrative procedure.

V: Now, to sum up, you believe that a juvenile correctional system *can* rehabilitate, that's fair to say, right? And that the current system is not rehabilitating.

M: Right.

V: Okay. But there's room within, without incredible sweeping changes, there's room even I might say within the statutes—to run a viable system, is that correct?

M: I think so, yes.

V: But you're opposed to the whole method of doing business in juvenile court, that's where we have a real problem.

M: Yes, that's the major problem. I'd say that's the major problem in Pennsylvania.

V: How far would you want to go, Jerry? Would you want a trial by jury?

M: I would want both. I would want to offer an option. I would use a model—there are some models—you know, there are some European countries that have never had juvenile courts. Sweden, Holland, Denmark.

V: Russia.

M: Russia, yes. Scotland, China, Scotland, East Germany, Yugoslavia. And there are variations on that and I think that what I would do is offer the kid an option, of having something akin to community councils which themselves would be only allowed certain options. I think the law would have to be very clear that they couldn't be sending a lightweight kid away, that sort of thing. He'd be offered the option of a community council, or he'd be offered the option of a regular adult proceeding, with all those guarantees.

V: Wouldn't this evolve to the current adult system, whereby, if I've got a guilty client I'll go before a jury, and if I have an innocent client I go before a judge?

M: Well, there's that danger. There's that danger. But in the juvenile area, the tradition is "everybody's guilty." I mean you really have to look hard to find any one who's ever found innocent.

V: Then it's fair to say that the juvenile advocate—be it attorney, social worker, or whatever—his major thrust is on disposition, right?

M: Yes. Yes. And see if we said "Look, this is a council that you're going to meet and it's all disposition, we aren't even going to talk about guilt," then it would be interesting.

V: What about the polygraph, Jerry, do you have a position on that? So many people advocate the use of polygraph on disposition alone. In other words, if there's already been a finding of guilty, and the kid—still insists that he's innocent—and it's one of these "too close to call" kinds of cases, the polygraph would be heard by the judge, and if of course the kid passes, the disposition would be a suspended sentence.

M: It's interesting. I'd never thought of that. I really haven't thought—

V: We have been advocating this for a couple of years now. Because you do have cases where the only actual eye witness was a seven year old, and let's fact it, some things we lack.

M: That's interesting. The reason I guess I've never heard it is because you'd never get the advocacy kind of lawyer involved in juvenile crime that would even think about that in most cases. You'd have to look through months of proceedings in this state to find a case that's been appealed ever. It's just routine. And then you have a very bad public defender situation, particularly in the smaller counties, where the public defender practices law before the same judge most of the time and then public defends part of the time, he doesn't want to alienate the judge so he doesn't really defend much.

V: Isn't that the problem with a lot of court liaison people want to pretend they're lawyers?

M: Sure.

V: Are you saying that kids would need the same kind of aggressive defense that any adult would need?

M: I think so, if you're going to go that route.

V: But if you go whole hog to defend a kid—really put on a full trial—

M: Then the judge will put it to the kid.

V: Yes he will.

M: Yes, but I would say that if they were strictly like adult proceedings, not the juvenile court at all, you'd probably have a better chance. You know, it's an awful thing to say, because I would not want to be on record as saying that I think all kids ought to be tried in adult court, because I don't. But, on the other hand, the experience in Massachusetts was, when they started binding kids over to adult court because we didn't have training schools, and there was about a 30 percent increase in kids being sent to adult court, the later research showed those kids did not end up in adult prisons. Because they were usually found not guilty in adult court, or they were returned back to the youth department, or they were put on probation. The adult court—given all the guarantees of an adult court, versus juvenile court, most of the kids got off.

V: And I also had that experience. I've represented a number of those kids that had the experience that because a place like Andros existed as another option, the judge . . .

M: Sent them there.

V: Another reason why a maximum-security or a secure setting has to exist for juveniles is, I think, that there's a waiver provision.

M: There's a waiver, and if you're very clear on your intake, because the danger is what we're finding now with the closing of Camp Hill. Well, for instance, in Weaversville at Allentown, we've set up a ten or twelve bed unit—a locked unit for kids. Well, now a judge goes out and looks at that and it's very nice. I mean it's a small little building really nice staff, a lot of things going on, kids well dressed, things looking good. Then the judge wants to send there kids that he'd never have sent to Camp Hill. But kids that are a pain in the ass to him and he wants to put them in a lock facility, he feels too guilty putting them in an adult prison, now we've got a juvenile locked facility and we'll fill it up. What's not realized is that the juvenile locked facility should be for kids who would normally go to the prison on serious violent crimes, period.

V: In other words, the one-step diminution of penalty right down the line.

M: Because otherwise, if you just create facilities and don't clearly define the target population that's going in them they'll just fill them up as fast as you build them. If you create group homes, they'll take kids out of their own home and put them into group homes. They won't take them out of the institutions. If you make more institutions, they'll take kids out of the group homes and put them in the institutions, and if you make maximum security places, they'll take kids out of the training schools and put them in maximum security because most maximum-security lock facilities for juveniles are not full of violent kids. They're full of kids who have been management problems in other facilities, and rather than hold those facilities responsible, we stash the kids.

V: That brings me to a very important point. I've had a lot of people in the business tell me that if a viable maximum-security institution were created for juveniles, that would take so-called hard-core kids, it would take the weight off the entire rest of the system. That one particularly rough kid can contaminate a whole program.

M: Well, that's a possibility, but I don't think it's particularly true because— that can happen, but generally the kid who so-called contaminates the program is not the violent kid. That happens now and then. But usually what will happen, is a kid will be a management problem, he's not a violent kid, he's just a management problem, doesn't like the institution, he might be a runaway, or a kid who's called incorrigible. But he doesn't get with the program, he's sassy, he throws something now and then, he won't stay, and those are the kids they'll want to lock up. And if you get into that it never ends because there are as many management problems as there are institutions. As soon as he leaves, someone replaces him. Now, if you're talking about a really violent kid who's killing or raping that's a different thing and that kid should be in a locked facility.

V: But what I'm saying is that you have a facility in New York, maybe it has four hundred children. I'm saying that if you took four kids out of that institution you could run the whole institution differently.

M: Yes. I think there's some truth to that, although you have to watch it. Institutions have a way of making roles so that those four will be replaced as soon as you removed them. It's like the current fad which holds that if we could gather up all the repeat offenders on the street á la Gerry Ford's recommendations and put them away, that we'd cut the crime rate. Hell. All those repeat offenders will be replaced almost the day you remove others.

V: Have you looked at the situation nationwide? Can you give me some predictions as to which way the juvenile legislation is going to go?

M: Well, right now it is in a repressive stage. The more liberal states are bottoming out on that, I think, we'll find they'll get more enlightened again in the next year or so. The less liberal states are just getting into it. Because of the cultural lag they are two or three years behind, so I think we'll have a fair amount of repressive legislation over the next year or two in many of the more conservative states. And we'll find New York looking better again in a year or so, I think.

V: You do?

M: Yes, I think so. Less repressive. I think there'll be a lot of reasons for that. I think we'll see a fair amount of slaughter as a result of the Supreme Court decision on capital punishment and that will, after fifty or sixty people have been killed, people will start to feel guilty again, and we'll be in era of reform and rehabilitation. People haven't understood and realized what's really meant when people say let's get back to capital punishment, let's throw away the key and all, and I have enough trust in people that if they understood that they would move away from it again.

V: Well, it is a fact that Massachusetts could execute a fourteen-year-old boy under the statutes, isn't that right?

M: I don't think you'd see it happening right now, but it's a fact.

V: The fact that it could happen is perhaps more important than whether it is happening.

M: I think what will happen, is that you'll see enough people dragged off to death row on television. I remember very vividly the last one that Ronald Reagan had executed and that will have an effect, I think, not the effect that capital punishment proponents think it will have. I think it will rebound. If there were too much of it done, however, it will have the opposite effect. People get a little bloodthirsty. If we had public executions it would turn out crowds unbelievably, it would become a circus, so that there's always that danger. But I think we have hopefully advanced enough as a society to be able to avoid that.

V: What about the idea of protecting society now with a more far-sighted view. For example, how do you respond to the statement that virtually every heavyweight criminal in this country is produced,—from Manson, to Panzram to Speck to anybody you want to name—virtually grew up in a juvenile institution? Do you think that's an accurate statement?

M: I think it's accurate. I don't think people understand it, yet, I think it's very accurate.

V: Do you think if people did understand it, they would respond to this whole problem of juvenile corrections differently?

M: Yes. And for a while they do understand then they forget. And then someone hits someone on their block and they forget. Yes, I think that's very true. And I think the only way people will understand really is if you have enlightened correctional administrators who expose their own system.

V: Do you think there's something about this country that makes it criminogenic as to juveniles, for example the fact that we now have tremendous violence problems with Chinese youth in New York, which were not there five years ago?

M: Yes, well you know the old story that has to do with the dissolution of family life, I think there's some truth to that. But there's also a tremendous tradition of violence in this country and the correctional system is a distillation of societal values in many ways. When you have a captive, you have freedom to do whatever you wish with and to that person particularly if they've done something pretty bad. The worst impulses of society will be right there. If you have a violent culture and a violent society, you'd have to anticipate that the corrections will have to be the worst of that, and I think that's very true.

V: But you think the fact that this kind of harsh treatment, this kind of brutal treatment especially produces increased criminal behavior—is lost on the general public?

M: Sure. I think it's lost on them now. Otherwise they wouldn't be calling for more incarceration to handle the crime problem. What they don't realize is that we incarcerate more per hundred thousand than any country in the

Western world now with the possible exception of South Africa. And we also have the highest crime rate and the biggest recidivism rate. You'd think they'd draw that sort of connection, but it hasn't been drawn. The solution still is to lock up more. Eventually that will collapse on itself. You just can't continue to lock up the numbers. Now I notice in the South there was some impetus toward releasing people early, but the legislative impetus is toward building more prisons. Eventually I think that will collapse on itself. I think there was more hope for it in the late sixties when with the advent of the drug culture, you had a lot of middle-class kids being locked up. If we could have prisons with middle-class inmates, the prisons would go out of business fairly soon.

V: But even in New York where they have the harshest drug penalties in the entire world? Most of the appellate courts are finding ways to set aside convictions, like life sentences for possession of LSD.

M: That's one reason why—I notice in Carter's platform, or not his platform, but a Jack Anderson column on his crime committee task force, they were going to stress more middle-class, white-collar and executive crime, as they should go to jail.

V: Does Carter have clean hands to talk? Is the juvenile system in Georgia anything that he'd be bragging about?

M: I don't know much about it. I know the correctional system, vis-à-vis other states in the South isn't that bad. At least he made some attempts.

V: Well look at the rest of the South. You're certainly not talking about North Carolina—

M: It's just awful. And South Carolina, Alabama . . .

V: Louisiana, Mississippi . . .

M: I'm saying next to them, Georgia isn't as bad. And I'm saying at the time he was governor, at least he visited all the prisons and showed some interest in that field. If you were to lock more middle-class people up, if they were really to go after white-collar crime, then I think you'd see a tremendous change in the prison system.

V: Wouldn't they just build more Allenwoods and Danburys?

M: That's the danger. But others would have to be put in those places too. I think that somewhere along the line in the next decade or so, some governor is going to see the political advantage of suggesting the abolition of most prisons.

V: Where would you suggest that might happen? In what kind of state?

M: Well it would happen in a state like Wisconsin or Washington or Oregon, one of those states. And if it were to happen there, then it would have a lot of meaning for a lot of other states as time went by. It could be put aside by states like New York and New Jersey who say that doesn't apply to our kind of urban multiracial society and all, but I think what they'd find is that it could apply. The reason it will happen in those states is because prisoners in those states are more like the people who put them away. They're basically white, some approach being middle class, they're rural, and that's why it'll happen there. When prison reform is instituted by a power structure that feels that they are superior or different from the people they are treating you never have it. The best you have is some sort of paternalism. But if you can get something that's closer—I guess that the key to prison reform is to have the prisons full of people like the people that run them.

V: And in this case, you need prisons full of the children of the people that run them?

M: I never went out of my way in Massachusetts, for instance, to get a middle-class kid out of our system. In fact we tried to hang onto them. I can remember sitting with a couple of kids and saying "Look, I'm going to try to fight to keep you here because you will add something and your folks will add something to this system, of getting us some change, and I hope you understand this," and the kid would understand it. I remember talking to a youngster out at Roslindale sitting there reading Tolstoy, and I said "It's really good to have you here. I hope you realize this is all a game and you're not going to be mistreated, but you can help us in changing this whole damn thing," because his folks were up the wall over the possibility of his being mistreated, whereas a poor kid might not have a family around to help with that.

L: Let me ask a question. Once you implement these programs and let's say that they are successful in the institutional environment, and then you return this person back to his jungle-like environment, the thing that really initiated his troubles in the first place; what kinds of programs would be provided in regards to the family structure, community structure, to continue right on the kind of programs?

M: Well, first off, the majority of kids that we're presently removing and placing out here as you look out the window, I wouldn't remove. I'd leave them in that community, because they're going to want to be there anyway. Most kids want to return to their own community. Now there are exceptions and I'd like to talk about that, but the fact is whether we like a family or not or whether we think a family's good or not, most kids return to that family, and they prefer it over anything else. For every kid that's removed from Philadelphia and placed in a state institution, I'd say we are spending thirty thousand dollars which could otherwise go into that community. Now let's find some resources in that community. Now that might include some kind of family help, it might include assigning someone to help keep the family together, it might include assigning someone full time with the kid, it might include assigning someone all of his free time, evenings and weekends. It might include vocational training, it might include bussing arrangements, so he can get out to the suburbs to a decent school and back, to a private school and paying for it. It could include all sorts of things. We're spending twenty-three, twenty-four million a year primarily to remove kids from inner city areas. We're paying people out in rural areas to give them care that doesn't work, and then we return them to a survival setting. That's not helping anybody. I would put that money back in there you know.

V: I think that makes perfect sense, and I think it's also fiscally sound because it wouldn't disturb the specific gravity of the budget. What about the single exception, though? You go back to the secure setting. You're only going to have one, or maybe we'll have two or three, but they're small, obviously we can't locate each one . . .

M: Back at home. Well, there's some kids who shouldn't go back home. Like kids in the gang situation for instance. I'd be very leery, and if you've talked to kids from gangs, some of them don't want to go back. It doesn't have much to do with the family, as it does with fear of getting shot, or fear of what's going on, and I think you've got to have that flexibility for some kids to set them up elsewhere. Like in Harrisburg, it's a different situation. It's kind of a rural small town problem, but there are some towns like York, for instance, where there's a heavy gang problem, kind of an old Appalachian "hit 'em on the head" gang problem, among the white kids. We've got some kids living in Harrisburg, which is far enough away from York, it's like thirty miles, to keep them out of it, but it's close enough so they can go back now and then and see the family and the family can come see them, but we've got them set up with a foster home in Harrisburg. The worst thing we could do for those kids is place them down in York. And I'm sure the same thing's true in Philadelphia with some black kids in the black gang areas. Unless you've got a really good program, like we've got the House of Umoja in Philadelphia that's worked real well. Sister Fatah works with gang kids and kids from that area. They are in their own area and still be a bit protected.

V: What about using the secure setting to reverse the usual problem of reentry. Here's what I mean: Let's say when you build the secure setting you don't make it a typical setting. It has an olympic swimming pool, it has a basketball court, it has a theater, it has an emergency ward kind of hospital setting, with actual interns. It has, in other words, a whole spectrum of facilities that the surrounding community does not have, and instead of taking the kids and saying "can we use your YMCA?" we say "you can use our facilities," and start the reentry in that fashion.

M: Well, that's another way to do it. I think that would work if it was done by the right people. The danger in it is that—like large training schools have often done that, in the past . . .

V: I don't think so. Any institutions that I've seen have had superior athletic facilities and that's it. They have no other kinds of facilities.

M: I think the more you can bring the community in the better. It helps as a watchdog way too.

V: In fact, in a Pennsylvania, in most fully nonurbanized settings, even the poorest, dirt poor communities will have athletic facilities. So that really isn't that much of a hook.

M: The number of violent kids are so relatively small that I would think any small institution you develop for them ought to have with it the kind of outreach whereby you could get the kids out of there with someone on his arm to go to a lot of places.

V: In other words, you would concede that such an institution couldn't be "community based?"

M: It could be.

V: But it could only be one community, it would be to the exclusion of another.

M: Unless you're going to have them settle in that community when they leave. You know, and that isn't going to happen. That's why I think the smaller facilities closer to the area that the kid's going to return to are better, and also allows you the option that if a kid has to get out of a community you have a place farther away that he can go to for a while.

V: Are you—optimistic or pessimistic about the future of juvenile corrections in this country?

M: I'm neither, you know. At times I'm very optimistic, at times I'm very pessimistic.

V: Is it going to get worse before it gets better?

M: In some states—I think it's bottomed out in the East I think it will start getting better about the first of next year. I think it's about as bad as it's going to be right now. But you can never tell—

V: Do you think it's the public that's changing or because there's Jerry Millers running around?

M: No, no. It has nothing to do with me—I think it has to do with the political climate, and I think people will be preoccupied with other things. Durkheim said a long time ago that when people aren't taken up in a war with an outside nation, for instance, they turn inward and they scapegoat, and they generally look to the criminal to go after. And I think we've been through that period now. Vietnam's over, and there's no huge conflict to point at. There's a whole kind of inner scapegoating. For a while it was people on welfare, recently they've kind of gotten off that, now it's the criminal. Now we're all after the criminal, and interestingly, it's the juvenile offender, the dangerous juvenile offender, there's a big preoccupation—

V: The reason I question you about bottoming out and public opinion is the *Daily News*, which, regardless of your opinion of its intellectual pretentions, has some pretty accurate straw vote polls, and in one 79 percent of the respondents said lock them up and throw away the key as far as kids are concerned . . .

M: Well, I'm sure that's true. But, see, that's always been true. I can remember the *Daily News* when I first went to Massachusetts in 1969, I can remember reading a thing they did on capital punishment, and they had to stop the series, it was so violent. They wanted suggestions, and people wanted kids fingers cut off on TV, and they wanted maiming, and it got really ridiculous.

V: These are people that haunt Times Square, but they're different kinds of folks.

M: But see, that underlay is always there, and I don't think any society ever gets away from that. I think every society's potentially a Nazi society. At the same time they're potentially the best of a Greek society. It depends on interplay of fears and all, as to what happens.

V: But you think the good guys will win?

M: No, I hope [laughter]. No, I don't think so.

L: I want to say something. It might not be that important but it's from my own personal experience. When I went into prison my background was shabby places, broke down, run down, no electricity, and going through prison, the various sattelites of prison, through college, going to a modern place like Leesburg [State Prison]. In fact, the place was better than any place I lived in the street—and coming back out into the street, I was despondent, because I had to live in a rat-infested area. I had to work in greasy factories. I went to school. And mentally, I think, I was thinking better than a lot of people that were in the community, not necessarily so, but I think mentally I had the right frame of mind, and I wanted to do something constructive, but around me was nothing to initiate that.

M: But if they've given you the supports—in other words, if you had available to you the amount of money that was spent to lock you up, you could have been in a very fine position, not to live in a rat-infested place. You know what I mean. It's probably costing the state twelve to fifteen thousand to keep you in any jail. And this idea, of that when you finish your term you go back to whatever's there, is nonsense.

V: And it's worse on children than it is on adults, right?

M: Yes, In many ways it's a sadder commentary on the society that a prison would be nicer than the community.

L: I said that in reference because options seem to be a very important part of what's been going on here. When I came out there were no options. The option that I was given in prison for an education, for social interaction with people, wasn't there. This guy that I know that came out had been in school, he had been doing good, inside, and he started throwing bricks.

M: Yes, and that's where the prison system impinges on the whole societal thing because we obviously aren't spending enough in the whole area of poverty programs and straightening out the cities!

**Interview between Andrew Vachss (V) and
T. Robert Clements (C), on July 21, 1976**

T. Robert Clements has been confined to penal institutions for most of his life, beginning when he was about ten years old. As a result, "Clem" is in a unique position to observe changes in correctional philosophy and procedure over the past decades.

He received the B.A. degree in community services from Trenton State College in 1972 while incarcerated, and has held a number of vital positions on committees and rehabilitative programs in the prison community. He is one of the founders of the Rahway Lifers Group Juvenile Awareness Program, which brings juveniles who have first come into contact with the criminal justice system inside a maximum security institution to give them a brief experience of their future if they continue along the path they seem to have selected. This program has received national recognition and is a model for similar efforts in many other states.

Clem has served as director for the Ad Hoc Parole Committee, law clerk in the prison law library, coordinator for the New Jersey Prisoners' Art Colony, and as consultant to the Juvenile Justice Planning Project. Paroled from a New Jersey life sentence, he is currently awaiting release from his last remaining prison sentence at Graterford Prison in Pennsylvania.

V: Would it be fair to characterize you, prior to your coming here on this bit, as a life-style criminal?

C: Yes.

V: Would it be fair to say that you have no compunctions about stealing?

C: My conscience left me when I was about ten years old.

V: Okay. Would it be fair to say that you would use violence to achieve your ends?

C: Yes.

V: Would it be fair to say that the only rules that you lived by were a sort of a criminal code?

C: Rules of the street. See, I started in crime when I was about ten years old, the first time, right? I got busted for a stolen car, which I was riding in. That may sound funny: you might say how does a guy ten years old reach the pedals. I was riding in it, I got picked up by two other guys while I was standing on the corner, and they said, "Bobby, would you like to go for a ride?" And I said, "yeah." Went two blocks, cops busted us, it was a stolen car. The oldest guy was seventeen, he got two to three years in the penitentiary, and me, and the other kid who was fifteen, got eighteen months in the Camp Hill Reformatory.

V: You got eighteen months at Camp Hill when you were ten years old?

C: Right.

V: Tell me about Camp Hill.

C: I guess, well it was back in the forties.

V: Right.

C: It was, it's hard to describe vermin, dirt, really bad there.

V: Did they still have the military model there?

C: Yes. You had to carry sticks, march with sticks, anywhere you went you marched.

V: I don't think it has changed much, from what—

C: Well they've done away with all military stuff.

V: In the last two or three years is all.

C: Right.

V: Well, look, let me put it this way. How did a ten-year-old boy survive at Camp Hill? What was the top age?

C: Twenty-one. I was put in a cottage, and the oldest guy in the cottage was the duke of the cottage, he was the toughest guy, he was nineteen. The second day that I was in the cottage I had a fight with this guy. I got my ass beat, but they respected me.

V: Because you were willing to fight him?

C: Because I was willing to fight him, not that I beat him. Alright. Now, as far as sex, the first time I was involved in a sex thing, I was in the shower, and a few guys came in and jumped me in the shower. Now, I picked up a mop wringer, I put one guy in the hospital, and I went in the hospital myself, because I got beat up real bad too. But after that, nobody bothered me anymore. Sex wasn't worth the fight.

V: Did you know what was going down when you went in the shower?

C: No, I had no idea.

V: So what motivated you to pick up the mop handle? Did you think this was a regular assault that was starting?

C: That's right. I thought it was a regular fight at first. Because everybody was in the shower nude, and what I mean by a mop wringer is the thing you wring mops out in. When I got done, all I had left was the handle, and I was all cut up. Our fighting made such a commotion that the cops came.

V: Okay, now you called it a sexual assault, but at the time you didn't think it was. When did you discover it was in fact intended to be a sexual assault?

C: After I got out of the hole. I got put in the hole. I went to the hospital first, to the infirmary, nurse looked at me said, "He's alright" then they took me to a lock-up, what they call an isolation cell. When I came out of the hole, the guys I hung around with told me they were trying to rip me off, but after that I never had any more problems with it.

V: Simply because of your willingness to be violent.

C: Right. To fight.

V: There were no previous overtures made to you?

C: No. Because I'd only been there about five days, six days when this happened. I was still in what they call quarantine cottage. Then when I did leave there and went to the other cottages my reputation preceded me. That's what kept people away from me.

V: What happened, did you observe other ten year olds, eleven year olds? What happened to them, did they have the same experiences?

C: Well, you get a lot of kids that are passive, you got to remember kids ten, eleven, twelve years old, when they go away, this is the first time being away from their family. Not being use to this for they are use to their mother or their father, whoever may be at home, telling them what to do, and they accepted that. Alright, now you got a kid that's fifteen or sixteen years old in a cottage with you, who's street-wise. This is maybe his third time of being down. So he knows how to get over on these kids. Knows what to say to them, knows how to con them. He might give them a half a pack of cigarettes. Smokes were "swag." If you got caught with cigarettes you were going to the hole, but if you had a smoking jones [habit] you might be apt to take them regardless of the hole. He might give the kid a smoke or something, and then tell him, "You owe me two smokes back." And the kid says, "I ain't got them, I don't know where I'm going to get them." And he'll say, "Well you can take care of business" and the next thing you know the kid is blowing the guy or being used as a woman.

V: Well, how do you separate—it happened to some kids and it didn't happen to others?

C: Mental attitude. It didn't make any difference how big you were. You could weigh two hundred pounds. You know that you've got kids fifteen years old that weigh that much. It was the way they carried themselves, the way they presented themselves. You could pick them out. It's the same way in the penitentiary, you can pick out a weak person easily.

V: Speaking of that, when you pick people out in the penitentiary, do the ones that are picked out as weak tend to be the ones that haven't done time before?

C: Yes.

V: Okay. So that kind of apprenticeship is in the juvenile joints?

C: The new guys are the ones who are taken advantage of, because the guy that's been there once or twice knows the ropes, he knows what he's got to do, he knows how to carry himself, he knows how he's got to talk, what he's got to say to get over.

V: Okay. Now, you did eighteen months on that first stretch?

C: Yes.

V: So you were still only eleven and a half years old?

C: Right.

V: Were you rehabilitated in there?

C: I was forced to go to school. That was in the A.M. I went to school from about eight o'clock in the A.M. until about eleven thirty. They had women and men who worked the cottages and they were called cottage mothers and fathers. These people took care of the teaching. All they wanted was for you to be there. We had a couple of teachers that did try to teach us, but when you have thirty-five or forty kids in the classroom who just don't give a shit about nothing, nobody learned anything. Rehabilitation, no. You learned how to hate, how to hate all authority, but worst of all you learned how to hate yourself.

V: Were the classrooms mixed as to age?

C: Oh, yes. You might have a kid in there twenty years old, and another kid eight years old, so the teaching level was geared only to teach you how to read and write, ABC's, things of that nature.

V: Okay did you think you were in prison?

C: Not prison as the word *prison* denotes. The first couple of months I was there, I was scared, lonely, sick. I got colds, and I didn't know what to do, because my mother always took care of this. I hadn't ever gone to a doctor myself. I didn't know how to do this, I didn't know what to tell the doctor. I used to tell my mother what was wrong and she'd tell the doctor and the doctor would know what was wrong. Many things like this.

V: Did you find that emphasis on people trying to convince you that a life of crime was a negative thing? Who were the big influences on your life there? Was it the other kids, or was it the staff?

C: Kids. The staff didn't have time to talk to us. It was either "don't do this," "get over there you son of a bitch, you bastard," always profanity. "I'm going to kick your ass if you don't do this, I'm going to bust your ass," and they would! They had what they called a bindle stick, four pieces of plywood nailed together. "Bend over and grab your ankles," and they would beat your legs right up to your ass. We were forced to march around the area for hours at a time if we did something wrong. You may have to go down and wash a cow down with a hose. That may sound funny, but you got a cow in front of you and you are standing up on a stool scrubbing with a scrub brush. Your pride is taken away from you, you're humiliated to the point where you begin to think and act like the dumb cow you are washing. Things like this. There was nothing said as to what you had done wrong, or why you were there, nor was there any help offered so you wouldn't come back. You were just doing time. In the afternoons you worked in the fields. You either worked in the dairy, or the piggery. You might work with the chickens. Now this may not sound too bad, but if you are shoveling cowshit or pigshit all afternoon, or you are cutting hay out in the hot sun and you are only ten or eleven years old, this isn't fun. It is the work of grown man. But we all had to work or else it was the bindle stick and the hole.

V: So what happened at night there?

C: Well, you had recreation there. You could play baseball or handball if it was good weather, or you could sit in the recreation room and play checkers or ping pong or rap with a friend or two. But at the end of the day you were always too tired for anything but sleep. You always wound up laying on your bunk reading a comic book until lights out which was nine o'clock. Do you want me to speak about how the kids cry?

V: If that's what they did.

C: Sure. Believe me, I'm talking about kids who were twenty years old. There were many strange noises at night. Many of the kids would cry at night, but this was never mentioned in the morning.

V: Now this was a cottage-type system, this wasn't cells?

C: Right. It was a cottage-type system. But they did have cells there, called them isolation (the hole). If a kid had a disease, they would put him in a cell.

V: If the kid had a disease they put him in a cell?

C: Yes. Isolation cell. If he had the measles, the mumps, because the hospital ward didn't have any separate area for these kids that had these communicable diseases.

V: Even if the child had a communicable disease, he didn't leave the prison?

C: No.

V: What kind of advice did the older kids give?

C: How to get over. How to get a smoke, how to get something extra to eat, how to sneak around the man.

V: How to jail, then, right?

C: How to jail, right.

V: Were there young people in there who had committed more serious crimes than yours?

C: The majority of the kids were in there for truancy from school. Playing hookey. There were kids in there for armed robbery, burglaries, but in those days there wasn't too many kids involved with drugs. If the guys who hung around the corners knew a guy was a dope fiend they'd chase him. I don't think there was anybody in there for murder, but there were kids in there for rape.

V: Did any murder take place in there? Were people stabbed in there?

C: Yes. But nobody died while I was there.

V: Nobody died? Was that a tribute to luck or what?

C: Just luck. Dumb luck, was all that kept them alive. I've seen guys cut with a sickle, the thing that you cut grass with. Banana handles, a knife used to cut down corn stalks with, I saw guys cut with them.

V: What were they fighting about? What were the fights about?

C: Stupid stuff. Maybe one guy had borrowed a pack of cigarettes or a couple of candy bars and was trying to get over or beat the other guy, or maybe they got into an argument over some kind of ball game, or a bigger guy may have taken advantage of a little guy, maybe mugged him or something, pushed him away. The little guy waited his chance and then stuck him.

V: That was what he was supposed to do, right?

C: Yes. This was the accepted thing. If you didn't do that you were branded "punk" and everybody would start to take advantage of you, and the next thing you know, they would be trying to fuck you.

V: So, in other words, if you failed to use violence in your daily activities, violence was used against you?

C: Yeah. If your people brought you something on a visiting day, they couldn't bring you much, some candy or fruit, you had to hide it, if you was a punk. Now if you were accepted by everybody, you could leave the stuff out and nobody would touch it because they know you would come back with a knife or something and get it back.

V: I don't hear anything that you tell me so far that would convince you that a life of crime was something negative?

C: No. Everything was positive, Andy. Like this bravado, like this tough guy thing was the accepted thing. Now I'm going to jump ahead. When I left the reformatory I went back to the street corner. Now I had been away for eighteen months. When I went away, and this is the truth, I didn't know nothing about nothing as far as reform school goes. When I came home, believe this, I was a good burglar, and I knew what armed robbery was. I knew what rape was, I knew what sex with a woman was. Although, I wasn't old enough to have these kind of things. At least I thought it could happen, but it couldn't really. I became twice as smart as I was as far as living on the street. Now here I was almost twelve years old and here's guys fifteen and sixteen looking up to me like a tough guy.

V: Because you had been in the joint?

C: Because I had been in the joint. I use to go to dances when I was twelve years old, school dances, and had girls sixteen and seventeen years old shooting on me, because I was a tough guy. But the good girls and guys would stay away from me. Maybe I'd go over and ask a girl to dance and she'd say, "Well I can't dance with you" and I'd say "Why?" and she'd say, "Well my father told me you're dirty" yet the clothes I had on her father probably couldn't buy.

V: Well how did you get the money for these clothes?

C: Stole it. I use to steal tires. I had a connection with a guy who would buy all the tires I could get, car batteries. This was right before the Korean War. Clothes. I had a great connection for clothes. I knew how to boost clothes right out of a store, I lucked out on these jobs. I'd put three suits together and put them under my coat. I knew how to boost toasters and stuff out of the sharpest stores. I knew how to create a disturbance at one end of the store and at the other end we'd rip off the stuff.

V: All of this you learned inside?

C: Right. I learned all of this inside. There really wasn't much to do at night before lights out so the guys use to sit around and brag about their capers.

You listen to their stories and their mistakes and you learned what was needed to be known.

V: The guys who were giving you this information inside. What was their attitude about the future? Did they expect to do more time?

C: Mostly what we talked about is what we'd like to do when we left, got out. I was too young to drive a car, but the older guys talked about getting money to buy a set of wheels. Somebody would say how are you going to get the money and they would say, "We know a bakery where we can get such and such, and we can sell it to Joe over here who's making hooch. We even knew who was making illicit alcohol. We knew all the bookmakers in the neighborhood. My personal experience was with a bookmaker. This guy's name was Lefty. Now all the time I'd ever seen Lefty, he was immaculately dressed. Nice clothes, nice shoes, always had a big Cadillac, always had a nice looking woman with him. I'd wash his car for him and he'd throw me two dollars. I'd go get him coffee and donuts, he'd throw me two dollars. I hung around this guy, I idolized, believe me, I idolized this guy. In the pool hall I went to work for him.

V: Did you know this guy was a crook?

C: Yes. He was in the loan shark business, he was in the real estate business, he was a bookmaker, he owned a restaurant, a piece of a restaurant, he owned a nightclub, was into hijacking.

V: Did you know him before you went down?

C: I knew *of* him. But I didn't associate, you know, I was too young. When I came from the joint I started going to the pool hall. I began to hang around with the older guys. They would bring me into the pool hall. Now the guy who owned the pool hall was a Jewish guy, a guy called the Jew. Now he said, "Look Bobby you can't hang out in here," and Lefty said, "Well, he's with me." So after that I had no trouble getting into the pool hall. And I'd have watches, rings, I might have some swag clothes saying, "What do you need?" Then I started to go to work for these older guys. They would boost me into a warehouse through a window, and I'd come around and bust the door for them and they'd come inside and they would throw me fifteen dollars and I'd split, and I didn't know what they got, but this is how I got involved with things.

V: Do you think, prior to your getting caught on the stolen car, the first time, at ten years old, is it just possible, in all sincerity that you would have ended up an eagle scout?

C: Oh yeah. I came from a fairly decent family, although we didn't have a lot of money. I was the oldest of seven children. I started working a legit job when I was fourteen, but prior to that I use to work with my father, and he'd give me a few dollars.

V: So that your father had a legitimate job?

C: My father had his own business.

V: And it was a stable family unit?

C: Yes.

V: Father didn't drink or anything like that?

C: No. No problems like that with my father.

V: It wasn't a broken home?

C: No.

V: Do you really attribute that your future life-style, to doing that time?

C: Yes. If I hadn't went to that reform school, who knows what would have happened when I became an adult. I probably, maybe I would have been involved in wise guy crime, like gambling, things like that. This was a natural thing in the street at the time I grew up. But I don't think I would have been involved in armed robbery, or B&E. You know I pulled armed robberies when I was thirteen. I remember walking across the street with a topcoat on and the shotgun hidden underneath and the corner cop stopped me. I dropped the gun and ran like hell, I got away that time.

V: When did you go back and do more time? How old were you?

C: Thirteen.

V: Didn't last very long.

C: Six months I stayed this time.

V: What was the beef this time?

C: Armed robbery.

V: Now isn't that something? You're a passenger in a stolen car at ten years old, you do a year and a half, you're thirteen you do a stick up.

C: I went before a different judge. This judge was very lenient towards juveniles, and he had seen my record where I had done eighteen months for the car thing, and since then this judge has died, but everyone wanted to get before this man, because nine times out of ten he'd give you probation. I was on probation six times, juvenile probation.

V: Where did you go back on the second stretch? Back to Camp Hill?

C: Camp Hill.

V: Did you see any of your old friends there?

C: Yes. There were guys from different sections of the city. Guys from different sections of Pennsylvania.

V: How did you feel going back there with a heavier beef?

C: Good. Nothing to it. When I walked in I was accepted like a god. I was already, for my reputation preceded me. The cops knew me. "Here he is again," we know what he'll do and what he won't do." I got a decent job this time.

V: How were you treated?

C: Better. I knew my way around. I was jail wise.

V: But you came back there with a heavier beef.

C: Right.

V: With a much more heavy commitment to violence in your life-style and yet

you were treated better than you were when you went there as an innocent
ten year old.

C: Right.

V: So what did that say to you?

C: That whatever I was doing was okay. All the cops I saw in there said,
"You're back again, huh? We'd figured you'd be back long before this."
Well I said, "I would have been if I'd been caught." You know this was my
attitude. I did the six months, went back out and I got busted again for
bookmaking. Don't laugh, this is the truth. I was a bag man for a
bookmaker. That charge was dismissed. I took a hell of a beating for that
too.

V: From the police?

C: With a telephone book placed on my head while a cop beat the book with a
blackjack. My head was this big [obvious gesture] when I left the police
station. A captain of police got me out of the precinct. This guy Lefty, I
was working for him then. The captain of police came and got me out after
Lefty called him.

V: What was the beating all about?

C: I had five bags on me when they caught me. Money bags with bookmaking
slips inside, about eight hundred dollars worth of plays. They wanted to
know who the bags belonged to and the names of those who gave them to
me, and I wouldn't tell them. Because I knew that once the word got out
that these bags were picked up by the cops everybody would be claiming
that they had hits.

V: So you were protecting Lefty?

C: Right. Because of the respect I showed him, and because of the money he
gave me, and because this was supposed to be done. You were not supposed
to talk.

V: Where did you learn that?

C: In the joint. Anybody that's a snitch or a rat is a punk. It's not like that
today. Okay, we're going back twenty-five years ago. It's like when I first
came to the state prison and I seen cons talking to cops, I said to myself,
"What's this?" You know, I was sick. Because nobody ever talked to a cop.
Only in the course of your work or whatever it maybe, but no personal
conversations. These guys were all having personal conversations. There's
people like me in jail today, not many, I'm not going to talk about it or
brag.

V: I notice very few people like you in the jail today. In some ways you're
a dinosaur, right?

C: Well, I'm not involved in homosexuality in or out of jail. Not that I despise
it. I realize there are guys that have certain needs or weaknesses that have to
be taken care of. I despise a rat. Although I do talk to rats, out of necessity,
you know? I just don't talk about certain things with them. My reputation

in the jail with the authorities is that they won't question me if anything happens.

V: Because they know that you are not going to say anything.

C: I will say nothing at all.

V: Let me take you back for a second. When you said you don't condemn homosexuality, when you spoke before about prison homosexuality, your attitude was one of contempt mixed with understanding, okay?

C: Yes.

V: You wouldn't participate yourself, but you understood it?

C: Well, let me clarify that for you, Andy, right? When I say homosexuality, the rip-off of another young kid, this is a test of that kid, in a way, to find out whether he'll stand up for himself. Now the kid will stand up for himself nine times out of ten. The kid will have a friend there or somebody that knew him from the street, and they'll back him up, saying "Leave him alone, he's okay," but that doesn't mean that the kid ain't gonna get ripped off. If they get him down in the barn or someplace, and they figure they can get him, they'll get him.

V: Let's understand the sequence. A kid is ripped off. Okay? How is the kid then treated by the rest of the population?

C: Bad.

V: Unless he does what?

C: He'll get back in good graces, to a certain extent, if he gets a pipe or a hammer, or whatever is available, and goes to work on the guys who took advantage of him. But he'll still be branded no matter how many times he goes home or how many times he comes back. Kids, even adults in the adult prisons will remember this kid as one who was sexually molested.

V: There's no distinction between a kid who gives it up voluntarily and the one who is ripped off?

C: There's a big distinction. Now the kid who gives it up voluntarily, well he's just naturally the jailhouse punk. A lot of these kids go into homosexuality, and they carry it on with them when they go off to the street. And when you see them the next time around, whether it's two or three years from now or ten years from now, they're very effeminate, they don't go out with women. They associate with people who are like themselves, which I'm not knocking, if this is what the guy wants to do then it's his thing. But the kid that defends himself, and it's maybe only one time the kid got ripped off. Now in the course of the years, whether it be coming back and forth to jail or out on the street corners, he may turn into a really bad son of a bitch, really a tough guy. Now guys will shoot at him to get even with him, by talking about what happened to him while he was in the juvenile joint. Regardless of whether he killed those three guys that raped him, or if he beat the shit out of them, and the fact that he was little and young and they took advantage of him doesn't mean a damn thing. This is something that stigmatizes. That stays with him and it's something he's always got to fight against.

V: Well, given, just the difference in the physical sizes, and the bad odds, isn't it a fact that any kid can be taken off?

C: Any kid. At any given moment. Regardless of how tough you are, or how bad you think you are, you may be laying on your bed sleeping, and then somebody comes and throws a blanket over your head and ties you to the bed. What can you do?

V: Does this engender in most kids a desire for revenge?

C: Oh, yes.

V: It's supposed to, right?

C: Oh yeah. If it doesn't, if you accept it, then the next time there's no fight; now one guy comes there and says, "Let's go, you're gonna take care of business." And the kid goes, because the kid's spirit is broken.

V: What do the guards do about this?

C: Nothing. If they catch you doing it, they'll lock you up. Now if the kid gets ripped off and goes to the guards and tells them, "So and so ripped me off," they'll come and lock the guys up. Then the kid is branded "rat" and they will have to put him in protective custody (punk city) and he'll spend the rest of his bit in there. Today this isn't the case. Rats have the run of the jails by working for the man. Now I never saw anybody taken to court or anything like that for it. I've seen them write letters to the parents that the kid was involved in a homosexual act, but they don't say whether he was pitching or catching. Just that he was involved in the act. Another thing of the past. Today homosexuality is encouraged, but not the rape part. It is hard for me to describe all the in's and out's, except that you are a loser no matter what.

V: Well what does that do to the kid's parents?

C: In most cases the parents don't give a shit. If the parents gave a shit, first off, the kid wouldn't be there. A lot of these kids don't have any parents.

V: What about if you had a son, your son's going to Camp Hill. What are you going to tell him? You can't go in there with him.

C: Well the first thing I would tell him is to stand up and fight. The first thing he should do whenever anybody starts to bother him is to pick up something, and smash their head in. Then I would tell him that when you do this, you're gonna get locked up, put into the hole. When you go to the lock up think about little things, don't think about anything important, don't think about your family, don't think about why you're there. Think about whether it's raining outside, whether it's night or day time, because you really can't tell, or think about when you're gonna eat, try to count how long it's been between your meals, because they don't give you anything to read or write with.

V: What if your son were to lose the fight and he was to be homosexually raped, then what's your advice to him?

C: My advice to him then would be to try to get even.

V: This is your own son, now.

C: This is my own son.

V: Okay, how would he get even?

C: Like I told him how to take care of himself when he first got there. But inside of me is this thing about telling on people. I couldn't tell on them regardless of what they did to me. I would tell him to take care of it himself. If it took six months, if it took a year, but he should get even. If he wanted to knock the guy down and fuck him in return, I'd go along with that too.

V: Would you go along with his killing one of the attackers?

C: Yes, Andy. Because how else was he going to get even? I just can't picture myself telling my son to go tell the man that this kid did that to him.

V: Do you think it would do any good?

C: It wouldn't do any good for the simple reason the kid might wind up getting thirty years for sodomy, would go to the state prison and he's just going to look around for somebody else to rip off. But if this kid gets his ass busted or gets his head beat in real good, he's going to say, "Whoa, I got to stop this shit."

V: There's an expression that we used to hear a lot. That "a wolf is nothing but a punk looking for revenge," and it simply means that a guy who is getting involved in this heavyweight rape stuff is probably a former victim of the same thing.

C: I'll go along with that too. I've seen guys who were ripped off who in turn, turned around and ripped other guys off.

V: Alright. You looked up to people in the joint right? You had to. The guy you looked up to, the real man, in the joint, even though he maybe wasn't a grown man yet, maybe he was sixteen or seventeen, did he engage in this type of behavior?

C: No. The guys that I looked up to, and most of the guys looked up to them, were the guys that didn't tell on anybody. They maybe hung around with one or two people, and they didn't clique up with anybody. They wasn't involved in any kind of sexual activity with another person. As far as a man goes they were jail wise. They were into things, they always had something to smoke, they were into gambling. Don't get me wrong they would rip somebody off as far as conning them or stealing from them. They wouldn't steal outright from another con, but from the man, yes.

V: What about their willingness to deal with violence?

C: They were willing to take your back if you had a legitimate beef, if you stepped out front first. Then they would step behind you. When I say step behind you, I mean that everybody had a knife, or a hammer, or a hatchet.

V: Were they willing to get down with the guards too?

C: Oh yes. If they figured the guard was wrong, they'd grab him. There was five of us who hung around together, we were all from the Philadelphia area, and one guy was from my neighborhood. The other guys were from different sections of the city. We hung together for the simple reason that we protected each other. We looked out for each other's interest. If you seen one of us, you'd see another one of us. When one guy left another guy would move into the group.

V: Was it necessary to be that way in there?

C: Yes. It was absolutely necessary. A man, a kid couldn't survive by himself. He just wasn't strong enough, nobody could fight five people and win. So you join together.

V: Did this mentality carry over to the street when you left??

C: Yes. Same thing when we went into the street. It's like I said before, I used to go to dances, and what we thought were the kids from the other side of the tracks, wouldn't associate with us because their parents, told them that we had been in reform school, because they knew, they lived in the same neighborhood with us. We were branded dirty, bad, all these things. Here the criminal was stigmatized.

V: Did you accept the label or reject that label? I mean were you ashamed of it or proud of it?

C: At first I was ashamed of it. I wanted to be accepted by these kids, and I really wanted to go to school, because my father was harping on me, and my grandmother. Not so much my mother, for she had too much with all the other kids. Like I said from ten years old, I was on my own, and I stuck up for myself. After these so-called "good kids" rejected me, I went to the kids that accepted me. It is like I said before they looked up to me as a tough guy. But in all reality, I wasn't really a tough guy, but I accepted this because it gave me something to relate to, to relate with.

V: You went down when you were ten, you did a year and a half, you had a few months on the street and went back down for six months, you wrapped that up, then what?

C: The next time I fell it was burglary. I did eight months.

V: You're still a juvenile?

C: I was fourteen.

V: After that bit? Meanwhile, by the way, let me ask you this. Are the bits getting easier and easier?

C: Easier as they go along. No trouble. The first one was the hard one. That was only hard for like seven or eight months.

V: So the prospect of going back and doing more time at Camp Hill didn't shake you?

C: Didn't scare me at all. I wasn't worried about it. I didn't even think about it. I knew eventually that sooner or later I was going to get caught again, not so much to get caught myself, but somebody was going to tell on me. And the cops they would be watching me and the next time or the next I was going to get popped. A couple of times I got popped because the older guys got busted that I was working with and they snitched on me. They (the cops) would ask them how did you get in? And these guys would say, "Well this kid Bobby opened the door for us, we pushed him through the window." I got busted a couple of times because of this. I didn't always go away for this, sometimes I would get probation because I was involved with older guys.

V: While you were doing time, and in between times that you were in the joint, you were on probation. So you were pretty much in the hands of the law from the time you were ten right on, right?

C: From the time I was ten until I was sixteen, I was always under some kind of supervision, as far as some authority like the police department, the probation department. I went to the Catholic protectorate one time for five months. I was under the supervision of St. Joseph's, the priests.

V: Were you actually living there?

C: Yes.

V: Was it different there?

C: Oh yes. I'd rather be in the joint.

V: Tell me why.

C: Well first off, the priest, the first thing he did when I went in there was to cut all my hair off.

V: When we talk about cutting all your hair off, we're going back a few years now, do you mean they shaved your head?

C: Shaved my head. Completely shaved my head with a razor. Okay? I had to pray from six o'clock in the morning until eight o'clock in the morning on my knees in the chapel. This was suppose to take the badness out of us as this was pounded in our heads each waking moment in this dump. After coming out of the chapel it was breakfast which was the same every morning, a bowl of oatmeal, two pieces of toast. I was forced to attend school. If I didn't complete a homework assignment, or something like this, I was a kid, I just didn't like this shit, you know (church-school)—I was beat, really beat, by the priests, brothers, punched, not slapped, punched. I had to scrub the bathroom floor everyday with a tooth brush. They did things to me to humiliate me, to myself. They told me I was a Catholic boy, which I was, they told me I had to go to church, I had to believe this and I had to believe that. I'll tell you, I wouldn't send no kid to any Catholic protectorate, I wouldn't care what the kid did. That's how bad they are.

V: Now, when you got out of there, then what?

C: I made sure I didn't go back there.

V: How do you make sure?

C: I made sure that the next time I got in trouble I'd tell the judge that I didn't want to be there, that I would rather go to reform school, and that is what they did to me, they sent me back to reform school the last time. The last time I was busted, I got busted for armed robbery, I was fifteen and a half, almost sixteen. I was a junior in high school, and the judge told me it was either back to reform school until I was twenty-one or I could go in the service. So I tried to join the Marines, the Marines wouldn't take me. I didn't want to go in the Army, so I joined the Navy. My father signed for me. I went into the Navy and I was in the service about seven months and I was called back to court where my papers were processed for me to have my juvenile record wiped out. While in the service I got my high school diploma from the high school I had attended. I didn't give up crime while I was in the service. To me the service was one large black market. I was in the service almost four years. I received a dishonorable discharge from the service for larceny. It was armed robbery, but it was broken down to robbery then larceny. I was placed on three years federal probation for this.

V: So nothing really changed?

C: No.

V: You took the service to get out of doing more time?

C: Okay. I went in the service to get out of doing more time. While I was in the service I was associating with what I called the good people, what I considered the good guys. Now very few guys in the service were as smart as me (street wise) at least this is what I thought. I turned my street knowledge into a profit while in the service. The cause for my troubles in the service. I knew what marked cards were, I knew what shakes was with the dice, I knew how to bet the ponies, I knew how to turn a quick buck. So I went into the loan shark business. I use to run gambling, I'd cut the games, I had marked cards, hot dice, in other words I took advantage of these guys, because they didn't know what the hell was going on.

V: And that's what they taught you in the juvenile joints?

C: Anybody that's a sucker. Like the saying goes, there's a sucker born every minute, and there's two born to take him, well I was that two who was taking him. Now I can tell you about this kid who was a friend of mine.

V: No, I'll get to that in a second. When you left the service, okay, you expected to do what with the rest of your life?

C: First off, I got kicked out of the service. I got a dishonorable discharge. In fact I still got it. A dishonorable discharge means that you can't vote, you can't own property, in other words you are a citizen in abeyance. In other words I'm a citizen of the United States but that's it. I don't have any of the rights or privileges of a citizen, but this didn't discourage me. I had a lot of money when I came out of the service. When I say a lot I mean about fourteen thousand dollars.

V: That was a hell of a lot of money then.

C: It was. It was back in the fifties.

V: And it was illegally obtained money, right?

C: Yes. This was money, not stolen money, but this was money I had earned through gambling.

V: Well it wasn't your service pay.

C: No. At the time I was in the service I had gotten married. It was a girl from the other side of the tracks, by the way, who I was in love with. I had a son while I was in the service. I came out and went into the plumbing business with my three brothers, into the plumbing business, and for about two years we made some big money. Now I'm talking about the first year, we grossed quite a few thousand dollars. I worked sixteen to eighteen hours a day, seven days a week. I didn't drink nor did I gamble or fool around at all. I came home to my family each night. This went on for about a year and a half.

V: You weren't stealing?

C: I was stealing, but I was stealing legitimately.

V: Okay, I understand.

C: I was doing what they call "white-collar crime," I was using other people's money to make money for myself, and this was all legitimate. To me it's stealing, but I didn't use a gun. For two years after I was out of the service, like I said I stayed legit. My wife, because of me being away from home so much, I guess it started while I was in the service, I don't know, because I didn't pay much attention to it, became involved with another man, who since that time she has married after divorcing me, which is one of the things—well, after my wife left me, I just gave up. I don't know whether it was her influence that made me do the things I had been doing to stay legit, but I just quit, I started drinking. For the next year, like I said I had plenty of money, so I went a whole year with no work, my brothers continued to work, but I just broke away from them, and for a year I was really bad, Andy, really bad. I don't think I drew a sober breath in that year. Then I started getting involved in petty stuff again. I started taking numbers, I started getting involved with burglaries, I was fencing things for different people.

V: Did you feel that you had given the straight life a chance and it had failed you or what?

C: Yes. I was looking for an excuse and I guess I blamed it on my wife leaving me, but it was my fault too, because I didn't devote enough time at home because of the way I was working. But I don't really—it's hard for me to describe why I went back the way I did. The reason I came here, I was involved with another girl, I still had plenty of money, I had a nice boat down at the seashore, I had two cars, but this was money I had made through illegal things. I had been to New York City to this party and from New York City I went to the seashore, and I found her on the boat with two other guys. I became enraged, I beat her, and threw her in the ocean and she drowned and that's how I got the murder rap.

V: Your response to seeing her on the boat with the two guys, was that a response that you think you learned a long time ago?

C: I became enraged. In other words, because of my street knowledge, I thought that these people were taking advantage of me. So actually from the time I was ten years old until the time I was twenty-five my whole life revolved around crime except for maybe a year and a half where I wasn't involved in any crime at all which you would call "crime" crime. I made bids on contracts, and underbid people because I had seen their bids, things like this, but this was part of the business.

V: You've seen, in all the years that you've been up and down—you've seen some of the same people over and over again, right?

C: Yes.

V: Have you seen people that you did time with back when you were a little kid?

C: Yes, I have. Originally in reform school I became very friendly with a guy, I'm just going to use his nickname, Moe. Now Moe, when he was fifteen years old, weighed 230 lbs and he was one of the best football players around. Even today some pros would have to go a long way to come close to him, but Moe was like three days behind everyone else. He was really retarded, he is retarded, in the sense his thinking ability wasn't up to par with the rest of us. He was, and is, the best stand-up man I ever knew. Moe took a liking to me when I was ten years old and he was about eleven. We met in reform school and hung around together. Now, going to reform school and coming back out and going back to reform school and being involved with crime I started hanging with Moe. He wasn't the only guy I saw over the years coming and going. Those seen are to numerous to mention, but it seemed that once you hit the joint it became a revolving door. Moe and I done a lot of time together. We done burglaries, we went from Philly to California doing B&E's and back again. Our thing used to be doctors' houses, that was our specialty. Because, we knew that doctors kept money. We use to steal their drugs for we knew who we could unload them on. We done just about everything together. Presently Moe is serving a sixty-year sentence in the federal penitentiary for killing, he killed a U.S. marshall and beat another, trying to escape from a two- to three-year sentence. Moe has been in and out as much as I have. He didn't have as much free time as I had because Moe never went in the service. I went in the service and Moe went back to reform school.

V: But you went in the service to avoid more jail, right?

C: Yes. That's the only reason I went in the service.

V: In listening to you talk, let me ask you some questions then to put things in perspective. When you were a young boy and even as a young man, did you see the world like divided into two kinds of people?

C: Yes. Those that had and those that didn't.

V: And you were one of those that didn't?

C: Didn't.

V: Your attitude towards those that did have was what?

C: To get their's, to take it. After the first time I left reform school, my attitude was to get what I could and it didn't make any difference to me who I got it off of.

V: And did subsequent trips back there change that at all?

C: No, it didn't change my opinion, all that did was to teach me how to become a better criminal. How to get away a lot easier, how to con people. It's like I said, the first time I went away for eighteen months, the second time I went for six months, because I had money to hire an attorney and go before a lenient judge. I went to see this attorney that I knew and he said for eight hundred I'll get you six months. I said you've got it. The six months didn't mean anything to me. I just didn't want to go for two years, or an indefinite sentence, until I was twenty-one. I learned that money could open a lot of doors.

V: So reform school didn't have any negative connotations to you after the first time; you weren't afraid of it?

C: No. No fear of it at all.

V: You think that the fact—you know you're sitting here now doing a life sentence. And listening to how the crime went down it sounds like an accident, do you feel that had this particular accident not taken place you would not have gone back to jail?

C: I would have eventually come back to jail. I'll tell you if I had any idea that I was going to commit this crime that I got convicted of, I would have went to the police. Now this really goes against my grain, and told them I did a burglary at such and such a time.

V: Just so they'd lock you up?

C: Just so they'd lock me up, and get that two to three, or eighteen months, or six months in the county jail, whatever it may be.

V: To summarize the position that you've taken in order to describe the juvenile joints, would it be fair for me to say that might makes right?

C: No, Andy. In the past years—see, like I am messed up here when you ask me a question like that. We're talking about what it was like when I was there?

V: Yes.

C: What it's like today? It's still the same situation. Might makes right, but as a person, no.

V: Okay. No, I'm not asking for your personal philosophy. Have I summed up the way things are in a juvenile prison?

C: Yes. Yes.

V: Okay. Alright. Now, let's say you take a kid, now, he's a veteran, he's been down, two, three, four times. You want to put him in a rational institution. You want to put him in a place where he can be worked with. But he's got that "might makes right" mentality. Do you think you can simply talk him out of it?

C: No. First off, let's use me as an example. It's like I told you, you smack me, even now, you get nothing, but I also know that certain kids need a backhand once in a while, but this isn't the answer to the problem. I'm not advocating the beating of anyone. When I say a backhand, what I mean is a slap. I know beating don't work. I was beat and seen plenty of others beat in these joints, but we still kept coming back or going out and doing the same things over and over. Tell these kids, show them, say look, I know what you are thinking, I thought the same way, so get it out of your head. Now let's start fresh. I'm going to come back tomorrow, next week, next month, next year, if necessary—you ain't going nowhere, and don't try to con me, because I'm going to know when you're full of shit and when you're not. This is the only way you're going to reach these kids. You can't use things like "Look kid, be good kid, go to school," these are things they don't know anything about. You've got to be able to get inside of them, find out what makes them tick, why they are doing the stupid things that keep bringing them back and forth.

V: Do you think the kids have a constitutional, moral, ethical, social, any kind of right to be protected from each other?

C: Depends on the crime. If it's a certain type of crime. Let's take a kid that's involved in drugs. I wouldn't want to put him in with kids that don't know anything about drugs. I would like to put kids together, well let's say that we have four kids that are involved with drugs. Let them associate with each other. Let them learn from each other. One kid may have been really sick and strung out, and another kid hasn't reached that point yet. Who could better relate than their own peer influences. Same way with kids who are into alcohol. Let's try to group likes together in order that they might be able to help one another.

V: So eventually, if we follow your plan, we're going to have the violence artists all together, right?

C: In one place, right. Regardless of whether those kids are in for murder, rape, arson, where people die.

V: It's still violence, right?

C: It's the violent kids. These are the kids that we must really worry about.

V: Agreed. That's where society's willing to make an investment. Much more so than car thieves, or in dope fiends.

C: You spoke about Charles Manson. That's what we're creating, more Charles Mansons.

V: Do you think you can stop the creation of a Manson before it starts, while it's going on, or do you have to wait until it's already started or gone down before you intervene?

C: Manson's trick, con or whatever you want to call it was love, concern, but he used his con to turn these young people the wrong way. They wanted this affection for a lack of a better word and he gave it to them, but in the wrong way. I really believe and I'm no master of life: everything I know I struggled to learn. I've learned from my own experiences, which most of them were bad. I would like to be able to make these bad times, poor experiences available to these kids in a way where I would or could use myself as a poor example showing that foolishness only leads you into loneliness and unhappiness. Let us take a kid who's in high school that's not in trouble, never even heard of trouble, but maybe he's hanging around with a kid who's into smoking grass or other things of this kind. His so-called friend may say, "Come on, try this." Just maybe if this kid has had the chance to speak to someone like myself who's been through the mill and his eyes and mind has really been opened to the fact of what crime is all about, he might say, "No, I listened to that guy Clem talk, and he got twenty-five years in jail for stuff such as that and I don't want to end up like him.

V: Don't you have a problem with that Clem, because in order for the kids to listen to you—and I do believe they *would* listen to you—they have to respect you, and part of that respect is admiration. So while you're telling the kids, "Don't be like me" they're also looking to you as someone they might like to emulate. It's very tricky.

C: I realize that situation too, and that emulation—I would explain to them what I am. I would tell them what I am. I'm thirty-eight years old, I have no family, I have no friends, I would like to have a couple of children like you for my own. These are things I'm never going to have, because I have put my life where these things are beyond my grasp. I can't raise a child when I'm fifty-five years old. If I had a kid now, by the time he's fifteen I'm fifty-three years old. What good could I do then? How would I relate to his life? I'd be an old man in his eyes. Imagine me beside the T.V., I can't go out and play baseball with him. I would try to explain these things to these kids and much much more, and I would try to explain that they don't have to have a lot of money, that the basic thing is to try and find happiness and love in life.

V: What about the kid who says, "I'd give it all up if I could just have two years on the street with an El Dorado and a diamond ring.

C: Then I would explain to him exactly what he's letting himself in for. This kid doesn't know what he's talking about and nobody ever really told him what he's talking about. He's listening to that bullshit he hears in the jail house, it's bullshit. Jails are full of pimps, the hustlers, the bookmakers.

V: That now leads us to a pretty logical point. Right now you, and some other lifers here in the institution, have formed an organization to work with juveniles, is that right?

C: Juvenile Awareness-Project Help. And it's three-fold. Let me explain to you what we're trying to work at. We are trying to work with those kids who are in juvenile institutions. In other words we are trying to destroy the peer relationships between them and us. Stop them from looking at us as bad guys when really we are sad men. The second part of it is to work with children who have just started to get involved with crime, who've been put into an institution, but who have been put on probation, or maybe been arrested for vandalism, playing hookey from school, or are hanging around looking up to some guy who's been away thinking that he's a tough guy when really he's a punk. The last part is a question and answer session with junior and senior high school students and first and second year college students, explaining exactly what prison, crime and its ramifications are.

V: Alright. Now, you, right now are not able to leave the institution?

C: That's right.

V: The plan is to bring these children inside the prison?

C: We are bringing children inside the prison from those communities which surround the institution. We are also working with police and probation departments throughout the entire state trying to reach as many kids as we can before they wind up in circumstances such as ours.

V: Why are they doing this?

C: They believe and have seen that it works.

V: So you persuaded them.

C: We've persuaded them. Something must be done and everything that's been tried thus far has failed. Most of these kids are multiple offenders, but still haven't been to the institution, for it's mostly minor stuff. They stole a radio out of a car or something like this, played hooky from school, never made big trouble, but they're back in and out of the police station four or five times. They are talked to by their parents, by social workers, some of these kids have seen psychiatrists and psychologists, but they still continue to go back to what they have been doing. Now, the reason for this, I believe, and a lot of the members of our group share the same feelings that these people, although they are trying to help these young people, aren't really aware of what they are trying to help them with. They are only going by what they have read in a book or what they may have learned in school. Our's is an experience that cannot be learned in a book or any school. We would like to try and show these young people through our hard earned experiences that crime isn't where it's at. We're experts. We've lived it so we feel that there isn't any crime or a problem with it that we don't know about. You name the crime and you'll find that a member of our group knows something about it. Whether it be drugs, misuse of alcohol, or whatever it may be. There's nothing these kids can tell us that we can't possibly talk about. Now, if we can't help them. We've already contacted over three hundred organizations. In the five surrounding counties about Rahway State Prison, and over two hundred of these outside groups have given us their written permission to contact them to help these kids. Now a lot of these people to myself are full of bullshit, but I've made a lot of phone calls talking to these people, and I explained to them that if we send a kid to them for help and you don't help him or her that we'll contact the newspapers telling them exactly what they are not doing. The majority of these people are really sincere about helping these kids. If the kids got a problem where his mother or father is drinking too much and this is why he's running wild, we'll help his parents, by turning them on to some people where they can get help. Maybe the kid's got a problem inside of his head, he messed up a little—we'll get help for him with this, or maybe it's one of his parents or maybe his father beats him up, we'll get him help with this and more.

V: So you see yourself as part of a team?

C: Right.

V: Not doing the whole thing yourself, but being both a referral service and advise and counselling, some pressure. What's your motivation for this, why are you doing this? It would seem—I'm sitting here talking to you in this filthy room with roaches running over the desk as we're talking—it would seem to me you'd be spending all your energy just trying to get out of here?

C: Can I talk personally for myself?

V: Sure.

C: Like why am I motivated?

V: Sure, why are you motivated?

C: I came to Rahway Prison in February. Prior to that I spent most of my time in Trenton State Prison. Now all my time—my first ten years in jail—I've got to give you a little background so you can understand.

V: Sure.

C: I was what they called the perfect prisoner. Now the reason for this is I'm jail wise. I know how to get over, I know what I'm supposed to say, I know what I'm supposed to do to get over, to get by. For my first ten years in jail I got by. I didn't try to help myself as far as seeing a psychiatrist or seeing a psychologist. I still had that juvenile thing in my head that I couldn't talk to any one in authority because I was afraid of opening up myself and showing my weaknesses to these people, because I figured they would take advantage of that. In 1970, I escaped from Leesburg Prison Farm. I escaped, I came back, and I got another sentence, twelve to thirteen months, and I realized that I wasn't going anywhere. I escaped from prison without having any idea why I escaped, where I was going, or what I was going to do. I still had this jail house bravado inside of me and I thought that this is what you're supposed to do when you're doing a lot of time. You get out any possible way you can, but like I said I came back. I went to work as a runner in six wing at Trenton, a wing used to house older men in the prison. I began talking with an older man in this wing. This guy had about thirty-five years in prison, and we became friendly. He told me that I was an asshole. I respected this man because he was jail wise like myself. He'd been in four or five institutions around the country. He wasn't a homosexual, he was a good

thief and would stand up (no snitching) although he had spent a lot of time
in jail, and he told me, "You're just being foolish, with that shit. Your
trying to impress the people around you is a waste of time." This sunk in. I
went to school. First I started college, I graduated college, I began to study
law, then I went to work in the prison law library. When I started working
in the law library I did a lot of jail-house law. I was doing writs and things of
this nature for guys. I started talking to young kids in the joint, these young
guys were twenty years old, nineteen years old, and I had to get some
background from them to try and prepare their briefs, trying to get them a
time cut or some relief through the courts. Sometimes I had to get into their
personal lives. I listened to these kids and it was like listening to myself. It
was as though I were talking with myself. I began thinking to myself why?
"Somehow, couldn't somebody grab these kids before they ended up here."
Then I spoke to you Andy, and then I got in touch with some other people.
All this took place over a number of years, because I was involved in trying
to straighten my own life out, plus I was pretty sick at that time, when I
found out through a routine x-ray that possibly I had cancer and had to
have my right lung removed. I had cancer and had the lung removed. While I
was in the outside hospital I met a little girl, who was twelve years old who
was dying of leukemia. Of all the people I have ever met in my life, this was
the most alive person I ever met in my life, was this little girl. She showed
me what life was all about. She knew she was dying yet she was very much
alive. She showed me what a flower really was, what grass was, what the rain
and the sun really meant, not just things that I just walk by all the time.
When I was released from the hospital I was granted a furlough by the
prison authorities to recover from the operation as the prison didn't have
what was necessary to insure my recovery. I went to the home of one of my
younger brothers. I had been away from my family almost eleven years. I
couldn't have been treated with more respect, with more love from all my
nieces and nephews, and my brothers and sisters than anybody else in the
world, but I was the loneliest person in their homes. I felt so out of place, I
felt like I didn't belong there. I looked at my nieces and nephews and I
started talking to them. They asked me questions about what it was like to
be in prison. And I told them. They talked with their mothers and fathers,
and they got mad at me, for telling them, but I said, "Isn't it better for
them to know from me, than to wait for them to get older and to try and
find out for themselves." I tried talking to my brothers and sisters, but, I
was never really close with them because I was always away. While on
furlough I got into trouble and one of my brothers said, "Bobby this isn't
1955; this is 1973." I thought to myself, "Wow, where am I at? Where am I
going?" I returned to Trenton State Prison and started on a self-help project

for myself, turning my efforts also towards helping others. In all the things that I have been involved in, both in and out of prison, the lifers' group Juvenile Awareness-Project Help program is the first thing in my life that I'd felt that I can sink my whole self into. That's why I guess I became involved with kids.

**Interview between Andrew Vachss (V) and
William J. Jesinkey (J) on November 4, 1976**

William J. Jesinkey has worked extensively with socially and emotionally
disturbed children, adolescents, and young adults since 1955. He began his
career with the New York City Board of Education as a truant officer and then
served in the mental hygiene clinic and stockade at Fort Meade, Maryland as a
counselor and group worker. Upon return to the board of education, he helped
establish New York's first "public" school inside a correctional institution
(Riker's Island). Bill Jesinkey then worked as a teacher and guidance counselor
in the New York City's "600" Schools (for socially maladjusted children) for a
decade. In 1972, he founded a specialized program for suspended school
children, "Advocates for Children" which presently serves over 400 families per
year. He also founded Martin de Porres Services, which consists of an Educational Day Treatment Program and two Group Homes. Like "Advocates for
Children," the goal of this program is to prevent the child's involvement with the
juvenile justice system through a program of special education and counseling.
He is the author of an in-depth analysis of New York City's special education
programs entitled *Lost Children* (1974), which is available from the John Hay
Whitney Foundation of New York.

V: Bill, in all the interviews we've had so far someone has always been trying to
   put the blame somewhere else for the juvenile violence problem that we
   have now; but one kind of consensus that has seemed to emerge has been
   that people are saying that it's possible to identify the children that later
   end up being major criminals while they are still quite young and still in
   school.

J: I would generally agree with that. From my experience, the kids that I work
   with, I wouldn't be as surgically precise as to say they'd be major criminals,
   but there are kids that you work with that you can see are just already bent
   to the point that they are going to hurt somebody or do something that's
   seriously antisocial. The distinction I would be making is that there are some
   kids that you can see that circumstance and poverty are going to draw them
   into it and you can work with them and there are other kids that, even in an
   operation like ours, which I think is a fairly integrated and complete service,
   I am really not sure yet how to intervene. I have a particular kid in mind
   that I've been working with for the last four years who's on a path, into a
   couple of muggings already at fifteen, at sixteen taking off taxi cab drivers
   with knives: I could see it coming when he came to us at eleven or twelve,
   and for the life of me I really did not know what to do or where to go for
   help for this particular kid.

V: Assuming that you have identified such a child, are you saying now that there are no resources to which you could turn?

J: I would say that as much as I know about the field, I don't know one. That's the fairest way I can put it. And my experience has been that these children are very difficult to work with and that society and responsible professionals have never made the effort to find out how to work with those particular individuals. So you come to a point where nobody knows anything about what to do with this particular child, and you find he becomes a ping pong ball. With the particular kid that I mentioned in my first response, we went through a whole series of things with him and he finally wound up in the Division for Youth; we made an arrangement with the court for the child to be placed in a group home but we warned them that we weren't sure that he could be contained and they dropped him as too difficult for their group home program. We thought that he would therefore move to a more confined intense program. No, he was just back out on the street, and we are now still working with that family to get some kind of services to this kid before he really gets—you know, he knows what's going to happen to him one night with one cab driver.

V: Is this a Catch-22 situation, you can't get really hard-core treatment for a kid unless the kid proves himself hard-core, making it thereby too late?

J: I would say that that's a fair statement. I would say that right now that the level of the art is not such that there are generally mental health workers who can pick it up and begin to work out a really intense plan to work with the kid. It's mostly after-the-fact responses to this type of child.

V: You're talking about mental health professionals, right?

J: I'm saying that I think that I've been doing what I've been doing long enough to spot this particular child, but what I'm saying is that it's not something that you can teach somebody else to do yet. We haven't gotten it down to that kind of a science where you can teach somebody or where we can give some tests, or do some other kinds of things that with a reasonable degree of accuracy will predict this child's behavior. It comes instinctively to some people after they've put the time in.

V: You've had a chance to field test your astuteness as a predictor over the years?

J: Yes.

V: But a lot of your prediction is based on your almost daily observation of the child?

J: Right.

V: So you would at this time state that you don't know of any diagnostic tests that you could give a child in the absence of observation?

J: No. In fact I've seen students that I've worked with that, at least from my daily observations, that you could pick up that had genuine cruelty, genuine antisocial behavior in their makeup who went through, breezed through

mental health tests, for whatever reason. Either they were threatened or just
didn't want to get involved with the mental health people and they gave
them their full cooperation and came through with flying colors.

V: Can we, for the purpose of this discussion, separate the violent children
we're talking about into two categories: one is the child who is involved in
basically economically based criminal activity, that ends up being violent;
it's a stickup and a gun goes off that shouldn't; it's a purse snatching, and
the victim gets her skull cracked. Let's differentiate those kids from the kids
who seem to get some kind of personal gratification from violence. Of these
two, which are the easiest to pick out at an early age?

J: In my experience, it may be just the nature of my work, it would be the
first category. That type of situation you could see coming because there
are predictors. We've worked with guidance counsellors in the school system
and developed a pretty good sort of checklist. If you have a child who's
from a multiple-problem family where you've had not only problems with
this child but with other children, where you know that there is family
disorganization, where you know there's poverty, where you know there's a
high level of ignorance operating in the situation, that child is pretty much
almost predestined to get involved in what you were describing as economic
criminal activity.

V: And enough of that is going to eventually produce violence.

J: Right. But I'm saying on that level. Those people aren't picking out the kid
who is in the second category you were describing. But when we get that
first undifferentiated category, and you start to work with them, you can
see those kids, as you put it, who get a personal satisfaction. You know that
they're not going to just take the pocketbook, they're going to kick the
person down the stairs, just for the sake of it. After they've gotten what
they wanted, they're still going to smack somebody around or hurt
somebody, that kind of thing. You can see that. But what I'm saying is for
us, and the way we're set up, we essentially spot the kid in a general group
as kids who are headed towards criminal activity because of a whole series
or set of circumstances. Most of the time I've worked in New York City and
most of the time I've worked with poverty-level children. I have had some
glimpsing experiences with kids from middle-class backgrounds who had this
kind of vicious personality syndrome and I don't know too much about it
except I saw it right away. I mean I said "Wow, that kid has got it to even a
higher degree than the poor kids do."

V: But you've seen enough to be able to state that there's no correlation
between economic class and this propensity for viciousness.

J: No. I would say that that's a fair statement. Except I guess I would say
though that my inclination is to believe that the child who is raised under
those three vectors of poverty, prejudice, and ignorance has a greater
possibility of coming up as a vicious individual than from the other groups. I

just think that you're talking about tolerance levels. He's just subjected to so much more pressure for such a longer period of time that the possibility of developing that kind of personality increases, but I don't think it comes directly out of poverty, I think it's something that's inherent in the individual and his reaction to what is going on. It can very easily happen with a middle-class kid, and you obviously see it a lot with well-to-do children for other kinds of psychological reasons.

V: You work with kids who have been previously institutionalized. Do you find it a fact that children who have been previously institutionalized are more prone to violence than children who have not been?

J: To be specific, I worked in what we'll call New York City "600" schools for a period of time and the children who came back to me from institutions and the Division for Youth definitely were more violence prone for their age level than more of the other students I was receiving.

V: If we're going to develop a juvenile justice service delivery system that's going to at some point intervene in this whole violence syndrome that we're seeing, is it not necessary to have some isolation area available to treatment personnel? In other words, at some point, do we not have to take certain children out of the system that you're working in and put them someplace else?

J: I would say yes. And you have to have very carefully planned systems of reenty into the mainstream of life if you want to work with that kind of child. You just can't say suddenly "You're ready to go back." It's a real support process back in and there will be falls, and you bring them back and you have to be prepared to move along a continuum of services. And the school that we run in a sense is based on that principle, that this child will be better served if you remove him. One of the paradoxical things about that need for certain kinds of children is that if you leave them in the mainstream, you add to the possibility of fermenting the problem or exacerbating the problem, because they are earmarked. It's a paradox which is hard to describe to somebody that hasn't gone through it, that you can create a more normal role for that individual in the community of an isolation setting than you can when you leave him in the so-called normal community. He's earmarked, he's branded, there are all kinds of subtle designations that he's a pariah within the society. Of course, this is going to arouse further hostility and further anger in him.

V: So the unisolated kid who has committed serious acts stands out from his peers?

J: Yes. I mean you can see it in the school system, in "opportunity classes," "academy classes," whatever other kinds of designations that individuals wind up with, they quite frequently, if they remain in the mainstream, are earmarked, and this creates greater anger in them.

V: Do they tend to try to live up to this earmarking?

J: Yes. I think they do. But I'm not even sure it's illogical. I think what you get is a reaction. If you're going to hold me at arm's length then I'm going to come at you, that kind of thing. I'm going to get angry and I'm going to explode.

V: What effect do we get if we take a child that in your professional opinion should be isolated, when this child is not isolated, when he's left in the conventional mainstream, what effect does he have on other children?

J: Well, I think what he does is that he blows apart programs. One of the things that I've never seen anybody talk about in terms of language that I could understand, is that programs have so many ergs of energy, in terms of staff, in terms of the intensity and training of staff, and they have a maximum level of what they're able to handle in terms of number and in terms of quality. Qualitatively these children go beyond that and start to draw all energy towards them and the rest of the system starts to collapse and you see morale go down among kids, among staff, and programs sort of disintegrate down to the least common denominator which is absolutely the opposite of what you're supposed to be doing which is rehabilitative and corrective where you're bringing people up to a higher level of functioning. So I feel for the sake of the public school system, for example, that it is better to remove these children and work with them and move them back into the system on a planned basis. I think though, just to clarify, that to some degree the child reaches that stage in mind somewhat unnecessarily. Because there is no early identification and no early intervention in terms of this child when it might have been possible. I wouldn't say with precision that it was absolutely so, but identifying him earlier when your energy levels and your energy inputs could have met his needs would have helped. But because we don't, and we tend to handle him legalistically, we start to treat his aberrant behavior as something that's to be punished. I'm talking about at a very young level, and something to be reacted to rather than to draw help to him. The problem expands to the point that there really is no other alternative but to take him out and to try to rehabilitate him because to leave him there is just to destroy him and to draw other children into that destructive pattern.

V: So we in effect have a precipitated system at which you've intervened at some point. For example: most of the men that I've interviewed who are now doing life sentences, and who began as juveniles, first did time for things like truancy or acting out in school. Your program takes those kids—but they are not institutionalized?

J: No. The whole feeling on our part is that institutionalization, unless it were really very carefully planned, and traditionally "institution" has meant the large warehouse-type response, is a loss. You've almost set up a situation where you've started to set up a series of self-actualizing prophecies, of no response to that individual which is going to draw him deeper and deeper into the system. So our whole idea, our whole philosophy, is to try to hold the line and maintain him. You're removing him in some aspects from some parts of his normal community life, school, maybe some recreational activities, and concentrating on rehabilitation that would be greater than could be normally provided in a school situation or normal recreational programs.

V: Can we take that a step further? We have a school system that's supposed to function. Certain kids are unable to function in that system. Rather than put them in institutions, they come into your program. So we've taken some of the precipitate, we've been allowed the original school system to function more intelligently. Now within your system though there are kids that precipitate out of your system, right?

J: Yes.

V: Where can they go now?

J: Right now, nowhere that I know of. Ours is as intensive a program as exists, and there are children who are just too much for us.

V: Because of the lowest common denominator aspect—

J: Because there is just a qualitative difference somehow in that second category of kids that you've mentioned as opposed to the first category of kids which you say in the wrong circumstances with the wrong pressures, they're drawn into a violent act, but they would avoid it if they had the choice. I think that hopefully there are people who are at least beginning to be able to work with that particular child, or at least some experimental or demonstration programs to work with that child should exist but I can't find any of them right now. In other words, if we can't handle them, they can't be handled and that's what we live with. Fortunately, we've devised some flexible systems within ourselves and we have sufficient staff ratios that we've found some ways. Maybe we don't help him to the degree that we'd like, but we can maintain him without disrupting the life of the other students. But it's a strain.

V: So it would be a service to you if a closed secure setting existed that could handle the so-called hard-core megaviolent kid, that would take pressure off your system the same way your system now takes pressure off the conventional school system?

J: Right.

V: So the continuum in fact is not a continuum at all, is it?

J: Maybe just another way of saying it is that you have a continuum but it's not a plane geometry continuum, it's a solid geometry continuum. At each point there needs to be a vertical continuum complementing the horizontal continuum, so that if you get to a particular stage along a line you have a level of services, up to this intense service for this megaviolent kid. That doesn't exist now. You're lucky that you got the plane geometry continuum. We're talking about the other kind of continuum that is really terribly missing at this particular point.

V: Is it a fact that all the programs you know of have the option to reject the intake of any kid that they don't want? Do you know any program other than a prison right now that has to take every kid referred to it?

J: I don't think so. I would think that our program attempts—we will take any child in who is not mentally retarded and not physically handicapped—

V: But you *will* take him in. You're doing it as a service, right?

J: Right.

V: You're taking kids that you don't really want that don't fit your program.

J: Right.

V: And you're keeping kids that don't fit your program, right?

J: Right.

V: Because there's no place else.

J: Right.

V: If there was another such place, would you keep those kids?

J: There would be some children we would not try to serve. What I think our technique would be is we would bring the child in and we would find out rapidly that this child would need more than we could offer and then we would look for that "out" for that particular child. For two reasons obviously, because of what it would mean to us, but obviously of course what it would mean to him. Because the great reality is that we may not have the firepower or the knowledge and the experience in that particular child's needs—

V: Or the physical facilities either, right?

J: Right, or the physical facilities.

V: Just to set the record straight, the kind of institution I'm talking about to take pressure off your thing would be limited to those children who committed criminal acts. Would that be a problem for you? Would you want to put kids in there who have not committed criminal acts?

J: That's a good question. What I would see as an enclosed treatment community kind of program, a therapeutic community—I don't mean that in the sense of the drug community—

V: But without the right to leave.

J: Right. Well, yes.

V: How do we justify that kind of detention for noncriminal activity? Or isn't it a fact, and this is my opinion, you can correct me if I'm wrong—that programs like yours, the best programs, tend to almost absorb criminal activity to the point where you're not running to the authorities every time you see evidence of criminal behavior, so in fact a lot of criminal activity simply isn't reported,—isn't acknowledged.

J: Right. I think that's definitely true of the school system and it's to some degree true of us. I think the question that you pose is a very good one because—quite frequently a child comes from a family that's also disturbed, so holding him is very hard because he's usually able to manipulate the family. I've seen so many programs set up where the kid manipulates the family to take him out and everybody plays into the whole thing and he's back out on the street. So I guess with all things weighted and with our political system and so forth you may have to do it in a case. But I think that what might occur is that if you had a treatment program, you might have more willingness on the part of the police and the courts to pick up kids for criminal activity that they're now saying "Geez I don't even want to look at that, what am I going to do with that kid?" kind of approach to the problem.

V: I think that's accurate. I think that it's in fact a police response. I've interviewed policemen and they've said just what you've said. I'm talking about concerned cops that really want to do something but just feel that continually arresting a kid does nothing.

J: But you see, my feeling is that truancy should be a tremendously powerful indicator that society has an early warning system to respond to, and yet we've gotten to the stage where the courts just don't respond to truancy.

V: Isn't it a fact that the schools are sometimes happy for truancy?

J: Right. In fact, one of the things that I am saying now is that they're opening up this really great confusion in this particular area and there are very few people that I can talk to about it. These children are now classified as handicapped children in the school system, so they're opening up classes for the emotionally handicapped and putting these kids in there. And in that particular setting, the point that you were making about disrupting programs, is particularly true. They're almost unable to run any kind of real quality program for emotionally handicapped children because they have not sought it out at all. Not even the first category of kids we were talking about, not to mention the second category, belong with kids who were having emotional difficulties or withdrawal or acting out behavior which has nothing to do with criminal activity at all. I mean it's just not in that kind of direction, it has a different cause and it's going to go in a different direction. Their acting out behavior is not being able to sit still, or talking too much, or moving around too much, but it's not going to result in criminal activity. As a result those programs in the public system are not working at all that I see. They just can't handle this particular child.

Well, I'm sorry Andy, I was starting to make a point and then I got a little tangential and missed it. What I see happening in the public school system in New York City, which is obviously a tremendous source of this kind of child because of the size of the city and the social situation in the city, they're making a very great mistake. They're having no sense of any continuum. They're taking out attendance teachers. They're taking out all the early warning, all the early intervention systems to put the kids into C.E.H. classes that consist of one teacher thrown in a room somewhere with ten kids and no real capacity to respond to these kids. So they're helping nobody, certainly not helping the child that they could help with such a system, as I was calling him, the emotionally handicapped as opposed to the delinquent if you want to use that, or precriminal kind of syndrome. And we have the worst of all possible worlds now. No early identification system, no routing of kids to appropriate systems, so you just helter-skelter put kids into these classes, and resources are being shifted to these classes. What they're running into is terrible attendance levels in these classes, so they're arguing that they can put more and more kids into these classes. What we wind up with is a lot of kids on paper registered who never attend programs and we're carrying them for three or four years until they do a big number and show up somewhere in family court or criminal court.

V: In line with that, if we were going to design a prescription, I need some of the ingredients. We've got a boy fifteen years old, he was a truant at ten, maybe he was institutionalized for six months, he stole some pocketbooks, he's been involved in some fights, now it's four armed robberies, and the last armed robbery a man was shot. The man didn't die. Now we've got this kid. He's in the family court. No question about it, there is a finding against him. He's got to go some place. Now wiping the slate clean of the Goshens and the Elmiras and all those places, what ingredients should the place this kid is sent to possess if this kid is to have a fighting chance to ever return into these streets?

J: I answer that question with caution because I haven't worked in design programs. I've thought about it but it's all on a sort of hypothetical level.

V: Based on what you observed with kids—let me put it this way: does he need a closed setting?

J: I would say yes, I would say he does. And I would say obviously he needs a closed setting in which he can be protected from himself. You don't set up the closed setting where you have big areas at the end. I've seen this at Riker's Island and other places where there are big areas where nobody can see in and kids can congregate and the next thing you hear is a rumble and you find somebody lying under a table, or somebody bleeding on top of the head. Or you have showers, in which people can carry out acts, that amount to an "attractive nuisance," if you want to put it that way, the design of the physical area. I'm not an expert in that but I've seen it in my couple of years that I spent working on Riker's Island.

V: The buildings are designed in such a way to facilitate negative behavior, no question. If we have a secure building, in which the child is safe from himself, and from his peers—

J: Actually, what real experience I have with this is the design of the school that we have now which makes it very easy to operate the school and, what is very important, (it gives all the kids in the school a sense of security which is absolutely important to give all the members of the particular program a sense of security) is a single corridor operation. For us, in a day school, where all the rooms come into the single corridor, into which the people who are responsible can see the entire corridor at all times, and any kid who has a problem, all he simply has to do is step into the corridor and he's in a sheltered area. He's in a protected area, he doesn't have to fight. If he's moving in the direction you want, you just have to teach him, if something starts to go wrong to just move to that corridor, you don't have to call us, it's automatic, somebody will respond. Because we're set up to do that. As opposed to with L-shaped and other kinds of things you start to have kids who lose their sense of security and who start to, in a sense almost justifiably, say "But I've got to be able to fight, I've got to be able to involve in this whoofing behavior and facing behavior and all this other kind of stuff otherwise they're going to walk all over me," you provide me in other words with no alternative. I've come across that in schools and in our own design. That's the reason we set the place up. We have two facilities, one which is not as ideal in which we have several levels and it's much more strain on the staff to maintain that sense of security for the kids. The way I approach it is that all the kids in the rehabilitative setting have to have a sense of security, that they don't have to fight, they have alternatives. Not that they have to be cowardly, but they know what the sense of the place is and they're not going to get drawn into some unnecessary thing because there is no alternative to them.

V: In terms of personnel as well as structures, do you try and engender the attitude that it's socially acceptable to step into the corridor? In other words, sure it's physically safe if he comes into the corridor, he doesn't have to fight in that sense, but what about the peer pressure to fight regardless of options?

J: I'm just trying to think of how we've actually handled it. Empirically it's acceptable in the school and in fact empirically what happens is the other kids respond to the kid who tries to cause the fight. Now I'm not exactly sure what we've done to engender that. One of the things that I did do when we first opened the school—and when you open a situation like this, until your staff gets experience and your physical layup gets out, you need somebody who really is the gorilla, kind of does the gorilla number—and one of the things when everybody came into the school I said, "There will be no bullying. I mean I will eat you up alive if I find you—" We did that, but after a while that got internalized and program took over. That's not an ultimate, that gorilla number, that's a stop-gap thing until program takes over. Or, hopefully, you had the resources that the program's there in the first place, you need very little of that kind of initial honcho number to be done at all. That's my empirical experience.

V: But although everybody agrees that this is necessary at first, your experience has been that after a while—

J: Very definitely. If we were facing a possibility of corporal punishment with younger children and the first year there was a fair amount of corporal punishment, by the second year, we had to strain our memories to find one kid who got hit, and during the third year, one kid who got a spanking for something when there was just no alternative or the person felt he had no alternative except to spank the kid. There possibly was one during the whole third year. And we're now to the point where we will say that we feel that there is practically no reason now to get involved in corporal punishment. Also what we found, for example, when we decided when we were going to open the second facility, we came in and trained staff in the first facility, but we not only trained staff, but we opened the second facility with some kids from the first facility so you didn't have that wild peer situation where nobody knows what to expect. The basic group of kids sort of said "Well this is what is expected of you," so it was much easier for the new kids to fall into place when they came once they—in other words you took your atmosphere with you to the second facility that you opened up. So we did not have, by the end of the first year, we were almost to where we were by the end of the third year with the first facility in terms of the hold the program had upon the kids.

V: If we take it as a premise that the children that we're talking about for this institution are nothing more than the same children you're working with, maybe a couple of years older or maybe a couple of more steps advanced down the same road, would you be willing to theorize that the same kind of methods could work in a closed institution?

J: Yes.

V: That after an initial period of asserting control there would be no necessity for this constant confrontation around violence?

J: I would predict yes. I mean all my experience indicates that that's true.

V: That was our experience in the institution. The conventional wisdom of course is that the fist must rule a closed setting, I don't find that to be true.

J: No, I don't think that that's true. I think that what you do have to have though, you may find as we move up into that closed setting, that you have to have highly trained people who have faced, I think particularly in themselves, the fear syndrome—becoming fearful when there's the possibility of attack. In other words, you sort of have to get your personality—I'm back to teaching these kids after a long absence, twelve years, and my first reaction I find is to get uptight, and it's taken me a full month to get myself back to the stage where when I'm confronted with violence my inner emotional reaction is calm, not weakness but calm. I convey to the individual that I will bring order, that I will do whatever I have to do to bring order to the situation but I'm not challenging him, I'm not uptight, I'm not confronting him, I'm not myself confronted or challenged. Quite honestly it was there again when I went back to it because I hadn't been in that kind of situation for a long time and I think you have to, as you go up the continuum, you have to get people who either naturally have that or who you put some time into it.

V: But that quality is trainable in the sense that people can acquire it.

J: I believe they can, but I believe that because of the traditional university outlook, they have not gone about it. These are things that I've really thought about, it's not a spur-of-the-moment kind of thing. I've thought of subjecting people to self-defense courses, to physical involvement courses, to situations that demand a certain amount of physical courage whatever you want to call it, like those outreach programs or Outward Bound programs where you go out and do some things that require some physical courage because a lot of people in our culture have been able to live a life where you never had to admit that kind of thing to yourself and work your way through it. It's a perfectly natural reaction, and their situation is healthy in a sense, "Yeah, I'm afraid" but they've never been put in a situation where they've had to say "Yeah I'm afraid but I still have to do something about it" so you have to find a way to train it, and I think it's trainable. But I don't think that just taking a course in it is going to train you in that kind of thing.

V: Our experience in that was, the rule was, there was no one-on-one behavior. We would say to a child "If you have to go in a room and you refuse to go in a room, if one of us has to put you in the room, the proximate result of that is that you will be injured. If six of us put you in the room, you don't have to be injured." Because we can absorb all the strength you have among the six people, we don't have to counter it with greater strength. So the only requirement among my staff was that they be willing to defend themselves and other people, be it inmate, resident, staff, anything else. But in terms of courage we always said there is no courage unless there is fear.

J: Right.

V: So you could have your full-race karate expert, but this is not gladiator behavior we're talking about.

J: What I was trying to say is what you were trying to say. I've worked with very difficult kids and the staff worked in unison. In other words, if a kid began to become violent the entire staff moved toward that situation. You found that after a while that the level of violence of the whole operation died, whereas if it was left to a one-on-one situation, there were alot of face-offs, there were alot of challenges.

V: And there's a pecking order that emerges and certain staff are not challenged, which is absolutely no good.

J: Right, and in fact it becomes demoralizing to staff because you get, as you say, a pecking order which sometimes actually becomes a power order in terms of decision making in the school, on a machismo basis rather than intellectual, professional response to what is being done. In fact, when you were asking me what content the program would have, what I have found is where that was allowed to happen, very seldom does the program get developed. I'm using program maybe in a narrower sense now. For us, in a day-treatment program with the age kids we work with, education *is* our program. I mean our education is precise, it's complete, it's all-absorbing as far as the kids concerned. We try to make it balanced, we try to make it enjoyable, but when he comes in he goes to homeroom, where he makes out his schedule for the day, which is not helter-skelter any day, but it is made out with his homeroom teacher, and he's encouraged to have input, but he'll also be told "That's not a practical suggestion." He has a program for the day that he knows he has to follow. Then, when he has the homeroom at the end of the day, it's monitored as to whether he's followed that particular program, and people during the day will merge with him and say "You scheduled yourself for this, the decision was made, you were there, people are waiting for you." There's material, and he's supposed to go to work, and you find after a while that this becomes the power that becomes the hold. That's part of a whole staff working in order, and a staff realizing, as I say, whatever the age is, what we're trying to accomplish with these kids is five things: that they learn to read as well as they can; that they learn to do math as well as they can; that they build a general fund of information on which they can develop their capacities as either a blue-collar or white-collar kind of profession; that they can express their ideas orally; and that they can express their ideas in writing.

V: Those are survival skills more than they are academic skills.

J: But I think they're also fundamental academic skills at the same time. If you distill what is a basically elementary education, those are the elements of an elementary education.

V: I agree with you in that they are building blocks to any kind of profession, but on the other hand, subtract those from any human being and you have somebody that almost has to commit crimes to make a living.

J: That's why I have no patience for people who talk to me about therapeutic education which doesn't make any demands upon a kid. I say "Yeah, except someday you're going to drop him at seventeen or eighteen years of age in a corner somewhere. Do you think ye's going to go and fill out an application to become vice president of AT&T?" I say "No, he's going to go into a store and get a knife or figure out how to take pocketbooks or something because he can't even fill out an initial application." So there's no such thing as therapeutic education; it does not get you a minimum set of survival skills because you have no options at that particular point in time.

V: Could a school like yours plug into the kind of institution we are talking about, because the skills that you teach, we agree are the absolutely most vital. We plan to have a kind of vocational orientation around money-making activities, for example, things like body and fender work, letter press printing, that kind of thing, because all communities need these skills. But without the base you are talking about those skills are not even teachable.

J: I am not sure that it is not teachable. I think it is harder. Let us say he took body and fender, you would almost have to teach body and fender one-to-one—I mean you *could* do it. The reason I am mentioning it is even *that* provides enough substance—this is the point I was trying to make before. It seems to me that many treatment programs fall down, ones as intense as you are talking about and ones even less intense, because they never get substance into the program, they think once they have gotten a kid under any kind of control, that they are doing their number. But unless he is faced with the pressure of having to put out, you don't know what kind of rehabilitation is taking place with this kid. He can take a low profile in a maintenance-oriented institution and you do not know what the hell is going on with him because you are not creating any life pressures for him. Life pressures for him should be knocking his head against the technique and you could do that, I think, with body and fender work, but the problem is that if you did not have the building blocks we were talking about before, you would have to stand there with one guy and say "Now do this, now do that."

V: It may come to that, though. Because we cannot go backwards in time. By the time we get these young men—

J: I also find that one of the reasons that you might have to confront that—my experience is that if you get them to master the body and fender skills (I don't even want to use magic words like their ego goes up) something occurs which gives them enough to go back and attack this area which obviously they are very panicked in, which is the academic learning. And they now say "If I did that, then I can do this." I have had that kind of thing occur, but I haven't had enough programs to really test that idea out, which would take the kid through the fact that he is really doing a good job at something so that you could now go back and see what kind of rehabilitation he is open to. Someone once told me, and I think it is applicable to this situation, that if you trace the history of rehabilitation movements you could work successfully with students until they moved into their adolescence and then it wasn't until twenty-five or twenty-eight before you could work with them again. And I really think that what they were saying was that with those programs that existed, that was the best you could do. Because what we are saying now is that those people who survived long enough to be twenty-five or twenty-eight had said "At least, God, I have survived at living, what have I got to lose if I go back and try to improve myself in some fashion?" But I have heard some frightening statistics on how many of those kids survive to make twenty-eight and thirty; it is frightening.

V: Just actuarily in terms of their involvement with crime if they get past twenty-six, twenty-seven, the curve just drops completely in terms of their potential. But that's not enough—

J: The point I was trying to make is that if you had programs that could introduce the same level of experience during their adolescent period, you could accelerate that time where you could really get them back to a point where they are open to rehabilitation. In other words, with an adolescent of sixteen, you can't choose how you are going to get into rehabilitation, or if you are going to go into a reading program, math—it may just be too late to come at him that way. So you find out what he can do but you hold him to it, to succeed at it and then once he succeeds at it the other things may open to you again. I have had that experience, as I say, but I haven't had enough of it or I have not seen enough of where people have had the ability to hold this kid to something that he succeeds at it in any fashion to the point that the other rehabilitative things open to him again.

V: Well, you cause me to rethink in a way. It may be that what we may want to do in the institution is have the same kind of fundamentals training that you have, maybe coexisting with the body and fender work. Maybe not go before or go after, but may be coexisting because it is a fact of life that a kid could be the best body and fender man in the world, a genius at it, but without these basic skills the most he could do is work for somebody else.

J: I would say you would probably have to have them coexisting. I think though that in some way what you would get into—I'm fantasizing a little bit now—is that setting in his mind some requirements for him to graduate from your institution, where you emerge from your institution—

V: We've already aimed at that.

J: And that the order in which he accomplishes those tasks, it may be that with these individuals it will vary. One guy will start to succeed with body and fender and then you can swing him around into making the other kinds of things that he is just sort of going through the motions at now. That I would suspect is the kind of thing you are going to find, that until you get success in one area, the most difficult area to succeed in will be the sort of pure academic area. Although, that depends to a great degree on the precision of the learning program. We are finding, which I think is a perfectly reasonable thing to expect, that as we refine what we are doing academically, we get more and more capacity to help kids. It is really a high-level professional activity. It is just not a matter of going in there with some mimeographed sheets and handing them out. It takes planning, it takes analysis, and it takes constantly getting feedback from this kid. It is not "What am I going to do today?" but "Based on what I did *yesterday,* what am I going to to today?" kind of precision that has to be built into what you are doing and that takes skilled leadership and it takes skilled people to be willing to carry that out.

V: To summarize what you have said so far, would it be fair to say that you are not ready to call any kid a hopeless case at this point?

J: I would say that that's fair, right. And I think that that's also in the whole tradition of Western philosophical scientific thought, right? I mean that you don't say "This is an incurable disease, that's a hopeless situation." It just has never proven to be true. We have always found a way of handling those problems if we set our mind to them and begin to put the problem in some kind of soluble fashion, then we find a solution. And I also say that empirically. I also find that there are kids who I never thought I was going to make it with that I make it with. The judgment that it's a hopeless case is frequently a matter of your own limitation on humanity. These are things that make enormous demands upon you and humanly you wish somehow the demand wasn't being made, so you say it's not possible to respond. You have to discipline yourself not to get caught into that trap.

V: And you would say that at least from your experience, which is a long period of time, with these type of kids, it is possible to design a program that wouldn't fail?

J: I would say with a very high percentage of kids, right. To a degree of success that everybody would be happy with, yes. I don't think that you are going to be able to help every child. But I would say that you could devise a program that would be cost-effective both in human and in fiscal terms. I would say it's certainly possible to do that.

V: We haven't done it yet, right? I'm talking about, not with your kids, where you demonstrably *have* done it, I am talking about with the kids that end up being institutionalized full-time. These are the kids that return to Attica. We haven't done it with them.

J: I haven't seen it.

V: Can you give some gut feeling as to why we haven't succeeded with these kids. When programs like yours have succeeded with kids that most people agree are harder to work with?

J: One of my initial gut reactions is that the pressure of economics on the mental health science has never made it very attractive economically to work with this kind of child. One does not develop a profession of a practice, or that kind of thing, in terms of really saying "This is a problem that I've got to put my back to solving." Go through the literature and you see very few social scientists, or real people I would classify as scientists in the sense that they were attempting to find a solution to the problem. There are not just that many. We have not put that much effort into devising a system or an approach to these particular children and we have just not been willing to say we've done this much and it's not enough so we'll do more. There seem to be a lot of artificial cutoffs as to how much we'll do. We'll provide this, if it doesn't help the kids then so we'll throw him away.

V: What's your per capita cost on kids?

J: Our program costs between $4,500 and $5,000 per child.

V: Well, how do we talk about money then when a stinking dump of a juvenile institution will cost $7,000, $8,000, $9,000 per kid. A warehouse costs that much.

J: It costs the New York State Division for Youth $21,000 per child.

V: First we say that there haven't been enough resources, then we turn around and we have a statement that the warehouse business is pretty damn lucrative.

J: It is an interesting point and a kind of decision by attrition as to where you use resources. In other words, the education people will say "Aha, we don't spend anymore than this per child." So a program like ours is looked at where we are, in the educational realm, as being expensive. But next month the kid is in an institution costing $21,000 a year per child and in *that* framework it's not seen as expensive at all. So, by attrition, he had to move from one system to the other system. One of the first things our agency did was a report called *Lost Children* in which we basically said that in New York City, the system is so fragmented that talking about how resources are used is meaningless because they are used in no coordinated way, nobody is making any attempt to say "If you apply resources systematically this is what you can achieve, and if you apply it so much more, this is what you can achieve." I sat in the guidance office of a "600" school from 1965 until 1969; I had maybe some eight hundred kids come through the institution or the school and I think I saw one probation officer and one social worker from the Department of Welfare come into my office, and I would say at least eight out of ten kids in the place was known to welfare, probation, bureau of attendance. From attendance officers I at least got phone calls, but I saw nobody else. These people were all doing their own thing with this kid. At tremendous cost. And one of the things that we did when we set up the school was to say "Screw that. *We* are responsible for this kid." Our attendance runs 96 percent. People say to me "How do you achieve that?" And I say "We don't accept absence." They say "What do you mean?" I say "the kid's not here; we go get him." We got a guy who doesn't have four degrees who is a very substantial reliable person. We pay him a fairly decent salary, $9,000 to $10,000 a year and he does a lot of things in the school. One of the things he does is make sure the kids come in the morning, and he very simply knocks on the door and says, "Harry you didn't make the bus," or "Harry you didn't get there, let's go." And Harry has to have a very good reason or Charlie has him in the car. It doesn't seem to be that profound, but if I don't have the kid 90 percent of the time then he is not going to grow.

    I looked at the records of these kids. I looked at two things and I think maybe it's worth putting it in the record. I see the statement "These kids can't learn" and I analyzed that from two points of view. One, I went into the classroom and, because of something you were saying before, because they had inappropriate kids in the class, 80 percent of the teacher's time was in control behavior and only 20 percent, and I think that is a conservative estimate, was in teaching behavior. So if you really analyze, the kids had one fifth of a year's school. He had 20 percent teaching time over a full year. The other thing is, if you looked at his record, he didn't come to school. He was there ten days, twenty days, and the system then says "This kid can't learn." He's been in school four years, he's not reading on a fourth-grade level, so if you put everything together, the amount of teaching time that actually took place when he was in the classroom and the amount of time he actually attended, he probably was in school eight months in four years if he was lucky, and if you look, he had made eight month's growth. And I think it in a sense establishes your hypothesis: that if you do not have the appropriate program, then you are taking money and throwing it up in the air or just burning it, and that's what I watched in that classroom. The teacher who became a successful teacher was the teacher who had great control skills. And the kid didn't learn. So what were you doing, you were running a maintenance baby-sitting program.

We have gotten away from that. We have a program in which little girls can teach. They have to have the skills, but the environment allows them to come in and apply their expertise to the learning situation if they have it. I don't mean necessarily for you to think that all teachers are women, that's not the case. But we have women who come in who obviously are not martial arts experts or anything; they're sweet little girls, and yet they are able to work because we got out of that box of throwing one person in a classroom with ten kids. We have a situation where on certain days a certain kid is just too much for the situation. So you have a way of working with him individually that day, you don't leave him there to blow up the other nine kids and that also has a very therapeutic effect, a positive effect upon what you are doing because there is consistency for the nine kids and there's also a desire for this one kid to get back to the class. He hasn't broken the pattern of the situation so he feels, "I'm outside, I want to get back in," but if he stays in there and takes it apart, it's *his* world, he's controlling it and he's happy with it, I don't mean really happy, but he's meeting whatever perverse needs he has in the situation, and it is not apparent to him that they are perverse needs because there's some gratification which is as much as he can understand. He's getting some gratification out of taking the class apart and he does that successfully every day, so what more can he want? It's a way of getting attention. I see it with the kids, it is an attention-getting device. We have ways of dealing with attention-getting behavior without allowing it to disrupt the learning situation and I think that that's critical. I think you have to have techniques that are more intense as you go up with the level of the problem of the child to achieve that, whereas if you let the program disintegrate, you do nothing.

V: Let me ask you one question that people always ask me. I want to see if you can answer this because it is one that really is the underpinning of all the opposition to programs that people like you and me want to have. How do you answer this question: What happens if you take Bill Jesinkey personally out of the program? Does it still go?

J: In the programs that I am involved with now, I am no longer directly in the programs. That's why I said when I had to go back to teaching this year it was a change. I am really an administrative fund-raiser, I am not in the schools, I am not in the group home—and it's functioning without me there.

V: And you believe it could even if you were to take a job driving a cab?

J: I think it's very likely that I might not be able to maintain myself, that I'll have to get away for a while, get a rest or a break, or—

V: It is very intense work—

J: Right, and I don't have any worry that the program will continue itself, except maybe fiscally. But from the point of view of staff, that kind of thing, they are perfectly capable of running the school at this point in time. Perfectly capable.

V: So you believe that even though initially a very powerful personality, even a visionary personality, comes in and takes charge of a situation and makes almost cosmic changes, if done properly, that person can disengage himself.

J: Yes. I think that's true. I think that that happens in many levels of activity. That there has to be somebody with a particular energy to initiate it. There are just, quantitatively, problems involved with start-up that maybe exceed what a lot of people can do. But once the start-up is accomplished, if what you have envisioned is valid, and has it's own integrity, then in fact—one of the things that I have consciously done over the last couple of years is to depersonalize it. I mean it seemed to me it was my responsibility, once I get it established to depersonalize it and to get that aspect of the program out, that this was a potential weakness. If it depended upon me being here, that was an absolute sign to me that you had created something that didn't have its own validity. For us it's worked. In fact I'm not sure they'd *let* me back in sometimes.

V: One final question for you. You took a population of children, juveniles that had been completely characterized by a lack of success in the conventional system, right?

J: Yes.

V: You've had certainly a great degree of success. Not the success you would want because you want perfection, but much more than was anticipated.

J: Right.

V: We are now talking about a population of juveniles, also kids that have been in trouble, perhaps they have committed more overt acts, their criminal behavior has accelerated somewhat. Do you see any reason at all why the principles, and values and philosophies of your program could not be translated inside a maximum-security closed unit for these type of kids?

J: No I don't, and my basis for saying that would be that for years I watched other programs as well as mine. I've seen kids who supposedly had to go to institutions and had to be put in foster homes and had the whole series of other things that had to be done who were able to function in our school. In fact, I think we have, trying to look at the learning levels in our school now, more than 50 percent of the children have more than one year's growth in a year. Now if you had a normal population 50 percent of the children should have a year or more's growth, right? And we've exceeded that with *this* population. I know the amount of input. If we did that with an average class, obviously all the children would maybe grow two years, but I don't care about that with this particular population.

V: The payoff is greater though because these are the kids who potentially could cause damage disproportionate to their numbers—to themselves and to others.

J: Cost and expense, and disruption of society, all the people in the Bronx, I mean whole segments of your population living in fear. The cost is immeasurable in human and fiscal terms.

V: And you are having trouble raising money for your school?

J: Yes. We are having a great deal of trouble because the [city] board of education is saying that they *have* programs for these kids, and I was explaining to you before, their idea of a *program* for these kids is that they have a *placement* for the kid. There is no sitting down with the board, they become defensive. My argument, just as you were saying before, is that what is the reason to be defensive? We are able to do what you can't do at a school of twelve hundred and you shouldn't have to try to serve this kid as one of a population of twelve hundred. It's our job to get him ready to come back into your situation of twelve hundred but it's certainly not your function to try and hold him in there. But that's what we're into now, and it's going to be very tragic. I think we may lose this entire program within a year or two unless we can convince the powers that be that the program is worth funding under whatever rubrics they want to fund it. What I was particularly interested in and committed to doing was prevention, as I said to you before, trying to intervene before the stage of the megaviolent kid occurred or the institutionalized kid occurred. And that requires an integration of child care, education, and mental health in a very tight, coordinated package. Well, it can't be done in a school system. They can't even figure out how to deliver mental health services, obviously you can't be reaching this particular kid if you're arguing whether the mental health service should be delivered in the school or in the community.

Ours is strictly empirical. You give him as much as he needs, as he needs it. And if there are things we can't do, we go out into the community and find someone who can do it. But we still keep control. There's one other thing that occurs to me that has to do I think with your underlying hypothesis and what you're trying to accomplish in terms of a particular kind of isolation. Very frequently I have found in working with these kids that a negative syndrome builds up between this child and his parents or whoever are the most important people in his life, that has to be broken.

And the way we break it at the school is our policy that no negative reports go home. The kid does forty-nine thousand things wrong and he blows his nose in a tissue, the note goes home "good health habits." At least at the age level we're working at, it's absolutely critical because the way, for some reason, we respond in society is the way we expect the family to respond. But when a kid is in a family situation that *can't* respond, all we do is to put further pressure on that situation until it absolutely dissolves. Till the mother looks at the kid as he comes in the door—"What happened today?" She's waiting for the note or she's waiting for the phone call, he feels that tension in her. What we've seen happen, it's almost a classical thing to watch, we cool it, and positive reports go home, and we get the kid working, and the work goes home, no negative reports go home, suddenly a head peeks in the door—"I'm Johnny's mother, How's Johnny doing?" "Well, he's doing very well, would you like to see him in class?" And she goes in and she sees Johnny working. Human nature is human nature. She begins to see (sometimes it's the father but in our situation it's mostly mothers), begins to feel some ability to be proud of her child, to see that he has some worth, that he has some value, and also, herself—"I haven't produced a loser, which means I'm not a loser either." You break that whole kind of thing.

I would say on an older level that the removal may have to be more complete, that you have to get the child totally out of that situation and then see what you can do to rebuild it or provide a different environment for him to return to. Our goal is always to maintain, as much as is possible, the family relationships. But we don't fool ourselves. There are some kids that we have in a group home, that we have no plans for them ever to go back home. We don't want them to deny their parents or to lose total contact with their parents. We don't have the illusion that those parents will ever be able to provide this child with rational support. So I would suspect that one of the underlying reasons that your proposition may prove to be true is that this is a necessary component of treatment. To break all of those negative expectations of parents, and negative expectations of children of parents which are operating in this kid's life and get him into a situation where you have enough control to see that most of the response to him is positive, and most of the expectation of him is positive.

V: Well, one thing I have to say, is that if I were you, I would just take this interview, and I would show it to anybody who is sincerely interested in doing something about children in this miserable city of ours: I would not write a proposal, I wouldn't do anything else. I would just show them this interview, and anybody that is sincerely motivated should know what to do from there.

Interview between Andrew Vachss (V) and "Gypsy" (G), on October 23, 1977

Gypsy was first incarcerated at the age of twelve on minor, noncriminal charges that would not even cause his arrest today. After a thorough indoctrination to youth gangs in various detention centers and training schools, he became a leader of one of New York City's major gangs, and was sentenced to a life term in adult prison following his conviction for homicide at the age of sixteen. The homicide took place during a gang fight.

Gypsy was eventually paroled but, upon his release, he was convicted of an armed robbery and returned to prison. Since his release from that sentence, he has been surviving in his home community. Gypsy's comments on the street gang scene in the 1950s are especially valuable because of his participant-observer status at that time.

V: Gypsy, how old were you when you first started to get involved with the criminal justice system?

G: I was around twelve, twelve-and-a-half years old.

V: What was the nature of the first involvement?

G: Truancy.

V: What happened as a result?

G: I went to Warwick. First I went to the youth house, from the youth house I went to Warwick.

V: For being truant from school?

G: For being truant from school.

V: How long were you at Warwick?

G: A rough estimation, around eighteen months because when I was in Warwick I ran away. I ran away once.

V: Then you returned to the streets?

G: Right.

V: When was the next involvement with the law?

G: The next involvement was a pocketbook snatching and that was around thirteen-and-a-half, and I went to Otisville.

V: How much time did you do at Otisville?

G: About a year.

V: About one year? Again you returned to the streets?

G: I returned to the street.

V: The next involvement with the law.

G: It happened in '59. I was just turned sixteen, and I was the President of Junior Knights and we had a physical confrontation with an opposite group, and I was accused of stabbing Junior Rodriguez. And that was the third confrontation with the criminal justice and the charge was homicide. And I went to court, the whole thing, pick a jury, and the verdict came it was murder in the second degree about a week later I was sentenced to twenty-five years in prison, twenty-five to life, and I went to Elmira Reception Center.

V: Did you stab Junior Rodriguez?

G: Well, it's very hard to say because there were around fifty individuals, and we all had knives, some had guns, and I know that I was stabbing somebody, somebody cut me in the leg, a few of my friends were stabbed, and some other individuals, so to say that I stabbed Junior Rodriguez up to this day, I don't think that I stabbed Junior Rodriguez.

V: Were you the only one convicted of a homicide?

G: No, there was another brother.

V: How large a group was the Knights in total?

G: I would say, in my division, it was around fifty.

V: How about in the Seniors?

G: The Seniors there were possibly fifty or forty-five.

V: And you also had Midgets?

G: No, we had Debs. And there were maybe around fifteen or sixteen sisters that we had.

V: But this rumble was just for the junior gangs?

G: This rumble was just for the junior gangs.

V: What was the name of the rival gang?

G: The Suffolk Street Boys.

V: So this was on the Lower East Side?

G: Lower East Side.

V: Both gangs were Puerto Rican?

G: My gang was mostly blacks. We had Puerto Ricans but it essentially was black and a mixture of Puerto Ricans and maybe three or four white boys. And the opposite gang it was all Puerto Ricans.

V: Were you involved in gang activity before the time you went to Warwick?

G: No.

V: When did you start to get involved with the gangs? Did you meet people in the institution?

G: Right. When I went to Warwick, particularly, you know I was beat up because I was not a member of the Chaplains, I was not a member of the Bishops, I was not a member of the Viceroys, I was not a member of the Enchanters, so when I went in, this was a total new thing to me. The most serious crime that I had committed was playing hookey, and maybe snatching a banana from the fruit stand on the corner. And this is what I was confronted with, "I'm a Bishop" and then in Warwick, remember, you had to march, and in formation and they used to call cadence, and I used to remember the fellas, the Mighty Chaplains, the Mighty Quintos so this being young, being an impressionable mind, when I went out, I wanted to join a gang, so I came out and I joined a gang and I realized that I had to build up a reputation to become a President or War Counsellor or what have you, and I did, I built a tremendous reputation, I became a War Lord, a War Counsellor of the Junior Knights, and did the most daring things. In retrospect, I look back at it now, it was silly but at that time that was the in thing, if you was in a gang, and plus if you went outside your territory you was beat up, so for protection, and perhaps for ego thing I joined the gang I became President of the Junior Knights.

V: When you were in Warwick, did any rehabilitation go on?

G: When I was in Warwick, the most vivid thing that I can remember, because you had a cottage parent, and the most vivid thing I can remember, was my cottage parents fighting, and coming in drunk, and when I look back, her husband, was somewhat sadistic because for the slightest little thing he would jump on particularly the oldest fellas of the cottage and just beat them up, for no particular reason. And [it was] this sort of animosity, sort of hate, which led to my running away from Warwick. And I ran away. And then I got caught in Paterson, New Jersey, and the process of reaching me from Warwick to Paterson, New Jersey, we burglarized a few houses because I was hungry and needed something to eat, and it was getting cold and we needed some clothes, but as far as me getting some rehabilitation of learning, and you know, I went in ignorant and I came out ignorant. I learned about gangs and I learned about reefers, I learned about how to making a lineup in a raping system, because usually the members of a gang would get a girl, and then one would go first then another would go, and second and third and what have you, and things of that nature. Everything was negative. I didn't learn anything positive in Warwick. As a matter of fact, I think it left me with emotional and psychological damage to this day. And it was the cause I think that led to my other criminal activities.

V: Was Otisville any better?

G: Otisville was a little better than Warwick. And the fact that it was better in the sense that it had pacification programs—basketball, T.V., but as far as teaching an individual a trade, or something constructive or productive, it lacked this also.

V: Was there a lot of violence in the juvenile institutions between inmates?

G: Yes, very much so. Particularly in Warwick. Gangs, Chaplains would be fighting the Bishops. A few of the fellas that I met up there, some of them were stabbed, I think two of them died as a result of stab wounds, and particularly on B-4 and D-1, where they have the bigger fellas, I was in A-1. The stuff that you heard up there was frightening, but I know that violence was very prevalent.

V: What was most of the violence about? What caused most of the violence?

G: When I went into Warwick, they put me in A-1. And when you're new, usually each cottage has a bully, a guy that can beat up anybody in the cottage, which everybody looks up to and respects, and he usually was a member of a gang, and he has members up there in that particular cottage to reinforce him, so when you go into the cottage for the first time you usually, if you get packages, and if you're weak, they'll take it away. It's like the survival of the fittest, you know the survival of the strongest. The strong would survive. And if you didn't fight, for me I had to like fight every other day. For my survival. And you had to fight the toughest guy in the cottage. And sometime it went on for days, one time even when I went to the cottage I fought this guy and one day he beat me up, and of course this guy was big, some guy would sneak around and get something and hit him in the head, and then his boys would jump me and then it went on that way until I was accepted into the group, because I was an outsider, as one of the members and everything sort of subsided, and I was accepted and so forth.

V: You were accepted because you were willing to fight?

G: You had to fight.

V: What happened to those who wouldn't fight?

G: The money that they received from home, the cigarettes, the packages were taken away from them, but usually they lost their manhood, you know what I mean, they were raped.

V: Did the staff know this was going on?

G: They had to know. Because not to know, would have showed a gross ignorance on their part. They had to know, but I don't think they were too concerned. What they were primarily concerned with was receiving their paycheck, and coming, and making sure that everything works, as far as the structure of the institution goes, with working correctly, but as far as sitting down and trying to talk to you and resolve a personal problem or like that—

V: Could the weaker prisoners look to the staff for protection?

G: No, because if they went to the staff they were considered rats. And then they really had to go through changes then. And that was like they were ostracized. To be considered a rat that was the lowest thing that you can possibly be stigmatized with. There was violence at Otisville but the thing is that the discipline was more regimentating. It wasn't as relaxed or lax as it was in Warwick, and in Otisville, if you contravene one of the regulations, your cottage parents or your supervisor would come up to you and smack you in the head, or bash your teeth down your throat if they had to go to that extreme. So the individuals here, they knew that they took disciplinary action against you, but the violence was still there because—

V: Sexual attacks were still there?

G: It was there. Even in my cottage. I remember this even today. He's dead now. Morganfield, little Morganfield. He was accused of raping a certain individual in the cottage, and that night they got us all out of bed, because this guy went—he couldn't take it no more, he went and told the supervisor that so and so had raped him, and this was going on for some time, and they got us all out of bed, and I had my hand in a cast, because I had had a fight with another brother, and I was saved because my hand was in the cast, and this guy just went berserk, beating everybody up, because he thought everybody had took part in this, but it went on.

V: When you left Otisville, in fact when you left Warwick, you intended to get involved in gang activity.

G: That was the thing, when I left Warwick, that was sort of like the magic word, that was the in thing. If you wasn't a member of the gang, you wasn't in to anything, you couldn't walk out your territory where you lived at—

V: Where did you live at the time?

G: I was really hanging out on Avenue D.

V: You knew of course, that if you got involved in gang activity that you'd probably have to do some more time right?

G: Those things didn't enter my mind. Because all I knew was that I was the President of the Junior Knights and if I said "We're going down tonight, listen, something happened we're going down to Forsyth, or we are going down to the Project," I knew that my orders were carried out. One doesn't think about if I'm going to get caught like so frequently did happen, that Joe Dokes is going to be killed, is he going to be shot tonight, or is it going to be me tonight because usually everytime we had a rumble somebody got shot, somebody got killed, so I don't think about those things. When a guy come into the neighborhood and started shooting and I go towards him and I don't be thinking about if I'm going to die, all I'm thinking is my reputation, it's a thing that cannot be explained. And it becomes addictive. The more I was involved in this thing, the more the reputation got involved, it was an ego thing, and it just took possession of me. So these things never came to my mind about being caught, and if I did get caught, like so many of my members did it was like a great thing. It was like "I am a member of the squadron and I did so and so" and it was a thing that was embedded in your psyche you were proud to be of a certain territory, you were proud to be a member of a gang you were proud to wear a certain insignia, and you were willing to die for these things, and these young brothers, when I look back, they were willing to die for their insignia. They were Knights, and they believed they were Knights, and they followed the Knights code.

V: Did your gang have an initiation?

G: We used to have what they called sham battles. Where you had to, there was made-up sort of fighting between members of the same gang. Like we would maybe fifteen individuals and John Doe would take fifteen individuals, he would call himself so and so and I would call myself so and so and we would fight.

V: So it really wasn't a sham battle, it was a real battle.

G: It was really a battle. But the thing was if you ran, well this guy can't be a member of the Knights, and usually we would have these sham battles with the older members, I was maybe fifteen, and the older members were maybe twenty-five, twenty-six and they would come because to be a Knight, you had to live up to what they had established, and they would come in and these were the guys that knew how to fight well and they were between jails, and you had to stand there and fight these guys and you couldn't run, and that is how it was determined that you had what it took to be a Knight.

V: Did any of the Hispanic brothers that were involved in this thing, were any of them into a pachuco thing?

G: No, I knew a few brothers that had that, they had the little flower—on their hand. These brothers, though, they really became addicted to this thing—

V: I don't want you to name names or anything like that, but give me an idea of what happened to most members of the Knights. Where are they now?

G: Most members of the Knights that I can recall now, a substantial number of them are dead as a result of being a Knight. I would say another great number of them are dope fiends and the rest are in jail. Very few that I know personally have made something productive out of their lives. Matter of fact, I haven't met anyone that lived, that was reared or came from the same neighborhood that really made something of himself or is doing something productive now. If they're not selling drugs, they're using it.

V: But almost all of them did time?

G: When I went into Auburn, it was practically like the whole neighborhood was there.

V: Well tell me how you got to Auburn. You were sent to Elmira Reception Center. And then what happened?

G: There I was reevaluated, they call it a reevaluation process and they give you a few tests that I couldn't see the relevancy of it, and then they decide whether they're going to keep you in a reformatory, or what prison they're going to send you to, so they sent me to Auburn.

V: So you didn't get to stay at Elmira?

G: No.

V: Even though you were only sixteen?

G: I stayed in Elmira three months.

V: Then you went to Auburn.

G: Right.

V: What kind of people were at Auburn? Were they your age?

G: No. I was one of the youngest. There was some my age, but very few and I was one of the youngest there. Then later on they start coming in, Dragon Lord and the Umbrella Man they start coming in. But there were a number of us that were young and we stood together. We were white and we were black, it was a mixture of various ethnic groups, but we stood together because we were young and we knew that these guys, we heard not to hang out with this individual because if you hang out with this individual or that individual you're going to wind up killing him or you're going to be killed, and we stayed together, man, because I definitely thought that I didn't belong there.

V: Why did you feel that you didn't belong there?

G: Because the crime that I committed was a crime of passion I felt, but not only was it a crime of passion, it was a crime to stigmatize me and call me a criminal and at that time I was thinking useful thoughts, if I get beat up, if five individuals beat me up, why shouldn't I go back with my five individuals and get him, and I called for a fair one [no weapons] anyway—

V: It wasn't a fair one, was it?

G: I know when I went down there I know there was fifty others and they were waiting for us and we met and we collided, and some of my people got killed, some of the people got hurt, and the next thing I know, twelve o'clock I was arrested, and I was being accused of stabbing Rodriguez.

V: You didn't go there with the intent to kill Rodriguez?

G: I didn't go there with the intent to kill Rodriguez. I know that I went there, I had a knife on me, and I went there to cut anyone, but my intention was not to kill, I didn't want to kill no one. I've seen people get stabbed and come out all right, so I figure I stab this guy and whatever, but I know that in my mind it wasn't calculated that I was going there and I was obsessed with it and I was going to kill this guy. There was none of that. There was a fight, and it was "Get your boys and I'll get my boys" and that sort things had happened before and some a few individuals got stabbed and got hurt and even a few individuals got killed, but it was never a thing where anybody knew who it was, nobody talked—

V: But this one somebody talked.

G: Somebody talked. They knew my name and knew where I lived. And then they had a witness that claimed that she saw the whole thing—

V: One of the Debs from the other side.

G: From the other side. And at that time she said she was going out with Rodriguez and she said that she saw me and it was me that stabbed Junior Rodriguez, that I confronted him first, we had a little dialogue, and something happened, he went for his pocket I went for my pocket—

V: Did your attorney argue self-defense?

G: No. I had a Legal Aid. Personally I felt that I was improperly represented, at that time, during my trial, I felt that my constitutional rights were violated from left to right.

V: Did you know that you had constitutional rights then?

G: No, but the way the whole thing happened I knew that there was something, the way I was arrested, and plus in the precinct they held me for twelve hours, and I was telling the individual this, that I didn't do it, I was with my girlfriend, I didn't do it, I didn't do it, and I knew that my mother was there and they didn't allow her to see me. And then when I went to prison and I started to hang out with other individuals, and I started to get into law books, then I realized my rights were violated, I was held incommunicado.

V: But at that time you just knew something was wrong, you didn't know what it was.

G: I knew that something was wrong. My lawyer came to me and told me "Listen these people are really trying to give you the chair what would happen if I get you twenty- to life? I said "Twenty to life, twenty years in prison, you expect me, I say no man, I'd rather be dead than to spend twenty years in prison." I mean right now if I really had to die I'd take the twenty years becuase I know that I'm alive, and once I'm dead there ain't no hope and there's nothing, but at that time I was young and I said "No, man, are you kidding me, twenty years."

V: Well twenty years was already more than you have lived right?

G: Not even that, because I had just turned seventeen.

V: Did any incidents happen to you once you hit Auburn that convinced you that Auburn was the same as Warwick?

G: When I went to Warwick, the first thing that was my reception I seen a gang of guys that was standing outside, that were homosexuals, and I knew that these must be the pimps, and these must be their whores or what have you and then I looked towards the yard and seen people gambling. Then my first day there an incident broke out, and the only consolation that I got was that I knew a few individuals, a few faces that were there, but other than that, I think I would have cracked up because I was really frightened, and the guy told us, man he really put this in our mind—"When you go up there there's going to be guys that were doing from now 'til forever and they're going to see you young guys and you're going to look like Marilyn Monroe, Jayne Mansfield, so accept nothing, don't take nothing"—

V: Who told you that?

G: Elmira Reception Center, they call this an orientation thing. But instead like helping you they planted these fears in me, so when I got there, any guy that tried to come near me—"What you want man?" Even up to this day I don't trust anyone because you can't trust no one in prison, man, unless you know them personally from the street. So when I went there I went to the tobacco shop, and it's nothing but a concentration camp. The school that they had before they built the new school, now, everything was obsolete, all the equipment they had as far as teaching you a trade were outmoded, archaic. So I stayed in the tobacco shop for a little while and then when they built the school I went into the dental laboratory and I learned some dental technology, I got my high school equivalency diploma, and I did this not because in the prison I suddenly saw the light, I did this really because of me. There's something in me that kept telling me "You don't belong here, you're not a criminal, and get out of here." And I said to myself "Listen I'm only going to do ten years, I'm going to get me my high school diploma, and get me a little trade when that school is built, and go back to court and get some kind of reversal and reduction in time." And that was my only hope, that was the only thing that I lived for, and I worked and I worked, and I seen guys that came in with me they started playing basketball, they played with cars. I went to my cell, to the law books, wrote here, wrote there, I got a little help here, and next thing I knew I had a reversal.

V: Do you feel that this progress that you made and this self-improvement that you went through was strictly self-motivated? Did anybody in the joint try to help you?

G: All this was self-motivated. I think maybe it was the stuff that I seen in the prison, the whole scene. The cruelest aspect of prison life is being deprived of your manhood. I think the most strongest force that a man has is his libido. His sexual energy, and that entails a whole lot of things, your ability to procreate, ability to bring someone into the world, and this thing was taken away from me, and I think that's what I missed most, was the opposite sex.

V: Well there's plenty of sex in prison though, right?

G: But the thing is I was never oriented to that. Some individuals can deal with that. Some individuals can go into prison and be a homosexual. Even today I respect homosexuals if that's what they want to be. I respect individuals for being that and I would even struggle for him to be that and even die for him to be that, but for me to engage in that, to look upon another man as a sexual object, it's not within me. I did nine years and it wasn't in me. I took some dirty books and I masturbated and relieved myself that way, but it wasn't in me. I missed it. I dealt with it, and even that left psychological scars. Because when you come out on the street like so many of us do and try to reinforce that thing that was taken away from you, you try to fuck everything in sight. And some individuals develop hangups and problems behind that.

V: Was there any counseling in the institution?

G: The people were so mechanical, they showed no concern. If you had a problem you go and they say "Next, come in" and it was like a robot. How can you when you're dying you go in there, you want to cry. And when you go in there "Yes, yes." Like a robot. As far as counseling goes and any kind of therapy, the only time I felt that they had some therapy with some sensitivity and they had some humanity was when they had some of these drug-oriented programs, and that was later on.

V: While you were up in the institution, did you run into other people that had been involved in gang-related homicides? Did you run into the Cape Man, the Umbrella Man?

G: Oh yes. As a matter of fact—this is odd—because the individual that I was
fighting against, you know the President, here's an individual that jumped
me, and I'll be back and as a result our meeting together which led to me
fighting him and which led to this guy getting stabbed and this guy dying
and resulted in me going to jail and getting twenty-five years and resulted in
him going to jail and getting natural life, this individual up here was the
cause of all this because if I had met him for that Sunday I would have, you
know, I seen him on the stairs of the library in Auburn and I don't know I
saw him, and next thing I know, I had no hate for him, and the next thing I
know we were talking, we became friends. When I came home he go to my
house and tell my mom that this is this and this is the case, and them I saw
as far as Umbrella Man, I met all them brothers, and like I said to myself,
they do not belong here, they are not criminals. You have individuals in jail
who are criminals, who are confirmed criminals.

V: Describe to me that kind of person. What would you call a confirmed
criminal?

G: A confirmed criminal is an individual that is first of all he is psychologically
unbalanced and he's one that goes out and a week later he's back in. And
this has happened, you know this recidivism thing. You just left and the
next week you're back. And not only that, he's back for the same crime.
You strangle your wife and you went up there and you strangle another
woman. And this man has a pattern for these things and the man is
criminally insane.

V: And these were the same people you were doing time with?

G: I was doing time with some individuals that were utterly psychotic. Some
individuals you see would be talking to themselves. They are unkempt. They
don't bathe. You go inside a cell and it's like going into a barn. And you can
see the difference between this inmate and that inmate. When inmates in a
particular gallery get together and say "This individual is not feeling well, he
don't belong here with us" you know that there is something wrong with
the individual. But a criminal—I have witnessed conversations between
inmates and I remember "When I was out there and I had this and I had that
and I told John Doe to bring me the money he didn't bring me the money
and I blew him away." This is what he talks about and then when he clearly
says "When I go out I'm going out and sell some drugs." They'll tell you
man "I'm going out and well some drugs, and the first individual I see with
some money I'm going to take them off" without saying let me see if I can
try this first, and they'll tell you "I'm going out to sell drugs, and I'm going
to do this and I'm going to do that" and one thing about these men they
have the criminal predisposition to become criminals. But when I was up
there I went to school and these people like Salvador and the Umbrella Man
went to school. We were young, our society, because when I got busted, I
was still going to school; I was in high school.

V: When you left Auburn, you went back to the street again.

G: I went back to the street again. I was again busted. For a robbery.

V: Was it an armed robbery?

G: Yeah, It was with a knife.

V: And what was the result of that bust?

G: The result was I got five years for that.

V: Where did you do the five years?

G: Greenhaven. I went to Greenhaven. And how does one explain that? After an individual does nine years, and has studied and has read a little, acquired an education and comes out and just like everything has fallen apart. And just can't adjust. Can't attach to the mainstream of the community or whatever. When I came out, personally, I can only talk from a personal point of view, when I came out, I had nothing, I had no help. I had no money first of all. I was living with my sister, she was poor. It's a bitch man, coming out of prison. It's hard, man. It's hard for me now, I'm going to school now, and many a time I've been tempted to do wrong, it's because I've been up tight. It's been an economic need. And it's not because I want to do wrong, because I want to do right. I want the good things in life, I want to live comfortably, I want to get married, I want to have kids, but with all these pressures that I have even right now, and as far as having any economic stability to do these things, maybe in another year I might think of taking the chance of getting married.

V: Where are you getting the self-control from now? How come you don't go out and stick somebody up now?

G: Because my last time, the last time that I was, that I went into prison, particularly, when I went into The Tombs, to me I've always maintained that the prisons do not rehabilitate the individual. Prisons are there for castigation, not for rehabilitation. When I went, this time that I was detained in The Tombs, I couldn't stand it. I don't know if I was scared or what, and five years ago I could have done that on my head, like nothing. But now, from my personal point of view that's how it affects me. And when I went to Greenhaven I don't know if I was maturing or what, but I kept saying "wow, man," I looked at them bars I said "I do not belong here, man" and like I say, one commits the crime and during the commission of the crime, one does not think about getting arrested or the consequences of it. I mean you really have to be very stable man to really say "I'm going to go in here and I'm going to take this guy off. Now I realize that if I get caught I'm going to get arrested." And there may some things about those things but it happens in a flash, but with all the other pressures that are constantly bombarding the individual, I got social problems, I got economic problems and all I know man that a few hundred dollars can mitigate and ameliorate these problems, and if I can get it, maybe individuals just put things in the way and say "Maybe it's worth it." If I get ten thousand dollars and sometimes I dream about this, if I had a stick-up with ten thousand dollars man, that would set me up for life. That happens through a dream, man, with ten thousand dollars I can buy me a piece of dope, I can sell it here and there and be cool about it. All I want to do is do something productive, whatever it may be, man, and try to get into counseling work if I can, or get into dental technology if I can, and just get me a job man, $175, $150, something that can help me pay my rent. I don't ask nothing astronomical you know.

V: Do you think that if you hadn't gone to a juvenile prison when you were twelve years old your life would have been different?

G: I definitely think so. I think my whole outlook would now have been different, because now when I left for Greenhaven, I knew if I studied I could retain man, and all I had to worry about was application, I know that I have met individuals that got positions. You know even if it is counseling, that I can do, and perhaps I have the competency and the ability to do that better than they can. I can't go into that field because of my record. So there are a lot of setbacks. A lot of civil disabilities, I can't go here because I'm an ex-con or I have a record, so I'm disbarred from going here.

V: But it all began in Warwick when you were twelve years old.

G: I say that it began earlier than that. I say it began in the society that I was brought up. I think that that was a prison. I recall what I had to eat, was cereal in the morning, cereal in the afternoon, and cereal in the night. And sometimes I didn't have that. I recall when I used to go downstairs, man at Christmas and see the kids, man, and they had new toys and I didn't have any I don't recall a Christmas where I received anything from my mother and my father; I never seen my father. So it's a deeper thing than that—

V: And the Knights gave you that? Gave you all those things?

G: You can't blame my mom, because she was part of another process also, part of another system, and she, I know she tried her best to bring us up, and there was eight of us. But I know like when I went out of there and I left home and I met a different crowd though, I was treated like *Gypsy*, man, and it gave me a sense of pride though, and it made me a new person, and I liked it you know, and it was one of them things.

V: Gypsy, we've been talking pretty much about the past right? Now I want to talk a little bit about the future. If we were to have a juvenile justice system that was to do the job, if Warwick was to have done the job with you, what would have to be different about it? How would we have to change those institutions?

G: First I think that primarily what has to be done there must be a radical change in the entire structure, and I mean from the acceptance of the individual until he leaves. The individual, when he enters the facility like a prison like Warwick, or Greenhaven, or Auburn, I think he should feel that he is going to an institution that if he has done wrong, he's going in not to be castigated, but to be, and this is a myth, rehabilitated, and a feeling should be given, and a feeling should be instilled in him that he's going to learn something while he's there and again the confidence and the sense of pride with it that he's going to go back into the community and be part of the mainstream of his community and be productive. This is something that's been lacking in the training schools, and it was lacking in the prisons. When I went into the prisons, I felt that I was going into a dungeon, as far as education, until they built the school in Auburn, that it was nothing, all the machines were outmoded. Why should I go in there and learn to become a shoemaker when they don't use those machines any more. I feel that you have to give an individual, if you're going to rehabilitate an individual, and we're talking about rehabilitation in the total sense of the word, you're going to have to give the individual a new perspective in life. I'm thinking about a new perspective in conjunction with education, something he can use when he comes back into the community, and I'm speaking about a new perspective that goes with a sense of pride, a sense of confidence that you are not going to tell an individual once you have opened on all the doors in the institution and you tell him, "yeah, go and get your Ph.D." "Go and get your Masters." "Go and get your Bachelors or what have you—" when he comes back into the society and it tells him "No you can't be this" or "You can't be that because you're an ex-inmate" or "an ex-prisoner."

V: All the things that you spoke about as being important like status, self-confidence, place to belong, you got all that from the gang, right?

G: I got that from the gang, but in a different sense. I felt that the things that were denied to me in the family structure like I didn't have no father, my mother when I came home it was twelve o'clock, I barely saw her, and when we did meet it was a verbal confrontation. So in the gang when I got like self-status, and I felt important, this was an ego thing and I don't know and yeah, I'd say that it was basically an ego thing.

V: Is there a way to give young kids that kind of ego boost without gangs? Is there a way that the justice system, in fact, can do that?

G: I think it can.

V: Let me put it this way. Let's say we had an institution and we hired some people like yourself. And you're working there. Are you going to be able to step in and motivate those young people?

G: This is what I'm saying. Who can understand another inmate better than another inmate? Who can understand a drug addict better than another drug addict? Who can understand better a prostitute than another prostitute.

V: I'll agree with you about prostitutes and prostitutes; even dope fiends and dope fiends. But not prisoners and prisoners because there are different kinds of prisoners. You said it yourself. Now are you trying to tell me that you understand a guy that rapes little babies? Do you understand that?

G: I'm not speaking about that—no—those kind of people they don't even

belong in prison. They belong in mental institutions. They are individuals
like I stressed before that have some sort of emotional and psychological
problem. And they do not belong in prison. And believe me when I tell you
that prisons are full of these individuals.

V: Even juvenile prisons?

G: Juvenile prisons. You can see. When I was there, at that time I didn't
understand this. You seen a guy that's constantly being beat up or was
raped, you know you just say "He's a punk" and just cast it aside, but the
fact that he didn't fight back or the fact that he withdrew, it was maybe
that he has some sort of problem, some emotional problem.

V: What about the people that beat him up and raped him? Didn't they have a
problem themselves?

G: Yes. But I'm saying. But you must understand that when you went to
training school, the ethics or whatever, the code, is eat or be eaten. And
even in the training school, the concept of the gang is there.

V: It sounds like the training schools just train you to be a criminal.

G: That's what they train you for. Training schools are only breeding grounds
for crime.

V: Does this have to be like this?

G: It doesn't have to be, but you just ask me how do you change this and I tell
you this is what has to be done. Could this be done? I don't know. How can
this be done? I don't have the answer. But I'm saying for an individual to
deal with these problems or to reform the training reformatories or the
prisons, you got to bring some sort of radical change and you got to bring
people that can identify with the needs of people.

V: The gangs that we had, the Chaplains, the Bishops, the Enchanters, the
Sportsmen, the Kings, the Forsyth Street Boys, any gang that we had,
because we had them all over the place in the fifties, they seemed to
disappear when heroin came on the scene right?

G: Right.

V: Now the gangs seemed to disappear overnight. I remember, I'm a couple of
years older than you, I remember that it was gang or nothing, right? In New
York City.

G: Right.

V: But in the sixties there was no gangs, just junkies—wall-to-wall junkies. Why
did that happen?

G: When I was coming up, gang was the thing. Being a part of a gang, the
insignia, you know "Gypsy," "Outlaw," whatever his name was, that was it.
Later on, like when I was in prison I started inquiring about two of my
homeboys, my buddies that came up, "Why did you get busted?" "For
selling drugs" or "For direct sale" or whatever, and they come in and you
say "What are those things there, man?" "Those are tracks, man, I've been
using drugs." "You been using drugs?" This thing was foreign to me.

"What's happening in the neighborhood, man?" You know cause you're concerned. "Joe Doe is OD'd, and so and so is shooting dope, and you know that sister there, she died of OD." And you realize that the gang thing has been wiped out by the drug scene. And you ask what happened. "My next door neighbor came to my house man and he was a dope fiend." Like these brothers, man I considered them potential revolutionaries, I considered them with so great minds that were going to have an economic upheaval. Like they were potential revolutionaries. What would happen, man, if these individuals, instead of fighting against themselves somehow got together and some mind came and told them "Man you're not the enemy, you're fighting among yourselves, man, the enemy is this, this is the enemy man." And directed that hate and that animosity towards another channel. Next thing we know we're being saturated with methadone. The whole community. And nobody was caring or showing any signs of solicitude until it started hitting the suburbs, and the little white boys were coming to their mamas and then they started to get concerned, but before that, man, our community was saturated with dope any kind of drug you can think of, man we had it, and now all of a sudden it's methadone. And now they have a drug to get you off methadone and we understand that individuals using heroin are using a drug that's more powerful than heroin and now you're going to use another drug to get you off methadone. To me that's not fighting the problem, that's running away from the problem, and what we got to deal with is the social conditions that led to my going to prison and today the same economic and social conditions that were materializing when I was coming up are materializing now.

V: So we see the gangs coming back don't we?

G: And the gangs are coming back. Broken homes. Mothers, and the fathers are leaving home and you have the moms taking over all the business and the kids are out on the street. And like in the Bronx. And not only the gangs are coming back, but it's not like we were coming before, we maybe had a gun, maybe one of us had a thirty-eight, but now them kids out there now, they all got thirty-eights, and particularly in the Bronx. Myself, there are certain spots that I wouldn't go because I know that I would be putting myself in a precarious situation man.

V: What's the difference between a gang like the Knights and a gang like the Savage Skulls.

G: A gang like the Knights, we, I would say that it evolved, it was a family sort of a thing. People in the neighborhood, in the community, from the same community, from the same neighborhood, went to the same school, more or less had similar ideas, experienced the same economic and social deprivations, and we just hanged out in a certain areas and that was our little territory and we protected that if necessary with our lives. And it was sort of like—there's a word I'm looking for to describe this—

V: Something that set the Knights apart from the Savage Skulls.

G: And the thing is like the Savage Skulls, they get their orientation, and their ideology from the Hell's Angels. And the Hell's Angels, man, and the Nomads, the Shing-a-Ling Nomads, the Savage Skulls, the Nomads, like the Shing-a-Ling Nomads, man, like when I went to see this, and we were going to use and do some organizing work, and we went to see them and man this is pathetic, this is really pathetic. He says "We are the Shing-a-Ling Nomads and we are fighting the Nomads because they carry our names and they're using our insignia and we're the Shing-a-Ling Nomads because someone from the Hell's Angels gave us our first insignia" and they were very proud of this. The Hell's Angels, man, I read about some of the things that they do, and man these guys they got to be psychotic.

V: The difference seems to be, if you try to put in one word, was that the Knights were organized about the concept of defense—

G: Defense of territoriality

V: Whereas the Skulls and some of the other groups seem to be organized around the concept of offense. You see?

G: Yeah. I see. That's applicable. But I think there's another thing involved. I think it goes deeper into an emotional and psychological thing.

V: Let me give you an example. Gangs very often—fighting gangs—got involved in pulling trains, okay. They'd do lineups. But these wouldn't necessarily involve force. You'd just have a girl that was willing to take on an entire gang. That's not the same thing as snatching a girl in the cellar and everybody raping her.

G: Right.

V: Now that seems to be what's happening today.

G: Exactly. Exactly.

V: And that's the difference.

G: Exactly. Usually when we put one of these on a girl, she came willingly, and maybe there were five of us and then we open the door, maybe there were twenty niggers over there. But today man these kids, I don't know where they get their . . . sometimes I think these guys, man, they got to be crazy. And then we talk with them man, and you're in with them you realize that they're not crazy. When you get back to basically the same thing, man. That being in a gang gives you a sense of importance man, a sense of pride and to be different and to act different and to behave different, even if you got to do weird shit, they want that. And I'm telling you it gives a sense of that thing that they're missing at home or whatever is reinforced by joining the gang. I don't know man, it's weird.

V: So you're saying, in other words we can conclude by saying that we're back at square one. Nothing's really changed.

G: Nothing has really changed. The more things change, the more they remain the same.

V: The big programs, the federal grants, narcotics, nothing has changed in this whole thing.

G: Nothing, nothing, nothing. Not a thing, not a thing, you know, not a thing.

V: Let me ask you one final question, then Gypsy. Do you have any hope for the future for our young people.

G: Yes, but in the family. As far as like society per se doing something for the individual, as far as prisons—First of all I feel that you should do away with prisons, I feel that word is a misnomer. There shouldn't be prisons at all. Call them maladjustment centers, call them correctional facilities, although they don't correct, what do they correct? If an individual contravenes or violates or breaks the law, to me like he's in a sense maladjusted. Maladjusted in the sense that he's not thinking correctly, he's a criminal, and he, you got to incarcerate him, and he stole a car, and there's many reasons, and then you know like the economic, the social, the political and what have you. If you're going to incarcerate an individual and then turn him back into the community you should give him something worthwhile to do while he's in prison and give him some sort of hope, while he's coming back into the community.

V: But right now you think that the system in 1976 is no different than the system that you were involved in in 1956.

G: I think it's worse, you know.

Interview between Andrew Vachss (V) and
Dr. Daniel Jacobs (J) on November 10, 1976

Daniel H. Jacobs, M.D. is a psychoanalyst on the faculty of the Harvard Medical School who formerly worked at the federal prison in Milan, Michigan. Dr. Jacobs is also director of the Cambridge Court Clinic, which treats a large number of juvenile offenders.

V: In your experience over the past several years as a therapist, how would you characterize the willingness of the average young resident in psychiatry to work inside a penal institution?

J: Well, I don't think there's any willingness at all, or very little. There are several reasons. In most psychiatric residencies little or no attention is paid to the impulsive violent individual or the antisocial character. These disorders have not been well studied in most psychiatric training programs. In my own residency training for instance, when offenders were referred from the courts, most residents and their supervisors labeled the people as "not motivated" or "not treatable" because they had court actions pending. They were fairly readily dismissed in terms of treatment or learning possibilities. I don't think that residents would have much exposure to working with these kinds of people. There are other issues involved too. One of them being fear. There are a lot of concerns and fantasies among mental health professionals about what harm they may come to in working with the violent individuals. They have no basis for knowing what the realities are. Another issue, I think, is that most of us who read have some idea of what penal institutions and correctional institutions are like. They are not places where it's easy to do therapy under even the best conditions. There are many, many restrictions, not only on the freedom of the prisoner, but on the freedom of the mental health worker. I think frankly most doctors can find work that's interesting and financially rewarding in other areas. They're not going to choose to work in a situation that is so encumbered.

V: So basically we're talking about the problems of individual motivation, on the part of the therapist, their interest; we're talking about the treatability of the patient himself, and the attendant possible dangers, and then we're talking about difficulties inherent in an institutional setting.

J: That's right.

V: Let's take them in order. The first thing then: motivation. Would you say that it's possible to motivate therapists while in the course of their schooling towards such a career?

J: I don't know about a career. I think it would be hard to expect that people were going to do this for a long period of time. I think you can motivate residents to begin to understand something about the dynamics of antisocial behavior, about what causes people to be violent. You can ask them to get over some of their own irrational fears and to sit and talk with people who have committed crimes—murder, rape, or whatever. In fact I know that it can be done; at Cambridge Hospital I've been able to convince a number of residents to see people who they ordinarily would not see—people who'd been convicted of rape or very violent assault. The residents are always surprised and gratified when they find these offenders are after all human beings with feelings who are often willing to talk about their problems. In order for the residents to be able to treat these patients it requires that they have a model of someone who's already done it, and survived, and maybe even learned something. In addition, they need a good deal of support and supervision. If they feel apprehensive or anxious or if they feel like they're making a mistake, they must have somebody to turn to who'll say to them "Well, let's see what's going on." They need a supervisor who's going to say to them that the dynamics of violent or antisocial behavior can be understood; that it's like any other form of behavior that we, as mental health workers, try to understand. If we patiently listen, the patient will tell us what's troubling him and why he's acting the way he is. Residents can be motivated, but it takes a good deal of effort.

V: That's motivation, and that's even treatability. What about the inherent nature of the institution itself? Do you believe that that's a necessity, that institutions have to be built constructed and managed in such a way as to make the therapeutic experience difficult to attain?

J: I don't know if they have to be built that way. That's the way they are, for the most part. I think that it's never easy to work in an institutional setting where people are coerced into being there. It's particularly difficult when the mental health people usually don't have administrative control. Then the decisions are being made by people who are not mental health workers. Often the mental health professionals view themselves as "outsiders" and are often viewed that way by the administrative staff. Psychiatrists often take a more liberal, flexible position, and are often seen by other staff of the institution as "bleeding hearts" or "do-gooders." It becomes a very, very difficult situation in which to work. I don't think it has to be that way, there may be some models in the country where it isn't that way. In this state, however, it would be hard to find a prison or juvenile home that was really run by mental health professionals.

V: Can you envision a balance of power, if you will—

J: Yes, I can.

V: Between security considerations—

J: I can. I think there can be a clinical director and an administrative director who share responsibility and who try to work together. One should not be given more authority than the other.

V: How long is a normal psychiatric residency?

J: Three years.

V: That's a fairly long time. If we in fact ran an institution where largely the therapeutic staff consisted of people doing their residencies, there would still be long enough time for them to acclimate and become quite useful.

J: Yes.

V: It wouldn't be like a six-month turnaround where once you got used to something you were leaving already.

J: The difficulty with that might be in finding training programs that felt this use of the residents' time was valuable in terms of the residents' overall training needs.

V: Well, aren't there a number of compensatory factors such as the opportunity for research, that you just really can't find. You said yourself that very little is known about the violent individual, the violent personality. Wouldn't this be almost an ideal laboratory?

J: It would be, but I don't think you'd find a lot of training programs that, for instance, would make it a compulsory part of a resident's training. I think it would more likely be seen as an elective. It could be made more attractive to training programs, if in fact there was a salary connected with the residents' work. Training programs are always looking for ways to fund their residents, to pay their residents' salaries. You might get more of a response if you could pay them.

V: Could you give me a ball park figure as to what would be an attractive salary to a new resident?

J: No, I really can't. That you'd have to negotiate with each residency program. You'd have to say, "Well, look, how much do you pay your residents? How much time is he going to spend out here? This is what we can help pay for." Another issue, good residents will not work in that setting unless they feel that they have good supervision. They are going to have to see this as a learning experience. I can guarantee you that most of the supervisors in the traditional residency programs aren't going to know anything about this field. So you're going to have a problem about how you're going to provide the kind of supervision that these residents would want and should have. It would mean that you'd have to have a very experienced and good clinical director who could attract other good supervisors.

V: But isn't it a fact that if such people were attracted and a viable program then built, that residents would be the recipients of a level of knowledge not generally shared by the rest of the profession.

J: That's right. They would really be able to develop—begin to develop an expertise which is much needed and would be for them, or could be, a particular field of interest. I think that's right.

V: Isn't it a fact that today, the so-called "aggressive violent youth" has virtually no institutional treatment options. Nonpsychotic, aggressive violent youth. Isn't it a fact that many programs would just reject a child on the grounds that he is in fact violent or a security problem?

J: We have a tremendous problem in this state in trying to find a placement for children who clearly can't remain in the community and who should not remain in their homes for a variety of reasons. There's no place to put these children, unless they end up in jail, or in some kind of detention center, which really doesn't do them any good. There's no public treatment center in this area that I know of.

V: How much differentiation is required in a program? For example, therapeutically, would you want to have a broad population mix or a rather narrow population band in terms of the kind of disorders you were going to treat.

J: Well, I think that depends on your physical plant, your staff-patient ratio, and your own goals. It's always easier to work with a more uniform population. But again, that would depend on what your own goals were and how much money and staff you could expend.

V: Let me pose this hypothesis to you then. The goal is to work with violent aggressive male juveniles. By violent aggressive, they've committed crimes such as murder or atrocious assault in the act of a robbery, a burglary, or a rape. The goal is to de-escalate their propensity for violence as a problem-solving tool. The goal is to isolate them during the period of treatment. The goal is to protect the community from them and to protect them from each other. There would not be financial constraints at all within reason. Given that particular population, and those goals, would you say that there is a need for the kind of therapeutic input we're talking about. Would they need in fact psychiatrists in such a program?

J: Yes. They would need an extensive diagnostic work up. That would have to be done very carefully. It would probably have to include in my thinking, a multidisciplinary approach. I don't think one discipline certainly can get an overview. I visualize a team approach. You need a mental health professional to take a good history of the child's development and of the kind of emotional problems which he faces. What kind of defenses does he use? When does his aggression show up? In what forms? What's been the texture, the quality of his life to date? What have been the losses he's sustained—the emotional losses—separation from parents, deaths, moves, etc.? I suspect these children have often themselves been abused. You'd want someone who could get a history of the way in which they've lived to date and the kind of coping mechanisms that they've tried to use, not always successfully. I think you ought to have psychological testing to help understand the vicissitudes of this youth's aggressive and sexual drives. How are they handled? Sometimes you can get that by just taking a history. With very dangerous youths, however, I would, as a clinician, feel more comfortable if I had psychological testing. Also you want psychological testing that could help rule out any kind of organic problem. A third area which would need to be explored, and which we're doing in my clinic, is cognitive functions.

We find more and more delinquents who come to our clinic either have real learning disabilities or severe learning problems. We find often, that these childrens' abilities to learn in the formal ways that school teaches is markedly impaired. We have one boy, for instance, who cannot assemble things—he can't do block designs at all. He has a severe perceptual motor handicap that is frustrating him in terms of employment because of his deficit. He can't even pass the test for entrance into the army! This is not just an emotional block. It's a perceptual motor difficulty that has to do with some kind of minimal brain damage. I suspect a number of the children you would see will have some kind of perceptual motor problems or other learning disabilities that would need to be carefully evaluated. This evaluation will be an aid in further vocational or educational planning with the youth. I mean, you can't ask a boy to be an auto mechanic if he has some kind of spatial relations problem that precludes his assembling things. This kind of cognitive evaluation is often overlooked. These youths, unless they have some way to earn a living, unless they have some way of gratifying themselves, of increasing their self-esteem through useful work, are not going to do well. Vocational planning is essential.

Institutions also need to involve the families of these youths. Careful evaluation of the families from which the child has come, and if he's a fourteen year old, to which he may return, is essential. Too often—I know in adult prisons—the individual has been worked with, but his wife is rarely seen, often she comes on visiting days, usually weekends, when the staff isn't there. No one gets to know her. These men go back to their wives and have incredible problems, marital problems that may precipitate antisocial behavior once again. For adolescents particularly, one needs to very carefully evaluate the kind of placement after the institution that is best for them. Can the boy's family provide the structure and support he needs? I think a good deal of family therapy would probably be indicated. Certainly a family evaluation by a social worker is essential.

V: You're talking about an outreach kind of thing now.

J: Yes, definitely. You have to have outreach. What we've found in our outpatient clinic is, the parents are often so overwhelmed by social and emotional problems of their own, that they have practically nothing to give to the child. If you take that child away for a period, help him, but then return him to parents who have not been able to give him much and who are still overwhelmed by problems, the chance that he is going to regress is quite likely. My impression is these children, despite all their toughness, suffer from a great deal of separation anxiety. Often they haven't got enough good mothering in the first place. They therefore have a lot of trouble separating from their environment. What you would do in an institution is separate them temporarily. They may then look as though they're doing well because they can put a car together or because they learn, but you may not have dealt with their emotional attachments to the parents that raised them. Often the parents are not willing to let go of the children either, even though they may neglect them or abuse them, they have very strong ties to these children. Unless those ties are examined, and emotional separation and individuation for the adolescent aided, you may find that the delinquents leave after looking successful in the program and be right back into antisocial behavior.

V: So even if this information was in part gathered by social-work kind of personnel, at some point there has to be an evaluation done at a level commensurate with an education such as that of a psychiatrist.

J: No, I think a good social worker could do much of it.

V: You do?

J: I do. I don't think it has to be done by a psychiatrist at all. I think that probably what you would need is a team with a psychiatrist, a social worker, a psychologist, an educator, and, maybe, a vocational specialist. Five people.

V: Well, five categories, anyway.

J: Yes, five categories. In addition, you would have to have a good physical and neurological work up on each child. That would require a pediatrician, who had some interest in neurology. EEG's might be necessary and other neurological tests. A good medical history and physical examination is important because these children may have all kinds of somatic problems that have not been discovered before. They need glasses, their teeth are falling out. They may have other somatic problems that have just not come to light and which often worry them even though they can't tell anyone about them.

V: Should this take place outside the final institution or within it?

J: You mean geographically?

V: Yes, physically. In other words we have two ways that we can intervene. We can have the courts refer children that they've targeted to a diagnostic center and have the diagnostic center make some of the preliminary work-ups, and not have the actual history taken until the child actually goes to the institution. Or we can have the institution do the bulk of the work-up itself.

J: Well, I think the institution ought to do the work itself. If you're going to accept the child into the institution, your staff might as well do the initial work-up. It isn't very helpful to have a diagnostic center ten miles away tell you that this child is good for your institution. The child may show up and your staff have a very different view. Your own staff ought to do it. If, then, they feel that the child is not appropriate to the institution, they can send him elsewhere.

Turning youths away may be a difficult problem in itself. Your staff, if they're good, are going to feel some commitment to finding placements for children you don't accept. You can't just expect a good staff to do an evaluation and then say to a boy, "Tough, you can't come here. You've got to go to this jail down the road."

V: Well is it possible to get some kind of consensus around the criteria with the staff before any children start to arrive?

J: Yes, I think you're right. I think you need to really get a consensus. But that doesn't make it any easier for the staff to turn people away. And that—after a while—I think would be a major frustration for your diagnostic staff. "What do we do with the kids that this institution is not appropriate for?"

V: Is that really the problem of a diagnostic staff, to worry about them?

J: If they're good, they're going to. If they really get involved with the kid and understand his problem, and they put in hours of diagnostic time, you can't expect them to say "Well, tough."

V: Yes, but wouldn't their commitment to the other children they are treating override—

J: Yes, I'm not saying that they're going to admit these children. All I'm saying is that you may hear a lot of frustration from this staff who says "For every one we admit we're turning away three, and these kids are going to jails or they're going back out on the streets, or they're going here or they're going there, and what about Johnny who's the epileptic, he's over in the county jail, and he's having seizures everyday"; your staff is going to get involved in doing these evaluations, if they do good evaluations they're going to have some problems with whom they turn away.

V: Would I overcome some of that anxiety on that score if I tell you one staff position within the institution will be that of an advocate for children, generally, so that this person's task and the task of his staff is to assure the proper placement of children that you don't accept.

J: I don't envy that person. That does allay my anxiety, and I think you might need someone like that just for the diagnostic center. Somebody to just work on placement of kids who were not accepted into the institution. I think that would help your staff a lot. They could say "Hey, that's Joe's job. We've done ours, now that's his job."

V: Joe should be a nonaligned person so that his simple task is to find the best placement for each child.

J: That's right.

V: Because otherwise we have political problems too, don't we, with whom we accept and whom we don't accept?

J: That's right.

V: Political questions like "If you don't take this boy, he's going to go to Attica." Then some feelings that you have that are nontherapeutic—

J: That's exactly right. Humane. There may be pressure to accept youths. For instance, you may hear, "If you don't take him, he's going to have to be out on the street and if he kills somebody, how are you going to feel, because you closed the door on him?" You have to have somebody who's going to relieve the diagnostic staff of those kind of worries. An advocate for the child. A placement counselor.

V: Let me give you some very very brief, sketchy profiles and I fully understand that they're not intended to be in-depth, but you could tell me whether or not this group could be comingled for therapeutic purposes. We have a kid who sets fires, is a bedwetter, and has shown a history of torturing small animals; we have another kid who's committed about fifteen armed robberies, and the weapon was a piece of pipe, with which he physically attacked all his victims; we have a kid who has made sexual attacks on young children; we have a kid who shot another boy during an argument; we have a kid who came home one day and wiped out his parents; we have a kid who was a homosexual prostitute on the street; we have a kid who was a narcotics dealer. Can we mix any of these kids together?

J: Well, you know you're asking a question that is very hard to answer because my feeling has always been that you can't tell much about a person merely by the symptom. You are describing different individuals with different symptoms. I don't know anything about them. I think often, one of the problems that we have in trying to get mental health professionals to see offenders is that as soon as they hear what the crime is, they say "Oh my God, a rapist, not for me. I can't treat him." What the person *does* doesn't always tell you a lot about them. It tells you the degree of stress they're under maybe, and the kind of abnormal symptoms they develop, but it doesn't tell you whether they're workable or not, or whether or not they'll be able to get along in a group setting. I would think that those people might be able to get along but I'd have to know a lot more about each person. I don't think the symptom can tell you very much.

V: You're rejecting the criminal offense for which the individual is indicted and convicted as a diagnostic tool in and of itself.

J: It's not a diagnostic tool in and of itself. Absolutely not. I don't believe so.

V: Do you think there would be problems with juveniles in terms of what we take now to be an insanity defense?

J: Can you explain that?

V: We're running the institution here for people who are not criminally insane. There are a number of "legal" tests for insanity. The usual one being "Are you able to distinguish right from wrong?" Do you think there are people who would be legally insane yet treatable within the kind of program we're talking about?

J: Well I guess it might be a matter of whether they were temporarily insane, if they were on drugs, or drunk or had a brief psychotic episode. I don't think that the insanity defense in itself would, again, indicate to you whether in fact, the person was treatable or not in your institution.

V: Do you buy into the standard paradigm—well it's not standard although it probably should be—that you have to look at whether a kid is dangerous or not dangerous; treatable or not treatable; and deterrable or not deterrable, and make an institutionalization decision based on those criteria?

J: Let's take them one at a time. Treatable or not treatable? How do you know? If he's never been treated before? It's very hard to know who's going to be treatable and who isn't.

V: Well, some of the assumptions are, for example, that a person who is a homosexual is not treatable.

J: I don't necessarily agree. In any case, you may not be treating him for his homosexuality. Hopefully, he isn't being incarcerated in a place like you're proposing because he's a homosexual. He may be a homosexual who gets into a panic at certain times and who kills somebody because he feels overwhelmed. That might be treatable. Whether his homosexuality is treatable or not I wouldn't know. Again, you'd have to evaluate the case. I don't often think you can tell in advance who's treatable and who isn't.

V: You'd have to be exposed to a course of treatment before—

J: At least a good diagnostic workup. A good diagnostician should see somebody two, three, four, six times, in order to get some idea about whether a relationship can be developed with the youth. If a relationship can be developed, if the child responds in some reasonable way, then maybe he can be treated. What were the other things?

V: Dangerous or not dangerous.

J: I assume all the people you would be incarcerating would be dangerous in terms of their past activities.

V: So clearly, you would say that nondangerous individuals should not be incarcerated.

J: I don't see why they should be.

V: What about deterrable versus not deterrable?

J: What does that mean? Is that different from treatable?

V: Absolutely. It's different in the sense that the punishment will produce a change in behavior. I shouldn't even say a positive change in behavior.

J: I think there are some people—this may be off the point—who need to go to jail for brief amounts of time. Jail probably, not a treatment center, in order to understand that their behavior has consequences—that they cannot continually be excused by the society. Because they get messages from the courts and the probations department, at times, that "you're doing bad things, but, there's always some excuse or reason for your behavior and you don't really have to be responsible for your actions." I have seen some people whom I thought a short stay in jail helped. It kind of got them to realize that if they continued their antisocial behavior, there might be serious consequences. They got a taste of jail and they decided they'd better work with a therapist on staying out.

V: That's not what we call deterrence for this particular—

J: I don't see how that fits in with the treatment model that you're proposing.

V: All I'm saying is that a person that's deterrable—purely deterrable—doesn't need to be in such an institution.

J: Yes, I agree.

V: One of the problems that we've seen—and maybe you can comment on this—is that a child is recommended to this kind of an institution. And he's rejected on the grounds that he's not suitable behaviorally. That child tends to return at a later date and now he's qualified. At what point can we intervene without stepping on people's rights.

J: Well, can you give me an example?

V: The first kid I spoke about, the kid tortures small animals, which, although that's an abominable act, would probably not cause incarceration. He wets the bed—that's certainly not incarceratable. And he sets fires, which probably is. But the fire he sets the first time, the first fire, he's playing with matches, and he burns down a shed. Now the standard criteria would tend to indicate that this child's potentially very dangerous, with those three things coexisting. Yet, his criminal behavior so far really doesn't merit incarceration in this type of institution. So how do we respond?

J: If I were doing the diagnostic work up on this child, one of the real questions I would have is could this child, who has not exhibited antisocial behavior other than fire setting, be treated in some other center which was equally good. Does he have to be put in with murderers, and very severely assaultive people?

V: He's the one type of kid that no group home will touch. Especially those made of wood instead of brick.

J: If I were evaluating him, I would look for a different setting. If there were none available, then I'd say "well I guess he has to come here." Maybe fire setting is not the best example. I think if it can be picked up early there may be no need for institutionalization. Outpatient treatment may suffice. By the time a fire setter got to you, however, he probably would have set more than one fire.

V: Oh, sure.

J: And he probably would have endangered people's lives. You know fire setters if picked up early may be treated as outpatients. You're talking about somebody who's really been doing it for a while and been ignored.

V: But that's in fact the standard pattern of the juvenile courts, though. It's very unlikely, very unusual that a child's first criminal act brings him inside the institution right?

J: Well, certainly—It's very hard, unless you do the individual evaluation, and know what the child is like, to know whether he would fit into your institution or not. It's certainly conceivable that a fire setter would. How violent do they have to be in order to qualify for your setting? Who decides that? Are admission criteria going to be by statute, or is it up to the diagnosticians?

V: Well, we contemplate a statutory scheme by which certain children are excluded from even the possibility of being committed to this institution, and the pool that is left is the pool from which the diagnosticians select. Let me ask you another question. How would an institution deal with the problem of a therapist being justifiably physically afraid to work there?

J: I'm not sure. You mean he's justifiably afraid—

V: When I say justifiably, I mean there are youth in there that are physically dangerous.

J: Well, in order for the therapist to work well, he has to feel sufficiently protected. He should be able to concentrate on what the child is saying without worrying about whether he's going to survive the interview.

V: Well, isn't that a question of the individual therapist's attitude more than the—

J: Well, it's probably partly that. However, once in a while you do see somebody who's so dangerous that you have to ask some one to sit in with you, or you have to leave the door open. You have to say to them, "If we're going to continue, you'll have to take some medication." The institution has to work out some safeguards, not just for the therapist, but for the child too. If the child is assaultive, if he's been allowed to get out of control it isn't good for him either. Some fears of the therapist may be irrational ones which can be dealt with through supervision. Nevertheless, there has to be a system where the therapists feel reasonably comfortable, so that they can walk down the hall and not feel that they're going to get whacked from behind, or be stabbed in a therapy session.

V: I've noticed from watching you over the years that you've either resolved that problem or else you're not particularly afraid of people.

J: No, I just trust my judgment. Every once in a while if I get afraid, then I call for help in one way or another. I say "I think we ought to leave the door open," or I say to the person, "frankly I'm beginning to feel a little scared. Is there any reason why I should be?" Even if the guy says "no" and I'm still scared, I take whatever precautions are necessary. Otherwise I'm going to sit there and worry and I'm not going to be able to listen to what the fellow's trying to tell me.

V: Yes, but—I'm no therapist or diagnostician—I know for a fact that you've been in confrontive situations with people that I know for a fact are nuts. Dangerous nuts. People I know personally. Heavyweight crazos. And you must have known that. And it didn't seem to bother you.

J: Well I guess I trust. You see, I think that if you form a good relationship with people, and if you really listen to them, and if you're interested, most of the people won't be violent with you. Unless they are absolutely psychotic and hearing voices and being told to—by the devil or somebody— to do you in. Most people, if you are reasonably concerned about them, even violent people won't hurt you. People become violent, I think, often because they have suffered some kind of narcissistic injury, some blow to their self-esteem. They've been cornered or trapped in some way. If you as a therapist are careful not to degrade them, not to humiliate them or trap them so that they feel the only way they can regain their sense of themselves is to strike out, I don't think you're going to usually find yourself assaulted.

V: One of the big troubles that we have at any kind of juvenile institution is the problem of non-consenting homosexuality. The standard theory being offered to explain this is that they are adolescent males deprived of female sexual outlets. Now I personally don't believe this, but I'd like to have your views on it.

J: Well, that's part of it. And I think there's a real problem in keeping adolescents away from heterosexual experience from the ages from say fourteen to seventeen. I do think that these are formative years for children. Their own sexual identity is not very clear to them, not cemented. If you put boys in an environment where they can't have any kind of heterosexual experience or exploration, the chances that they'll turn to homosexuality at least temporarily, if not permanently, are greater.

V: I'm talking about homosexual physical attack. And if that theory is accurate—they're deprived of normal outlets—how do you account for rapes that take place within three hours of incarceration? How do you account for rapes that take place in the sheriff's van on the way to the jail? Is there any component of homosexual violence that's in fact assaultive, that has nothing to do with sex?

J: Oh, yes. A lot of it has to do with restoration of one's esteem. I mean here you are on the way to jail, and you're feeling so terribly vulnerable yourself, and probably frightened. You're feeling as though your own masculinity is being threatened by the loss of freedom, so you try to restore it by assaulting someone else, and saying "I'm a man and I still have some control over my life."

V: Right now, in juvenile institutions, of all the areas that are therapeutically ignored, in my opinion that's number one because a male child that's been homosexually raped is given one of three institutional options: he can go to solitary confinement, and accept the kind of ostracism and deprivation that goes with that; he can accept that he has been thrust into, become a practicing homosexual vessel; or he can kill his attacker.

J: Right.

V: Those are the options that he's offered.

J: Right.

V: Can you postulate any kind of therapeutic treatment for a child that was in fact homosexually raped, that's outside those options?

J: A treatment?

V: Well, is there a way that a child can be made to look at what happened to him in such a way that he can not accept it but live with it, so that he doesn't have to act out either against himself, or against another? Does it have to be a choice between suicide and murder? Is there something else?

J: Yes. I think that there is a way, over a period of time, to help the child see what's happened to him and try to find solutions to it. That requires though that the child have enough space and not be under intense pressure. I mean there's no sense in talking to a youth twice a week about his problems when after he leaves your office, he has to face this gang that's around the corner, and either submit to sexual attack or get the crap beaten out of him. The child has to have enough freedom from fear to be able to think through what's happened.

V: Alright, so you're at the point where you're in agreement with the fact that if a therapist is going to have an even chance at success, there has to be a certain degree of institutional control and custodial observation and security—

J: Absolutely. Absolutely. Absolutely. That is essential. If a child is in an institution and is under constant anxiety, about very real, not imagined, but very real threats to his identity, and to his body integrity, you're not going to be able to do any therapeutic work with him. I mean you know, it's like in the middle of the battle where bullets are flying, trying to analyze with someone, "Well, how did you get into this situation? What do you think about war? What are your aggressive feelings?" I mean the guy is ducking and dodging and trying to survive, and as long as that kind of environment is created even unintentionally for a child, I don't think there's any possibility of rehabilitation.

V: As a matter of fact, that is the environment in the average juvenile institution.

J: Well, that's unfortunate.

V: That's my feeling. To what extent would the psychiatric staff need to have input into the administrative decisions?

J: A great deal. As a matter of fact I think that you have to give the clinical director as much authority as any other administrator. I think they should have a great deal of authority in the institution. Traditionally, as you know, it's always been the guards or the security forces that could veto whatever therapeutic endeavors were made if they didn't like them. There's one other thing I wanted to mention in terms of treatment of these kids. In our clinic we were using, for a long time, a traditional model: that troubled male adolescents usually didn't have a strong male model, and, therefore, we would assign them to male therapists. I think in institutions there are often many more males involved than females in therapy roles, or custodial roles, whatever. This year we've begun to realize that many of these youths also had defective mothering, and that it might be just as valid to assign some of these rough and tough characters to a woman therapist and see what happens. We're finding really amazing results. They take to it very very well, and they open, many of them open up to women quite readily. If I were thinking about running an institution, I would think about using quite a number of female therapists, who were experienced and who knew how to deal with adolescents. But I think the model has always been for them to stick troubled adolescents with strong men, and it gets into a macho model that even the staff may have. There isn't the kind of softness and the kind of maternal quality that women can add. I think that they have a very important role to play in these kind of institutions.

V: What about the problem of—for want of a better term—"lay therapist" overstepping his or her bounds. One of the constant complaints I got from juveniles, is that—one guy who's now doing four life sentences for four separate things, told me that when he was a juvenile, when he was in an institution, the therapist, who was a B.A. social worker, asked him questions about his relationship with his mother, in such a way that really flipped him out. He couldn't deal with it. And I heard this complaint a lot. That nonpsychiatrically trained staff get into analytical areas that they really don't belong.

J: Well, that's true, not only institutions, but also in clinics throughout the country. Less experienced people often don't do as good work. I think that the only safeguard against that is a very careful screening of who you hire, and very close supervision in the beginning. By very close supervision I mean for the first year or two of their work in the institution, they should be closely supervised and, after that, as they seem to do well, be given more freedom. I hate to see people without supervision. I think it's very very important. Often staff are put out on a limb with patients that really nobody knows very much about in terms of the profession, and they just kind of psychologically roam around trying to get a handle on the case. They make a lot of mistakes.

V: There's been a tendency in the profession, and one that as you know I've subscribed to rather heavily myself, to use former prisoners as counsellors. I think, I'm afraid, that it's gotten out of hand. I don't know, and I'd like to have your comments on that.

J: I think it's gotten out of hand, very frankly. Some of the former prisoners, I think are talented and good. Others have used being a therapist as a way of not having to look at their own problems. They've quickly jumped from being "a problem" to being "a therapist" without any intermediary request that they look very carefully at their own lives and the ways in which they handle their own problems. Then they get into all kinds of trouble. They may not have resolved their own antisocial problems. These problems get acted out in the therapeutic environment. They may overly identify with the kids and be unable to get enough distance to really be helpful. I think there is certainly a role for people who've been in trouble, but I would not hire someone who was an ex-con who had not been in therapy after release from prison. I would require that they either had been in therapy or be in therapy.

V: You wouldn't make that an across-the-board requirement for all therapeutic staff though?

J: Well, I assume that most of the people that—well, I think that's hard to do. I mean you have a huge staff, you can't ask everybody—

V: I'm talking about the treatment staff, now—

J: Treatment staff, I assume that most people who are going to do therapy seriously are sooner or later going to want some therapy themselves. You know, the problem you mentioned of inexperienced people asking the wrong questions is going to be true for residents too. I mean a second-year resident doesn't know very much, and that's going to be a problem. With supervision, it can be overcome.

V: Alright. Let me take you all the way back down to the bottom line. Do we need a maximum-security closed secure setting for some juveniles?

J: Absolutely. Absolutely. I think it's not fair to them and to society not to have it. And particularly to them. I mean it exposes society to what they may do, but a kid who's clearly out of control that's killing or assaulting, needs some help. To ignore that request is really a tragedy—they wind up either in prison, or dead, or in some unfortunate situation.

V: So you would—

J: There are definitely youths who have to be removed from their home and from the society; who need a highly structured setting for a fairly long period of time.

V: If we accept that as fact, and if we also accept as fact that juvenile institutions in the past have been almost completely criminogenic in and of themselves, we're faced with the problem of designing an institution which will exist which is not in itself criminogenic. We've talked a lot about the therapeutic inputs that would have to be part and parcel of such place. I would like to just briefly ask you some architectural questions from a therapist's point of view. I'm told that in Japan they have gardens that actually induce people to commit suicide. That suicide is a revered thing in Japan, and that there are specific places in Japan to commit suicide. That the atmosphere and the setting is suicide inducing. Do you find that concept possible? Can you envision such a thing?

J: Well there are atmospheres that would lend people to think about committing suicide. I don't know if in our country it would be gardens, but certainly—

V: In our country I'm saying it might be institutions.

J: That's right, exactly, and when I worked in a federal prison, a number of people were put into isolation. They didn't have enough cells for everybody, they crowded four or five people into cells designed for one or two, the suicide gestures anyway increased tremendously. There are institutional settings which, no doubt, push people to think about suicide.

V: By the same token, are there institutional settings and designs which push people towards violence?

J: Yes, I do think so.

V: Do you think that those are to some extent architecturally correctible?

J: To some extent, yes. I think the external environment is a factor in why people become violent, there are internal issues too, but certainly the external environment can make a difference.

V: One of the things that we've been experimenting with—and I'd like you to comment on this, is the idea of having the wall that contains people actually contain all the structures of the institution, and that inside the wall, there would only be living units so that it would be possible to "escape" from the living unit and yet still be within the wall. We're postulating that there are certain people who have a need to control their environment in negative ways, such as escaping. That they could do it here with a certain measure of security.

J: I think that's very important. Because when people escape it's not just that they want their freedom back. They usually escape from some type of intolerable feelings that are beginning to emerge. That—whether they're murderous feelings, or suicidal feelings, or feelings of longing for somebody they miss on the outside, they are some feelings that they can't tolerate, that they have to get away from through action. I think it's important that people have room to escape a little. Not a lot. Not over the wall. But to have room to escape. That's one of the ways in which they try to control their feelings. That activity can be analyzed in the therapeutic environment. "What made you have to escape? What made you run around the grounds?" whatever. But they need the room to do that. And I think violence escalates and suicide attempts escalate where there are not escape hatches for people within the environment.

V: Right. And what we propose architecturally is provide the escape valve without the reality of an actual functioning escape.

J: That would be nice. That would be very nice.

V: You spoke of a highly structured setting. Does a highly structured setting necessarily mean maximum security in the context we're discussing?

J: Maximum security has had, it seems to me, a bad connotation. We always think of the worst prisons. If by maximum security we mean maximum security for each youth in the setting, where he can learn, develop, explore his problems without having to worry about being raped or assaulted—that kind of maximum security I would certainly be in favor of. If we also mean an environment in which youths understand that if they cannot control their own violent or aggressive behavior, there are people and environments which will help them control it; so that nobody need feel that their crazy, violent, suicidal, inclinations will get out of hand, so that they can feel secure that somebody will be there—if things do get out of control. That kind of maximum security I'm all in favor of. I guess also if you're going to deal with very, very dangerous people, the surrounding community is going to have to feel that you're in control of the situation. If you just mean guards who are going to patrol up and down, that kind of maximum security has not been very effective.

V: So you're really saying security is a double-edged sword. The resident, the inmate, the prisoner is also secure.

J: That's right. I mean that's the reason for having maximum security—all that is done in an institution like the one you propose should have a therapeutic effect. We should think of the youth first. An environment that is not maximally secure for each youth is not the best kind of therapeutic environment. You know, you can justify maximum security on the grounds that it's best for the youth. It doesn't have to be an external force that's imposed on the youth because society's afraid of them.

V: Well, that ties in very well with what we want to do architecturally because we believe that we can heighten the individual's sense of security by the design. Simple things like each child will have his own toilet and bathing facilities. And that's not the way it's done in institutions. I think that would go a long way toward heightening the sense of security, the sense of privacy.

J: That's right.

V: We think the visiting arrangements can be made physically better. We think that the cafeteria, the restaurant, whatever you want to call it, can be made more like the way people eat in the real world, than one long institutional table. Our intent is to design these things that have a therapeutic value as well as just being nice.

J: Let me ask you a question. You design a place that is maximally secure for the child. You take kids from urban ghettos, and you put them in a place where they have a shower of their own, and a room of their own, something maybe they haven't had before. They have all kinds of facilities and people interested in them, things they may not have had before. What's going to make them want to leave to go and be a mechanic earning maybe ninety or one hundred dollars a week? How can we encourage them to re-enter an environment that is not nearly as caring? I think that's really a problem for good institutions. That children and adults become institutionalized and the outside world doesn't seem nearly as nice as these institutions are.

V: I think that has to be on the therapists' head. I think that part and parcel of the therapy is that this separation thing is dealt with from the beginning. Because, sure, we can make a perfect institution, and there would be, maybe very little desire to leave. But part of an intelligent therapeutic program would be to have the individual understand that there is a certain inevitability here.

J: That means you have to run your own after-care program. You have to have continuity of care, so that a child who has seen a therapist for a year or two maybe, doesn't think he has to sacrifice that relationship by leaving. That therapist should follow him in the outpatient setting, not necessarily turn the treatment and after-care over to new people.

V: You put your finger exactly on it, on what we think is one of the strongest points of the institution. We want to put the kind of facilities in this institution which do not exist in the outside community. And, rather than the standard thing of bringing the bad kids into a local YMCA and saying "Can we use your gym," we want to have a much better gym. But part of what we want to have is an outpatient clinic. But not just for our children that have been released, you see what I'm saying? For people in the community too.

J: Well, that's fine. I think one of the problems I've experienced is the patients seen went to very disparate geographic areas. It was tremendously difficult to provide after-care for kids. I assume that your institution would take from a large geographic area and have a similar problem.

V: Statutorily yes, functionally, no.

J: The smaller the geographical area the better. I think if you have somebody from Albany and somebody from all over the state—

V: That's probably going to be very unlikely, Dan, because practically 90 percent of our kids would come from the five boroughs. You're talking about a federal institution and that's an endemic problem with federal institutions.

J: Even with state institutions I think.

V: Depending on the size of the state, right.

J: Yes. I think that can be a problem.

V: The final thing I want to ask you is this. Can I sit down with you at a future date and bring the actual architectural blueprints.

J: I don't know much about architecture.

V: You don't have to. I'm not asking you about architecture I'm asking you about therapy.

J: Well, one of the problems that I've seen in institutions is how you allow people the kind of individual living space they need but also not have those spaces become areas that are unsupervised, where kids can assault or rape one another. If you have private rooms, well, then somebody has to know who's in them and whether anyone's being forced into them. That's a terrific problem: to have the kind of room that kids need for privacy to be by themselves, but to supervise them so they don't abuse it.

**Interview between Andrew Vachss (V) and
Raymond K. Gilyard (G), on October 26, 1976**

Raymond Kiidh Gilyard grew up on the streets of Corona, New York and
surprised most observers by his graduation from high school in 1970. Yet, by the
time he graduated from college, he had won numerous creative writing awards
and had several poems published in various anthologies including *The Treehouse*
and *White Paper/Black Poem: A Black Tornado*.

After a period as a street worker in a community-based anti-narcotics
program and work with the Friends of Walter Lee McGhee Committee and
Advocacy Associates, he received the Woolrich Memorial Fellowship to attend
the writing division of the School of the Arts at Columbia University. He
received the M.F.A. degree in 1978.

He currently lives in College Park, Georgia and is concentrating on writing
fiction.

V: Kiidh, you've been involved, either as a participant or an observer, with the
youth gang phenomenon in New York for quite a number of years, right?
G: Right.
V: Have you perceived any change in the attitudes, in the codes, in the
methodologies of youth gangs in the past ten years? Are they any different
now than they were?
G: Well, basically they're the same in that there's a group of frustrated young
people that get together bonded by some type of ties that they didn't find
elsewhere, outside of the so-called traditional environment. What I find is
that things are really going in cycles. In '76, '75, you have the same type of
gangs that you had in '65, '66, '64, but in between those two cycles, you
had a period of heavy drug use, and it seems that that's the way the cycles
run. They run from youth gangs to drugs, to youth gangs to drugs, so right
now I would say we're just ending another cycle of youth gangs and it seems
as though we're going into another period of heavy teenage drug addiction.
V: In the fifties we had the same cycle didn't we?
G: Well it was the same thing, from what I understand. The late forties there
was a lot of morphine and heroin usage. Then in the fifties the gangs, the
bebops. Then in the early sixties it was heroin, then drugs again, then heroin
again in '68, '69. I guess that was one of the high points, '68, '69, '70 for
youth. That was the first time I think that the drug movement was basically
a youth movement in New York. Prior to that it was mostly so-called
veterans that shot dope. But in the late sixties it was youth. Then you had
in the early seventies the gang movements; again, I think, started first in the
Bronx. A gang called the Black Skulls was one of the first of the new gangs

out. Then that ran till about '74, early '75, but now from what I understand, there's a lot of heroin back out in the streets.

V: Do you see a connection between the two phenomenons?

G: The gang movement is a self-destructive movement, in that people from rival gangs often harm and in some cases kill each other. But also they do great harm to property in the neighborhoods which they war in. It seems to me that whenever there's too much gang involvement, too much gang activity, too much destruction of property, it seems as though drugs become available.

V: Can you give me a profile of a typical gang leader? For example, has a typical gang leader been incarcerated before?

G: Most of them. As a matter of fact, in some of the youth gangs, the leader is the one who has had the most adult experiences in life. He was the one who first went to reform school or first went to jail, or first got busted. Because the whole mores of that game point to that whole macho masculinity thing, so the one who's had the greatest amount of that experience at a relatively young age usually becomes the leader, from what I've seen in gangs.

V: Do the juveniles that you know appear to fear the prospect of incarceration?

G: Not that I see now. It seems like they romanticize it more than they fear it. Based on legends they hear from the old-timers. And a lot of them think jail is a learning experience anyway, because going back to that leader thing, the leader when he has spent some time in jail, when he comes home he seems to be somewhat more crafty and cunning, than other people who were out on the street, though it would seem the other way around. A lot of people, youth, they romanticize that whole jail experience. Like they don't really fear it.

V: You don't see the juvenile institutions as being essentially rehabilitative?

G: No. Not at all. They seem to be another type of school. Where you learn another type of trick. How to deal with the street.

V: Now there's been a heavy move, which has been reflected in the media and the legislature, about returning to the old ways of doing business—longer periods of incarceration for various juveniles. The perception of the general public being that juveniles can pretty much do what they want and get away with it. Do you find this perception to exist at the street level?

G: If you're speaking in terms of community citizens? Yes, I find that this is a prevalent attitude. To me it's a basically ignorant attitude also, because there are other ways of dealing with the so-called juvenile problem, because actually it's an adult problem, it's not a juvenile problem at all. They are only responding to things in the environment so I don't like to use the phrase juvenile problem at all. As far as some of the legislation that's been proposed within the last year, I find it to be very extreme measures. They are talking about adult incarceration at age fourteen with a minimum sentence. I don't believe that any youth at that age can be sentenced to a long-term sentence, because you have to understand that the things that led to his behavior to the point where he was arrested, those only occur over a period of months maybe and the downfall of the juvenile may take place in only a period of months. So if he can, say in a period of six months, go from being a so-called average juvenile to becoming what you would call the worst juvenile, how do you sentence him to two years? You seem to leave out the fact that maybe in six months you can turn his life back around. But in these provisions that I've read, there is no provision for six-month or nine-month reviews. It's a straight four years. From what I heard it was a straight four-year sentence but I don't recall the exact bill. I familiarized myself with the material somewhat and it called for four years straight sentence, which to me seems to be totally harsh and illogical.

V: When you talk about alternative ways of dealing with juveniles what would you do instead of incarceration?

G: I would—I lean toward community-based facilities or in some cases I can see that you need a certain type of incarcerating facility but I think that it's not the building that determines incarceration. In some cases you need a maximum, I would even say secure detention facility but that is only to get the individual into a place where you can deal with him, constructively. What I find happens now is that you have cold buildings, cold structures, and cold administrators. I think that the building alone is not what determines incarceration. So I feel as though you can have a secure detention facility, but if it's run by sensitive and understanding administrators, that an effective job of rehabilitation can be done.

V: Do you know any institution where that's going on now?

G: No I don't.

V: Have you heard from any of the kids you work with about any such place?

G: No. I've heard about Goshen and places like that, which I certainly wouldn't put in any utopian category.

V: Can you expand on that a little bit more? What have you heard about Goshen?

G: Well, I've not only heard, I've visited it, and It's seems—well, on the day that I visited Goshen was in respect to interviewing two clients for a program in Queens, and it seemed to me like half the clientele was on some type of drug. You go into the blocks you see people laying on floors drugged.

V: These are drugs administered by the authorities?

G: I would imagine so, I don't think they have a large-scale smuggling operation there, fourteen-year-old kids. In the middle of upstate New York. I don't think they could get this themselves. I assume that it was administrative. The administrators themselves, they don't talk to the kids on any kind of counselor-client level. How they talk is like people talk on the street. The older and physically bigger, they "wolf" the younger weaker specimens, and this is the way these counsellors spoke to these kids. And most of the counsellors were physically larger, they had belligerent voices, that type of thing. It was like a street environment, it was like another gang only instead of your leaders being El Macho on the street, it was Mr. Jones or whatever his name was inside there. So you weren't really taught any respect, you were again taught to fear what was more powerful than you that whole physical—

V: So might makes right in there?

G: Might makes right there, as it does in the street culture.

V: Before you said, and I think it was extremely on the money in terms of an observation, that you wouldn't call it a juvenile problem that it's an environmental problem expressed in juvenile behavior. Now give me an example of some of these environmental factors that bring about what we have been calling a juvenile problem.

G: Well, you look at broken homes for example. People—social workers you find want to go to homes and deal with kids without dealing with the home situation. Not realizing that maybe if the home wasn't a ghetto maybe the kids wouldn't have these acting-out problems that they have. You have people talking about proposals where they want to spend sixteen, twenty thousand dollars to incarcerate a kid for a year, but do they ever stop to realize that if they gave that twenty thousand to that family, that kid might not have those type of problems. You look at the whole street environment. How a child looks at his elders, the type of things that he sees them do, the type of role models that they set. The pimps, hustlers, drug addicts, dope fiends, you have the traditional educational environment, junior high school, high school, which is insensitive, in the large part, speaking from my point of view, to black children, the traditional educational environment is insensitive to their peculiar cultural needs. Really between those two forces—the home and the school—which is where they spend, let's say in school they may spend 33 percent of their life at home they may spend another 40-50 percent of their life. So 85 percent of their lives are spent in environments that they cannot cope with in some way. Where there are deficiencies that are beyond their control, because at the age of thirteen, sixteen, they are in no way responsible for those structures in which they are involved.

V: Who are the heroes in the community? What type of people are the heroes to the average kid who's just hanging out?

G: The average—the biggest hero I guess would be somebody who's one of the big numbers runners or something like that because he got money, and he never goes to jail, so he's a lasting type of hero because he's always around. You have some people that see a lot of so-called up stick-up kings that they admire, but you never know when they're going to be around. You have pimps, they're admired. Whiz kids, and so forth. Those are the heroes. In the black community you don't have too many professionals, so-called professionals that you can look up to.

V: Even if there are professionals, they're not very visible in your community?

G: No they're not very visible; where they usually choose to do business is outside of the community, because most of them don't want to identify with the neighborhood, so they are not around.

V: In your own situation, you seem to represent a contradiction to your own words. You came from a broken home right?

G: Yes.

V: Your father wasn't in the house, right?

G: No. Not after the age of ten or eleven.

V: And I know you grew up on one of the worst blocks in Corona.

G: That's true.

V: I know you got in plenty of trouble yourself as a juvenile.

G: Right.

V: But you're in the Master of Fine Arts program at Columbia. How do you explain that? What do you say when someone says to you, "Well, look here, Kiidh Gilyard made it so what's wrong with the rest of these suckers?"

G: I can't take all the credit for that actually. I've had some people that have helped me along. I think that my problem is not basically different from the problems of people out there today. The juveniles that we were just speaking on, I don't think it's a contradiction, just that I did get a break—

V: Are you attributing it to luck? Are you saying that there but for the grace of God you could be in the joint too?

G: That's true, but I'm not attributing it to that. What I'm attributing it to is some people that happened to take an interest in me. That I can call luck because if certain people had not taken an interest in me, what you just said could in fact be true because I'm not very much different, nor do I consider myself of having too much more potential than a lot of the kids I see today; it's just that, and there's other people who came through things such as I, but it's so small in comparison to what needs to be done, it just so happens that I ran into a few people—

V: When you say people there, you're not referring to community institutions—

G: No I'm referring to individuals, you know, who my meeting them was just a chance matter, it was just like one of those matches that occur in life. So basically I'm trying to avoid sounding heroic or existential because that would be a false representation of what you call my present success. On the other hand I realize that a lot of those people out there, they don't have anyone that come in touch with them to help them and you mentioned that when I was referring to help that I meant community institutions, where in tact there was no community institutions, so if it wasn't for my chance in life through a certain few individuals, I really can't see myself not being in jail somewhere, or maybe dead somewhere.

V: Well, let's be more specific. Are your friends in jail?

G: Most of them. Most people that I grew up with are in jail or dead. Or the few that's out are on drugs.

V: But you say that you don't exist as any kind of living refutation of that meat grinder in the community.

G: What I do think is that I exist as an example of what can be done with a child if he's taken at an early enough age and given some kind of proper guidance.

V: When you say early enough age, at what age would you begin to intervene in the lives of these young people on the street?

G: I would intervene with them as soon as they appeared on the street. As soon as they had chosen the street as a place where they wanted to spend a lot of time, because if you look in communities today you can find that at ten, eleven years old. Nine even. You find kids hanging out in the street at hours which even as fast as we grew up, you didn't see anybody nine years old too much hanging out; so now you see it today, so as soon as they showed up on the street exemplifying problems, things like that, I think is early enough to start intervening, but on the average, I would say that they come out at thirteen or fourteen, that type of age.

V: In working with kids, do you have more success working with kids who have been previously incarcerated or kids who have never been incarcerated?

G: I don't know. I've never really thought about it statistically. I think you can have success with both. But it seems to me that if you have one that has been incarcerated for a long period of time it seems that it's more difficult to work with then because there seems to be some type of—I don't want to call it brainwashing, but some type of attitude that gets set and rigid the more you send a person to jail so I think that a person who's not been in jail or a person who's had what I call light experience in jail is still flexible enough to work with.

V: Isn't it a fact that most of the more advanced forms of crime tend to be committed by juveniles who have been incarcerated? For example, if we see a kid involved in an armed robbery, aren't the chances pretty good that he's been in the institution before?

G: I would say so. I would say the chances would be something like four out of five. What you see then is juveniles being used, like I said earlier, it's another type of school.

V: Well, they call those schools training schools.

G: That's what they are. But they don't train them for what you think they do.

V: Is the public then getting value for its money out of these training schools?

G: The public is not getting any value out of them for what they're spending. It seems to me that if they wanted to invest money properly, they would do it by investing in better institutions that would cut the recidivism and graduism rate, graduating being a juvenile who goes on to become an adult felon, recidivists are felons who leave jail and come back, which I think the national rate of recidivism is approximately 70 percent. It's not hard to see where that's a great waste of taxpayers' money.

V: What about people at the community level? Are they cynical about this? Do they believe that the juvenile prisons are doing any good?

G: What you got to remember is that people at the community level don't have a clear understanding of the problem. All they see is the immediate threat. These kids hanging on my block, where they might break in my house, or that type of thing, so anything that can remove them from their visual sight is good. I would say that it would be a very rare example of a community resident who has been to visit one of these institutions outside or if one of their own family was there, so I don't think they have any idea of what's going on.

V: Even as a visitor, to visit a member of their own family, they don't see the inside.

G: They don't see the inside of the institution. So I think the community is being duped at large. They think it's helping the kids to get sent up to Goshen or whatever.

V: So the community actually believes that it might be beneficial to the child to go away?

G: Yes.

V: Do the conventional religious organizations believe this?

G: I find that to be strong amongst them also. They accept it. They seem to have a blind acceptance of this type of justice. They seem to say "Well if you're caught doing something, you must pay your dues or whatever to society" that whole type of concept. And "May the Lord bear with you while you're doing your time," that kind of thing. They're basically ignorant, I find, to the problem.

V: Do you think the people—you say ignorant, so when you say ignorant, you don't mean stupid—

G: No they're not stupid, just uneducated—and uninformed. I don't mean stupid.

V: Do you think there's any potential for educating the general public?

G: I believe that of course they can be educated. It would take a lot of things, they would have to be shown a lot of things. That's the way people learn the most is if they see things, like they say "seeing is believing" sometime. I've become skeptical about educating the public because it seems that as though the public is fooled so many times by so many simple things, that I think I would rather focus on getting into letting legislators and things like that see, maybe the change can come from them because they're in a more direct position to do something about the type of institution that exists in this state. I think that education of the public, I think you can do it but I'm not that optimistic about it that part of the solution even though I admit that it should be done. I don't know exactly how to go about it I don't want to say that I do.

V: That's interesting because one of the arguments that we've heard—let me say this first—we've been proposing a new service delivery system in juvenile justice. Basically it would be anchored by a maximum-security institution which would house for the whole state only fifty to seventy-five young men. The rest would be in a variety of community facilities, be it foster homes, group homes, halfway houses whatever you want to call them. The argument that I've heard from some people is that the community would never go for this because they are opposed to any kind of maximum-security prison. Now do you think that's accurate based on what you told me?

G: That the community is opposed to maximum security? I think that's completely false. The community is not opposed to that at all. As we have just spoken they tend to favor it. I just had a thought, while we were talking about education that's possible one way to do it is that if you could have a community-based facility at least, like I was saying before, you have to show people things. If you have a facility in their community that seems to be doing an effective job that gives it a good image, maybe some of the attitudes will change.

V: Do you think that there would be community resistance to such a facility?

G: I don't think so. Not if you're using it under the guise of corrections. I know that with the drug problem, during that era, you had a lot of drug programs being set up, that a lot of people resisted that because of the stigma of drugs. They said "junkies are going to be around." But I think that if this is a state-run type of institution that is dealing basically with corrections and juveniles, runaways, that type of thing, I don't think that there'll be too much resistance in the community. Whatever resistance it is, I think that it can be easily overcome, with a few months of decent performance.

V: In a community like yours, if you were going to put a community-based correctional facility for juveniles in that community, how would you go about getting people to accept this facility if you were to approach them in front?

G: Well when we say community-based, that has to be what we mean. We can't say community-based and then import workers in from all over the state. So when we say community-based we make it that and we make it responsive to community input, we stay open to community suggestions and ideas, we try to find community personnel, they should get first priority as far as employment is concerned. I'm not saying that they have to be from the community because we may not find enough qualified personnel in that locale, but I think they should be given the first chance if they are indeed qualified.

V: What about the population, what about the inmates themselves? Should they be from the community?

G: In the community that we speak of, there's certainly going to be enough inmates to fill the place so I don't see why they can't be from the community. And if you see that that makes the whole thing more familiar to the community, they know that their neighbor from across the street's son is there. And their neighbor's cousin works there. That type of thing, if you really make it community-based, I don't see why it can't work.

V: One of the things that has concerned us is this. We feel that juveniles have certain ethical and moral rights that are largely ignored because they can't be articulated constitutionally. For example, we believe that juveniles have the right to be safe, physically safe, even while they are doing time, and we feel that it's a fact that they're not safe right now. That kids do get taken off in the institution. Kids do stab each other and rape each other and suicide is committed. One of the methods that we want to use is to isolate a small percentage of highly dangerous juveniles in a closed facility. Now do you have any reaction to that? First of all, do you accept the premise that there are some juveniles that need to be isolated?

G: Yes, I accept that premise because even though going back to my basic approach that there's a lot of kids that are victimized by things that are beyond their control, you can't negate the fact that once victimized they are changed into other types of beings in some cases. The victimization is so great, plus a lot of people, some kids, we can't rule out that they have personality disorders also. In a certain number of cases, I'll accept that premise. I won't accept it on a large scale, and I hesitate to, because like most people, once you accept a premise, they try to flood you with cases to prove that this person fits into what you've just accepted. I think at best it's a small percentage of people, and you did mention small percentage so I accept that. There is a small group of people that do need to be isolated. You just mentioned the whole safety factor, we know about that whole horror story that goes on inside the institution. I would ask how—you said you're going to take a small group and isolate them. I would ask how, individual cells, or what? It seems to me like if you just took the worst and just threw them together, you would only intensify the violence. And I don't know what kind of housing situation you are talking about.

V: We're talking about people security not mechanical security. In other words, we believe, like take a homosexual rape—that is not going to go down if personnel are on the job. Those kind of things happen because you rely on mechanical security. Like you lock two boys in one cell. And you look the other way. Now two kids are going to go at each—

G: I've seen that—

V: Sure. But it doesn't have to be. I don't agree that that kind of activity has to take place inside every institution.

G: I don't think so also. From my experience in what we call remand shelter I've seen things happen that could not have happened had there been more correction officers around, or if there had more of a screening process about who has put into a cell block with who, that type of thing, so I think that it's a good idea to do that type of screening and pick out the people that need to be isolated and given more people security, like you say.

V: We call what we have going for us a juvenile justice system, right? In speaking to the thousands of kids that you've spoken to over the years is it their perception that the system is just or not?

G: Most of the juveniles that you find that can articulate I find overwhelmingly they can point out the injustices in the system.

V: Do most of them have a kind of stoic acceptance of the whole thing or what?

G: Yeah, they seem more or less to accept it as a whole, to me they seem to accept it but at the same time I think they're aware of some of the things that's wrong. It's hard for them to put it logically and articulate it but they can see different systems at work. That whole physical thing we were talking about before, how come this person gets certain privileges as opposed to that one, but this is the same type of thing they seem to accept on the street also.

V: So their ambition is not to change the system but to move up in it?

G: Right. That would be a good way to put it.

V: Is that because they perceive that changing the system is just an impossible task? I mean is that part of it or what?

G: At that age, probably so. When I was adolescent I thought that that would be my ambition, to be the king, not to try to change any system. I really didn't think that deeply. I guess if I did I would have felt some kind of hopefulness about it. I guess I just accepted it. You want to be king when you're that age, I feel.

V: How do you get to move up in the hierarchy of the street? What is it you have to do?

G: What you have to do to move up is establish a reputation. Not really establish, you have to take somebody else's reputation, that's the way you move up. You watch someone who is held in high regard and is supposed to have a reputation for being a "bad nigger" and what you have to do is try to dominate him, which nine times out of ten means a physical confrontation. If you turn out to be a winner, you assume his spot. It's something like what they do in orchestras, if you want to be the first flutist you have to challenge the first flutist, and if you can outplay him you get his chair.

V: But it's not a very permanent chair, is it? In the street?

G: No. Well, there's always somebody else learning how to play the flute. All the time.

V: When we're talking about changing the system, you seem to indicate that even if we were to have a more responsive, enlightened juvenile justice system, it wouldn't really be dealing very much with the problem.

G: It's a complex thing, but I feel as though with a different system you can reach children's heads and make them deal with it because for me to grow up the way I did, and I managed to escape a lot of things, the system wasn't changed at all, it's just that I was enlightened and made to accept certain realities that helped me to stray away from the dominant environment because the system is the same as when I was growing up. So I feel that it's not futile to change the juvenile justice system just because the total society at large—that's like a fatalistic concept to say "Because we can't do this, there's no use even trying to do this." I think that it's just the other way around because if we can effect a change of attitude in these juveniles they won't be tomorrow's adults.

V: We mentioned gang problems leading historically into addiction problems and then back into gang problems. We've had very little luck with the gangs it seems; in fact, some commentators have indicated that heroin was the solution to the gangs. Whether or not that's true isn't important, but you have had experience working in narcotics programs, and you've observed a lot of them. They were there to solve a specific problem of youth on the street and it would seem to me that it failed. Can you comment on this at all?

G: Yes. I would agree that they failed, especially, in fact, not even dealing with juveniles you see a phenomenon in the street now where people who were drug-free for as much as five, six, seven years are beginning to shoot drugs again, and I couldn't imagine that before. I thought they'd have someone who was seventeen who had kicked by the time he was twenty-four, I didn't see no way he could go back to drugs but I see it happening now. The reason I think a lot of programs do fail is because they don't really address themselves directly to the person's problem. They seem to think that the problem is merely drugs, that if they can keep a person detoxified for a certain length of time, then let him out into the street and tell him "Drug addicts are greasy, and they hate people, and they don't like themselves," if they do that enough the person will go out and be cured when in fact the person knew all that before he came in the place. Like you see people going to jail, they go to jail for nine months and they write you and they tell you they have kicked. Well, they really had no choice in most cases. But when they come home, as soon as they hit the environment they are shooting dope again. Or in programs where you have the whole rhetoric structured around "dope-dope" and nobody really deals with the fact that the drug problem is a larger psychological and social problem that's coming; and the programs that were set up that were funded by the state really couldn't avoid getting into this syndrome because they had catered to the dominant theories in effect. Those doctors who pioneered a lot of therapeutic communities and the methadone maintenance programs, the theories they offered—there was a theory called metabolic deficiency. They stated that if you begin using heroin, that a certain chemical change that was created in you that made you crave for that drug so that the only way to cure you of that was to deal with that chemical reaction in your body. These experiments are what led to the rise of the therapeutic communities and the methadone maintenance clinics in New York. What they're dealing with is something basically that has never been scientifically proven but it's been accepted because, I feel, it was economically expedient.

V: So in other words, what you're saying is that if community organization had a certain theory, a certain concept, and they wanted to fight, combat juvenile delinquency, they would be forced to buy into the dominant theories of how to fight juvenile delinquency in order to get funding?

G: That's right. Because that is what was getting funded. It seemed to me like you had to have a certain line in your proposal, a certain rhetoric that the office of the Drug Abuse Commission wanted to hear, and if you didn't conform, I guess you didn't get funded, and if you were funded, in order to remain funded you couldn't be too radical, which all that means is getting to the roots of things, you couldn't be that. And that's another reason programs fail because they have to rely on that funding and I think that if the funding wasn't so precarious and people in certain programs were made to think they could stretch out and do some innovative things and I think then some innovative things would be done. But as far as I look at it now, the drug programs, the maintenance, and so-called therapeutic communities have been largely a failure.

V: Do you think that the problems of the community narcotics programs would end up being the same as the problems of community antidelinquency programs? The same demand to follow existing theories, the same funding problems?

G: Yeah, I think that's the key. That you have to have a secure funding base so that these community-based facilities could indeed be made most responsive to the community around them and the community's problems. I think that if the funding is in jeopardy, if you have to rely on year to year funding, the programs will always be in jeopardy.

V: In conclusion, I'd like to ask you to speculate if you will about the future. We talked about the juvenile gang phenomenon running in cycles, interrupted at approximately half-decade periods by onslaughts of heroin. What do you think the future's going to be in terms of the juvenile crime picture in New York City?

G: Depends on the kind of outlook we take. We can look at it as if nothing is done. If nothing is done, we can see the cycle going on, with this heroin usage thing. In another few years we can look for another onslaught of juvenile gangs. We can look for this until the whole thing becomes sort of

self-consuming and there is practically no society. We can look at it if
something is going to be done, I think that certain institutions can be
instituted, man, that would help a lot. I can see programs that kids are taken
into that are responsive to them, that teach them certain skills, that educate
them in a way that they weren't in school, that don't teach them how to use
machines that went out of existence twenty years ago. They are learning
some real valuable things about how to survive in this world. I think if that
type of thing can be done we can look for a lot of progress. I think if that
type of thing is ignored we can look for nothing but more chaos.

**Interview between Andrew Vachss (V) and Lieutenant
Arthur Holsborg (H), on October 5, 1976**

Arthur M. Holsborg received the B.A. degree from Fordham University and was
a member of the Yonkers (New York) Police Department for over twenty-one
years. He retired in 1977 with the rank of Lieutenant, at which time he was
appointed director of the Westchester County Office of Criminal Justice
Planning, where he currently serves.

V: Lieutenant Holsborg, how long have you been associated with law enforcement work?

H: I've been a police officer for twenty-one and a half years.

V: During that period of time, which is approximately the last two decades,
have you perceived any change, have you perceived any change in the type,
quantity, and quality of juvenile crime?

H: Oh, yes. Very, very dramatic change. From the days of my early police
career, as a street officer, a radio car officer, it's gotten worse, it's gotten
much greater, and the problems seems to be with the police department and
its patrol activities, primarily with juvenile crime.

V: You would say that juvenile crime is the number one problem with the
police force?

H: Absolutely.

V: Let me ask you this. Is this a new thing or is this a return of a cycle? In the
fifties we had a big youth gang problem in New York, right?

H: Yes, that's correct.

V: It seemed to die out with the onset of heroin addiction . . .

H: Yes.

V: In the sixties.

H: Yes.

V: Now it seems to be returning.

H: It's returning with respect to the gang situation, seems to be reoccurring.
But in the fifties we did have a problem, but it was an isolated specific
problem. We were able to create specialists who would handle gang
problems. They got close to these gangs, and I believe they were very, very
instrumental in breaking up the problems these gangs were generating in and
around the city of New York. But that is only one small portion of the
problem today. You have the general problem of juvenile crime, which is
not related to the gang structure. These are individuals or small groups
ranging in age from seven or eight years on up. I've seen case histories of
juveniles brought in at eight, nine years of age, charged with burglary.

V: What happens in this case?

H: Generally nothing. They're brought in, if they're brought in—more often a child in that age category will be brought home—When and if they do wind up in family court, generally it's nothing more than that one and only one appearance in family court where the parent or parents or guardian are warned to straighten the kid out. It's considered a very small incident, a burglary committed by a juvenile.

V: Is that a change from perceptions of twenty years ago?

H: Very definitely. A drastic change. Burglary used to be considered a very serious crime, and if you recall, prior to the change in the penal law in the state of New York, the police officer could shoot a burglar if he failed to stop, say, in fleeing. That's how serious the crime was. Today it's so commonplace I think it's classified with the petty larceny shoplifter.

V: When we're talking about burglary, are we talking about actual house invasion?

H: Yes, of course. Also commercial establishments, at night. It's not uncommon to find a group of ten or twelve year olds breaking into a building at three o'clock in the morning.

V: Do these ten or twelve year olds, or eight or nine year olds generate their own leadership, or are they led by older boys?

H: Generally they're self-sufficient in their own age group. It's not too common a practice for them to be led by the older individual. It does happen. You do get this type of thing, but I think more often it's among themselves.

V: How about the propensity for violence, which is what most concerns us. Has this increased?

H: Yes. Extremely. In fact, the street crime problem with the juveniles, muggings, pocketbook snatches particularly, and most particularly against the aged. Whether it's coupled with the act for the purpose of getting the pocketbook and getting away before the individual can take notice of who is doing it or not I don't know, but almost always now, the attack is made from the rear, the individual is pushed to the ground usually, a hand goes behind the head and forces the face into the sidewalk, they remove the pocketbook and run before the person has a chance to recover even slightly, to see what happened, the perpetrator or perpetrators are gone.

V: We've always had the kind of juveniles that would throw gasoline on a sleeping drunk and set him on fire, or will torture a small kid, or will commit some wanton act of brutality. We've always had this type of kid.

H: Yes.

V: Not in very large numbers. Have you seen this particular type of incident increase?

H: Yes, very wantonly, and seemingly for no reason. Those isolated instances that we used to become aware of years ago such as you cited are now cropping up more often than not. I'm speaking of what I know of what's going on throughout the United States. I read a number of police periodicals, I travel to a number of seminars and conferences and throughout the country, I speak with a lot of people in the criminal justice sector, and I feel that it's not just happening here, it's happening all over.

V: The police are routinely accused of making crime statistics bend to their will. They are routinely accused of manipulating crime statistics. Do you think that's accurate? Only in respect to juveniles, that's what we're talking about.

H: I would say that it's almost nonexistent today. It did happen years ago. I don't believe there's a progressively minded police administrator anywhere who in doing something like this doesn't have in the back of his mind that whether it's for good or bad, initially, he'll be uncovered in the long run. There are too many watchdogs. So I believe the reporting of events is as honest as it can be.

V: So that we can take it as fact that juvenile crime is definitely on the increase?

H: I would offer that as a definite fact.

V: To what do you attribute this? Some people have said it's the restrictive Supreme Court rules, some people have said it's a lack of incarcerative alternatives for youths, some have called it a breakdown in the family structure, some are blaming the schools. Where, if anyplace, would you place the blame for this?

H: All of those. And probably more that you and I are both unaware of but I think in my personal opinion, the problem lies with the revolving justice that affects these juveniles. Particularly the incorrigibles, the ones with the highest recidivism rate, and unfortunately if the records are perused you'll find that they are the ones that get the most lenient application of justice. I think they're getting more and more brazen, their egos are being fed, there's nothing to restrain them. They very often will tell a cop, "Go ahead take me in, I'm only gonna go right back out on the street, there's nothing you can do to me," and this is a very prevalent attitude in these juveniles.

V: You're talking about children under sixteen?

H: These juveniles are under sixteen. Those that we cannot charge with a crime per se.

V: The new laws seem to indicate that a protracted period of incarceration is possible, now under our new legislation. Are you in favor of that?

H: Very definitely, if the application of the law is done properly and professionally. If it's a professional application of the justice that's been built into the law.

V: Let me go further than that. We're proposing a single maximum-security treatment unit. This will be secure. Minimum incarceration will probably range from a year to eighteen months. The problem would be who goes to such a place. How would you want those decisions, as a professional law enforcement officer to be made?

H: Well, it would have to be a professional making the decision, but all factors would have to be included. I think the juvenile probation system is good, but it has to be more regulated. There has to be less prerogative allowance. There have to be more determined facts as a guide to the probation department in their dealings with these incorrigibles or these hard-core juvenile criminals.

V: How can we go with a definition of that? Let me postulate a few types of behavior and you tell me whether or not this kind of individual would fit, okay? A kid who B&E's a gas station. Does he fit?

H: He could and he might not. It would again depend on the total factors involved.

V: I'm talking about—each of these things I'm going to posit to you would be a first contact with the law.

H: Right.

V: You would say, even such a crime, the kid must be a factor for the institution?

H: He could be, yes.

V: Okay. An arsonist.

H: Most, probably definitely.

V: A rapist.

H: Definitely.

V: A homicide.

H: Definitely.

V: So you'd say without equivocation then, homicides, rapes, armed robberies—

H: Yes. These are the violent people. No matter what age, these are the violent people capable of committing these horrors against society time and time again.

V: Now this is just the crime without any other factors. If we were to take all juveniles convicted of such felonies and incarcerate them, I'd assume you'd have in the four figures.

H: Probably.

V: And I also could say, probably accurately, that New York State's not prepared to do that.

H: Not to my knowledge. And this is one of the reasons why they're walking the streets today.

V: Do you think that routine incarceration, incarceration as we've known it for juveniles for the last twenty-five years, is productive of rehabilitated human beings?

H: Absolutely not.

V: Do you have any—I always pose this question to professionals I interview— can you name a single major heavyweight criminal this country has produced that did not do time as a juvenile?

H: No. I think in every case, as you say, a major heavyweight criminal, you'll track him back to ages of five, six, and seven when he first came into contact with the law.

V: Right, and what seems to be a pattern with such individuals is that they were incarcerated in the early years.

H: Very definitely.

V: So now we're on the horns of a dilemma, are we not? Can you accept as a hypothesis that we have to isolate certain children, but that isolating the large number that we do isolate is in fact detrimental?

H: I definitely would accept that as a very valid hypothesis.

V: We're talking now, I think you'll agree, about a predatory-type human being, who has to have other human beings to prey upon.

H: Right.

V: Isn't it a fact that such individuals find a natural pool of victims inside the juvenile prison?

H: Always. The natural thing.

V: For example, the crime of homosexual rape, have you ever heard of that occurring on the outside?

H: No. I've never heard of it in any of the reading I've gone through.

V: Yet it's common in the institutions.

H: Very common. It's a daily occurrence, I guess.

V: Suicides are common in the institution.

H: Very common.

V: And of course, violence is common.

H: Very common.

V: Isn't it a fact that we have to isolate the average delinquent from the heavy delinquent?

H: I think this is a very important key to rehabilitation of the average delinquent.

V: Do you agree that these populaces cannot be mixed?

H: Most definitely. The mixing of the population does nothing more than foster the continuance of the bad guy and make bad guys out of possibly good guys.

V: Isn't it a fact that in a juvenile institution, as in an adult institution, the bad guys are treated pretty well.

H: Oh yes. The institutional caretakers are definitely going to see to their operations because they assist in the regulation and operation of the institution.

V: So, in fact, what we call isolation is nothing more than mixing victim and victimizer.

H: Very definitely.

V: Would you agree that the first priority, if we're going to prioritize, would be to isolate the heavyweights?

H: I would say if we tried that as a first step, it would be the right way to go.

V: The problem being that at one time we routinely incarcerated juveniles. It didn't seem to work.

H: It has never worked.

V: There has been a wave of what we're calling de-institutionalization.

H: Yes.

V: Which is to incarcerate nobody.

H: Right.

V: That doesn't seem to work.

H: Not according to our crime statistics.

V: There seems to have to be some kind of happy medium. Now we get to the problem of having a small institution. Just for the genuine heavies. Again we have the problem of making the diagnosis. I would pose to you that we cannot put every child involved in a robbery in New York State in such an institution. Just on sheer numbers we can't.

H: Right, right.

V: Do you believe that we have to look at more than the rap sheet before we can make that decision?

H: Most definitely. The rap sheet will tell you something, but definitely not everything. You've got to talk to people that know this kid, and you've got to talk to this kid in depth, I mean a professional who knows what the kid is saying when he does reply. So many areas have to be covered and approached to establish a profile of this individual. The rap sheet is just one part of it.

V: Are the police becoming cynical about juveniles, are they getting the attitude that it doesn't do any good to arrest them?

H: I believe it's past tense already, Mr. Vachss. They have become cynical.

V: Has that affected their performance?

H: Very definitely. At the risk of sounding very cynical myself, sometimes it's better to kick the kid in the rear end and tell him to get the hell out of there than to bother going through the paperwork. Particularly when you know you've bagged him about a dozen times before and he's still doing what you bagged him for.

V: Are the police the first line of diagnosis? Can they see an escalating pattern of criminal behavior?

H: I think in most instances, if we're not the first, we're the second. I believe the schools would probably detect these things faster than the police.

V: But the schools just throw them out, right?

H: Well, they throw them out or they hide their dirty linen in the closet. They don't even want us to know what's going on behind those rosy walls.

V: I've been on the street with cops and they've pointed out a kid and said

"That kid will kill somebody." Some say that about half the kids they see, but some appear to be real diagnosticians. What does the cop do with this information? Is there anybody he can bring it to?

H: Not really. Quite often the cop who has that little extra push and possibly envisions a small degree of hope for a kid will speak to a probation officer in the juvenile probation department. I would say we're fortunate in Westchester, particularly in the Yonkers office, to have some good staff in the juvenile probation department, but there aren't enough of them, to do a really good job. And if the cop does go up as a personal effort for an individual, very often it's lost in the flow of papers that ensues.

V: Is it true that the police and the probation staff are especially handicapped by the fact that, in speaking to a kid the kid can always point to another kid, who's done some pretty heavy stuff, and has either walked off or has gone away for three months and is back home, as evidence of the fact that there's no point in them worrying about it?

H: Very definitely. This is done constantly to my knowledge. They're citing parallel situations where nothing's happened.

V: Is it true that the street cop is more physically afraid of kids than he is of adults?

H: Very definitely. Because of the fear that if he does use force in whatever the problem is, there's a stigma attached to dealing with the kid that way. Particularly if a firearm is used and if he's fully justified in the use. There's always that fear, whether it be real or imagined that somebody's going to call him down for it.

V: We have a cutoff age in New York of sixteen—what do you think a realistic cutoff age is?

H: In my personal knowledge of the types of crimes and the quantities of crimes being committed by juveniles, I'd move it back to fourteen.

V: Most states do have it at fourteen.

H: I would here too.

V: So you would put a fourteen-year-old boy in Attica?

H: No, I wouldn't put him in Attica. I would still keep him out of the mainstream; I would call him a criminal, but I would isolate him from the adult criminal and the adult I would say is over twenty-one. I think if we miss them initially at the juvenile level, which I hope a plan such as your plan is could correct, but if we do miss them at that level, we'd have this second opportunity to redirect them.

V: I show you this clipping, I'd like your comments on it. This clipping describes a twelve-year-old boy who allegedly murdered a nine-year-old boy with a knife, and may now face trial as an adult in the state of Florida. You'll notice that his stepfather, an ex-con, is requesting that the boy be tried as an adult, allegedly because of his claim that the juvenile justice system will do the kid no good. Do you have a comment on it? Look at the picture of that boy. Now imagine that boy in Raiford State Prison, what's going to be the result?

H: You may as well build a tombstone for him.

V: So what's the answer for a kid like this?

H: Nothing today. We don't have it today. There is nothing that we could do for this kid today, really.

V: So you would agree that there does have to be an institution designed to deal with such children?

H: If we ever hope to salvage any of these people from where they've gone or where they've arrived at, or to protect the rest of society and their peers, from the ravages of their contagion.

V: I have been told from many, many sources, and I agree with this, that a twelve-, thirteen-, fourteen-year-old boy who commits a serious crime, and is sent to an adult prison and lives through it, is almost guaranteed to be a vicious killer.

H: I'd agree with that. I think he quickly learns because of his age, and physiognomy, to either defend himself or become bait for these animal traps that they have in prison.

V: Those are in fact his alternatives, are they not? To kill or to be raped?

H: Absolutely. It's survival of the fittest.

V: And when you say fittest, one could be perfectly fit and still be a raving psychopath.

H: Of course.

V: In fact, it might be a help.

H: Very definitely.

V: Are you aware for example, that Charles Manson, the last time he was paroled, this was in the federal joint, begged not to leave?

H: Yes. I think he knew what he was capable of. I think the one spark of sensibility came through. This quite often is the case with the psychopathic mass murderer. They'll send notes to the authorities, asking to be caught, giving clues, they want to be caught, but they don't have it in their power to give themselves up. He knew that what was happening to him was eventually going to wind up being what did happen.

V: What does it say about our system, that Manson could know, and yet the whole system couldn't know?

H: It stinks, in plain English. There is no other word to describe it.

V: Let me ask you a very tough question. I've asked everyone else this. You can not answer it if you choose. If your own son, say at age fourteen and a half, was to commit a homicide, what would you want to happen to him?

H: Well, I'd like him well taken care of. I certainly wouldn't want him walking around on the streets for fear that he might commit more homicides or worse, not worse but bad crimes. And I would want to know in my own mind, that he was in an institution or a place where he could be helped, not just rotting behind four walls. And isolated from those that he could hurt again.

V: And protected from those that could hurt him?

H: And protected from those that could hurt him, of course that goes without saying.

V: Do you think that that's a fair thing for any parent to want for their kid?

H: Absolutely.

V: Do you think that parents in New York State get this?

H: Not at all. Not at all. They haven't ever in the juvenile justice system.

V: Well, a man of limited income, and by that I mean an income certainly such as yours, any income below six figures, really, can't really get anything else for his child can he?

H: No. No. Not really. The average individual as you say, could not even approach this kind of alternative.

V: Do you think it's a fair alternative that everyone should have?

H: Very definitely. It's a part of life, and good or bad, it's something that's required because we know what's happening without it.

V: Now you're into planning. You've seen plans come and go, some are implemented, some are not.

H: Yes.

V: Do you approve of the way in which grants are made, I am talking now strictly about by the federal government?

H: Not entirely. In some areas, yes, but in the major designed areas of federal funding in the criminal justice sector, their priority seems to be a little bit backward in my opinion.

V: The police have been routinely accused by other professions, or I should say other professionals in criminal justice, of making bad use of LEAA funds. Buying gas grenades, antitank weapons, two-way radios. Yonkers was unique in that you used a federal grant for civilianization. Has civilianization worked?

H: Very definitely.

V: Has it been institutionalized by the city of Yonkers?

H: A great deal of it has. Sixty percent of it has, and we have been fortunate in receiving third and final year funding recently.

V: What do you anticipate for next year?

H: I expect that 80 percent of the program will be institutionalized.

V: Is that unusual?

H: It's extremely unusual.

V: Haven't we then put our finger on the defect with most federal funds?

H: Very definitely.

V: Federal funds for juvenile justice work, appear at first analysis to have produced nothing but a lot of plans.

H: Right.

V: Would you go on record as strongly recommending that any federal funds for juvenile justice now go towards that which will be state institutionalized?

H: Yes. Yes. Definitely.

V: For example, the institution we're talking about constructing, I believe we could get federal funds to run it for two, three, or four years.

H: Right.

V: Don't we run the risk, unless we contractually agree in front, that the program will be—disappear after that time?

H: Absolutely. If there isn't a well-tied-up plan to institutionalize, why even bother? The most successful program can be buried by a poorly structured budget, or by the economy of the times. This is something that a program that we're embarking on and using public sector funds, we should determine in advance that if it is successful that it will be continued. Otherwise why even begin it?

V: We've had actuaries look at the costs of incarceration. They give us various figures, let's say it costs fifty-five hundred a year to keep a kid locked up, fifteen thousand a year. We don't have any problem with facts and figures. But what I wanted to ask you is this: We have a hypothesis that regardless of what we spent on a certain small percentage of kids, if we spent fifty, sixty, seventy thousand dollars a year, the community would still reap a return if the program worked.

H: Absolutely, whatever the investment, it's worth it. And I think society in general is getting smarter. We've long gone past the stage where government funds are being dealt out indiscriminately to anyone and all, and no production at all can be evaluated from any of these investments. People want to see productive investments and they want it for a good cause. And I think the best cause would be today, in the juvenile justice sector, because the majority of people I think if questioned today, particularly in the urban centers, would tell you that the main problem lies with youth.

V: That brings me to another point. One thing that we have always been accused of is not being sensitive to the community. I've been accused, for example, of recommending a maximum-security institution for a number of kids and I've been told that as a result, the community would be up in arms, they don't want their children locked up.

H: You're not going to be locking up "the children of the community," you're going to be locking up the isolated few who are the troublemakers, whom the community knows as the troublemakers. You'll have a long line of backers in getting them off the street, because they're corrupting not only their kids, but they're destroying their way of life. They're the ones that are making prisoners out of these elderly people. They're the ones that are ruining commercial areas, such as in Yonkers, the Getty Square area of Yonkers has been totally destroyed by these roving gangs of toughs, who harass merchants, commit street crimes; they're scaring people away. They've destroyed a commercial area in the city, which is the fourth largest city in the state of New York. In fact as part of the profile of these incorrigibles, if you would, you'll find that parental responsibility has been totally absent since the kid was born. So you're not going to get much of a hue and cry from the parent factor, and the community I think, to a person would be wholly in favor of such a program.

V: How about the reentry problem. Right now, there doesn't seem to be any reentry program at all for juveniles coming back from the institution.

H: No, they're just cut loose and brought back to the streets that they were arrested on.

V: Isn't it a fact that the police department doesn't even know when these kids are returned?

H: That's absolutely true. Unless they happen to spot the kid on the street, the cop who made the original bust.

V: And if he does, he doesn't know if the child escaped, or what—

H: That's right. There's practically no line of communication between the police agency and the institution that the juvenile had been incarcerated in.

V: In the institution we're talking about constructing, wouldn't we have to set up some kind of liaison with local police, so that—remember that at most, each police department would be sending two or three children to this institution—wouldn't they want to be kept informed—

H: Absolutely. I think it's a must. It's a whole part of the criminal justice system. It's so fragmented now, I don't believe any one factor in the criminal justice system knows what the other is doing, or planning or accomplishing. And this is, I think, a big problem in the effort that's being employed.

V: Do you think that if the police were given this information and given this input, if you will, they would be more cooperative in terms of helping the child reenter?

H: I think so.

V: It's a fact now that they're hostile, right?

H: Very definitely.

V: Do you think that we could change that if there was communication?

H: Very easily.

V: What kind of individual would we need as a promoter or salesman, if you will, to the police departments around the state. We need a guy, or a woman, it doesn't matter, to go around the state and sell individual police departments on increased cooperation/participation in this kind of diagnosis, and definite participation in reentry. What kind of person do you think it needs?

H: Well, first of all, in speaking to the pessimist that a cop is, they usually don't believe anything that officials, particularly tell them, because it never really materializes. I think it would have to be another cop. Someone that they could relate to immediately, whom they could feel believes in what he's selling them. And I think that would be the greatest part of the battle.

V: Do you think it could be sold though, if we had the right person?

H: I definitely do. I think what's happening here is these police officials are hungry for something, for some solution. The problem is there, it's not being abated, there's no solution on the horizon, at least anything that sounds good to these police officials. There has to be something that they can realistically consider as some hope in causing an abatement to the problem, and it is a big problem.

V: Aren't the police right in the middle? I mean aren't they the ones that really get blamed for the increase in juvenile crime?

H: Always. And I don't think there could be a greater mistake made in this blame being placed at the feet of the policeman. There are quite often incidents where the police can be blamed for perhaps perpetuating a condition that could have been more simply resolved and would have helped individual juveniles, but in the main I think the police are being used as whipping boys.

V: So the police would in fact look forward to some way off the spot that they're on?

H: Hungrily. I think there wouldn't be any sales problem here whatever. What are we offering them here? We're offering them a solution or hopefully a solution to a condition that we know exists, will exist, and will continue to exist unless something can be done to abate it.

V: One final question. Do you think we'd have a problem in terms of the police, with them being satisfied with what we're offering? In other words, we're offering a simple institution for the real superheavyweight kid. And that's it. We're not offering incarcerative possibilities for fifteen hundred to two thousand kids. We're not. We're saying we're going to take the worst you've got. The biggest problems. But we're not going to back to the way we were twenty-five years ago. We're not offering that. Do you think that would be a problem? For example, let's say there were seventy-five open beds in this institution. Do you think one jurisdiction would try to fill it all by itself?

H: No. Knowing that this was an opportunity to clear up the condition of the real pain-in-the-neck juvenile criminal, they'd jump at it. They wouldn't overreact to say this availability of beds, although this does present a problem in itself. The availability of institutionalized beds for other juvenile problems that come before the police, they would know where to draw the line, I don't think they would abuse a situation like this.

V: Then you're in effect, placing the police department in terms of maturity and intelligence above, say the district attorney's office?

H: Yes. I think there's more clear thinking down at the police level than there is at the DA's level in that respect.

V: Is the police department in your opinion any less political?

H: Very definitely, less political.

V: The thing that we would want to avoid is that say Yonkers has more clout than say Poughkeepsie, so Yonkers gets more beds—

H: I don't think there should be any fear of this ever happening. I really don't. I think proportionately every community will be afforded what it is hoped they will be able to utilize. There will be the occasional exception to the rule which can be accommodated, but more usually than not, as long as they do have an avenue for distributing these kids away from their jurisdiction they are going to appreciate it, whatever is offered to them.

V: So in the final analysis, you believe that this institution, and it's allied programs, could in fact be sold?

H: I feel it would be an easy selling job in my personal opinion.

**Interview between Andrew Vachss (V) and
Dr. Walter Stewart (S), on January 2, 1977.**

Walter A. Stewart, M.D. is a training analyst and teacher at the New York
Psychoanalytic Institute. He is the author of *Psychoanalysis: The First Ten
Years, 1888-1898*, and *The Secret of Dreams* (with Lucy Freeman). He is
currently working with the re-entry problems of individuals who previously
served long prison sentences for homicides.

V: Dr. Stewart, the whole concept of juvenile justice is built around the
premise that juveniles can be "rehabilitated." People are now tending to
write off not only the juvenile justice system but the very concept of
rehabilitation as nonexistent, as something that doesn't function, something
that doesn't work. Before we go further, can you give us your definition of
rehabilitation?

S: The idea would be to make the children more like us. Responsible to
society, capable of having tender feelings for other people with sufficient
self-restraint so that they wouldn't be violent, so that they could talk over
their problems rather than act on them. Exactly the opposite has been their
whole experience in life. They've never been in touch with anybody like
that.

V: Is rehabilitation a possibility for anyone regardless of their intellectual
capabilities?

S: Within fairly wide range, I would say that intellectual capability is not the
essential issue. The capacity to form a relationship with another person is
more significant. I think it's better of course if you're articulate and if
you're intelligent and can relate verbally as well, but even the sort of
nonverbal character with some damage due to a lowered IQ, if he can be
reached emotionally and personally, he still could be rehabilitated. The
terrible thing about rehabilitation is just what you said earlier, it's either
everybody's for it, and it's a wonderful thing, or then they get disillusioned
and it's no good, and it's never been done sufficiently, the issues, the criteria
for rehabilitation have never been sufficiently delineated.

V: Well, speaking of those criteria, could you give me an operant percentage as
to the number of individuals, or the percentage of individuals that might be
open to the very prospect of rehabilitation? In other words, if we have a
hundred kids that are getting into some serious trouble, can all of them be
rehabilitated?

S: That's for sure not. And the percentage I would think is smaller than
anybody really wants to admit. But you'd have to find somebody that is
still flexible, who can still form a relationship, who can still after all, change

the major aspects of his character, the nature of the ideals that he strives for. We think that if you read a book or if you write something, or if you restrain yourself, or if you have tender feelings for somebody else, or are glad to do favors for other people without the expectation of compensation, you don't believe in violence. Now exactly the reverse is true with so many of the juvenile delinquents. They have been trained to believe violence is the only manly way to do anything. And now you're going to change this around: instead of their admiring Al Capone, or James Cagney, they're supposed now to admire a college professor? That's crazy. And to bring that about must be one of the hardest things you can do. Now that far you wouldn't literally have to do. If you could get them into the general stream of social responsibility, they don't have to become students, or professors, but they would have to not admire violence and they would have to have something else to admire. You've got to substitute. You can't just take away the violence, because that's the ego ideal that they've got. You've got to substitute something else.

V: Let's talk now strictly about hard-core delinquents. Children who have been involved in serious, repetitive acts of violence. They are the ones on whom we would want to focus most of our rehabilitative thrust. Are they as good candidates as other children?

S: Harder, I would think. You've got an interesting problem. It's hard to describe it. In a given case you would have to measure something about the capacity to learn, the willingness to change, and you take a leader in one of the groups. Is that a better person to try to rehabilitate or would a follower be better? It's very hard to say. You know you can't really say ahead of time, which would be better.

V: But that gets outside the analytic area and more into the sociological area. We found for example that if you can defuse the sociopathic core the gang tends to fragment and just defuse itself. But I don't know if that's a crime control measure or a rehabilitative measure.

S: Crime control I would think, not rehabilitative. The only essential thing in rehabilitation is going to be an identification that the youngster's going to make with somebody that he admires, who follows and pursues certain goals. Like Pirate in your interview, obviously is a very tough customer and he's admired because he's meaner than most. Now you're going to try and find somebody that is going to be more attractive to the young fellow than a tough hard-core criminal.

V: Is it possible to be a tough hard-core rehabilitative agent?

S: Yes. But they're very few and far between. Think what that means. You've got to have had some street experience. You've got to have been able to surmount it, and you've got to change. Those typically are the ones that do most of the good work. They've been on the streets, they know something about it. Just like alcoholics are probably, in Alcoholics Anonymous, the best way to treat alcoholism. So I think the simple-minded liberal who doesn't really know what the hell he's talking about is the worst because he is a laughing stock with these people.

V: In what physical setting would such treatment be optimized? Could you see such people on an outpatient basis? Would it be better in an institution?

S: I would think in an institution. It requires more than an hour a day. It really requires a relationship over a sustained period of time. But you've got a hard problem, because the minute that they're in an institution against their will and you're the administration, you're the enemy.

V: It's a fact that the children about whom we're speaking are going to end up institutionalized one way or the other?

S: Sure.

V: And an institution would at least have some kind of environmental control that you'd lack on an outpatient kind of basis.

S: No question about that. But I think even more important than that is that you could possibly build up a human relationship of some trust. That's absolutely essential.

V: You read the interview with Pirate that I gave you. Can you tell something about him from the interview?

S: A very successful young man.

V: He is successful, I agree with that.

S: And he's learned—apparently there was a period of time when he really decided that he would hurt instead of be hurt. I think it was ten or eleven, that's probably rather characteristic. They're more at home at that time, then they begin truanting some, and at some point they figure they'd better be aggressive rather than the victim. That was one thing. How he used the term "hurt" was interesting. And it meant really the freedom. Because you spoke one time in the interview about justice, and I would say not so much "justice" as the rules controlling aggression. And there are rather clear rules, when he talked about hurting you. He talked about if he saw you and you waved to him, fine, he might not wave back. He had no reason to hurt you. But you give him any trouble he'll hurt you. And you asked about suppose someone raped your wife. And he said in effect as I understood it, you have to come down there, you have to talk to the gang, and you have to say this is the fella that did it and they have to give you permission to kill the fellow. Otherwise you kill him without their permission then they'll kill you.

V: That's his fantasy of what would happen. But even as speaking he knew damn well that that's not the reality. That was his fantasy of an all-powerful . . .

S: Sure. Some braggadocio quality to it. But it's an interesting fantasy and it's important because it becomes part of the ego ideal—the way the world *should* work. And you have to study the way their world works and they think it *should* work just as you would have to study the way we think it works. And all their training is the opposite of ours. But it has something in common with ours because the control of aggression is a much more rigid . . .

V: Well it's more chanelling than control, isn't it?

S: Yes. Except, remember if the President and Vice President [of the gang] vote differently from the other four, then they have to reconsider. So there is some respect for senior people, there is an agreement about mutuality. You're not allowed to be an individual.

V: But it's a veneer respect because Pirate was quite clear in saying that his ambitions, his personal ambitions, included attainment of that particular office for himself.

S: Right. And the respect that goes with it.

V: But doesn't vote in these elections to obtain this office.

S: No. Well, I don't know how the six get there. Do they fight their way in?

V: Oh yes.

S: But out of some admiration for the other people you don't just kill everybody around you. And get to the top. You have to earn their respect. And there are initiation rites. It's a band of brothers, and very strict unwritten rules govern it.

V: So as you said before, then with that allegiance, as skewed as it might be, we don't have the traditional psychopath here.

S: That's right. Because the psychopath is a person who has no allegiances. No loyalties. No band. Superficial emotional life, looks good on the surface. Never any deep contact. No obligation to anybody else. Not even awareness of the consequences of his own behavior. Just apparently is oblivious to the fact that some rules might apply to him. He thinks that they don't. And so you're a friend of his, and if you have money out on your desk, he takes it. It wouldn't occur to him not to. Whereas this man, if he took it you would have to be the enemy. He wouldn't take it from a friend.

V: Of course he's capable of creating enemies whenever it suits him.

S: Like anybody, I think. I wouldn't swallow what he says whole. I see his statements as an ideal, that he's working toward some understanding of human relations, just as you and I are. But, and you're right, it's very skewed, but he's not crazy. He's an ambitious person who's profited from experiences of life and has adapted himself to them.

V: Where would you put his IQ on a scale?

S: One hundred and twenty.

V: It's considerably better than normal, isn't it?

S: Yes. Maybe even 130.

V: Is he rehabilitatable? I'm asking you to make a judgment based on an interview, but . . .

S: Sure. And just an opinion on it wouldn't be a very serious opinion. You can't tell. You see that's the whole point of it. He's intelligent enough, he's ambitious enough, he's leader enough. I wouldn't say he's cruelly warped. He's not a sadist. He's not getting his kicks out of that. He likes the sight of blood he says, he likes the fact that he's an excellent man with a switchblade. But those are all skills. You like being a lawyer, I like being a doctor, he likes being a man with a switchblade. If you could make contact with him and show him that there is another way to live that's more admirable, but you've got to be his ideal at some point.

V: That's the problem, because you say you like being a doctor. If the coin came up the other way, you'd be just as happy being a farmer wouldn't you?

S: Right.

V: And I know for a fact that there's other things I would be happy doing. Pirate doesn't have anything else that he would be happy doing that can be conceptualized right now. So it would be necessary to make that real to him, not to just speak of it.

S: Absolutely, and real to him and then not laughable. You see, because it would be as hard to change me into a switchblade thug aged sixteen, as it would be to change him into somebody who's going to become a doctor. I just wouldn't have been able to do it anymore, I couldn't have learned the street life. And people have finished their growth in many ways, particularly in the structures of their conscience, of their ego ideals of their ambitions in life, what they think is admirable. Those don't change too quickly.

V: Who should call the shots, doctor, in a therapeutic institution that is designed first of all to securely contain certain violent juveniles, and then perhaps even as a secondary requirement, rehabilitate? Who should call the shots? Should it be an analyst, should it be some kind of program director, should it be the floor staff, who should call the shots?

  Suppose somebody says that the kid made certain mistakes, he should be in solitary confinement. You say that solitary confinement is therapeutically contraindicated for this kid. Who should decide? How should those decisions be made?

S: Be nice if it could be a group decision.

V: Be nice. But you know practice has proven that . . .

S: Right, not very likely . . .

V: We have our own professional aggression . . .

S: Although there again you meet the same point. I'm sure you won't succeed unless there is a band of brothers that runs the institution, then you get something working back and forth between them. If the people that run this thing are all rivalrous, and angry and uncooperative and backbiting, they won't hit each other, but it will be the same thing, and the children will pick that up in no time at all. There will be nothing to admire.

V: The extent to which the staff isn't unified will be readily communicated to the population.

S: Right. Right. Now to answer your question, I really don't know what their answer would be. I haven't had that much experience. I would think the person who was in charge of the overall business, the top person there. That everybody works under him.

V: But who is that top person? Is he a doctor?

S: No. An administrator-criminologist. The one closest to the street experience. My own feeling, were I in a group like that, I would much prefer to have a voice in it, in the decision, but only my opinion, and if people didn't like my opinion, I'd rather drop it or I'd go somewhere else. But I wouldn't want to have the responsibility alone for that. My specialty is understanding the unconscious, not necessarily how to take care of these violent people.

V: But you have a specific unique skill that in our multidisciplinary approach, to use a term I'm not crazy about, could be heightened, could function better.

S: Yes. Presumably I'd learn something if I were working in that setting.

V: Well, in a proper setting, wouldn't all the staff's ability be heightened?

S: Yes. Yes. Should be.

V: And that's a difficult coordination job is it not?

S: Yes.

V: In New York there's been a special unit allegedly designed to take care of children like Pirate, that has not been successful. It's supposedly been a working relationship between the Department of Mental Health, and the Division for Youth (Corrections). Instead of any kind of intermeshing between them, there's been conflict. That's why I posed the question "Who calls the shots?" It seems to me that these decisions have to be made before the institution is opened.

S: Yes. But I think getting good people must be an extremely important point. Because most of the people working in rehabilitation have had very little experience. Most of them are just police officials with the notion that if the child doesn't obey, they'll beat the shit out of him. And that isn't rehabilitation by any manner or means. Nor is "Look, I trust you, I love you, so be good for me because I love you."

V: Well, describe the consequence of those two approaches on our subject here, Pirate. What is a Pirate's response if he is subjected to continual physical abuse?

S: He's used to that. That's no problem. It's just that he's in the unfortunate position that he's been hurt instead of being able to hurt. When he gets out from that, then he'll hurt back.

V: That's right. Pirate can live with it. And just wait for his time to come.

S: Right.

V: But in fact Pirate has not even progressed to the point where he wants to seek physical revenge on those that hurt him. It's any member of that group, which is the rest of the world.

S: A stranger you see. There again I love to pick up what is the sort of philosophical-sociological dynamic view of his comments, even allowing for the grandiosity. You're quite right. He believes that there are bands of brothers, there are rules governing aggression on the inside, there are rules governing aggression on the outside. You are going to hurt some of the time, you try not to be hurt some of the time, if you're hurt, there's a way you can try to get your revenge, but you can't do too much independently, because there are laws governing these things.

V: Now what about the opposite. What if Pirate is confronted with people who say "We love you, there's no such thing as a bad boy . . ."

S: First, he knows that they're full of shit. Which he also says in this, "Anybody comes up to me and says look I trust you, I love you, I respect you," and right away he figures what do they want. Not bad. And why should they love him? He's not that lovable. He's not in the love market. The attitude towards women is extremely interesting. The rape. Then the fact that you said something about, "suppose there's a fight over that, that's stupid." You repeated it and he said, "that's stupid, men don't fight over women. That could make trouble." Now as they get older, then something about laying their lady, which I gather means their girl—

V: No it means laying *up* with their lady, which means not just sex but spending full time in a male-female relationship becomes important. The gang becomes less important.

S: Which is interesting in itself. Also there's their less criminal activity, or does the criminal activity itself change?

V: It's less, and that which does survive is more sophisticated.

S: One would guess that this has an adolescent quality of the boys banding up together, the girls being not so important.

V: Pirate sees that for himself; he knows that it's a trap that he personally can avoid, that he has the skill to avoid.

S: Laying up with a lady and getting out of the gang? That would be interesting to see. And it may well be that he idealizes it.

V: Well the full-race nuts that I know that run gangs in the city are not sixteen, and they are not eighteen. They're in their twenties, some of them are in their thirties, and they have avoided what Pirate sees as a trap and the focus is still entirely in the street with the younger kids.

S: Now the interesting thing, why have they so little regard for women? Ordering them to get the food, remember, and the rape. And the thing is, anything smacking of femininity, of tenderness and of love is out. That's a weakness.

V: You see that most exclusively in kids that have been institutionalized because without women a kid that loses a fight is suspected of femininity. The constant homosexual harassment at best, and rape at worst that goes on in these places, tends to draw the roles from the exclusively male population. So you see what you observed in Pirate much more heavily.

S: He refers to it. He said "they will think something about me which I know isn't true," obviously referring to whether he can be screwed, run around, beaten up, treated like a woman.

V: Yes. That's exactly the way he sees it. Let me just ask you to take a guess. Now you've never met Pirate. How big would you say he is physically?

S: Medium height. Not too big. Probably not as heavy as I am.

V: That's right.

S: One forty, one forty-five.

V: Almost right on the nose. He's not an imposing physical specimen at all. What would you think about his appearance? How would you think he'd look? I don't mean his features, but how he keeps himself.

S: I don't know, but I'd just hazard a guess, sort of a natty way.

V: That's true also. He's immaculate. Not in the sense that he wears very fancy clothes. He wore blue jeans. They were starched. They had a crease in them. Extremely clean.

S: A marine sergeant.

V: Right. Also in the institutions, the way you distinguish yourself from the others, is how good your institutional clothes look. Because you don't have the clothing options.

S: It's pathetic.

V: It is pathetic. But unfortunately it's also dangerous. Now another thing that I'm curious to have your insight into. While I was talking to Pirate, and I spoke to him for a few hours, I got the impression that at some point I was getting along with him. I don't mean that we became buddies or anything like that, but we were communicating very well. I felt very unthreatened by this kid. There were other people in the room who did feel threatened by him. Can you explain how that works, how that happens?

S: Yes. You've got to be firm enough and clear enough and with no horseshit, because hypocrisy, fear, stupidity, (like tenderness) are all marks against you. And you came across as somebody who's had some experience in the world, you were also vouched for by someone else, right?

V: Right.

S: That helped. But the way you talked, except for a couple of occasions, one time you said "incarcerated," you remember and changed it right away, and he might have noticed . . .

V: I wanted to watch his face when I said it. There was no reaction then I changed it.

S: Another was "justice" where I think it was not really so much justice that was sought there but the control of aggression.

V: I used justice because it is a very very common term that you hear. It's a euphemism for revenge.

S: Right.

V: Very often when I'm talking to someone from a specific small subculture I use words to see if they respond to the words. If they don't, I would be sufficiently flexible. The problem with Pirate is that he really tries hard not to respond. But towards the end of the interview he was doing so.

S: Yes, I think so and also that he obviously trusted you and liked you enough and he wanted to show off in front of you.

V: He did want to show off.

S: And that made him more grandiose towards the end.

V: As a matter of fact, he had the knife with him. Whenever he was done he opened the knife like he was going through a whole routine with the knife. And when I ignored him he just put the knife away. I don't really know if that was . . .

S: Well, I think it was to show off. The way somebody who knows algebra comes home and says "Look daddy, $X_2 + Y_2$." He wanted to get your good approval. And that would be the road to it, you see, and the more you tell me that sort of contact he made with you the more he might be capable of rehabilitation. But you'd have to start by saying "You handle that blade very well." You'd have to admire him.

V: I wonder. See, that sometimes is very smart. And then exactly what you wonder is whether he was deliberately mishandling the knife, so that I'd say "you handle the blade very well," and then he'd say "No I don't, chump." On the other hand, though, to be deliberately provocative and say you handled it badly, if that's the best he can do, I've insulted him needlessly. It's a very difficult decision to make on the basis of one contact.

S: You wouldn't have to have any judgment on it. The thing to do would be to say, "show me what you've learned with the knife." That sort of thing. "How do you use a switchblade?"

V: The reason I wanted to avoid that, and there's a point there, this kid was nervous, and he was really leery of being challenged at all, and afraid, and he might have taken that as a direct insult. You know, I'm bigger than he is, maybe I thought that in spite of the knife he couldn't hurt me. You see that a lot in juvenile institutions, "you think you're a tough guy, you want to box with me?" kind of thing. It doesn't communicate very well.

S: I was thinking more that he would show you something. You have to let him have some virtue, and the most that the rehabilitation says is that "we're going to do you good, we're going to change you," and nobody likes that.

V: I told him that the reason that I wanted this interview was that he could give me some valuable insight as to how to do something about the juvenile justice system. Which I don't like. And he saw this as kind of a revenge trip, and he seemed to go along with it—

S: That would be the way.

V: He didn't have a bad time with it. After the interview was over, he told me that in so many words that he was impressed with the fact that I didn't press him for details about the sexual episodes. That he talked to what he called a social worker, and I have no idea who that could be, who had been obviously vicariously interested in the whole process. And he got very turned off, very queasy about the whole thing.

S: Even if the social worker wasn't that turned on by it, it still would turn Pirate off and he would be suspicious because men don't talk like that, or sex isn't that important, or you don't talk—you talk dirty, but you don't talk sexually.

V: Right, although you'll notice his language was free from profanity by and large, and it would not have been so free from profanity on the street. He did make some kind of adaptation, which does lead me to believe that he's somewhat more rehabilitatable.

S: That wouldn't be a good indicator. That could be clever, that could be sly, that could be flexible. What you're looking for is somebody that can begin to admire you. And not because you're the leader of the gang. To come back to your earlier questions about who should make the decisions, I think I could define it more in a functional sense. Because it wouldn't be a bad system where you had a sort of big brother arrangement. You've got to have somebody there who can talk their language, and who is admirable, and who has a different set of ideals, that's the only way to reach them. And so somebody like that in relationship to him would be the thing. The doctor could be in the background. Now if it turned out the doctor was admired by somebody, fine, you'd be using all the people in your institution to try to reach him.

V: Alright. So they wouldn't have a hierarchial kind of importance. They'd have individual kind of importance, as to each individual resident of the institution.

S: Right. Some people are going to be marked because they're the policers, and they are not going to be close to these boys at all. The doctors might not be because either they're not around that much or they're not that experienced. So you try to find somebody then that can work directly with the boy with some advice from these other people.

V: What do you think about the idea of defusing the essentially all-male character of a juvenile institution by the more or less extensive use of female staff?

S: I don't know. I should think it could be quite a source of turmoil, and it's a little bit mechanical. I'm all for women being around, I think they make a difference to the boys, it depends on what age, what experiences they've had, what sort of people they are, what sort of functions they serve, I think if you could get away with it it would be dandy. I think there could be a lot of problems in it.

V: My position has always been that we have to take more risks than we'd like to with kids like this, because the holding action, the warehousing . . .

S: Is nothing. But the change is going to be not so much. Of course if they admire a woman, that's fine, and that's an interesting thing here that the only people he really had respect for were his mother and father. Very different from either schizophrenics, manic depressives, psychopaths. There again was an order here, the mother kicked him out and he must have disappointed the mother, he has some respect for her.

V: He's still disappointed in her too. He still can't understand why, he just wanted to be himself, and the rules were that he wouldn't hurt her—

S: And this is a sort of generation gap, the equivalent of the adolescent quarrelling with the parents.

V: Yes, his mother is my age.

S: Right. And he says "look, she doesn't even know what's going on in the streets."

V: Do you think that's accurate?

S: Yes, I think she doesn't know as much as he does. I don't know what her background would be but I would guess that she wants him to work and to be responsible. And in that setting, this is the ways those boys are going to turn out. Most of them.

V: What are society's options with a young man like Pirate?

S: I should think you could always kill him, otherwise you incarcerate him or you rehabilitate him.

V: That's it?

S: That's it.

V: There's no medication that would stabilize this kid on the street, right?

S: No. That's a nice point. You see this is not a mental illness. This is a way of life, of growing up.

V: His entire milieu is functioned along a certain kind of line and has been sufficiently rewarding for him to continue it.

S: And determine it. You see, Freud said that our dispositions are inhibitions in development. His whole disposition has been brought about by the experiences that he's been through, and the ego ideals he's seen, and the method of adaptation when he stopped being hurt and began to hurt people, then he was a man for the first time. He said "Fuck it, I'm not going to put up with that." So this isn't a mental illness, this is a way of raising people. You take if I may, a tribe whose adults cuddle their children, mother them, and the minute they're hungry they feed them. Their children turn out to be sweet, adaptable, loving, affectionate children. Whereas if they beat the children, never feed them, and do a long list of things they shouldn't do, the children end up as headhunters and cannibals, and they kill each other. It's a predictable thing. You can take a child born in that setting, adapt him to a good community, and he'll come out fine.

V: That's sort of the back door, though, that's diagnostic. In other words, now we have some insight, in a very simplistic way, into why Pirate is what he is. But we have no ability to give him a family.

S: No. Now the rehabilitation is the question. It's a variation on that theme. It would be nice if there were a family, and a community, and it would be a whole different thing. But you've got to do something like that or you're never going to succeed. You see, what does rehabilitation mean? Nobody defines it. It means a change in their ideals, their conscience, their purpose in life, what they believe is admirable. That's a big thing to change.

V: Is the word a misnomer in and of itself? Doesn't it imply kind of a return to a former state?

S: Yes. I would think it carries the quality that they were habilitated and now they have got to be returned. It has the quality of making them have to admit that the're bad. So that the first thing is the disowning of the self. They're not going to do that. It's been hard enough to achieve that integrated picture in that setting and they're not going to turn around and say "Yes, I realize now that everything I've ever learned and done was bad."

V: Is there a better term? Is there a more functional term? A more acceptable term?

S: Whatever term you use is going to be misused pretty soon so it doesn't matter. What term were you thinking of?

V: Well, habilitation is one. Adaptation.

S: Adapted they are.

V: Yes, adapted to a life style and a milieu that's so socially unacceptable that the larger society countenances violence against it.

S: Right. Right. And for good reason. And they would mug us, and we don't want to be mugged so we hire people with guns to shoot them.

V: Actually the worst part is they wouldn't mug us. Pirate was very, very clear. He prefers old ladies. Younger children. Very, very good target selection. He's not running amok. He's a fairly cold-blooded kid. So I think that he's more dangerous than some lunatic that's going to run out here in the street and stab anybody he sees.

S: Right.

V: I don't see Pirate assaulting a cop. Although he would certainly do it to resist arrest. But he's not a political person at all. His politics are very simple—us and them.

S: Right.

V: And you're saying that what differentiates him from a psychopath is that it's "us" not "me."

S: *Group Psychology and the Analysis of the Ego*, by Freud would be a good book to read. How a group is formed. Because you said if the head is cut off then the whole thing disperses. Which is quite true. There has to be somebody you admire when you come into the group, and you are willing to do things to become like him, to improve yourself. That's education. You could say that at Harvard too, right? You come into Harvard. You want to do things like the professor.

V: Isn't some of the education that we'd have to do as habilitative agents in effect debunking the mythology that this child has built up around himself.

S: Yes. I think so. But there, very delicately, and terribly important, because what you're showing them is that this is defensive, and his grandiosity is obvious. And you're trying to get him to admit that he's frightened. Well, that's what his whole life has been to avoid.

V: But it's okay to be frightened, you see, it's more than getting him to admit that he's frightened, but that it's okay to be frightened, that everybody's frightened, and that you can't be brave unless you're scared in the first place. I'll give you a good illustration. There was a street gang in Chicago called the Conservative Vice Lords. Conservative, by the way, referred to their way of dress, not their politics, and the Vice Lords professed this incredible allegiance to members who had gone to prison. Remember Pirate said they'd wait for him. Actually their allegiance was highly symbolic but not very functional. For example, every time they'd drink wine, before they'd ever drink, they'd pour the initials of the group—like Vice Lords Nation, or Vice Lords, or Conservative Vice Lords—they'd pour it out in the street with the wine. This was some kind of symbolic tribute to members that were dead or in jail. It didn't get anybody out of jail and it didn't bring anybody back from the dead.

S: Right. Not meant to. Its meant to allay the rivalry. It's a symbolic way of trying to control the aggression from the in-group. There has to be a leader, there have to be rituals, there have to be rules about controlling aggression, just like the incest taboo, there has to be some kind of taboo about aggression on the inside, otherwise you've got no group. Then the aggression has to be turned out. The nazis know it, the fascists know it, the communists know it. You get an enemy, and you get a leader that you admire and you aspire to be like him, then you're functional. And that mostly controls the homosexuality, which is one of the frightening things, by making ideals instead of object relations and by the rituals of the happy few.

V: Do you think that these kids are worth the investment? Let's say I told you it would cost us $125,000 per child per year, per Pirate per year. Are they worth that investment?

S: I don't see that there are many options. It would cost more than that to incarcerate them forever. I don't know how to figure it out in financial terms. I think this is hard to do at this age. It's almost impossible. The better way would be to get them earlier.

V: The way the juvenile justice system is constituted now we can't get them earlier. In fact, when you see a Pirate, he's been created by that system that intervened earlier, the intervention being a form of institutionalization. So what people have tended to come up with in the past five or ten years is "No more institutions, institutions are bad, they are criminogenic."

S: Most of them I imagine are.

V: Right. And what we're saying the Pirates are the precipitate. When you institutionalize them, you have no choice any more with him. He can't function out here anymore, in a way that we can accept, that we can live with.

S: I think the answer to your questions is if you could develop criteria to select the people that you have a real chance at being successful with, it would be worthwhile. They're saveable, it's a life involved, it's only money that's being spent, that the terrible thing is to spend all the money, not choose the right people, do a lousy job. Which is the history, I presume . . .

V: It *is* the history of the juvenile justice system for sure. Let me ask you these series of questions in summation. We're going to put an institution together. We're going to attempt to treat, to habilitate young men like Pirate. Does the population mix of this institution have to be very, very narrow in order for it to succeed?

S: Population mix in what sense?

V: Could we put an arsonist in there with Pirate? Could we put a child molester in? Could we put a kid that hears voices in?

S: No. That's part of what I meant by criteria. If you're hearing voices, you're schizophrenic, that's not a rehabilitation problem to begin with. That's much closer to a medical problem. And this is really a teaching problem. And therefore you want teachable people.

V: What about putting Pirate in an institution for car thieves? And runaways and truants?

S: Not so good, it depends, here again we're taking too much to the behavioral level. A car thief maybe so. Maybe he's beginning on the Pirate business and if you really felt you could work with Pirate and he wouldn't do damage to the car thief, and teach him more ways (which part of your institution would have to see didn't happen), then it wouldn't be a bad mix. And of course the more you've got people who are leaders that you can put in the institution and have on your side, then they're doing your work for you. There's only one route, through human relations.

V: And perhaps the biggest danger is not that we fail to see this, but that we've invested all kinds of buffoons with the mantle of knowledge in this area.

S: Right. I'm sure that's extremely important in two ways. That the people who go into this work generally are not particularly the talented ones, plus also they've got some notions that they're important, because they're doctors or lawyers or indian chiefs. If they don't *work* with the people they should go home.

Interview between Andrew Vachss (V) and Judge
Shirley Wohl Kram (K), on January 26, 1977

Judge Shirley Wohl Kram, a graduate of the College of the City of New York and Brooklyn Law School, began her professional career as a staff attorney with the Legal Aid Society of New York City in the Civil Division. Later, she became assistant attorney-in-charge of the Society's Harlem Office and then attorney-in-charge of the Narcotics and Mental Health Division where she instituted the patient representation program in Bellevue Hospital certification hearings.

Judge Kram was a family court judge from 1971 to 1978, the court which then had exclusive jurisdiction over juvenile delinquency proceedings in New York. She currently sits as a judge of the civil court.

Judge Kram has published numerous articles on juvenile delinquency and matrimonial law and is currently preparing a book on the law of custody and visitation in New York State.

V: Do you anticipate that there is going to be a designated felony part in the New York Family Court?

K: I think there will be an attempt to comply with it in substance in that it will probably be incorporated with a regular trial part as they've had to do with those parts handling child abuse petitions, simply because we are so limited as to the available number of judges.

V: Would you say that in your opinion the new juvenile laws render themselves less amenable to plea bargaining than their counterpart felony laws in the criminal courts?

K: Well, I think that there might be more of an impetus to plea bargaining in a limited sense with the "designated felonies" because there is ostensibly some assurance that a juvenile can be placed for a specific period now.

V: But you wouldn't imagine that a juvenile defendant would plea bargain out of the "designated felony" category?

K: I think that it might be possible.

V: What is your reaction to legislators, who want the designated felonies tried exclusively in the supreme court and not in the family court?

K: Well, I think that their objective is an understandable one. There is tremendous public pressure for something sensible to happen with violent juveniles, but I think that trying them in the criminal division of the supreme court is not the answer. The criminal courts are not doing that well with the adult defendant, so that what would be happening over there is not an improvement. Secondly, if there were adequate resources in this court I think we could do a much better job.

V: Isn't it a fact that the family court has probably seen these children before, and has much more experience working with juveniles than the supreme court could be expected to have?

K: Well, I think that we have a very superior bench. So far as the quality of the judicial work in the area of juvenile delinquency, the number of published opinions, and the kind of decisions the judges on our bench have written, there has been a very scholarly thorough approach. The problem has been that the court has had inadequate resources, it's been in the dispositional phase where we've had the problems.

V: That brings me to really the key of the interview. As a family court judge in the city of New York, what dispositional options are available to you in the case of a juvenile who has committed say a number of serious physically violent felonies?

K: Well, they're rather limited and actually as has happened in the past, it is either an Elmira placement, which for all intents and purposes simply isn't happening anymore, or placement under Title III, and the terrible problem there has been that the responsibility has been that of the Division for Youth. So the judges have had the experience of placing a dangerous or violent child and finding out within a brief period of time that child is out on the streets again, and this has been happening because in many instances social workers involved with that child have made an unrealistic assessment of the situation. The judges have not been consulted.

V: Do you agree with the assessment that if a child is incorrectly placed, it not only does harm to that child and to the larger society, but to the other children with whom that child is placed?

K: Well, yes, because I think that these children are at a formative point in their lives. It is essential that the placement be a constructive one for them, otherwise it's just damaging to everyone.

V: In an overall evaluation of the constructiveness of placements that you have personally been involved with, how would you rate such placements?

K: I would say they've been extremely ineffectual. Children come back here, they've absconded, it seems to be that Division for Youth has an enormous number of children who have absconded, warrants are outstanding for them, they sometimes discover where the child is and do nothing about effectuating the placement, and it's only when the child is brought back into court again that we realize what has happened. Some of the children have been staying at home and continuing to get into trouble, and the Division for Youth has done nothing about it. From what I can see, even at this point, the Division for Youth [DFY] has been most ineffectual.

V: When you have a hearing on the issue of disposition, isn't it a fact that this hearing only consists of whether or not the child will be committed to DFY and not to what specific institution or to what specific program?

K: Well, we don't have the option of deciding what DFY does with them. They have the primary responsibility, they are an independent department and it's been just a matter of form in more recent months that they have even sent us any kind of a report on a child. Which I, as I indicated earlier, don't take exception to, but I think that they are really operating on a disorganized level.

V: Does New York State—not just New York City, but the whole state—have a definite specific felt need for a secure treatment facility for violent acting-out male delinquents?

K: There's no question about it. We've had that need all along and for one reason or another it is not being met and DFY has not been successful in meeting this need, and the problem just continues on.

V: In view of the new legislation, wouldn't it seem apparent that such facilities must be constructed?

K: Must be. And I think that something has to be done about DFY. Now what I have been hearing is about various new programs, about various reorganizational plans that DFY has; well I hope they have them and I hope they materialize, because from what I've seen so far, nothing of that is apparent to me.

V: DFY would attempt to defend its lack of secure facilities on the grounds that it is a largely rehabilitative rather than punitive deterrent, incarcerative kind of agency. In your experience, does the agency function in a rehabilitative fashion?

K: Well, if you turn these kids, violent kids out, kids who've been involved in homicides, you turn them out on the streets within six months, eight months, you haven't even taught that child how to read during that period of time. This is not rehabilitative or constructive. I recall one discussion with a worker when I took him to task about paroling a particular boy that I had placed because of a very serious offense, and he said to me, "Well we promised him that he would be paroled by a certain date, and we had to keep our word"; I really find that many of the social workers or supervisors that are involved in these situations with these children either because of limited experience, limited life experience, are making ridiculous judgments, and they are jeopardizing the children and jeopardizing the community by such nonsensical judgments.

V: But of course these judgments are not tested in a proper arena, in an adversarial arena, because in fact the only thing litigated, if you will, is whether or not DFY is going to have custody of the child.

K: Well, what's litigated is whether he will be placed under a Title II or a Title III. And when a child is placed is under a Title III, it's because the child has violent propensities as indicated by past performance and other considerations at the time of dispositional hearing, then I find—I had one boy, last week I think it was, who after a Title Three placement was placed with the Lt. Kennedy Home, which is a completely open setting, he promptly absconded and had been living at home all along with full knowledge of the

Division for Youth. It wasn't until he was brought in on another serious crime, involving a homicide, you turn them out on the streets within six that we found out where he was and what he had been doing.

V: Let us say that the state was to provide a small secure maximum security facility, a rehabilitative facility, that would in fact also be incarcerative. How should the decision be made whether or not to send a child to such a place? I ask you this because Senator Marino and others in his particular field, feel that the crime should determine the time, there should be a strict correlation.

K: I think there is some correlation.

V: You think there is some correlation?

K: Yes, I do think there is some correlation, and I think it is wrong to disregard this. We had one situation where a child was involved in a homicide and after a finding was made, and he was found to be guilty of the allegations, he simply was paroled and walked out of this court.

V: What kind of effect does that kind of activity on that young man's cohorts?

K: I don't think it has a good effect, on him or on them. It makes the whole judicial process a joke.

V: Do you think in fact that this perception of the judicial process filters down to the street level where these children—

K: Absolutely. Absolutely. I think it's destructive to the children, I think it's destructive to the community.

V: Would you agree with the assessment of other professionals that I have interviewed in that there seem to be very little if any consequences to acts?

K: Yes.

V: For New York juveniles?

K: Oh, yes. And they have been aware of it, and I think this is an unrealistic approach, and I think it's an outmoded approach, an idea that should have been buried long ago.

V: Is *parens patriae* still viable?

K: In a limited sense.

V: Not to the extent perceived in 1899 when this began?

K: No, and I think that we're still operating under a social theory of the 1930s and I think most professionals in this area no longer consider this valid. The reality is that people have to face the consequences of what they do. I think that of course this is moderated by a child's age, by a child's background, all sorts of mitigating circumstances, but I think an important consideration is the value of the act. One must also consider what treatment the child himself requires. All of these are considerations.

V: So chronological age, in your opinion, is not automatically exclusionary of culpability?

K: No, I think it's a mitigating factor, it's a consideration; I think the welfare of the child is important. Concern as to how to turn this child around and make it possible for this child to live a constructive, fulfilled life so far as he is—so far as the child is concerned, and so far as society is concerned is the principal consideration. But I think that the severity of the crime is a consideration. I think that a definite period of removal from the community is necessary, and then rehabilitation can take place.

V: Would you agree with one train of thought that we see emerging and that is that the child, if you will, first comes to grips with the criminal justice system in reality when he's sent away as an adult at sixteen? In other words, we have kids who are in family court fifteen times, and are not really participatory. Then at sixteen, they commit again a serious felony, and the next thing you know they are in prison.

K: The sad reality is, and I have realized this after talking to a number of the probation officers, who at various points in their career were first in the family court and then in the criminal court, that most of the defendants in the criminal court have had prior family court records, which would indicate to me that we've been almost ineffectual in accomplishing anything.

V: How would you respond to this: In the past we've had a fairly comprehensive network of juvenile incarcerative alternatives. We've had training schools, we've had juvenile prisons, etc., etc., throughout the country. They seem to have failed, they seem to have been criminogenic, more than they have been rehabilitative.

K: Well, I don't know whether that's really quite fair. In one sense, I don't think that adequate funds have really been made available for many of these places to do a proper rehabilitative job, in that I don't think that proper educational opportunities were made available to these children. They haven't had adequate psychiatric and medical attention. I don't think they've really had adequate vocational training. I think there has to be a commitment to do those things for them.

V: So you're saying, that in effect, I'm not trying to put words in your mouth, but that the whole idea of rehabilitation in a closed setting really hasn't had a fair trial.

K: I think to some extent it has not had the kind of trial that it should have had, but I think that from what we've seen of it, we know that it's not wholly a valid idea either. I think there has to be a combination of things. I think that rehabilitation has to remain as the primary objective, but there has to be a realistic understanding that violent juveniles must be confined for an adequate period to effectuate treatment.

V: We're not really talking about a lot of children, are we Judge?

K: No. We're talking about a small group of really seriously violent juveniles, who are extremely dangerous, dangerous to themselves, and dangerous to the community. So far as the bulk of the children are concerned, I think it's really the commitment to them that's important, that there be adequate rehabilitative alternatives available to them.

V: Would I be summarizing your position fairly if I said that you favored incarcerative alternatives for the violent offender and community-based nonincarcerative alternatives for the truant, for the nonviolent offender?

K: Well, I don't know that I go with the term "incarcerative." I think that there have to be closed settings for these children, I think that we have to be committed to a period of time that will make it possible to really do something constructive for them. I think what we've had is a big joke, just pushing children through a system which is not benefiting them or the community.

V: How do you think, aside from a commitment of more money, which seems to be almost mandated by the new legislation, but assuming that we were able to free up the family court judges to do the kind of job that they are fully capable of doing, assuming that we had money for adequate training for support services, for corporation counsel, even assuming that we had viable institutions, how would we handle the problem of who goes to the institutions? Who would, if you will, perform the diagnosis? You find a child guilty of crime X. That wouldn't automatically put him in institution Y. You see.

K: Well, not really. Today for example, when we're making a determination that a child is to be placed with a Title III setting, we are making the determination that it's within a certain limitation of facilities that that child should be placed. But I think there has to be more control over what DFY is doing, and there has to be more independent judgment. Having DFY being run by a director perhaps is not adequate, perhaps there have to be representatives from various aspects of the community who operate as a board and have some control over what's going on with DFY. The community has input into many areas that concern citizens, so why not this important area?

V: Your view, interestingly enough, was completely echoed by Dr. Jerome Miller, who is the commissioner for juvenile corrections for the state of Pennsylvania, which actually has a more extensive juvenile prison network than we do.

K: Well, I have really found in my contact certainly with the previous director, more than Mr. Edelman, with whom I have not had any extensive contact, that it was a unilateral decision in almost every situation, and there was no outside opinion as to an evaluation with each of the children. I think that they committed themselves to a limited philosophy and I think there's no room for that really. I think the whole problem is really too serious. It's of too much importance to the entire community.

V: Well, could the judiciary have a more extended role? For example, could the family court judges entertain more writs of habeas corpus than they do regarding suitability of incarceration?

K: I think that's really starting from the wrong end. There has to be a wider input into policy for the Division for Youth, and more control over what that agency is doing. There has to be a board of professionals and lay people who set policy and review these decisions. A board consisting of such a cross-section should make all decisions as to when a child is ready to be paroled or whether everything suitable is being done for a particular child.

V: To what extent are the family court judges participating in the informational flow. Do you for example, visit when DFY opens a new facility?

K: Well, we're notified, but you have to understand that family court judges are not given any time to visit these facilities. I have gone to visit some on my vacations, but there are too many places I have never seen.

V: Well, then are you recommending a watchdog agency for DFY?

K: I think so.

V: Would it be—

K: Either a board, or some control.

V: Do you perceive DFY, as I have heard it referred to as a closed corporation?

K: Policy is being made by a small group of people. I think that in a way we only see what's wrong by seeing the end results of individual situations that come to the attention of an individual judge. The feeling I'm already getting even about the present DFY set-up is that it doesn't seem to be functioning as it should.

V: This is not, I take it, a new opinion of yours.

K: No, I hesitate to be too judgmental about the present setup because it isn't very long since Mr. Edelman took over. And I believe he's well-intentioned, and I would like to see more of what he plans to do. So far I've not seen anything that I felt was impressive.

V: What, for example, do you know about the special unit at the Bronx State Psychiatric Hospital?

K: Well, we did have a great deal of information about it originally, but I understand it is no longer functioning. All sorts of administrative problems arose, and the whole thing, unfortunately, petered out.

V: That's not a pun? Was this information you received projected information or information about what actually was happening? Was it in the form of copies of proposals to LEAA, what they planned to do, or was it information as to what was actually happening?

K: Well I'm afraid we really just heard about the end results of what was happening, but I assume that [the Administrative Judge] might have been more involved with the actual planning stages. I don't know whether he was but he should have been consulted and he should have been involved.

V: You seem to be saying, and correct me if I'm wrong, that the role of the judiciary has got to be almost like a one-time role, like there can't be this constant judicial supervision of facilities—

K: Well, judges can't be all things. I think that personally I would think it would be fine if there were enough time for me to do my job in these other areas as well. I would like to go to every one of these institutions, I would like to personally see what's happening. I have not. I am tied to a calendar five days a week. The institutions I've seen, I've seen on a vacation when I've been in the area, or I've seen on a weekend. You know, there are limitations to what people can do in the course of their work. We simply don't have the time or the opportunity, and so frankly taking on more responsibility that we can possibly assume in a constructive way doesn't make any sense.

V: That's doubly depressing because it appears to me as someone who's been in this field a long time, that the changes in juvenile justice have come about via the intervention of the judiciary.

K: I have spoken out on every occasion that I could publicly, because I felt it was my obligation as a judge, and as a citizen, as a human being to do that. It's really been a complicated problem. There are differing points of view to a great degree amongst the judges themselves.

V: Would I be overstating if I said though that there was consensus that the current system is not working?

K: I think everyone agrees with that.

V: Let me digress for one second and ask you a question that's been on my mind after some other interviews with other people: If you were sitting in family court and it was a homicide case and there were very difficult problems with proof. No real witnesses, so-called circumstantial evidence, but there was a finding against the child. Would you be open to a polygraph examination of this child?

K: No.

V: You would not?

K: No. Because it's my position that when we make a finding, that finding is beyond a reasonable doubt. If there is any question, then that kind of finding cannot be made, and I think that certainly where I make such a finding, I am extremely careful, I think that's true with my colleagues as well. I would go on the basis that there has been overwhelming proof that the child is guilty of the crime alleged.

V: Would you be open to the results of the polygraph on disposition only?

K: No.

V: Not even on disposition?

K: No.

V: So you basically feel that that particular device has no real future in the family court?

K: I do not feel that I would see any real purpose for it.

V: Is part of your response now colored by the fact that your disposition options are so limited?

K: No.

V: Even if we had several different types of institutions?

K: No, because I think that if you know anything about the hearings in our court, they are made with all of the constitutional safeguards, and with everyone's rights being fully protected, and a very careful trial and hearing and the judges are very careful about this despite our time limitations and despite the pressures of their calendars. These children are represented by the 18B [court-appointed] Counsel or by Legal Aid. They scrupulously examine the situation to see that their client's rights are fully protected. If there is a finding I accept that as the truth of the issue.

V: On disposition would you be open to expert witnesses, psychiatric testimony?

K: Yes, I think that's important. I think that all of the professional disciplines have a great deal to learn from each other and any assistance in this area that the judges can have, is important.

V: Let me conclude by asking you a few questions about the future. Are you at all optimistic that the new juvenile legislation will produce a pragmatic effect?

K: You mean do I feel that the community will be safer if more of these violent children will either get the appropriate treatment or—

V: Yes. Are we going to lower juvenile crime?

K: The new legislation will be given an adequate opportunity, but I really am not impressed that the public or the bar really understands the limitations. Firstly, the act refers to a Class A designated felony which includes murder one and two, kidnapping, and arson. I have never had one case of a kidnapping, before me, and only one arson case. The public is of the opinion that under this designation a juvenile can spend up to five years or even up to the age of twenty-one in secure detention. This is not so. The act calls for one year of secure detention for a perpetrator of any of the above acts, another possible year in an open setting, and then a period of parole. Under the non-Class A acts, the period of required secure detention is only six months. These acts include such serious crimes as rape, sodomy by force, assault one, robbery one, attempted murder one and two. Under the old statute, an Elmira commitment for a violent juvenile of fourteen or fifteen was possible. We no longer have this. I do not believe the public really understands the limitations of the new legislation.

V: I don't want to make you comment on other people's draftsmanship, but would you think it's a fair statement if I were to say that the new legislation is going to promote a flood of appellate litigation?

K: Well, I think any new legislation does. But I do think this new legislation will, because there are great gray areas and no one really understands what was really intended or just how to proceed in certain instances.

V: Don't you think that the legislative history of this act is somewhat infirm.

K: Infirm?

V: Yes, weak, shaky.

K: Yes, I think it was a series of compromises.

V: One final question. As far as people being worried about new legislation, new juvenile laws. Would you agree with the statement that unless we, for want of a fancier phrase, tighten up our ways of dealing with juveniles, in our courts and within the legislature, sooner or later we are going to have a tremendous pendulumistic swing back to the old ways and we are going to eventually see younger children incarcerated with adults?

K: Yes and it's one of the reasons I feel so strongly about a more realistic approach to juvenile delinquency, because if we don't, or the system is not meeting its responsibilities what we're going to see is more oppressive legislation that is really going to be destructive to the children and I would not want to see that happen.

**Interview between Andrew Vachss (V) and David
Guy Baldwin (B), on July 28, 1976**

David Guy Baldwin was fifteen when he accidentally shot and killed a young
friend. Placed on probation, he was soon sent to a juvenile training school largely
because of problems he was experiencing over the death of his friend. He became
an accomplished escape artist, and was eventually sentenced to Trenton State
Prison at age eighteen. His (attempted and successful) escapes continued and he
was later convicted of homicide and committed to Trenton to serve a life
sentence.

At age forty-two, he now awaits a hearing with the parole board.

V: David, how old were you when you first went to a juvenile institution?
B: Fifteen years old.
V: You had never been in trouble with the law prior to that?
B: I was on probation for a year prior to that.
V: For what?
B: Numerous amount of juvenilistic charges, which consisted of a stolen car,
and basically running away from home.
V: But no heavyweight beefs?
B: No.
V: You went down at fifteen for what?
B: Burglary, carrying a concealed weapon, and just general juvenilistic-type
stuff.
V: How long did you stay on that first bit?
B: It developed into several bits after that. I was at Annandale, and I escaped
and went to Bordentown, and I escaped and I wound up in Trenton State
Prison.
V: For what?
B: It originally started for, like I said, running away from home, burglary, and
the stolen auto.
V: You ended up in Trenton State Prison for what crime?
B: Escape.
V: You did a bit at Trenton and you got out?
B: Right.
V: You later returned?
B: I returned to Trenton three times.
V: What were the charges those three times?
B: The first time was the escape, the second time was for three to five for
burglary, and then I came back for another escape from a penal institution
which was called the workhouse, and then I was later returned for life.

V: For what crime?

B: The crime of murder, first degree murder.

V: Before you went to the juvenile prison the first time, how would you characterize yourself? What kind of a kid were you at fifteen?

B: I came from what you might call an average middle-class family; my father was in business, and I was active in what they call police athletic league (PAL), which was the boxing for the local area; I fought several times for the PAL, and I had what was considered a good school record, and I was just what was considered an average individual.

V: Well, what changed you? Now you're considered a major heavyweight escape artist, a bad guy, right? You've done an awful lot of time.

B: Well, I suffered an emotional trauma when I was younger which consisted of a death, I was involved in an accidental shooting and later on it was proven to be an accidental shooting. Prior to its being proved an accidental shooting, it was discretionary whether or not I would be tried, at that time, as an adult, and if I had criminal tendencies, and should they then send me away for life. I went through all those stages prior to my coming here.

V: How were you treated during those stages?

B: I think that at that particular time I was fortunate to the extent that my father was influential in the local community area, because he was so active in all community affairs, and he felt as though he was responsible for whatever it was I did at that particular time, and I was given basically, like I said at that time I was placed on probation, and it just developed from there to where he would like seem to get me out of whatever I got into. I later was given a suspended sentence from Jamesburg which was never even recorded on my record, with the understanding that I would go to California and stay with my father and never return to the New Jersey area.

V: When you were in the juvenile prison, was that the first time that you came into contact with other juveniles that were involved in crime on a full time basis?

B: My first encounter with people in confinement consisted of what they call, it's referred to as a juvenile shelter, and it's like a home away from home, it's not completely jail, and you're not completely free, but we were allowed to attend school classes, and things of that nature and return to this particular home, something similar to a foster home, and at this particular institution, because this was for the accidental death thing, like I said it was an emotional trauma and I was like pointed at and you know singled out; nobody had a charge of that nature in all the time I've been in that particular institution and they had invented this particular type of confinement for juvenile offenders so they didn't use to send us to the county jail, and they had no such thing in the Trenton area where I come from.

V: You were in Annandale?

B: Annandale and Bordentown.

V: While you were there, were you helped?

B: In no way. I didn't stay there very long anyway.

V: You escaped, right?

B: I stayed there approximately thirty-some odd days, and then escaped. But I was put in the hole.

V: Why did you escape?

B: Well, there are a number of reasons as to why I actually escaped. I didn't really understand confinement to the extent that I was confronted with it at that particular time, although I felt that because of that initial incident that I had that I was receiving an extreme amount of difficulty in my home life. I was receiving definitely a lot of trouble at school. One of the things was racial, because the other individual was black and I was white and although I lived in a mixed neighborhood, it still had a real major effect on me, and by coming to a place of confinement, which at that particular time was half black and half white, and I was a rather frail individual, I was kind of small, and I was definitely considered not aggressive, although I was in the PAL, I still was not an outward person. I was kind of like more or less to myself, and I suffered a lot of what they call setbacks as a result of my passiveness.

V: Can you give me an example of some of the setbacks?

B: Well, particularly the fact that there wasn't a lot of black movements so to speak, but it was still racially mixed up and they said this was a white guy that killed a black guy and that's what they said at fifteen, and I had to live with that, and anyplace I went from that point on, even some adults, and when I say adults, I mean people that were of the ages of twenty to thirty and up, you know, they resent the fact that I killed a black kid and this is the type of racial conflict that I went into. It caused me fights, it even got to the point like they came out to my house, they stoned my house, they fought my brother and I had to go out—they fought my sisters, in fact it was so bad at one point my probation officer took me out of school and allowed me a year's absence from school, as a result of it.

V: Did you find this type of racial difficulty followed you all through your prison career?

B: It did follow me through my prison career, but it took an undercurrent when I became outward and more aggressive; plus the fact that I was successfully articulate enough to explain to people that it was accidental, the man was my friend, and that time he was a boy, he was my friend, and he and I, was childhood friends and that we went to school together, we did everything together. My family understood it, and naturally were the most excusable for it. But it ended there. Everything outside of the families, his and mine, it was not excusable.

V: How old were you when you actually started to do time, and sat down and did a real stretch?

B: I would suspect that would be Bordentown, is where I stayed for approximately a year, before I escaped from there and that was where I did the time, and at that particular time I really tried to seek help; I went to social workers, I went to psychiatrists, psychologists, most of all it was required of me at this institution that you see all these people, and I would be openly honest with them tell them these here things like I just explained to you about how I underwent emotional difficulties and I went through the racial stuff. For some reason, like the reports that I had an opportunity to see, through the classification department, through illegal means as a matter of fact, somebody had snuck me my folder to show me just what it was they were saying about me, they said I was too—that I spoke too freely about my family because they—I would sit down and the psychiatrist would tell me "Now look I'm here to help you, I want you to tell me exactly what you think of your mother, your father, your sisters, your brothers, your friends, I want you to lay your cards on the table there's no record or nothing." I believed that wholeheartedly, and I thought that's what they were there for. And everything I said was derogatory, interpreted as derogatory, and it worked against me, they said I was too hostile, they said I was too aggressive, and they said I was too outward, I was too easily influenced, and I became—I got a stigma at that time of being suicidal, homicidal and everything else I could think of.

V: How old were you when you went to Trenton the first time?

B: Eighteen years old.

V: So you were still in effect a juvenile, you were less than twenty-one years of age?

B: I really believe that I could say I didn't successfully reach the point of maturity until I was approximately thirty-five years old.

V: So how did you handle the first ten years in there?

B: Mostly physical. Because there was never no intellect involved. It was strictly based on a physical basis, and that's how you could only survive. My whole struggle would consist of surviving my confinement. Education-wise they had nothing to offer me. Psychologically they couldn't help me. And as far as you know any type of program that they had adapted in the lower institutions all proved to work against me.

V: Give me some examples, if you can, of what you mean by having to survive physically in there.

B: Well, I was extremely young, and I didn't shave, I had what was considered a fair complexion, I was approximately 118 pounds, and when I first walked into Trenton State Prison they made me face the wall because there was a mass movement going on and I had to stand at what they call the control center, while the entire population moved about. Now when you reach an institution such as Annandale or Bordentown or even prior to that in the county jail, they say never go to Annandale, now this is with respect to homosexuality, they say that you go to Annandale and you have two or three choices: you either commit a sex act, or participate in a sex act, or break out. That's what they said were your two choices, or you could fight. Now you felt that if you couldn't win the fight then you escape, and if you couldn't do that then you're submitting to whatever events it was against you. And so I came—and I was believed by all the others to be young and I considered myself to be born a male and I was into that physical thing at that particular time and I was going to defend whether it was my honor, my masculinity, and so on. And that was my biggest problem when I first got to Trenton State Prison, I received numerous amount of notes, packages came to my cell, some came to this particular area of the cell block with, "I'll look out for you, all you got to do is be my kid," be my friend, or whatever they considered you to be. If you didn't want to accept the packages or the food or whatever it was, you didn't want anybody to look out for you, help you get a particular job in the institution, or hang around with them in the yard so to speak. There was a particular man there that knew my father, when he was younger, and he came to me and asked me my relationship with this individual, and he asked if it was my brother and I said no it was my father, and he said well I know him real good. He said look, the only real advice I can give you is to take this, and he had something wrapped up in a magazine, he said the first trouble you have pull his head off, go to the lock-up for a year and you'll have no more trouble. So when I took this particular item that he handed me it was wrapped up in a Life magazine and a piece of old newspaper, I laid it on my bunk, and when he later went away and I opened it to see what it was and it was a twelve-inch knife. And he said this was the only way I could survive Trenton State Prison at that time.

V: Did it turn out that he was right?

B: It turned out that he was right. Because of the fact that I was new in Trenton State Prison, it was required that runners that worked for the institution they give you your clothing, and they come and they ask you alot of questions, as far as like where do you come from, and a lot of personal information that they are supposed to need for their records. And then it would get from this particular information to parts like where do you come from where do you live, you got any sisters, you know anybody here, which I didn't know anybody there, and then the next thing out of their mouth would be well was you doing anything, and what they meant by was you doing anything was were you performing any sex acts. So the first individual that ever approached me with this, he was really an outright homosexual I didn't know it at the time, and he wanted to be the passive individual and he wanted me to be the aggressor. But I didn't take time to read the whole contents of the note so I just went to my little stash where I had been told to hide my knife, and I got it out and I jumped out on the tier and he saw me coming out with the knife and he ran and from that moment on I was tagged as "don't bother me." Although I did have some other problems after that. I guess I had (maybe) one other real serious incident where a guy actually did challenge me physically and I had to fight back, and of course I was successful and I won the fight so it didn't go past that. These were necessities and you couldn't survive otherwise.

V: Did you think it was worse in Trenton or worse in the juvenile joint, in this one aspect?

B: Well, if you was in the reformatories you had more of an opportunity to fight it out fair, it was a more fair situation. The fairity left with Trenton State Prison, there was no fairity involved, you had no choice in the matter, you had to fight and you had to resort to a weapon, because like I said, I was rather young and I was kind of small, and half the guys that approached me were big guys, and they had all been in jail before, and they were what you call seasoned-type criminals and they weren't about alot of talking and they weren't about saying "Well meet me down the back and put your hands up." They would pipe you in the head first and rip you off and when you woke up you would ask what happened to you, something of that nature. But in the reformatories I found that you would at least have an opportunity to go into the back, or to step into a room and fight it out. And if you won the fight, you were allowed to walk out, and if you lost the fight, you would have to subside to whatever it is they wanted. And if you confronted the institution with it, then they would put you in a protective custody status and you would have a bad name from that point on and that worked against you, more so than if you had the fight and took the beating or whatever.

V: What happens if you were forced to submit? What was the proper response for you to take then, later on?

B: Well, there was only one thing. If you lost the fight on a fair basis and, say, had to commit some sexual things or whatever, then your only alternative was to sneak up on him like later on. If this was in your make-up, if you felt as though you tried to fight and you wasn't successful, and the guy took advantage of you, then the only other outlet you have is that if you knew alot of guys who could get with you and give it a gang fight in the yard or something like that and they would support you, or you could wait till he was eating his breakfast and pipe him in the head and sometimes I chose to do that too.

V: Again you thought that these were necessities—

B: It wasn't that I felt that, I knew it, it was a fact. They were necessities.

V: Can you say that jail helped you, prison helped you, juvenile joints helped you in any way to deal with your problems?

B: I feel that if at the time when I was more susceptible to what you call education, and really what I felt later on is that nobody at that particular time was either sensible enough, educated enough, to sit down and realize that society was losing me they was going to lose me to a confined environment.

V: What kind of person would you have listened to, David? I mean, describe the kind of person you might have listened to, at that time.

B: Like I said, I was easy to convince that people was trying to help me because I needed help so bad—I was open to almost anybody that would sit down and tell me that this was it, they're going to help me. And they said that this was their job, there was a particular social worker down there who I remember distinctly, who came in and told me that he was really going to help, because he thought it was really such a shame, so I gave him my background, I really had a good background, other than the fact that I had underwent this here, like I said this here trauma, with this here accident thing, and he really said he felt sorry for me and I believed him, because he sat there and he was almost as emotional as I was, I became extremely emotional because I was in such desperate need of help and I wanted to get out of there, and I came right out and what you call opened my heart up and I opened my mind up, and I told him everything, I mean if they ask you a question like did you ever peek through the keyhole at your mother, did you have any sexual desires for your sister, and then he just goes on. And then I remember a certain psychiatrist ask me did you ever see two dogs hung up and I said of course I did, and he said what kind of feeling did you get? And I said man sign my pass and let me out of here, I said I'm not gong to sit here and listen to this here, this is pure unadulterated garbage, and he said I have to ask you these questions, you don't have to answer me nothing right back, and I got up and walked out, and as a result of my walking out he gave me a report that said that I was extremely uncooperative, I was hostile, I got really got a writeup like you wouldn't believe, I would never want to get a writeup like this again.

V: After a while did you find out that the things that they said negative about you eventually came true because they treated you as though they were true?

B: Definitely they came true because like I said I wasn't aggressive you know, and because I had such an ability to prove to somebody or to at least get somebody to listen to me they gave me this here title of being a con man and I never even in my whole life tried to con anybody out of anything, but because of my desire to want to express myself and to really give them the depth of the true feeling of what I thought in my mind, because you very seldom tell anybody what's really on your mind. You don't meet no other prisoner that you confide in. You don't meet anybody, like I said, prison staff that even cares what you are you know. All they're interested in is that you don't cause them no trouble and if you don't cause them no trouble then you just survive prison like the best that you can.

V: Same in the juvenile joints?

B: It was definitely the same in the juvenile joints. At that particular time, now, since this time, because I think, I was extremely involved in what you might call politicalness as far as institutions is concerned, I do note now that they do have some acceptable programs where they have available to you. Now I don't of course know if it's been working or not because I haven't been down there but in being at the age I'm in now, in other words, when I entered the institutions I couldn't read nor write, eighteen years old I came in Trenton State Prison I couldn't read and I couldn't write. Comprehension was bad and I guess depth perception was almost nonexistent, and as far as knowing anything intellectually my depth perception was so shallow that it was pathetic. I just took it upon myself, I had to survive prison, so I had to spend a lot of time by myself so I had to do whatever kind of reading I could, or to educate myself any way I could. Trenton at the time we entered, when I say we I mean some of the guys that were down at that time, had no education process, we had no social worker no psychologist, no nothing, and I think that it's a little late then to grant us that because they was all, as I said seasonal and I think that anything after that was game playing, you know it was like [you] wanted to play what they called it, the rehabilitation game, because that was what was expected of you, that put it on the records and it's all a game, and it really was a game at that point. Now, I'm not saying that your ideas, your personal ideology doesn't affect how you feel at that time because you do want to get out of prison, so maybe, even if you play, you may say, that even if you go to church enough you know something will come to you, so if you play the game enough something will come to you.

V: Do you think something that might rub off in spite of yourself, even though you're treating it as though it's a game?

B: But, on the institutional level that I came from unless you really got a sincere individual that meant what he said to you, when I say a sincere individual I mean a psychiatrist or a psychologist, or an educator, or anybody from a professional staff that really meant what they said, and that what did happen to you as far as like I say if you could give them a sensible and logical conclusions as to why you wound up in the institution and that they was going to really help you. They saw I needed education, they saw I needed guidance, they saw I needed consultation; they saw I needed all this. But now they said they offered it to me which was true they did offer it to me, but then they neglected it and they abused it in the sense that they abused me because what they told me later proved to be false, and they weren't really doing what they said they were doing. If they did that I don't believe I would be here today.

V: You were involved in a homicide after you left Trenton, right? Do you think that could have been avoided if your original experience inside had been different?

B: I think the clearest way to give you an understanding is if you got accused and blamed for everything so much that you just got tired of it and said the hell with it, "I might as well be that person that they think I am," so I adopted the character or the tag they put on me and that's the person I became. I became the aggressive, hostile, uncooperative, unmanageable, and disconcerned and high security, I became all this because I was young, I was idealistic, and that kind of thing at that time attracted me, you know like all I heard about the underworld, was all like attractive to me, and they couldn't see, when I say they I mean the professional staff members, they couldn't see that this was the direction I was taking; that they were aiding me in that direction. I was extremely influenced at the age fourteen when I read an article in the paper about a certain case about a gang. And it ranged with boys from eight years old to fourteen who had stolen a car and gone on a joy ride, they even had a dog with them, and I really felt like that was superfantastic at the time because they made headlines, they made the front page, they even had pictures at the time and I really felt that was fantastic.

V: Well, you made quite a few headlines yourself later right? Did that satisfy you?

B: To a degree, yes, I can say honestly that nobody likes to feel that they're nobody, and that they're being left out of everything and I found that the only way to survive is not to be left out of everything.

V: When you were in jail, especially when you were younger, what kind of people did you look up to? What kind of people did you respect and admire among the other inmates?

B: The outward aggressive, you know, tough, what you call the tough kid or the tough guy or something like that. They impressed me because I saw once how they survived that like the tougher you were the more respect everybody treated you with. They either did one of two things. I found out later on that there were two things that people respect around here and that's either an ass-whipping or plenty of money. If you had either one of these two—

V: Well, you could use one to get the other.

B: You could use one to get the other and that's what it was, and you see that became the manner of survival as well. If I'd had a lot of money, people would like kiss my ass to get my money you know and if I was a tough guy, they would like shake my hand to keep them from getting kicked in the ass, and that would be your survival method.

V: So might makes right.

B: Right. That's what it consisted of.

V: You see a lot of kids come in here, right? You've been here a long time, you've seen a lot of kids come and go?

B: That's right.

V: I assume that a lot of them have done juvenile time before they got here. Is that true?

B: Most of them I know from other institutions.

V: What's wrong with the juvenile prison system, in fact with the whole juvenile justice system? What's wrong with it?

B: Well, looking back at it, because like this is hindsight now, because like obviously I've been through it and I look back at it, and I can use myself as an example, and I also saw other people. Now there was a young fellow down that I knew at the time, he was there for the same type of crime or the same type of incident that I was involved in where he accidentally shot another juvenile, and he was given a life sentence for that particular crime. And he had the same identical situation that I had where he accidentally shot this boy and he later stood trial and they had sent him for evaluation programs and they felt as though he could have avoided it, and they adjudged him guilty of that particular crime, whereas I was fortunate where I was given like I said a probation period, and—

V: Why do you say fortunate, David, because the end result is exactly the same?

B: Well, to a degree it was, however, you know like if at the time, through the probational period, I had received guidance—

V: That's what I'm saying—

B: I received none whatsoever—

V: So what use did the probation really do for you? It was supposed to be a period where you could get help right?

B: Well, you see, maybe you just look at it in this sense, right. There was the psychological effect it had on me to know that I almost went away, that I almost did—

V: Okay. But did you have any sense of what doing life meant at the time?

B: No.

V: Would you have wanted to talk to somebody who had already done a life bit?

B: I definitely would have—

V: Would you have listened to such a person?

B: I think I would have listened. See anybody that I think would have been intelligent enough to know that I had a problem because I was being evaluated to see whether or not I would be tried as an adult, so that would have meant at that time they had the death penalty or I could of got time or sent away for life. Like this other particular kid, he did get sent away for life. He got sent to Bordentown and he stayed there until he was eighteen or nineteen years old and he was later transferred to the prison, and I saw him later on there because I as I said I came back on other sentences, most of them were for escape and he stayed in the prison system until he was like I think thirty-five years old, and I met him when he was eighteen. I know that he was like completely a wreck, and at the time like I said although I was fortunate in that I was given a probational period, I did like you said end up here as a result of not receiving proper guidance, not receiving the treatment if you so will, or anything else where it would give me incentive not to do anything where I would be confined.

V: You've had all the time you've been confined—leaving aside the last few years because I think you've gone through some changes—but before this last few years, is it fair to say that the only restrictions on your behavior were whether or not you'd be caught? When you were in the institution would you hit somebody in the head with a pipe?

B: Oh, definitely.

V: Would you steal?

B: Oh, definitely.

V: Lie?

B: Definitely.

V: What wouldn't you do while you were in the prison? I assume you wouldn't inform on anybody, but outside of that, was the line drawn anyplace?

B: No. There is absolutely nothing I wouldn't do if I probably could get away with it.

V: And you're not really very different from the majority of people in here right?

B: I'll say this here. People don't actually tell you exactly how they think and feel, but based on most of the individuals that I've hung around with we've contemplated robbing the store, we've contemplated escape, there's one thing that I don't particularly get involved in is rip-off of a kid, and I'm not that type of person myself because I despise that type of person. I don't particularly care for somebody who robs another prisoner. When I'll say I'll rob I mean I'll rob from the state or from the system itself. I'll bullshit the man if I think that's the only way you can get out. I'll lie to a parole officer if need be, and anything to do with respects to getting out then the line is not drawn, except like you said about becoming a police informer. And I've been offered that and I've turned it down.

V: Why did you turn it down, David? I mean you wanted to get out more than anything in the world, right? You were willing to risk your life, because you risk your life when you go over the wall, right?

B: Yes. But if you recall, in the earlier interview I told you I was extremely impressed with the underworld stuff, and I thought that at this particular time this was glamorous to me and this was the Mafia, and later the Cosa Nostra, and so on, and so I grew up in this type of environment, and I had been around people where your code of ethics in prison consists of one thing: You don't tell. Everything else was excusable and acceptable except the fact that you did not tell, and you did not break any trust or confidence of anybody that put it into you. In other words, if another person trusted you, you go to his home, and he would trust you with his wife or his children you gave him that, you know due respect. And these were the things about which they said death before dishonor, and I think that I would die before I ever let anybody say that I was an informer or that I messed with their family. Anything else was excusable, acceptable, and even expected.

V: I know you've learned a lot of negative things in the institution—you also learned these things in the institution too, right? You didn't have this attitude before you came?

B: No. I don't think I had any what you call sense of value on freedom, I had no sense of value on money, I had no sense of value on materialistic things. Later on I had what you might call capitalistic ideas because I wanted a lot of money because you know like I said life was glamorous and played up to be glamorous and I thought that the only way that you could have this type of life was to get as much money as possible as quick as you could and due to the fact that I was starting from behind, I just thought that I would have to go rob it to get it. Because you know to work till I was sixty years old and then retire I couldn't enjoy my money, and I wanted to make it up for all the things I missed. I'll say this here: At twenty-eight years old I was fifteen years old and I was outside in an environment that was violence-prone where I was barhopping where kids barhop at eighteen, nineteen years old, I was barhopping, twenty-five years old, getting into fist fights, and playing tough on the pool table, and things of that nature. Things that I know kids go through when they're fifteen, sixteen, so I went through mine at twenty-eight.

V: Let me ask you this final question to kind of sum things up. Are you ready to leave?

B: No, I'm nowheres ready to leave.

V: You're not?

B: No. I have twelve years in on a life sentence—

V: I mean are you emotionally ready to leave, are you mentally ready?

B: Oh, I am prepared if that's what you mean—

V: That's what I mean.

B: I'm prepared I'll say as far as the intellectual work, as far as my ideas, my future, prospective ideas, my aims, my goals, my objectives, I'm ready on all of that.

V: You don't consider yourself a violent person anymore?

B: You know, anybody is prone to be violent. Now as far as anybody saying will you rob and kill, you know how could you say that, you could say no you could say yes. And the thing is that anybody put in a certain situation, given a particular opportunity having to respond or react to something, well then you could become potentially dangerous, as can anybody, but just to go out and contemplate murder, or just to go out and say well, I'm going to rob to stick up a bank and kill a couple of people, well, no this has never entered my mind.

V: So you're at least able to say that you could defer gratification for the things that you want. You could go about it at a normal pace?

B: Definitely.

V: You missed a lot of time on the street. You don't think you'd have to make up for it in a week or anything like that?

B: No, not now because see my valuations have changed. Now I know the difference between what you call materialistic ideas and materialistic views with respect to emotional feelings and the ability to just want to live a life. I don't have decision power here. One thing confinement does is take away decisions. Now although I said the fact the decision to survive, you have that, that's three decisions that you've got. In life, you know you have many many decisions. Every day, every day, you walk life, right from the beginning of going to work, going home getting married, and this decision power has been taken away from you and I want to contemplate I have a good family if you want to call it that, I have somebody else's family, I have a girl and some children and that to me is my family and I have some children of my own, also, but their mother's married. But now I know what I can do to survive and I know what I want to do to survive and just break restriction, break confinement, that's all I really need now.

V: How many more years do you have before you're eligible to leave?

B: I see the parole board in approximately two years.

V: So you could go home in two or three years?

B: I think it would be safe to say that I could go home in five years. That would be giving it almost the maximum. I could go out in two, as a matter of fact, but I'm saying that looking at it realistically, because of the type of record I built up for myself, it's going to take a couple of years to prove to the parole board, which has recently changed, that I'm prepared for release.

**Interview between Andrew Vachss (V) and
Yitzhak Bakal (B), on July 28, 1977**

V: Dr. Bakal, you're largely associated at the Northeastern Family Institute, with various kinds of programs that have nothing to do with maximum security. You're associated with shelter programs, diversion programs, counseling programs, intervention programs, right? Do you have a position as to the viability of maximum-security incarceration and/or treatment for any juveniles at all?

B: I think there is no doubt that we need maximum-security settings. And I think there is no doubt also that there are certain youngsters that need this. The question that is always disputed is "What percentage of the kids?" "What is the process by which the kids enter and get out of these institutions and these programs?" "How are the programs supervised?", "What do the programs offer besides security?", "How the security is being offered?", "What constitutes security and what constitutes treatment?", and how these things get interchanged and overlapped, but there is no doubt in my mind that setting is important if not for the sake of society then for the sake of the youngsters, and possibly for the sake of everybody.

V: Is your statement that such settings are required founded upon political reasoning or therapeutic reasoning or both?

B: Both. Political reasons we will have—there is no doubt in my mind that we have to satisfy certain judges, certain community leaders, if not only for the general political reasons for satisfying those people, at least, and consciously many of these people have to be reassured. I feel that society by and large has to be assured that violence cannot be tolerated, and young people, even if they are young, can be stopped, because without this, the level of anxiety of people will be vastly increased. And we will unleash much more destruction if we don't provide this type of security. This is, by and large, the framework for the political reasons. I can see the whole process by which a child is found to be in need of this secure setting is largely political. Some people say that he needs it, others say he doesn't need it, and out of this whole battle a compromise is reached. There is no such thing as black and white. It is all going to depend on the level of tolerance of that particular community, the professionals, and what advocacy they develop for that kid or for kids in general.

V: So it is by no means cut and dried. In other words you're saying that regardless of the crime committed, disposition could vary depending on the climate?

B: Bravo. Depending on the climate. Depending on the socio-political-economic factors.

V: If we could isolate political factors, if we could imagine a pure kind of society in which politics did not play a part, would you still advocate secure settings for certain juveniles?

B: I would definitely advocate it. This is found in all psychological theory; every individual needs a feeling or a setting at one point or another that can stop him, and with the violent youngster he might need to be safe from his own impulses, to be assured that he can be stopped no matter what, to be assured that he can't rule the roost, if you will. So if we dismissed all kinds of environmental, sociopolitical considerations there are still children that grow for whatever reason without the ability to control their impulses, and they actively seek this control with outside environments and outside settings. If the symbols that society has, which is the symbol of jail, or the symbol of court or police does not help, we might need a very much more confined and secure setting. In fact, if you take it with a little child, take the same analogy with a little child, who is growing up in his own home, if the child is putting up a temper tantrum because he wants something, the family, father, mother, others can restrain him, or they put him in his room, and physically can restrain him, so that he's assured that even his own impulses cannot get completely out of hand. Now if this child grows, and his immediate family can't restrain him, he needs a secure confined setting that can restrain him. And I see this by and large the reason why we need some secure settings.

V: What happens to such a child if instead of a secure setting, he is placed in a non-secure setting, a group home, if you will, a shelter care—

B: Well, there are a variety of processes that are going on there. First of all, if the child and everybody knows that he needs a secure setting and yet he's put in somewhere else, it's another victory for him, another victory for his impulses. It's a victory that one side of him wants and that another side of him doesn't want. It's a victory that leads further to his destruction. And he knows damn well, that that's what it's going to lead to.

V: Is it a fact that if we do not apply certain kinds of restraints and controls, during a maturation period, it would almost inevitably commit this child to maximum security incarceration as an adult?

B: Yes. I agree with that. Every child needs to feel and every person needs to feel, for that matter, that there is a power that is above them, that can restrain them; I am not saying a power that smashes him—I don't believe in that either—but a power that can restrain him and if he gets constant victories by overpowering every other power, he'll get himself destroyed in the end.

V: Do you think the children have a sense of this inevitable destruction?

B: They do. Definitely. And this is why by committing more and more violence, they are pressing society, pressing the environment, pressing everybody to come up with another restraining factor.

V: So the constantly escalating violent behavior that we observe in some juveniles is, in your opinion, a demand on their part for additional restraints?

B: Definitely. There is something in psychology that is called a feeling of omnipotence. Everyone of us has some feeling of omnipotence. But when this feeling of omnipotence takes over to the point that one feels that he is completely omnipotent, it becomes chaotic, and gets out of hand.

V: Can you typify for us the type of juvenile that would require such a setting? Can you typify perhaps, the kind of acts he would be committing, the type of behavior he would be exhibiting?

B: Again, if we are talking solely from the point of view of psychological reasons, because we have to accept that people are not living in isolation, and therefore many of these behaviors can be triggered by destructive forces, by oppressive forces from outside and thus much of the violent behavior could be reactive rather than really a demonstration of psychological problems within the kid. However, by and large I would say, that a child that's been constantly again showing this kind of thing, impulsive behavior, and has been winning all along the way.

V: So you would postulate a repeated pattern of acts as opposed to a single act?

B: Definitely, yes.

V: So would it be fair to say that you would be more concerned about the child who began stealing and ended up in physically violent robberies, than the child who is involved in a homicide one time and has no prior history.

B: Yes.

V: You wouldn't be talking then strictly about the type of crime defining which children go in the secure setting? Then it would be simplistic to say that the type of crime that the child commits would indicate the setting in which he is to be treated.

B: That is an oversimplification. But, again, this distinction between the one-time homicide versus the long-standing kind of problem is a very important one. It is a very important distinction, and it should be elaborated on.

V: How do we separate acting-out violent behavior from the kind of heavy psychopathology that perhaps cannot be treated in the setting that we're talking about. For example, we have one child whose criminal career has eventually peaked to the point where he has been involved in repeated armed robberies with violence. He's not only taking money, he's perhaps slugging people over the head with the pistol, he's firing the gun when it's not necessary. His behavior does not seem to be related to a desire for money. He's contantly acting out. When this child is institutionalized, he's involved with violence within the institution. That's one kind of child. Another kind of child is involved in sexual abuse of little children, much smaller children. Now I think their pathologies are distinctly different. Would you treat them within the same setting?

B: Of course not. I don't think it would be helpful to treat them in the same setting. First of all, based on your understanding of the situation, the child who has been constantly acting out needs a setting in which you work on his ability to control himself.

V: Is he a participant in this training or a recipient?

B: He is participant and recipient. I would say he would maybe start by being a recipient and then moving little by little into being active participant. But we are not going to compromise on violent behavior. This is not acceptable. And it will be dealt with once he's willing to play. Which means when he's willing therefore to recognize that here is another factor that he has to reckon with and we are going to have then to negotiate the process of learning, and that's going to happen between us there.

V: Do you want to continue this to the extent that we're going to stop violence at all levels. For example, many institutions are somewhat capable of controlling resident violence against staff and ignoring intraresidential violence.

B: I think violence against everybody. Definitely. I see the problem as working with violent behavior, as not so much the problem of the people who have the violent behavior as much as the problem of all the people involved in the treating of it. It's not so much really dealing with violence that is the issue, it's the variety of disagreements, high emotions, incompetency of staff. In psychological terminology, it's the feeling maybe that is evoked in us to deal with somebody who is violent and either one is going to be completely subservient and frightened of the person and build him up even more, or one is going to be completely suppressive and kill the person. The problem of working with the violent behavior, again, if I want to rephrase it, is not the problem of the behavior. They are people like everybody else, who have some problem, and it's fairly easy to constitute a treatment plan. The problem is with the variety of disagreements, discussions, and the feeling that evokes any kind of treatment modality in doing anything of this sort. People are so much in disagreement on how these things should be handled and they are also untrained because society by and large does not know how to deal with violence.

V: Is this transmitted to the child himself? Does he understand?

B: Definitely, it's transmitted to him. Let's take this issue another step further. The way society deals with violence also comes out the same way. You can go and kill in Vietnam, or be completely all-out destructive, let's say; that's okay, or you can be completely liberal and beautiful, which is "Step on me and kill me it's okay." There is no such a thing as a whole plan on how to deal with violence. And many of these people need an "in-between" dealing with violence. It means you train people how to deal with violence, with their own violence, those people who work with kids, violent kids, and what it evokes in them, before they can even come close to those kids because these kids smell it and are in tune to it. This is why you have almost like two sets of people who deal also in society in all these institutions with all these violent kids. They're two kinds of people, either fuzzy-headed liberals, as you call them, that ignore violence completely, and believe everything is beautiful, or the completely ugly destructive suppressive kind of people who beat the hell out of the kid, even without provocation.

V: How do you reach that midpoint in terms of training staff? Because you seem to be saying that a staff member who is fearful of the juveniles he is to treat is incapable of anything other than the two responses that you're talking about, to deny the violence because of his own fear or to suppress his own fear or to suppress his own fear with violence of his own. How do you train people not to be fearful?

B: You start first by having the right people. And when we do hiring here at Northeastern Family Institute, almost the first thing we look at when we interview people, is how comfortable the person is, what kind of a person is he, how does he deal with his own life, what kind of life experiences does he have, whether there is a big gap or discrepancy between the words and the actual living. What I mean by that is, is he a fuzzy-headed liberal that talks about how he "loves" kids or is he realistic and does he know how to really hit if there is a need to hit, and stand up for himself, defend himself, to be firm to be strong as well as to be compassionate, and loving. And I would want people who had some life experiences, who have some living experiences, who grew up with many things, including with violence, and how to deal with violence, with violent people and who learned how to communicate. The next step is really developing a whole training program that is geared to increase staff abilities that already exist, and not to just take people who believe that they are going to save the world but who really don't know how to deal with themselves. The training program—the only way I can explain it—is an action-oriented, experimental kind of a program. We do a lot of encounter group techniques, we teach people how to confront one another, and how to get the garbage out as much as possible, and let people deal with feelings and fight with each other.

V: Is there a danger there? In this part of the country encounter groups are almost an art form and many people are comfortable in an encounter group because they know that the rest of the middle-class oriented people in the group have made a commitment to nonviolent behavior physically, and there's no physical fear involved. In the institution, of course, there *is* physical violence. How do you make that transition in your training?

B: There are other issues of training. These would be to get the person to work with senior staff, expose him to all kind of activities. For example, we are considering hiring somebody as a clinical director for the shelter care. We have someone already, who is somebody who has already proven himself, has been with kids in a variety of levels. So the director is taking the clinical director, who is going to be his assistant, to one of the intensive security settings. They are going to spend a day there. The guy is going to be interviewing some kids, which is also going to expose him, and see what kind of reaction does he have to this thing. That's part of assessing the capacity of the person. But that's also another part of exposing the person I imagine that some people after fifty years might not be trainable. I would say that there are a good number of people that are completely untrainable. And I'm not going to destroy a kid's life to do that. I'm impatient in those things. I want a good person and I want a good person from the beginning. In fact, many of the trainings do not occur at the beginning. I don't even believe in doing a lot of training at the beginning when a project starts. You make the program experiential again in the same way, because otherwise you are playing the same facade you're putting another veneer of behavior on top, that is based on some kind of notion that he's taking from somewhere that we don't know where from. And we use kids in the training. Let me give you another example. I feel, we have a very interesting program, a foster home program in which we place kids. Some of them are violent kids, angry kids, a variety of kids, anxious kids awaiting trial, and when we started we couldn't even believe that we will have many foster parents that will stick. Right now we have about twenty foster parents, even more than we need. But the key to that was the regular training session with these foster parents. We started foster parents by putting the kid there for a day or two. And if they didn't lose their interest, we followed that by asking them to talk about their experience, bring them to regular weekly foster parents' meeting. In the home, having a kid that doesn't belong there, in your own home is a most difficult experience. It's really a very difficult experience.

V: So the conventional method of simply farming the kids out just isn't going to work. Let me ask for you for two levels of analysis then in terms of this whole business of staff suitability. Let me ask you first on a personal level and then on a professional level. I've seen you Yitzhak, personally, in a maximum-security institution and you appear to be utterly fearless, willing to confront very dangerous violent people, yet somewhat relaxed and confident, without any kind of bravado. Now what do you attribute this to, because physically, of course you would be no match for the average kid in there?

B: My answer to that is that in my own work, working with families, counseling, and a variety of things, I learned that many of these anxieties are based within me and within the person. You can also take it to an extreme and say that there is no such person that is a dangerous person. Of course, there is a person who is a dangerous person. But usually, they are dangerous because they are dangerous to somebody or to something, not across the board dangerous. But if I were a woman, and they were sexually frustrated, they might want to rape me; but I'm not a woman, so I'm not going to have problems with rapists. And also, there is no across the board all-out craziness. I learned this in working and being around people in mental institutions, and I learned this in being around people in prisons and other institutions. But the scary feeling that I get is usually tuned into my own fears and anxieties. If I am out of my fears and anxieties, then I can talk and assess the person. The easiest way to handle somebody who is aggressive is just telling him that he looks scary. Is he trying to be scary? And many times they are not aware. I was working with a father the other night, and the father is a complete bastard because he beats up on the kids and so on. I made him listen and hear how scary he was to every one of these kids. And he wasn't fully really in touch with that and he's mainly feeling that he's been victimized by everybody and therefore he's not going to take this shit, and beating up everybody is his way of saying that. He was in many ways scared of his own shadow, and his own fears, and his own inadequacies, and once I got hold of that, I couldn't be scared of this guy because I knew he was a little frightened guy. All that I need to do is to protect him.

V: That's the point because I've seen you use this confrontive technique and implicit in your challenge, which is "Are you trying to be scary?", is that you yourself are not scared.

B: That's because I realize who the person is. The minute you realize who the person is and who you are dealing with and you are connected with him rather than with your own fears and anxieties, then you don't have the fear and the anxieties. You are dealing with a person, with another human being.

V: Alright, now, on the secondary level, you observed, if not on a daily basis, at least the proximate results of the initial staff at Andros, which was subjected to an extraordinary amount of violence by the kids. Analytically, why did this happen?

B: First of all, the haste with which we went into the business of intensive care. That, I would say, is number one, and I would say that by and large the lack of vision, the lack of ability really to see what they were into.

V: Well, it wasn't supposed to be intensive care originally, right?

B: Nobody was listening to the fact that what was going to make the whole de-institutionalization thing work or fall was the intensive secure units. I made this point regularly. This is going to make any program, any kind of changes possible or not, any closing of institutions or any new programs work or not work out. What happened was right after the statement of closing institutions and so forth there were furious telephone calls from some judges, then immediately the assignment at that time was said "Oh, please, Yitzhak, let's get this thing going, let's get an intensive secure unit," and since I was talking about the need for these things, I was assigned the role. Now the next step, number two in this thing, so that there was no adequate planning to get any program off the ground, and I saw this Andros thing the way it was put together at this time, as an ingenious way of doing something very quickly and very good. I mean quickly. There was no time for research. Now, number two—now we needed an organization that also we can hide behind, if you will. We wanted to get out of the bag of institutions and the containments and controls, but I felt at that time that's it's better to be under the so-called "auspices," the "good auspices" of the psychiatrist, psychiatry in general. Because you know, even if you are labelled that you are a little crazy and dangerous, that's okay, that's much better. At least they don't use the whip. And we were making the point that we are humanizing things, so you need a liberal, a good name. So at that time, the only one that was really available, at a moment's notice to get something off the ground was the private agency. Number three was that the private agency despite its failures and limitations, was ten times more equipped than many other psychiatric institutions and I didn't want to put kids in all kinds of wards, being destroyed by these doctors who are completely aloof and just using drugs. This private agency, at least at that time, was talking about doing all kind of community meetings, therapeutic meetings, groups, a variety of things. So that they were more equipped but even they had no knowledge as it turned out. Not much knowledge. But they were much more equipped, they were at least versed in these things that you try to control behavior through groups, in community meetings, and you also provide a setting for that. The biggest bungle that I see, the biggest problem, is that they tried to pull this very fast and therefore recruited staff that weren't well equipped, and I told them they were all young and inexperienced and they spent too much time in putting them in all kind of training, which they were—which was really a waste of time because they were mainly working on their *own* issues, rather than learning how to deal immediately with kids, and by the time the kids were moved there, they were completely bored. They also brought in their own system of operation. They moved it from the private agency up to the institution. That system again worked okay with middle-class people who accepted order, but didn't work out with the kids who needed a much more bouncy and active program.

V: What was there about the staff specifically though that made itself so prone to this type of violent response from the kids?

B: Well, the staff, there was something almost like printed on their forehead that said "we're liberal, we're nice guys, take advantage of us." To tell the kids—they came to where they thought they are going to handle everything with love in the beginning. Their intention was to handle everything with love, and not to put any pressure. And I remember that at the time I was talking to them about the need to start with a very strict structure. I told them to even make it as difficult as institution. It's much easier to give in after that. And you know their attention wasn't there, they were supervising the place just from afar, and maybe they didn't show much interest in it.

V: Would you have selected that same staff?

B: The staff? No. I would not have selected that staff. There was too much inexperience. I mean they were very much inexperienced. I would have put them through a test of seeing how capable are they to extend to kids, how unafraid are they of dealing with kids, and from that sense you were almost like magic in straightening out the staff. It was tremendous, because the minute you came to that program, you put your finger on the problems. You realized that the staff was completely afraid—

V: Well, by that time the problems were exacerbated to the point where they were quite clear.

B: Yes. But when you say "to the staff, I wouldn't take anyone who wouldn't defend himself, they would be fired immediately, and I also would fire anybody who will brutalize kids." You made the most remarkable statement, "I will fire you if you don't learn how to stand up for yourself, and I will fire you if you brutalize kids."

V: Those are fair parameters though aren't they?

B: Bravo. Excellent parameters.

V: And they are parameters that regardless of your particular orientation towards treatment that you could buy into.

B: Definitely.

V: Okay. Do you think that the population at Andros—the original population—all belonged in the secure setting?

B: No. Definitely not. Andros has been misused and abused—

V: This is the point that I wanted to talk about. In other words, Andros, for a period of time, was generally perceived to be as a success.

B: Yes.

V: The judges liked it. The community liked it. The profession liked it. DYS liked it. Within a relatively short time, historically speaking, many many more kids were referred there, more secure units were planned and built. Do you think this is a danger when we construct secure settings? A universal danger?

B: Well, I would want to see some kind of coherent system of secure settings. But let me just tell you my philosophy about secure settings. I can say that Andros was misused but I want to put it in a different way. I feel that really, generally it's going to be very difficult to establish criteria as to which kid should go where. You'll always have problems with that. You can say, well, the physically violent will go here and this one will go there and there is one unit that will do this and will do that. I would rather, if you asked me, I would vote for a place that would be so well endowed, and so

well budgeted and so well staffed and so well programmed that they almost
take care of any kid that would be there. I'm saying *almost*, I'm not saying
everyone. What I would have wanted to see in Andros was this possibility of
being really an advocacy center in the true sense, for the kids. And you take
every kid, no matter how off the wall he is, and work with that kid to assess
where the kid is at and what you have to do in terms of programming on a
long term basis, to be really truly the expert and the center for those kids
that nobody else wants. And develop a variety of programs that are geared
to help every one of these kids. So you must be well endowed and well
staffed to do that. They do that, in all kind of hospital settings, middle
class, upper class, I mean it doesn't matter if you have something wrong and
nobody can find out, you go there and you stay for about a month, two
months, three months, and every specialist in the world will come just to
diagnose, and to help you, and there is a whole plan. I would want to see
that, rather than say "Okay, we are going to have one program, or we are
going to have one institution that will deal with this kind of kid, and
another to deal with this kind." And all they get is to turn them into
machines. Now to me that's the failure of the intensive secure unit in
Massachusetts. It was based and conceptualized wrong from the beginning.
People start to feel right away that there is this kind of kid and that kind of
kid, and I agree that there are this kind and that kind, and it's good in
theory for you to be able really to reach out to the problem. But on the
level *of working* with kids, you have to basically construct a setting that is
full of good people, committed people, with a lot of budget and resources
that can handle situations. And in the long run you might find that this is
cheaper.

V: In the concept of a maximum-security institution, one thing you seem to be
saying is that the maximum-security institution, or the secure setting, or
whatever you call it, has to be integrated as part of a therapeutic whole with
the rest of services that are given to children; that it cannot exist by itself
off in a corner.

B: Definitely. And this is the key to making an intensive secure system a
success or a complete disaster. That's what makes the difference, really. And
the history has always been that these semi-institutions, or whatever you
want to call them, being a dumping ground and becoming completely
isolated from other services. I like also to look at two things in every
program, especially intensive secure units: the intake, who is being put in,
and outtake, the outside, where are they going after that? If the force of
putting youngsters in is very strong, and without any selectivity, you are
just creating masses of people that are being victimized many times without
hope and without expression, like most of the detention centers. If the kids
are not getting out, if the release is a problem, you are creating a condition
which explodes.

V: Does a proper secure setting have, if you will, a therapeutic effect on the secure setting as a whole? Does it take pressure off the other kinds of treatment modalities? For example, you're running a group home. Is it an advantage to you to be able to have an institution to which to refer a given juvenile that cannot function in that setting?

B: Yes. It should be a secure setting. It could be one of interdependent, interrelated complex of systems—it's one of the options, yes. And it should be part of the total system. Our goal here in the Northeastern Family Institute is to create an interrelated system of service delivery to kids. I don't want to have just one program. I'm not a "Macdonalds operation" as I call some of those programs that are run this way. We offer just this: a human being is multifaceted. He also needs to grow from one thing to another. I want to see the intensive secure unit as one of a system, it could be that the kids will stay there just for a while because he's completely out of control, but it definitely should not be the end of the road, because if it's the end of the road, it's very destructive. Ideally it could be sometime, the beginning of the road. They take kids to jails to listen to a lecture. These kids have never been in crime, and all of a sudden it opens their eyes to what this means to be delinquent, to be criminal, and so on and so forth. Whether he wants to do that or not. Similarly, for example, we favor one program that we were involved with for a while which was taking a few kids on trips, weekly trips, bimonthly trips to Walpole [State Prison]. They go and visit some inmates that are interested in working with kids. And, of course, we had to control it. We had to know exactly what's going on there. But in some ways it had some very effective sobering influence on some kids. Now I don't see anything wrong with some kid just winding up in an intensive secure unit for a very short period of time and as a way of almost like gaining some insight.

V: That's a completely new concept in the use of secure units.

B: It's almost like you can even use it as a prevention device. At the same time you are not completely isolating the population, just the destructive kids in one place, but you are intermingling, and the key really to bringing the heavy delinquent back into society is by *not* isolating him, by making him *part* of society, even if he is doing everything he can to be put in the corner, not being part of society, the key is how you are dismantling the roadblock that he's put, and still get him to be part of society.

V: In other words, you're saying the child is not dumped there, yet he may need an injection of this kind of treatment on a very temporary basis, perhaps.

B: Yes. And also, by doing that, we are not completely isolating the one who is already labelled and putting him there. Let me just give you one example that talks to this whole issue of stigmatization and isolation, because I see this as the key to the destruction or rehabilitation of a youngster. And how many times this works. It's actually a very interesting thing that happened here. We have one office in Salem and it's in a respectable kind of business area. And some of the kids came out of some kind of art working session in which the person in art was playing with balloons and doing all kind of things with balloons. And two of the kids that came out from this were still high and they had two balloons in their hand. They were these long balloons that had a phallic symbolism to them, they looked like a phallus, and they were going around in the street and just playing with this as if it's a penis, shocking everybody. And I was coming in with one of my staff and they were doing this on the streets and some phenomena occurred that was so interesting and really says something about the human behavior. They passed by a person who was in his late fifties or early sixties. He looked a somehow respectable guy but you can see from the way he walks that he's half drunk or something. So the kids, in their mischievous way, they were trying to embarrass him, or to embarrass everybody with this gesture they were making, and all of a sudden, they said "Hi" to him and he turned and said "Hi" and then he started to talk to them and he was talking in some mumbo-jumbled way, in a very bizarre kind of discussion, and he was making sounds and jumping up and down, and it was really embarrassing them to stand and talk to him. This embarrassing kind of behavior almost like shocked these kids into reality. They all of a sudden straightened out this thing, they threw the balloons away, and they started to talk like perfectly respectable human beings. This really says something about what happens if we isolate one behavior. Like all the rest, if you take this example, the rest of the straight people on that street were reacting to them with embarrassment, therefore the kids were constantly misbehaving and not even being totally aware of their own behavior and what impact it had until somebody came that was supposed to behave in a certain way and behaved in a completely shocking way to them and shocked them right into reality, which really has implications for these units. If we are just going to isolate people and put labels on them, they will behave according to the label; they live up to the label. But many times in order to make the person behave differently you might need to show them that there are others who have different behaviors and maybe even as bizarre and as different as theirs. For the violent kid, you might also need to show him that there is a person who can be even more violent.

V: This is something that we did at Andros.

B: Yes. There is a person who can be even more violent. There are people who are so much more violent that it could even shock, or there are people who even much more bizarre in their own behavior, and the same impact you might receive by having some of the kids who are in the beginning of negotiating with violence, or entertaining violence, and you bring them to a violent place where there are many "heavies" and this shocks them into reality in terms of not wanting to be in this situation.

V: On that basis, are you an advocate of using therapeutic agents who have in fact have done time in prison, or who in fact have had criminal careers?

B: Definitely. I advocate for that, but I would be very selective. I would want definitely to see whether the person's completely stable in his new behavior. Let's say if it's somebody that has been violent and now he's not violent, but he's really not stable in this new behavior and just being around violent kids he might need to compete with them and to show off and to be even more violent than ever, or he might need all kind of gimmicks, which is reverting back to his own thing, which is to be a model for them. The other criteria I have is that I would want somebody that is going to *learn* in the process of working with kids, and is going to *grow* in it. I mean let's say that if I, as a new staff, who had some past experience in working with kids, I'm even helping myself more and more because I'm getting more and more convinced that being anticriminal and antiviolent is better. Those people who grow, those with past criminal records who grow in this process are usually people who exhibit the "mirror effect" as I call it; they see their own past behavior in these kids, and this will help them to control these behaviors more in themselves. Just by helping kids. By helping the kid overcome some of his own problems, they are essentially helping themselves further in the process of growth.

V: So you make a very important point. Whereas there is universal agreement with your initial point which is that you must screen staff more selectively than is currently done, there has been a current liberal trend to simply hire the so-called ex-offender.

B: That's enough. That makes him, if he's an ex-offender, that's enough to be hired, or that's enough for him to hired, but that's not true—

V: And of course the same highly selective criteria have to be applied.

B: Definitely.

V: Do you see in the future of juvenile corrections—I'm going to ask you now for a prediction—do you see it becoming more enlightened or more repressive?

B: I really think that it is going to be more enlightened. I don't see it reverting back to being more repressive. I feel that some of the cry for toughness with the kids, and so on and so forth could be a challenge to the professionals to come up with something better. Which is not giving all the same old jargon which is you cure everybody with love and acceptance and so on and so forth. It's a challenge to come up with more constructive kind of programming and programs for kids, and if we are tough enough we will be able to really find more solutions for kids, and I see many more people with brains getting into our profession.

V: So it's a viable task for our profession, it's a fair task for our profession?

B: Yes. And I don't think there have been many good thinkers or workers in the field of corrections, especially juvenile corrections, in the past. It has either been some theoritician who through some jargon or something, or some people in the field who have never been able to theorize, and I see hope coming from people who have both ability to theorize and as well as working constantly in the field. By the way I didn't feel I had anything to say as long as I didn't have programs of my own. It makes me real, I know what I'm not talking about, I'm talking about kids, I'm talking about real people that I'm seeing here, or working with, that makes things more real.

V: Let me ask you this then. In terms of making things more real and having the profession respond, one of the advantages that you do have now that you did not enjoy before is you're not locked into a civil service continuum. You talked extensively about criteria you would use to hire staff. Obviously you do not have to take everyone who passed the state test. Obviously you can fire somebody who does not meet your standards. Do you see the future in juvenile corrections being more in the area of private contracting for services?

B: Definitely. I agree with you. That's the future. However, I can conceive also that private vendors can develop also the same kind of inflexibility, this disease of the blood, this arterial sclerosis, that the state has. I can imagine that they can develop all kind of bureaucratic systems in this field, and therefore they should be changed. I see this as a continuing change. They should be constantly prodded. Especially in the field of human services. Constant change. But the new system of private vendors allows that. Why couldn't we have good competition to work with kids?

V: The problem with competition as I see it is this, and I'd like your response: The profession is largely infected with the proposal-writing mentality. You develop a system and this system has produced grants of a quarter-million dollars for you. There is a reluctance to change that system for fear of tampering with your funding source.

B: Well, you see, the monitoring and evaluation should come from the state or from whoever is giving you the money.

V: But if the monitoring and evaluation comes from the state which has of course at the bottom line the self-interest in defeating the private vendors—

B: They don't *completely* have this desire of defeating because despite the fact that they are not running the show, they take either credit for it or they will be held liable, for it too, so they are in many ways wed to these programs. I don't fully believe that the state should be the only one who will go on and try to get money for us. I can conceive of people in youth services or mental health being comfortable with their paycheck, because they are monitoring staff, and they wouldn't fight for the private vendors to get more money to do more programs. That's basically the problem that I conceive. I don't think that will try to destroy the system. However, I would say that the private vendors should be also not stick all their hopes in the state. They should also fight their own battles. Open the system, find multiple ways of funding, they have to be flexible.

V: Isn't it a fact that many private vendors, and the state too, treat LEAA money as play money? By this I mean simply that the level of performance required is not very high. Because the state itself is treating federal money as not coming out of its own pocket. In other words I see no future for this profession until the private vendors are paid directly from the state from the state budget, with a budget line, for such services.

B: Bravo.

V: We're living in Fantasyland now. When you write a proposal to some omnipotent federal agency which gives you a half a million dollars to do a program that the state thinks so little of that it does not even institutionalize that program into its own budget.

B: Yes.

V: See, before I can believe there is a commitment to specialized care for children, by a state, I want to see the state put its own money up. To put federal money up, what does that say?

B: Well, you're right. The problem like in many other bureaucratic institutions that you have a variety of interest groups, a variety of departments, and political systems that you have to contend with. Let's say a very good person sitting on the state level who is fighting for delinquent kids, trying to get more money, the question is what's happening in the economy recently and what's happening on the level of the state legislature, and what's happening with the governor and what's happening with everybody?

V: To make a point. Do juveniles have their own lobbyist?

B: They don't. And I don't think they will ever have. I wish they could. However, the new vendor system for the private institution systems is much better in the sense that we have many, many more people lobbying for the kids, than we had in the past system.

V: Partly based on the desire to raise funds, right?

B: Partly based on the desire to raise funds. Let's say for example, let's take our program. If we are putting eighteen kids in foster homes, we have already gone to about fifty or hundred families who either in some way or another had worked with some of the kids. They had, many of them have had good positive experiences, they know what we are talking about, they know what behavior problems are, what a delinquent kid is, they know that he's not a terribly bad person. And also we have all kinds of people who are volunteers and are interested people.

V: So you've created a constituency that would respond, in effect, to a lobbying effort.

B: Yes. And creating in many ways, inadvertently, much more support. And I imagine many many, many programs, every program that has some kind of contract with DYS has this type of reverberation effect. There are people much more educated to the needs of kids, and to DYS, much more so now than they were five or six years ago, when kids were in institutions, out of sight and out of mind. And there is much more exposure, lobbying, and knowing the kids, and people are responding; and there is a constituency, if you want to call it that, much more so than it was in the past, but it's in the beginning stages. Many more university people have been involved, many more students have been involved, before that, up to six years ago, if you are a student, and if you are interested in that, you have to travel about an hour and a half to get to an institution to see a kid, to go to Roslindale, go through this harrassing experience, but right now you can see a kid, and there have been many, many programs in which you can take a kid. I mean we had about twenty students from Salem State College who had been involved with us and who will be with kids, taking kids on a trip, driving them somewhere, working effectively with kids, being conned by kids and learning from that. So it has a ripple effect. And many, many people are looking at themselves seeing themselves as becoming professionals in this field of working with kids. That's good.

V: The final question I want to ask you is this, and it's almost a purely a kind of fiscal question, don't you feel that the LEAA grants and other forms of grants should be written for longer periods of time? Don't you think they should be written for even ten-year periods? Of course with the possibility of cancellation for nonperformance. But to have to write a proposal each and every year—

B: The same thing with the state. With the state we have yearly contracts. Of course you know that the contracts can be expanded, but it makes you in the position of almost like being a little child who has to perform rather than having to stand on your feet and believe in what you want to do with the program. There are two problems, two concerns I have there. (a) That it is not on a long term basis and (b) it's so inflexible. You have to follow "line items." And you can spend money only in a certain category and then you have to get into a big hassle if you want to change categories. It can destroy even your ability to develop a system of staff training and recognition in terms of salary. You have to give the salary exactly the way you wrote it. And you can't here develop a step system. And therefore you almost have to put a high salary that to insure yourself that you are going to get the right person, but if you got a person with good potential, you can't put him on lower salary because immediately they will grab the difference and you are left without it. It is very inflexible. That's one area. The other area, is really to deal with kids, with human services you have to have so-called flexible funding, flexible funds so you can take the ten dollars to buy this and this if that's necessary, if that's important to the kids' self-image. And you have to go through a variety of things. Of course we are a private agency. We have much more flexibility because I can always maybe get some private donation to supplement us.

V: But there is an investment in time to get that private donation is there not?

B: Investment of time and also you have to sing and dance and destroy some idea that you are working for. By that [I mean] you have to involve so many people in just the process of decision making and get through a variety of kind of issues.

V: In the final analysis then, although you're optimistic, and although you feel that the future definitely lies with the private vendor, and the private contractor, it would be fair to say that you think progress is being impeded by the system of doing business that we have now, in terms of funding.

B: Definitely. Definitely impeded, yes.

**Interview between Andrew Vachss (V) and
Nicholas Pileggi (P), on April 20, 1978**

Nicholas Pileggi is a journalist and author who has been writing about the
criminal justice system since 1956, when he was first hired as a police reporter
by the Associated Press in New York City. He covered police headquarters,
crime, corruption, labor, organized crime, the courts, DAs, corrections, and the
judiciary for the AP in New York for twelve years.

Since 1968 he has been a contributing editor at *New York Magazine* and has
written for numerous publications including the *New York Times Book Review*,
the *New York Times Magazine, Esquire, Life*, the *Saturday Evening Post*, and
McCalls.

V: Nick, you spent quite a number of years, decades in fact, on the police beat
in New York City. You've kind of had your finger on the pulse of New
York in terms of the public's response to crime and violence. What's the
current feeling of the average person in this city towards juvenile crime and
juvenile violence?

P: I think that juvenile crime seems to disturb people more than just about any
other kind of crime. When I talk about juvenile crimes I'm talking about
particularly gruesome attacks, especially on older people, by kids who are
under an age where they are really felt by the adults to be made to pay for
their acts. And that would be the kick-in burglars, the muggers, the
senseless kind of violence that goes along with snatching a seventy-four-year-
old woman's pocketbook. And the feeling among people is there seems to
be a greater visceral anger about this kind of crime than there is about
organized crime, then there is about crooked politicians, white-collar
crime—all of the other illegalities you deal with. You don't seem to trigger
in people the outrage in any of the other crimes that you do in the violent
juvenile offender.

V: What's the public perception of what happens to a violent juvenile criminal?

P: From the people you talk to when you're working on stories in that area
they all laugh at you. They say all those kids they all get away, nobody
bothers them. And it always goes back to people who have personal
problems: We have two kids in our neighborhood, we have three kids in our
building, we have the kids upstairs in the project they've been mugging
people, they've mugged my grandmother—they wind up going home, they
go out and their mothers go and get them and they come home. I mean
they're fully aware of the fact, or feel that they're aware of the fact, that
there is no punishment or rehabilitation or anything for these kids.

V: Is that the general perception too?

P: As far as the general public is concerned, they never even heard of them. The public is not aware of Goshen or the difference between Goshen and Spofford, they have no idea of half-way houses, in-between houses, summer camps, family farms, and all of those places that DFY [New York State's juvenile corrections agency] has available for rehabilitation of some of these troubled kids. People are not aware of those generally.

V: How about people being aware of whether or not DFY is functioning? Do people think DFY is doing the job?

P: Are you talking about real people or are you talking about people in the system? Real people, people in the street, never heard of DFY. I mean, God, DFY, for all they know it's some kind of neutron bomb.

V: Is it true that the general public, the average guy in the street, thinks that being a juvenile is just a license to commit a crime and get away with it?

P: I think yeah. I think the general perception is that there are kids who take advantage of that situation and the more sophisticated people on the outside are not only aware of the kids taking advantage of that situation but since they develop a pattern of fulfilling their needs by these kinds of violent and illegal means, they see these sixteen-, or fifteen- or fourteen-year-old kids down an avenue that's going to keep them doing that when they're eighteen and nineteen, they'll be sticking up liquor stores and eventually killing somebody, getting killed themselves. Nobody will know. It will be irrelevant, the fact that a guy gets killed.

V: What's the difference between the public attitude towards juvenile crime now and in the fifties when we had an absolute scourge of gang wars in the city?

P: Well what I did when I was doing pieces in this area, I went back and I read all the newspapers from the fifties and it's fascinating. It's as though the papers were the same. There was more of a gang orientation at the time. The papers quite often played the stories down to some degree. It didn't get the kind of play it gets today. And also the kids themselves seemed—the acts were not as bizarrely described as they are today. But if you read between the lines you can guess that some of the more bizarre acts were committed then as they probably were in the Roman times. I mean that's just man's inhuman nature.

V: What about somebody telling you in a bar that in the fifties kids fought other kids, in the seventies they're attacking older people. Do you think that's valid?

P: Well in going through the stories in the *Times*, in the *Post*, in the *News*, or the *Telegram* or the *Journal American*, I was not as struck by the number of violent acts on old people. I mean, that may be new. There were incidents where older people were mugged. But two things happened. It didn't get the kind of play it does today, and at the same time you were not as aware of a whole criminal social pattern of activity.

V: How do you respond to this? There's a theory that in the fifties most of the perpetrators of juvenile crime had organized crime aspirations, that there was a place for them if they distinguished themselves correctly as juveniles. But that today's juveniles have no such aspirations and in fact organized crime is not really open to them.

P: Well in the fifties there was very little written about organized crime in the papers, and almost nobody recognized that it existed. The FBI at that time had not yet recognized that it existed, and you got judges like Nathan Sobel saying that there is no such thing as organized crime in Brooklyn. He says that right in the middle of Murder Incorporated. So there was no pattern of organized crime in the sense of big-shot hoodlums; and labor racketeering was another world. I mean these kids could just as soon try to become board members at Chase Manhattan as become members of the mob, the major mobs. One of the things that was fascinating during the period was the people and the kids themselves were involved much more in gang activities and it was the warring over turf that was very important. You've got to remember, there was still the beginning of the southern migration into New York City. Boundaries had not been defined, the whole Bedford-Stuyvesant, Navy Street, operation was still very fluid. Bed-Sty was not a wholly black area at the time. And you had white gangs in Navy Street, you had the Socialistic Dukes of Bed-Sty, you had the Robins—and playgrounds were still being fought over on a block to block basis. And so a lot of the adolescent activity was fought over that kind of stuff and maybe to that degree there was an emphasis away from the simple stick-up mentality that we have today.

V: There's more individual acting out today you think?

P: I would guess—what's happened is that there's no money, everything is dried up in the street. And those kids were violent and they were bad, and they'd stick up people. I remember when I went to elementary school a guy got electrocuted. I mean everybody knew somebody who was going to the electric chair or had already been.

V: You don't read about that at all. I mean you don't read about a Tarzan Santana, or Cape Man, or anything like that right?

P: No.

V: We don't read about a heavy significant penalty being visited on gang kids?

P: No, no longer today, no, there's none. There was in those days. But it didn't make any difference.

V: It didn't seem to, did it?

P: No, the guys who always went to the chair are the guys who wound up like [name deleted]. They were always slightly oafish anyway. I mean they were never the worst guys in the area. They were the ones who were slightly retarded, just a little slow.

V: Okay, now your story about George Adorno [see chapter 1, note 10] probably had the greatest impact on public perception of this kind of situation of any other piece that's been written in the last several years. Do you think George Adorno is some kind of aberrant, genetic mistake, or do you think there's others like George Adorno?

P: I would place George in the extreme 5 percent of those potentially dangerous homicidal kids. I mean a guy who has been convicted of very calmly pulling out a gun and shooting somebody and not having too much remorse about it or even thinking about it, a half-hour after killing a cab driver he was dancing in Mr. Soul's. I don't think he's typical. I think most of the kids up there who I talked to who knew him were afraid of him.

V: Do you think he's a completely isolated phenomenon? Do you think there's other guys like him?

P: Oh, I think there's a lot of guys probably like him. You pick a city with so many millions of people in it. But you can't think of him as typical in any way or even a little typical because he was usually isolated even by his peers. Nobody wanted to get near him. Even the kind of cuckoo motorcycle gangs up there, they'd come walking down the street, and these are bad guys, guys with earrings and chains around their knee caps and stuff, they'd come walking down the street and they'd see George Adorno, they'd go to the other side of the street. They didn't want to tangle with him because they would think of him as totally irrational. His sister told me a story: she was saying that she was very proud of the fact that she had gotten to be eighteen years old and she was still a virgin. And she claimed that she was one of the only girls in her whole area who was. Because it is quite accepted, she says, up in 111th Street and that area, that a girl cannot get past puberty without getting raped. Somebody grabs her and drags her into a building, there's no recourse, the cops do not really make a serious effort to find out who it was. There is no such crime as rape of adolescent girls in that kind of ghetto community. It's tragic but it's true. She hadn't been, and was very proud of the fact, that she hadn't been because she was George's sister. And she told a story about once walking down the street, usually George met her at the subway so he could escort her home so nobody would mess with her. One day she was walking down the street and a guy grabbed her and started to shove her into one of the abandoned buildings and another guy came running over to him and said "You're crazy, that's Atta's sister, that's Atta's sister" (Atta was his nickname) and the guy just froze. He was in terror, that struck him when he realized that he had been manhandling Atta's sister, he just took off and ran. And it gave her great pride in a way in the fact that she had a brother who was such a terrifying creature up there.

V: Is part of the terror that George was able to induce in other people based on the fact that he seemed to have no perception of consequences whatsoever for his own acts?

P: I think that's part of it. I mean he was free. Since he had no perception of consequences he was totally free to do anything he wanted to. There's this confession that he made (although there may be questions about it) but you can hear a boy in his own voice, a nice little, soft little voice, talking about being on the roof and seeing this guy walking across the street. The fellow who was standing next to him said "he owes me," and George simply took a rifle and put one right through the guy's head. And you can hear George describing that with calmness, and then George grabbed the rifle and went down the stairs to unload the rifle to give it to somebody's sister. And he said "I sprained my ankle going down the stairs." And his whole concern, his whole perception of life was upon his ankle. I mean the fact that just two seconds earlier he had described pulling a trigger and killing a guy on the street; that was totally irrelevant. What was really bothering George was the fact that he had kind of pulled his ankle a little bit and he had to hippity-hop all the way to the girl's house.

V: You pointed out once that George went into a homicidal rage at the thought of anybody stealing from his family?

P: Yes.

V: And yet George stole from everybody?

P: Yeah, but that was his family. And it was not only George, it was all of those kids I talked to. They cannot conceive of anybody stealing from them, it really gets them angry and they do not put the two things together. They do not put together somebody's going to steal from you like you're stealing from them. That's not the same. It's as though you're discussing two entirely different concepts, two different worlds.

V: Let me ask you something about the juvenile court or family court, as we know it, in New York as it relates to George Adorno. Would you say that George gave off any warning flags before he was brought in for the homicides?

P: Oh, I think there were any number of warning flags. There was just a series of warning flags. But how would you be able to perceive them? These are the prehomicidal warning flags, how would you be able to distinguish between George's warning flags and maybe my warning flags. If I was a bad kid raised right next door to George, we would probably both be giving off terrible warning signals.

V: But we know them in the system right?

P: Yeah, sure. But the system is incapable of discerning who they are. They are evaluated by a series of people from psychiatrists to parole officers. There are certain quotas, although they will never acknowledge it, but these probation officers—you have to prosecute cases. You're getting paid. You've got to process cases; you cannot spend three days trying to figure out exactly how George works. I mean it is part of the assembly line of the civil service system. And although everybody does as good a job as they can, it's obviously not good enough to deal with the problem. Then you get into the deeper psychiatric area and you find out whether or not indeed psychiatrists can really deal with these kids. The second part of that question is that the psychiatrists that the City can afford are not necessarily those men in the forefront of the system to begin with, and quite often they are the kinds of psychiatrists who find it difficult to match that salary in the outside market because of language problems, cultural problems; they come from other worlds. So you wind up with, let's say a refugee Viennese psychiatrist who's approaching age seventy, being paid something like, maybe $30,000 a year, $25,000 a year on a part-time basis to analyze what is going on in the head of a fifteen-year-old junk-addict kid, whose mother is a hooker and who's never seen her and who's never seen his father. I mean, the psychiatrist doesn't even know the language the kid is talking about and the kid has no idea who Freud is. Freudian problems? This is not Vienna in the first third of the century. And so the whole psychiatric process that the City has to deal with these kids I think is pretty faulty.

V: Okay, what if I were to tell you a scenario went something like this in the Adorno case. The Judge says the confession is no-good, Corporation Counsel says "that's our case." Would that surprise you? Knowing that they had this kid for days and he was talking to them? Would it surprise you if I told you that scenario?

P: No, nothing would surprise me.

V: Of course, I understand that. Let me ask you this. You were in Supreme Court when George was sentenced. He got 15 to life. Do you think George's age was a factor?

P: I think he [the judge] had a rationale. At that time it was enough of a rationale that it did not disturb me in the sense that it was—what the heck—George was now something like nineteen or so—he would, if he got out, he wouldn't get out for fifteen. I think that part of the rationale may have been the fact that he would probably be pretty much burned out by then anyway.

V: Do you believe that?

P: I don't know. My personal feeling is that I don't know what kind of time George is going to do. I mean I don't know whether fifteen or five or ten is going to be—I don't know whether George will make 3. He's not a big guy. George is a tough kid, but he's short, he's a wiry, tough, good fighter. But if he's going to go up to a place like Attica or a real prison with real bad guys and he keeps the sort of tough quality to him, he's not gonna have access to a gun.

V: No, but they do make shanks up there.

P: Yeah, they make shanks and so does everybody else and he's going to be in with very bad guys. He may psychologically be incapable of making the fifteen, that's what I'm thinking.

V: But I've got guys in my files who got seventeen, eighteen, nineteen to life for *attempted* murder.

P: Yeah, it's amazing. There was another factor. I think it also had to do with another case—I think it had to do also with his age. There was a question as to whether he was really under age when that first thing went down. He may have used his brother Miguel's birth certificate.

V: I know Judge Roberts did say that. That he had reason to believe that George was in fact sixteen or better when he was actually tried in the family court.

P: Yes. And yet they could never really work that out. They tried to go through the schools to find out how old he is but the schools do not require birth certificates and people who come in and say this is my child, and this is his age, especially children who might be born or parents who were born out of the country, say in Puerto Rico, in a small town in Puerto Rico, they do not have the same kind of multi-xerox copies of birth certificates. You know it might be on a small piece of paper or in the family bible.

V: Now let me just ask you this to wrap it up. We're going to talk about solutions just for a brief period. What's the solution to this? These are the ones that have been proposed. I'd like to have your comments. Both your personal comments and those comments you think of the man in the street. The first solution is we're going to drop the age so that thirteen or fourteen year olds can go to state prison if they commit certain crimes. The second solution is that we're going to provide a system whereby each child will be individually evaluated and those kids that don't pass the evaluation will then be tried in the adult system. Okay. The third solution is to eliminate the family court entirely. Just to do away with it we'll have a "crime equals time" kind of set-up. And the only kids who will be handled in family court will be dependent and neglected kids. The final solution is our current solution which is a designated felony act, which is certain kids, certain classes of felonies, will do certain time in certain places. Do you think any of them have any viability?

P: I think the only thing that has viability is the whole series of combinations of a number of those things, plus all sorts of things that they haven't even dealt with. I think first there has to be a tremendous separation when possible, between violent acting kids and kids who are in need of supervision but are actually the victims rather than the victimizers. And that's at least I would say three quarters of all the kids in DFY facilities are those types of kids. They're the victims; not the predators. Of the really troubled kids, now these are the kids who might start as PINS [Persons in Need of Supervision] but go on to be really bad kids, they are not a lot of kids. That's what's so fascinating. We're dealing with maybe at any given time frame, a few dozen maybe at the tops a hundred kids. The thing is that some of these kids have got two hundred appearances in family court before they're sixteen. This is actual appearances and lots of times they're kicked in the ass and sent away by a cop, the times that they get caught is like 143 times for this one—I don't think the answer is to take a fourteen-year-old- or fifteen-year-old-bad-acting kid like that and send him into Attica. First he would just be totally brutalized and come out, (because eventually he's going to come out) and he'll come out and be so much worse than anything you put away that you wouldn't know what to do with him. So I think as long as they are young and there is some hope a really serious program has to be set up. Not one of these things that's set up today or even remotely like DFY's evaluation. There is no evaluation of who these kids are in DFY. The kind of guards (and that's essentially what they are, even though they're referred to differently), they can't figure out who these kids are. They don't know who the kids are. You go upstate in Goshen where you've got a lot of nice men, they're hard-working guys, they live in the area, they're not very well-paid, they're almost all white, they come from a basic Slavic background, they're not super-educated men. Their whole concept of decorum, social values, etc. are quite different than the kinds of kids who go up there to be evaluated by them. And the kids are savvy, they know how to con the guys, and the guys are looking to get home anyway, they've got three kids of their own, they've got to fix the television antennae, so as long as he don't make any trouble he'll be out of here in three weeks. He's home on his weekend leaves.

V: Do you think a program that was specially designed for the George Adornos that holds them a minimum of eighteen months, two to three years, that worked only with those kids and there was no mix in the institution, would have any chance of impacting on his life-style?

P: I think it might, especially if it was very carefully done and very intelligently handled. All of these kids, they're fascinating. When you talk to them, kids that mug people when you're one-on-one with them and you're not after them for anything—they have a little bit of pride. In fact, a number of them have a lot of pride. And they're ashamed of things like not being able to read. Almost none of them can read. I'm not going to say that because kids can't read they are criminals, because a lot of our best readers are the biggest crooks. A lot of those Watergate types, etc. But we're dealing with violent kids. And violent kids have a tremendous sense of their own worth. I mean they don't want anybody to have a bad attitude about them. They want to have class. They want to move in the street. It's one of the reasons why they're involved in all that stuff. Because it gives them some distinction on the block. And any set-up, any structured society, or prison or whatever you want to call it, rehabilitation, that was able to give them some tools with which to assert that pride along lawful means would be valuable. And I think there are all kinds of triggers in these kids that can be pulled, that could very well take them away from that kind of a street life. Especially if there was real after-care services for them. Somebody really watching over them.

V: Do you think, the final question, that it's worth the investment? Assuming we could set up such a program and say it cost $50,000-$60,000 per kid per year.

P: Well, God, it costs you almost that amount now. But what would happen of course, it would take oh, at least a minimum of seven to ten years to really get these operational, by the time things are planned. And by that time the age curve would probably have passed. So the population thing that has created a lot of this situation, according to some people, will have passed and the real concern will be about senior citizens who are going around mugging people. And the kids will have come in a dip in the population curve and there might not be a need for this kind of a facility.

V: So you say if we're going to have this and it's going to work, it has to be done yesterday?

P: Yes. I would think so. I mean certainly according to the cab drivers that George Adorno killed, it should have been done four days ago, four years ago.

V: Do you think that same population would rather have the death penalty than new institutions?

P: What population are you talking about?

V: The guy in the street, the guy who drives a cab?

P: I think a lot of them—I think there's a lot of rhetoric about the death penalty. Yeah, the death penalty, you know there's a lot of the people who are screaming about death penalties and yelling about them are also people who are very committed to the right to life. So there's an interesting ambivalence in a lot of those people's hearts. Whether they really do want to take somebody's life, whether they're unborn or just poorly born.

**Interview between Andrew Vachss (V) and
"J" (J), on October 27, 1976**

"J" first ran into trouble with the law at age thirteen and was put on probation. His first sentence to a juvenile training school began a criminal career that resulted in numerous incarcerations as an adult on charges involving robberies, weapons possessions, and assaults.

A gifted legal scholar, talented musician, and skilled craftsman, "J" has hurt himself through his quick temper far more than any of his victims. He now supports himself in his own business.

V: "J", how old were you when you first made some negative contact with the criminal justice system?

J: About thirteen.

V: Prior to that there had been no problems?

J: No, I didn't have any problems. The only problem I had was home.

V: Were you in school at age thirteen?

J: Oh yeah.

V: How old were you when you were first incarcerated?

J: Sixteen.

V: And what was the charge?

J: Atrocious assault and battery and violation of probation.

V: So you were on probation for a previous charge?

J: Yes, I was.

V: And that charge was?

J: Larceny of a motor vehicle.

V: How old were you then?

J: That was when I was thirteen.

V: You were on probation three years without incident?

J: I had minor incidents, brushes with the law. That's like I said when I first got in trouble I just continued.

V: Okay. When you were incarcerated at age sixteen were you treated as a juvenile or as an adult?

J: As a juvenile.

V: And you were sent where?

J: Annandale. I did a year and a half and then I was released.

V: What happened after you were released?

J: I got busted again and went to Bordentown.

V: Is Bordentown a juvenile institution?

J: It could be considered juvenile, but they had men there at the time also.

V: Was it a youthful offender sentence?

J: Yeah.

V: What was the charge that time?

J: Atrocious assault and battery and breaking and entering.

V: When you were released from Bordentown, what then?

J: I was trying to make up for lost time, and I got busted for atrocious assault and battery with intent to kill, kidnapping and armed robbery. I was sent to Trenton. I stayed in Trenton for a year and then spent the balance of time at Rahway.

V: And how many years was that?

J: I spent six years.

V: Before you went to the juvenile institution, before you were incarcerated for the very first time, what had you planned to do with your life? Did you have any, at age thirteen, career goals?

J: No, not really. I didn't have anything. I had just gotten married when I was fifteen, and I had problems with the in-laws.

V: So you had problems at home and problems with in-laws.

J: Right.

V: Were the people at the school aware of these problems? At the school you attended?

J: No. There was not anything really. They had schooling more or less, or the job that you were supposed to have done. I was doing electrical work there and I had no intention of doing it when I got out.

V: What about inside the institution, did anybody talk to you about the problems that you had had with the family?

J: No. Never.

V: Can you describe for me briefly what institutional life was like? The first time you went down.

J: Yeah, it was sort of scary. There was a bunch of guys there. There was older guys, and there was all kind of stories you heard when you first went in. But after a while you adjust to the life and follow along with the pattern.

V: You adjusted to the life.

J: I adjusted to the life.

V: Is everybody adjusted to the life?

J: Oh, no. You can't. You got too many people that, the way I feel, shouldn't even be in the place.

V: Did you feel you should be in the place?

J: At the time, no. I didn't.

V: Was your ability to adjust to life inside the institution in any way predicated on your own physical competence?

J: No I don't think so because I was kind of small at the time. I guess it was the will to survive.

V: What did you have to do to survive in there?

J: Well, you had to hold your own more or less. You couldn't take all this—when you're in a cottage—this is Annandale—when you're in a cottage, you've got your dukes, more or less their cliques, their followers and everything else, and if you didn't go along with what they had going you always got an ass whipping, and I got a couple of them and that was it. I wasn't going to take anymore.

V: What did you do? Just personally retaliate?

J: Of course. I had to. I started fighting. And after that, they found out that they couldn't come up to me and tell me "Well kiss my ass," because I'd fight back ⌐.

V: And tha. ⌐nough to let you do your own time in peace there?

J: Oh yeah. After that. I mean you find a lot of guys though that couldn't hold their own. And when you can't hold your own, you do what they tell you to do. Just like these fine looking kids that used to walk around there.

V: Did the authority, the administration, the guards, social work personnel, did they all know what was going on?

J: Well you had to know what was going on. Especially if you were in a cottage because they had steady cottage officers, and very few times you would get a relief, and if they didn't know what was going on, then they're dumber than some of these people that they say are dumb.

V: Did they intervene in any way?

J: In physical violence, yes.

V: You mean if the violence was actually happening, they'd step in?

J: Right. That was it.

V: Were you in a dormitory kind of situation?

J: No, I was in a cell. I was always in a cell.

V: By yourself.

J: By myself.

V: Was that the usual way things were done there?

J: No, they had dormitory cottages also.

V: Well how did they decide who was in a dormitory and who was in a cottage?

J: Classification committee.

V: Did you see the classification committee?

J: Oh yeah.

V: And what kinds of questions did they ask you?

J: That's kind of far back. I don't even remember. They asked me what type of work I did before, and I told them, and they put me in the electric shop anyway. And I was afraid of electricity.

V: You were married at the time?

J: Yeah.

V: Was your wife able to visit you?

J: Oh yeah. She did. And the baby, she'd visited me for the first four months and that was it.

V: And then what happened?

J: I didn't hear from her no more.

V: Did the institution personnel ever attempt to work with your wife and help your wife adjust to the fact that you were incarcerated?

J: Never.

V: When you left Annandale, had your attitude in any way changed from the time before you went in?

J: Yeah. Like I said, I wasn't much of a fighter or anything else before I went in, but when I got out, I knew I could beat the world. Plus when I got there also, the guys that have never been there used to like look up toward me even though I was smaller, because I had the experience now. I was one of these bad asses that come out of a jail.

V: So that didn't discourage you in any way from criminal activity?

J: No, no. In fact it enhanced my thinking.

V: Did you learn any new criminal techniques while you were in the institution?

J: Of course.

V: Would you describe yourself as a relatively unsophisticated criminal before you went to Annandale?

J: I didn't consider myself a criminal before I went to Annandale. I never thought of really ripping people off like that. Whatever I did used to be petty except for the fighting. Although I did go there for fighting, it was more or less in self-defense, because the guy I did fight was bigger than I was. But after I got out, it was always fighting, and it was always when somebody would assert authority at me, I'd rebel and I'd go right back to the same attitude I had when I was in the joint.

V: When you left Annandale, did you feel yourself in any way better prepared to cope with the problems that you had before you went in?

J: No. If you're talking about my family problems or anything, no. There was nothing there.

V: Was there any education at Annandale? Was there a school?

J: Yes, I guess you could say that it was a school. They had a something like vocational training there. But it was really minor.

V: You returned to Bordentown about a year and a half two years later, for a similar kind of offense, another assaultive offense?

J: Right.

V: Was it a more serious assault?

J: No, not really, it was the same thing. Self-defense at the time it was.

V: You didn't at anytime see a connection between your own attitude and the fact that you were constantly involved in fights?

J: I didn't pay no attention to it. Like I said, I thought that I was the bad ass. Or I had a reputation and I had to continue with that reputation at that time. I had to prove something to everybody else, including my family. Because I always get a negative attitude from my entire family. I was more or less the black sheep. I had a run-in with my uncle one time, it was the same thing, it was "Oh you're blackening up the [family] name, you know, nobody's ever been in trouble except you, why you doing this, why you doing that?" But it wasn't to sit down, "Well, what's the problem? How come? Why did you do it?" I never got that.

V: Did you have any relationships while you were in either Annandale or Bordentown with any staff members, where you would speak with them about your problems?

J: In Bordentown, yeah, there was—I forget what the doctor's name was. But they come up with these—to me I thought they were off the wall questions, some of them—like one of them was "Did you ever have intercourse with your mother?" which of course kind of gets you mad, then after that anytime they come up with something— I used to come up with a reverse answer and they finally got to the point that they put down that I wanted to kill my father, which maybe in the back of my mind was true, but I doubt it. I never did like him. I didn't get along with him, not until after he died anyway, or just before he died, but there was always a negative attitude like I said between my family and myself. And that extended into the reformatories and the prisons.

V: Subsequent events while you were at Rahway proved that you in fact had an extremely high IQ and you were able to make rather extraordinary educational accomplishments. Did you realize while you were in the juvenile institutions that you were in fact intellectually gifted?

J: No I didn't.

V: Did anybody tell you that you had potential to achieve?

J: No.

V: What was your self-concept at the time? How did you see yourself? What did you think of J then?

J: What did I think of myself? I didn't think of nothing of myself. Like I said, I really didn't care. I didn't give a damn. I didn't care for the people around me and I didn't care for the people outside.

V: When you left the institution was the hostility toward the larger society or towards specific individuals?

J: Toward society in general.

V: Did you learn that in the institution or did you have it before you got there?

J: No I didn't have it before I got there but I sure and the hell had it when I come out.

V: When did you start the weightlifting program?

J: In Bordentown.

V: What was the motivation for that at the time?

J: Release hostilities. Instead of fighting I figured I'd take it out on the iron pile.

V: Did that work?

J: Sometimes. Not all the time.

V: You saw a lot of different kinds of juveniles when you were locked up right?

J: Yeah.

V: All different types?

J: Oh yeah.

V: You said before that you felt some kids did not belong there. Can you describe more fully the type of kid that did not belong there?

J: Sure. There were kids there—now this is going back to Annandale again—there was kids there because they were playing hookey from school and their parents said they didn't have any control over the kids so they threw them in Annandale for a period of time.

V: How did these kids make out in Annandale?

J: Nine times out of ten, they picked up the same attitude I did. Other ones, they became the little girls of the joint.

V: You said at first you were frightened at being in the joint, right? By the time you left were you still frightened?

J: Oh, no. I knew I could do time anywhere.

V: So you weren't worried about going back?

J: No, I wasn't worried about going back.

V: Did you expect that you might be going back?

J: No I didn't but I did.

V: There was no deterrent as far as you could see? You didn't say to yourself "I'm going to make sure I do right so I don't end up back here?"

J: No, for what? And as I said after you got used to the joint it was a picnic. Really it is.

V: For certain people.

J: For certain people. For other people it's pure hell. You read your suicide rate. While I was there they had a guy hang himself.

V: You never thought about hanging yourself?

J: No.

V: Because you can survive there, right?

J: No, I don't like being hurt.

V: And you saw suicide as a form of hurting yourself?

J: That's right.

V: When you eventually as an older person got involved in armed robberies and stickups, what was the motivation then? Was it purely economic, was it partly hostility and economics?

J: It was a combination. It was the easiest way to get money and I was still getting back at the people.

V: When you say it was the easiest way to get money, isn't it a fact that after a while you began to realize you were a pretty intelligent human being?

J: Yeah, but you're asking me about then. Then my motivation was the easy way to get money and I'm still getting back, like I said.

V: What did you want the money for?

J: Anything I wanted to get.

V: So you were really weren't prepared to spend a lot of time getting the things that you wanted.

J: No.

V: You talked about making up for lost time.

J: Right. I felt, like I said, I felt that somebody owed me a living. And I was getting that living, and that was the easiest way possible.

V: Even though the risks were much higher.

J: I didn't think about the risks.

V: You didn't at all?

J: No.

V: You would probably, in my opinion and in the opinion of others, qualify as a rehabilitated human being. You've got a means to earn a living, you've made educational accomplishments in your life, you have fairly stable relationships with people, you're considered to be a man of your word; when did this take place? When did this change take place and how did it come about?

J: The last six years I spent between Trenton and Rahway. I found out that I couldn't keep on going that way. And I didn't expect to get out in six years. I expected to do more. But through friends and a couple of breaks I got out.

V: Are you saying that Rahway rehabilitated you?

J: No, not Rahway. *I* did. I did with the help of my friends. Because I still had a negative attitude while I was there. And I had—the only thing I had on my mind was revenge. Even though I was still going to school and doing different things to occupy myself. That's all it was, to occupy myself. To keep me from climbing the wall, or to keep from climbing on somebody's frame over there. So I stayed in the cell or whatever I had to do, and I did it. And I thought about what I'd do when I got out. In fact, while I was in quarantine in Trenton, I sat down with my partner, and I started figuring out at twenty-four hours a day at time and half and double time and holidays how much they owed me. And it started coming up into a pretty good price there.

V: And originally you determined to exact that price?

J: I was going to get that price. And I didn't care who fell. There's a saying, and you've probably heard it many a time "I'd hold court in the street."

V: I think that accurately describes your attitude several years ago.

J: I guess it does.

V: So you're saying that the change that took place was almost entirely self-motivated?

J: No, it wasn't self-motivated . . .

V: Well, in terms of you and the prison. You may have gotten help from other people, but you put yourself in a position to (1) get that help and (2) take advantage of that help.

J: Yeah. But, like I said, when I was going to school there I didn't do it because I wanted to get smarter, I did it because it was a means of passing the time.

V: Didn't you have a motivation to do something about your own case?

J: Oh, yeah. I was working to get myself out but that had nothing to do with what I was taking up while I was going to college there. Because I studied the law on my own, but everything else was like I said a means of passing the time. I did enjoy psychology because it helped me know a little bit more about the people that were around me and the people that were supposed to be running the joint.

V: You would agree, I assume, that juvenile institutions are just losers, they're just negative things?

J: Sure they are. They don't work with people.

V: Do you think this is because they're institutions or because of the way the institutions are run?

J: I think it's because of the way the institutions are run. Number one, like I said before, alot of people don't have to be in a place, but they don't take the time before they go to court to find out just what the reason is that they did what they did, or whether there's any extenuating circumstances either the family, or the society, or whether the kid has an inferiority complex or what or feels demeaned all the time, to where you go in, then you have authority always asserted over you, and if they go in because of that, then it really gives them a negative attitude. And there's no way that they work with inmate in there because nine times out of ten, you've got four to five hundred inmates in the joint and they don't have the staff that will take care of that. And even if they do find someone that has a problem, they don't take the time to stay with that guy to find out just why, how come, where, who.

V: So you think that institutions might be indicated for certain juveniles?

J: Oh definitely.

V: Give me an example of the type of juvenile that you would definitely incarcerate.

J: I would say someone that really goes after the violence kick. You would have to do something, because there has to be something wrong, there has to be a reason for him doing. But you can't say, slap on the wrist, and so back out on the street. When I was doing that, like I said, I had something that I had to prove. And if I had to take it out on other people I was going to do it. Well, this is maybe the way some of these people feel, but you have to find out why, what the reason is.

V: Would you agree that if a child under the age of sixteen was involved in a homicide, that it's probably necessary to lock him up?

J: Of course.

V: A rape?

J: Of course.

V: A string of armed robberies?

J: Of course. You have to. If it's armed robbery, there's a potential.

V: So anybody that really is involved in an armed robbery is going in there ready willing and able to do heavy violence if necessary?

J: Anybody that puts a gun in their hand is going to use it sometime, if he keeps it there long enough.

V: Now we've got a joint that contains this type of young man. Are we going to put in that joint a homosexual?

J: How can you?

V: Are we going to put in there a kid who compulsively and constantly steals cars?

J: How can you?

V: What about a kid who's involved in narcotics?

J: There's altogether different crimes. You've got to categorize now. If you put a guy in there that's a potential killer with a person that's going out there and getting their kicks because he's a homo, how are you going to put these two together? The homo might like it and the guy that's doing the armed robberies might like it. But he might get his jollies off trying to rip this guy apart. There's too many different things, there's too many different crimes, and I can't see building a joint for each crime, but after a while, it's going to come down to that sooner or later. Maybe not in our time but it will. Because they figure that prison offers an education now. It does, it always did though. It still offers an education whether they got school teachers there or not because every inmate in there is a school teacher. One guy learns one thing, another guy learns another.

V: If we're going to build a juvenile institution to take strictly the heavyweight felony beefs, and that's all, do you think we could have such an institution, containing say fifty, sixty young men, that functions, that could work, that could help and motivate them?

J: Yeah, you could build a joint like that. And like you say if you were going to classify the crime and put the person according to his classification, but you still have to find out the reason why he did what he did.

V: Right. There's different kinds of murders right?

J: Sure there is. There's spur of the moment because of anger. And there's the one that's almost planned. You never know, and then there's the one that's an accident because the guy's going in to rip a joint off, he gets scared, the other guy makes a false move, and the next thing you know he blows him away.

V: So it's not sufficient simply to categorize by crime.

J: No it isn't. You have to find out what motivates the person. What the reason is behind it.

V: Do you think it's necessary in a juvenile institution to have a whole bunch of different rules? Are a lot of rules needed for this type of young person?

J: No, they've got too many petty rules.

V: Give me an example.

J: Because you didn't pass inspection, you have loss of privileges, and that's because you might have had a speck of dust on your bed or something. Or your floor wasn't shined the way they wanted it shined. This is Annandale, now, used to be a buff job, you used to wax and buff your floors.

V: In an institution that we ran that you know about and that we'll talk about later, we had three rules—no sex, no violence, and no drugs. Do you think those rules are enforceable, even among what we're going to call the worst of the juvenile population? Do you think that's enforceable?

J: Well you've always got somebody that's going to break a rule no matter what you have, but I think it's generally enforceable. Because the majority of guys don't want to get in trouble, they want to get out, unless they're doing such heavy time that they don't give a shit anymore.

V: Well, among juveniles we wouldn't have that problem?

J: No, you got guys in there that go in there that don't care.

V: How would you enforce such rules? Let's say you're in charge of an institution, and you've got about thirty-five young men in there, and the rule is that there can be no homosexual rape, no rip offs. How do you want to enforce that rule, how would you enforce that rule?

J: Well, first of all, I think any guy that rips off another guy off, he ought to be charged with the crime and given more time for it. Whether or not he was in there or he had the mentality or he had the thoughts at the time of being a hard core criminal, he goes in there and he does something like that, it's there automatically. Somebody that comes off with something like that, you have to do it.

V: Let's assume that charging him with the crime is a limited deterrent, now, more important, how do we prevent this from happening?

J: A juvenile, then you have to stick that guy into an adult situation and let him go through the same thing.

V: Again, that's still a punishment thing. Even a treatment thing if you will. But not a prevention thing. How do we stop this kind of activity inside the institution? Stop it before it starts?

J: How to stop it before it starts. That's a hard one. That's a tough one. If you've got the guy, and do you know he's a potential—

V: No, these are kids we know nothing about. Although they've probably done time before we can assume that, and we know they have done serious heavyweight crimes, and we know that, and that's it.

J: You're going to have to come across with the guy himself that's getting ripped off, whether he should be there himself—I don't know. That would be like me going to the joint and somebody coming up to me and saying

"I'm going to rip you off." "You're a fine looking fool, you got to be kidding."

V: Not everybody's in the same shape you are, J. I mean there's people that can't defend themselves.

J: I'm not talking about the defending, I'm just talking about looks. Now who the hell would take *you* and try to rip you off in the joint? But how to prevent it. How do you know what's running through a guy's mind unless you try to find out?

V: Well, we can assume, can't we. Can't we look at a population and point out three or four kids and say "They're going to be targets" and look at three or four other kids and say "They're going to be the arrows?"

J: Well, this is what I'm saying. You can look at the guy and figure that he's a potential victim. You're going to have to take this guy out, but he's still classified according to that crime isn't he?

V: Yes.

J: So why should he placed in the situation other than someone else.

V: So we're getting to another point also. We're saying that not just crime, and not just treatment, but certain people, certain juveniles, are going to present a security problem in and of themselves, just by being excellent victim types.

J: Right. A lot of times you can be around a guy and you can tell just what type of person he is, whether he's going to be a rip-off artist, or whether he's going to be pacified by what's going on and just stay there and say "Look I got my time to do, I'm going to do it and get the hell out of here." But it doesn't always work that way. I mean no matter where you got, if you get a bunch of guys together, there's always going to be some sort of trouble. There's always going to be a fight, I don't care, whether it's the garden of Eden someplace, you're going to have a fight. So you always have potential danger.

V: So you're saying that the institution personnel, whether you call them guards, or treatment specialists or anything else, really have to be on the scene constantly?

J: Sure they do. They have to be there so they know what the hell's going on. I mean they have to see what's going on. They got to see how a guy's acting. Number one, they have to be qualified to take care of people. They have to have some sort of training to say "Well look, this guy here, he looks like he's a little keyed up there all of a sudden, now what's running through his mind. What's his first idea? Is he going to be to beat this guy's ass, rip him off, or just come back at us?" But these guards that they have now, they have no training, not really.

V: Let's talk about training. You know that at the institution you visited in Massachusetts, Andros, a large percentage of the staff were former prisoners, that had no "formal" training, yet they were trained.

J: They had on the job training. They'd been through the situation before. They knew what was going on, they knew how to handle the situation, nine times out of ten. But even them, you can't say that they're the greatest either, because everybody's fallible.

V: It's more a question of attitude than success. I mean we expect people to fail, but we do also expect them to try.

J: Of course, but the thing is there, you get these guys out there that have got a job. They've got eight hours a day that they're going to put in. They're going to come in and they're going to punch the time clock. When they leave, that place is behind them, they're going home. When they walk out of there, there are no bars around them or no walls around them. These other guys are in there twenty-four hours a day. And nine times out of ten, they're mingling with each other for a good fifteen hours a day, at least. So there's bound to be trouble unless it's caught before it happens.

V: So prevention is more important then?

J: Sure it is. You have to have prevention.

V: Now when we're talking about hiring former prisoners, as staff, and this is a pretty hot topic today, I've always maintained that it can be done, and I've done it, and it has worked, but there are certain criteria that you have to have. I'd like you to share with me your own observations here. If you and I were going to run an institution, and we were going to hire staff, we were interviewing today in a state prison, what are we going to look for in terms of potential staff.

J: My feelings would be to find somebody that's already started doing something for himself. That knows a little bit about people or that can understand people a little bit. He doesn't have to be no Freud or any of these other guys, but find somebody that knows a little bit about people, that can judge people. And you take it from there.

V: Alright. But let's add some things to that though. We talked about putting juveniles in specific institutions based on the acts they committed.

J: Right.

V: Are we going to use the same criteria in hiring staff?

J: Why not?

V: Can you give us some examples now. Are there certain types of prisoners that we're not going to let work here?

J: Okay. You've got murderers that are getting out, a lot of guys that I feel shouldn't be doing the time, because they get screwed in the end, because of the seriousness as they say of the offense. But if you got a bunch of juveniles, whether it be felony murder, accidental murder, murder by automobile, the thing is now you get a murderer, because he's been though it, he knows what's going on. He did the time already, and he's got the most time in, nine times out of ten. He can handle them. Where if you put a guy in there that went to jail for stealing a car, or for drugs, and then he tries to handle somebody that's facing possible life or is doing life at the time, how the hell can he handle it?

V: That's a good point. But we are going to have kids in the institution that have been involved in rapes, and various sex crimes. Would we use sex criminals to work with them?

J: No, I don't think so. You better use a doctor there.

V: Why do you say that?

J: Number one, why should there be any rape in the first place? There's too many broads out there giving it away.

V: So you're saying that ipso facto, anybody that rapes is a sick person?

J: Sure.

V: So you wouldn't then hire a former rapist to work with them?

J: No I wouldn't. Well I'm prejudiced against rapists anyway.

V: Okay. A lot of people are prejudiced against rapists and perhaps properly so. I think the underpinning of what you're saying is this. The institutions don't rehabilitate. Some people manage to rehabilitate themselves. I've not known the institutions to be particularly successful with sex criminals in any way.

J: No, because while I was in Rahway, when they had five of them inside the joint, nine times out of ten, guys that are doing thirty years or getting out in a year and a half two years, and they're right back in and they're getting right back out again.

V: You're talking about the one prospect in Jersey for fully indeterminate sentencing, the sex offender?

J: I'm talking about the sex offender, right. And this is to me, a big laugh, the whole sex offender thing that they got now, because they were protected more in the joint than the average convict, they had their own medical staff and everything else, which the regular convict didn't have and although they didn't have the staff, they were still coming back, so what the hell was the deterrent there? What was the object, if it wasn't to cure, or help these guys. Instead sending them back out and they come back in for doing the same thing to a seven-, eight-year-old-kid.

V: What about the problem when you're working with former prisoners as staff, what about the problem of the tendency of former prisoners to clique up?

J: Well, that goes with your screening in the beginning. You have to find out just how the guy feels first.

V: Well, there are very friendships in prisons now that reach across racial lines, right?

J: Yeah, I'd say that.

V: Well that's a big problem in juvenile institutions. You know racial attitudes are a big problem. If we have a staff that's racially divided, it seems to me it would exacerbate those problems.

J: When you got a bunch of kids there, you're going to always have your mixture, you're going to have your Spanish, you're going to have your black and you're going to have your white. And there's no way you're going to get out unless you start segregating again, and there ain't going to be no segregation. So you have the same type of staff, but you have to find staff members that get along, and they can set an example for the kids that they got there. An example, Mack and I, we got along beautifully. But I'll tell you what, there's white guys and there's black guys that I wouldn't want nothing to do with, and if I'm prejudiced, then I'm prejudiced against both. The thing is now, you're always going to have a racial problem now because it's started out here, it's not because it started in the joint. Guys always got along in the joint. It started right out here on the streets.

V: So you're saying that the institution, be it juvenile or adult, is going to reflect the society anyway.

J: Sure it is.

V: And it's pretty pointless to talk about no racism inside the joint as long as it's going to be here outside?

J: Yeah, unless you can block the outside away from the inside.

V: What kind of programs would you like to see for juveniles who are in fact incarcerated?

J: You have to have an educational program. You have to evaluate how far the kid went in school, what his potential is, and try to find out just what the kid wants to do. And you can't—like when they go into the joint they ask you what you did and you say "I was a carpenter outside" and they throw you in a kitchen while you're in there. You have to give the kid a chance to find out what he wants to do himself. And if you have the facilities, then give him what he wants, or give him another choice. I mean you can't say "You've got to do this" and "you've got to do that" because right there, you upset the whole thing. Guy comes out and says "I don't have to do a damn thing except die."

V: Besides educational programs what do we need? Is that enough? What else do we need?

J: Most of the joints, they got sports. That's all you got is sports. But besides educational, you have to have something there to give the kid a chance to find out what's the matter with him, what his reason is for being there, and give him enough time to think about it. They come up with these group therapy classes, but they don't amount to a diddly-shit. Because there's one con here he's talking about this then you got the con over there "Well, I don't think we should go into this form of talk, or questioning," or whatever the hell it is, and you end up with chaos around the whole thing.

V: Well, but you think that some kind of counseling has to be part of . . .

J: Sure it has to be. But it has to be individual, it can't be a group thing.

V: So you think that each child needs the opportunity for individual counseling . . .

J: Sure he does. And it can't be just one period. It has to be over a period of
    time, because if you just sat down with me one time, how the hell could
    you tell me what I'm like or what I'm going to be like, or what I even think
    about. I could sit here all day and tell you I think about one thing and go
    out and do something else.

V: You're talking about an ongoing program now, not one or two individual
    opportunities.

J: Well, if the guy's locked up for two years, why shouldn't he have two years
    of counseling. Doesn't have to be an everyday thing, once, twice, a week,
    but at least he finds out that "Well, these people might be trying to do
    something for me" or even if they don't do anything, it'll give him enough
    to think about and maybe he'll find out for himself, what the hell's the
    matter.

V: When you visited the Andros institution in Massachusetts and you talked
    with all the kids there, did you notice anything different about these kids
    from other kids that you'd seen in other institutions?

J: There was a little contentment there, and there wasn't the thing that they
    had to fear authority, because authority wasn't exerted there. You could
    tell the difference between the person now and the inmate. But there was
    no animosity. The kids didn't feel, "That's my watchdog over there. I got to
    watch what I do." It was a free spirit program, that's what it was.

V: When you say free spirit do you mean kids do anything they wanted to do?

J: No no, everybody has rules and regulations. Even at Andros you had rules
    and regulations. But there was a different type of enforcement, I felt, than
    there is at a regular institution or a prison. It was that the kids felt that
    there was somebody there that they could talk to if they had to talk to
    them.

V: You do realize that the kids at Andros were all involved with serious
    felonies, right?

J: Yeah.

V: You had no trouble talking to them right?

J: No, I didn't have any trouble talking to them.

V: Did that surprise you?

J: I guess in a way, because I was still an outsider coming in, whether I was a
    con or not. Whether they knew I was a con or not I couldn't tell. But the
    thing was . . .

V: They knew.

J: They had, that there was a different feeling there at that program than there
    was at a prison or a reformatory, plus there wasn't that many guys. There
    wasn't a big population. It was a limited number of men, and there was
    more chance of each guy to get to know each other, and to get to know the
    staff also. To find out what they could do, what they couldn't do, and how
    they would go about doing what they could do.

V: When you visited the program, you were in fact out of prison yourself only a very short time, right?

J: Two days.

V: And you had been somewhat cynical about the prospects of this program working, although you'd been very supportive while we were trying to get the program started. Did you find the cynicism justified when you spoke to the kids?

J: No, weil, cynical yes. But I had faith in you and people that you had for your staff, and after I spoke with even the staff, it wasn't like any other place. That's all I could say really. There was a harmony there, there was a harmony like you'll never find in any joint.

V: But in fact the joint itself was very physically bad, it was rotten, it smelled bad, it was ugly, it was in a bad part of town . . .

J: What prison isn't?

V: I think the most important thing that we get out of this is that the problems with people have to be solved by people—we can't build anything to solve it.

J: Sure, but you've got to have people to start with that understand the problem.

V: There's a lot of people like that running around who in fact aren't involved in this rehabilitation game at all?

J: Sure there is.

V: Let me give you a good example—yourself. You were very very interested in this whole thing yourself for years and years, right. You followed the development of Andros, you visited the place. Yet, is there any opportunity for a guy like you to get a job working with kids?

J: No. I've got a record. How could I become a cop? That's just like when I was in there; I was studying. I would love to have become a lawyer. But I couldn't become a lawyer because I'm not ethically qualified.

V: Based on the fact that you have a prison conviction.

J: That's right. But how do you classify ethics?

V: Pretty good question. Ethics are classified simply in terms of whether or not you're honest.

J: Yeah, but according to the ethics of an attorney, it's their rules and regulations, it's different, it's what somebody else said sometime before. How they wanted it run.

V: Well, in terms of the way we treat juveniles, I don't think we've progressed fantastically far. There's a number of new laws which indicate, strongly, in fact, that juveniles have got to be treated as adults. Fact is there's a twelve-year-old boy going on trial for his life in Florida now.

J: But the thing is though, I feel that before a kid is sent away, he should be evaluated out there, but they don't want to take the time either. When a kid gets in trouble the first time, there has to be a reason why, not going up in front of a judge and putting him on probation and saying "Okay now you come see this guy once a week" because I'm on probation right now, and what do I do, and you know what the guy talks about—my car, how I'm doing, what am I doing, that's all. It's a hassle, that's what it is. And it's only to make the kid say "I got to go there once a week, I got to be there, or I got to be there every two weeks." But there's nothing, he's not saying "Well, look, I can do this for you" or "How come you did this" some of them might be qualified, they might have their B.A.'s in psychology and everything else, but that still doesn't tell the kid what's the matter, why he did it.

V: Could you work with a kid on probation?

J: Yeah, I think I could. In fact, a lot of the guys that I hire now are on probation, or on parole, or ex-offenders, and we have a beautiful relationship.

V: As a summary, do you have any hope for the future of juvenile corrections? Do you think we can have a juvenile justice system that delivers justice, that does rehabilitate, that does offer opportunity to actually turn a kid around?

J: Sure. As long as these people get rid of these outmoded ways that they have right now.

V: But you believe it can happen and you are optimistic about it. Do you think it can be sold to the public?

J: Sure it could be sold to the public, but the first thing the public wants to hear is how much it's going to cost. That's their main concern.

V: Could the public understand—you're a businessman and a taxpayer now—if I told you something would cost a lot more than it does now for a couple of years, and then a lot less, from then on, would that appeal to you?

J: Sure it would. Show me how to save money, even if it costs money in the beginning. They say you have to have money to make money. But how can you have anything if you don't try it? They try prisons. They don't work.

V: So you think the public is ready to try something else with juveniles?

J: I don't know if the public is, but they should be.

Interview between Andrew Vachss (V) and
Ramon Jimenez, Esq. (J) on April 19, 1978

Ramon J. Jimenez, Esq. received his law degree from the Harvard Law School. He has worked extensively with labor organizations as coordinator, organizer, legal consultant, and counsel/negotiator. He has also served as adjunct professor at various colleges in New York, and currently teaches a course in "Racism and the Law" at New York University School of Law.

Ramon Jimenez was recently a grassroots candidate for state senator from the South Bronx and is currently engaged in organizing and representation of citizen groups in that community on issues of health, housing, and employment.

V: As a community leader in the South Bronx, where would you place the juvenile crime and the juvenile violence problem on a scale of priorities in the neighborhood?

J: I would place it very high among, either 2, 3, or 4, I would place it very high.

V: What are the other problems that would rank in the same league as juvenile crime and violence?

J: Housing and jobs.

V: And juvenile crime is right up in that area? With one of the most poverty stricken communities in the entire Northeast?

J: Right, most definitely.

V: Okay. Have you any insight in years of working out there as to why the Bronx, particularly the South Bronx, has been so notorious for a juvenile gang problem?

J: I think that the South Bronx would breed juvenile gangs. The conditions in the South Bronx create organizations of youth to attempt to deal with the conditions that they're in. I don't mean *correctly* deal with the conditions they're in but to deal with the condition they're in whether it be a necessity for material things, for property and so on, or whether it be to rip people off. In other words those conditions breed those type of organizations.

V: You seem to be implying that if there were more alternatives for youth in the South Bronx there would be less of a juvenile gang problem. Is that in fact your position?

J: Yeah, most definitely. I mean like there are no alternatives [for] youth in the South Bronx. When they announced jobs a year ago there were about four thousand youths on 149th Street and Courtland, there was almost a riot and then all those youths found out that was the wrong office—the newspaper had given them the wrong information. So everybody was hung up for nothing. And I also remember the day of the blackout; I was having a meeting and as soon as the lights went off we all went downstairs and the first place that was ripped off, believe it or not, is this place that sells sporting goods supplies on 149th between Morris and Courtland. And you saw basketballs and sneakers and bats all gone—people running down the street with them.

V: Well you've spent a lot of time with juvenile gangs on the street, in their clubhouses. Are you really saying that if there were jobs and other kinds of alternatives all juvenile gang members would give up the gang activity?

J: No, I think that every juvenile gang has a very small minority of young people who have been so twisted and turned that they'll be into violence for a very long time. I think the vast majority, given alternatives, would stop that activity. In fact two weeks ago I was walking down my street and I saw a few members of the Savage Skulls and I stopped and I spoke to them and I told them about the organization I'm a member of and you know after about a half an hour of talking, next Monday they showed up in the office at 8:00 o'clock in the morning and waited—you know it wasn't open until 10—and waited there and then talked to us. They're searching, as soon as they find about something they're searching for something.

V: Well how do we differentiate between the hard-core gang member and the kid who's drifting in and out of delinquent behavior because of lack of alternatives? What are the characteristics that separate those two different types of kids?

J: There's kids who are hard-core organization-wise, in other words to be part of an organization or to be part of something. While there are also hard-core gang members who are into continuing violent activities and I think that honestly speaking I think anyone who spends a little time with these youths can determine it through their actions and so forth.

V: Alright, the average gang member in the South Bronx, tell me some things about him? Is he in school?

J: The average gang member—there's a debate about that right now because we always had the concept that he was not in school and recently in our interaction with some of the people from the Savage Skulls they contended that the majority of their members were in school and then we spoke to some other people that had been in gangs, like Louie Olivo used to be the head of a gang in the South Bronx, and Amos Torres, and their position is that believe it or not, the average member in the gangs in the South Bronx is in school.

V: Okay, now we hear headlines all the time, a juvenile gang rapes a thirteen-year-old girl, stabs a retarded boy to death, sets fire to a building. Are these accurate stories?

J: I think that those stories are definitely accurate stories. I mean I think the gangs are involved in a lot of violent doings. I don't think you ever hear stories though about maybe some of the positive aspects or the complexity of gangs—I don't think that gangs just spend every day raping people or putting fires to buildings. There's a little more complexity to gangs and I think that when actions like that take place, I think again there's a small minority inspiring that and creating these negative standards. When I learn about some of the gangs in the Bronx, some of them try to do some positive things and sometimes it depends on who's in the leadership. I think that the newspapers oversimplify it, although I think that all that kind of stuff really has to be punished and stopped.

V: Okay, when you say punished and stopped, isn't it a fact that the average gang member in the city of New York and certainly in the South Bronx, has already been to family court a number of times? Has already been convicted in family court a number of times and has probably been institutionalized a number of times?

J: You know I would say that there is a significant number of people in the gangs who have gone through that process but I think that process just hasn't been able to do anything but dehumanize people even more. And therefore make them subject to doing more when they come out. The Family Court and the whole juvenile system just dehumanizes people more, and so when they come out it's natural that they do something even worse.

V: In the profession, we've talked a lot about how we can service these kids and what they need. Do you have a position on victims? When these kids do act out, they act in a predatory fashion; they hurt human beings. Most of the time they hurt human beings that we would characterize as helpless, old people, crippled people. What about the victims?—What is your solution?

J: Well my solution to some of these things would be to develop meaningful alternatives. A meaningful alternative might be like developing recreational things and jobs and part of the jobs might be working with older people and helping older people or helping retarded people and getting youth involved in that kind of stuff. There are no real alternatives now and I'm saying that real alternatives would deal with 90 or 95 percent of these youth.

V: What about the remaining 5 percent?

J: I believe that for the 5 percent there would have to be some form of effective incarceration—with a heavy psychiatric input. But obviously that's unlike the model that exists right now.

V: You're not taking the position that there's no such thing as a bad boy?

J: Oh no, definitely not.

V: Or saying they're just basically harmless kids or anything like that?

J: No, like I said I think there's a small minority that has been so twisted and turned that they're dangerous to human beings, dangerous to my mother, your mother, and therefore I'm for letting them being incarcerated.

V: Are you in favor of them being executed? I mean are you in favor of the death penalty?

J: I would only be in favor of the death penalty if the death penalty was to be objectively carried out for rich, poor, black, white and so on. I've never seen it objectively carried out so I couldn't be in favor of that if it's going to just strike down certain classes and certain ethnic groups.

V: Do you believe that if it was objectively applied it would be effective?

J: I don't know whether it would be effective or not but I think when a human being kills two or three human beings you know they have no right to exist any longer as far as I'm concerned.

V: You know there's proposals now to bring fourteen or fifteen year olds into the criminal court arena, take them out of family court. Are you in favor of that?

J: Well, again, I don't think that's the solution because I think that that just puts them into the bigger prisons where the same kinds of things happen. So, if it means that you put them into the Supreme Court but you put them in institutions that are modeled differently and operate differently, okay. But if you put them into Attica or something like that, I don't agree.

V: Many years ago you conducted some classes basically for Hispanic youth at the institution that I ran in Massachusetts. Would you say that those juveniles that you interacted with then are any different than the juveniles that are running around the streets in the South Bronx today?

J: No.

V: But how did you feel about the kids that were in the institution? Did you feel that they were dangerous, out of control and crazy?

J: No, I thought that for the first time they were in an environment (a) where people were very concerned about them, and (b) where people didn't also allow them to push people around, you know where they had to confront and respect everyone that was around. And where they were given a lot of responsibility at the same time, they were forced to comply with that responsibility. So, I think that they were in the process of receiving some good treatment.

V: Would you distinguish in terms of treatment between the type of juvenile who commits a basically economic-motivated crime such as a mugger or a thief, from the type of youth who commits a crime that's motivated by other forces, such as a rape?

J: Yeah, most definitely. I think that you have to deal with economic crime in a different way especially when you understand the background of these youth. You have to deal with it in a totally different way, because it's more a problem of the social situation than it is with anything else.

V: Wouldn't the alternatives you suggest have an additional benefit in that they would expose the truly violent juvenile? In other words if we had a lot of alternatives, isn't it a fact that some of the kids still wouldn't participate?

J: Sure, I agree. I would agree it would expose that small minority.

V: Your organization has members in it that were formerly heavily involved in the gang scene, right? They're no longer involved and they're working productively? Have you any insight into the process by which this happened?

J: One is a process of just maturing after a while, I mean, I'm talking about people who were very much heavily involved in the gangs, you know from Louie to Amos to Efrian of the Viceroys.

V: Efrian is probably the best example I can think of. Efrian was not only a major gang leader but in fact committed a homicide, right?

J: Right.

V: And served thirteen or fourteen years in prison?

J: That's right.

V: Yet, I know Efrian, you do too, I think most people consider him to be a very responsible human being at this point. Are you giving the prison system credit for Efrian's rehabilitation.?

J: No, I'm giving Efrian credit. Efrian is a rarity. Efrian is a young person who was caught into no alternatives, was caught into like the whole rules and regulations of the gangs, the whole macho thing, he got caught into a situation where violence ensued. But I don't think that Efrian is a violent creature. So therefore I think that he got caught into that whole thing and part of it was because there was no alternatives, no real alternatives.

V: So we can't really distinguish by type of crime can we, because in fact Efrian committed the ultimate crime, homicide? Yet we both know that Efrian is basically not a violent human being and certainly not a vicious one.

J: Efrian's was a gang fight if we had to differentiate between the different types of violent acts. But some violent acts you can say something's really wrong with that person. And something has to be done.

V: Okay would you say that there are certain crimes that once having been involved in such crimes, the prognosis for rehabilitation is greatly decreased? For example would you agree with the premise that a kid involved in a homicide is perhaps a better candidate for rehabilitation than a kid who's been involved in sex crimes?

J: Yeah. I would agree with that.

V: Do you think that if Efrian had been offered the alternatives that you've spoken about he would not have participated as heavily in the gang thing?

J: Right, definitely, I agree. I mean I don't think Efrian had the alternatives that should exist. I think that the alternatives could possibly begin to create different channels for people. You got the Renegades in Harlem and although we understand the Renegades now have gone away from the whole gang-like concept and so on but some of the Renegades were real heavy gang members and when they found the alternative—to deal with buildings and so, they got into it. [The Harlem Renegades now operate a sweat-equity building rehabilitation agency.] Even like a gang in the South Bronx, like I said this gang called the Savage Nomads. They're trying to figure out how do we fix this building where we live in.

V: As a person that has moved heavily into various political arenas, how do you respond to this: Somebody says well, look, you're interested in all these rehabilitative services and all these alternatives for youth, okay. But why should we waste any money or any time on these people when the real issue is the people they're victimizing? How do you respond to that?

J: Well I always think that the real issue is the future victims and the way to deal with that is to create situations where there's few future victims. So therefore I'd like to deal with the future rather than dealing with the past victims.

V: Okay, what about the present victims? As we're going through the process of providing alternatives, the streets are not safe. The apartments are not safe; the schools are not safe. What can we do about that in terms of the juvenile problem?

J: I think that juveniles that commit violent crimes should be put into situations, environments where they're going to be there for a while and where they're going to receive a lot of psychiatric help, counselling, education, and so on and where the resources are sufficient to be able to do something. But I mean creative, innovative programs maybe run by different community groups. Something by and which they really get help rather than the type of institutions that exist right now. I really don't know how to respond to you as far as the economic crime. Because I really don't know in other words, if this summer in New York City there's no jobs for youth and there's so many youth on the street, you know there's no way I can respond to you about economics.

V: Okay, let me ask you this when you talk about a different model of treatment, what kind of setting should this occur in? Are you talking about a halfway house, a group home, an actual penal institution?

J: I'm talking about a penal institution. I have to talk about penal institutions. I'm not talking about a halfway house for people who have committed some violent crimes.

V: Okay, so you think that part of the solution is to transmit a message so that juveniles who commit serious violent crimes are in fact institutionalized? And that that message will get down to the street?

J: Well I think that that's one, but I think that it's also to create a creative, innovative penal institution also. We're going to have the youth there for a long time—that deals in the way they should, I mean from education to psychiatry. I don't think that this is an impossibility, I think that it's a good possibility. The people who have been running these places have been so ill themselves, so out of it, they're the ones who've contributed more to increased victimization than anybody else.

V: So you think that you endorse the principle that the juvenile institution of the past has caused criminality?

J: Definitely.

V: Okay, now how do you respond to this. Someone says that your position is essentially a racist position because if we do build specialized penal institutions for violent juveniles most of the kids in there are going to be nonwhite. How do you respond to that?

J: I don't know if that's true or not. I live in a black and Puerto Rican community. Everyone has to have three or four locks on the doors, everyone has to have a dog, when you walk down the street you've got to look real tough because if you don't look real tough someone might rip you off. So our community *wants* to deal with that problem. At the same time it wants to deal with the type of lack of services, jobs, and so on that we don't get. You know those are the things that we don't get to stop that problem from continually popping up.

V: Well do you think that the pulse of your community is in favor of actual incarceration, in favor of more liberal treatment, more harsh treatment?

J: Incarceration without a doubt. In fact, probably more harsher treatment.

V: Okay, when people, say up in Scarsdale, say that we need all these specialized services for youth because the poor communities want specialized services, is that true or isn't it a fact that the poor communities just want retributive kind of violence themselves?

J: Definitely.

V: Well what's the response of the average young Hispanic male who finds out that his mother's been victimized?

J: Hey, that person should be killed whoever did that.

V: And you think that's a truly universal response?

J: Yeah, sure.

V: Does that response translate all the way down to the level of police protection? Do people want more police interaction in their community?

J: Sure, I think that they would want the police to be more involved in those major things that happen in the community rather than in the minor things or not being around that much, definitely.

V: So you would expect the community would endorse a higher emphasis on gang-related activities by the police?

J: Yeah, definitely.

V: Okay, do you remember the old street worker programs? Those haven't been operating for a long time. How do you feel about such programs?

J: Again, if there's no alternatives, the street worker program doesn't mean a thing. It's like sending a chaplain out there to try to pacify the youth.

V: So if he doesn't go there with something tangible and material, it's a useless endeavor?

J: Right.

V: Do you endorse what I've heard from other leaders in minority communities which is that the street workers were in effect missionaries, that they were from different ethnic groups and different classes than the people that they were supposed to serve?

J: Yes.

V: Do you endorse the position that a street worker requires a certain physical strength and mental toughness just to do the job?

J: Most definitely. But again no street worker's going to do any job unless there's a resource that's available.

V: And right now in the South Bronx are there resources available?

J: No.

V: Do you think the school systems have been responsive to the problems of juvenile violence? Isn't their response just to suspend a kid that has any problems at all?

J: Yes, the school system produces it's own juvenile delinquents with its lack of meaningful teaching. You know what I mean, it turns people off; it turns those youths off to education and to learning. You know I was in an elementary school yesterday and just seeing the way they deal in elementary schools, you know they break kids easily. You know, they ruin kids' minds easily.

V: Well what about the gang? What does that do for a kid's mind.

J: What does it do? It makes him feel like he belongs to something, it gives him a sense of solidarity with other people, it gives him a sense of protection, gives him a sense of power.

V: Dr. Stewart, who I believe you know, who is one of the consultants to the project, told me that there's a certain mentality in a gang that's healthy. That there's a certain cooperativeness, a certain kind of sharing. He said that it sometimes gets perverted with the use of violence. He says that young people have always banded together.

J: Yeah, I would agree totally.

V: But the kids that we're talking about are beyond Little League, right? They're beyond the Boy Scouts?

J: Oh, yeah. I think there's gang members of all different ages. I mean they go from—at least from what I know, from 9 on.

V: Isn't it a fact that some gang members are in their thirties too? Just maturing past a certain chronological age is no guarantee that they're going to stop gang activity?

J: Sure.

V: What about the stories we've been hearing about juveniles being used to cooperate with adult criminals? For narcotics dealing, for arson, even for homicide? Do you feel those stories have validity?

J: Most definitely. I mean it's an alternative, it's an economical alternative. The people in organized crime or in dope *are* offering juveniles some economic alternatives.

V: So you're saying that if the competition is so weak, alternatives like that are going to be accepted?

J: Sure.

V: What do you feel it would take, on a more sophisicated level, besides simple jobs? Let's get past jobs, now we've jobs for kids. Is that enough?

J: No. First of all, when we talk about jobs that's an issue within itself because traditionally jobs for youth have been "no-show" or "no-do" jobs. And right now if you check out the summer programs coming up they'll be fifty thousand no-show or no-do jobs.

V: Who will control those jobs?

J: They'll be controlled by poverty agencies and those poverty agencies will put on the youth who are very close to them, and hire their cronies as the top administrators and those youth will maybe clean the sidewalks once a week, they can go to Coney Island once a week, and listen to music and hang out on the corners the rest of the time. Except when somebody's coming from downtown and then they'll put on a show as if they're doing something heavy, serious. There's no meaningful education going on that could be, no meaningful training going on, and the welfare mentality is created and reproduced. There are a tremendous amount of problems with that.

V: Well speaking of the welfare mentality, are most of the kids who are involved in gangs supported in one way or another by a social agency? Are their parents on welfare?

J: I wouldn't know. I would assume so but I couldn't answer that.

V: Do you see any correlation between the strength of the family structure in gang activity?

J: Yes, most definitely. Most of the people I know who are involved in gangs have some really messed up family situations, therefore the organization of the gang takes the place of the family.

V: Isn't it a fact that this kind of kid who's supersusceptible to peer pressure is going to go with the flow even in an institution? It's going to take a much more specialized institution to turn this kid around than a standard kid?

J: Yeah, sure, but it depends on what type of flow the institution creates.

V: So you're saying that in fact in the right institution this kid might be even easier to work with?

J: Of course.

V: Just give me as a sum-up a little forecast of the future for the South Bronx? What's going to happen to the South Bronx?

J: Well unfortunately the South Bronx is due for its next rip-off. A billion dollars is coming in, that billion dollars is going to supposedly create new housing but we're not even sure who's going to get those jobs and those buildings that are going to be built, what the rents are going to be. So we're going to have a lot of people probably pushed out of the community. They're going to renovate factories, build new factories when, in fact, the majority of those factories have Puerto Ricans and Latins working for $2.65 an hour with no benefits. So again business and construction companies and so on are being subsidized while there's nothing—the youth problem is not even considered part of saving the South Bronx, I mean no one talks about it, like they don't talk about the college, they don't talk about the health services. The only part of saving the South Bronx is putting up new factories and new housing.

V: So, in effect, that's not going to have any material change on the quality of people's lives.

J: No, unless there's a significant pressure put on by a lot of different groups.

V: So if I were to tell you that the kind of juvenile institution we've been working on that we want to construct would cost $3 million to build, and would cost $50,000 a year to keep each juvenile in there, those figures wouldn't strike you as being excessive?

J: No.

V: Do you think that there's anything that people can do in the final analysis, people, citizens, to turn around this juvenile violence problem here in New York City and especially in your community?

J: I think that the things that they can do is be trying to deal with the overall problem in terms of jobs and meaningful alternatives and really organizing behind that kind of stuff. And I think that's more important—that will begin to deal with the problem. Because what I'm saying is that unless you deal with some of those roots the problem will continue.

**Interview between Andrew Vachss (V) and
William Madaus (M), on September 22, 1976**

William C. Madaus, Ed.D. graduated from the College of the Holy Cross with a major in education. He received the M.A. degree in counseling from Assumption College and was awarded the Ed.D. in counseling and guidance by the University of Massachusetts.

Dr. Madaus was assistant commissioner of the Massachusetts Department of Youth Services during the 1970-1974 de-institutionalization period and has had extensive experience in counseling and guidance of socially and emotionally disturbed juveniles. He is currently director of the North Shore Guidance Center in Salem, Massachusetts.

V: Dr. Madaus, you were one of the people originally associated with the de-institutionalization effort in Massachusetts, right?
M: Yes, but now I'm out of the Department of Youth Services, I'm now with the Department of Mental Health and a community mental health clinic. So I'm not sure that the populations would be that similar, but yes, I'm still involved with courts and with the Bridgewater Diversion Unit at Danvers State, and with the adolescent day program at Danvers State. But with those kids, that are not only delinquent but their degree of emotional disturbance would be greater in terms of outright psychosis in many instances.
V: Did you find as a practice that overtly psychotic juveniles were committed in DYS's normal course of doing business?
M: Yes. In fact it was true to such an extent that it was not even really admitted by the Department of Mental Health as being a problem until Dr. Goldman came in as commissioner, and said point-blank that they didn't have the facilities to handle these kids, that they had done nothing with them, and that gave impetus and advent to these Bridgewater Diversion Units that are now being set up in every area. It's interesting that Judge Baker Guidance Center or McLeans Hospital might say that a child was psychotic but the Department of Mental Health usually used the label "severe character disorder, needs control, return to DYS." Usually what would happen is that the child would be brought in to a hospital after maybe an attempted suicide, or mutilating his arm, or some type of crisis. There'd be a doctor on duty, the doctor would do a cursory ten or fifteen minute interview, they knew that there were only two orderlies up on the floor, they knew that this kid might attack another patient, that he might be unmanageable, or even if he was not, the fantasy that he could be, and usually the diagnosis right on the spot was severe character disorder, needs control, return to DYS.

V: Is it a fact the conventional mental health facilities would not take a child in Massachusetts if the child was physically violent?

M: Yes. And that became increasingly more of a problem as DMH [Department of Mental Health] also moved to open up their units, and in most state hospitals there were no closed units that could contain this child, and also they were not equipped to handle them. And the other thing that happened within DMH is that since most of their admissions were voluntary, they had difficulty. And because they set up standards to divert to community mental health clinics or go out-patient, the population usually tended to be more of the chronic or burnt-out schizophrenics. The mean age on the wards was probably forty-five or fifty, and an acting-out adolescent really represented, with some justification on their part, a threat to other patients or orderlies on that unit. The fact is that they should have set up programs, but given the structure that they were operating within, it was difficult for them to handle the types of kids that were being referred.

V: In a purely de-institutionalized system, where do you put the acting-out psychotic, where do you put the dangerous child, where does he go?

M: Well, I don't know. I would have to take a step backwards and see what kinds of labels and definitions they were going to place on kids to make that determination.

V: Would you concede that in a normal population of juveniles committed to any youth service agency, half of one percent are usually dangerous?

M: I think that would be a low figure.

V: But you would concede at least that many?

M: Yes.

V: Where would you place these children? In what kind of facility?

M: In a specialized kind of facility that would meet their needs.

V: Would it be a closed facility?

M: Yes it would be.

V: So you would not have a hundred percent de-institutionalization?

M: No.

V: Did Massachusetts have complete de-institutionalization?

M: No.

V: Yet the media perception of it is that all the juvenile institutions were closed.

M: I think it's safe to say that all of the training schools for youth were closed, but, my recollection is that two weeks after the Lyman School was closed, which was the last training school for boys to close, a private agency opened a secure unit at Roslindale Detention Facility at the time of the closing.

V: Was this a coordinated effort? In other words did DYS anticipate and in fact solicit this proposal from the private agency?

M: No, I think that there was a lot of controversy within the department as to the best way to handle the kids. I think that as I look back at it historically,

I think that 1970 was very different than 1976. In 1970, you might have one child committed on murder, for the total year, and I am not talking about other children that were committed for a murder offense that went adult. You might have one, two or a maximum of three of those types of offenses per year. What happened was that when Bridgewater was closed, there were approximately fifty youth there that supposedly were the most dangerous kids in the state and the Department of Youth Services contracted with—and I don't recall whether it was Judge Baker or with a private psychiatric group—to get evaluations of the kids there. And after evaluating those forty-six to fifty kids, they saw twelve kids there that represented either a threat to themselves or a threat to the community, and what was clear was that Bridgewater represented the ultimate control and back-up for the institutions. There was also the feeling at that time that perhaps the notion of dispersal made the most sense. That those programs that were handling whatever labels I want to put on "moderately disturbed" or just "delinquent" or "acting out" kids and doing a good job and had a milieu of positive care culture within the program, that they could tolerate one more difficult kid, the notion being that staff and kids collectively could do a job in managing behavior and turning the kids around. And that somehow the notion that labeling kids as the worst and congregating them as the worst somehow becomes a self-fulfilling prophecy where that kind of label and diagnosis brings about the kind of acting out within the facility that you don't want. I would say that initially our inclination was dispersal and that the political reality of the final closing when they were all closed, was that we would have to operate at least one secure facility to handle the kids. But my feeling is that if everyone had their druthers at that time, there probably would have been dispersal and maybe supplementation of existing rates and programs.

V: Well, if there was in fact dispersal as the sole option, isn't it a fact that in this state, particularly, as well as in other states, this would have resulted in more juveniles going to adult prisons?

M: I think that that's probably the greatest misnomer that's been created about de-institutionalization, that de-institutionalization has meant that fourteen year olds through sixteen year olds, in this state are housed in adult institutions. That does not say that there were not more bind-overs, and the district court judges did not use the threat of sentencing this child as an adult, but my experience has been that superior courts are much more tuned in to the rights of indigents and delinquents than are district courts. There is almost a presumption of guilt in district court, so that the bind-over rate certainly increased, but the number of juveniles going into adult prison did not increase, and in fact—and I only have the figures up through 1974 or 1975—declined by a very marginal percentage point.

V: Well what happened, what disposition was made of these juveniles once they got to superior court?

M: Well superior court still has the right to commit the child to DYS. That happened in some cases, and I don't have the exact statistics, but my hunch would be that probably about 60 percent were committed back to DYS and the other 40 percent, as the ultimate sanction, were placed on adult probation, so a further—

V: We're talking about probation for crimes like murder and rape?

M: Murder, rape, armed robbery—

V: Children were placed on probation as a result of these crimes?

M: In some cases, yes. The notion being that a subsequent offense would mean that the child would be incarcerated as an adult.

V: What are the chances in your professional opinion of a child who has already moved through the system, he's already a veteran, he's now committed a homicide, what's the chances of this kid surviving probation?

M: I don't know. I have an interesting theory that with some of those kids, that sanction was meaningful, that the fact that he knew that if he did commit another offense, that he would go adult, and I'm not sure how successful the sanction was, but maybe he was much·cooler about the type of offense. Also, that ultimate threat would not be carried out unless there was a subsequent violent offense. I mean if that child went out and stole a car or did a B&E, no they're not going to send him to Walpole or Concord, but a subsequent violent offense, they would.

V: So you really believe that to this particular adolescent population, the existence of the state prison system was a sufficient deterrent to change their behavior?

M: To some of the kids, yes.

V: To some of the kids. Are these kids that actually could have been worked with anyway? In other words I'm postulating that a kid's sufficiently tuned into himself and his environment to be deterred by anything as vague as the possibility of going to a prison he's never visited, is a kid that could be worked with.

M: Yeah, they were workable kids. The majority of the kids—the vast majority of those kids—were workable kids and kids the programs could have responded to. But I guess that I'll still stand on the statement that I think that that sanction could be internalized enough by kids that they recognize the reality of what's going to happen to a sixteen year old in a prsion.

V: Okay. But you spoke of politics before. How politically viable is it to give a sixteen year old boy probation for a murder?

M: Well, in the cases of murder, that would not have been a probated offense. Those kids—again, one has to make distinctions about the types of kids that would be bound over to superior court. It was not always a crime of violence against a person. It had a lot to do with how much deviancy the community could tolerate and as you moved away from Boston a fifth stolen car in a town like Orange could mean a bind-over to superior court. A fifth stolen car in Boston, the kid might not even be on probation, it might be a warning to the parents, and a lot of it depended upon how much the community could tolerate deviancy, and what the attitude of the judge towards rehabilitation versus punishment, exclusion, and example to community—

V: Well are you saying that a commitment to DYS was rehabilitative?

M: Yes. And certainly not as destructive or dehumanizing as a commitment to the old institutional system.

V: Prior to the new system, would you say a commitment to the Middlesex County Training School was less dehumanizing than one to Walpole?

M: Yes.

V: Simply because of the physical abuse—

M: Physical sexual abuse—

V: Alright, a sixteen-year-old kid who's 225 lbs. and a very vicious kid. Is Walpole going to be any worse for him than Middlesex County?

M: No but then one again cannot make the exception to the rule. Although I'm not sure, Andy, that I want to accept that training schools per se were prisons.

V: Why?

M: Because I really feel that they were more benign than the prison system for a kid. One had to make the distinction and look at the controls within an institutional setting. In some ways, the message was very clear to the kid, "Keep your mouth shut and do your time, keep your nose clean and you'll get out of here." The abuses within the institutional system occurred when the kid did not respond to that system, they occurred within the Cottage Nine, within Wachusett Cottage at Lyman School, within Bridgewater, when the kid refused to respond to the benign neglect that he was getting within that institutional system.

V: Well wasn't part of that benign neglect homosexual gang rape in the institution? Wasn't part of that benign neglect the fact that the tougher kids ran the institutions?

M: Yes. Certainly. I feel that I'm getting caught up in a trick bag, because I'm saying that training schools are more benign. You're now making the argument, that they were not destructive. I am comparing them and equating them with the fourteen or fifteen year old at Concord or Walpole, and to me it was a much more benign setting.

V: Right, but you're saying it's a more benign setting simply because a fourteen or fifteen year old is less physically equipped to deal with Concord and Walpole. I'm asking you to consider the hypothesis, and I'm basing this on interviews with hundreds of guys who have done time in both places, where they say that if they had to do time again they'd much rather do it at Walpole. Now they're speaking of course as adults. I understand that. But the "privileges" you enjoy in a prison are much more extensive than those you enjoy in a juvenile institution.

M: I guess what I'm having problems with is a stereotypic response to institutions per se. I can talk about my feelings about institutionalization. To me the worst training school of all was Oakdale, for the nine to twelve year olds. And as far as public acceptance, it was because it was a brand new facility, and a very nice facility, except for the dormitory area which resembled Roslindale, but it had lots of glass and windows, and gyms, and a library where kids couldn't use the books. But it gave to the public that came through it a feeling that since the kids said "yes, sir" and "no, sir" and had their heads shaved and were passive and docile, that somehow that represented rehabilitation, and the recidivism rate, Jerry always used to claim was 95 percent, I don't know if it was 95 percent, sometimes we pull figures out of a hat. But it certainly was 85 to 90 percent. Yet there were very few instances of physical abuse there. The abuse there was far more psychological. It was a male-oriented and male-dominated facility. There was marching, there was not allowing kids to be kids, there was no spontaneity. And that was an extremely destructive system. Lyman School on the other hand, before it closed was probably the more progressive of the training schools there, I mean they had volunteers in and out, the superintendent did not tolerate any physical abuse and if he got word of it from kids, would investigate it, and would take action, so I would have to make distinctions between the training schools. I mean the fact that they were in rural areas, the fact that they were exclusionary, the fact that you could not attract minority staff, the fact that you couldn't do integration and after-care planning, all of those kinds of things, the fact that they were dehumanizing, the fact that they were not democratized, all of those things were negative aspects. Yet I can think of some of the changes that took place before they closed, when we did make an attempt to break the control systems, some of the things that were happening in the cottages where we handpicked some staff, were as good as what was happening in some of the community-based programs. Community-based programs can become insulated from the community also.

V: But isn't it a fact that that was merely a response to a portent of change? I mean isn't it a fact that the Nazi concentration camps, just before liberation, got to be pretty decent places, compared to the way they used to be, because the Allies were marching down the road. Isn't it a fact that Lyman and Shirley cleaned up their act to some extent anticipating that if they didn't, for the first time there would be some pretty severe penalties, such as loss of jobs?

M: Oh, sure. And I think that Jerry [Miller] and Yitzhak [Bakal] and others that were there, myself included—that we were going to break those existing negative controls within the institution. But I don't think that the changes took place because there was the recognition that they were going to close.

V: You don't think anybody believed that they were actually going to close?

M: I don't think that *we* believed initially that they were ever going to close. I mean we had Maxwell Jones in. We had Harry Voraff in, guided group interaction. We were going to open and democratize and develop after-care plans, and student government, and they were going to be really neat places—

V: So I have to assume then because of the statement as well as the tone of your voice that this did not prove to be a feasibility.

M: No it didn't.

V: So the institutions were closed not because you came in there with the intent to close, but because you didn't feel that they were salvageable? The institutions, if you will, couldn't be rehabilitated?

M: Yes. And our feeling was that the more good programs that we instituted, the more window dressing we were putting in, and the more we were supporting the system that none of us really accepted. That there were high points within it, and I really believe, that I can think of two or three cottages that were really as good as any community-based program operating today. Somehow we were getting caught in a trick type of bag that by doing this we were justifying something that none of us believed in.

V: Isn't it a fact that these "good" programs that you characterize as "good," always had the shotgun at the kids' heads to the extent that if they didn't work out inside the good program, they could go do time at the IJG [Institute for Juvenile Guidance, a maximum security juvenile prison at Bridgewater, Massachusetts] ?

M: That's not true in all the programs.

V: Well, where was there a program where they *didn't* have this? If they had a program at Lyman, they always had a "disciplinary" cottage—

M: I think one program when it was operating well at Shirley—

V: And what happened if a kid didn't work out in that program, didn't he go to Cottage Nine?

M: Cottage Nine was closed by that time. But there were two kids that went from this program that I remember to Wachusett Cottage at Lyman.

V: All I'm trying to suggest to you is this: that if you have an open system with no bottom line whatever, so that each program has to deal with everybody inside that program, how many programs would survive?

M: My guess is very few if any that I know of.

V: Isn't it a fact that the concept houses routinely lost 50, 60, 70 percent of the people that originally came there?

M: Yes.

V: Do you think it's possible to design a service delivery system for juvenile justice, never mind juvenile delinquency, that doesn't at some point contain a secure setting?

M: No, I don't.

V: When you close institutions, you have staff that are not assigned to any task, is that right?

M: That's right.

V: What do you do with that staff?

M: Well this was an ongoing problem during the whole time that I was with DYS. I'll jump ahead a year and then come back, because I think that if one canvassed the staff after they left the institutions and were working in regional offices and community-based programs that there was no way that you could get them back into an institution.

V: So are you saying parenthetically that all staff that were moved from institutions got other jobs?

M: Yes.

V: So that in fact the much-vaunted savings of de-institutionalization, which were largely staff costs, did not materialize?

M: They materialized through an attrition policy which was started in 1974 without the filling of staff positions which resulted in some savings, but also resulted in a system where new blood was not coming in, which also had disadvantages.

V: But you could have an attrition system without de-institutionalization. They are not necessarily married to each other. You could simply decide not to hire any staff, and, there will be a diminution in staff at some point?

M: Well, my point is that DYS used that as a mechanism to convert those "01" positions into "07" purchase-of-care monies which could purchase community care for youth. But it did present some problems within the department. The most difficult staff to deal with were those purely institutional positions, I'm thinking of some crazy titles we had such as swineherds, which was an existing position, it's not being made up, seamstress, stockroom operator. Cooks did very well because they usually had kids working with them and could respond and relate with kids. But those titles where they had really limited or no access to kids, no relationship with kids, those were the most difficult. And in the end the decision was made to terminate those people, and I think that was probably was the worst decision that was made within the Department of Youth Services because the political payback from that decision to in the end get rid of sixteen people cost the department in my estimation—I think there were other factors contributing to it—but a 22 percent cut in two years with an inflationary rise of 22 percent, or a real cut of over 40 percent in terms of services. It also bothered me because it negated the promise that I made the staff when institutions closed, that no one would lose their job.

V: When you made that promise though, you believed you were telling the truth?

M: Yes.

V: And you were told that that was in fact the case?

M: Yes.

V: If you were to do this again, if you were called in, let's say that New York was going to de-institutionalize, would you refuse the position unless you could guarantee that all staff would be retained?

M: My feeling is that if you have a human services system that works, with a secretariat, that many of those positions that we ended up terminating could have easily been absorbed, if it had been integrated into the Department of Corrections and the Department of Mental Health. The problem was that Jerry started a movement within the state, where other human service agencies were also starting to de-institutionalize. DMH, Corrections, and it was not very attractive for them to pick up those positions. The problem is they didn't do it with the same kind of speed, and in some ways adult de-institutionalization, with adult corrections, and people's fears or fantasies have been more problematic than it even was for delinquent kids. But as I look now at institutional populations that they're all overcrowded, that they easily could have absorbed those positions, so that there might be some types of swap-offs within a human services system where some of those people could be assimilated and perform a function within other human service agencies. There was not the clout and there was resistance from other human service agencies to pick up these people. That would be those who have no contact with kids and whose jobs were mainly institutional and could be easily converted over to another facility.

V: Let me ask you this. We were talking percentages before and we were saying that there was an identifiable percentage of juveniles that required institutionalization. By the same token, talking about the staff, was there an identifiable percentage of staff that should have been terminated regardless of de-institutionalization.

M: Yes.

V: Did that percentage in any way coincide with the percentage of people that had to lose their jobs?

M: No it didn't because no one lost their job.

V: In fact, no one lost their job. I'm saying if you were to start again, you were to close institutions, you were going to have some people that were excessed—

M: I think, Andy, I have just got to point out one fact. It is my understanding that before Jerry [Miller] came, no one got a job unless they were politically referred, and someone that they wanted to hire, they would tell the person to get a sponsor, and again, this is hearsay, and they kept a card file as to who was hired, and who the referral politician was. What happened was that it was also a political decision because Mrs. Murphy's seamstress was referred by senator X or representative Y, and as soon as the notion of possible termination came, and then you add on to that the civil service system, and then you add on to that the unions, that the decision to retain staff and to transfer was a political decision, and I very much understand the decision that Miller's successor made to terminate those employees, from the moral point of view that they had no useful functions, that they were sitting in some cases in closed-down institutions, that the money should be converted, but within a system's change, the political payoff and payback for that, to me really destroyed services for kids. So one also had to see how one operated within that political structure that was the funding source for the department. If one were to operate it like IBM, and had complete control over staff without any other constraints, my guess is that as high as 80 percent of the staff would have been let go.

V: Is the solution almost complete purchase of care? Is the solution to do *away* with civil service?

M: Well, there's kind of an image that purchase of care provides—it's cheaper and provides better quality care. I think that in the long run that's true. The costs for institutions in 1971 when we closed them was about $11,000 per child and that did not include capital expenditures to the buildings to administrative costs for support. My best guess is that was probably about fifteen thousand dollars. What I think a state has to assume is that the cost *initially* is a cost and a *half* to *de-institutionalize*. There are transitional costs which states have to agree that they are going to assume and that the payback is going to come down the line, either through an attrition policy with staff, through conversion, through other kinds of fiscal machinations— and that, that financial payback would not be realized probably for five years after a state deemed to close those institutions.

V: That's a pretty quick amortization though isn't it?

M: Yes, it is. But the problem is that given the recession or whatever you want to call it, of 1974, 1975 and 1976, that states did not want to make that initial investment of a third. We went from an $11.0 million agency to $16.7 in three and a half years. There was a one-third increase in the budget of DYS.

V: Before I get into the problem of federal monies and failures to institution- alize federal programs, I want to talk to you about costs for a minute. You're saying, even speaking conservatively, we could fiscally amortize the cost of this rather expensive overhaul within five years.

M: Yes.

V: What I want to know is this: what is your postulation on the other cost benefits involved, let's take for example just "crime." In fact just take "crime against persons." In a system that was redesigned from the ground up, could you sincerely postulate that we would have a decrease in criminality by the graduates of this system?

M: My hunch is—no one's done it, and I've suggested a lot of times—is that what they're saying in Massachusetts is that there was a small drop in the recidivism rate. However, my hypothesis is that although that kid might have stolen another car, that the graduation from more violent to less violent crimes was probably the greatest accomplishment of the Department of Youth Services. I'm not saying that he didn't steal another car—and that's a very difficult argument to sell, that he's only stealing another car and he's not holding someone up, or he's not stabbing someone and he's not going through the gradations of the offenses or behavior that one saw in a kid going from Oakdale on "stubborn" to Lyman on cars to Shirley on B&E's to Concord on armed robbery. And that to me was the greatest success, that we were not turning out more violent kids, which I believe the institutional system did. Now, needless to say, politically, it was very difficult to get up and say, "He may still steal cars, but he's not going to stick someone with a knife." But to me in the rehabilitative process, the fact that I didn't have an angrier more violent kid leaving that facility, going back with no kinds of plans or supports, that all of that was kind of built in, the kid might have stolen another car, he might have done another B&E, but as for the graduation to more serious crime, my hypothesis is that it was substantially reduced.

V: If that's a fact then, the benefit to society is far greater than the simple financial savings that you were discussing.

M: That's true. That's very difficult to get a handle on and to get some kind of formula that would take that into consideration.

V: Well, do you think it's a decent working hypothesis? For example, I think it's fair to say professionally that the old juvenile institutional system was criminogenic, I think that's fair to say.

M: Yes.

V: In fact, I often ask people I'm interviewing if they can name me one major criminal the country's produced that didn't get his start in juvenile prison. I've yet to come up with a name. I don't care if you want Charles Manson or Joe Barboza. I don't care how you are politically, I don't care if you want George Jackson, every one of them. That's something that I think is very very important. That if we're going to do a cost analysis, then we have to say what it's going to save us in human lives.

M: Really what the recidivism is based on when they do their analysis are those kids committed on felony charges. And those other kids committed on noncriminal or "stubborn" or truant or wayward are not included in the populations they're doing their recidivism study on. The other thing that bothers me is that it does not take into account the rising in street crime and violence that has been going on within society—

V: Do you know for a fact that it's going on? Are you basing this on the FBI uniform crime reports or what? I mean do you know for a fact that so-called street crime is rising in society?

M: That's a good question. I tell you what I base it on. I base it on my experience over a five-and-a-half-year period with DYS, and the changing patterns of offenses that the children were committed on. Over 40 percent of the kids in DYS when I was there were on stolen cars. Stolen cars represented less than 15 percent of the commitments by the time I left. Unarmed robbery and B&E, crimes against property and person, were the crimes the kids were being committed on. And what I'm comparing it in Massachusetts is on the pattern of commitments to the department, the decrease in crimes against property, particularly stolen cars, and noncriminal, which I'm calling wayward and stubborn, and the rise in more violent types of offenses and offenses against person and property.

V: But we have a big problem here, right? If you're not going to incarcerate young children, as truants, stubborn and wayward, those are the kids that would steal cars if they had been incarcerated at eight, nine, ten or eleven years old. If you're not going to incarcerate them, you see, it may be that you're eliminating people from the stolen car pattern without really changing the crime rate at all.

M: That's right.

V: Now you're aware of course that there's a lot of LEAA money around. And you're aware that a police department that doesn't report its share of crimes is going to get less money.

M: Right.

V: I'm not ready to accept as an affirmative fact that there's more crime. J. Edgar Hoover told me that there was more crime every year.

M: All I can do again, Andy, is the pattern of commitments over the five and a half years that I was there, and what is more significant, although I don't have the reason for it is offenses by girls. They were getting girls committed on what were normally "boys' types of offenses." That has been a dramatic shift.

V: I'm not sure we can attribute that to a change in criminal behavior as much as a change in our whole society as it has to do with girls.

M: I guess I believe we're a more violent society and we're becoming increasingly more violent. I guess that I do accept that.

V: I personally don't. I think that this society's always been a very heavily violent society, and what happens is that when violence goes on inside the institutions, we don't call it violence.

M: Right.

V: I think probably more violence was committed inside the juvenile prisons that we never saw. That never saw the light of day. That wasn't crime, that wasn't violence. So as long as we had those kids locked up, their sphere of possible new environment in which they commit crimes was very limited so we said it wasn't happening.

M: Right, right.

V: With de-institutionalization you're naturally going to have more reportable types of crime.

M: Right.

V: The question is what type of crime is it?

M: Right.

V: Also, years ago, if you had a kid who had committed a murder he was going to get bound over, so that doesn't go as a juvenile crime does it?

M: Right. No. No, it would not have been reported. It would have been reported as an adult statistic.

V: So I think these are real problems in looking at it fairly. What we're talking about is we're trying to set up a system that we can stop producing the Charles Mansons. That's what we're talking about now. It's not some pie in the sky thing where we can stop kids from stealing cars. And the solution is not to clean up the ghettos. In other words, what we're saying is that there's a certain percentage of children that are going to grow up to be major heavyweight adult criminals. We're trying to deal with formulating a kind of system that will identify and treat these kind of kids. Now everyone has so far agreed that the bottom line is they have to be isolated from the other kids, regardless of how you're treating the other kids. What's to be done with them is another story. The diagnosis is very difficult. For example I assume that you're opposed to the concept of crime equals time.

M: I am.

V: I assume then that you're also opposed to the concept that if you do a man's crime you do a man's time.

M: Right.

V: What diagnostic criteria would you use? We have an institution. It's a small institution. It's going to treat a certain type of child, the child who is dangerous. We can't say *will* be because we can't be predictive here. So we need certain overt acts before we can put him in there, do you agree with that?

M: Yes.

V: What kind of acts?

M: My initial one would be crimes of violence against a person involving a weapon.

V: Regardless of motivation? Is there a difference between a guy that likes to stick four-year-old girls with a knife and a guy that stabs another guy in a fight?

M: Yes.

V: They're both crimes of violence against a person with a weapon. Is there a difference between a guy that sticks up a liquor store and a guy that shoots his mother during an argument?

M: But I guess what I am saying is, yes—

V: You're saying you want it as an exclusionary category?

M: Yes.

V: In other words everything outside that you'll leave alone?

M: Yes.

V: Okay. Crimes of violence with a weapon. Everything else goes?

M: Oh boy, now we're really getting into—

V: Well, we've got to have some answers on this, that's the unfortunate part, but . . .

M: For example, in hindsight I think it was for political reasons we didn't do the job with girls. Mainly because we didn't have any women in the department with decision-making positions, number one, but number two because girls tended to be more self-destructive than outer-destructive.

V: In the home instead of the school?

M: Yeah. And once you get into a category of just outer-destructive behavior, so it's persons involving weapons, then one has to decide what one is going to do with that kid at Roslindale who's eating glass, who's mutilating his arms, who's—I hate the labels—who's borderline psychotic or is in and out of psychosis, is he in and out of touch with reality.

V: What about an arsonist?

M: An arsonist. Okay. However, the type of program that you're talking about, I don't really see many of those kids in that program.

V: I don't either.

M: But that doesn't mean that I would negate that they need specialized kind of care, that they might not need security. But that the care might take a different form. I'm not big on medication, but I *would* give antipsychotic drugs to someone that was in psychosis.

V: Most people, when they reluctantly come around to the fact that de-institutionalization across the board can't happen, start to fight you on the number of places you're going to build.

M: Right.

V: But it appears to be a fact that you're going to have to have two, maybe three separate, small different kinds of secure settings.

M: Right. Let me give an example. I think that intensive care as it was constructed, was totally destructive to what I'm going to call that self-destructive, fragile kid who was in and out of touch with reality. It was based on a lot of peer pressure, on a lot of group process, on a lot of outdated concept kinds of models, and for fragile kids to be in that kind of intensive situation is destructive to the kids. I am talking about a different population that really we were unable to handle well, and really did more to discredit the reform in Massachusetts than the move towards de-institutionalization. And that was the kid that we couldn't hold in any intensive care unit.

V: We've got an exclusionary sort of framework. We're saying that unless a kid needs this, we won't even consider him to start with. And for the purposes of our definition, we can say that arson is a crime of violence with a weapon. The matches being the weapon, right?

M: Yes. I also see this program as kind of the ultimate catcher's mitt. That this would be a kid who has not responded to any traditional kind of treatment and he may have been, and probably has been, given the political realities, placed in some highly expensive kinds of programs that do very well with motivated kids and sometimes with nonmotivated kids, if they can motivate them and turn them around. But he has not responded to any traditional modes of treatment. In fact, the kid as I see the kid would be a kid who not only has committed those types of offenses, has not responded to treatment, but probably picked up another offense while he was in treatment of a similar kind or nature. It would be those kids that we used to blow up programs.

V: Define what you mean by blowing up a program with a kid.

M: Intensive care program is going fairly well. They've developed what I'm going to call a positive peer culture within it. Relationships between staff and kids that are fairly sound, but in all of those programs it's never that sound, it's always fairly fragile, they're always fighting to maintain it. And Joey Jones has bounced out of three other intensive cares, has a record of seven escapes, has run with two other kids who have a similar pattern of behavior. It's clear that we aren't going to be able to hold this child in X, Y, and Z program. The three of them go in. Sometimes one of them can do it. One of them can destroy that culture almost overnight. Through overt and covert intimidation of other kids. So that they no longer feel a sense of security within the program. Through overt or covert intimidation of staff, so that what happens is that there is a buying-off process that goes on where a kid is made a junior staff member because no one can deal with him. Where he gets extra cigarettes, or he can watch T.V. late or where he gets to go to the store with a staff member. And the other kids see this, and the real thing is that people are afraid to confront the behavior and afraid to deal with it. And it's even worse when you magnify it and you have this grouping of kids of three or four or five kids in intensive care—I'm taking about in the Massachusetts experience—ten to a max of fifteen kids. You move three or four in. What you've done is you've moved a delinquent culture into that program and you've destroyed it overnight. And then you say "Jesus, it was a good program, Christ, they're having problems now. I wonder what's going wrong with that program" and then the other thing is that programs, once they're operational get smart also, and they start to have some say as to whose going to come into the program and they start setting up their own exclusoinary process in terms of these kids not able to get in and destroy their program. Or when they're in and identified they want them out.

V: So in your catchers mitt analogy, there would be no such option.

M: This is the end of the line for these kids.

V: It's also the end of the line in the sense that the program itself would not have this rejective mechanism available to it. They'd have to take every child.

M: They would have to take every child and they would have to hold and treat every child.

V: You're also postulating that maybe two or even three such programs might have to exist, one to handle kids whose problems are emotional-psychiatric, if you will, another whose kids' problems are more sociopathic, more acting out violence as opposed to self-destructive.

M: I would make that distinction, yes. I don't see this program as handling the kids in and out of touch with reality, that brain-damaged child, that retarded child. I don't see—I think there are better mechanisms, and I think that kid responds, also. In some ways he might be more damaged, but there's a lower incidence. And he can be treated and he can respond.

V: Let me ask you about population mix. Now I'm going to mention names on this tape just to provide references for you but they will be deleted from the tape. At Andros we had a [name deleted], we had a [name deleted], we had a [name deleted], we had a [name deleted], we had a [name deleted], we had [name deleted, name deleted]. Is this mixture at all possible? I mean could you possibly have a success with this kind of mixture?

M: The success of that program was based on the personality of the director, and the dynamics of the director. Whether it could have been sustained over a long period of time with that kind of mix, I'm not ready to make a judgment on.

V: In effect, Andros was two or three units, so your point is actually well taken, although the general perception was that Andros successfully worked with this many kids, what Andros did was it put some kids, such as [name deleted] in effect in the cooler. I don't mean in physical isolation, but he wasn't part of the program. The bottom line was he couldn't leave. So it was a success. And nobody could brutalize him. But that's as far as it went, that's what I'm trying to tell you, the success was a political success. But when we talk treatment, I don't think that mix is viable anymore.

M: I don't think it's viable either. I never thought it was—

V: The department must have had a sense that it was somewhat viable, because the department assigned every kid—

M: Well, and also because it was the only option available at that time.

V: Now how do we deal with that. Let's say we have this system to bring us back to right now what we want. We have this, we're going to call it a maximum-security unit, right? And it is working. How do we protect ourselves from the department saying "Goddamn, those guys have something that really works," let's give them another five kids. Let's give them another ten kids?" Andros went from eight kids to thirty kids.

M: I don't have the answer to that question. There is also, in my estimation, an underestimation of the length of treatment that some of these kids, given the amount of damage, actually need. My guess is that the mean length of stay would fluctuate from twelve to eighteen months. Consequently when you have a program that's functioning for twelve to eighteen months and there's not much movement out, there's always the political pressure, and the real pressure, this kid's on his way to Walpole [State Prison]. If you don't take him, he's going to Walpole. I know that Johnny Jones is doing well. Is there any chance there's an unease on the part of the program, because really his gains are based on relationships within that program, and placing him in the community even though you're trying to build support mechanisms. He's not ready for it. And there's an uneasy feeling and usually what it comes down to is maybe he could do it, maybe if we tried—but no one really believes that. And no one wants to see that kid go to Walpole. The problem with that though is that as your mean length of stay increases, the number of units have to increase, and I have some problems with the proliferation of units. I've seen the best and the most humane become brutal. I've seen people that I liked that were friends of mine are still friends of mine, do things to kids that I would never believe that they could do to kids because of their frustration and internalized feelings of failure and rejection from these kids. And then what you get is the proliferation and the proliferation bothers me. Because to maintain consistent quality and humaneness is a task in and of itself. To keep them humane, let alone treat them, becomes a paramount kind of task. And as the length of stay increases, the options for more kids getting out and then the proliferation—I don't have an answer for that. I don't have an answer to that question.

V: Well perhaps we have to adopt a triage mentality, Bill.

M: I think one thing that insures it is to provide to the agency that's providing the treatment a continuum of care and not to make them depend upon existing resources that have been unable to deal with these kids and to let them form their own continuum of care so that maybe the mean length of stay is reduced but the relationships have been maintained and the kid's working toward continuum care, security to group home, to supervised foster care, to independent living to supportive work, to whatever would be in their continuum of care for that kid, out of that host facility, because you get them dependent on other community agencies, that really don't know the kid, don't know how to respond, are threatened by the offense, really don't want the kid in the program, fulfill the kid's prophecy, because it comes across to the kid that he's a risk, that he's a danger, that he really isn't accepted there and that maybe, and I know this is jumping the gun, but maybe it just isn't a secure facility, but also the availability of funds to develop a continuum of care to move that kid out more quickly but consistently.

V: Look, there's no question about the correctness of that because we had the situation where kids wouldn't leave Andros, that wouldn't go home, because they knew, better than we did. Also, another problem with the de-institutionalization which I think you've already spoken to is that it's proponents say "You have to go to the community, you know, there's resources in the community." Some communities don't have any damn resources.

M: That's true. And if you want to look, if you wanted to do a demographic study of where group homes located you would find out that the majority located in poverty neighborhoods, where there aren't any kinds of consistent services, where there's a breakdown in services, mainly because the neighbors there were so fragmented that they couldn't organize to keep them out. They didn't go next to a community mental health clinic. They didn't go into an area where there was a college or a university or a lot of resources. They couldn't get into those areas. So they generally located in areas that were going to give them the least hassles about zoning, where they could hide the program and I think that's fairly accurate.

V: That's right on the money, sure. Well, if we're going to do this, and I think there's pretty much a consensus that it has to be done, more so in New York than in Massachusetts, where things have really gotten out of hand, if we're going to do this, and we have an idea about how we want to do it, do you think it's fair to say that even a very limited "success" would bring about some drastic change in the system overall? Let me put it another way. If I could take that 1 percent, out of the system as it currently functions, do you think that would take enough pressure off the system to allow it to humanize?

M: I think that it would reduce it, but I think that the notion of community-based care has not been accepted, by legislatures, by courts, by communities, by school systems, by the whole range of either social service or political networks. I think that it would negate some of the strongest arguments against it, but I see other things on the horizon, like they can't even get a group home for the retarded into Salem. Retarded kids, that represent no danger to the community. They finally got a positive decision from the Massachusetts Supreme Judicial Court. And it seems that the only way that they're getting into any neighborhoods now is through litigation. And that costs money. I believe when Tom Wicker and Ted Kennedy are both saying "I give up" both coming from the same place, with a Buckley thrown in, that we're going to go to determinate sentences, that rehabilitation has not worked, does not work, that we've got to separate and hold, and you know I'm saying, and liberals are saying, for a shorter period of time. But that even liberals have soured on the notion of rehabilitation and community-based care, that I see some more ominous clouds on the horizon, than just what we do with that kid.

V: But isn't that based on kind of a liberal petulance because things haven't worked the way they want them to work so they're ready to scrap the whole concept? You know to say rehabilitation doesn't work is one thing, to say it doesn't work in Attica is another. They're not the same thing.

M: I think it's stronger than that, Andy. I'm saying that they're saying it doesn't work period.

V: That's what they're saying. But I don't think that the people we're concerned about have ever had that opportunity.

M: I don't think they've ever had that opportunity, and I agree that it would negate and dull some of it, but had we done it in Massachusetts and done it well, de-institutionalization would have been accepted a lot more readily by other states than it is now. But that's not the only thing that's impinging on a network of care for kids within the community.

V: But doesn't the existence of a tiny network of small secure units take a lot of pressure off the system politically as well as rehabilitatively?

M: Sure, I'm not questioning that. It still might not be enough because I don't believe that the judges are by nature vindictive, I believe that they send kids to training schools because there's no other option and because the kids are poverty kids, and they can't get services, and—

V: Well they used to send them to the army, right?

M: Yeah. But I believe when the judge makes that decision, he's made a decision on separation. And the fact that the kid that's caused this kind of fury is being held and hopefully treated and is being handled humanely is a relief to him. I think it dulls it, but I still think that the notion hasn't changed much from separation and punishment for all deviants, be it mentally ill, retarded, delinquent. This is still a strong fabric within society that many people are ascribing to: it bothers me that more and more people seem to be ascribing to it.

V: Well that's a fear-generated kind of response, I think.

M: I do too.

V: But you don't have to be any kind of brilliant clear-thinking professional to realize that punishment's been dysfunctional. Straight punishment. The most vicious kids I've ever seen were products of the training schools. By far. Also the most physically tough kids. The ones that have built up almost an immunity to physical violence. To the point that there was no kind of physical threat that would really accomplish anything.

M: But there is something else to be said for this notion. Because I believe that those mechanisms that are worked out within that program that are successful, and have more ability to say what doesn't work than what does work, may be really applicable to a much larger percentage of the delinquent population in terms of care. I'm excluding now the notion of security. But the kinds of things that might be built in in terms of treatment methods, you can rehabilitate and deal with these kids, they're going to give us some better hunches and ideas of how to deal with kids in general, delinquent kids.

V: If your son killed somebody when he was fourteen years old and couldn't even explain to you why, what would you want to happen to him?

M: I'd probably get the best lawyer around, and I'd probably have him go to the children's unit at McLeans Hospital. I have private insurance, I could pick up six months of it on insurance, it would cost me another eighteen thousand dollars and out of my own pocket, which I could mortage the house and pay for, I could work closely with the psychiatric and clinical staff there, and I could probably have my child hopefully rehabilitated, and back home within a year. That's what I'd do.

V: That's what you'd actually do. Right. The difference between you and most other parents, do you think it's strictly that you're economically able to do this?

M: I think that number one I could probably manipulate the court system through getting the best lawyer around. And I could probably convince the judge that another option is available. I think that I could probably do that.

V: Would you say that if we took these one-percenters, that we'll call them, and we simply contracted with McLeans [a private psychiatric hospital], that we'd have something successful?

M: No.

V: Why not?

M: Because then you've got to draw the parameters around my son or daughter's behavior a little differently. You've got to say that not only did my son kill someone, but two years before he had pulled an armed robbery with a sawed-off shotgun, he had almost strangled someone before, his violence was almost uncontrollable, he had very little if any moral values or social conscience, he didn't form relationships with people, or if he formed relationships he used them as manipulative and destructive, and that there had been a whole pattern of history of poor impulse control, of violent behavior, of lack of social conscience and moral values, of inability to relate, of fear of intimacy—

V: So you would have interceded many, many years prior to this incident if you'd seen the warning signs, and that's the difference.

M: Yes.

V: Simply an injection of cash is not going to do it.

M: Not at that point in time. But see what I know is that if the child had committed that offense without those other things, that I can get a psychiatrist to say that my child is psychotic because his behavior is so out of touch with past behavior, and so unexpected, that the behavior by definition becomes psychotic and therefore, I mean that's the way you make the legal case.

V: You wouldn't have a particular problem with that I agree with you. In fact Jerry told me the story about some famous senator's daughter who's killed somebody. And how she will never be exposed to a real institution. That's all very well and good, but I don't think the political arguments are the answer here. In other words for somebody just to say "If we had enough money we could solve it," I think it's a little late for that, that's what I'm saying.

M: I don't believe that anyone has a solution.

V: But even if we're going to intervene. Take the classic murderer's triad, right? You have a kid who sets fires, wets the bed, and he tortures small animals for no apparent reason, we got a kid who's probably going to do something seriously bad here before long, right?

M: Yes.

V: But what crime has he committed right now that would allow him to be locked up? Much less treat him? That's a problem too, isn't it?

M: Oh, it certainly is. However, so is our inability to predict and so is the notion that that has to then be done within a physically secure facility. And I guess that in some cases it should be and that I would agree with you, if our predictive abilities were that good. Judge Baker did a predictive study on the most violent kids in Massachusetts when institutions closed. As to predictability of future violence, no correlation. I mean we're not that good at it yet. The people that are good at it never do it and those are the people that are working in the programs with the kids. I mean I would rather trust a child-care staff member's judgment who's working with this kid that this is a violent son of a bitch and you better watch him, than I would the psychiatric community trying to put the labels on this kid.

V: Let me ask you to briefly summarize what you feel the future holds for juvenile justice. I mean have we got a chance, are we just treading water, is there going to be some serious change?

M: Well I'm not sure because I don't read as much as I should but there have been some studies done that show correctional reform and delinquency reform take place when the society's most affluent. And that the greatest amount of anger comes toward "the deviant" when times are bad. I think times have been bad the last three or four years.

V: I do too.

M: I think there has been a political structure that has played into emotions and fears and unleashed a lot of fantasies in the mind of the average citizen as to what works and what doesn't work. I really don't know. One can look at things and become somewhat of a cynic. That when LEAA says that they're going to put lots of money into secure treatment and intensive care, does that to me mean more separation, more facilities that abuse kids, more facilities that don't treat, more facilities that label them the worst and lets them act out their expectations, or does it mean that it's an honest effort on the part of LEAA to try some new and innovative approaches with kids within a secure facility and to do some research on whether they work, not just in terms of recidivism, in terms of self-concept in terms of changes every day, in terms of carry-over. I'm not sure that it meets that need now, or that it's not feeding into the political social structure that we find ourselves in.

V: So you would not attempt then to separate the political-social-economic climate from the so-called treatment profession. In other words, we're a more responsive than we are an innovative profession?

M: Of course we are.

Interview between Andrew Vachss (V) and
Richard B. Child (C), on September 24, 1976

Richard B. Child is a professor of law at New England School of Law in Boston, where he has taught criminal law and commercial law. Professor Child is a graduate of Harvard University and of Harvard Law School, and is a member of the Connecticut Bar Association and the Massachusetts Bar Association. He founded the *New England Journal on Prison Law* in 1972, and has served for several years as a consultant to the Juvenile Justice Planning Project in New York City.

V: Have you perceived any change in public, legislative, or judicial attitudes toward juvenile crime in the last several years?

C: Well there certainly has been more skepticism in the last several years, than previously about the juvenile courts and the juvenile correctional institutions and I would say a growing feeling generally that the problem of juvenile crime seems to be pretty much out of control.

V: Do you think that's a media perception or do you think that's actually the case? Do you believe juvenile crime has in fact escalated to the extent to which the media would have us believe?

C: I can't say with any definiteness myself, as far as incidence of antisocial activity by juveniles. I think it's a fair statement, though, that lawyers and other professionals in the area have real perceptions that the problem is getting out of control, so that that is not purely an invention of the media.

V: We have seen in the past, a wave of progressive attacks on conventional methods of doing business in juvenile justice. There's been a lot of court decisions, there's been attempts at de-institutionalization. There have been a number of things designed to improve or reform, if you will, the juvenile justice system. All of these efforts are now being characterized as failures. Do you think that's a fair characterization?

C: I think it's a little too early to characterize things as failures that have only been tried in the last decade or so. It's even too early to characterize as failures experiments that took place twenty or twenty-five years ago because you can't really tell what impact a correctional program has had until you can trace offenders through more or less their whole life cycle to see what impact it's had. It's certainly too early to characterize the success or lack of success of programs that have only been tried in the last decade.

V: In fact, though, regardless of whether or not the characterization is unfair, the whole concept of de-institutionalization is now under heavy fire.

C: Yes.

V: Do you think that this fire will continue? Do you think that there is going to be a trend towards a return to the old ways of doing business?

C: I think there is already.

V: Are you personally, philosophically, politically, whatever, opposed to institutionalization? Of criminal offenders, now we're talking about.

C: I would say I have a fairly open mind on the subject at the present time. Unlike the death penalty, institutionalization does not give me a strong gut feeling of revulsion, so I basically am looking at institutionalization in terms of being highly skeptical of its efficacy but not rejecting it philosophically outright.

V: How would you respond to a statement such as "There is a certain percentage" without naming the percentage and admittedly a small percentage "of juveniles, who for their own safety and the safety of society need to be temporarily removed from society?"

C: I would agree with that statement.

V: Would you agree that this removal from society also has to mean removal from conventional institutionalization for juveniles? In other words, do other juveniles, less dangerous to self or others have a right, be it constitutional or simply moral, to be isolated from such people?

C: Yes. I would agree with that too.

V: How would you characterize a statement such as one that blames the large percentage of megacriminal behavior, serious criminal behavior, on previous juvenile incarceration? Nonpsychotic criminal behavior? If I were to say for example, that our more sophisticated bank robbers, professional murderers, people involved in life-style criminality are more likely than not to have done time as juveniles?

C: That certainly I would agree with. Strongly. What the causal relationship is is less clear to me.

V: Do you think that that statement was, in effect, taken at face value about a decade ago, that institutionalization as a result was decreased, and that that concept has pretty much had a fair trial?

C: Do you mean because institutionalization has decreased, therefore we're going to have less heavy criminal behavior because people are not going to have had the experience of being messed over in juvenile institutions? No, obviously, it's much too early to draw that kind of conclusion.

V: Would you think that the proximate results of such a conclusion being correct are worth the risk of increased de-institutionalization?

C: Not if it's applied to all juveniles across the board including the ones who are most dangerous to other juveniles and to the society in general.

V: If we were going to construct such an institution and we were going to fill it with, say in a large state like New York, only fifty to seventy young males, in this case, what diagnostic criteria would you like to see applied and who would you like to see apply it in terms of controlling the intake of such individuals?

C: Well I would certainly want to see a combination of legal professionals and treatment professionals establishing and enforcing any criteria that might be appropriate because if you have legal professionals alone establishing such criteria they relate insufficiently to the chances of a successful treatment program, but if you have treatment professionals alone establishing and enforcing the criteria, there's not enough concern for the societal interest that the criminal juvenile law is intended to protect. In other words, treatment professionals alone might give insufficient attention from society's point of view to an armed robbery and a murder.

V: Is the legal profession in trouble in terms of defending juveniles, professor? In other words, as an attorney, what is your real responsibility in defense of a child who's already committed a serious violent act and in your sincere opinion is likely to commit more? What is your actual responsibility to this child?

C: Well, now of course there's a serious ethical problem that lawyers have to face. It's a lot more serious problem today than it was ten years ago because of all the procedural protections that the courts have come up with and applied to juvenile trials since the *Gault* case. From my own practical experience in juvenile defense work, there's a strong inclination not to get into heavy involved procedural defense tactics because (1) it tends to seem like a waste of all your time (2) especially with regard to serious antisocial activity the lawyer is left with a feeling that it's a—especially in terms of the bottom line in juvenile trials—that it perhaps simply doesn't make sense to make a strong defense as a legal matter and yet, we've got the code of professional responsibility which indicates that the lawyer has a strong ethical obligation to his client to make a strong a legal as well as factual presentation as possible, so what I think happens in fact is that lawyers don't make as strong a legal presentation as they might in an adult criminal trial where the consequences in terms of institutionalization seem more severe to the average lawyer but they end up with a really bad taste in their mouth as a result, so the lawyer is left in a very difficult position which I'm sure affects the morale of lawyers actively involved in juvenile defense work.

V: To put it bluntly, is it a fact that if you put on a heavyweight legally sufficient defense, you decrease the child's chances, if he's found guilty of a better disposition?

C: That is correct.

V: And wouldn't that be a primary deterrent to lawyers in terms of putting on such a defense?

C: That is correct. And another factor that has to be faced is that the lawyer's also faced with the frustrating feeling that he or she ought to confront a system, which in effect penalizes the juvenile for in effect making a strong legal and factual presentation, and yet really the safest thing to do is to kind of cave in and only make a strong presentation on disposition.

V: Do you believe the philosophical and moral underpinning of the juvenile court which is normally expressed with the words "parens patriae" is in fact realistic? Do you think that the juvenile court can continue to function, as it has been designed to do in this country for about the last seventy-five years?

C: It really depends entirely upon the quality of the personnel involved. I don't think that by definition it's unworkable.

V: How do you respond to people who are now saying "the only way we're going to have justice in juvenile justice is to have jury trials, to have the full panoply of rights, to run it exactly as you would in an adult court?"

C: Well I can't see how either a jury trial or any other extension of procedural rights not yet available in juvenile trials is going to help juveniles.

V: That's been pretty much the response to that. In cases outside the juvenile justice field, the court seems to be slowly establishing, particularly in the mental health-civil commitment field, the right to treatment. Do you think juveniles have a right to treatment?

C: I think juveniles have nearly as clearly a right to treatment as civilly committed mentally ill adults and clearly more of a right to treatment than adults within the correctional system, so I would put—now I'm really talking not so much in constitutional terms as in moral terms or ethical terms of what the society owes different classes of people—I think that the right to treatment might be more ethically owed by society to mentally ill adults but the distinction between mentally ill adults and antisocial juveniles isn't a strong one.

V: Isn't it a fact that any distinction that would be alleged to exist tends to blur the more the one buys into the whole parens patriae mentality?

C: That's correct.

V: That in fact is a medical model, isn't it?

C: Right. Exactly. Where the parens patriae notion for juvenile courts came from, in my recollection of having read this somewhere, is there is a typographical error in sixteenth or seventeenth century edition of some English treatise and as a result a doctrine which had previously been applied only to mentally ill individuals was applied more or less accidentally to juveniles but it was originally a model intended for the mentally ill.

V: How far can we take the separation doctrine in terms of treatment? Juvenile courts, in fact juvenile institutions, evolved in this country out of a sense that to mix juveniles with adults, regardless of behavior, was in effect productive of crime. Juveniles deserved to be separated. Lyman School in 1846 was built for that reason. The Juvenile Court Act of 1899 in Illinois was written just for that reason. Now can we carry separation further? In other words, do juveniles involved with stolen cars, smoking marijuana, truancy, crimes like that have a right to be separated from juveniles who are mass murderers, arsonists, rapists?

C: I would agree with that. And of course the whole trend in terms of adult correctional classification is towards making that type of segregated treatment program available on a more limited basis even for adult offenders.

V: If we were to adopt that though, isn't it a fact that we'd be in some very difficult diagnostic trouble? For example, who's more dangerous: a child who is a participant in the gang fight in which a person dies, or a child sho sets small fires, tortures small animals, and has a problem wetting the bed. Who's more dangerous?

C: I'm not prepared to draw a conclusion.

V: But as to the law, it is clear that the child involved, even tangentially in the homicide is more dangerous, right?

C: That's correct. And that raises all sorts of problems with regard to procedural protections in the juvenile justice system as well, because if you can't get a pretty specific information as to the degree of participation of a juvenile in a gang fight, and if you get serious Fifth Amendment problems, you're not going to be able to get such information, how can you draw a safe diagnostic conclusion about almost anything, especially crimes involving more than one juvenile?

V: Well it is a fact that the quality of the legal defense varies with the economic class of the individual, correct?

C: That is correct.

V: At least that's a commonly held perception.

C: Right.

V: It also appears to be a fact that our juvenile institutions are largely filled with people from the lower socioeconomic strata?

C: That's correct.

V: However, in hypothesizing a specialized juvenile institution to deal with only serious acting-out kinds of violence, I think that these distinctions would tend to disappear. So that might be a democratizing kind of technique that nobody's even looked at? Do you agree with that?

C: That is possible.

V: For example, what I mean is this: juveniles from lower socioeconomic strata tend to be involved heavily in crimes of violence around robberies and thefts and fights. But the child that rapes and kills a five-year-old girl cannot usually be economically correlated. They tend to come from all areas of the socioeconomic strata, right?

C: That's possible. I'm not really in a position to answer the question, but that certainly sounds like a reasonable hypothesis.

V: Well what I'm trying to isolate is whether or not there would be opposition from an element of the community that we did not expect. For example, a child from a wealthy family who is involved in a serious violent crime may end up at McLeans [a private psychiatric hospital]. Because there is no special institution to deal with such children right now.

C: Right.

V: If such a secure treatment unit existed, sure the kid from Roxbury's going to go there. Is the kid from Belmont going to go there?

C: I think you've got a good point there. To the extent that violence and antisocial activity by juveniles is not classified or not classified to too strong a degree, you're certainly going to have more equal treatment when an institution is available for juveniles of all economic strata and when the nature of the dispositional system is such that juveniles ought and are going to be treated equally with regard to the likelihood of being institutionalized.

V: It's a fact that a crime of particular violence that appears to be motiveless tends to be characterized as viciousness if committed by a person from a lower economic class, and as insanity if committed by a person from a higher economic class.

C: That's quite possible. Certainly it's much easier for a juvenile of the upper class to successfully make that argument because of the difference in the quality of representation, among other things.

V: As an advocate representing a child who is in fact guilty of a serious violence crime, say a torture-murder, a motiveless crime, what would I have to assure you exists within a given institution before you would abandon the child's procedural legal defense and fight for a disposition to *this* institution?

C: I'd mainly have to believe in the quality of the personnel in the institution, and if I believed in the quality of the supervisory personnel and I had some notion as to the nature of the supervision, I think that would be sufficient.

V: Do you think the writ of habeas corpus could be effectively utilized by counsel in this case as a methodology which you would verify the quality of treatment?

C: That would seem true to me, yes.

V: Do you think that's a viable tactic that we might see in the future?

C: That's quite possible, yes.

V: We have not seen it in the past, even the famous cases, Jerry Gault was doing time all the while that his case was being appealed, right?

C: Right.

V: I think that's a distinct problem. And when you, as an advocate, say you want to be reassured about certain qualities in effect we cannot give you a track record if we are going to build the institution tomorrow. I can't say our graduates have such and such—

C: Right.

V: I can say to you: "You can visit the institution" but what good is that? By utilizing the writ it would seem to me that you could in effect get an evidentiary hearing on the quality of care.

C: Right.

V: How do you feel about the child being a consumer and the various programs, institutions, programs whatever you want to call them being the vendors of juvenile treatment? In other words should the child have the right to elect between vendors?

C: I don't think that is an accurate characterization of the function of the juvenile justice system.

V: How about an accurate characterization of the fact of the juvenile justice system. Let's take Massachusetts, we have dozens of "community programs" each of which receive a "per head" grant, they get so much per kid per year. They compete for these kids. But in effect it opens up whole avenues of political corruption. I was told about a judge in Pennsylvania who owns a nearly controlling interest in a certain institution and in fact sentences every kid to that institution.

C: Well that's certainly not the way the system should run.

V: I'm saying that I think the system does run that way to a certain extent. If there were, leaving aside right now the question of the very serious heavily violent kid, but if there was a kid involved in repeated thefts, and there were four programs set up specifically under contract to the state to deal with such children. Should the child be said to "Well we're going to give you the fifteen thousand which we would pay the program and you pick the program and you may try this program for three months, and you may shop around," how do you feel about the viability of this?

C: It doesn't seem to be viable to me.

V: The hypothesis by which this is advanced is that people tend to pick what's best for themselves, and people are not generally self-destructive, and that even if a program were to be set up to deliberately allow kids to do whatever they wanted to do, a high percentage of kids would reject this program. That they would perceive in and of themselves that they need some help.

C: That doesn't stand psychologically a plausible approach to the problem.

V: What about the argument that if we run a viable institution a functional institution, a good institution that we have, in effect, declawed the juvenile. That when he has to return to his own community, he's less equipped for survival in that community?

C: Well if you look at the problem that way, there's really no way to deal with antisocial activity by juveniles except to destroy whole communities. I just don't see that as a viable approach to the problem either.

V: What effect do you think it would have if we could functionally remove from the juvenile justice population the committed population, whether institutionalized or not, this 1.0 percent or 0.5 percent of heavily dangerous children. If we could just remove them from that population? Whether we remove them, isolate them, institutionalize them or whatever? What effect would that have on the rest of the population?

C: It would probably have a calming effect and would make whatever rehabilitation is going on a lot easier. And it might also, and probably would, cut down on any tendency institutions have to be breeding grounds for future adult criminals. I understand that that theory is predicated on the notion that there is a hard core of highly antisocial juveniles who are kind of seducing or forcing other kinds of juveniles into more antisocial juveniles, and that is a fairly well-established perception that underlies the notion that de-institutionalization should take place and this really is another alternative approach to that problem.

V: The three major problems in a juvenile institution so far have been homosexual rape, physical violence, either between staff and residents or residents and residents, and suicide. Is it not possible to design, build, run and maintain an institution in which those things did not happen?

C: It's certainly possible to design an institution in which it would happen much less frequently and in which all of the problems you mentioned other than suicide could be cut to a absolute minimum.

V: Well isn't homosexual rape almost exclusively an institutional phenomenon? It's not something we see very often on the street.

C: That's correct.

V: So do you think it's fair to lay the blame for that particular aberration directly at the door of the institution?

C: Yes. Of course that's different conclusions, one the notion that institutions should be very designed and another the notion that institutionalization per se is harmful to individuals. It seems to me that you could go in either direction and that it would indeed be possible to design institutions in which that type of aberrational antisocial conduct would not take place.

V: Isn't it in effect possible to combine both arguments by building one single institution only for the type of children we've been talking about and basically eliminate institutionalization across the board for others?

C: That's correct.

V: What about a theory that I heard advanced which I would like you to comment on. If we build such an institution, staff it very heavily, provide really the best kind of care and treatment, that we're open for an equal protection argument because people who have not "qualified" by committing serious major felonies don't get this kind of treatment.

C: I can't see where anybody would be in a position to want to advance that argument and even if it were advanced, I don't think it has much constitutional merit.

V: So in effect, you think it's viable to tailor, even custom-tailor treatment to offense, or treatment to individual without getting into any kind of equal protection problem?

C: I think it's completely legally and constitutionally viable.

V: When we talk about staffing this special institution, we have the conventional kinds of staff. Do you think that there should be an attorney on the staff? In other words, should the institution have its own advocate?

C: That might be appropriate, yes.

V: Here's the reasons that have been advanced for that. The attorney could appear as *amicus* in cases where there were dispositional arguments to be made. Second of all, when you have fifty of these type of juveniles committed to one institution, the odds are absolutely overwhelming that each kid will have a dozen to twenty other pending cases. Perhaps of less weight, certainly, but he'll have these cases. He will have been in trouble with the law, he certainly will have been on probation, or perhaps parole from another institution, so that we could have a thematic kind of defense.

C: Well at least there ought to be an attorney somewhere in the state legal system whose work is predominately dedicated to the institution, and on the basis of what you've just suggested it seems to me it would justify having at least one attorney full time.

V: The intent is to write purchase of care contracts that are performance oriented. Now, we obviously cannot write them and say "If you fail to rehabilitate X number of kids you won't get paid." That's obviously out of the question. But I think it's possible and I'd like you to comment on this, to write contracts so that certain things are guaranteed. You will have if you will X number of hours of therapy, X number of hours of vocational treatment, there will be X number of staff hours assigned to each kid. There will be a certain nutritional content in food. There will be certain safeguards in terms medication. Do you think these contracts are possible and should be used in the future?

C: Yes. I think so. Such contracts can be written with sufficient specificity as to provide for a meaningful kind of quality control and I think that they certainly offer a lot better hope for quality control than running the institution as part of the state bureaucracy.

V: Would it be fair to summarize your position at least thus far as being not only not opposed but perhaps in favor of heavier institutionalization for a small percentage and decreased institutionalization for the remaining percentage of juveniles?

C: I think that would be a fair statement.

V: How do you feel about the use of former prisoners in therapy?

C: I think former juvenile offenders are particularly well positioned to understand juvenile delinquents from their own personal experience, so I would feel that past juvenile offenders might conceivably be a very good group to draw on.

V: There have been some problems with this.

C: Well I can imagine that there would be serious problems depending on your personnel selection. I'm just saying that is not a group which I would immediately exclude.

V: We've actually come to the conclusions in our work that we do exclude based on type of crime, because we've found that certain types of criminality, the purveyor of such criminality tends not to be effective, and I'm being charitable, and I'm particularly talking about sex offenders or people with addictive problems.

C: Well I can well understand that. I can understand that there would be whole classes of offenders that you would not want to use in that setting. All I'm saying is that I would not automatically exclude all ex-offenders. I certainly don't think that they're going to be your first or even your tenth group to draw on but that's certainly a possibility.

V: Can you offer, in conclusion, any hints as to where we might be going wrong? You know the direction we want to go, we want a small institution, for certain types of megaviolent juveniles, in order to take pressure off the rest of the system and we do want to give rehabilitation a serious shot within this institution. Can you foresee any particular problems that we might run into in attempting to implement this plan?

C: I foresee a number of difficulties in your being able to *sell* this plan but I think that if you're successful and convincing as I stated before it's a good plan, that it can and would be implemented without great practical difficulties. I can just see most of your problems in being able to convince people that it's the right way to go.

Index

Index

About the Authors

Andrew H. Vachss, Esq., is the director of the Juvenile Justice Planning Project in New York City and a criminal defense attorney specializing in juveniles and youth. His broad-based field experience in community organizing, criminal justice, and law includes positions with the United States Public Health Service (Ohio), the New York City Department of Social Services, the Community Development Foundation (Connecticut), the Calumet Community Congress (Indiana), the Uptown Community Organization (Illinois), Libra, Inc. (Massachusetts), the Medfield-Norfolk Prison Project (Massachusetts), director of Andros II (a maximum security institution for "aggressive-violent" juveniles), the Department of Youth Services (Massachusetts), the Office of the Crime Control Coordinator (New York), Advocacy Associates (New York and New Jersey), and numerous special consultant assignments.

A graduate of the New England School of Law and a member of the American Bar Association and the American Society of Criminology; his publications include "Parole As Post-Conviction Relief: The Robert Lewis Decision," and "Ad Hoc Parole Committee Public Information Report #1: The Parole Denial Process in New Jersey."

Yitzhak Bakal, Ed.D has devoted many years of work and study to the field of juvenile corrections, both in Israel and the United States. He served as assistant commissioner in charge of institutions for the Commonwealth of Massachusetts during the 1970-1973 de-institutionalization period. He also edited the book, *Closing Correctional Institutions*, published by D.C. Heath.

Presently, he is the director of the Northeastern Family Institute (NFI), which he founded as a nonprofit organization engaged in developing community-based programs for delinquent youth.

DATE DUE

APR 1 0 1980			
ILL 2760386 12-22-95			